Learning Disabilities and Challenging Behaviors

Third Edition

Learning Disabilities and Challenging Behaviors

Using the Building Blocks Model to Guide Intervention and Classroom Management

Third Edition

by

Nancy Mather, Ph.D.
University of Arizona
Tucson

Sam Goldstein, Ph.D.
Neurology, Learning and Behavior Center
and University of Utah School of Medicine
Salt Lake City

and

Katie Eklund, Ph.D.
University of Arizona
Tucson

with invited contributors

Baltimore • London • Sydney

Paul H. Brookes Publishing Co.
Post Office Box 10624
Baltimore, Maryland 21285-0624

www.brookespublishing.com

Copyright © 2015 by Paul H. Brookes Publishing Co., Inc.
All rights reserved.
Previous edition copyright © 2008.

"Paul H. Brookes Publishing Co." is a registered trademark of
Paul H. Brookes Publishing Co., Inc.

Typeset by Scribe Inc., Philadelphia, Pennsylvania.
Manufactured in the United States of America by
Sheridan Books, Inc., Chelsea, Michigan.

Cover image © iStockphoto/michaeljung.
Photograph of Dr. Goldstein on p. ix courtesy of Michael Schoenfeld (www.michaelschoenfeld.com).

The list from Jones, 1994 found at the bottom of p. 120 is from *Attention deficit disorder: Strategies for school-age children.* Copyright © 1994 NCS Pearson, Inc. All rights reserved.

All examples in this book are composites. Any similarity to actual individuals or circumstances is coincidental, and no implications should be inferred.

The information provided in this book is in no way meant to substitute for a medical or mental health practitioner's advice or expert opinion. Readers should consult a health or mental health professional if they are interested in more information. This book is sold without warranties of any kind, express or implied, and the publisher and authors disclaim any liability, loss, or damage caused by the contents of this book.

Purchasers of *Learning Disabilities and Challenging Behaviors: Using the Building Blocks Model to Guide Intervention and Classroom Management, Third Edition,* are granted permission to download, print, and/or photocopy the assessment tools in Appendix 1A, Appendix 8A, and Appendix 10B for educational purposes. None of the forms may be reproduced to generate revenue for any program or individual. Photocopies may only be made from an original book. *Unauthorized use beyond this privilege is prosecutable under federal law.* You will see the copyright protection notice at the bottom of each photocopiable page.

Library of Congress Cataloging-in-Publication Data
The Library of Congress has cataloged the printed edition as follows:

Mather, Nancy.
   Learning disabilities and challenging behaviors : using the building blocks model to guide intervention and classroom management / Nancy Mather, Sam Goldstein, Katie Eklund.—Third edition.
      pages   cm
   Summary: "This third edition shows teachers and specialists, such as school psychologists and speech-language pathologists, how to support children in Grades K-12 with learning disabilities and behavioral challenges in the era of high-stakes testing and accountability. An innovative framework is included to help professionals identify areas of strength and weakness and to determine the types of educational and behavioral interventions needed and to develop meaningful, realistic educational goals. Even more comprehensive and user friendly than the popular previous edition, this text follows the same basic format: the Building Blocks model targets 12 factors and abilities related to school success and gives teachers practical strategies for helping students succeed as well as a detailed questionnaire that pinpoints student strengths and needs. The reliable, up-to-date research makes this an essential textbook for any course focused on learning disabilities and behavior problems, and the practical advice and guidelines will be a lifeline to in-service teachers year after year. The new edition explains the same philosophy and model for intervention, but it also includes information on multi-tiered systems of support, positive behavior interventions and supports, and social-emotional learning. This new edition has a new third author, Katie Eklund, who will bring a fresh energy to the author team. As in the previous edition, there are a few invited contributors as well, including Robert Brooks"—Provided by publisher.
   Includes bibliographical references and index.
   ISBN 978-1-59857-836-2 (paperback)—ISBN 978-1-59857-840-9 (pdf ebook)—ISBN 978-1-59857-837-9 (epub ebook)
   1. Learning disabled children—Education.   2. Behavior disorders in children.   3. Classroom management. I. Goldstein, Sam, 1952– II. Eklund, Katie. III. Title.
LC4704.M374 2015
371.9—dc23
                                                                                          2014042845

British Library Cataloguing in Publication data are available from the British Library.

2019   2018   2017   2016   2015
10   9   8   7   6   5   4   3   2   1

Contents

About the Downloadable Materials vii
About the Authors ix
About the Contributors xi
Preface xiii
Acknowledgments xvii
A Note to Teachers xix

I Introduction
1. The Building Blocks of Learning: A Framework for
    Understanding Classroom Learning and Behavior 3
2. Theoretical Foundations 31
3. The Learning Environment 55

II Foundational Blocks
4. Self-Regulation: Understanding and Managing Students with
    Hyperactivity and Poor Attention, Planning, and Impulse Control 81
5. Understanding and Managing Challenging Behaviors 123
    with Lauren Meyer

6. Emotions: Understanding and Managing Anxiety, Depression,
    Trauma, and Stress 155
    with Gretchen Schoenfield and Jennifer M. White

7. Strategies to Promote Resilience 181
    with Robert Brooks

III Processing Blocks
8. Specific Learning Disabilities and the Processing Blocks 207
    with Deborah A. Schneider

9. Instruction for the Processing Blocks: Decoding and Encoding,
    Reading Fluency, Calculating, and Handwriting 273
    with Breanna Sherrow

IV Conceptual Blocks
10. The Conceptual Blocks: Verbal, Nonverbal, and
    Executive Functions 351
    with Ann M. Richards

11   Instruction in Reading Comprehension, Written Expression, and Math Problem Solving..403
with Ann M. Richards

V Conclusion
12   The Classroom Environment as a Microcosm of the World...................................463

References..475
Additional Resources..513
Web Sites and Professional Organizations...523
Index...527

About the Downloadable Materials

Purchasers of this book may download, print, and/or photocopy the assessment tools in Appendix 1A, Appendix 8A, and Appendix 10B for educational use. These materials are included with the print book and are also available for download at **http://www.brookespublishing.com/mather/materials** for print and e-book buyers.

About the Authors

Nancy Mather, Ph.D., University of Arizona, College of Education, Department of Disability and Psychoeducational Studies, Education Building 409, Tucson, Arizona 85721

Dr. Mather is a professor at the University of Arizona in the Department of Disability and Psychoeducational Studies. She specializes in the areas of reading, writing, and learning disabilities. She has conducted numerous workshops and presentations both nationally and internationally on assessment, instruction, and issues that affect service delivery for individuals with learning disabilities. She has written many books and articles on topics and issues in the field. Dr. Mather is a coauthor, along with Dr. Fredrick A. Schrank and Dr. Kevin S. McGrew, of the Woodcock-Johnson IV Tests of Cognitive Abilities (WJ IV; Riverside, 2014). Dr. Mather has also coauthored two books on interpretation and application of the WJ IV: *Woodcock-Johnson IV: Recommendations, Reports, and Strategies* with Dr. Lynne E Jaffe (Wiley, in press) and *Essentials of WJ IV Tests of Achievement Assessment* with Barbara J. Wendling (Wiley, in press). In addition, she has coauthored *Essentials of Dyslexia: Assessment and Intervention* with Barbara J. Wendling (Wiley, 2012).

Sam Goldstein, Ph.D., Neurology, Learning and Behavior Center, 230 South 500 East, Suite 100, Salt Lake City, Utah 84102

Dr. Goldstein is a board-certified forensic and clinical neuropsychologist, certified school psychologist, and member of the faculty at the University of Utah School of Medicine. He is Clinical Director of the Neurology, Learning and Behavior Center in Salt Lake City, Utah, and on staff at the University Neuropsychiatric Institute. Dr. Goldstein is an adjunct assistant professor in the Department of Psychiatry at the University of Utah School of Medicine. He is Editor-in-Chief of the *Journal of Attention Disorders* and sits on the editorial boards of six journals, including the *Journal of Learning Disabilities*. His publications include 47 professional and trade texts on subjects including genetics and developmental disorders, intelligence, executive functioning, autism, depression, classroom consultation, learning disability, and attention. He has coauthored six psychological and neuropsychological tests, including the Cognitive Assessment System, Second Edition (PRO-ED, 2014), the Autism Spectrum Rating Scales (Multi-Health Systems, 2009), and the Comprehensive Executive Functioning Inventory (Multi-Health Systems, 2012). Dr. Goldstein speaks internationally on a wide range of child development and forensic topics.

Katie Eklund, Ph.D., University of Arizona, College of Education, School Psychology Program, 1430 East Second Street, Tucson, Arizona 85721

Dr. Eklund is an assistant professor in the School Psychology Program at the University of Arizona. She received her doctorate in counseling, clinical, and school psychology from the University of California, Santa Barbara. Dr. Eklund has worked in public education for 14 years as a school administrator, school psychologist, and school social worker and is a Nationally Certified School Psychologist and licensed psychologist. Dr. Eklund has authored a number of publications on childhood risk and resiliency factors, including early identification and intervention for behavioral and emotional concerns, school climate, and positive psychology. Her teaching interests include school-based academic and behavioral interventions, crisis response and intervention, and school-based consultation and problem-solving skills.

About the Contributors

Robert Brooks, Ph.D., 60 Oak Knoll Terrace, Needham, Massachusetts 02492

Dr. Brooks is a faculty member at Harvard Medical School. He also has a part-time private practice and provides consultation to several educational institutions. His major professional activity is conducting workshops and presentations nationally and internationally to groups of educators, health care professionals, business people, community organizations, and parents. The major themes he addresses in his writings and workshops pertain to motivation, resilience, positive school and work environments, and balancing personal and professional lives. He has coauthored or co-edited 12 books with Dr. Sam Goldstein, including the second edition of *Handbook of Resilience in Children* (Springer, 2013).

Lauren Meyer, M.A., University of Arizona, College of Education, School Psychology Program, 1430 East Second Street, Tucson, Arizona 85721

Ms. Meyer is a doctoral student at the University of Arizona pursuing a Ph.D. in school psychology and a minor in rehabilitation counseling. She teaches undergraduate psychology and developmental mathematics at Mesa Community College. Much of her work has involved curriculum development and schoolwide programming targeted to improve retention rates and campus connectedness in high school and early college. She has worked as an advocate for multiple organizations at the local and national levels promoting suicide prevention, sexual assault and domestic violence awareness, and treatment alternatives to high-risk behaviors among students. Her research interests include crisis response and intervention, positive psychology, and emotional and behavioral concerns, specifically how they intersect during the high school to college transition.

Ann M, Richards, Ph.D., West Virginia University, 508G Allen Hall, Morgantown, West Virginia 26506

Dr. Richards is an associate professor at West Virginia University, where she trains teachers of special education at both the graduate and undergraduate levels. Much of her work has been done in the areas of transition, schoolwide positive behavior support, collaboration, and learning disabilities. She has provided several professional development workshops on characteristics of special needs learners and the need for differentiated instruction within general education classrooms. She is also an active volunteer for West Virginia Special Olympics, providing preservice teachers with experiences working with individuals with disabilities.

About the Contributors

Deborah A. Schneider, Ed.S., University of Arizona, College of Education, Department of Disability and Psychoeducational Studies, Education Building 409, Tucson, Arizona 85721

Ms. Schneider is a doctoral candidate and Department Fellow in Special Education at the University of Arizona. She earned an Ed.S. in language, reading, and culture; an M.A. in educational psychology; and a summa cum laude B.A. in English at the University of Arizona. She has also studied English literature and linguistics at the graduate level at the University of Fribourg in Switzerland. She has coauthored several book chapters on the identification and remediation of learning disabilities. Her research interests include testing and measurement in education and the identification and remediation of learning disabilities. In addition to her departmental fellowship, she has worked in various capacities at the University of Arizona for a combined total of more than 7 years. In that time, she has contributed to several research projects, including research concerning literacy, the adoption of instructional technologies, and strategies to promote the success of veterans with disabilities in the higher educational environment.

Gretchen Schoenfield, Ph.D., Neuropsychology Limited, 2650 North Wyatt Drive, Tucson, Arizona 85712

Dr. Schoenfield is a licensed psychologist in private practice specializing in neuropsychological evaluation and brief model interventions in inpatient rehabilitation and outpatient settings. She received her doctorate from the University of Arizona in school psychology with an emphasis in pediatric and adult neuropsychology. She has coauthored several book chapters on the topic of diagnosis and treatment of anxiety disorders in childhood and adolescence. Her clinical interests include neuropsychological assessment of individuals with medical conditions having neuropsychiatric sequelae and assisting patients and families with their adjustment to cognitive and lifestyle changes.

Breanna Sherrow, M.A., University of Arizona, College of Education, Department of Disability and Psychoeducational Studies, Education Building 409, Tucson, Arizona 85721

Ms. Sherrow is a doctoral candidate at the University of Arizona pursuing a Ph.D. in special education and a minor focusing on behavior and positive behavior supports. Because she had specific learning disabilities in reading and writing in elementary school, she has a personal connection to the field. Ms. Sherrow's research interests include assessment, instruction, and intervention for students with specific learning disabilities and emotional behavior disorders. She is also interested in parent and teacher supports for students with learning disabilities.

Jennifer M. White, M.A., University of Arizona, College of Education, Department of Disability and Psychoeducational Studies, Education Building 409, Tucson, Arizona 85721

Ms. White is a doctoral student at the University of Arizona pursuing a Ph.D. in special education with a minor in school psychology. She has experience as both a reading specialist and special education director. Much of her work has focused upon training teachers in research-based reading instruction and implementing accommodations and modifications in the classroom. Her research interests include evidence-based interventions, assessment, and diagnosis for students with high-incidence learning disabilities, as well as how to effectively prepare teachers to provide effective reading instruction to students with learning disabilities.

Preface

Most children enter kindergarten feeling excited and ready to learn. They are instinctually optimistic and intrinsically motivated. They are of an age during which they believe they are capable of achieving anything they set their minds to accomplish. The very experience of success is all the reinforcement they require to persevere. Yet within a few years, a significant minority become disenchanted and turned off to school not because of the challenges they face but because the educational system has failed to understand and address those challenges. Many children struggle with learning, behavior, or emotional problems at school. School experiences for these children further reinforce their perceptions of inadequacy. The instinctual optimism that children bring to life must be nurtured at school if all children are to make a successful transition through their educational years.

What variables contribute to this change of heart and view of self? For example, despite failing to complete a puzzle, most first-grade students confidently report that if they were given another chance, they would be able to complete the puzzle successfully. Yet by the end of elementary school, many students do not predict that they will experience future success following failure (Dweck, 2006). Some scholars would suggest that this transformation in attitude is simply a process of maturation. Young students are unable to assess their capabilities accurately and, when facing a problem, they are naive about the probability of success. Yet this very same research can be viewed from the perspective that school experiences negatively alter students' self-confidence (Goldstein & Brooks, 2007). If this is the case, we are missing a valuable opportunity to help children develop self-discipline; confidence; and a resilient, optimistic view of self—essential components for life success (Brooks & Goldstein, 2001, 2007, 2013).

Although the next decade brings promises of unlimited technological and scientific advances, as a society, we are experiencing increasing problems in preparing our youth for this future. Violence, vandalism, increased school dropout rates, and mental health problems among our students remind us daily of this fact. The burden of preparing children for their future has been and must be increasingly borne on the shoulders of educators. Our schools must find a way to educate all students efficiently and effectively, providing them with knowledge and instilling in them qualities of hope and resilience. These qualities will help them be confident and overcome the challenges and adversities that they will face.

To accomplish this goal, educators must begin looking at children differently. Rather than viewing the learning, emotional, and challenging behaviors that some children experience as somehow making them different in a fixed and stable way, educators must view these problems as malleable and responsive to environmental manipulation. This requires a shift from a categorical model of differences to a model that acknowledges that most children's school problems result from the combination of variations in abilities and environmental influences. Children with slower learning rates, for example, learn through the same processes as others but may require more time. They respond to the same types of strategies and interventions that other children do but often require more assistance.

The third edition of *Learning Disabilities and Challenging Behaviors: Using the Building Blocks Model to Guide Intervention and Classroom Management* marks more than 18 years of collaboration between the first two authors and is the result of a chance meeting at an educational conference in Saskatoon, Canada. We were each speaking on different but related topics concerning children's development, learning, and behavioral challenges. Although our backgrounds and training were quite different, we immediately found common ground in our conceptualization of children's development as well as in our understanding of how to help children who struggle in the classroom.

Our first joint book, *Overcoming Underachieving* (Goldstein & Mather, 1998), was written as a guide to help parents foster their children's school success. In that volume, we took a novel approach by suggesting that an appreciation of a finite pattern of skills and abilities could help parents understand the reasons for their child's successes and failures in the classroom. Of note, these skills and abilities, which we organized into the Building Blocks of Learning model, could be used to evaluate and then address children's difficulties in school.

A number of years later, we were fortunate to meet an editor at Paul H. Brookes Publishing Co. who asked if we would be interested in creating a book for teachers based on our Building Blocks model. The first edition of this volume was published in 2001 and then the second edition in 2008. In this third edition, we have made the following changes:

1. We have added a third author, Dr. Katie Eklund, who has additional expertise and experience in social-emotional development, school climate, and educational policy changes, such as implementation of the Common Core State Standards and multi-tiered systems of support (MTSS). In addition, we have several colleagues who have made significant contributions to specific chapters of this edition: Robert Brooks, Ph.D., Jennifer M. White, M.A., Lauren Meyer, M.A., Ann M. Richards, Ph.D., Deborah A. Schneider, Ed. S., and Gretchen Schoenfield, Ph.D., and Breanna Sherrow, M.A.

2. We have revised all chapters to include the most up-to-date research available.

3. We have added information on school climate and the importance of teacher–student relationships.

4. We have added information on MTSS, positive behavior interventions and supports, and social-emotional learning.

We have also modified the Building Blocks model, as well as the questionnaire used to assess a student's environment, behavior, and abilities. Although our model still emphasizes the underlying behaviors and skills that contribute to efficient learning, it has been revised to reflect the most recent educational, psychological, and neuropsychological research. Since the publication of the first and second editions, an increased emphasis has been placed on assessing the effectiveness of educators to teach basic skills in the areas of reading, writing, and mathematics. Terms such as *curriculum-based measurement, Common Core State Standards, high-stakes testing, accountability,* and *merit pay* are common terminology in the educational landscape. In an era in which educators are warned of the consequences of "leaving a child behind," some still fail to understand and appreciate how children learn, how they differ, and what are the best ways to help them when they struggle.

We are confident that the revised material in this third edition enhances and expands on the content presented in the first and second editions. It is our hope that this book will increase your understanding of children's learning and behavior difficulties. Throughout, we suggest many specific strategies and interventions to use to ensure that more struggling students are successfully educated and prepared for their futures. It is our belief that throughout this educational process, all children can be nurtured and guided to develop a resilient, optimistic view of themselves and their surrounding world, thus preparing them academically and emotionally for their future lives.

REFERENCES

Brooks, R., & Goldstein, S. (2001). *Raising resilient children: Fostering strength, hope, and optimism in your child.* New York, NY: Contemporary Books.

Brooks, R., & Goldstein, S. (2007). *Raising a self-disciplined child.* New York, NY: McGraw-Hill.

Brooks, R., & Goldstein, S. (2013). *Handbook of resilience in children* (2nd ed.). New York, NY: Springer.

Dweck, C. (2006). *Mindset: The new psychology of success.* New York, NY: Ballantine Books.

Goldstein, S., & Brooks, R. (2007). *Understanding and managing children's classroom behavior: Creating sustainable, resilient schools* (2nd ed.). New York, NY: Wiley.

Goldstein, S., & Mather, N. (1998). *Overcoming underachieving: An action guide for helping your child succeed in school.* New York, NY: Wiley.

Acknowledgments

We would like to express our gratitude to Lynne Jaffe, Nicole Ofiesh, Deborah A. Schneider, Michael E. Gerner, Jack Naglieri, and Connie Rissen for their helpful comments regarding revisions to the Building Blocks model. We would also like to thank our contributors for their assistance with this revision. Thanks also go to Rebecca Lazo at Paul H. Brookes Publishing Co. for her guidance throughout this project, as well as Danny Constantino, Michael Kingcaid, and Michael Miller at Scribe Inc.

We also wish to thank and express our admiration for the many inspired and dedicated educators who are the charismatic adults guiding children in their learning and development.

I would like to thank all the teachers and school psychologists I have known over many years who are determined to understand why students are struggling and the ways that school personnel can help. The lives of these children and their parents were made better because they were at your school.

—Nancy Mather

I want to thank the thousands of families over the past 35 years who have entrusted me with the diagnosis and care of their children. Helping them has gifted me with a lifetime of learning.

—Sam Goldstein

I would like to thank all the teachers, psychologists, social workers, counselors, principals, and other school staff I have worked with over the last 15 years. Your level of dedication, creativity, and commitment to the field are remarkable and continue to fuel my passion for this work.

—Katie Eklund

A Note to Teachers

Your best efforts in working with challenging students will be inspiring to other teachers and parents, but your efforts will give special encouragement to the students themselves, as illustrated in this letter from Andy, a 9-year-old boy, to his teacher.

Dear Ms. Caseman. Thank you for helping me with my writing this year. You listened to my ideas. Have a great summer.

To my son, Daniel: What a marvelous young man you have become! And to his fairy godmother, Vesta Hammond Udall, an extraordinary teacher who knew that the way to reach students is through sincere caring and respect. Thank you both for a lifetime of love and support.

—NM

For my grandchildren, Isaac and Avery, and my wonderful wife, Sherrie.

—SG

For my grandmothers, Phyllis, Florence, and Adele—all strong and beautiful women who dedicated their professional lives to teaching.

—KE

I've learned that people will forget what you said, will forget what you did, but will never forget how you made them feel.

—Maya Angelou

Tell me and I forget. Teach me and I remember. Involve me and I learn.

—Chinese proverb

I am not afraid of storms for I am learning to sail my ship.

—Louisa May Alcott

No one has yet fully realized the wealth of sympathy, kindness and generosity hidden in the soul of a child. The effort of every true education should be to unlock that treasure.

—Emma Goldman

SECTION I
Introduction

CHAPTER 1 OUTLINE

BUILDING BLOCKS OF LEARNING

The Learning Environment
Foundational Blocks
Processing Blocks
Conceptual Blocks
How the Blocks Work Together

COMMON PROFILES

Strengths in the Processing and Conceptual Blocks, Weaknesses in the Foundational Blocks, and a Disadvantaged Environment
Strengths in the Foundational and Conceptual Blocks, Weaknesses in the Processing Blocks, and a Supportive Environment
Strengths in the Foundational and Processing Blocks, Weaknesses in the Conceptual Blocks
Strengths in the Conceptual Blocks, Weaknesses in the Processing and Foundational Blocks
A Significant Strength or Weakness in One Block

BUILDING BLOCKS QUESTIONNAIRE

Completing the Building Blocks Questionnaire
Ryan's Profile

PURPOSE, OVERVIEW, AND AUDIENCE

APPENDIX 1A: BUILDING BLOCKS QUESTIONNAIRE

CHAPTER **1**

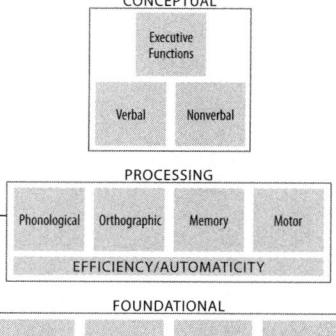

The Building Blocks of Learning

A Framework for Understanding Classroom Learning and Behavior

The last day of school at the Harper Unified School District was a cause for celebration as well as a time for reflection. Although both the teachers and students were looking forward to the summer break, the students were sad to leave their teachers. The teachers also had mixed feelings about the school year coming to an end, as they were worried about certain students. The teachers wanted all their students to be successful in school in the coming years, but they were most concerned about the children who had learning and/or behavior difficulties. On some days during the past year, these students were their teachers' greatest source of fulfillment; on other days, they were their teachers' greatest source of frustration. There were many days when thoughts of these students and their chances of being successful in school occupied their teachers' minds.

Veteran teachers know that students with learning and behavior difficulties face a challenging journey and that their education requires constant attention and fine tuning throughout the school year if they are to succeed. One such teacher, Ms. Abram, recognized this fact when working with Andy, one of her third-grade students. Although Andy could talk up a storm, he struggled with both fine and gross motor tasks. On the playground, balls would roll past him. He often tripped going up or down the school stairs. When the class played kickball, Andy usually wound up on the ground after attempting to kick the moving ball. Andy still could not tie his shoes, nor did he attempt to ride a bicycle. Although Ms. Abram had worked with Andy diligently all school year to improve his handwriting, he seemed to have made little progress. His spacing was still poor, and the size of his letters was inconsistent. One day, Andy left the following note on Ms. Abram's desk: "I'll see you later." (See Figure 1.1.)

Ms. Garcia was concerned about Beto, a fun-loving 8-year-old in her third-grade class. Beto was born and raised in New Mexico to Spanish-speaking parents who arrived in the United States just before his birth. Beto spoke only Spanish until he attended kindergarten, at which time he was placed in an English-only classroom. He received English as a second language (ESL) support services in kindergarten through second grade. Beto had always struggled with reading and writing in English. Each year, his teachers noted

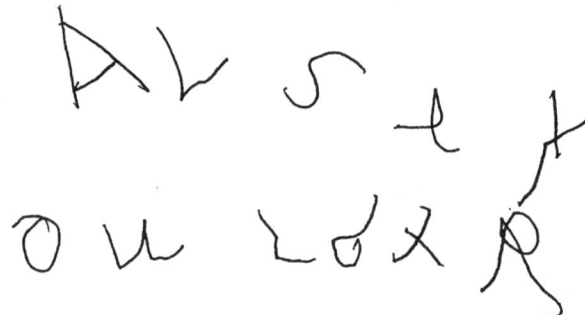

Figure 1.1. Andy's note to his third-grade teacher: "I'll see you later."

concerns. He had never been referred for testing because each teacher concluded that he was behind because he "was still acquiring English." At the end of second grade, he received the designation of "fully English proficient," or "FEP." As a result, he no longer received pull-out ESL services. By mid-year in third grade, Ms. Garcia knew that Beto was falling further and further behind.

Mr. Steen, a fourth-grade teacher, was thinking about Ryan. At the beginning of the year, Ryan entered Mr. Steen's classroom with very limited reading and math skills. Ryan seemed to have difficulty memorizing information; he knew few multiplication facts. He also had difficulty completing assigned tasks quickly. He complained about how hard tasks were and how much he disliked school. He was quick to tell others that he was "dumb" and that school was "stupid." Because of the daily visits to the resource room for individualized instruction and an adapted classroom program, Ryan's reading skills, attitude, and self-confidence had improved somewhat. Nevertheless, Mr. Steen was well aware that, because Ryan was so far behind, he would continue to struggle with reading, writing, and math tasks in the years ahead.

Whenever Ms. Taylor, a fourth-grade teacher, saw Stephanie on the playground, she was concerned that Stephanie did not interact with her peers appropriately. Stephanie often ran up to other children on the playground and pushed her way through them. When they told her to stop, Stephanie would look at them and move closer. Finally, the other children would walk away as a group, with Stephanie lagging behind, trying to get their attention. Ms. Taylor tried to create situations that would help Stephanie develop friendships, but nothing seemed to work. In the classroom, Stephanie spelled, memorized rote facts, and read words with ease. She talked quite easily about situations and information she knew well. At times, she seemed to go on and on with little point to the conversation. In contrast, when questioned about a story she had just read, Stephanie was unable to provide any answers. When she was asked to predict an answer or follow several directions, she often forgot what she was doing and was unable to complete the task.

Ms. McGrew, a fifth-grade teacher, was most concerned about Katy. Unlike Stephanie, Katy had several good friends, but she also struggled to learn new concepts and vocabulary. Although she memorized her spelling words easily, she had trouble using the words in sentences. She had memorized many math facts, but, after reading a story problem, she would ask, "What am I supposed to do? Add, subtract, or times it?" She often volunteered information in class, but her answers usually missed the mark. In the

The Building Blocks of Learning

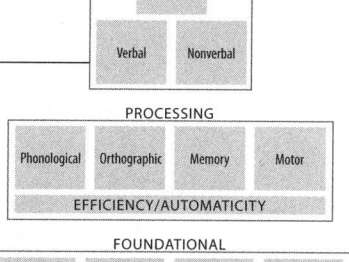

last month of the school year, when Ms. McGrew asked her students what they knew about the animal, a jaguar, Katy raised her hand and stated, "It's a car." The following year, Katy would start middle school and would work with six or more teachers each day. Ms. McGrew worried and wondered how Katy would keep up and obtain the individualized attention and support she would require in a new middle school environment.

Ms. Jones was thinking about Anthony, who had been in her fifth-grade class. Throughout the year in her classroom, he appeared withdrawn, quiet, and inattentive. Over the first few weeks of school, the quality of his work declined and he often appeared sad. One day, Ms. Jones found Anthony hiding in the closet. When she asked him to join the class, Anthony said he did not feel like it and would rather stay in the closet. Ms. Jones talked Anthony into coming out of the closet, but he refused to join the class, so she finally sent him to the nurse's office.

Mr. Chavez was preoccupied by thoughts of Jeremy, a fifth-grade student in his class. Jeremy's first-grade teacher had described him as a "moving target who can't control his movements." Although Jeremy had been diagnosed with attention-deficit/hyperactivity disorder (ADHD) and was receiving medical treatment and counseling, he still had trouble following directions and completing tasks. Mr. Chavez believed that Jeremy could do his schoolwork if he could only concentrate for longer periods of time and think through situations before he acted. One day, after blurting out a response in class, Jeremy explained, "I just can't keep the words in my mouth."

Ms. Perry's thoughts were on Mark, a sixth-grade student. She secretly wished she could adopt Mark. She knew the boy had a lot of potential, but every afternoon when he left school, he returned to a chaotic, inconsistent homelife. Mark, his two brothers, and one sister were living in a trailer with four adults. As Ms. Perry learned more about Mark's homelife, she came to understand why he never completed or handed in any homework or studied for the weekly quizzes. Knowing that she had no control over his home environment, she stopped assigning Mark homework and instead arranged a special daily study time for him at school. She even spent 2 days per week with Mark after school, helping him keep up with his assignments. One afternoon, Mark thanked Ms. Perry for liking him.

Mr. Arnold, a sixth-grade teacher, recognized early in the year that Maria was having trouble with reading and spelling. When reading aloud, she skipped words that were difficult to pronounce. Some of her attempted spellings bore little resemblance to the actual sound structure of the words. Mr. Arnold had asked Maria's mother if Maria's hearing had been checked and was assured that Maria had no difficulties with hearing. Maria's mother did mention, however, that Maria had experienced many ear infections during her preschool years. Her mother also reported that they typically spent 3–4 hours each evening completing her homework. Mr. Arnold recognized how hard Maria was working and how willing she was to attempt any task, but her reading and spelling skills were nevertheless far behind those of the majority of her classmates.

Thoughts of Samuel, a sixth-grade student who seemed to get in trouble for something every day, were never far from Ms. Handler's mind. In the past, Samuel had taken jewelry from other students, stolen lunch money, and even plucked the doorjambs from the classroom wall. Ms. Handler had to check Samuel's backpack each day to make sure that all the contents inside were his. He had been suspended twice during the school year, once for lighting a firecracker in the school hallway and another time for bringing a pocketknife to school. Recently, when he was asked by a student teacher to remove a hat from his desk, he refused. When the request was repeated, he picked up his chair and threw it at the teacher. Last week during lunchtime, he locked two children in the art supply closet.

Ms. Roberts, a middle school English teacher, was thinking about Ben, an eighth-grade student. Ben loved physical activities and sports. He excelled in soccer, baseball, and tennis. In school, he enjoyed challenging math, science, and computer activities. He loved to draw intricate sketches of machines and cars. Ben did not, however, enjoy activities involving reading and writing. Although he read fairly accurately, his reading rate was extremely low. When most of the students had already read 10 pages, Ben was just starting the second page. He often misspelled short common words, such as writing *thay* for *they*. He tried to avoid writing tasks by any means possible. Ms. Roberts wondered how Ben's high school teachers would respond to his limited writing skills and his negative attitude toward writing tasks.

Mr. Kelly considered how to help Marta, a freshman in high school. A shy girl with an amazingly sweet smile, Marta had arrived in the United States from Honduras 2 years earlier. According to her mother, Marta read and wrote well in Spanish, and there were no concerns about her school performance in Honduras. Once she began attending middle school in the United States, however, she received pull-out ESL services to support her English development. She learned how to speak English, but her reading and writing skills remained limited. Because there was no ESL teacher in her new high school, Marta received some help from the special education resource room teacher. The rationale for the provision of services by the special education teacher was that she was the teacher most qualified to provide scaffolding and support for literacy. Marta's history and language arts teachers were also concerned that Marta was not able to keep up in their classes.

Dr. Mantell's thoughts were on John, a junior in her American history class. Although John was enthusiastic about learning and always completed his homework assignments, he appeared to possess very poor study skills and had trouble grasping concepts. He received As on his homework assignments but never passed in-class tests. When he volunteered a response in class, his answers revealed his limited understanding. In fact, it seemed as though he possessed "Swiss cheese" knowledge. He appeared to understand some things but lacked basic knowledge in other areas. One day in class, when he was asked to name the country that bordered the United States on the northern side, he responded, "England." When asked what material was used to make paper, he responded, "Sodium." John had extreme difficulty understanding the concepts introduced in his science class, such as the difference between meiosis and mitosis. Even with tutoring three times a week, John could not understand or retain the concepts to pass the classroom tests.

For general and special education teachers who have been teaching several years, and school psychologists who have worked with children with learning and behavior problems in some capacity, the characteristics of these children are likely to sound familiar, and educators in training will soon come to recognize these characteristics as well. All children possess different learning styles and abilities. The reasons why one child struggles typically differ from the reasons why another child struggles, and learning and behavior difficulties are rarely resolved quickly or easily.

The Building Blocks of Learning

This is not a typical introductory textbook about specific learning disabilities (SLD) and classroom behavior problems. Although various learning and behavior problems are explained and informal ways to assess these difficulties are described, the main focus of this text is on identifying the developmental, learning, and behavior skills of children and then determining the practical strategies and techniques that will be most effective in helping them succeed in school. As illustrated by the brief descriptions of these students, each child has an individual style of learning and a unique set of circumstances. Increased awareness and understanding of a child's unique profile of strengths and weaknesses can help educators improve school-related outcomes.

BUILDING BLOCKS OF LEARNING

When a child struggles in school, teachers must first determine the underlying factors contributing to the learning or behavior problem, because when a child acts out, the reason may not be readily apparent. Similarly, when a child fails or refuses to complete work, it is rarely because of poor motivation. Lowered motivation in students is often a secondary symptom resulting from chronic failure and school difficulties. Over many years of working with students, school psychologists, special and general education teachers, and parents, we have developed and revised a simple framework for explaining why children experience learning and behavior problems in the classroom. This framework is called the Building Blocks of Learning (Goldstein & Mather, 1998). Although similar in intent to our original framework, this third edition contains an updated model and a revised questionnaire.

Our efforts to develop a working model of classroom problems and the reasons they occur, combined with our professional experiences, led us to conclude that the classroom behavior and learning problems of children could be represented using a three-level, triangular framework with the bottom of the triangle reflecting foundational skills, the middle of the triangle representing processing or perceptual skills, and the top of the triangle representing conceptual or thinking skills. The remainder of this chapter introduces the Building Blocks of Learning model. Chapter 2 reviews the theoretical foundations for the model.

Although the model has not yet undergone large-scale evaluation, we believe it is consistent with both past and present research and with the observations and reports from parents, teachers, and specialists throughout the years. The model offers a bridge between research and educational practice. Its intent is to help educators increase their understanding of the various reasons why children struggle in school and, more important, the ways in which professionals can help these students.

This model, presented in Figure 1.2, contains 12 Building Blocks stacked into the shape of a pyramid. At the base of the pyramid is the learning environment—an external variable that includes a child's home and classroom environments. The 12 blocks of the pyramid are divided into three distinct groups. At the base are the four Foundational blocks: *Self-Regulation, Behavior, Emotions,* and *Resilience.* The middle level contains a set of four Processing blocks: *Phonological, Orthographic, Memory,* and *Motor.* Underlying these four blocks is a support block: *Efficiency/Automaticity.* Automatic and easy processing facilitates all learning. The top level contains three Conceptual blocks: *Verbal,* for thinking with language; *Nonverbal,* for thinking with images and spatial reasoning; and *Executive Functions,* the top block, for thinking with strategies. The abilities in the Processing and Conceptual blocks affect different aspects of academic performance and learning.

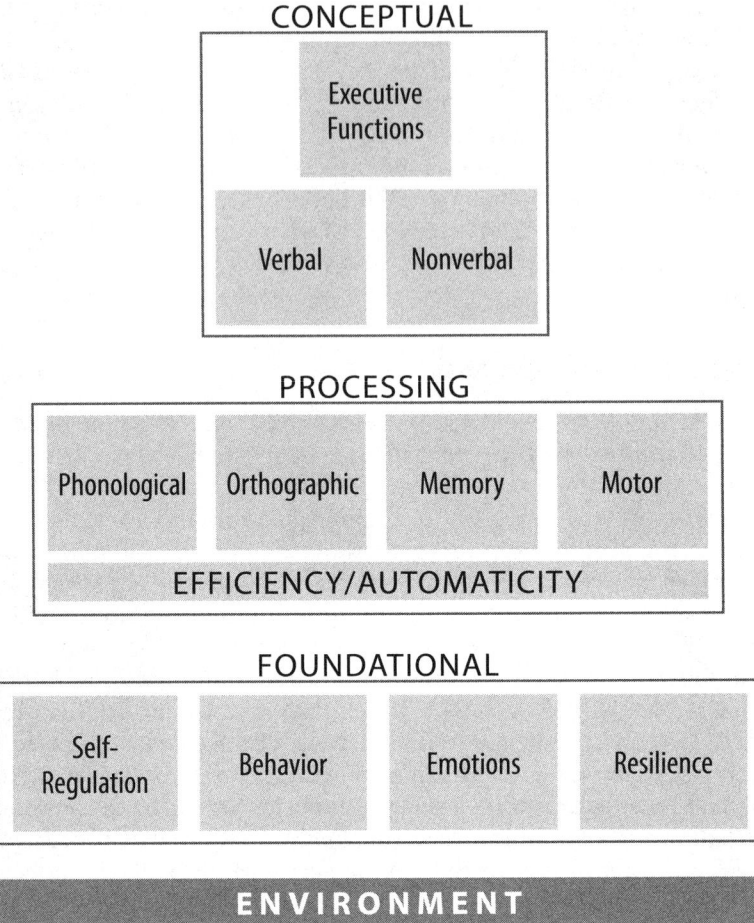

Figure 1.2. The Building Blocks of Learning model.

Many of the most common classroom learning and behavior problems can be represented clearly, described, and subsequently understood through the use of this model. We acknowledge that not all important school abilities are accounted for in this model; we also recognize that these blocks are not discrete units but rather encompass interrelated factors and abilities. Certain abilities do not fit neatly into one block, and some degree of overlap exists among the abilities in different blocks. For example, aspects of morphology, the meaning units of language, are relevant to the Phonological and Orthographic blocks, such as the skills needed to decode multisyllabic words by breaking words apart into prefixes, roots, and suffixes. Other aspects of morphology are more related to the Verbal block, such as how knowledge of the meaning of word parts can influence vocabulary development. The Memory block really affects all types of learning and is involved in the Processing blocks, as well as extending into all the Conceptual blocks. Different demands are placed on memory depending on the nature of the task. Working memory is involved in the earlier perceptual processes but also in the network of executive functions (Gathercole & Holmes, 2014). For example, memory is involved in learning multiplication facts or following the series of steps in a long division problem (Processing blocks) but also involved in retelling a story or planning a strategy to solve a problem (Conceptual blocks). As another example, some overlap exists among

The Building Blocks of Learning

the attentional demands within the Foundational block of Self-Regulation and the attentional control that is required in the Conceptual block of Executive Functions. As we explain the model, we will attempt to clarify these overlaps and distinctions. Although learning does not consist of isolated skills, identification of the unique affective, behavioral, cognitive, and linguistic variables that influence development and school performance can help educators understand a student's challenges and subsequently design appropriate behavioral and academic interventions.

The Learning Environment

Symbolically, the base of the pyramid is the learning environment. This includes the supports provided for the student in the home and school as well as any special services such as speech-language or occupational therapy that the student receives. Clearly, children's learning and behavior problems can be exacerbated by factors within the home and school settings. For example, lack of parental support coupled with chaos at home was having a significant effect on Mark's self-concept and his emotional availability to engage in academic tasks. Although Beto had a stable home environment, neither one of his parents spoke English. Thus, when he entered an English-only classroom, he was at a distinct disadvantage. Despite the fact that the home environment exerts a powerful influence on school adjustment, our focus in this book is on the learning environment at school. Classroom teachers have the primary responsibility for creating a nurturing class environment in which students feel respected, valued, and supported academically, socially, and emotionally.

Foundational Blocks

The Foundational blocks provide the support system for all learning. Just as the foundation of a house must be strong enough to support the structure, these four blocks must be strong for efficient learning to occur. A brief description of the skills in the Foundational blocks follows.

Self-Regulation

The Building Block of Self-Regulation includes a child's ability to pay attention, regulate behavior, and control impulses—all skills that are critical to learning. Mr. Chavez knew that the basis of many of Jeremy's attention and behavior difficulties stemmed from poor self-regulation and that his problems with impulse control prevented him from focusing on the relevant requirements of classroom learning tasks. Jeremy had trouble maintaining persistent effort and was easily distracted when attempting to pursue a goal. He had difficulty sticking with a plan for completing his assignments and rarely turned in work. He would often disturb other children.

Behavior

The Building Block of Behavior includes a student's covert and overt actions, including social skills and compliance. Conduct disorder, oppositional defiant disorder, and insufficient anger control all are examples of externalizing disorders and behaviors that influence interactions with teachers and peers. Samuel's behavior caused negative reactions from his peers. He would often shove another student or, without provocation, knock a student's books onto the floor. Ms. Handler had tried to implement several interventions, including moving Samuel's desk away from other students or sending him to time-out, but his disruptive behaviors continued.

Emotions

The Building Block of Emotions includes a child's general temperament as well as his or her moods. Problems in this block are sometimes called *internalizing disorders*—conditions such as depression, anxiety, and poor motivation. These disorders can significantly affect a child's availability to learn. Difficulties in school also affect attitude and performance. Ben had always struggled with reading and spelling, for example. These difficulties affected his attitude and his willingness to persevere on tasks requiring reading and writing.

Resilience

In our model, the Building Block of Resilience focuses on how students perceive themselves and to what factors they attribute their successes and failures. These are learned attitudes, developed in part through feedback from parents, teachers, and peers. Resilience is a quality that reduces risk and vulnerability while simultaneously enhancing functioning and development.

Poor academic self-efficacy can affect a child's resilience and willingness to persist on difficult tasks. Maria, the sixth-grade student, wrote about this in her journal (see Figure 1.3). Clearly, her struggles with spelling and writing were affecting her self-concept and perceptions of self-efficacy. Because of these difficulties, Maria was beginning to believe that she was not good at anything at all.

To succeed in school, a child requires a supportive classroom environment, the ability to sustain attention, self-discipline, healthy emotions, and a positive view of self and school. Strengths in the Foundational blocks help a student compensate for other difficulties and learn to persevere even when faced with difficult tasks. Weaknesses in the Foundational blocks affect school performance, and adverse factors such as anxiety or depression reduce a student's mental availability for learning. Strong Foundational blocks do not, however, guarantee school success. Some children have support at home and school, pay attention, and are happy and well adjusted but struggle because of specific cognitive and/or linguistic weaknesses in the Processing or Conceptual blocks.

Processing Blocks

The second level of the Building Blocks model involves the processing of information through the senses. The abilities in these blocks help children gain access to, produce, recall, and retrieve information about the symbolic aspects of language. Many terms have been applied to the deficient school achievement of this group, including SLD, underachievement, learning difficulty, dyslexia, and specific developmental disorders (Hinshaw, 1992).

In general, the abilities in the Processing blocks are conceptualized as secretarial in nature because these difficulties primarily affect basic skill development or the mastery of the coding systems of language: decoding (i.e., word identification), encoding (i.e., spelling), and motor coding (i.e., handwriting). Isaacson (1989) aptly distinguished between the roles of the secretary and the author in the writing process. The secretary manages the mechanical concerns of writing, such as spelling, punctuation, and handwriting (i.e., skills affected by strengths and weaknesses in the Processing blocks), whereas the author formulates, organizes,

The Building Blocks of Learning

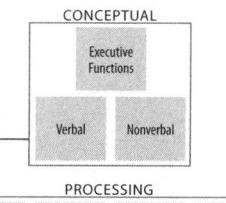

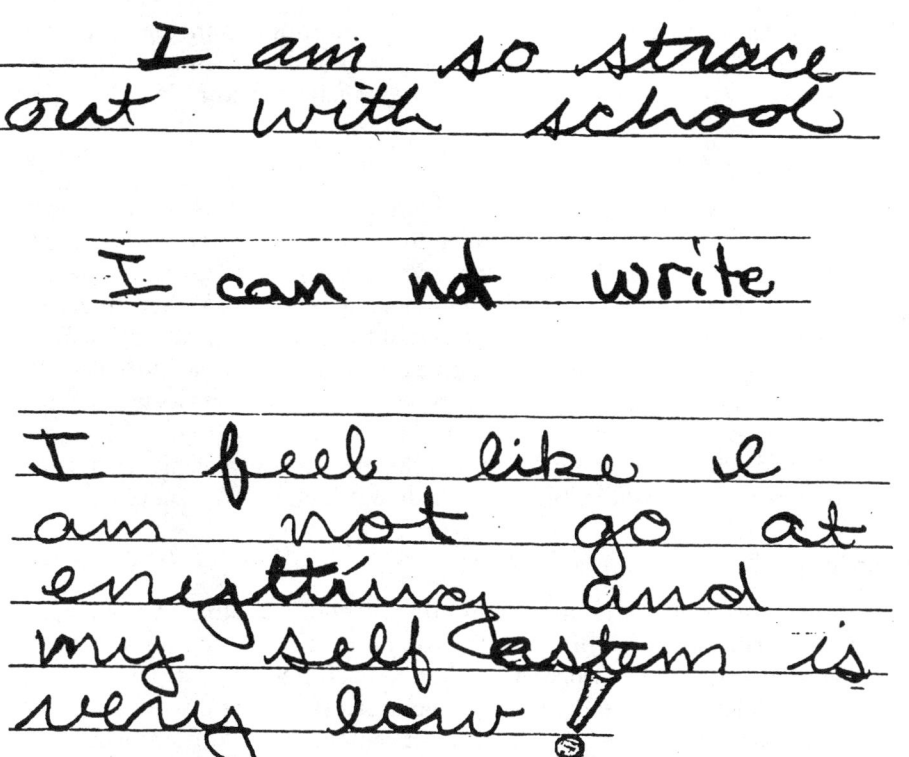

Figure 1.3. Maria's comments from her journal.

and expresses ideas (i.e., skills affected by strengths and weaknesses in the Conceptual blocks).

Some children have trouble with phonological processing tasks (e.g., rhyming words, identifying the discrete sounds in words). Other children have trouble with the orthographic or more visual aspects of learning to read and spell, such as remembering which way to write the letter *b* or how to spell the irregular element in a word. Certain children have trouble with aspects of memory, such as learning to say the months of the year in order or memorizing multiplication facts. Still others do poorly on the motor aspects of learning and, like Andy, have trouble cutting with scissors or learning to form letters. Eventually, these abilities become increasingly more automatic (with little thinking involved) as performance becomes more effortless and efficient. Children with marked weaknesses in these blocks are often diagnosed as having SLD. A brief description of the skills represented in these blocks follows.

Phonological

This block encompasses phonological processing, an oral language ability that helps individuals to understand the sound structure of speech. Phonological awareness allows the individual to manipulate language sounds. As students learn an alphabetic language such as English, a critical first step in prereading is becoming aware that speech can be divided or sequenced into a series of discrete sounds, words, syllables, and phonemes, or the smallest units of sound. In most children, this awareness develops gradually during the preschool and early elementary years. Maria's difficulties with reading and spelling were caused by poor phonological awareness. She had trouble discriminating similar speech sounds and often would omit sounds when spelling a word or confuse certain sounds, such as writing *f* for the /v/ sound.

Orthographic

The next block is orthographic processing. In a general sense, *orthography* refers to the writing system of a language, including the punctuation marks, capitalization rules, and spelling patterns. In a narrower sense, orthography refers to the perception and recall of letter strings and word forms. This ability, referred to as orthographic awareness, allows the individual to form a mental representation of the appearance of a letter or word. In addition, orthographic sensitivity helps one become aware of the common spelling patterns and word parts as well as the rules about legal letter strings or combinations that exist in a language. For example, most first-grade children quickly learn that the letters *ck* can be placed at the end of a word to make the /k/ sound but not at the beginning of a word.

Memory

Several different types of memory can affect school learning. In reality, aspects of memory permeate all learning. Verbal short-term memory refers to the ability to repeat in a serial order information that has just been heard. This type of skill is needed to follow directions in a classroom or take notes during a lecture. Difficulty with memory is also associated with remembering rote information, such as learning the letters and their names or memorizing multiplication facts. This type of memory is often referred to as paired-associate learning or associative memory.

Some memory abilities are more complex and include aspects of two or more blocks, such as working memory. Working memory refers to the ability to apprehend information and then rearrange it in a specified way. A simple example would be to ask someone to listen to a series of digits and then ask him or her to say the digits back in a reversed order. This type of ability requires verbal short-term memory as well as the ability to visualize and rearrange the digits (nonverbal) and the ability to use strategies (executive functions). In some cases, a student's academic difficulties are primarily related to a weakness in some aspect of memory. In other cases, poor performance on tasks involving memory is more related to weaknesses in self-regulation or verbal ability.

Motor

This block includes fine motor tasks—tasks involving small muscles such as those used in writing or drawing. Although it also includes gross motor skills, or skills involving the large muscles, such as jumping and running, fine motor skills are more related to school performance. Fine motor skills can be broken into two types: 1) symbol production (i.e., writing letters and numbers) and 2) artistic expression (i.e., drawing a picture). Some children can sketch or draw wonderful illustrations but are stymied by the production of symbols. This difficulty with producing the motor patterns needed for writing is sometimes referred to as dysgraphia. Andy possessed weaknesses in motor planning that made it difficult to perform most types of fine motor tasks with ease; however, he was an excellent artist.

The Building Blocks of Learning

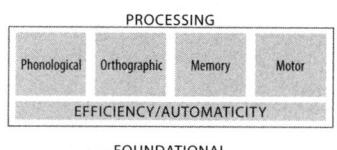
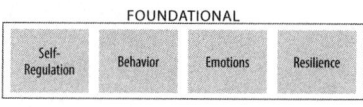

Efficiency/Automaticity

This block, at the base of the Processing blocks, involves automatic and efficient retrieval, or the speed of recognition and production of letters, numbers, and words. This ability is needed to recall quickly basic sight vocabulary for both reading and spelling and to solve a page of math facts quickly. A child with initial weaknesses in this block is likely to have a slow reading rate and poor spelling in later years. In fact, Ben's major problems with reading and spelling were due to both his poor orthographic awareness and his slow speed of word perception. Often a student with a weakness in this block will have low scores on measures of processing speed or rapid automatized naming (RAN).

In general, as skills become increasingly automatic, students are more able to perform secretarial tasks such as accurately and fluently identifying words, taking notes, and memorizing math facts. Once a child has learned a task, which may require repeated practice, these skills become increasingly automatic, or *automatized,* and are performed with little thought and effort. For example, when a child has learned to read a word, the word is recognized instantly when it is encountered, and, as a child learns to write letters, the speed and ease of writing these symbols increase. The best way to become an expert is through practice—the more practice the better (Rosenshine, 2012).

Skills in the Processing blocks help children perform various tasks, but these skills alone do not guarantee school success. Some children have no difficulty learning to read, spell, write, and solve math computations. These children perform automatic processing tasks with ease; however, when the curriculum begins to accelerate and the children must read to learn, they may struggle because of weaknesses in language or reasoning skills. They may be capable of mastering basic mathematical processes but struggle with more complex mathematics because of difficulties with spatial reasoning and concept formation. In our model, these types of difficulties relate to the abilities of the Conceptual blocks.

Conceptual Blocks

The top of the pyramid includes the Conceptual abilities: Verbal, Nonverbal, and Executive Functions. The abilities in the Conceptual blocks help students to understand meanings, comprehend relationships, visualize complex designs, apply previously acquired knowledge, and evaluate their performance as they engage in academic tasks.

Verbal

The Verbal block includes tasks that involve thinking with language, such as understanding what is heard, comprehending written text, expressing ideas through speaking and writing, learning and using new vocabulary, and solving mathematical story problems. Students with strengths in language tend to speak easily and possess an expansive vocabulary. Students with weaknesses in language often have trouble with tasks involving both comprehension and production of text. Katy had weaknesses in language, and, consequently, her answers often missed the mark. One day, Ms. McGrew showed Katy a picture of four trees and then asked her, "Half of these trees would be how many?" As she drew a horizontal line across the trees, Katy asked, "You mean if you cut them this way?"

Nonverbal

The Nonverbal block includes tasks that involve thinking with images, such as the abilities involved in reproducing complex visual patterns and designs as well as understanding and judging spatial relationships. Some children have more difficulty with tasks of a nonverbal nature than with those involving language. These children tend to have particular difficulty grasping and acquiring mathematical concepts. They also may have trouble with developing social competence and recognizing, evaluating, and interpreting gestures and facial expressions. Stephanie had a lot of trouble interpreting facial expressions and could not readily assess how others were feeling. This block represents some problems associated with what is often referred to as nonverbal learning disabilities (NVLDs).

Executive Functions

The top block on the model is Executive Functions. Executive functions encompass the abilities to monitor performance and act strategically to solve problems and complete tasks. These skills and abilities are used to direct all cognitive activities and include the abilities to plan, organize, monitor, evaluate, and reflect on one's own learning. This block is placed at the top of the model because of its importance to all learning and behavior. Strengths in this block help students to be purposeful and engage in goal-directed behavior. Ultimately, if students can be strategic, they are better able to maximize their performance while compensating or adjusting for weaknesses. This block includes thinking about thinking, or what is referred to as metacognition.

How the Blocks Work Together

In thinking about the learning and behavior of students, one can understand the role that specific weaknesses in one or more of the Building Blocks can play in creating school difficulties. Ryan had weaknesses in the Processing blocks. These contributed to his reading difficulties and consequently affected his self-esteem. Katy had weaknesses in the Conceptual blocks, and she struggled to comprehend tasks that involved using language and reasoning. Jeremy struggled with weaknesses in the Foundational block of Self-Regulation. Although Ben could produce intricate sketches of machines and rebuild a motorcycle engine, he had trouble spelling even common words. Ben's weakness in orthography affected his ability to store and retrieve a mental image of the appearance of words. His marked difficulty with spelling contributed to a negative attitude toward all types of writing tasks. Mark came from a disadvantaged environment in which little support was provided for learning in the home. Marta had weaknesses in English but not in her native language.

When the blocks are stacked together as a model, it is easy to understand how a student's unique learning and behavior characteristics, as well as the child's support system and environment, can affect school success. When considering the unique characteristics of each student, the first goal is to identify specific strengths and how these abilities can be used to enhance performance; the second is to identify weaknesses so that appropriate accommodations and instructional plans can be developed and implemented.

The Building Blocks of Learning

COMMON PROFILES

Children's difficulties result from qualitative differences, and many different combinations of skills are possible. "One size fits all" does not apply to the learning abilities or disabilities of children. When designing academic and behavioral interventions for specific students, a more accurate adage is "One size fits one." We have, however, encountered a few frequently occurring general profiles. We describe five of the most common profiles in the following sections.

Strengths in the Processing and Conceptual Blocks, Weaknesses in the Foundational Blocks, and a Disadvantaged Environment

Some children have the language, reasoning, and processing abilities needed for school achievement but are hampered by emotional or behavioral issues. The difficulties that some children experience in school can be related directly to weaknesses in the Foundational blocks. Students who experience trouble with self-regulation or have serious emotional or behavior problems may be mentally unavailable for learning. Other children, like Mark, return home each evening to a chaotic or extremely stressful home environment. This constant disruption at home can reduce the child's ability to profit from instruction. In most instances, once their attentional, emotional, or social issues have been addressed and resolved, these children can succeed in school.

Strengths in the Foundational and Conceptual Blocks, Weaknesses in the Processing Blocks, and a Supportive Environment

Some students possess above-average language and reasoning abilities and the ability to sustain attention, and they live in supportive homes and participate in nurturing school environments. In spite of their many capabilities, their marked weaknesses in the Processing blocks affect their ability to learn and memorize specific types of information. Although these children may be well adjusted and highly motivated, they struggle with school tasks that require rote learning and memory, such as reading words, spelling, or calculating. They are slow to develop automaticity with word reading and spelling and may be diagnosed as having dyslexia, dysgraphia, or dyscalculia (specific reading, writing, or math disability). With understanding and systematic, intensive interventions, as well as curricular adjustments and accommodations throughout their school careers, these students can be successful.

Strengths in the Foundational and Processing Blocks, Weaknesses in the Conceptual Blocks

Students with weaknesses in the Conceptual blocks have trouble with tasks involving reasoning and language. These students have particular difficulty with tasks involving comprehending and expressing ideas and problem solving. In contrast, because of strengths in the Processing blocks, they can memorize spelling words and math facts easily but have trouble applying these skills to real-life problems. A modified and adapted curriculum coupled with direct instruction in the use of language and the application of strategies can help these students improve their chances for school success.

Strengths in the Conceptual Blocks, Weaknesses in the Processing and Foundational Blocks

Some children with strengths in thinking and reasoning have weaknesses in processing and attending to information. For example, some students with SLD often receive the dual diagnosis of SLD and ADHD. In other cases, students with SLD lack resilience or have emotional or behavior problems. These problems contribute further to reduced motivation and school failure. With appropriate, often intensive, long-term interventions, these children can succeed in school.

A Significant Strength or Weakness in One Block

Some students excel in one area. Although Ben was having trouble with reading and writing, he was an extremely talented athlete. His success in sports helped him maintain a positive view of himself. Maria had trouble with the sounds of language but not with tasks involving thinking with language. Her strong ability to reason with language enabled her to learn through listening and compensate somewhat for her phonological processing problems.

Other students possess a significant weakness in only one area that often results in a specific diagnosis and eligibility for special services. For example, a student with a specific weakness in phonology or orthography may be diagnosed with dyslexia. A student with severe problems in motor skills may be classified as having a sensory motor integration disorder or dysgraphia. Similarly, a student with serious behavior problems may be classified as having an emotional or behavior disorder. A student with persistent problems in self-regulation may be diagnosed as having ADHD. A student with a significant problem in language acquisition or use may be classified as having a language impairment. Students with severe weaknesses in one domain often require intensive and systematic interventions to succeed in school. Maria, Jeremy, and Andy are all examples of students with marked weaknesses in one area. To compensate, these children must learn how to rely on their strengths in addition to receiving accommodations and interventions designed to mitigate their weaknesses.

BUILDING BLOCKS QUESTIONNAIRE

The Building Blocks Questionnaire, presented in Appendix 1A and available as a download, is designed to help educators pinpoint a student's strengths and weaknesses and to provide an overview of school-related skills and behaviors. This questionnaire has two sections. Part 1 provides 13 questions—1 question for the environment and then 1 for each of the 12 Building Blocks—which are intended to provide a general overview of a student's strengths and weaknesses. For example, under Foundational, for the Emotions block, the general question would be, "Does the student appear to be sad or anxious more often than not during the day?" The user would indicate whether this was true by checking the options *Rarely, Sometimes,* or *Frequently.* Part 2 provides an additional 10 items for the environment and then an additional 10 items for the other 12 blocks in order to provide more in-depth information about the behavior or ability.

Completing the Building Blocks Questionnaire

When concerns exist about a certain student, a teacher can make a copy of the Building Blocks Questionnaire and then complete it. A parent also can fill out the

The Building Blocks of Learning

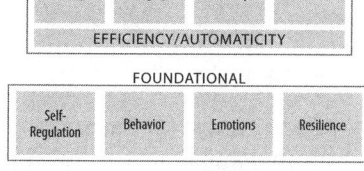

questionnaire, or a teacher or school psychologist may interview the student and complete the questionnaire. The purpose of completing the questionnaire is to gain a better understanding of the factors contributing to a student's successes and struggles in school. When teachers are able to understand the reasons why a student is struggling in school, they are more efficient at determining and designing appropriate interventions. In addition, when teachers are aware of a student's strengths, they can build on these abilities in designing programs and selecting interventions.

Ryan's Profile

Mr. Steen, Ryan's fourth-grade teacher, thought about Ryan as he answered the 13 questions in Part 1 of the Building Blocks Questionnaire (see Figure 1.4). He had noted that on occasion, Ryan seemed inattentive, so he checked *Sometimes* for Self-Regulation. Ryan usually followed school rules, so Mr. Steen checked *Rarely* for Behavior. At times during the day, Ryan seemed sad, so Mr. Steen checked *Sometimes* for Emotions. Ryan often complained about how much he disliked school and was quick to tell others that he was "dumb," so Mr. Steen checked *Frequently* for Resilience. Ryan had started the year with very limited reading and spelling skills, so Mr. Steen checked *Frequently* for both the Phonology and Orthography questions. Ryan had difficulty with memory, so Mr. Steen checked *Frequently* for the Memory question. Ryan did not seem to have difficulty with motor tasks, so *Rarely* was checked for that block. Ryan did, however, work slowly on most tasks, so Mr. Steen checked *Frequently* for the Efficiency/Automaticity question. Ryan enjoyed science and math activities and had an adequate vocabulary, so Mr. Steen checked *Rarely* for the Verbal and Nonverbal questions. Ryan was, however, inconsistent in devising and sticking with plans, so Mr. Steen checked *Sometimes* for the Executive Functions question. He then completed Part 2 for the questions that were answered *Sometimes* and *Frequently*. The completed questionnaire helped Mr. Steen get a sense of the kinds of tasks that would be easy for Ryan and the kinds of tasks that would be difficult. As a result, Mr. Steen was able to develop an effective educational program to help Ryan improve his self-esteem and attitude as well as his basic skills in reading, spelling, and math.

PURPOSE, OVERVIEW, AND AUDIENCE

The information in this book does not address all the learning and behavior problems experienced by children. Its purpose is to help general education teachers and specialists—such as school psychologists, speech-language therapists, and special education teachers—to increase their understanding of the factors that influence a student's school performance. The goal is to help professionals involved in education increase their knowledge about the ways that developmental, behavior, and academic problems influence school performance and the ways in which these problems can be addressed.

As we have discussed, the Building Blocks model was developed, in part, through our many years of consulting, teaching, and counseling children and their families. The first requirement for helping a student is to form a clear understanding of his or her unique characteristics by evaluating his or her strengths and weaknesses. The next step is to determine the types of educational and behavioral interventions needed and to develop meaningful, realistic educational goals. A student's strengths and weaknesses in these 12 blocks can affect multiple areas of learning. Before reading further, you may wish to review the Building Blocks Questionnaire in Appendix 1A (also available as a download) and complete it for one or more students. When learning and behavior are viewed through the lens of this model, it is easy to understand why children such as Andy, Beto, Jeremy, Katy, Ben, and Marta are struggling in school and, more important, what can be done to mitigate their problems.

Building Blocks Questionnaire

Student's name **Ryan** Grade **4th**

Teacher's/Parent's name **Mr. Steen** Date **5/30**

PART 1

The 12 questions composing Part 1 are general and provide an overview of the student's school-related skills and behavior. For each of the Building Blocks described with questions in the left-hand column, indicate with a check mark whether the student exhibits the behavior rarely, sometimes, or frequently. Once you have completed Part 1, for each of the questions you have answered *Frequently* or *Sometimes,* proceed to Part 2 of the questionnaire and complete the additional 10 items corresponding to that Building Block. For example, if you answered *Frequently* to "Does the student appear inattentive or impulsive?" under the Foundational Self-Regulation item, then you would proceed to the second section of Part 2 and answer the additional 10 items under the category of Self-Regulation.

FOUNDATIONAL	Rarely	Sometimes	Frequently
Environment: The student's school environment is not conducive to learning.	✓		
1. *Self-Regulation:* Does the student appear inattentive or impulsive?		✓	
2. *Behavior:* Does the student have trouble following the rules?	✓		
3. *Emotions:* Does the student appear to be sad or anxious more often than not during the day?		✓	
4. *Resilience:* Does the student appear to cope poorly in the face of problems?			✓

PROCESSING	Rarely	Sometimes	Frequently
5. *Phonological:* Does the student have difficulty hearing or applying letter sounds when speaking, reading, or spelling?			✓
6. *Orthographic:* Does the student have trouble reading or spelling words with irregular elements (e.g., *once*)?			✓
7. *Memory:* Does the student have difficulty repeating information just heard?			✓
8. *Motor:* Does the student have difficulty forming letters or writing legibly?	✓		
9. *Efficiency/Automaticity:* Does the student have trouble completing tasks quickly?			✓

CONCEPTUAL	Rarely	Sometimes	Frequently
10. *Verbal:* Does the student have trouble using or understanding oral language?	✓		
11. *Nonverbal:* Does the student have difficulty creating mental pictures?	✓		
12. *Executive Functions:* Does the student have trouble forming or following a plan?		✓	

Figure 1.4. Building Blocks Questionnaire, Part 1, as completed for Ryan.

The Building Blocks of Learning

This book is also designed to serve as a text or supplement in undergraduate and graduate introductory, characteristics, and methods courses in SLD and behavior problems. In addition to school psychologists, special educators, and counselors, preservice and in-service general education teachers can use this book to increase their understanding of the types of problems that their students will face and the specific teaching techniques and materials that they can use to help students overcome these difficulties. Unlike many other texts and resources outlining SLD and behavior problems, this text focuses on developing an understanding of the underlying causes of a student's problems. We stress the importance of identifying an individual's underlying strengths and weaknesses for the purpose of designing an effective intervention program.

In Section I, the introductory section, Chapter 2 provides the theoretical rationale for the Building Blocks model. Chapter 3 discusses the importance of a positive, nurturing learning environment.

Section II addresses the Foundational blocks. Each chapter addresses a specific Building Block: Self-Regulation, Behavior, Emotions, and Resilience. If a student has problems in any of the Foundational blocks, we suggest that you turn to the questionnaire, answer the 10 additional items, and then read the relevant Foundational block chapter.

Section III addresses the Processing blocks. If a student has problems in any of the Processing blocks (Phonological, Orthographic, Memory, Motor, or Efficiency/Automaticity), we suggest you turn to the Processing blocks section of the questionnaire, answer the additional items about the student's skills and abilities, and then read the chapters in this section.

Section IV addresses the Conceptual blocks. If the student has difficulty with any of the three Conceptual blocks (Executive Functions, Verbal, or Nonverbal), we suggest you turn to the Conceptual blocks section in Part 2 of the questionnaire, answer the additional items about the student's conceptual abilities, and then read the chapters in this section.

Finally, if you are in training, working as a consultant with teachers, or working in a classroom with many children, we suggest that you read through this entire text. Many of the ideas and techniques presented in this book have been used for years by special educators and school psychologists working with students who are experiencing school problems. The techniques are practical, supported by evidence-based research, and are relatively easy to implement.

One conclusion from research is clear: For children with learning problems, learning is hard work; for their teachers, instruction is very hard work and requires an enormous amount of training and support (Semrud-Clikeman, 2005). Effective education for students struggling with learning and behavior is dependent, however, on the individual actions of competent and caring professionals (Kauffman & Landrum, 2012) and the implementation of an individualized approach that provides effective teaching strategies (Zigmond, 2004). It is our hope that all children struggling in school will receive instruction from caring, sympathetic teachers who understand learning, behavioral, and temperamental differences and know when and how to intervene to help support these students in their growth and development.

APPENDIX **1A**

Building Blocks Questionnaire

Building Blocks Questionnaire

Student's name _____   Grade _____

Teacher's/Parent's name _____   Date _____

PART 1

The 12 questions composing Part 1 are general and provide an overview of the student's school-related skills and behavior. For each of the Building Blocks described with questions in the left-hand column, indicate with a check mark whether the student exhibits the behavior rarely, sometimes, or frequently. Once you have completed Part 1, for each of the questions you have answered *Frequently* or *Sometimes*, proceed to Part 2 of the questionnaire and complete the additional 10 items corresponding to that Building Block. For example, if you answered *Frequently* to "Does the student appear inattentive or impulsive?" under the Foundational Self-Regulation item, then you would proceed to the second section of Part 2 and answer the additional 10 items under the category of Self-Regulation.

FOUNDATIONAL

	Rarely	Sometimes	Frequently
Environment: The student's school environment is not conducive to learning.	☐	☐	☐
1. *Self-Regulation:* Does the student appear inattentive or impulsive?	☐	☐	☐
2. *Behavior:* Does the student have trouble following the rules?	☐	☐	☐
3. *Emotions:* Does the student appear to be sad or anxious more often than not during the day?	☐	☐	☐
4. *Resilience:* Does the student appear to cope poorly in the face of problems?	☐	☐	☐

PROCESSING

5. *Phonological:* Does the student have difficulty hearing or applying letter sounds when speaking, reading, or spelling?	☐	☐	☐
6. *Orthographic:* Does the student have trouble reading or spelling words with irregular elements (e.g., *once*)?	☐	☐	☐
7. *Memory:* Does the student have difficulty repeating information just heard?	☐	☐	☐
8. *Motor:* Does the student have difficulty forming letters or writing legibly?	☐	☐	☐
9. *Efficiency/Automaticity:* Does the student have trouble completing tasks quickly?	☐	☐	☐

CONCEPTUAL

10. *Verbal:* Does the student have trouble using or understanding oral language?	☐	☐	☐
11. *Nonverbal:* Does the student have difficulty creating mental pictures?	☐	☐	☐
12. *Executive Functions:* Does the student have trouble forming or following a plan?	☐	☐	☐

Building Blocks Questionnaire *(continued)*

PART 2

In Part 2, the Building Blocks described in the questions in Part 1 are grouped according to the levels of the pyramid. In order to get more in-depth information about a student's strengths and weaknesses in these various areas, complete the 10 items for each corresponding block for the items for which you answered *Frequently* or *Sometimes* in Part 1.

FOUNDATIONAL

Environment

	Rarely	Sometimes	Frequently
Time is allocated inefficiently in the classroom.	☐	☐	☐
Student does not get along with peers in the classroom.	☐	☐	☐
When the teacher gives directions, the student does not comply.	☐	☐	☐
A standardized system does not exist for enforcing rules and consequences.	☐	☐	☐
The classroom is not conducive to learning.	☐	☐	☐
The teacher does not have a method for providing group instruction.	☐	☐	☐
Strategies are not in place to improve student compliance.	☐	☐	☐
Classroom expectations are unclear.	☐	☐	☐
Communication with parents is ineffective.	☐	☐	☐
A system is not in place to assign, follow up with, and collect homework.	☐	☐	☐

Self-Regulation

	Rarely	Sometimes	Frequently
Appears restless and fidgety	☐	☐	☐
Shows inconsistencies in behavior depending on the type of task	☐	☐	☐
Has trouble staying seated	☐	☐	☐
Seems to act before thinking	☐	☐	☐
Fails to finish tasks	☐	☐	☐
Has trouble making transitions	☐	☐	☐
Has difficulty working independently on schoolwork or homework	☐	☐	☐
Has trouble persisting on routine tasks for extended periods of time	☐	☐	☐
Has difficulty listening to and following directions	☐	☐	☐
Interrupts others	☐	☐	☐

Building Blocks Questionnaire *(continued)*

FOUNDATIONAL

Behavior

	Rarely	Sometimes	Frequently
Has difficulty getting along with peers	☐	☐	☐
Is frequently in trouble at school	☐	☐	☐
Lacks engagement in classroom instruction	☐	☐	☐
Does not respond to discipline as expected	☐	☐	☐
Disturbs or distracts others	☐	☐	☐
Makes inappropriate physical contact with peers (e.g., shoving, pinching)	☐	☐	☐
Insults others verbally	☐	☐	☐
Refuses to comply when asked	☐	☐	☐
Seems argumentative	☐	☐	☐
Hurts self or others	☐	☐	☐

Emotions

	Rarely	Sometimes	Frequently
Appears sad	☐	☐	☐
Changes mood quickly	☐	☐	☐
Worries excessively	☐	☐	☐
Complains of or presents with physical ailments (e.g., nausea, fatigue, headache)	☐	☐	☐
Appears tense and anxious	☐	☐	☐
Cries	☐	☐	☐
Isolates self from others / has poor peer relationships	☐	☐	☐
Has difficulty listening to and following directions	☐	☐	☐
Seems bored or disinterested	☐	☐	☐
Puts forth little effort	☐	☐	☐

Building Blocks Questionnaire *(continued)*

FOUNDATIONAL

Resilience

	Rarely	Sometimes	Frequently
Seems disinterested in academic tasks	☐	☐	☐
Complains about not being smart	☐	☐	☐
Complains that academic tasks are too difficult	☐	☐	☐
Has limited interactions with classmates	☐	☐	☐
Complains about not being liked	☐	☐	☐
Makes negative comments about self	☐	☐	☐
Gives up easily on tasks and assignments	☐	☐	☐
Seems overly sensitive to criticism	☐	☐	☐
Has trouble with stressful situations	☐	☐	☐
Seems to lack self-confidence	☐	☐	☐

PROCESSING

Phonological

	Rarely	Sometimes	Frequently
Has trouble rhyming words	☐	☐	☐
Has difficulty producing or pronouncing certain sounds	☐	☐	☐
Has trouble putting sounds together to pronounce words (blending) when reading	☐	☐	☐
Has difficulty breaking sounds apart in words (segmenting) when spelling	☐	☐	☐
Has trouble manipulating sounds (e.g., substitution, deletion)	☐	☐	☐
Has trouble distinguishing letters with similar sounds (e.g., /b/ and /p/, /f/, and /v/) in speech and when spelling	☐	☐	☐
Has difficulty sounding out words	☐	☐	☐
Has trouble ordering sounds in a correct sequence when spelling	☐	☐	☐
Has trouble pronouncing multisyllabic words	☐	☐	☐
Confuses words that sound alike	☐	☐	☐

Building Blocks Questionnaire *(continued)*

PROCESSING

Orthographic

	Rarely	Sometimes	Frequently
Forgets how letters look	☐	☐	☐
Confuses letters with similar appearance (e.g., *n* for *h*)	☐	☐	☐
Misreads little words in text (e.g., *were* for *where*)	☐	☐	☐
Reverses letters when spelling (e.g., *b* instead of *d*)	☐	☐	☐
Transposes letters when reading or writing (e.g., *on* instead of *no*)	☐	☐	☐
Has trouble remembering irregular words for reading and spelling	☐	☐	☐
Has difficulty copying from a book or board to paper	☐	☐	☐
Spells the same word in different ways	☐	☐	☐
Spells words the way they sound rather than the way they look	☐	☐	☐
Reads at a slow rate	☐	☐	☐

Memory

	Rarely	Sometimes	Frequently
Has trouble following multistep directions	☐	☐	☐
Has trouble learning the days of the week and months of the year in sequence	☐	☐	☐
Has trouble repeating sentences accurately	☐	☐	☐
Has trouble skip counting in math (e.g., 2, 4, 6 . . .)	☐	☐	☐
Gets confused when solving multistep problems	☐	☐	☐
Has trouble memorizing math facts	☐	☐	☐
Forgets previously learned information	☐	☐	☐
Forgets studied information for tests	☐	☐	☐
Forgets materials, due dates, and/or required assignments	☐	☐	☐
Has trouble with mental math	☐	☐	☐

Building Blocks Questionnaire (continued)

PROCESSING

Motor

	Rarely	Sometimes	Frequently
Draws pictures that seem immature for age	☐	☐	☐
Has difficulties with tasks involving fine motor coordination (e.g., tying shoes)	☐	☐	☐
Seems disinterested in learning to write	☐	☐	☐
Has trouble holding a pencil or pen correctly	☐	☐	☐
Forms letters in odd ways (e.g., starts from the bottom rather than the top)	☐	☐	☐
Has poor spacing between letters and words	☐	☐	☐
Has papers that appear messy	☐	☐	☐
Has unusual letter formations	☐	☐	☐
Has difficulty learning cursive writing	☐	☐	☐
Has a slow rate of writing	☐	☐	☐

Efficiency/Automaticity

	Rarely	Sometimes	Frequently
Requires more time to complete tasks	☐	☐	☐
Has difficulty naming things rapidly	☐	☐	☐
Requires more time on tests	☐	☐	☐
Has a slow speed completing routine tasks	☐	☐	☐
Retrieves information slowly	☐	☐	☐
Performs step-by-step processes slowly	☐	☐	☐
Completes detailed assignments slowly	☐	☐	☐
Has a slow rate of reading	☐	☐	☐
Has a slow rate of writing	☐	☐	☐
Has a slow rate of completing math computations	☐	☐	☐

Building Blocks Questionnaire *(continued)*

CONCEPTUAL

Verbal

	Rarely	Sometimes	Frequently
Was slow to develop and use oral language	☐	☐	☐
Has limited speaking vocabulary	☐	☐	☐
Has problems retrieving specific words	☐	☐	☐
Has trouble answering questions	☐	☐	☐
Has difficulty organizing and expressing ideas when speaking	☐	☐	☐
Has difficulty sustaining meaningful conversations	☐	☐	☐
Makes grammatical errors when speaking or writing	☐	☐	☐
Has trouble understanding what is read	☐	☐	☐
Has trouble expressing ideas when writing	☐	☐	☐
Has trouble solving math story problems	☐	☐	☐

Nonverbal

	Rarely	Sometimes	Frequently
Has trouble putting puzzles together	☐	☐	☐
Has difficulty distinguishing left from right	☐	☐	☐
Has trouble judging distances	☐	☐	☐
Has trouble with tasks involving spatial reasoning	☐	☐	☐
Has difficulty creating mental images when reading	☐	☐	☐
Has difficulty with the visual and spatial aspects of mathematics	☐	☐	☐
Has trouble understanding maps, diagrams, or graphs	☐	☐	☐
Has difficulty interpreting body language or social cues	☐	☐	☐
Has poor social skills	☐	☐	☐
Has difficulty understanding humor	☐	☐	☐

Building Blocks Questionnaire *(continued)*

CONCEPTUAL

Executive Functions	Rarely	Sometimes	Frequently
Has trouble monitoring performance	☐	☐	☐
Has problems initiating activities or tasks	☐	☐	☐
Has trouble developing a plan to complete a task	☐	☐	☐
Has difficulty sustaining effort when problem solving	☐	☐	☐
Has trouble identifying and prioritizing the most relevant aspects of a task	☐	☐	☐
Has difficulty revising or generating an alternative plan or strategy	☐	☐	☐
Has trouble evaluating the quality of performance	☐	☐	☐
Has difficulty selecting and using techniques to memorize	☐	☐	☐
Has trouble selecting and using techniques to study	☐	☐	☐
Has difficulty with generalization (i.e., taking what is learned in one situation and applying it to another)	☐	☐	☐

CHAPTER 2 OUTLINE

RATIONALE FOR THE ENVIRONMENT

RATIONALE FOR THE FOUNDATIONAL BLOCKS

Self-Regulation
Behavior
Emotions
Resilience

RATIONALE FOR THE PROCESSING AND CONCEPTUAL BLOCKS

Phonological, Orthographic, Memory, Motor, and Efficiency/Automaticity
Subtypes of Reading Disabilities
Subtypes of Math Disabilities
Verbal, Nonverbal, and Executive Functions

BUILDING BLOCKS MODEL AND THEORIES OF INTELLIGENCE

Planning, Attention, Simultaneous, Successive Theory
Cattell-Horn-Carroll Theory

BUILDING BLOCKS MODEL AND ACADEMIC PERFORMANCE

CONCLUSION

CHAPTER 2

Theoretical Foundations

This chapter provides an overview of how the theoretical framework for the Building Blocks model evolved. It begins with a brief historical overview of children's classroom problems. These include difficulties related to the environment, self-regulation, behavior, emotions, and resilience. Next, the neurodevelopmental skills of the Processing blocks and the Executive Functions, Verbal, and Nonverbal abilities of the Conceptual blocks are discussed. Two theories of intelligence are described to illustrate how they relate to the abilities included in the Building Blocks model. Throughout the chapter, relevant research is reported to substantiate the development and interpretation of the skills and abilities presented in the model. The chapter ends with a discussion of intraindividual variations and how these differences can be used to further understanding of a student's unique learning and behavior profile.

RATIONALE FOR THE ENVIRONMENT

The environment provides the base for the triangle of the Building Blocks model. Both the home and school environments can support or hinder learning. Multiple environmental factors play roles in explaining school problems. Learning is affected by the complex relationships among individual characteristics as well as family- and school-based influences (Meltzer, 1994; for a review, see Goldstein & Brooks, 2007). What are the factors that enable some children to achieve but cause others to fail? As Werner (2013) noted, even in the most disorganized, impoverished environments, some children still manage to develop stable, healthy personalities and function successfully in school.

Many environmental factors outside of the classroom affect children in the classroom. In 2012, approximately 16 million, or 22%, of American children under the age of 18 were in families living in poverty (National Center for Education Statistics [NCES], 2012). That means that nearly one in five children in the United States were living at or below the poverty level (Wight, Chau, & Aratani, 2010). The number of children living in poverty rose by 21% between 2000 and 2008; there were

2.5 million more children living in poverty than in 2000 (Wight et al., 2010). Up to 39% of African American children, 36% of American Indian/Alaska-Native children, and 33% of Hispanic children lived in poor families; the poverty rate was lowest for White children (13%) and Asian children (14%; NCES, 2012). Children who live in poor families appear to be exposed to significantly more risks than other children. The prevalence rates of physical and mental illness, child abuse, and parental problems are significantly greater in these families. Living in poverty decreases the number of protective factors a child has and increases the risk of classroom problems (Goldstein & Brooks, 2005).

The classroom is a child's central learning environment. Experiences at school may lessen or heighten the negative influence of family factors (Kauffman & Landrum, 2012). During the school year, children spend as much time in their classrooms as they do in their homes. They also typically spend more time with their teachers than with their parents during the school year. Students with learning and behavior difficulties require extra assistance and support to succeed. In discussing the efficacy of various service delivery models, Zigmond reflects,

> The accumulated experimental evidence to date produces only one unequivocal finding: Languishing in a regular education class where nothing changes and no one pays any attention to an individual is not as useful to students with learning and behavioral disorders as getting some help. (2004, p. 114)

Some classroom settings can foster problems, such as a class that has too many rules or a classroom in which too much talking is permitted. Specific class members who do not conform to rules within their classroom can cause disruptions or difficulties that interfere with academic tasks. In addition, when the task difficulty is not controlled and students are not given work in line with their capabilities, increased behavior and attention difficulties occur in the general education classroom (Liaupsin, Umbreit, Ferro, Urso, & Upreti, 2006). Sufficient data also suggest that when teachers have too many students requiring extra attention, classrooms do not function optimally and problems often escalate. Even something as simple as the organization of desks (e.g., clusters, rows) has been found to significantly affect classroom functioning. In one elementary classroom, the frequency of disruptions was three times higher when desks were arranged in clusters than when they were arranged in rows (Wheldall & Lam, 1987). Environmental modifications through a well-organized classroom are a preventive, whole-class approach to allow all children to access learning without interruption, reducing the probability that challenging behaviors will occur (Martella, Nelson, & Marchand-Martella, 2003). For example, the amount of time spent on task in direct and indirect reading activities predicts growth in reading for children with specific learning disabilities (SLD; Zigmond, 2004). Thus, one primary job of the teacher is to structure and order the learning environment "in such a way that work is accomplished, play is learned, love is felt, and fun is enjoyed—by the student and the teacher" (Kauffman, 2005, p. 441). The learning environment provides the foundation, support, and setting for students to have positive learning opportunities and experiences.

RATIONALE FOR THE FOUNDATIONAL BLOCKS

Childhood research increasingly points to a number of areas that appear to predict school success or explain why some children experience a lack of success even when they possess adequate cognitive abilities for good school performance. The foundation of typical achievement and learning is based on a student's Self-Regulation, Behavior, Emotions, Resilience, and Environment relative to school performance.

Theoretical Foundations

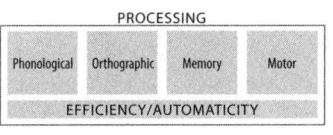
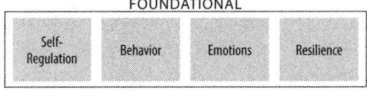

These five areas form the Foundational blocks, and problems in any one area can contribute to academic or social difficulties in school.

Self-Regulation

The essence of self-regulation is self-control; a lack of self-control often leads to attentional problems and challenging behaviors. Good self-control is also a key component for good executive functioning (EF). The concept of EF and its importance to school success has become increasingly of interest to educators (Goldstein & Naglieri, 2014). Across all grade levels, teachers' complaints about behavior most often relate to disruptive behavior. These complaints frequently contain behavior descriptions of inattention, impulsivity, hyperactivity, and poor planning, all symptoms of attention-deficit/hyperactivity disorder (ADHD). Since the 1970s, a significant issue in schools has been providing intervention for and behavior management of children with ADHD (Barkley, 2005). Within classroom settings, children with ADHD symptoms experience myriad impairments. Their temperaments often make it difficult for them to inhibit impulses and persist in repetitive activities that they perceive to be uninteresting. These children also experience difficulties as a result of their learning history—a history that often reinforces them for beginning but not completing tasks.

Frequently, teachers' efforts to manage the symptoms of ADHD and help children develop self-regulation result in negatively reinforcing interactions that tend to focus on the misbehavior itself rather than on extinguishing problematic behavior. These negative interactions often further disrupt other students in the classroom. Although at one time ADHD and SLD were considered to be different descriptions of the same problem, we now know problems with self-regulation and attention result from faulty performance, whereas problems with learning are often the result of inefficient processing, recall, or understanding of the material.

Behavior

Hostile, defiant, aggressive, and antisocial behaviors involving both overt (e.g., setting fires) and covert (e.g., lying, manipulating) acts cause significant classroom disruptions. These behaviors can form two types of behavior problems: oppositional defiant disorder and conduct disorder, both of which influence a child's chances for school success. These disorders are described as externalizing behaviors, as they manifest in children's outward behavior and are often viewed as disruptive or intrusive by teachers and students. A large volume of research has demonstrated that externalizing behavior problems may interfere with a student's classroom performance as well as his or her potential for academic and vocational success (for a review, see Goldstein & Brooks, 2007).

Emotions

Within the classroom, two main types of emotional problems—worry and helplessness—interfere with children's ability to achieve and succeed. Symptoms of these problems form the basis of depression and anxiety. These two conditions are closely linked with a variety of other disorders and may be episodic or chronic in nature (Kauffman & Landrum, 2012). These problems often are referred to as internalizing disorders because they are usually nondisruptive in nature and the symptoms are not as apparent to an outside observer. Students experiencing these problems may appear passive, withdrawn, or isolated in the classroom. Their behaviors, though not disruptive to either the teacher or nearby students, are nonetheless a cause for worry and concern. These emotional problems often interfere with a student's classroom performance and may occur along with other externalizing disorders.

Resilience

Resilience can be defined as a child's achievement of positive developmental outcomes and avoidance of maladaptive outcomes under adverse conditions (Goldstein & Brooks, 2013; Rutter, 2006; Wyman et al., 1999). One important aspect of resilience is self-esteem. Self-esteem encompasses children's feelings and beliefs about their competence and worth and whether they view themselves as worthy of respect. It involves such factors as having control over their lives, developing self-discipline, confronting rather than retreating from challenges, learning from both success and failure, and treating themselves and others with dignity and respect. Students' attitudes, beliefs, and perceptions of their potential for success that they bring to their classroom significantly affect their performance, independent of other skills and abilities.

RATIONALE FOR THE PROCESSING AND CONCEPTUAL BLOCKS

Skill and ability weaknesses in either the Processing or Conceptual blocks provide an explanation for the achievement problems experienced by the majority of students who are struggling in the classroom. The Processing blocks encompass the lower level perceptual abilities, whereas the Conceptual blocks encompass the higher level thinking and reasoning abilities. The abilities of the Processing blocks are related to lower order academic tasks that become automatic with repeated practice, such as memorizing multiplication facts, spelling words correctly, or reading tests quickly. In contrast, the abilities of the Conceptual blocks are related to higher order processes, such as those required in composing a letter, comprehending passages in a textbook, or solving a math story problem.

Historically, the *Illinois Test of Psycholinguistic Abilities* (ITPA; Kirk, McCarthy, & Kirk, 1968) presented a clinical model—an adaptation of Osgood's (1957) communication model. Within the adapted Osgood model, four basic processes were included: visual, auditory, vocal, and motor with two levels of organization. The first level was called the automatic level. At this level, the individual's auditory and visual responses are less voluntary but highly integrated, such as in tasks involving rapid symbol processing, verbal short-term memory, or blending sounds together to form a word. At the second or representational level, the individual engages in more complex mediating processes involved in tasks that require the comprehension of visual and auditory stimuli. Within the Building Blocks model, the automatic level is similar to the abilities of the Processing blocks, whereas the representational level describes the abilities of the Conceptual blocks.

Past results from analytic and related research on SLD appear to reflect two broad groups of skills necessary for efficient learning (Ingalls, 1991):

1. *Auditory and verbal processes:* Weaknesses in these areas result in reading and writing disorders and other language-based learning problems.

2. *Visual, perceptual, and motor processes:* Weaknesses in these areas may result in reading problems but may also affect handwriting, spelling, and mathematics.

Theoretical Foundations

Tables 2.1 and 2.2 present a model developed by Ingalls (1991) conceptualizing these skills. Similar to the model proposed in the ITPA, this model places learning skills on rote/automatic and conceptual levels. With repeated practice, the skills in the Processing blocks become increasingly automatic and are performed with little effort.

These levels of processing are also consistent with the distinction between automatic and conceptual processing (Schneider & Shiffrin, 1977). Once mastered, the automatic processes do not require attentional resources, whereas the conceptual processes are controlled and require the application of knowledge and strategies. Weaknesses in these cognitive and neuropsychological processes impede children's rate of learning and performing and can be used to explain SLD. However, instead of the generic term SLD, domain-specific labels (such as reading disability, math disability, and language impairment) more aptly describe the problem. As noted by Fletcher and colleagues (1998), a more appropriate approach is to describe domain-specific achievement skills and the abilities related to these skills. These domain-specific terms can occur in conjunction with other difficulties such as social, emotional, attention, or behavior problems. Part of the confusion regarding the heterogeneous term *SLD* has stemmed from the misuse of the terms *category* and *diagnosis* (Mather & Healey, 1990). In the field of SLD, the term *SLD* often is used erroneously to represent both the category of disability and the diagnosis of the disability. The categorical term is *SLD*, whereas the diagnosis needs to be a specific type of SLD such as a reading disability caused by poor phonological awareness or a math disability caused by poor working memory.

Phonological, Orthographic, Memory, Motor, and Efficiency/Automaticity

The Processing blocks include Phonological, Orthographic, Memory, Motor, and Efficiency/Automaticity. Essentially, these blocks are needed for efficiency in symbolic learning, such as learning sound–symbol associations, memorizing the times tables, or writing the letters of the alphabet quickly. Problems with any one of these areas can affect performance in basic skills in reading, writing, or math. Children with severe impairments in one of these domains often are identified as having SLD. As Bateman (1992) observed, children with SLD have more trouble acquiring, applying, and retaining information than would be predicted on the basis of other information about the child. The most common problem observed among these children is poor performance in basic reading, math, and spelling skills. Despite impairments in processing abilities, students with SLD often have intact conceptual and

Table 2.1. Skills necessary for efficient learning

	Auditory/verbal	Visual/motor
Conceptual	Verbal conceptual	Visual/nonverbal conceptual
		Spatial organization and nonverbal integration
Rote/automatic	Auditory motor	Letter perception
	Auditory perceptual	
	Rote auditory sequential memory	Rote visual/sequential memory and retrieval
	Rote and associated memory and retrieval	Motor sequencing / fine motor control

From Ingalls, S.I. (1991). *Skills for efficient learning* (p. 1). Salt Lake City, UT: Neurology, Learning, and Behavior Center; reprinted by permission.

Table 2.2. Levels of processing related to learning disability characteristics

	Auditory/verbal	Visual/motor
Conceptual	Language semantics (word meaning, definition, vocabulary)	Social insight and reasoning (e.g., understanding strategies of games, jokes, motives of others, social conventions, tact)
	Listening comprehension (understanding and memory of overall ideas)	Math concepts (e.g., use of 0 in addition, subtraction, and multiplication; place value; money equivalencies; missing elements)
	Reading comprehension (understanding and memory of overall ideas)	
	Specificity and variety of verbal concepts for oral or written expression	Inferential reading comprehension and drawing conclusions
	Verbal reasoning and logic	Understanding relationships of historical events across time; understanding science concepts
		Structuring ideas hierarchically; outlining skills
		Generalization of abilities
		Integrating material into a well-organized report
Rote/automatic	Early speech (e.g., naming objects)	Ability to assemble puzzles and build with construction toys
	Auditory processing (e.g., clear enunciation of speech, pronouncing sounds/syllables in correct order)	Social perception and awareness of environment
	Ability to name colors	Time sense (e.g., doesn't ask, "Is this the last recess?")
	Ability to recall birthday, telephone number, address, and so forth	Ability to remember and execute correct sequence for tying shoes
	Ability to say alphabet and other lists (e.g., days, months) in order	Ability to easily negotiate stairs, climb on play equipment, learn athletic skills, and ride a bike
	Ability to easily select and sequence words with proper grammatical structure for oral or written expression	Ability to execute daily living skills (e.g., pouring without spilling, spreading a sandwich, dressing self correctly)
	Auditory "dyslexia" (i.e., poor discrimination of sounds, especially vowels; auditory blend of sounds to words; trouble with distinction of words that sound alike [e.g., *mine, mind*])	Ability to use the correct sequence of strokes to form manuscript or cursive letters
	Poor phonetic spelling	Eye–hand coordination for drawing, assembling art projects, and handwriting
	Poor listening or reading comprehension due to poor short-term memory, especially of rote facts	Directional stability for top/bottom and left/right tracking
	Labeling and retrieving math facts (i.e., trouble counting sequentially, mislabeling numbers, poor memory for number facts and sequence of steps for computation)	Ability to copy from the board accurately
	Ability to recall names, dates, and historical facts	Visual "dyslexia" (e.g., confusion when viewing visual symbols, poor visual discrimination, reversals/inversions/transpositions due to poor directionality, limited recognition of shapes or forms of a word that has been seen many times before: "word-blindness")
	Ability to learn and retain new science terminology	Spelling (e.g., poor visual memory for the nonphonetic elements of words)

From Ingalls, S.I. (1991). *Skills for efficient learning* (p. 1). Salt Lake City, UT: Neurology, Learning, and Behavior Center; reprinted by permission.

Theoretical Foundations

reasoning abilities. In fact, many have average or even above-average performance in verbal abilities (Orton, 1966). Essentially, what distinguishes individuals with a reading disability from other poor readers is that their listening comprehension ability is higher than their ability to decode words (Rack, Snowling, & Olson, 1992).

Phonological and Orthographic

Many reading and spelling disabilities are caused by weaknesses in phonology (knowledge of the speech sounds) and orthography (knowledge of written language and spelling patterns). Early in the 20th century, many explanations of reading disabilities focused solely on the visual aspects of reading. Because the connection between the eyes and reading is obvious, the belief developed that reading disabilities are entirely a function of poor visual processing skills. Reading disorders have been attributed to faulty eye movements, problems with visual perception, slow fixations, failure of the eyes to work cooperatively, and poor scanning efficiency. In addition, many of the symptoms evidenced by poor readers also appear to be related to visual skills. Poor readers may reverse letters or transpose words when reading, such as pronouncing the word *was* as *saw*. Although various symptoms are apparent and a variety of explanations have been proposed, the exact visual mechanisms that contribute to poor reading are still not completely understood.

Although visual processes are clearly important to reading, many individuals with reading disabilities have difficulty pairing the speech sounds of language (phonemes) with the printed letters or letter strings (graphemes), which involves both phonological and orthographic processing. As Pennington eloquently wrote,

> Over and over again when we read we must translate printed letter strings into word pronunciations. To do this, we must understand that the alphabet is a code for phonemes, the individual speech sounds in a language, and we must be able to use that code quickly and automatically so that we can concentrate on the meaning of what we read. The difficulty that dyslexics have with phonics, the ability to sound out words, makes reading much slower and less automatic and detracts considerably from comprehension. (1991, p. 59)

Impairments in the child's ability to learn these phoneme–grapheme correspondences and then to recognize these patterns quickly impede the development of word recognition skills.

Further support for the Phonological and Orthographic Processing blocks comes from functional magnetic resonance imaging (fMRI) studies. These studies have indicated that children with dyslexia can have impairments that affect phonological processing in the temporoparietal cortex or impairments that affect orthographic processing in the word-form area of the occipitoparietal regions (Shaywitz & Shaywitz, 2003; Temple et al., 2001). Findings from an fMRI study indicated that developmental dyslexia has a neural basis and is characterized by both phonological and orthographic processing impairments (Temple et al., 2001). In the study by Temple and colleagues, children with dyslexia showed less left temporoparietal activation on a phonological task (e.g., determining if two letters rhymed, such as *d* and *t*) as well as reduced extrastriate activity—especially in the occipitoparietal regions—during an orthographic task (e.g., determining if two letters were visually the same). Although these skills appear to be separate components of variation in reading and spelling skills, orthographic competence may be based on already established phonological sensitivity and competence in phonological skills. Presumably, a child with limited sensitivity to speech sounds will also experience difficulty with the identification and production of orthographic patterns. Thus, a foundation in phonological awareness precedes and provides the foundation for the development of orthographic competence. Dyslexia is then characterized by difficulties with both phonological coding (using letter–sound correspondences to analyze and pronounce words) and orthographic coding (storing written words in memory and recalling word-specific patterns to aid in word recognition and spelling) (Berninger & O'Malley May, 2011; Pennington, Peterson, & McGrath, 2009).

Memory

Problems with memory are also common among children with learning difficulties. These abilities can be grouped under the label of short-term working memory, which includes the following three components: 1) memory span, 2) working memory capacity, and 3) attentional control. McGrew, LaForte, and Schrank (2014) explain that memory span refers to the ability to encode information and then reproduce the information in the same sequence in which it was represented, such as repeating a string of digits in order. Working memory capacity includes the ability to transform information within memory, such as what is required in repeating a string of digits in reverse order. While transforming the information, one has to be able to hold a small amount of information in the mind in a readily accessible form (Cowan, 2014). Attentional control, which is part of the Self-Regulation and Executive Functions blocks as well, refers to the ability to focus on the relevant stimuli and ignore irrelevant stimuli. Thus, weaknesses in memory can also be caused by problems in regulating and controlling attention.

Students with SLD tend to perform poorly on a variety of memory tasks (Mann, 2003). They may experience difficulty with recalling letters, digits, words, phrases, or sentences. These memory difficulties can affect the ability to follow classroom instruction, say the months of the year in order, or learn the multiplication tables. Working memory is also involved when the student has to juggle a lot of information at once. For example, when writing, a young writer must not only remember how to spell words but also think of the words to express meaning; organize those words according to the rules of grammar and syntax; and pay attention to the size, shape, and spacing of letters.

Motor

If the student has poor motor control, subsequent difficulty with handwriting affects written production. Although the importance of handwriting skill diminishes in adulthood, problems in motor control can affect the legibility and the speed of written production. Slow handwriting speed can then affect other aspects of writing. For example, the speed of letter writing appears to be a strong predictor of spelling outcomes for young children (Caravolas, Snowling, & Hulme, 1999).

Efficiency/Automaticity

This supporting block underlies performance in basic skills and encompasses the ability to work quickly with ease. Many students with SLD have slow production rates that affect performance on reading, math, and writing tasks. Often these problems with the rate of production result from difficulties with accuracy in basic skills. For example, if a student cannot pronounce words accurately with ease, reading speed and fluency are affected. If a student has not memorized multiplication facts, he or she will not be able to solve double-digit multiplication problems quickly. Similarly, if a student cannot form letters with ease, his or her speed of writing production will be slow and affect the quality of his or her written communications.

Theoretical Foundations

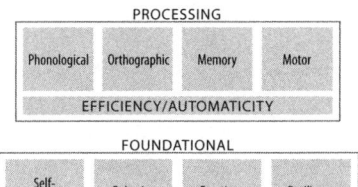

Subtypes of Reading Disabilities

An understanding of the history of efforts to subtype SLD can help explain why phonology, orthography, memory, and efficiency/automaticity are critical for classroom success. The majority of this work has centered on individuals with specific reading disabilities. Both Boder (1973) and Bakker (1979) attempted to classify and identify subtypes of reading impairments. Boder described three subtypes of children: 1) a dysphonetic group lacking word analysis skills and having difficulty with phonics, 2) a dyseidetic group experiencing problems with whole word gestalts, and 3) a mixed dysphonetic, dyseidetic group. According to Boder's research, the dyseidetic group included 67% of those identified as having LD and the mixed group included 23%. Thus, children with visual learning problems constituted a smaller percentage of this population. Although this research was subjected to numerous criticisms, the model provided a framework for thinking about different subtypes of learners.

A distinction concerning skill weaknesses exists between children with learning problems stemming from verbal skill weaknesses and children whose problems stem from visual weaknesses. Approximately 80% of children with a reading disability appear to experience some type of language-based impairment, with a much smaller percentage experiencing some type of visual problem (Denckla, 1972a; Mattis, French, & Rapin, 1975). Mattis and colleagues (1975) identified three groups of children with LD: 1) children with language problems, 2) children with articulation and graphomotor problems, and 3) children with visual-spatial perceptual disorders. Similarly, Phillips (1983) and Satz and Morris (1981) reported five distinct groups of children along the verbal–nonverbal continuum: 1) those with language impairments, 2) those with specific language problems related to naming, 3) those with mixed global language and perceptual problems, 4) those with perceptual motor impairments only, and 5) those in which no significant skill impairments could be found. Clearly, these pioneering studies on SLD support a multiple syndrome approach.

In the 1970s, a dual route model was proposed. This theory specified two interactive yet distinctive pathways for word recognition: an indirect, sublexical phonological decoding route for pronunciation of unfamiliar words alongside a direct, lexical route for automatic recognition of high-frequency words (Coltheart, 1978). A weakness in either pathway could affect the development of reading skills and result in two different subtypes of dyslexia: phonological dyslexia (i.e., difficulty with nonword reading) and surface dyslexia (i.e., difficulty with irregular word reading; Castles & Coltheart, 1993). Within our model, the symptoms of surface dyslexia would fall within the Orthographic Processing block.

An individual with phonological dyslexia experiences trouble with phonological awareness tasks and with the reading of nonwords, whereas an individual with surface dyslexia is able to read nonwords but experiences greater difficulty with exception words or words with an irregular element that do not have regular, predictable grapheme–phoneme correspondences (e.g., *once*). Although this pattern alone is insufficient to identify different subtypes, differences between performances on regular and irregular word reading and spelling may be indicative of different etiologies for reading and spelling difficulties.

Nearly 2 decades ago, Wolf and Bowers (1999) proposed a theory referred to as the double-deficit hypothesis, involving phonological awareness and rapid automatized naming (RAN) speed. Both phonological awareness tasks and rapid letter-naming tasks are useful predictive measures for identifying children who are at risk for reading failure (O'Connor & Jenkins, 1999). RAN measures account for independent variance in later reading scores and relate to distinct aspects of reading development, particularly reading speed (Bowers, Sunseth, & Golden, 1999; Manis, Seidenberg, & Doi, 1999). Measures of processing speed (i.e., the ability to perform simple cognitive tasks quickly) are also associated with both reading disabilities and ADHD (Pennington et al., 2009). Processing speed becomes an important predictor of skilled performance once students know how to perform a task. Thus, two third-grade students may both understand how to perform simple addition, but one has math facts memorized, and the other counts on his or her fingers (Schrank et al., 2014). Thus, RAN and processing speed are most related to the block of Efficiency/Automaticity. Both of these abilities are discussed more thoroughly in Chapter 8.

Subtypes of Math Disabilities

Some attempts have also been made to identify specific disorders of mathematics. Some students seem to have trouble primarily with computational skills, such as adding, subtracting, and multiplying; other students have trouble with the conceptual component, such as the abilities involved in solving story problems. Novick and Arnold (1988) found that some individuals demonstrated impairments in fundamental arithmetic operations even though they demonstrated adequate reasoning, language, and visual-spatial skills. Other individuals demonstrated preserved computational skills but experienced difficulties with the production and comprehension of numbers. Novick and Arnold defined *dyscalculia* as a "developmental arithmetic disorder, which refers to the failure to develop arithmetic competence" (p. 132).

Kosc (1974) described six different subtypes of developmental dyscalculia. One type described a disorder in performing computational operations; another described a disorder in understanding mathematical concepts. Although the results of subtyping provide mixed support for the differentiation of mathematics disability subtypes, two findings are clear: 1) some students experience difficulty solely in the domain of mathematics, and 2) these children appear to show differences in neuropsychological abilities and types of arithmetic errors (Keller & Sutton, 1991).

Geary (2003) explained that many children with SLD have weaknesses in the basic arithmetical competencies and have trouble retrieving basic facts from memory. In fact, the most documented research finding regarding students with SLD in math is that they have persistent difficulties memorizing and then retrieving basic arithmetic facts once they have been committed to memory (Geary, 2013b). Many of these students appear to have some form of working memory impairment or weak executive functioning in which they have trouble monitoring and coordinating a sequence of problem-solving steps. Most experts view memory impairments, specifically weaknesses in working memory, as the primary factor associated with SLD in mathematics (Watson & Gable, 2012). Although most individuals with a math disability have average intelligence, they may also have weaknesses in attentional control (Geary, Hoard, Nugent, & Bailey, 2012).

Geary (2003) described three basic subtypes of SLD in math: 1) procedural, 2) semantic memory, and 3) visual-spatial. The procedural subtype uses developmentally immature procedures, makes frequent errors, and has trouble sequencing multiple steps; the semantic memory subtype has trouble retrieving math facts and makes frequent errors on facts; and the visual-spatial subtype misinterprets and fails to understand spatially represented information. Similarly, Montague and van Garderen (2008) described students who have serious perceptual, memory,

Theoretical Foundations

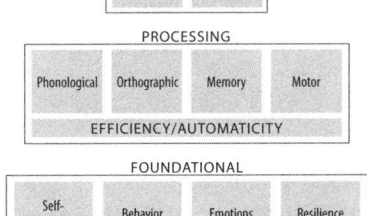

language, and/or reasoning problems that interfere with mathematical problem solving.

As with dyslexia, dyscalculia is a neurobiological disorder. In some cases, the localization of mathematics disability appears to be in the left hemisphere, causing problems in the learning and retention of facts. In other cases, dysfunction seems to be associated with the right cerebral hemisphere, causing problems in spatial organization, reasoning, and social-emotional functioning (Geary, 2003; Hale & Fiorello, 2004; Semrud-Clikeman & Hynd, 1991; Strang & Rourke, 1985)—key characteristics of a problem that often is described under the umbrella of nonverbal learning disabilities (NVLDs). Thus, the procedural and semantic memory subtypes are associated with the abilities of the Processing blocks, whereas the visual-spatial subtype is related to the Nonverbal Conceptual block.

Verbal, Nonverbal, and Executive Functions

The abilities of the Conceptual blocks can be thought of as representing higher order functions that support more complex learning tasks. These abilities primarily support the higher level academic tasks that involve reasoning and the use of strategies for problem solving.

Verbal

At the conceptual level, verbal abilities (thinking with language) affect performance in reading comprehension, written language, and mathematical problem solving. Many of the same receptive and expressive language processes contribute to the development of these abilities. In most instances, the comprehension of spoken and written language appears to be independent of word-reading ability (Aaron & Simurdak, 1991). In the Building Blocks model, poor word-reading ability is related to the abilities in the Processing blocks, whereas problems with the comprehension of text and the expression of ideas are related to the Conceptual blocks, particularly Verbal ability. Children who have difficulty understanding or using spoken language usually also have difficulty with aspects of reading, writing, and mathematics that require language-specific processes and involve higher order cognitive activities. Oral language, reading, and writing all form an integrated system with reciprocity in development: Verbal abilities provide the knowledge base for reading and writing, and what children learn from reading and writing enhances oral language development (Lerner & Johns, 2014).

Verbal abilities and acquired knowledge have a strong and consistent relationship with reading (Evans, Floyd, McGrew, & Leforgee, 2002), mathematical problem solving (Floyd, Evans, & McGrew, 2003), and written expression (McGrew & Knopik, 1993) across the lifespan. The most substantiated relationships are between oral language abilities and reading comprehension and written expression. Both reading comprehension and written expression are dependent on background knowledge, familiarity with sentence structures, verbal reasoning abilities, and the possession of a broad and deep vocabulary (McCardle, Scarborough, & Catts, 2001). Thus, words and the concepts they represent provide the foundation for advanced literacy (Cunningham, Stanovich, & Wilson, 1990; Perfetti, Marron, & Foltz, 1996).

In the Building Blocks model, the Verbal block encompasses the higher order aspects of linguistic functioning that allow students to understand what they hear and read and express their thoughts when speaking and writing. In some cases, students with reading disabilities have underlying oral language impairments and more pervasive disturbances of reading that contribute to low scores on measures of both verbal ability and reading; in other cases, students with reading disabilities have good verbal abilities but severe problems acquiring word recognition skills (Carlisle, 1993; Carlisle & Rice, 2002; Fletcher, Lyon, Fuchs, & Barnes, 2007).

Nonverbal

As mentioned previously, problems that are not primarily language based have been referred to collectively in the research literature as NVLDs (Johnson & Myklebust, 1971; Pennington, 2009; Rourke, 1989). This type of disability is characterized by good verbal abilities, with weaknesses in social skills and visual-spatial thinking. The neuropsychological hallmark of a NVLD is verbal abilities significantly higher than nonverbal abilities and visual-spatial skills; affected students tend to have strengths in word reading but weaknesses in reading comprehension (Pennington, 2009).

Strang and Rourke (1985) suggested that children with such disabilities may experience seven areas of difficulty: 1) problems with spatial organization, 2) problems paying attention to visual detail, 3) procedural errors in mathematics, 4) failure to shift psychological set (i.e., when two or more operations of one kind [e.g., addition] are followed by an operation of another kind [e.g., subtraction]), 5) fine motor weaknesses, 6) poor factual memory, and 7) poor judgment and reasoning. Although a number of the Processing and Conceptual blocks in our model relate to these skill areas, the primary problem seems to affect spatial skills, or the ability to think with images.

Many authors (e.g., Johnson & Myklebust, 1971; Pennington, 2009; Rourke, 1989; Strang & Rourke, 1985) contend that nonverbal learning disabilities (NVLDs) are much less common than language-based LD, occurring in only 1%–10% of children referred for learning problems. Some researchers have referred to NVLDs as reflecting a right-hemisphere impairment in the brain because the right side of the brain is considered to mediate or control visual, perceptual, organizational, and psychomotor coordination, as well as complex tactile perceptual skills (Harnadek & Rourke, 1994). At a conference of the International Dyslexia Association, a mother informed us that her daughter had just been diagnosed as "right-brained." Although the intent of this diagnosis may be clear, it is too simplistic. The connections between the right and left hemispheres of the brain are highly complex, and it is an oversimplification to speak of one hemisphere as if it exists in isolation from the other. Nonetheless, the organization of the brain appears such that, loosely speaking, the left hemisphere processes language and is more involved with the processing of rote, detailed information, whereas the right hemisphere processes novel, holistic, and spatial information (Hale & Fiorello, 2004).

Not surprisingly, children with nonverbal weaknesses are often described as having poorly coordinated gross and fine motor skills. They struggle with handwriting, mathematics, reading social cues, and managing emotions (Weintraub & Mesulum, 1983). Often, they also struggle with interpersonal relations—also not surprising, given estimates that 65% of communication is nonverbal (Mehrabian & Ferris, 1967). Nonverbal behavior appears especially important in communicating feelings, emotions, and preferences. Facial expressions, eye contact, and voice cues, such as pitch and volume, play significant roles in daily communications (Mehrabian & Ferris, 1967). Although much has been written about this disorder and its impact on academic and social skills, sufficient evidence does not yet exist to support NVLD as a valid disorder (Pennington, 2009; Spreen, 2011). After reviewing the research on NVLDs, Spreen concluded,

Theoretical Foundations

The concept has been adopted by many educators who see NLD as describing a child often encountered in schools: shy, poorly relating to others, with clumsiness, inner-directed, appearing depressed. But neuropsychologists have expressed skepticism about the concept. At this point, it must be concluded that NLD remains a hypothesis, but that it should not be used in clinical practice unless it is supported by solid research findings. (2011, p. 435)

Executive Functions

Executive Functions are located at the very top of the Building Blocks model. *Executive function* (EF) has come to be an umbrella term used for a diversity of hypothesized cognitive processes, including planning, working memory, attention, inhibition, self-monitoring, self-regulation, and initiation carried out by prefrontal areas of the frontal lobe (Goldstein & Naglieri, 2014). Pribram and Luria (1973) were two of the first to use the term *executive* when discussing matters of prefrontal cortex functioning. Since then, at least 30 or more constructs have been included under the umbrella term *EF,* making the concept hard to operationally define. Many authors have made attempts to define the concept of executive function using models that range from one to multiple components. Lezak (1995) suggested that EFs consisted of components related to volition, planning, purposeful action, and effective performance. It has been hypothesized that each component involves a distinct set of related behaviors.

Reynolds and Horton (2008) suggested that EFs are distinct from general knowledge. They suggest that executive functions represent the capacity to plan, make decisions, and generate novel motor outputs adapted to external demands rather than the passive retention of information. Naglieri and Goldstein (2012) based their view of the behavioral aspects of executive function on a large national study of children. They suggest that executive function is best represented as a single phenomenon, conceptualized as the efficiency with which individuals go about acquiring knowledge as well as how well problems can be solved across nine areas: 1) attention, 2) emotion regulation, 3) flexibility, 4) inhibitory control, 5) initiation, 6) organization, 7) planning, 8) self-monitoring, and 9) working memory.

Thus, the Executive Functions block contains the abilities that are needed for planning, organizing, and analyzing and solving problems. Several key components of executive functioning include the abilities to plan, organize, regulate thinking, and self-monitor performance (Cutting & Denckla, 2003). This awareness of how one is doing is critical to the learning process (Semrud-Clikeman, 2005). Executive functions are supported by verbal and nonverbal abilities, forming the three blocks in the model that compose the conceptual abilities. The relationship between verbal abilities and executive functions is ongoing and complementary; in fact, a student's use of language can provide insight into how that student is managing his or her executive skills (Gordon-Pershey, 2014). Executive functions have been described as the "supervisor of cognitive processing" that is capable of selecting, overseeing, and integrating information from several sources (Baddeley, 1986). These abilities apply to the awareness of how something is accomplished rather than just what is accomplished (Semrud-Clikeman, 2005).

Executive functions can be measured through ability tests such as the Cognitive Assessment System 2 (CAS-2; Naglieri, Das, & Goldstein, 2014a) or behavior inventories such as the Comprehensive Executive Functioning Inventory (Naglieri & Goldstein, 2012). Regardless of the assessment tools employed, direct observation of the student in the classroom is important.

Within the neuropsychological literature, metacognition is often referred to as a part of executive function or executive process (Torgesen, 1994). Metacognition has been described as knowing what one knows and knowing what needs to be known to achieve a goal (Wallach & Miller, 1988), or, more simply, the ability to think about one's own thinking. Metacognition contains two major components: knowledge about thinking and the ability to regulate one's thinking (Brown & Palinscar, 1982). Metacognitive knowledge is gained from experience and includes such things as monitoring, planning, and self-regulation skills (Torgesen, 1994). These variables appear to be most related to a student's ability to comprehend text, produce text, and solve problems. As an example, Baker and Brown (1980) specified five of the metacognitive behaviors involved in reading comprehension: 1) clarifying purposes, 2) identifying important aspects of a passage, 3) monitoring understanding, 4) engaging in self-questioning to determine if goals have been accomplished, and 5) taking corrective action when one fails to comprehend. Research during the 1980s and 1990s suggested that children with SLD performed differently from others in a range of situations that involve some form of metacognitive behavior (e.g., Torgesen, 1994).

BUILDING BLOCKS MODEL AND THEORIES OF INTELLIGENCE

Multidimensional theories of intelligence can help us understand the cognitive processes contributing to children's learning and behavior. Two theories of intelligence are explained briefly to illustrate the relationship between these theories and how the abilities in these theories relate to the Building Blocks model.

Planning, Attention, Simultaneous, Successive Theory

The Planning, Attention, Simultaneous, Successive (PASS) theory is one view of intelligence that aims to define four basic abilities—planning, attention, simultaneous, and successive processing, termed *basic psychological processes*—that underlie performance in social, behavioral, and academic areas. This theory is rooted in the research of A.R. Luria (1966, 1973, 1980) about how the brain works (Das, Naglieri, & Kirby, 1994). Das and colleagues used Luria's work as a blueprint for defining the important components of human intelligence. Their work represents an important effort to use neuropsychological theory to reconceptualize the concept of human intelligence.

Luria theorized that the four processes of the PASS theory could be conceptualized within a framework of three separate but related functional units of the brain. The three brain systems are referred to as functional units because of the unique neuropsychological mechanisms each contributes as they work in concert to achieve a specific goal. Luria (1973) stated that each form of conscious activity is always a complex functional system and takes place through the combined working of all three brain units, each of which makes its own contribution. This means that the four processes produced by the functional units form a working constellation of cognitive activity (Luria, 1966).

Each of the four PASS processes falls within one of the three functional units that can be associated with specific regions of the brain. The first functional unit, attention–arousal, provides regulation of cortical arousal and attention; the second analyzes information (using simultaneous and successive processes); and the third (planning) provides for strategy development, strategy use, self-monitoring, and control of cognitive activities.

The first of the three functional units of the brain, the attention–arousal system, is located primarily in the brainstem (Luria, 1973). This unit provides the brain

Theoretical Foundations

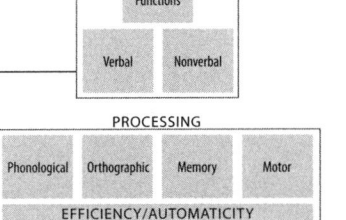

with the appropriate level of alertness as well as directive and selective attention (Luria, 1973). Moreover, only when individuals are sufficiently aroused and their attention is adequately focused can they use processes in the second and third functional units. The abilities to track cues, sustain attention, choose among potential responses, and self-monitor once a commitment has been made to a particular behavior are critical for effective academic and behavioral functioning in the classroom. These abilities are similar to the ones in the Self-Regulation block of the Building Blocks model.

The second functional unit is associated with the occipital, parietal, and temporal lobes of the brain. This unit is responsible for receiving, processing, and retaining information a person obtains from the external world using successive and simultaneous processes. Successive processing involves information that is linearly organized and integrated into a chain-like progression. This process is required when a child must arrange things in a strictly defined order in which each element is only related to those that precede it and the stimuli are not interrelated. For example, successive processing is involved in the decoding of unfamiliar words; the production of words in a specified order, or the syntax of language; and speech articulation. Following a command such as "Lilly, put your coat on the hanger, then put your book in your cubby, and then go sit in your seat" demands that the tasks and the order be remembered, which demands successive processing. Whenever information must be remembered or completed in a specific order, successive processing is involved. This process, therefore, is involved in the perception of stimuli in sequence as well as in the formation of sounds and movements in order. For this reason, successive processing is integral to activities such as phonological decoding, which involves working with sounds in sequence (Das et al., 1994). Successive processing has been conceptually and experimentally related to the concept of phonological analysis (Das et al., 1994). Successive processing is similar to the abilities involved in the Phonological, Orthographic, Memory, and Motor blocks of the Building Blocks model.

Simultaneous processing is a mental process that requires an individual to integrate separate stimuli into a whole. It involves integrating stimuli into groups such that the interrelationships among the components can be understood. An essential feature of simultaneous processing is the organization of interrelated parts into a cohesive whole. Simultaneous processing tests have strong spatial aspects for this reason. Simultaneous processing can be used to solve tasks with both nonverbal and verbal content as long as the cognitive demand of the task requires integration of information. Simultaneous processing underlies use and comprehension of grammatical statements because they demand comprehension of word relationships, prepositions, and inflections so the person can obtain meaning based on the whole idea. For example, the use of both sequential (recalling the directions) and simultaneous processing is necessary in order to follow this direction: "Get the book that is on the top shelf to the left of the door." Simultaneous processing is involved because this direction requires an understanding of the relationships among the different physical locations, the integration of the different parts of the direction into a single task, and the comprehension of logical and grammatical relationships. Thus, the Verbal, Nonverbal, and Executive Functions at the top of the Building Blocks model are similar to the abilities that are involved in simultaneous processing.

The third functional unit is associated with the prefrontal areas of the frontal lobes of the brain (Luria, 1980) and provides what Naglieri and Das (1997) called planning processing. The prefrontal cortex plays a central role in forming goals and objectives and then in devising plans of action required to attain those goals. This functional unit selects the cognitive processes required to implement the plans, coordinates them, and applies them in a correct order. Finally, planning processing is required for evaluating one's actions as successes or failures relative to one's intentions (Goldberg, 2001) and is one of the abilities that distinguishes humans from other primates. Planning, therefore, helps an individual achieve through the use of strategies and is critical to all activities in which the individual has to determine how to solve a problem. This includes generation, evaluation, and execution of a plan as well as self-monitoring and impulse control. Thus, planning allows for the solution of problems, control of attention, and simultaneous and successive processes as well as selective use of knowledge and skills (Das, Kar, & Parrila, 1996) and provides for the most complex aspects of human behavior, including personality and consciousness (Das, 1980). Both the Executive Functions and the Self-Regulation blocks of the Building Blocks model involve planning processes. Table 2.3 provides a comparison of the PASS processes and the Building Blocks model. As can be seen, the abilities portrayed in the PASS model incorporate in an interactive way many of the abilities represented in the Building Blocks model. PASS abilities and behaviors can be evaluated informally in the classroom or formally through nationally standardized tests such as the Cognitive Assessment System 2 (Naglieri et al., 2014a) or the Cognitive Assessment System 2 Rating Scale (Naglieri, Das, & Goldstein, 2014b).

Cattell-Horn-Carroll Theory

Another theory that can be related to the Building Blocks model is the Cattell-Horn-Carroll (CHC) theory of intelligence (Carroll, 1993; Horn & Cattell, 1966; McGrew, 2005). This theory evolved from the combination of *Gf-Gc* theory and Carroll's three-stratum theory. Historically, *Gf-Gc* theory, developed from the work of Raymond Cattell and John Horn, was an acronym referring to fluid (*Gf*) or more innate abilities and crystallized (*Gc*) abilities (i.e., those more influenced by learning and experience). Carroll's three-stratum theory describes human cognitive abilities from three hierarchical stratums: Stratum I, narrow abilities; Stratum II, broad abilities; and Stratum III, general intelligence, or *G*.

CHC theory provides an empirically based description of intelligence based on the analyses of hundreds of data sets that were not restricted to a particular test

Table 2.3. Relationship of Planning, Attention, Simultaneous, Successive (PASS) processes to the Building Blocks model

PASS process	Description	Relationship to Building Blocks model
Planning	Planning is a way of thinking that a person uses to evaluate a task, select or develop a way of doing something, monitor progress, and develop new strategies when necessary.	Self-Regulation; Executive Functions
Attention	Attention is a way of thinking that allows a child to focus on one thing and ignore others.	Self-Regulation
Successive	Successive processing is a way of thinking that a person uses to work with information that is arranged in order.	Phonological; Orthographic; Memory; Motor
Simultaneous	Simultaneous processing is a way of thinking that a person uses to relate separate pieces of information to a group or to understand how parts are related to a whole.	Verbal; Nonverbal; Executive Functions

Theoretical Foundations

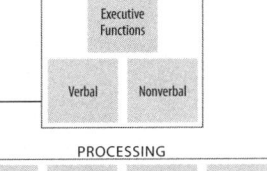
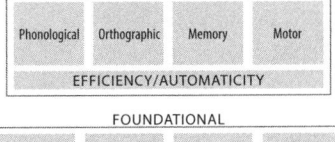

battery. This theoretical framework includes several broad domains of ability as well as more than 70 narrow abilities that can be measured successfully using tests. The broad abilities are abbreviated with G, representing intellectual ability, accompanied by one or more lowercase letters that indicate the specific type of ability. CHC theory includes the following cognitive abilities: comprehension–knowledge (Gc), fluid reasoning (Gf), visual-spatial thinking (Gv), long-term retrieval (Glr), auditory processing (Ga), processing speed (Gs), and short-term working memory (Gwm).

In a research synthesis of the existing CHC cognitive-achievement relationships, McGrew and Wendling (2010) explored how CHC factors are related to performance in basic reading skills, reading comprehension, basic math skills, and math reasoning. Depending on the specific area of achievement, as well as the developmental (age) status of individuals, the CHC factors had differential relationships with achievement. In several cases, a narrow ability, such as perceptual speed, was more significantly related to achievement than the broader CHC ability, processing speed. For example, perceptual speed—the ability to rapidly perform simple tasks that use symbols such as letters or numbers—was highly related to performance in basic math skills across all age groups.

Table 2.4 illustrates how the cognitive factors relate to the abilities portrayed in the Building Blocks model. In addition to the cognitive and linguistic domains,

Table 2.4. Relationship between Cattell-Horn-Carroll (CHC) abilities and the Building Blocks model

CHC ability	Description	Relationship to Building Blocks model
Comprehension–knowledge (Gc)	Ability to acquire general information, vocabulary, and knowledge	Verbal
Fluid reasoning (Gf)	Ability to reason, form concepts, and solve problems that often involves unfamiliar information or procedures	Executive Functions; Nonverbal
Visual-spatial thinking (Gv)	Ability to perceive, analyze, synthesize, and think with visual patterns, including the ability to store and recall visual representations	Nonverbal
Long-term retrieval (Glr)	Ability to store information efficiently and retrieve it later through associations	Orthographic
Auditory processing (Ga)	Ability to analyze, synthesize, and discriminate auditory stimuli; also related to phonological awareness—the ability to analyze, synthesize, and manipulate speech sounds	Phonological
Processing speed (Gs)	Ability to perform automatic or simple cognitive tasks with speed and efficiency and ability to visually scan efficiently	Orthographic; Efficiency/Automaticity
Short-term working memory (Gwm)	Ability to apprehend orally presented information in immediate awareness and repeat it back within a few seconds (short-term memory); ability to hold information in immediate awareness while performing a mental operation on the information (working memory)	Memory

two additional CHC abilities are typically associated with academic performance: quantitative knowledge (*Gq*) and reading and writing (*Grw*).

As with the Building Blocks model, some students will show patterns in which certain abilities are above average and other abilities are below average. For example, Ben has well-developed visual-spatial thinking (*Gv*) and reasoning abilities (*Gf*) but demonstrates inefficiencies associated primarily with orthography and retrieval of sound–symbol associations (*Glr*). Maria has strengths in listening comprehension (an ability classified under *Gc*) but weaknesses in phonological processing (an ability classified under *Ga*). Katy has strengths in memory (*Gwm*) but weakness in language (*Gc*) and reasoning (*Gf*).

CHC provides the theoretical basis for the development and interpretation of several test instruments, including the Woodcock-Johnson IV Tests of Cognitive Ability (WJ IV COG; Schrank, McGrew, & Mather, 2014). The WJ IV COG provides several types of intraindividual variation procedures that allow the comparison of many domain-specific abilities. Another instrument, the Kaufman Assessment Battery for Children–II (KABC–II; Kaufman & Kaufman, 2004), uses both of these theoretical models: the CHC model of broad and narrow abilities and Luria's neuropsychological processing theory. Using a subset of subtests from the KABC–II, the evaluator can interpret the test results from two different but complementary perspectives (Kaufman & Kaufman, 2004). CHC theory places emphasis on the interpretation of specific cognitive abilities and an understanding of how these abilities are related to performance, whereas Luria's neuropsychological theory emphasizes the way children process information when solving problems.

When considering the assessment of individuals suspected of having SLD, both approaches are useful for different types of referral questions. In clinical cases that involve the role of language as a factor affecting performance, application of the Luria framework de-emphasizes the role and importance of factual knowledge and allows the evaluator to consider mental processing while reducing the impact of low language performance. The Kaufmans state the following fundamental principle for understanding when to include or exclude measures of knowledge and language from an evaluation: "Measures of *Gc* should be excluded from any score that purports to measure a person's intelligence or overall cognitive ability whenever the measure of *Gc* is not likely to reflect that person's level of ability" (Kaufman & Kaufman, 2004, p. 4). For example, in an individual who is just acquiring English, measures of vocabulary knowledge and general information (*Gc*) administered in English would not provide an accurate measure of the person's intelligence.

In most instances, when assessing individuals suspected of having SLD, the Kaufmans recommend the use of the CHC model over the Luria model because *Gc* is an important aspect of cognitive performance (Kaufman & Kaufman, 2004) and is often a relative strength for individuals with SLD. Results from the WJ IV, the KABC–II, and the CAS2 (Naglieri et al., 2014a) can help identify an individual's strengths and weaknesses in cognitive ability and mental processing, making them valuable tools for identifying basic processing disorders, a key aspect of most LD definitions. In addition, the theories of intelligence that were used to develop these instruments provide further support for the more informal methodology presented in the Building Blocks Questionnaire (see Appendix 1A, also available as a download).

Clearly, human abilities are complex, and the completion of any task can involve the employment of numerous overlapping, interactive skills and abilities that theories of intelligence and models of performance can never fully capture. An

Theoretical Foundations

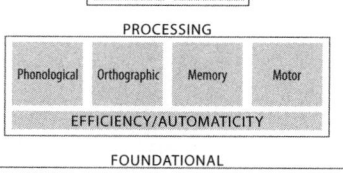

understanding of essential abilities, however, can help us appreciate and address individual differences in learning and behavior in students.

BUILDING BLOCKS MODEL AND ACADEMIC PERFORMANCE

The Building Blocks model reflects our efforts to interpret and integrate educational research and theory into a functional framework that directly connects to intervention. It is a model that can be practically and reliably used daily by classroom teachers. Although skills and issues that cause children's classroom and achievement problems are organized into 12 blocks, multiple skills, issues, and behaviors exist within each block that increase either the probability of success or the risk of classroom problems. Table 2.5, adapted from and based on the work of developmental pediatrician Levine (1990), lists basic skills necessary for achievement, beginning with the simplest and building to the more complex. These skills are hypothetically conceived as essential to the development of basic reading, writing, and mathematical abilities.

CONCLUSION

The Building Blocks model is an attempt to provide a relatively simple framework for understanding intraindividual differences in learning and behavior and the elemental factors that are needed for school success (see Figure 2.1). This framework is not to be viewed as a static model of discrete elements. Rather, elements of each block can be viewed as involving components or elements of another block. For example, elements of a concept such as Executive Functioning at the Conceptual level can also extend into the Processing and Foundational blocks. The basic level of executive function includes earlier developing abilities such as response inhibition and working memory; impairments in both have been associated with ADHD, whereas the higher order components are involved with organization and planning (Cutting & Denckla, 2003). Similarly, both phonological and orthographic processing are aspects of oral and written language, but they are more central to performance and acquisition of basic learning tasks, such as spelling, than they are to higher order tasks, such as those involved in reading comprehension or math problem solving.

As we have discussed, some important abilities do not fit neatly into the model, as they involve both lower and higher order abilities. For example, morphology, or the study of the meaning units in language, affects both spelling (lower level) and vocabulary (higher level) and thus cannot be neatly placed in either the Processing or Conceptual blocks. Essentially, morphology forms a bridge between spelling and vocabulary, and an interaction exists between orthographic development and morphological knowledge (Templeton, 2004). Thus, the abilities specified in the Building Blocks model are to be viewed as interactive, overlapping, and dynamic. Although the model covers many critical abilities related to learning, it does not cover all the abilities related to effective learning.

The purpose of this multidimensional model is to represent many of the most common cognitive, motivational, environmental, and behavioral factors that may impede or enhance a student's school performance. Once again, a multiplicity of factors and multiple developmental domains influence school success. The remainder of this book provides discussions of how problems in each of these areas can contribute to behavior and academic difficulties. In addition, specific suggestions are provided for implementing the most effective interventions and treatments.

Table 2.5. Basic skills necessary for successful academic performance

Subject	Skill	Result of skill deficit
Reading	Appreciation of language sounds	Language sounds don't seem very clear.
	Remembering sound–symbol associations	The sounds of combinations of letters are difficult to remember.
	Pushing together the sounds in a word	The sounds of letters are known, but it's difficult to put together the sounds in the right order to pronounce the words during reading.
	Reading fast enough	It takes too long to pronounce or understand each word.
	Understanding sentences	The vocabulary or grammar is too difficult.
	Understanding paragraphs or passages	It's difficult to find the main ideas and the important details, or it's difficult to understand the concepts, ideas, or facts.
	Remembering while reading	Ideas don't stay in memory during reading.
	Summarizing what was read	It's too difficult to decide and remember what's important and to organize important ideas in your own words and sentences.
	Applying what was read	It's difficult to use what you've read.
	Enjoying reading	Reading is too much work; it's not automatic.
Spelling	Remembering letters and sounds	It's difficult to remember that a certain combination of letters stands for a certain language sound. It's difficult to understand how sounds are different from each other.
	Picturing words	It's difficult to remember how words look. It's difficult to recall and sequence the sounds of multi-syllabic words.
	Spelling longer words and understanding spelling rules	It's difficult to understand what combination of letters is allowed. It is also difficult to understand spelling rules.
	Spelling consistently	It's difficult to recall the correct spelling.
	Writing and spelling at the same time	It's difficult to write and spell at the same time. It's difficult to remember how to spell when writing words in sentences or paragraphs.
	Avoiding mixed spelling errors	It's difficult to distinguish word sounds, remember the rules, and picture words.
Writing	Using fine motor skills	It's difficult to keep track of just where the pencil is while writing. It's difficult to get the right muscles to work together quickly and easily. It's difficult getting eyes and fingers to work together.
	Remembering and writing at the same time (i.e., mechanics)	It's difficult to remember punctuation, spelling, capitalization, grammar, vocabulary, letter formation, and ideas all at the same time.
	Thinking about ideas and writing at the same time	It's difficult to think quickly about ideas at the same time as one is writing.
	Planning and organizing	It's difficult to think up something to write about or understand what the teacher expects; decide who will read the writing; think up many good ideas and write them down; take all the ideas and put together the ones that belong together; know what ideas to put first and what ones to put second; get rid of ideas that don't fit; make sure that things make sense; and reorganize what has been written.
	Knowing how to translate ideas into language on paper	It's difficult to express ideas clearly when writing.

Theoretical Foundations

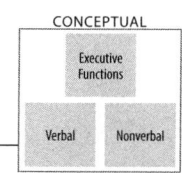
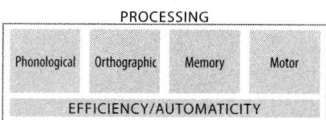
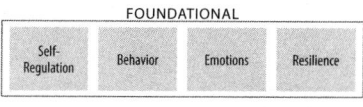

Subject	Skill	Result of skill deficit
Mathematics	Grasping the concepts	It's difficult to understand concepts that include things such as numbers, place values, percentages, decimals, and equations.
	Remembering mathematics	Mathematics is a big memory strain. Mathematical facts need to be remembered very quickly or you may forget something you need to do. When you finish doing one part of a math problem, you need to remember what it was that you were going to do next.
	Understanding the language of mathematics	There is a lot of language (e.g., labels) in a math class, which makes it difficult to keep up with what the teacher is saying and understand certain assignments.
	Using problem-solving skills	It's difficult to think up the best way (or ways) to come up with the correct answer. It's difficult to take time to think about a solution.
	Visualizing	It's difficult to picture what you are able to describe in words.
	Remembering things in the right order	It's tricky to understand some concepts unless you can see clear pictures of images of them in your brain.
	Paying attention to detail	It's difficult to be alert and tuned in to the many little details in mathematics.
	Recognizing or admitting a lack of understanding	It's difficult to recognize or admit that you do not understand or remember basic concepts in order to understand the new ones.

From Levine, M. (1990). *Keeping ahead in school*. Cambridge, MA: Educators Publishing Service; reprinted by permission. Copyright 1990 by Educators Publishing Service.

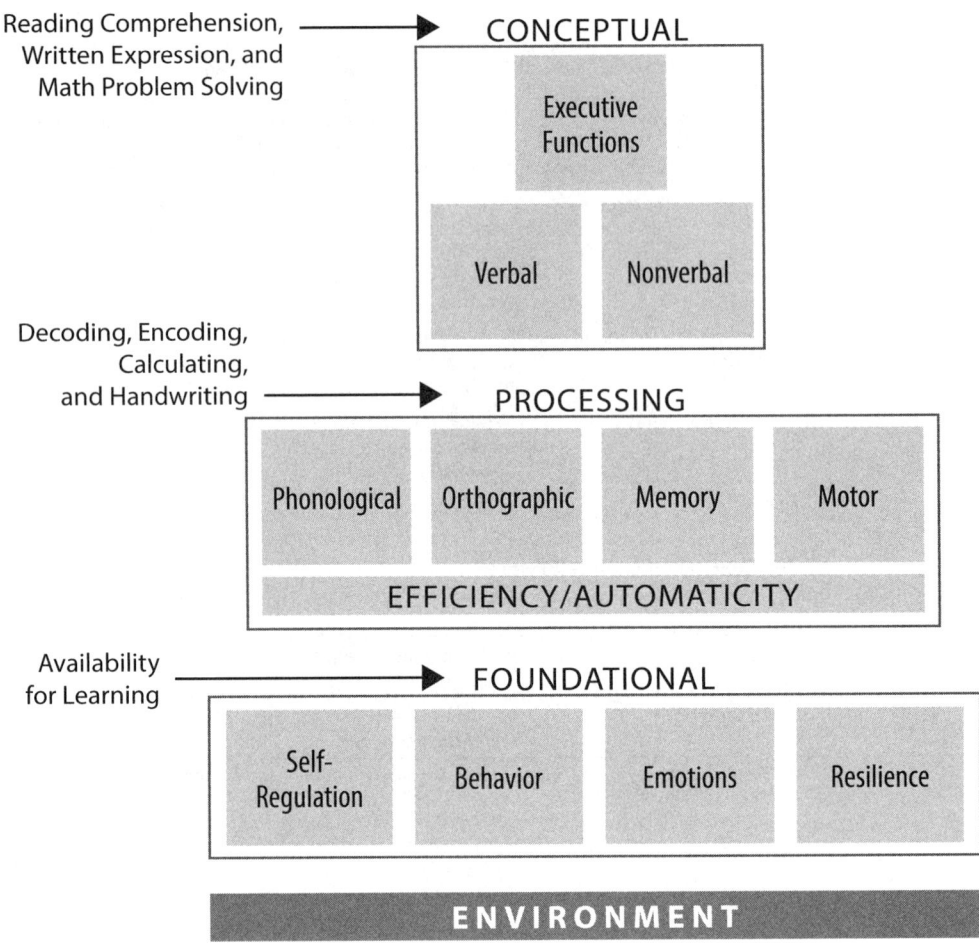

Figure 2.1. Building Blocks of Learning model that forms the basis for corresponding academic skills.

CHAPTER 3 OUTLINE

CREATING EFFECTIVE SCHOOL ENVIRONMENTS

- School Climate and Culture
- Positive Behavior Interventions and Supports
- Common Core State Standards

EFFECTIVE TEACHERS

CREATING OPTIMAL CLASSROOM ENVIRONMENTS

- Student and Classroom Variables
- Physical Arrangement of the Classroom
- Out-of-Classroom Services
- Student Expectations
- Transitions
- Student Engagement

CONDITIONS AND COMPONENTS OF THE INTERVENTIONS

- Individualized and Small-Group Instruction
- Principles of Instruction
- Relationships
- Communication with Students
- Communication with Parents

DIVERSE BACKGROUNDS

- Economically Disadvantaged Backgrounds
- Culturally and Linguistically Diverse Backgrounds

HOMEWORK

- Creating Assignments
- Meaningfulness, Difficulty, and Assignment Length
- Completing Homework

CONCLUSION

CHAPTER 3

The Learning Environment

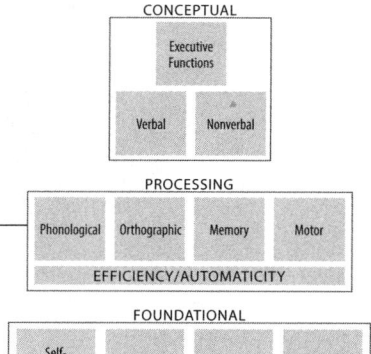

As a first-year, fifth-grade teacher, Mr. Patrick worked diligently throughout the summer collecting interesting posters and materials for his classroom. During the days before school began, Mr. Patrick spent many hours preparing his classroom, deciding where to place materials and how to help students have access to activities and supplies in the classroom. Mr. Patrick also attended a number of professional development trainings. During one of these sessions, the trainer explained a method for setting up materials and learning stations in the classroom. This arrangement would allow students to move between stations and obtain necessary materials with some degree of autonomy. Mr. Patrick was certain that he had designed his classroom for maximum efficiency and student learning. Yet within the first few days of school, he noted that students were moving around too often, and, as they moved, they often disrupted others.

Observing the increased pattern of off-task behavior in the classroom, Mr. Patrick's colleague, Ms. Jones, an experienced teacher, pointed out that sometimes too much of a good thing can become detrimental to student learning. Ms. Jones provided Mr. Patrick with a set of statements to consider about his classroom environment (see Table 3.1). After reviewing the statements, Mr. Patrick realized that some changes were needed in the physical arrangement of his classroom and his classroom management strategies.

The performance of even the most academically advanced, well-behaved, emotionally secure students can vary on the basis of environmental factors. The classroom environment includes all aspects of classroom function, setting, and structure. Such diverse factors as communication between teachers and students, issues related to discipline, size of group instruction, transition times, classroom rules, and the critical link between teachers and parents can be influenced by teachers.

The third edition of this book reflects a shift away from efforts to manage classroom behavior and structure toward the creation of a framework to develop sustainable classroom environments by shaping educators' mind-sets. Effective educators are capable of appreciating the forces that truly motivate students—even students with serious behavioral and learning challenges. These educators are capable of recognizing that the daily expectations of their classroom not only

Introduction

Table 3.1. Questions to consider about the classroom environment

Have you allocated time efficiently in the classroom?
Do you and your students get along?
When you provide directions, do students comply?
Have you developed a workable system for discipline?
Is there a workable system for seating and classroom space?
Do you have a method for providing group instruction?
Do you use a number of strategies to improve compliance?
Do you have a system for developing and implementing classroom rules?
Is a system in place to communicate effectively with parents?
Is a system in place to assign, follow up, and collect homework?

contribute to students' self-esteem and resilience but also provide an essential foundation for making a successful transition into adult life.

It is increasingly recognized that the quality of teacher–student interactions is a better predictor of how much children learn than the curriculum (Raver et al., 2011; Sabol, Hong, Pianta, & Burchinal, 2013). For example, high-quality classroom environments characterized by organization and emotional and instructional support reduce academic risks associated with difficult temperaments such as impulsivity, inattention, and worry (Curby, Rudasill, Edwards, & Perez-Edgar, 2011). Teachers enhance self-regulation in the classroom when they are able to employ a positive emotional tone and a higher ratio of approving to disproving comments toward students (Fuhs, Farran, & Nesbitt, 2013). Finally, teacher behavior toward students creates classroom conditions in which negative beliefs are minimized, and as a result, students demonstrate higher levels of achievement (Griggs, Rimm-Kaufman, Merritt, & Patton, 2013).

This chapter highlights recommended practice considerations for effective school and classroom environments, including classroom management strategies, modifications to the classroom environment, and teacher–student relationships. The discussion includes ways in which teachers communicate with parents about students' behavior, progress, and performance, as well as the means by which homework is assigned and collected. Effective teachers create positive, nurturing classroom environments that focus on positive student learning and behavioral outcomes.

CREATING EFFECTIVE SCHOOL ENVIRONMENTS

The educational climate of evidence-based practices and interventions rings loudly in the minds of school administrators, teachers, and staff and in the hallways and meeting rooms of schools. These are clearly times with increased accountability as schools work to ensure the academic, behavioral, physical, and psychological well-being of all students. Although many efforts have been made to bolster the academic needs of students (e.g., Common Core State Standards, Elementary and Secondary Education Act, No Child Left Behind), environmental considerations within both the classroom and the school at large play an integral role in helping students achieve academic and social-emotional success within the school environment.

The Learning Environment

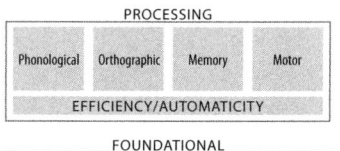
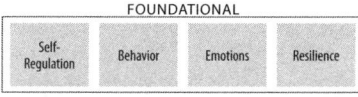

School Climate and Culture

School climate is defined as "the quality and character of school life . . . based on patterns of people's experiences of school life and reflecting norms, goals, and values" (Cohen, McCabe, Michelli, & Pickeral, 2009, p. 180). A sustainable, positive school climate fosters youth development, positive teacher–student interactions, and student achievement. The following are five key elements of safe and healthy schools: 1) positive and productive relationships, 2) awareness of and respect for diversity, 3) transparent and unbiased norms and expectations, 4) individual value and shared purpose, and 5) opportunities for growth and achievement (O'Malley & Eklund, 2012). These five elements have been found to promote improved school climate, result in lower rates of student problematic behaviors, and promote positive staff and student outcomes. Teachers and school staff are called upon to focus on these five elements when working to address school climate at the classroom, building, and district levels. Specific examples of how schools, staff, and teachers can embed these important elements in the classroom and school environment are described in this chapter.

Positive and productive relationships among staff and students can be fostered by using evidence-based programs to improve social and emotional skill development of students. This may include locally developed lessons to address the needs of a particular school, classroom, or group of students, as well as packaged programs such as Second Step or Promoting Alternative Thinking Strategies (PATHS) that are designed to help students develop appropriate problem-solving and coping skills (Edwards, Hunt, Meyers, Grogg, & Jarrett, 2005). Professional development opportunities should be provided for staff committed to the development of social and emotional competencies required to work with youth.

Awareness of and respect for diversity includes identifying curricula, classroom activities, and wall images that represent the demographics of the students in the school. Adults in the school should also communicate high expectations for all students, regardless of background.

Transparent and unbiased norms and expectations can be used by allowing students to participate in classroom and school norm- and rule-setting activities at the beginning of the year. Allowing students to have an active voice in creating rules can lead to increased student buy-in, as youth are more apt to follow rules that they have helped to develop. Eliciting student voices within the school can help promote a shared sense of community, where adults clearly value and recognize student opinions.

Individual value and shared purpose are further promoted by giving students an active voice in school governance councils, advisory committees, and service-learning projects. School staff members can also share a sense of responsibility regarding school activities, school improvement goals, as well as professional development planning.

Finally, *opportunities for growth and achievement* can be established by building in time for staff to attend professional development trainings and setting high academic and professional standards for students and staff that are also achievable, widely recognized, and celebrated. Table 3.2 provides a detailed list of additional strategies for promoting healthy working and learning environments.

Positive Behavior Interventions and Supports

Several programs and products are available that promise to erase or minimize challenging behaviors in the school environment. Unfortunately, there is no magic

Table 3.2. Key characteristics of safe and healthy schools

Positive, productive relationships	Social and emotional skill development of youth is supported using evidence-based programs as well as structured, natural opportunities for skill building.
	Collegial relationships among school staff are supported and encouraged through systematic school planning.
	Professional development opportunities are provided for staff to support the development of the social and emotional competencies required to work with youth.
	Caring home and neighborhood adults are encouraged to volunteer in classrooms and shared school spaces.
Awareness of and respect for diversity	Students can "see" themselves in school materials. Curricula, classroom activities, and wall images represent the demographics of the school.
	School staff members reflect upon their own potential biases and assumptions.
	Caring home and neighborhood adults from diverse groups are encouraged to volunteer at school and actively participate in school decision-making activities.
	Teachers reflect upon the diverse backgrounds (i.e., culture, language, family history, religion) of their students and modify curricula to meet their needs.
	School adults communicate high expectations for *all* students, regardless of background.
Transparent and unbiased norms and expectations	School policies are applied to all students, regardless of gender, race, socioeconomic privilege, or perceived sexual orientation.
	Students and caring home and neighborhood adults are provided opportunities to participate in classroom and schoolwide norm- and rule-setting activities.
	School rules and expectations are reiterated regularly and are visible within classrooms and shared spaces.
	Professional development opportunities are provided for staff to support the development of positive classroom management practices.
Individual value and shared purpose	School staff members share a sense of responsibility over school activities and goals.
	Staff members are given opportunities to inform decisions related to future directions of school activities, including professional development planning.
	Students are encouraged to participate in governance councils and advisory committees.
	Students are encouraged to make shared contributions to the school and neighborhood communities through a variety of experiences, including service-learning projects.
Opportunities for growth and achievement	Cooperative planning and professional development time for school staff is supported, encouraged, and expected.
	Curricula are rigorous and meaningful, emphasizing critical thinking, application of knowledge, and self-reflective learning.
	Academic and professional standards for students and staff are high but achievable.
	Achievements of staff and students are celebrated and widely highlighted.

Source: Adapted from O'Malley, M., & Eklund, K. (2012). Creating safe and supportive learning and working environments. In S.E. Brock & S.R. Jimerson (Eds.), *Best practices in school crisis prevention and intervention* (2nd ed., pp. 151–176). Copyright 2012 by the National Association of School Psychologists, Bethesda, MD. Reprinted with permission of the publisher. www.nasponline.org

The Learning Environment

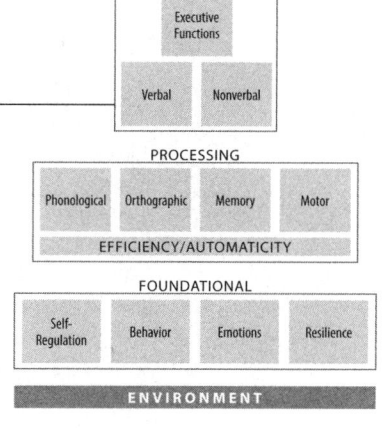

bullet to address all behaviors that may negatively affect the learning environment. However, advances in schoolwide discipline have emphasized systems of support that include proactive strategies for defining, teaching, and supporting appropriate student behaviors. Positive behavior interventions and supports (PBIS) have been implemented in many schools across the country to help reduce disciplinary infractions and increase students' sense of safety at school by promoting positive, prosocial behaviors and improving schoolwide behavior. The premise of PBIS is that recognizing and rewarding positive student behavior through continual teaching will reduce unnecessary discipline and promote a climate of greater productivity, learning, and safety (Sprague & Horner, 2007).

Whereas many teachers may believe that it is not their job to teach kids to be good or that students should already know what they are supposed to do, many students are coming to school unprepared to meet the behavioral expectations of individual teachers or the larger school context. Whereas punishment-based strategies, such as reprimands, loss of privileges, and office referrals, have been traditional responses to student misbehavior, research has shown that the use of punishment, especially when used in the absence of positive strategies, is ineffective. Instead, teachers are encouraged to use strategies such as preteaching student expectations, modeling, and reinforcing social behavior as one way to improve students' educational experiences. This should include behavioral expectations within the classroom (e.g., entering the classroom, transition periods, peer interactions) and addressing student behavioral expectations in each setting at school (e.g., hallway, lunchroom, bathroom). Schools that use PBIS apply a multi-tiered approach to prevention that not only identifies a universal mission to guide schoolwide behavior principles but also uses targeted and individualized interventions to improve student functioning and overall school climate. A PBIS approach should be used in conjunction with carefully delineated academic goals or standards that align with multi-tiered systems of support for student learning.

Common Core State Standards

The Common Core State Standards (CCSS) were developed to ensure high-quality academic standards in English language arts/literacy (ELA) and mathematics by outlining what each student should know and be able to do by the end of each grade level. The CCSS have been formally adopted and implemented by 43 states, four territories, and the District of Columbia. The goal of such standards-based reforms is to increase student achievement through the specification of academic content standards and assessments (Stecher, Hamilton, & Gonzalez, 2003). These content standards are ideally designed to inform curriculum development, guide instruction and assessment, provide clear goals for student achievement, and raise performance expectations (Troia & Olinghouse, 2013). There is hope that CCSS will help facilitate an increased emphasis on evidence-based classroom practices.

However, CCSS pose multiple challenges for classroom teachers. The adoption of the CCSS indicates a major change in the intended curriculum for all students. Whereas the national recommendation has been a staggered rollout by grade level, decisions on how to implement the standards are made at the state and local levels. As a result, some states and local municipalities have made alternative arrangements by mandating schoolwide implementation at each grade level (or multiple grade levels) within the same academic year. Additional stressors include inconsistent or nonexistent professional development for classroom teachers as well as limited guidance on how to select an evidence-based curriculum that will align with content standards. This has resulted in a large degree of frustration and panic among classroom teachers and educational support staff. Further, there is insufficient empirical support that the standards are accessible to various student learning styles and diverse populations (Tienken & Orolich, 2013). CCSS iterations indicate all students may have to demonstrate mastery of all standards at the same level of difficulty and in the same formats. Clearly, students with academic and behavior difficulties may be at a disadvantage until many of these new challenges are resolved. Whereas the standards establish what students need to learn, they do not dictate how teachers should teach. It is important teachers focus on effective instruction that is systematic, explicit, and intensive and promotes active engagement. Teachers can provide instructional support by ensuring students efficiently acquire, rehearse, and connect background knowledge to other knowledge. Teachers can provide additional support by chunking new materials into manageable amounts, modeling, guiding student practice, helping students when they make errors, and providing sufficient time for students to practice and review (Rosenshine, 2012). The continued focus of this chapter will be to provide guidance and additional recommended practice considerations for how teachers can create an environment that fosters and supports learning for all students.

EFFECTIVE TEACHERS

More than 40 years ago, Bushell (1973) eloquently wrote that teachers are powerful change agents of student behavior. This statement remains true today. Effective teachers exert a significant impact on children's achievement, emotions, and development. Bushell described teachers as the following:

> Purchasing agents, property clerks, and accident insurance salesmen; they are attendance monitors, playground monitors, hall monitors, lunch room monitors; they remain cheerful at faculty meetings and brave when caring for skinned knees and bloody noses; they are audio visual technicians, janitors, psychologists, revenue collectors for the lunch room, referees for athletic contests, and counselors to parents. (1973, p. 1)

Effective teachers exude an aura of authority and affection. Children do not learn well from people whom they do not like or admire. A teacher's mind-set about the classroom is critical in determining whether strategies, however effective in theory, work well or yield few benefits. The school environment, as the late Dr. Julius Segal (1988) reminds us, is a prime location for nurturing resilience. The mind-set of effective educators provides a framework for understanding the lifelong impact adults can have on their students based on daily classroom activities. Emphasis is placed on the importance of understanding, appreciating, and building assets and strengths as well as managing student concerns and weaknesses. An effective classroom teacher, who also can be called an environmental engineer (Goldstein & Jones, 1998), must carefully select curricula, structure and plan learning activities, involve students in the learning process, closely monitor students' progress, change and modify various interventions, and regularly provide feedback about student progress and accomplishments. The teacher must organize and maintain the learning environment of the classroom to maximize the time spent engaged in productive activity and minimize the time lost during transitions or disruptions requiring disciplinary action. An effective teacher must develop methods to elicit achievement from students, involve students in classroom activities, and teach students a means for self-management and self-control. Effective teachers use a workable set of classroom rules and are able to respond consistently and quickly to problem situations.

The Learning Environment

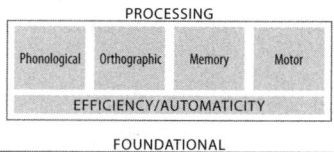

They have structured their classroom to minimize disruption and maximize educational experiences, and they respond to the needs of their students.

Teachers can increase the chances that all students will experience problems if they are intolerant and rigid in providing directions; condescending or uptight in relationships with their students; and able to recognize only the need for academic accomplishment. In contrast, effective teachers possess the attitude that they can be and are responsive to their students' needs for support and manage the classroom environment effectively while holding high expectations for students' achievement and behavior. Effective teachers are confident, realistic, and honest when they interact with their students. They accept each student as an individual. They understand human behavior and child development and know that vast developmental differences exist in the abilities and learning rates of children. The mind-set of effective teachers reflects a sense of patience, flexibility, and a willingness to accept that students work with rather than for them. Finally, effective teachers provide each child with a sense of security, making school a place that children desire to attend and the classroom a place where every child feels important and valued. The golden rule for being an effective teacher is to be a good human being. Strickland described a good teacher in this way:

> A good teacher should recognize that some children learn by listening, some by seeing, and some by feeling; and his classroom surely contains children with each learning style. The teacher should recognize that some children are facile with words, some with numbers, and some with neither; and that children vary widely in the amount of time needed to absorb knowledge. Most of all, an adequate teacher must realize that, if a child is doing badly in school, there is always a reason: and that reason is rarely laziness or willfulness. The child who is doing the very best she can and has no idea why she is not succeeding is depending on the teacher to find out why her struggles are in vain. If the teacher can't figure it out, then the child is in store for years of frustration. (1998, p. 132)

Some teachers blame student failure or behavior problems on internal characteristics of the student or home, believing that a child's problems are due to something within the child or caused by the parents. They place more emphasis on interventions aimed directly at the student, often suggesting the student needs to take ownership for the problem and solution. Athanasiou, Geil, Hazel, and Copeland (2002) noted that the internal attributional style of teachers is reflected in their beliefs about needed classroom interventions. Teachers tend to attribute lack of progress to students while crediting either themselves or students when progress is made. Other teachers or parents assume that there is a problem to be diagnosed through the use of formalized assessments designed to examine and describe the student. Although further assessment might be warranted in certain cases, teachers and school staff can address many of these concerns using an ecological problem-solving process.

Instructional consultation is one model that focuses on the interactions among a student's entry-level skills, the instructional design or format, and the actual task with which the student is presented, rather than a search for an internal student impairment (Rosenfeld, 2008). The use of this type of "instructional triangle" allows school staff to evaluate the effect of student–task mismatch, which can alleviate student behavior concerns. Effective teachers are called upon to focus on variables within their control—such as curriculum selection, instructional strategies, and interpersonal relationships with students—in order for meaningful student change to occur.

CREATING OPTIMAL CLASSROOM ENVIRONMENTS

For the purposes of this chapter, the classroom environment is determined by four key factors: 1) student and classroom variables, 2) physical arrangement of the classroom, 3) student expectations, and 4) student engagement. The effectiveness of the classroom environment is usually measured by student behavior, student engagement, and performance. When students are actively engaged in meaningful work, following the basic classroom rules, and communicating effectively with each other and their teacher, the classroom environment is effective and optimal. But optimal classroom environments do not arise spontaneously. Optimal environments begin with an effective attitude and a willingness to accept a basic premise—that classroom educators should first seek to manage the learning environment rather than the student. In a synthesis of empirical investigations related to the most effective instructional conditions, Foorman (2007) noted that researchers have identified the following seven characteristics of schools with outstanding achievement: 1) a positive social climate, 2) strong leadership, 3) increased time spent on instruction, 4) high expectations for all students, 5) continuous monitoring of student achievement, 6) ongoing professional development, and 7) parent involvement.

Student and Classroom Variables

Since the 1970s, researchers and educators alike have recognized that student and classroom variables play determining roles in the functioning of the classroom. Student variables such as home experiences, temperament, language skills, and social and interpersonal abilities exert a significant impact on performance. A student capable of following teacher directions and rules, completing classroom work, and responding appropriately to conventional management techniques is going to experience far more success and positive feedback from teachers than a student who does not use or has not mastered these skills. Furthermore, the structure of the classroom, the number of students, the range of student abilities and achievement, the size of the room, and the manner in which work is presented also contribute to successful educational experiences. Students are nurtured by educators who are competent in behavioral and educational strategies but who are first and foremost concerned with creating a safe, accepting climate. Thus, teacher, student, and classroom variables at any given moment interact with and contribute to, in varying degrees, the manner in which the classroom operates.

Physical Arrangement of the Classroom

For all children, especially those with learning or behavioral concerns, modifications to the classroom environment have been found to increase academic engagement and decrease disruptive behavior (Visser, 2001). Environmental modifications through a well-organized classroom are a preventive, whole-class approach to allow all children to access learning without interruption, reducing the probability that challenging behaviors will occur (Martella, Nelson, & Marchand-Martella, 2003). The allotment of space in the classroom is critical, as crowding at home and school can have a negative impact on behavior. Arrangement of the classroom exerts a powerful influence on teachers' abilities to praise, monitor, and supervise students effectively.

In addition to increasing physical space, teachers should attempt to minimize distractions. Although some schools have moved toward more open concept

The Learning Environment

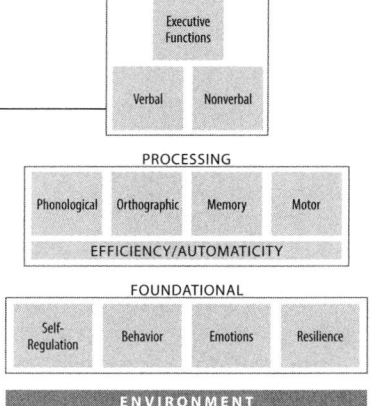

classrooms, research indicates that classrooms with more walls are associated with less student distraction from noise, less teacher distraction, more student satisfaction, and less restriction of classroom activities (Ahrentzen & Evans, 1984). Making changes to the structure of the classroom can include modifying the layout or design of the classroom so that materials are easily accessible and adopting seating arrangements that maximize attention while also minimizing opportunities for student distractions.

A three-stage process has been created to help teachers assess their classroom to improve student learning and behavior (Guardino & Fullerton, 2010). Step one includes having teachers observe students in their classroom, noting how areas of the classroom are used and where and when disruptive behavior is occurring. Step two includes identifying options for modifying problem areas, such as arranging furniture to define learning areas, delineating traffic patterns to minimize distraction from peers and the environment, and improving the availability and accessibility of materials. Finally, step three asks teachers to self-critique classroom modifications, addressing follow-up questions such as "Do students have all the materials they need throughout the day in their own space?" and "Do any modifications need rearranging, changing, or removal?" These strategies can help teachers begin to identify simple solutions for improving student engagement and learning.

Out-of-Classroom Services

In a chapter about the classroom environment, it may seem odd to address out-of-classroom services, but these options are important for some students. Many students with learning, emotional, and behavior difficulties spend the majority of their time in general education classrooms. A few students with the most severe difficulties are served within self-contained classrooms and may not receive any general education services. Others receive a portion of their instruction in small-group settings or in resource rooms. Although the goals of inclusion are philosophically sound, students with severe learning, emotional, and behavior difficulties require more support and intensive individualized instruction than can solely be provided within a general education classroom.

In the late 1970s, few, if any, argued with the spirit of the concept of the least restrictive placement. Cruickshank cautioned, however, that, for a student with SLD, the least restrictive placement might often be the most restrictive academically:

> A child [who is] placed in a so-called least restrictive situation and [is] unable to achieve, who lacks an understanding teacher, who does not have appropriate learning materials, who is faced with tasks he cannot manage, whose failures result in negative comments by his classmates, and whose parents reflect frustration to him when he is at home, is indeed being restricted on all sides. (1977, p. 194)

Given the increased responsibility and time restraints placed on classroom teachers, there is often insufficient time and resources to provide some children with the specialized help they require. Individualization in typical classrooms is simply not a reality; as Lieberman pointed out, "The barrage of curriculum materials, syllabi, grade-level expectations for performance, standardized achievement tests, competency tests and so on continue to overwhelm even the most flexible teachers" (1992, p. 15).

A further concern is the lack of academic progress for some students who spend all their time in general educational environments. Even when students with SLD are part of responsible inclusion programs, many do not make sufficient or acceptable academic progress in general education classrooms (Fuchs, Fuchs, &

Fernstrom, 1993; Zigmond et al., 1995). As Klingner, Vaughn, Hughes, Schumm, and Elbaum described,

> The students of greatest concern to us were those who were very poor readers at the start of the school year and as a group made no progress, despite being part of a responsible inclusion program that received substantial support. We must conclude that full-time placement in the general educational classroom with in-class support from special education teachers is not sufficient to meet the needs of these students. They require combined services that include in-class support and daily intensive one-to-one instruction from highly trained personnel. This is an expensive proposition but appears to be the only solution that will yield growth in reading for students with severe reading disabilities. (1998, p. 159)

This level of intensive instruction is necessary for helping students with reading disabilities become competent readers.

Placement decisions should not be dictated by political or educational trends but rather by the needs of an individual student. Mercer (1995) noted that teachers should not be discussing the least restrictive environment but, instead, the most enabling environment. The issue to address is where the student will receive the most appropriate and effective instruction, whether in a general or special education classroom. For the majority of students, effective teachers can create an environment in which even students with weaknesses in other Building Blocks can function optimally and successfully.

Student Expectations

Establishing expectations includes identifying and defining a small number of positively stated expectations or rules that are broad enough to include all desired behavior and are mutually exclusive (Simonsen, Fairbanks, Briesch, Myers, & Sugai, 2008). Teachers are encouraged to systematically introduce, teach, model, and reinforce such expectations so that all students receive appropriate supervision and feedback. This could include basic messages such as "Be respectful, be responsible, be safe" to more specific classroom rules or norms that students actively contribute in developing. Posting, teaching, and reviewing expectations have been associated with decreases in off-task and disruptive behavior as well as increases in academic engagement (Lane et al., 2003). Active supervision is also a key component of reinforcing such expectations. This includes teachers moving around the classroom, interacting with students, correcting errors made by students, and providing reinforcement for behavior that is consistent with classroom expectations. Active supervision of students within the classroom and nonclassroom areas (e.g., hallways) has also been shown to decrease behavior incidents and increase student participation (De Pry & Sugai, 2002; Schuldheisz & van der Mars, 2001).

Transitions

Of all the parts of the school day, transitions provide the greatest potential for disruption. Transitions account for close to one fifth of the time spent during the school day. Teachers can effectively manage this component of the environment by modeling appropriate behavior; signaling the beginning and ending of activities clearly; dealing with transition problems as soon as they occur; having students actually practice transitions; and providing ample reinforcement for quick, smooth transitions.

Transitions are particularly difficult for students with ADHD and attentional challenges.

The Learning Environment

Mr. Chavez struggled to help Jeremy come into the classroom, settle down, and begin working. Because of his problems with self-control as the result of ADHD, Jeremy experienced little difficulty getting off task or moving to an enjoyable activity but experienced much more difficulty than his peers with returning to and completing a structured task. Just walking from his classroom to the resource room was a difficult transition for Jeremy. Walking through the hallway afforded Jeremy a number of interesting activities, from stopping in the bathroom to visiting with other children in the halls. Punishment for arriving late to the resource room did little to alter Jeremy's behavior. Mr. Chavez decided to increase Jeremy's interest in and motivation for arriving on time to his classroom, using what he had learned in a workshop about reinforcement for students with ADHD. Mr. Chavez offered an incentive for all students, including Jeremy. Students arriving early or on time were given the opportunity to stop work early and spend the last 10 minutes of class working on a group jigsaw puzzle. Once the puzzle was completed, Mr. Chavez had promised an ice cream party for all his students. The solution worked effectively, and Jeremy began arriving on time to the resource classroom.

At times, rearranging the classroom can assist with transitions.

After reviewing the basic principles of class management and organization, Ms. Jones helped Mr. Patrick reduce the number of transitions by adjusting station locations. Ms. Jones also helped Mr. Patrick with a number of other issues noted. Mr. Patrick realized that even simple issues such as deciding where materials are placed in the classroom or how often students move from place to place can be powerful forces in determining student behavior, cooperation, and performance.

Student Engagement

Since 1975, research has documented that the proportion of time in which students are actively and productively engaged in learning best predicts their academic achievement and the overall quality of the classroom. As early as 1977, Good and Grouws reported that students make greater gains in academic achievement and like their classrooms better when minimal time is spent on discipline. A teacher's effectiveness in managing behavior and choosing instructional strategies needs to match the learning capacities of students. Though some have suggested that the nature and quality of time in the classroom may be used to create a formula to predict learning, no one has yet generated a formula that can be uniformly applied by each teacher. Productive classroom time is a function not only of students' abilities but also of the teacher's personality, teaching style, and management of the environment.

Typically, between 50% and 60% of the total school day is used for direct instruction (Strother, 1984). Time is often lost in organizing and beginning instruction, managing transitions, dealing with misbehavior, and responding to requests for assistance. However, if students are actively engaged in instruction, then it is difficult to engage in incompatible behaviors (e.g., blurting out, talking to peers, being out of seat). Teachers can increase active engagement in the classroom by increasing students' opportunities to respond. This teacher behavior includes prompting or soliciting a student response (e.g., asking question, presenting a demand). Two common methods used to increase the rate of presenting opportunities to respond in a classroom include choral responding, where all students answer a question in unison, and response cards, where all students write their answers to a question on erasable boards or papers and then hold up the boards for the teacher to see (Simonsen et al., 2008). Clickers, or student response systems, are another method whereby teachers can use technology to increase students' opportunity to actively engage in learning. Research demonstrates today's learners prefer to process pictures, sounds, and video rather than text (Hart, 2008). Implementing audio and visual learning tools in the classroom can add variety to the learning environment, such as the use of short video clips or podcasts. Using online discussion boards provides a broader opportunity for students to participate and contribute to discussions outside of class. Increasing the pace by presenting students opportunities to respond has led to increases in on-task behaviors and the number of correct student responses (Sutherland, Alder, & Gunter, 2003).

A second strategy is classwide peer tutoring where students are paired and assigned the roles of tutor and tutee. Tutoring could be used during tasks such as paired reading practice or teacher-directed activities, allowing students access to peer and teacher support. Classwide peer tutoring has been shown to improve not only academic engagement but also reading achievement (Simmons, Fuchs, & Fuchs, 1995). Even during independent learning time, time can be used productively if activities are of high quality. Many independent student learning activities for K–3 classrooms created by the Florida Center for Reading Research can be downloaded at no cost from the center's web site (http:/www.fcrr.org/Curriculum/studentCenterActivites.htm).

CONDITIONS AND COMPONENTS OF THE INTERVENTIONS

The conditions and components of an intervention appear as important as the selection and use of a specific evidence-based approach. Results from intervention studies suggest that the nature of the program is less important than its comprehensiveness and intensity (Fletcher et al., 2007). For example, Torgesen and colleagues (2001) found the same positive outcomes for two different reading programs that both provided intensive, systematic, one-to-one instruction. Effective instructional elements include small-group instruction with high response rates, the provision of immediate feedback, and sequential mastery of topics—all elements of good teaching (National Joint Committee on Learning Disabilities, 2005). In addition, several instructional principles can help inform decisions regarding diverse learners and effective early instruction: 1) capitalize and use instructional time efficiently; 2) provide interventions early, frequently, and strategically; 3) teach less but more thoroughly; 4) explain strategies in a clear, explicit manner to students; 5) provide teacher-directed and student-centered activities; and 6) evaluate the effectiveness of instructional materials and student progress frequently (Kame'enui, 1993). According to Hallahan, students with SLD also need "intensive, relentless, iterative, and individualized instruction that depends on a viable categorical approach to special education service delivery" (2007, p. 24). In addition, many types of interventions and methodologies are needed to meet the needs of the diverse learners in any classroom.

Individualized and Small-Group Instruction

Individualized and small-group instruction are effective and necessary components for learning and are research-proven techniques to enhance student achievement. Teachers often face the dilemma, however, of working with individuals or a small group while simultaneously managing the rest of the classroom. In this circumstance, some students may be disruptive. Other students may require assistance and must wait until teachers are available, thereby wasting valuable classroom time. In some circumstances, a parent volunteer or an aide can help with this problem. In addition, periodic praise directed at the larger group can be effective in keeping

The Learning Environment

students on task. The following four critical components can help teachers manage classroom instruction in groups: 1) moving consistently through the room, stopping for only 15–30 seconds at any one place while instructing or while students are working independently; 2) scanning the room to remain aware of what the entire classroom is doing; 3) praising students; and 4) following up with the groups (Paine, Radicchi, Rosellini, Deutchman, & Darch, 1983).

A master teacher, Ms. Delphine Woods (personal communication, September 1998), advises new teachers that one of the most important ways to establish respect in the classroom is to call students by their first name and use "please" and "thank you" as many times as possible each day with students. Effective praise should follow the *if–then rule:* If a student is engaged in a behavior that a teacher wants to increase, then it should be praised. Good praise should include the student's name; a description of the behavior being praised; and a varied, convincing delivery.

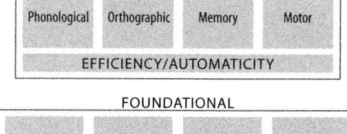

Although all teachers agree that praise is important, the amount of praise that students receive for exhibiting appropriate behavior typically decreases dramatically by third grade. Concomitantly, the rate of teachers' negative attention toward students who are off task or engaged in other nonproductive activities usually increases. Praise, however, is the fuel that helps the engine of the classroom operate efficiently.

Principles of Instruction

Research in cognitive science and on cognitive supports and investigations on the classroom practices of master teachers have revealed a number of research-based principles of instruction. The following 10 instructional principles are summarized by Rosenshine (2012), highlighting evidence-based strategies that teachers can use to ensure optimal student learning and achievement.

1. *Begin a lesson with a short review of previous learning.* Daily review can strengthen previous learning and can lead to fluent recall.

2. *Present new material in small steps with student practice after each step.* Only present small amounts of new material at any time, and then assist students as they practice this material.

3. *Ask a large number of questions and check the responses of all students.* Questions help students practice new information and connect new material to their prior learning (e.g., "How are ____ and ____ alike?" "Which one is the best ____ and why?")

4. *Provide models.* Providing students models and worked examples can help them learn to solve problems faster.

5. *Guide student practice.* Successful teachers spend more time guiding students' practice of new material.

6. *Check for student understanding.* Ensuring student understanding at each point can help students learn the material with fewer errors.

7. *Obtain a high success rate.* Up to 82% of students' answers were correct in classrooms with the most successful teachers, whereas least successful teachers had only a 73% success rate. Guided practice can lead to higher success rates during independent work.

8. *Provide scaffolds for difficult tasks.* Scaffold student work with temporary supports and provide additional scaffolds to assist students when they learn difficult tasks.

9. *Require and monitor independent practice.* Students need extensive, successful, independent practice in order for knowledge and skills to become automatic.
10. *Engage students in weekly and monthly review.* Students need extensive practice to develop well-connected and automatic knowledge.

Relationships

The more positive a teacher's relationships are with students, the more likely students will want to comply when the teacher provides an instruction or directions. Unfortunately, research suggests that relative to Latino and Caucasian children, African American children and their parents appear to have less supportive relationships with teachers, and the quality of these relationships affects children's motivation, engagement, and achievement (Hughes & Kwok, 2007; see the "Diverse Backgrounds" section for more on cultural and ethnic backgrounds). In addition, disruptive students often develop negative relationships with their teachers. This inadvertently contributes to differences in a teacher's relationships with different students. Research has demonstrated that students who teachers like and who are compliant are provided with more opportunities to respond academically; receive more teacher support, praise, and attention; and receive less criticism.

Unfortunately, teachers receive little professional preparation on how to build positive alliances with parents and warm relationships with students (Hughes & Kwok, 2007). To foster a positive relationship with students, teachers should consider the following:

- Avoid responding directly to student behavior that is provocative or confrontational.
- Provide genuine praise and encouragement to all students, making certain that each student experiences success every day.
- Use humor.
- Arrange opportunities for students to receive positive attention, contribute to the class, and feel that they are important classroom members.
- Work to develop positive relationships with all students in the class.

Feeling cared about by a teacher encourages students' investment and engagement in school and learning (Patrick, Ryan, & Kaplan, 2007).

Communication with Students

Teachers who rely on positive communication to interact with their students are less likely to have students who are noncompliant. In contrast, when teachers use punitive methods to discipline children, they are more likely to experience classrooms in which students resort to less acceptable forms of noncompliance, such as defiance, passivity, and oppositionality.

This chapter is in part devoted to strategies to help teachers develop effective communication with their students. The bottom line is that ineffective communication is more likely to lead to an escalating pattern of disruptive classroom behavior. As described by Forehand and McMahon (1981), when teachers provide a command directed to a student with whom they have not developed an effective means of communication, the child often interprets the command as aversive and does not comply. Teachers then give up, withdraw, or escalate coercive pressure for compliance. This may involve the teacher raising his or her voice,

The Learning Environment

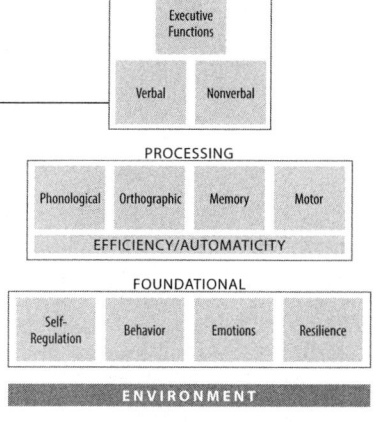

threatening, or intimidating the student. Then the student is rewarded for noncompliance if the teacher withdraws or terminates his or her request or if the interaction escalates, which provides the student with an opportunity to practice direct defiance.

Teachers usually fall into this trap with students because they themselves may have been rewarded for using coercive tactics if students eventually comply. Teachers must be sensitive to this escalating pattern of noncompliance, a pattern that often is driven by a negative reinforcement paradigm. To reduce risk, teachers should consider manipulating antecedent behaviors by anticipating problems and teaching students competent skills to deal with classroom issues. When a teacher acts in a reactionary manner after a problem has occurred and has begun to escalate, the probability that the classroom will be further disrupted increases. Unfortunately, most teacher interventions focus on manipulating problems after the noncompliant event occurs rather than manipulating the antecedents. Teachers use far more negative responses—such as punishment, time-out, and response cost—than positive consequences. Although antecedent manipulation is effective, most efforts to increase compliance and reduce noncompliance involve consequential events such as reward or punishment. Preventive interventions, however, are recommended because they reduce the potential number of negative interactions that arise between teachers and students. This mind-set allows a teacher to act in a proactive rather than reactive fashion.

Communication with Parents

One important proactive measure for teachers to take is establishing good communication with parents. If teachers make an effort at the beginning of the school year to communicate with parents and establish a workable means by which parents can communicate with them, students are much less likely to experience problems between home and school. Parents should be encouraged to write notes, call, or e-mail with questions. Most school districts have e-mail addresses available for every teacher. This is a particularly efficient means for teachers and parents to communicate. Although a teacher's communication with many parents may be minimal, setting this communication system in place is invaluable as problems arise. For students with chronic or ongoing academic or behavioral challenges, a daily or weekly note is an effective means of communicating with parents. Figure 3.1 provides a sample school–home note for elementary school students.

DIVERSE BACKGROUNDS

Almost every school population consists of children from many different economic, ethnic, linguistic, and cultural backgrounds. Children who live in poverty, as well as students whose primary language is not English, face additional challenges in adapting to and being successful in the school environment.

Economically Disadvantaged Backgrounds

Although the new millennium has brought promises of unlimited technological, scientific, and cultural advances, our society is experiencing increasing problems with preparing our youth for the future. Competency in reading, writing, and mathematics is simply not enough. Violence, increased school dropout rates, and mental health concerns among students signify this problem.

| Student Name _____ | Date _____ |

Teacher directions: Please rate this student in each of the following areas, using a 1 as the best score:

Came to class prepared	5	4	3	2	1
Used class time wisely	5	4	3	2	1
Followed class rules	5	4	3	2	1
Followed recess rules	5	4	3	2	1
Respected the rights of classmates	5	4	3	2	1
Completed homework	5	4	3	2	1
Followed directions	5	4	3	2	1
Displayed a good attitude	5	4	3	2	1
Participated	5	4	3	2	1

Homework _____

Comments _____

Overall, today was a
☐ great day
☐ good day
☐ average day
☐ mediocre day
☐ very poor day

Teacher initials _____

Figure 3.1. School–home note. A score of 1 is the best score a student can earn. (From Goldstein, S., & Goldstein, M. [1991]. *It's just attention disorder: User's manual* [p. 64]. Salt Lake City, UT: Neurology, Learning, and Behavior Center; adapted by permission.)

Many children do not have adequate educational opportunities prior to entering school and come from impoverished environments. Sadly, living in poverty often results in poor social and academic outcomes for children. In fact, poverty, with its many associated conditions such as inadequate food and shelter, exposure to violence and chaotic living conditions, and limited learning opportunities from nurturing adults, is the strongest predictor of school failure (Kauffman & Landrum, 2012). Teachers must consider each child's living conditions.

As described in Chapter 1, Mark, a fifth-grade student, lives in a crowded trailer with three siblings and four adults. There is little room for sleeping and no room for studying. It is not reasonable to expect Mark to complete homework at night or to always come to school with clean clothes. The challenge of preparing children for the future has and must be increasingly borne on the shoulders of educators. Our schools must find a way to educate all students from all types of backgrounds efficiently and effectively by providing them with knowledge and instilling in them qualities of resilience—qualities that will help them be confident and know how to overcome the daily adversities they may face.

Culturally and Linguistically Diverse Backgrounds

An essential aspect of understanding the role of the environment on behavior and performance is consideration of the diverse cultural and linguistic backgrounds of children. According to the 2011 Census, English is not the first language for about

The Learning Environment

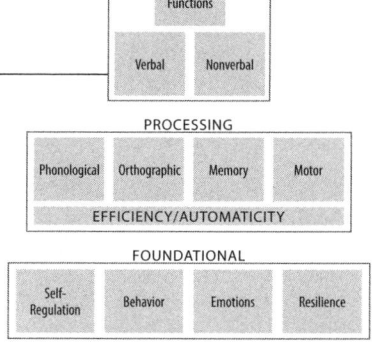

one fifth of the children enrolled in U.S. public schools (U.S. Census Bureau, 2013). In addition, teachers may respond to and interact differently with students from different racial and ethnic backgrounds. Results from a recent meta-analysis indicated that teachers have higher expectations for Asian American and European American students than for Latino or African American students and that teachers direct more questions and encouraging remarks toward European American students than Latino and African American students (Tenenbaum & Ruck, 2007). Clearly, this reality suggests that teachers must pay attention to and develop an understanding of the unique cultural values and beliefs of each student in the classroom. Based on this individually tailored understanding of linguistic and cultural differences, a teacher can then evaluate more readily the suitability of specific behavioral and academic intervention strategies for a specific child. All teachers need to address the myriad difficulties facing students from culturally and linguistically diverse groups and select interventions that are responsive to their needs (Klingner, Sorrells, & Barrera, 2007).

For decades, concerns have been expressed regarding the fact that certain racial and ethnic groups have been and continue to be overrepresented in the SLD category (Rueda & Windmueller, 2006). Many of these students may be placed in special education because they are not meeting school demands, even though they do not have a "disability" per se. Thus, the challenge becomes providing more appropriate instruction to children who speak different languages within general education settings. English immersion programs offer the least native language support, and the students enrolled in these programs are more likely to be placed in special education than students who are participating in other types of language support programs (Artiles, Rueda, Salazar, & Higareda, 2005).

School districts in California categorize English language learners (ELLs) into two subgroups: students with limited proficiency in English who are proficient in their native language and students with limited proficiency in both their native language and English (Artiles et al., 2005). Clearly, as long as they receive support, students with competency in one language, even if it is not English, are better prepared to meet the academic challenges of a classroom, whereas additional supports are needed for students with global linguistic weaknesses. An understanding of each student's unique circumstances can help a teacher create a classroom atmosphere where all children feel welcome, safe, and valued as individuals. In essence, the goal for all teachers should be to learn about the cultural and linguistic backgrounds of students in the classroom and create a classroom climate where differences are respected and shared while at the same time advancing the language learning and achievement of all students (Klingner et al., 2007; Nelson & Van Meter, 2006).

HOMEWORK*

Successful management of homework is a key ingredient of an effective classroom environment. Children differ significantly in their attitudes about homework and the methods they use to complete homework. Teachers also differ in reasons for homework, homework strategies, and types of homework they assign. Children with weaknesses in the Building Blocks often consider homework another opportunity to fail, so they refuse or resist. Students with attention concerns may also

---

*The material in this section was adapted from the text on homework by Zentall and Goldstein (1999).

find other activities to do that are far more interesting than homework. They also have trouble remembering to turn in their homework even when it has been completed.

Many children with weaknesses in skills and abilities struggle with the completion of homework. Andy completed his homework independently, but his teacher could not read anything he had written. Katy had difficulty because she rarely understood her assignments and could not complete them without a great deal of parental assistance. Jeremy's parents had to sit down with him in the evening or he could not accomplish anything. Even with constant nagging, Jeremy just could not sustain the attention and effort needed for homework completion. Even on the days when Jeremy had his completed homework in his backpack, he rarely remembered to place it in the homework box without his teacher's prompting. Ryan struggled with all homework involving reading and writing but completed his math assignments independently. Maria's mother spent several hours with her every evening, helping her with homework. Although Maria never had late assignments and always received high grades on homework, her mother had assumed a large role in homework completion. Ben could not keep up with the assigned readings, so he did not do any reading unless one of his parents read with him. In secondary school, John experienced problems similar to Katy's. He became overwhelmed with all the assignments from his different classes and often did not understand what he was supposed to do. Fortunately, his father spent a lot of time helping him complete the assigned work. Samuel and Mark never turned in any homework.

The purpose of homework is to promote independence, not to foster increased dependence on parents. Homework should be manageable and reasonable. For children who struggle, adjustments have to be made in the type and amount of work they receive.

In spite of these student-centered problems, some benefits can be derived from homework. Homework is a cost-effective means of delivering instruction that increases in importance as children move into junior high (middle school) and high school. Homework also can help foster positive attitudes toward school and provide an important link between home experiences and school learning. In the elementary grades, high levels of feedback and supervision are necessary so that students can practice their assignments correctly. For students in middle school and high school, homework should facilitate knowledge acquisition in specific areas. The average high school student in a class that was assigned homework outperformed almost three quarters of peers in a class without homework as measured by standardized tests, and junior high school students achieved half that gain (Cooper & Nye, 1994). Students devoting time to homework are thus likely on a path to improved achievement as well as a path of greater achievement motivation and better skill development.

In general, teachers' problems with homework can be grouped into three main areas:

1. Problems creating assignments
2. Problems in the meaningfulness, difficulty, and length of assignments
3. Problems getting students to complete homework

The Learning Environment

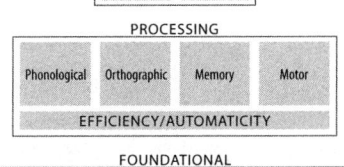

Creating Assignments

When teachers create assignments, clear instructions are critical. A teacher should consider the purpose of the assignment, the date that it is due, the format required, the materials that are necessary, and the requirements for good performance, which may include many steps in a complex task. The majority of teachers assign homework at the end of class periods, which may penalize younger students or students with difficulties in attention or behavior. These students often have difficulty attending at the end of the class or day. Other principles to adhere to include the following:

- Present assignments with clear directions earlier in the school day.
- Offer students the opportunity to volunteer to explain the assignment in their own words.
- Provide a brief time for students to begin assignments in class to make certain that they understand what they need to do.
- Post homework assignments in the classroom (e.g., on the blackboard, on a bulletin board) so students will have plenty of time to write down the tasks.

Meaningfulness, Difficulty, and Assignment Length

Assignments that are meaningful, at a moderate level of difficulty, and neither too repetitive nor too long are more likely to be completed. In reality, the most frequent types of assignments are unfinished class work and practice tasks (Polloway, Epstein, Bursuck, Madhavi, & Cumblad, 1994). Boredom is a frequent complaint of students with regard to homework. Boredom results in students completing less work, less accurately. To reduce boredom, consider using homework to reinforce what has been learned, alternate math and reading homework on different nights, keep repetition to a minimum, and allow students who struggle with assignments to begin homework in class to make certain that they understand the process and task.

Motivation to complete homework can also be increased by altering the meaningfulness of assignments. If an assignment is interesting and relevant to the child's age level and if elements of choice are included in the assignment, more homework is likely to be completed. Children who are able to understand how their schoolwork relates to their own skills and experiences have fewer homework problems (Nicholls, McKenzie, & Shufro, 1994).

Assignment difficulty is also a critical factor. For students to independently complete an assignment, they must have achieved a moderate level of understanding during class. When students do not understand homework material, they become frustrated while attempting to complete homework. When assignments vary in difficulty level and students vary in ability, the teacher should consider what additional supports may be available during homework. Some schools or districts offer telephone or online homework hot lines. Helping parents understand the nature and methods for homework assignments is also critical. Homework can be reduced in length to accommodate students with slower working rates or limited attention spans without changing the purpose of homework. A teacher may also specify the amount of time that should be spent on the homework rather than specifying the amount of material to be completed. For example, a teacher may ask students to read for a half-hour rather than reading a set number of pages.

Completing Homework

Completion of homework depends in part on a teacher's ability to communicate that finished assignments are important, valued, expected, and rewarded. Homework completion must provide some positive outcome for students. Positive outcomes could include feedback when homework is completed successfully and turned in for a grade. When teachers convey the significance of homework to students patiently and consistently, students eventually understand that completion of homework is important.

When students experience difficulty with some aspect of behavior and learning, modifications may need to be made in the homework. An assignment change involves alteration of the information, curriculum content, or lesson objective. If the lesson objective is solving math story problems, then reading the problem to the child or allowing the child to use a calculator does not represent a change of lesson objective. However, if the objective is math calculation and the child computes math problems using a calculator, then a change of lesson objective has been made. In this case, checking math calculations with a calculator would be reinforcing to the child after the completion of a certain number of problems. This would not involve changing the lesson objective. When a change in lesson objective has been made, a teacher may find it difficult to justify giving that student the same grade as others. Particularly in elementary school, grades should be based on personal accomplishments and not on peer comparison. When teachers compare students who have marked weaknesses in one or more Building Blocks with peers, the student's performance appears substandard and he or she is assigned failing grades. For a student for whom a task change has been made and who puts forth reasonable effort, a grade that reflects his or her abilities and effort should be provided.

Katy, one of the students mentioned earlier in this book, is several years behind most of her peers in academic performance. Katy has weaknesses in language and reading. Figure 3.2 presents a story that she wrote about her missing homework. Living in Arizona, she notes that a coyote ate her homework rather than a dog! By reading her story, you can see her weaknesses in sentence structure and vocabulary. If adjustments are not made for Katy, she will receive several failing grades. This would defeat the purpose and goals of education.

When students fail to complete assignments, consider talking to them about why the assignment was not completed, and assist them in developing a system

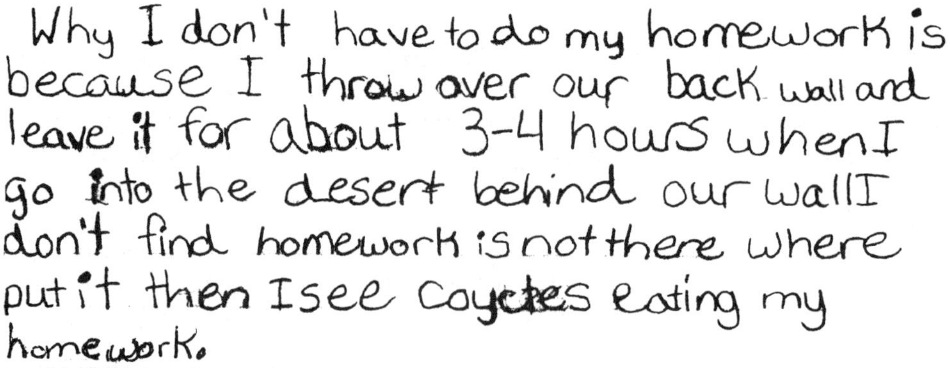

> Why I don't have to do my homework is because I throw over our back wall and leave it for about 3-4 hours when I go into the desert behind our wall I don't find homework is not there where put it then I see Coyotes eating my homework.

Figure 3.2. Katy's story about missing homework.

The Learning Environment

to make certain assignments are completed in the future. Also, consider whether too many assignments are being given. Assess adaptations, and actively involve parents by providing recommended homework strategies. Assignments are more likely to be completed and turned in when a routine has been established for homework, when reduced homework is offered as an incentive for completed homework, and when school privileges are used as incentives as well. As a general rule, homework assignments should not be used as punishment. When assignments become part of a behavior management system, students' attitudes toward these assignments become equally negative. Often this attitude spreads to all assignments. One of the purposes of homework is to foster an enjoyment of working during leisure time. If students find that their assignments are intended as punishment, then the proposed benefits of homework are not realized.

Increased parental involvement has also been found to increase homework completion, increase attendance rates of students who may avoid school, decrease disruptive behavior at school, improve students' attitudes toward school, and increase math and reading achievement (Bryan & Nelson, 1994). At the beginning of the school year, a teacher can meet with parents at an after-school meeting or back-to-school night and provide a brief, printed overview to parents about homework for the coming year. After the first month, a teacher can ask parents whether they are satisfied with the type and amount of homework their child receives, how much time the child is spending, how much assistance is provided, what kinds of problems are encountered, and what suggestions they could offer to improve the class's homework policies. Communication with parents is even more critical when children experience weaknesses in the Building Blocks that cause them behavior, emotional, or achievement problems at school.

Occasionally, it is unreasonable to expect children to complete homework. Because of limited home support, Mark never attempted homework assignments. Because Mr. Patrick, his fifth-grade teacher, was aware of his circumstances, he arranged a time for Mark to complete homework during the school day. Although it involved taking the late bus home, Mark was willing to stay at school with his teacher's supervision and complete his assignments.

Figure 3.3 presents a questionnaire about effective procedures for homework. This checklist offers guidelines for teachers to begin establishing policies, attitudes, and activities regarding homework. Teachers rarely take a class about homework, yet the management of homework is a significant factor in enhancing student performance.

In the elementary grades, teachers and parents often perceive the primary role of homework as the opportunity to review and strengthen basic achievement. Homework in the elementary grades is a critical activity that assists students in developing the independent learning skills, self-management, and responsibility necessary to become independent learners. When students struggle as the result of learning, emotional, or behavior problems, these important benefits of homework are jeopardized due to the increased stress and pressure that homework places on these students and their families. Teachers must not only make adjustments in homework for these students but also attempt to locate and provide other activities and opportunities for these students to develop independent learning skills.

Assigning Homework

☐ Yes ☐ No 1. Do you use an outline of assignments and dates?
☐ Yes ☐ No 2. Do you make sure students have assignment books, homework planners, or homework buddies?
☐ Yes ☐ No 3. Do you make daily assignments at the beginning of the class rather than at the end?
☐ Yes ☐ No 4. Do you make sure the directions given to students about homework are clear by asking a student to repeat them or checking what is written down in the assignment books?
☐ Yes ☐ No 5. Do you present instructions visually (e.g., on the overhead projector, on the board) as well as orally?
☐ Yes ☐ No 6. Do you provide assistance at the end of the period or end of the day to students who have trouble organizing their materials?
☐ Yes ☐ No 7. Do you provide assistance to students who have trouble sustaining attention by modifying the amount of work required of them?

Meaningfulness, Difficulty, and Length of Homework

☐ Yes ☐ No 1. Does the homework assignment overlap the lessons from the day?
☐ Yes ☐ No 2. Do you make homework assignments interesting to students?
☐ Yes ☐ No 3. Do you talk about the purposes of the assignment?
☐ Yes ☐ No 4. Do you communicate to parents what is being taught and explain how parents can help?
☐ Yes ☐ No 5. Do you avoid assignments that require self-teaching or new learning?
☐ Yes ☐ No 6. Do you involve parents, other family members, or community resources in homework projects?
☐ Yes ☐ No 7. Do you use in-class study periods for elementary students?
☐ Yes ☐ No 8. Do you allow students with handwriting difficulties to use adaptations such as computers, notetakers, taped reports, printing, or reduced writing and copying?
☐ Yes ☐ No 9. Do you give assignments that are active as opposed to passive (e.g., gathering resources, interviewing people)?

Collecting and Returning Homework with Feedback

☐ Yes ☐ No 1. Do you teach children who have difficulty returning homework how to graph percent of homework completed per day using colorful bars?
☐ Yes ☐ No 2. Are the rewards for completing homework as great as the consequences for not completing it?
☐ Yes ☐ No 3. Do you consistently grade homework or provide feedback to the student?
☐ Yes ☐ No 4. Do you give students incentives for completing homework, such as extra recess or class outings?
☐ Yes ☐ No 5. Do you have students turn in written excuses for missed assignments?
☐ Yes ☐ No 6. Do you allow a certain number of excused homework assignments (especially for students with special learning needs or with many after-school responsibilities)?

Figure 3.3. Positive teacher homework practices. (From Zentall, S., & Goldstein, S. [1999]. *Seven steps to homework success* [pp. 98–99]. Plantation, FL: Specialty Press; adapted by permission.)

CONCLUSION

By understanding the powerful role of environmental factors in the classroom, teachers can enhance each child's educational success and also create an effective and efficient setting for learning. Strengthening a student's sense of self-esteem and emotional well-being is not an "extra" curriculum; if anything, a student's sense of belonging, security, and self-confidence provide the scaffolding that supports the foundation for enhanced learning, motivation, and self-discipline. Teachers are called upon to provide social and emotional interventions hand in hand with academic instruction (Merrell, 2002; Weist, 2003). In fact, a sustainable school

The Learning Environment

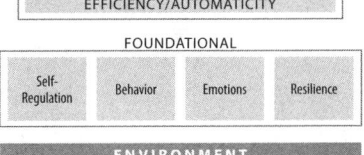

environment must be capable of meeting the social, emotional, and academic needs of all students (Elias, Zins, Graczyk, & Weissberg, 2003; Goldstein & Brooks, 2007). All aspects of the learning environment from curriculum and instruction to the student–teacher relationship and assessment of a school's climate play a role in achieving successful learning environments for all students.

SECTION II
Foundational Blocks

CHAPTER 4 OUTLINE

CHARACTERISTICS OF STUDENTS WITH HYPERACTIVITY AND POOR ATTENTION, PLANNING, AND IMPULSE CONTROL

- School Problems
- Attention-Deficit/Hyperactivity Disorder in Adulthood
- Biology and Environment
- Incidence
- Other Causes of These Problems
- A Cluster of Symptomatic Problems
- A Problem of Faulty Performance
- Core Symptoms
- Diagnostic Criteria
- Legal Protections

CAUSES OF ATTENTION-DEFICIT/HYPERACTIVITY DISORDER

DEVELOPMENTAL COURSE AND COMORBIDITY

- Early Symptoms
- Attention-Deficit/Hyperactivity Disorder and Language Disorders
- Attention-Deficit/Hyperactivity Disorder and Learning Disabilities
- Attention-Deficit/Hyperactivity Disorder and Social Difficulties
- Attention-Deficit/Hyperactivity Disorder and Behavior Problems

THE TEACHER'S ROLE IN THE EVALUATION OF ATTENTION, PLANNING, IMPULSE CONTROL, AND HYPERACTIVITY

MEDICATION

- Effects of Medication
- Neurotransmitters

A CLASSROOM MODEL FOR MANAGING INATTENTION, IMPULSIVITY, POOR PLANNING, AND HYPERACTIVITY

- Effectiveness of Interventions
- Behavior Management Strategies
- Planning Facilitation

INTERACTIVE ISSUES

- Be Positive
- Give Clear Directions
- State Rules
- Provide Cues
- Structure and Minimize Transitions
- Provide a Consistent Routine
- Keep Things Changing
- Allow Nondisruptive Movement
- Offer Feedback
- Pair an Undesirable Task with a Desirable Task
- Build Success
- Prepare for Changes
- Use Preventive Strategies
- Use Class Time Effectively
- Adapt the Curriculum
- Use Color-Coding

CONCLUSION

CHAPTER 4

Self-Regulation

Understanding and Managing Students with Hyperactivity and Poor Attention, Planning, and Impulse Control

As a 10½-year-old fifth-grade student, Jeremy had a history of impulsive, inattentive, and disruptive behaviors at school. According to Jeremy's family history, his father and mother had similar problems as students. Two nephews on his mother's side of the family had been diagnosed as having attention-deficit/hyperactivity disorder (ADHD). Jeremy reached his early developmental milestones at a typical rate, and he did not experience any serious developmental problems. At home, Jeremy's parents described him as inattentive and overactive, although he enjoyed watching television. He belonged to a scout troop but did not participate in any other activities. His grades at school were adequate, but every year teachers commented about his problems with completing work without significant prompts and supports. Although his grades were average, group achievement test data reflected that Jeremy's skills were in the top 10% for his age group. Clearly, he was not performing in school at that level.

Jeremy demonstrates a fairly typical history of an elementary school child with poor attention, planning, impulse control, and hyperactivity. Although these can also be symptoms of other serious psychiatric or developmental problems, most often they constitute ADHD.

The childhood cognitive and behavior problems characterized by inattention, poor planning and impulse control, and hyperactivity have long constituted the most chronic behavior problems of childhood (for a historical review, see Barkley, 2005). Since the early 1980s, these problems have composed the largest single source of referrals to child mental health centers (Barkley, 1981; Express Scripts Report, 2014; Jensen et al., 1999). It is not surprising, therefore, that these problems also result in the most common teacher complaints and may account for as many as 40% of referrals to special education services and child guidance clinics (Barkley, 2005; Goldstein & Goldstein, 1998; Wolraich et al., 2012). Referrals of boys have consistently outnumbered referrals for girls. In large-scale community-based studies, many of these children receive diagnoses of ADHD with the gender ratio for the diagnosis close to three to one (Barkley, 1990; Mouridsen, Rich, & Isager, 2014). The higher referral rate for boys may be a function of the greater prevalence of other disruptive problems, such as oppositional defiance and conduct disorder (Breen & Barkley, 1988; Goldstein & Gordon, 2003; Takeda, Ambrosini, deBerandinis, & Elia, 2012). Prevalence rates have also changed, as the diagnostic criteria have changed. Females are now diagnosed at a higher rate (Express Scripts Report, 2014). Because these problems make up the core symptoms of ADHD, this chapter will be organized by research related to this diagnosis.

CHARACTERISTICS OF STUDENTS WITH HYPERACTIVITY AND POOR ATTENTION, PLANNING, AND IMPULSE CONTROL

Even as educators learn about the diagnostic criteria for ADHD (*Diagnostic and Statistical Manual of Mental Disorders, Fifth Edition* [*DSM-5*]) comprising symptoms of inattention, hyperactivity, and impulsivity, data are being generated to support the hypothesis that, for the majority of affected children, poor executive functioning and planning leading to poor self-discipline represents the core impairment of this disorder (Barkley, 2005; Goldstein & Naglieri, 2006; Lopez-Vergara & Colder, 2013). The major consequence of these neuropsychological impairments is impulsive behavior. Problems with impulsivity can affect children's interactions in all environments, particularly in the classroom. Impulsivity results in a child's inability to meet situational demands in an age-appropriate fashion (Marx, Höpcke, Berger, Wandschneider, & Herpertz, 2013; Routh, 1978). Children with ADHD typically experience difficulty in educational environments. Their behavior is often described as uneven, unpredictable, and inconsistent. The unpredictable quality of their behavior—now you see it, now you don't—adds additional stress for educators and often leads to the erroneous belief that these problems stem from reduced motivation and limited desire rather than from neurologically based disabilities. It is easy to think that a capable student like Jeremy could just complete his work if he really tried, but this is not the case.

School Problems

Children with ADHD present an unpredictable variety of difficulties at school. For a significant percentage of children, problems observed in preschool progress as the child advances in school (Campbell, Endman, & Bernfeld, 1977; Schleifer et al., 1975). A review of the available literature suggests that measures of attention, activity, and inappropriate vocalization in the classroom consistently distinguish children with ADHD from groups of children without ADHD (Harvey, Lugo-Candelas, & Breaux, in press; Platzman et al., 1992). In fact, Jeremy's mother recalled the day when the kindergarten teacher asked her to come to school to get Jeremy because he was under his desk, barking like a dog.

In elementary school, school-based ADHD-associated symptoms include problems with activity level, problems with vocalization, negative peer and teacher interactions, and off-task behavior (DuPaul & Stoner, 2003; Loe & Feldman, 2007). For students at the secondary and postsecondary levels, the continued problems of ADHD combine increasingly with a history of negative school experiences to exert a cumulative negative impact on behavior, achievement, emotions, and self-esteem.

When considering the chronology of problems, it is important to review a child's experiences in the early grades.

Self-Regulation

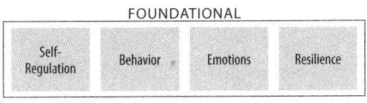

Jeremy was first diagnosed with ADHD in kindergarten. One of his teachers had a 15-year-old son with ADHD. Somewhat reluctantly, his parents, Mr. and Ms. Hanson, agreed to have the school conduct an evaluation. The summary from this evaluation is presented in Figure 4.1.

When the Hansons met with the school team, the psychologist noted that he had never tested a child before who had such a high intellectual level in addition to symptoms consistent with the diagnosis of ADHD. The Hansons then took Jeremy to a psychiatrist in town who specialized in ADHD. He interviewed Jeremy and his parents but did not do any more testing.

Jeremy began on a low dose of Ritalin (methylphenidate hydrochloride) in the summer before first grade. Although the medicine helped Jeremy tremendously, each year, new struggles emerged with behavior and academics. In fact, his school career to date was marked by performance inconsistencies. Jeremy went from the honor role in third grade to getting straight Ds in fourth grade. He also had an increased number of office discipline referrals, which began to worry his parents.

Over the years, Mr. and Mrs. Hanson saved Jeremy's report cards. The comments in Table 4.1 were taken directly from these cards. When reading these comments, several common themes emerge. Jeremy's class performance is marked by inconsistency; sometimes he can do the task and sometimes he cannot. He has a tendency to rush through assignments and make careless mistakes. He does not sustain enough effort and is often unprepared for exams. His assignments are often missing or late. At times, Jeremy demonstrates inappropriate behavior. He becomes overwhelmed when tasks involve too many details. These types of difficulties that Jeremy's teachers describe are very typical of students with ADHD.

Attention-Deficit/Hyperactivity Disorder in Adulthood

For many individuals, ADHD represents a lifelong disorder (de Zwaan et al., 2012; Kessler, Berglund, Demler, Jin, & Walters, 2006; Roffman, 2000). Research reflects the significant and pervasive effect that symptoms of ADHD have for the majority of children with ADHD as they enter into adulthood (Barkley, Murphy, & Fischer, 2010; Biederman et al., 1999; Hart, Lahey, Loeber, Applegate, & Frick, 1995; Lomas & Gartside, 1999). Years of ineffective interactions with parents, teachers, and peers and failure to meet the expectations of one's surroundings result in a long history of negative experiences (Leitchman, 1993). These in turn become a major force in the child's emerging personality (Brooks, 2002; Ungar, 2010; Wender, 1979). Clearly, the daily experiences of children contribute to their adult life outcomes, with even small successes building resilience and the capacity to deal with stress (Werner, 2013). Thus, educators must be concerned not only with the effect of ADHD core symptoms in the classroom but also with the significant secondary impact these problems will have on a child's future life and the lives of his or her family members.

Jeremy, a child functioning in the superior range of intellectual skill, demonstrates a history of mild to moderate disruptive behaviors. This pattern of problems is chronic and has caused Jeremy school problems since his entry into kindergarten.

Jeremy struggles to attend to repetitive, effortful, uninteresting activities. He experiences difficulties with restless, hyperactive behavior and often acts impulsively. This symptom profile appears consistent with DSM-IV diagnostic criteria for attention-deficit/hyperactivity disorder. This diagnosis is deferred to Jeremy's physician.

Despite exceptional intellectual ability and advanced academic achievement, Jeremy's problems with attention, hyperactivity, and impulse control have significantly and negatively affected his ability to succeed in school and benefit from his education. He does not experience specific physical disabilities, developmental delays, social difficulties, or serious psychological or emotional problems.

Figure 4.1. Summary of Jeremy's evaluation report.

Table 4.1. Teacher comments from Jeremy's report cards

Kindergarten
"Likes to hurry through rather than take pleasure in the process. Has difficulty paying careful attention to his written work."

Grade 1
"Tendency to rush through his assignments. When he takes his time with an assignment and does it carefully, it is handed in with very few mistakes. More often, however, he rushes through his work making careless mistakes."

Grade 2
"He will sometimes omit things in his math book saying he can't do it."

Grade 3
"There is a gap between his extraordinary knowledge and his output. Silly behavior and a need to socialize interfere frequently. When given a dictionary project to work on, he frittered away his time jumping from one silly topic to another and then gave minimum effort to the task of defining his list of words. This is just one example that shows how difficult it is for Jeremy to produce the same quality of work that he knows and can verbalize . . . easy exit into silly behavior. Sometimes he can get sidetracked by telling unrelated stories, at which point his behavior deteriorates."

Grade 4
"Needs to carefully check his work for mistakes. Jeremy can be easily distracted in class and needs to work on the necessity of focusing his attention on the task at hand. He needs to concentrate on staying on task and avoiding distractions. He must also be sure to do all work and assignments completely." [Language arts]
"Jeremy's performance on written tests has been uneven, and he has not been meticulous in his preparation of homework assignments. The caliber of his work can fluctuate wildly." [French]
"Jeremy is an enthusiastic participant in class activities, but he is not always focused on their purposes. He must pay more attention to what he is trying to find out and the methods that he should use to answer his questions." [Science]

Grade 5
"Jeremy is not doing as well as he should be. He needs to ask more questions in class when he does not understand what is being discussed and certainly put in more effort all round." [Science]
"He must now concentrate on listening to and writing French accurately. He continues to find exams very difficult." [French]
"Part of his problem is that he works very slowly and rarely finishes the set work." [Mathematics]

Grade 6
"Needs more focus and consistency. This may mean thinking things out more thoroughly before diving into an English assignment, reading the directions carefully before beginning a map in history, or being more attentive in math class. He usually has a problem paying attention to his work. He easily gets distracted." [Homeroom]
"At times, his attention span falters. I would urge Jeremy to guard against distractions in class and to refrain from occasional immature behavior." [French]
"Jeremy is an articulate boy whose success was limited by inappropriate behavior. He usually has a problem paying attention to his work. He easily gets distracted." [Art]
"I am concerned about the number of times that Jeremy's homework comes to me with sections that he does not understand. Jeremy needs to be more aggressive in asking questions during the day when the lesson is presented. If Jeremy can stay focused, he will find that his grades will improve. Jeremy needs to work more carefully to avoid making careless errors." [Mathematics]

Grade 7
"Jeremy is not really applying himself in history. He should prepare himself much more thoroughly for daily quizzes on textbook reading sections and for chapter tests. He should read the daily textbook sections more carefully." [History]
"Jeremy needs to be more consistent in his effort, especially on homework assignments." [Mathematics]
"Jeremy arrives at an understanding of concepts in a roundabout manner. He should focus on the purposes of experiments." [Science]

Self-Regulation

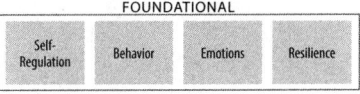

Grade 7 (continued)

"Sometimes Jeremy loudly overreacts to what he perceives as annoyances from his peers. He could still stand to improve his attention in class." [English]

"The quality of diligent preparation for class still varies greatly from one day to the next. During class, Jeremy spends too much attention on irrelevant matters, such as how much personal space around his desk he is entitled to. He can be a little too testy and prone to temper tantrums with boys whom he perceives as annoying." [Latin]

Grade 8

"He must study more thoughtfully and proofread his work. His homework is done in haste and the exam shows lack of preparation. Jeremy is quite often inattentive in class; therefore, he misses a lot of explanations. I (and some of his other teachers) feel that he can do better. Greater maturity and more focus are the keys. He is too often unfocused and insufficiently prepared." [French]

"Jeremy's exam was filled with numerical carelessness." [Mathematics]

"Jeremy is sometimes careless in the lab and this carries over into his lab write-ups." [Science]

"Jeremy is capable of good work when he is not distracted." [Computer]

"Jeremy is motivated by external forces more than by a desire to do things well." [Mathematics]

"His span of concentration in class needs to be improved." [Latin]

Grade 9

"Needs to be more attentive with respect to taking thorough notes in class, study the lesson to learn the material before starting the assignment, and then practice by applying this knowledge to the homework." [Mathematics]

"Needs to spend more time in preparing for cumulative evaluations." [Biology]

"Needs to be reminded to take notes and complete assignments." [Algebra]

"Jeremy has an average of 33%. His performance on the most recent test reflected absolutely no preparation as well as complete ignorance of the story. I cannot help but feel that I wasted 3 weeks going over the poetry." [English]

Grade 9 (repeated: went to boarding school)

"You should not be socializing in the dormitory or talking on the phone for long periods of time. The time between 8 p.m. and lights out at 11 p.m. is reserved exclusively for your academic work. With significant organization and effort on your part, you can improve. Please plan your time carefully. You need to carve out time for your homework."

"Though his room is not a community space, Jeremy lacks attention to this part of his responsibilities. It seems that he cannot keep this space clear and clean. There are always clothes all over the floor and his desk is a mess." [Academic restriction report]

"Does not like to ask for help. Did not show up to the extra review session the day before the final. He also left the exam 15 minutes early, which surprised me. His organizational skills still need work, as does his presentation of solutions." [Algebra]

"Jeremy reminds me of a good socket wrench set that's been spilled on the floor with sockets of all sizes rolling every which way. He needs time and opportunity to organize himself and stick to a task." [Latin]

Grade 10

"Sometimes I saw little effort, even when he had the opportunity to make up the work he had failed.... drifting off sometimes in class." [Latin]

"I think he had trouble filtering out other distractions and concentrating." [Geometry]

"He often seemed confused when asked to simplify expressions with more letters than numbers. Often he would work on a problem, realize he was stuck, but then could not see another way to solve the problem. From what I observed, Jeremy needs lots of support, he needs to be held accountable daily, and he needs to be pushed. In a classroom of 13 that meets 4 days a week, there wasn't enough time and structure for Jeremy to succeed.... To stay on task, to remain focused, and to absorb new ideas in class was a real struggle for him. I do believe that he was trying, that he wanted to do well, and that he cared. But his mind wandered regularly in class." [Algebra II]

(continued)

Table 4.1. *(continued)*

Grade 11
"Made no effort to correct his poor habits repeating over and over the same mistakes." [French]
"I think Jeremy needs to learn that if he puts the time in, what must seem like an overwhelming and confusing array of detail will actually fall into structured categories that are rational and meaningful. But it does take time." [Chemistry]

Biology and Environment

Although some have argued that the problems of ADHD may in part represent a cultural phenomenon (Aase, Meyer, & Sadvolden, 2006; Block, 1977; Diller, 2006a, 2006b), ADHD is a disorder in which the severity of the child's problems results from the interaction of temperamental traits and the environmental demands placed upon the child. The symptoms of ADHD reflect an interaction of biology and environment. Biology appears to set the risk for problems. The type of classroom environment, however, is likely to affect the number of teacher complaints and the severity of reported problems (Goldstein & Brooks, 2007). In addition, although culture makes a difference in terms of the expectations and tasks placed on children by educational systems, children worldwide with ADHD demonstrate a fairly homogeneous set of symptoms (Baydala, Sherman, Rasmussen, Wikman, & Janzen, 2006; Bener, Al Qahtani, & Abdelaal, 2006; Pierrehumbert, Bader, Thévoz, Kinal, & Halfon, 2006). For individuals who have ADHD or in fact demonstrate impairment from these skill weaknesses, often a poor fit results between classroom expectations and the individual's abilities to meet those expectations. Fortunately, in many cases, ADHD can be reliably evaluated and effectively managed and treated.

Incidence

As the tempo of society increases, a greater incidence of ADHD may exist (Diller, 1998; DuPaul & Stoner, 2003; McNamara, 1972). The reported incidence of diagnosis and medication treatment for ADHD has increased rapidly since 1985 (Express Scripts Report, 2014; Safer, Zito, & Fine, 1996). However, normative data for standard educational assessment tools do not support the hypothesis that children are increasingly less attentive or more impulsive (Naglieri & Das, 2007; Spring, Yellin, & Greenberg, 1976; Wechsler, 1991). In fact, as a result of children's early exposure to the media, their capacity for sustained attention may have increased at younger ages rather than decreased. A more likely explanation for the increase in diagnosis reflects increasing community, professional, and parental awareness of symptoms of ADHD, leading to more children being referred, correctly identified, and offered appropriate treatments (Goldstein, 1995). The consensus among researchers and professionals is that the core symptoms of ADHD affect a significant minority of the educational population, approximately 3%–5% of students. Statistics vary depending on the population studied, the thresholds, and the definitional criteria that are used (Faraone & Biederman, 2005). Studies have suggested a conservative incidence of 4% across all ages (Kessler et al., 2006). Recent surveys by the Centers for Disease Control and Prevention (CDC) asked parents whether their child received an ADHD diagnosis from a health care provider (Visser et al., 2014). The results show the following:

- Approximately 11% of children 4–17 years of age (6.4 million) have been diagnosed with ADHD as of 2011.

Self-Regulation

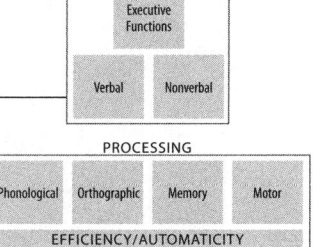

- The percentage of children with an ADHD diagnosis continues to increase, from 7.8% in 2003 to 9.5% in 2007 and to 11.0% in 2011.
- Rates of ADHD diagnosis increased an average of 3% per year from 1997 to 2006 and an average of approximately 5% per year from 2003 to 2011.
- Boys (13.2%) were more likely than girls (5.6%) to have ever been diagnosed with ADHD.
- The average age of ADHD diagnosis was 7 years of age, but children reported by their parents as having more severe ADHD were diagnosed earlier.
- Prevalence of ADHD diagnosis varied substantially by state, from a low of 5.6% in Nevada to a high of 18.7% in Kentucky.

Other Causes of These Problems

Multiple causes other than ADHD can be responsible for a child's apparent inattention, impulsivity, poor planning, and hyperactivity. Depressed, anxious, and even angry children at times may be described as inattentive in the classroom. Some medical conditions can cause these behaviors. Some children may be weak in just planning skills leading to poor school performance. However, if these patterns of behavior are observed frequently in the classroom, ADHD should be considered as a causative condition.

A Cluster of Symptomatic Problems

In part, the controversy and, at times, confusion concerning various aspects of ADHD may be the result of a tendency to view this disorder as a unitary phenomenon with a single cause. The symptoms of ADHD may be conceptualized most accurately as a set of symptomatic problems rather than one single, atypical behavior (American Psychiatric Association [APA], 2013; Voeller, 1991). The cluster of symptoms associated with ADHD makes it distinct from other classroom problems (Biederman et al., 1996a; Biederman et al., 1996b; Loe & Feldman, 2007).

Throughout his school career, Jeremy's behaviors were described in the following ways: "Jeremy fails to complete tasks"; "He appears not to listen"; "He loses focus easily"; "Jeremy acts before thinking"; "He bothers his peers when they are trying to work"; "He makes impulsive judgments." These behaviors were apparent both in school and at home. During the summer before second grade, the Hansons tried to take Jeremy off medication. The first week of summer break, Jeremy took off into the desert at dusk, chasing the family dog. The dog came back, but Jeremy did not. Several hours later, Mrs. Hanson found Jeremy wandering around. The next morning, she called the doctor to renew the prescription.

Over lunch, three elementary school teachers were discussing their views about ADHD. Based on her experience, the first teacher commented that ADHD is probably best defined as difficulty listening and paying attention. The second teacher disagreed, noting that, in his experience, children with ADHD were capable of listening and paying attention but never seemed to finish what they started. The third teacher commented that, in her view, children with ADHD were not completely different from other children; rather, their problems represented an exaggeration of typical classroom problems related to general behavior, conduct, and accuracy or completion of work. In different situations, for different students, all these perceptions are correct.

From an educational perspective, the concepts of attention and planning as executive or foundational skills required for classroom success have gained increasing popularity (for a review, see Barkley, 2005; Goldstein & Naglieri, 2006, 2014; Paolito, 1999). Sustained mental effort, self-regulation, planning, execution, and task maintenance are all considered measures of executive functioning (Daigneault, Braun, & Whitaker, 1992). In order for children to perform competently in the classroom, to meet expectations, to manage themselves, and to interact appropriately with others, the efficient use of these executive skills is essential. Thus, not surprisingly, children who are struggling with these skills experience problems with functioning effectively in the classroom, despite the fact that they may possess adequate basic achievement skills.

In our market economy, as a particular problem becomes popular, controversy and opinion concerning that problem, as well as a recommended diversity of solutions, come to the forefront (Goldstein, 2006). Many more lay texts are published on this subject so that the field continues to be overrepresented by opinion rather than clinical studies. In 1992, Goodman and Poillion reviewed articles and books about ADHD and identified 69 characteristics and 38 causes. At that time there was no clear-cut pattern for identifying the condition and little agreement about its cause.

Though it is true that many symptoms of ADHD share common ground with other psychiatric and developmental conditions (Gillberg et al., 2004; Jiron, Sherrill, & Chiodo, 1995), a solid body of scientific evidence demonstrates that the cluster of symptomatic problems used to define ADHD clinically represents a disorder distinct from other conditions (Biederman et al., 1996a). Multiple physical and biological differences (Dickstein et al., 2005; McConville & Cornell, 2003; Pliszka, 2005; Thome et al., 2012) as well as genetic differences (Faraone et al., 2005; Fisher et al., 2002) have been identified. As noted, since the 1970s, however, research has increasingly suggested that the core problem for ADHD is not excessive activity but impairments in executive functions (Douglas & Peters, 1979; for a review, see Barkley, 2005). Though the *Diagnostic and Statistical Manual of Mental Disorders, Fifth Edition* (*DSM-5*) diagnostic criteria continue to weigh heavily upon symptoms of inattention, emerging literature provides strong contrary evidence that difficulties with self-regulation and executive functioning offer a better explanation of this condition and its impairments (Goldstein & Naglieri, 2014; Barkley & Murphy, 2006). Yet the change in focus to problems of poor self-regulation and executive dysfunction—both likely driven by impulsivity—as the core symptom of ADHD causing the most serious impairment has not come easily. Just as the lay public begins to accept that inattentiveness is a problem for some, the preponderance of the research literature in the past 10 years suggests that in laboratory settings, the problem is not that these individuals cannot pay attention but that they do not pay attention efficiently or effectively. Their inconsistent attention occurs in repetitive, effortful situations in which inhibition, planning, and working memory are required. Converging lines of evidence including measures of physiological functioning, laboratory tests, and neuroimaging studies increasingly support disinhibition as a core impairment in ADHD (for a review, see Barkley, 2005; Harrier & DeOrnellas, 2005; Wellington, Semrud-Clikeman, Gregory, Murphy, & Lancaster, 2006).

Barkley suggests that "ADHD represents a profound disturbance in self-regulation and organization behavior across time" (1994, p. vii). These functions are subserved by prefrontal, midbrain, and cerebellar regions in the human brain (Fuster, 1989). ADHD appears to be a condition that affects the organism's ability to organize behavior over time and meet demands for present and future performance. To understand the condition, one has to look at the point of performance (Ingersoll & Goldstein, 1993). ADHD is a condition best captured

Self-Regulation

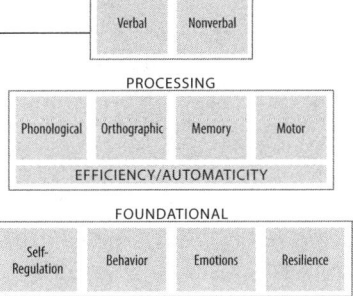

and understood by the observation and measurement of real-life behavior. Pervasive impairments caused by ADHD, as Barkley (1994) notes, are driven by the following:

- Difficulty fixing on and sustaining mental images or messages that relate to external events so that one can act or not act upon them
- Problems referencing the past in relation to those events
- Difficulty imagining hypothetical futures that might result from those events
- Problems establishing goals and plans of actions to implement them
- Difficulty ignoring stimuli likely to interfere with goal-directed behaviors
- Poor utilization of internal speech in the service of self-regulation and goal-directed behaviors
- Inefficient regulation of effect and motivation or response to situational demands
- Problems separating affect from information or feelings from facts
- Difficulty analyzing and synthesizing information

Thus, ADHD—a problem occurring at the point of performance—defines a disorder of executive functioning. The problem results from being capable of learning from experiences but incapable of acting efficiently on that learning at the point of performance (Ingersoll & Goldstein, 1993). It is thus a disorder of inadequate response inhibition—a problem of performance, not skills.

A Problem of Faulty Performance

Despite the seemingly different classroom definitions of ADHD, a consensus exists that ADHD represents a problem of faulty performance rather than faulty input. It is not that these children do not know what to do in the classroom but that they do not do what they know consistently. As a result, ADHD is a problem of inconsistency rather than inability (Goldstein & Goldstein, 1992; Stein, 1997).

In third grade, Jeremy pulled a switch that shut off all the power in the school. As a result, all the people working on computers lost their work. When asked why he pulled the switch, Jeremy replied, "I just wanted to see what would happen." Children with ADHD often act and then reflect upon their actions. One afternoon, Jeremy dug up all the potatoes in the family garden. Later, he asked his mother if it was time to dig up the potatoes.

All educators need to have a working understanding of the diagnostic criteria for ADHD and a practical perception of the ways in which the symptoms of ADHD affect a child's classroom functioning. The frequency and severity of symptoms fluctuate across educational environments and activities, and the perceptions of educators fluctuate also (DuPaul & Stoner, 2003; Zentall, 2006). Furthermore, the traditional disease model does not apply to the concept of ADHD (Ellis, 1985). ADHD is more like creativity or linguistic ability; individuals differ not in having or not having the traits but in the degree of manifestation. ADHD symptoms are also multidimensional rather than unitary (DuPaul & Stoner, 2003). Thus, interventions are needed when a child's attention skills and impulse control are markedly discrepant from those expected at a particular age (Kauffman, 2005; Kauffman & Landrum, 2012).

Core Symptoms

Agreement regarding which dimensions represent the most distinguishing impairments of the disorder, however, is not resolved. A general consensus is that symptoms of ADHD fall into two broad dimensions: those related to the behavioral manifestation of faulty attention and those related to hyperactivity and impulsivity. Symptoms of hyperactivity and impulsivity appear to co-occur at such a high frequency that on a statistical basis, it is difficult to separate them. However, hyperactivity reduces significantly with age (Barkley & Murphy, 2006). With regard to predicting future functioning, however, the level of impulsivity stemming from poor planning and other weak executive skills appears to correlate positively with impaired classroom performance and life outcome: the greater the degree of reported impulsive behavior, the more problems in the classroom and later life. Thus, it has been increasingly hypothesized that the core impairment in ADHD represents faulty inhibition or self-control, secondary to executive skill impairments leading to a constellation of related symptoms.

Key differences exist between the symptoms and consequences of ADHD. Symptoms represent a limited, research-based list that defines the problem and describes individuals. Consequences, however, represent an open-ended list of outcomes that can occur from living with the defined symptoms. Although the symptoms of ADHD may be powerfully influenced by heredity and minimally responsive to behavior management, the consequences of ADHD can be managed effectively in classroom environments with a variety of behavior management strategies. The first goal, then, is to describe the symptoms.

Jeremy's classroom teacher, his parents, his principal, and the school psychologist met to discuss Jeremy's difficulties sustaining attention in the classroom. Jeremy's teacher, Mr. Chavez, began the meeting by explaining that Jeremy struggled to begin tasks and stick with them until they were finished. He appeared to rush through his work. From a classroom perspective, his teacher could not identify a single activity to which Jeremy paid attention well. The school psychologist, however, commented that during her meeting with Jeremy, he focused on tasks reasonably well, was verbally engaging, and appeared to enjoy the assessment session. The principal added that he had observed Jeremy on the playground, commenting that it appeared Jeremy did not stick with any activity or play with any group of children for more than a short period of time before moving on to something else. Finally, the Hansons observed that at home, he paid attention quite well to activities that were of interest to him, such as watching television programs about science or playing video games.

Diagnostic Criteria

The *DSM-5* (APA, 2013) defines the range of childhood developmental, emotional, and behavior problems that appear to set children apart from their peers and cause impairments in daily functioning. The *DSM-5* diagnostic criteria, summarized in the following text, made an effort to correct the mistaken course that ADHD represents a disorder of only one type (APA, 2013). The field studies conducted for the ADHD diagnosis appear to be more comprehensive and better structured than previous efforts. Note that, using the *DSM-5* criteria, three subtypes of ADHD are identified: 1) ADHD, combined type; 2) ADHD, predominantly inattentive type; and 3) ADHD, predominantly hyperactive-impulsive type. As summarized next, the following must also be present:

Self-Regulation

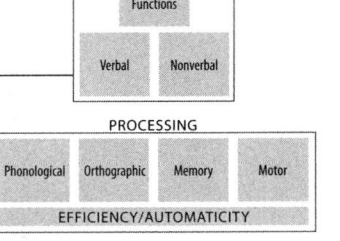

- At least six of the nine symptoms of inattention (e.g., not paying attention to details, showing careless errors in schoolwork) and/or at least six of the nine symptoms of hyperactivity (e.g., often fidgeting or wiggling when sitting) and impulsivity (e.g., having trouble waiting to take a turn)
- Symptoms present in at least two settings (e.g., school, home, work) before age 12
- Aspects of areas of functioning (e.g., social, academic, or occupational) are affected, and not as the result of other medical conditions or disorders

In the field studies completed for the *DSM-IV-TR*, approximately half of the children diagnosed had the combined type, three tenths had the inattentive type, and one fifth had the hyperactive-impulsive type (Lahey et al., 1994). Children with the hyperactive-impulsive type tended to be just entering school. It was hypothesized that this group would ultimately receive the combined type diagnosis when they were required to sustain mental effort in the classroom. As of this printing, such a breakdown from the *DSM-5* field studies is not available.

In the classroom, teachers are most likely to encounter children experiencing the combined type of ADHD. Children with the inattentive type are often overlooked or described as lazy, unmotivated, or withdrawn. Some researchers have suggested their problem reflects slow cognitive tempo (Milich, Ballentine, & Lynam, 2001). The children with inattentive-type ADHD are less easily identified because they have fewer behavior problems and are less problematic in the classroom. The child with combined-type ADHD experiences more disruptive problems in the classroom, thus increasing the risk that the child may be labeled by teachers as defiant or purposely misbehaving.

Jeremy's difficulties are better described as impulsive rather than inattentive. When Jeremy was in second grade, he went to the gifted and talented class 1 day per week. After he had attended this class for several weeks, the teacher called the Hansons and informed them that he could no longer be in the class because his behavior was too distracting and he was constantly bothering other students. Jeremy was taking Ritalin (methylphenidate hydrochloride) at the time, so the Hansons did not know what else to do. They pulled him from the program, as they were afraid that it was becoming another negative experience.

Unfortunately, the *DSM-5* criteria continue to focus on inattention as the core problem for the disorder, limiting the scope and focus on the impact of impulsivity due to poor planning and other executive skill weaknesses as the core impairment. This perpetuates a number of major misconceptions, including that the inattentive type of ADHD represents a subtype of the combined disorder (Anastopoulos, Barkley, & Shelton, 1994). Increasing amounts of research suggest that it does not (for a review, see Barkley, 2005). The more likely possibility is that the inattentive type represents a distinct disorder, primarily reflecting difficulty with organization and paying attention to repetitive, effortful tasks (Bauermeister, Barkley, Bauermeister, Martinez, & McBurnett, 2012). The problems that children in this group experience may very well be the result of faulty skills as opposed to inconsistent or inadequate use of skills; that is, children with the inattentive type of ADHD may well lack ability, whereas children with the combined type are inefficient and ineffective in using the abilities they possess.

Based on the work of Douglas and Peters (1979) and Douglas (1985), Goldstein and Goldstein (1990) first proposed a four-part practical definition of ADHD that was later expanded to five parts (1998). This definition, modified for this chapter, provides an educational perspective of the condition. It is offered as a way to facilitate understanding, measure impairment, and design effective treatment. Those with ADHD experience a constitutional predisposition to struggle with attention, effort, inhibitory control, and fully modulated arousal and have a need to seek stimulation (Douglas, 1985). They struggle with the executive processes defined by Barkley (2005). The five components of this definition include the following:

1. Impulsivity and Planning

This group of individuals experiences difficulty with inhibition leading to problems in planning. Planning is a mental process by which an individual determines, selects, supplies, and evaluates solutions to problems (Naglieri & Das, 1997). Planning requires the efficient choice of strategies and the ability to self-monitor, self-correct, flexibly shift, and adjust to feedback. These students have difficulty weighing the consequences of their actions before acting and do not reasonably consider the consequences of their past behavior. They struggle with rule-governed behavior, likely due to an inability to separate experience from response, thought from emotion, and action from reaction. Their behavior seems impetuous, and they seemingly do not appear to learn from experience. These individuals are often repeat offenders, a pattern that frustrates parents, teachers, friends, and spouses.

Scholnick (1995) reviewed an extensive literature of nearly 11,000 references concerning the development and implementation of planning. Planning requires an internal process of problem solving that precedes the external strategic action; requires the capacity to inhibit action while thinking through the best ways to obtain goals; and involves multiple stages, each of which is critical in designing, choosing, and following through with the problem-solving approach regardless of the nature of the task. Planning, first described by Luria (1966), is an active process. Clearly this process requires selective inhibition or impulse control. Planning relies on working memory to construct and anticipate a plan and to monitor its execution. Such a process requires prolongation, self-directed speech, and reconstitution at the very least (Barkley, 1997). For example, if an individual is unable to anticipate future consequences of his or her actions or reflect while acting, he or she is likely to be accident-prone. Adept planners make fast computations and think ahead several steps through the use of working memory. This skillful allocation of resources requires that attention be divided simultaneously between active construction and utilization of a plan. Planning is likely also influenced by long-term memory, motivation, personal attributes, and belief about personal capacities. Planning impairments have been repeatedly found to significantly discriminate youth with ADHD from those with other conditions and controls (Naglieri, Goldstein, Iseman, & Schwebach, 2003; Naglieri, Salter, & Edwards, 2004; Paolito, 1999).

2. Inattention

Individuals with ADHD have difficulty sustaining effort and functioning efficiently relative to their peers and ability. In new or novel settings and those that are less repetitive and effortful, they appear to function better, suggesting that the fault lies not in failure to know what to do but from inefficient actions. This reinforces an important point: ADHD represents an exaggeration on a dimensional basis of typical

Self-Regulation

problems such as too much restlessness or an inadequate investment in tasks that must be completed. On a dimensional basis, the behavior of these individuals represents the extreme of what is expected.

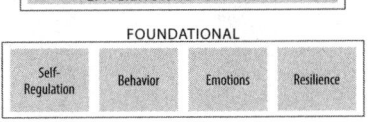

3. Hyperactivity

Individuals with ADHD often tend to be excessively restless and overactive and struggle in particular to control body movements when they should be staying still. Interestingly, even youth diagnosed with the inattentive type of ADHD demonstrate more restless, fidgety behavior than controls (Lahey, Pelham, Loney, Lee, & Willcutt, 2005).

4. Problems Modulating Gratification

Individuals with ADHD often appear driven toward immediate, frequent, predictable, and meaningful consequences. They demonstrate less sensitivity to changing parameters of reinforcement rate, which may be secondary to problems sustaining attention and/or faulty inhibition (Kollins, Lane, & Shapiro, 1997). They demonstrate an excess or exaggeration in comparison to peers in regard to these variables. They experience greater difficulty working toward a long-term goal. They often require brief repeated payoffs rather than a single long-term reward. They also do not appear to respond to rewards in a manner similar to others (Haenlein & Caul, 1987). Rewards do not appear to be effective in changing their behaviors on a long-term basis. They are quick to regress once the reward paradigm is removed. Impulsivity drives their behavior to remain consequentially bound. However, it also appears that given a sufficient number of trials and opportunities for generalization, their behavior—that is, the capacity to do consistently what they know—can be shaped in a way similar to that of unaffected individuals (Shure & Aberson, 2005). In regard to consequences and behavior development, for those with ADHD, the issue is not so much behavior modification as behavior management. The provision of a sufficient number of supervised, structured, and reinforced trials for everything from daily habits to social, academic, and work skills is essential.

Individuals with ADHD also receive significantly more negative reinforcement than others. Their interactions with others are often shaped by an effort to avoid aversive consequences. Negative reinforcement offers a plausible, experiential explanation for the diverse problems individuals with ADHD develop. Efforts of helpers tend to reinforce passivity and helplessness. Eventually the avoidance of aversive consequences tends to exert greater influence over behavior than the seeking of positive consequences. Individuals with ADHD—children and adults alike—learn to respond to demands placed on them by the environment when an aversive stimulus is removed contingent on performance rather than for the promise of a positive future reward.

5. Emotional Regulation

Individuals with ADHD become aroused quicker. Whether happy or sad, the speed and intensity with which they move to the extremes of emotion can be much greater than that of peers. This problem appears to reflect an impulsive inability to separate thought from emotion. When happy, they tend to be so happy that people are disrupted. When unhappy, they tend to be so unhappy that people are equally disrupted. Negative feedback from others and stressful relationships can exert a significant influence on the development of a sense of psychological well-being, locus of control, and personality style. Problems with ADHD typically cause significant and pervasive impairments in day-to-day interactions in the environment across the lifespan. Familial, social, academic, and vocational demands of a fast-paced culture require a consistent, predictable, independent, and efficient approach to life. Failure to develop, maintain, and use these abilities efficiently leads to uneven and unpredictable behavior, characteristically a function of knowing what to do but being unable to do it in a consistent, predictable manner.

Legal Protections

Students with ADHD first were eligible to receive services through the Individuals with Disabilities Education Act (IDEA) Amendments of 1997 (PL 105-17) under the category of other health impairment (OHI). This distinction was continued in the reauthorization of this legislation (IDEA, 2004, PL 108-446, 34 CFR). The term *other health impairment* includes chronic or acute impairments that result in limited alertness that affect educational performance. If the multidisciplinary team determines that a student's heightened alertness to irrelevant or environmental stimuli results in limited alertness with regard to educational performance, the criterion of the OHI category would be satisfied. Some students with ADHD are served under IDEA because they have another disability, such as learning disabilities (LD), a language impairment, or a serious emotional disturbance. Unfortunately, specific eligibility criteria beyond receiving the ADHD diagnosis have yet to be determined.

Many students with ADHD who are not served under IDEA are eligible for legal protections under the guidelines of Section 504 (Rehabilitation Act Amendments of 1992, PL 102-569). Under this civil rights law, disability is defined as a condition that substantially limits a major life activity, such as learning. Although the wording of both of these laws is broad in order to encompass a diverse group of children, the broad language also creates interpretive problems (Mercugliano, Power, & Blum, 1999). Under Section 504, accommodation plans, reviewed yearly, specify the adaptations and adjustments that the child will need in the general education classroom. For students with ADHD, examples of the types of adjustments include 1) preferential seating; 2) extended time on examinations; 3) increased teacher monitoring; 4) modified or reduced work assignments; 5) more frequent breaks; or 6) specific test accommodations, such as a quiet environment. Figure 4.2 presents Jeremy's revised 504 accommodation plan in fifth grade.

CAUSES OF ATTENTION-DEFICIT/HYPERACTIVITY DISORDER

ADHD is one of the most heritable conditions (Edelbrock, Rende, Plomin, & Thompson, 1995; Posthuma & Polderman, 2013). A number of genes and types of gene codes for brain chemistry appear to place individuals at risk to receive a diagnosis of ADHD. Recent studies suggest that genes on chromosomes 4, 5, 8, 11, and 17 may combine to contribute to risk for this diagnosis (Muenke, 2006). In addition, other genes when present may act protectively to reduce risk. The hypothesis of genetics as a contribution to ADHD is powerfully reinforced through the findings of concordance for this disorder among identical twins (Edelbrock et al., 1995; Zahn-Waxler, Schmitz, Fulker, Robinson, & Ende, 1996). Genetics set the stage for risk. Life experience then determines whether an individual ultimately receives a diagnosis of ADHD (Goldstein & Goldstein, 1998; Ingersoll & Goldstein, 1995). Sometimes parents are diagnosed at the same time as their children. Ms. Hanson, Jeremy's mother, was diagnosed for the first time when Jeremy was in kindergarten.

Self-Regulation

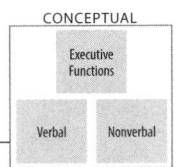

Section 504 Accommodation Plan

Name Jeremy H.   Date 04/05/08

Student ID# JL9998   Date of birth 10/20/04

School Hillworth Elementary   Teacher Mr. Glaser   Grade 5th

1. Describe the nature of the concern. Inattentive, hyperactive, and impulsive symptoms impair Jeremy's ability to succeed in school.

2. Describe the basis for the determination of disability (if any). School and physician evaluation

3. Describe how the disability affects a major life activity. Despite excellent intelligence and academic skills, Jeremy's inattentive, impulsive, and hyperactive symptoms impair his ability to succeed at school.

4. The Child Study Team/Intervention Assistance Team has reviewed the files of the above named student and concludes that he or she meets the classification as a qualified individual with a disability under Section 504 of the Rehabilitation Act Amendments of 1992 (PL 102-569). In accordance with the Section 504 guidelines, the school has agreed to make reasonable accommodations and address the student's individual needs by:

PHYSICAL ARRANGEMENT OF ROOM

___ Seating student near the teacher   ✓ Seating student near a positive role model

✓ Standing near the student when giving directions or presenting lessons

___ Avoiding distracting stimuli (e.g., air conditioner, high traffic area)

___ Increasing the distance between the desks

___ Additional accommodations: _____

LESSON PRESENTATION

✓ Pairing students to check work   ✓ Providing written outline

___ Writing key points on the board   ___ Allowing student to tape record lessons

___ Providing peer tutoring   ___ Having child review key points orally

✓ Providing visual aids   ___ Teaching through multisensory modes

___ Providing peer notetaker   ✓ Using computer-assisted instruction

✓ Making sure directions are understood   ✓ Including a variety of activities during each lesson

___ Breaking longer presentations into shorter segments

___ Additional accommodations: _____

ASSIGNMENTS AND WORKSHEETS

___ Giving extra time to complete tasks   ✓ Using self-monitoring devices

✓ Simplifying complex directions   ___ Reducing homework assignments

✓ Handing worksheets out one at a time   ___ Not grading handwriting

___ Reducing the reading level of the assignments

___ Including a variety of activities during each lesson

___ Providing a structured routine in written form

✓ Providing study skills training/learning strategies

(continued)

Figure 4.2. Jeremy's Section 504 accommodation plan.

Figure 4.2. *(continued)*

___ Requiring fewer correct responses to achieve grade
___ Allowing student to tape record assignments/homework
___ Giving frequent short quizzes and avoiding long tests
___ Shortening assignments; breaking work into smaller segments
✓ Allowing typewritten or computer printed assignments
___ Additional Accommodations: _____

TEST TAKING
___ Allowing open-book exams   ___ Allowing extra time for exam
___ Giving exam orally   ___ Reading test item to student
___ Giving take-home tests
___ Using more objective items (i.e., fewer essay responses)
___ Allowing student to give test answers on tape recorder
✓ Giving frequent short quizzes, not long exams
___ Additional accommodations: _____

ORGANIZATION
✓ Providing peer assistance with organizational skills
___ Assigning volunteer homework buddy
✓ Allowing student to have an extra set of books at home
✓ Sending daily/weekly progress reports home
___ Developing a reward system for in-schoolwork and homework completion
✓ Providing student with a homework assignment notebook
___ Additional accommodations: _____

BEHAVIORS
✓ Praising specific behaviors   ✓ Allowing legitimate movement
✓ Using self-monitoring strategies   ___ Contracting with the student
___ Giving extra privileges and rewards ___ Increasing the immediacy of rewards
✓ Keeping classroom rules simple and clear   ___ Implementing time-out procedures
___ Making prudent use of negative consequences
___ Allowing for short breaks between assignments
___ Cuing student to stay on task (nonverbal signal)
___ Marking student's correct answers, not his or her mistakes
✓ Implementing a classroom behavior management system
___ Allowing student time out of seat to run errands and so forth
___ Ignoring inappropriate behaviors not drastically outside classroom limits
___ Additional accommodations: _____

MEDICATION
Physician's name _____   Telephone _____
Medication(s) _____   Schedule _____
Monitoring of medication(s) _____ daily _____ weekly _____
                              _____ as needed basis
Administered by _____

Self-Regulation

```
SPECIAL CONSIDERATION
    ___ Suggesting parenting program(s)           ___ Alerting bus driver
    ___ Monitoring student closely on field trip  ___ Suggesting agency involvement
    ___ In-servicing teacher(s) on child's disability  ___ Providing group/individual
                                                        counseling
    ___ Providing social skills group experiences
    ___ Developing intervention strategies for transitional periods (e.g., cafeteria, physical
        education)
    ___ Additional accommodations: _____
NOTES



Participants (name and title) _____
                              _____
                              _____
                              _____

Case manager's signature _____
```

Researchers have also identified areas in the prefrontal cortex, basal ganglia, and cerebellum that are important in helping individuals with self-regulation. These structures have been described as the brain's "braking system" (Castellanos et al., 1996). A large body of research demonstrates structural, biochemical, and physiological differences in the brains of individuals with ADHD (Ernst, Cohen, Liebenauer, Jons, & Zametkin, 1997; Hynd, Hern, Novey, & Eliopulos, 1993; Wellington et al., 2006; Zametkin & Rapoport, 1987). Although results from these group studies have helped to develop an understanding of the causes of ADHD, these types of findings to date have not been found helpful for making the diagnosis of ADHD in individual children (Barkley, 2005; Goldstein & Goldstein, 1998).

ADHD may also be caused by a disease, illness, or other disorder. Genetic disorders, such as fragile X syndrome, neurofibromatosis, Turner syndrome, Noonan syndrome, and Williams syndrome, are all chromosomal and genetic disorders in which attentional problems and ADHD have been reported (Hagerman, 1991). Disorders resulting from fetal alcohol syndrome, cocaine exposure in utero, lead poisoning, vapor abuse, perinatal complications, certain medical problems (e.g., hypothyroidism, encephalitis), and radiation therapy secondary to leukemia have all been reported as responsible for creating problems with inattention and impulsivity. There are reported cases of children experiencing specific medical conditions, such as pinworms or thyroid problems, who demonstrate a sudden onset of inattentive and hyperactive classroom behavior. In the popular press, ADHD has also been attributed in the absence of research to a myriad of etiologies, including low birth weight, poor diet, and vitamin deficiency. It is currently estimated that these factors combined account for 20% of ADHD cases (for a review, see Barkley, 2005).

DEVELOPMENTAL COURSE AND COMORBIDITY

An increasing body of scientific data has been generated concerning the developmental course and adult outcome of children with ADHD. ADHD in isolation or comorbid with other conditions predicts a wide array of adversities in all major life areas. Even in isolation, ADHD is unfortunately a powerful negative force leading to increased risk for school, legal, substance, emotional, marital, and lifestyle problems (for a review, see Barkley & Gordon, 2002; Goldstein & Teeter-Ellison, 2002).

Early Symptoms

Infants that demonstrate difficult temperament do not handle changes in routines well and exhibit a low frustration threshold and a high intensity of response (Chess & Thomas, 1986; Gallagher, 2002; Thomas & Chess, 1977). In fact, in follow-up studies of such infants, as many as 70% develop school problems (Terestman, 1980). These infants appear at greater risk than others of receiving a diagnosis of ADHD and can negatively impact their developing relationships with caregivers—a relationship that is critical in predicting a child's life outcome (Katz, 1997). Toddlers and preschoolers with ADHD often fit the description of the child having difficulty with attention, impulse control, and aggression (Kauffman, 2005; Kauffman & Landrum, 2012).

Although early symptoms of ADHD may be viewed as transient problems of children, research data suggest that ignoring these signs results in the loss of valuable treatment time. Many children later diagnosed with ADHD could have been identified by their symptoms during the preschool years (Cohen, Sullivan, Minde, Novak, & Helwig, 1981; DuPaul, McGoey, Eckert, & Vanbrakle, 2001). Young children manifesting symptoms of ADHD are more likely to have language problems (Kim & Kaiser, 2000) and to develop a wide range of behavior problems (Cantwell & Baker, 1981; Cohen, Davine, & Meloche-Kelly, 1989; Mathers, 2006) than children who do not have those symptoms.

Attention-Deficit/Hyperactivity Disorder and Language Disorders

Research suggests that the comorbidity of language disorders with ADHD merits routine screening of children suspected of ADHD and language disorders, especially during their younger years. Children with ADHD relative to controls use fewer strategies of textual organization and more tangential language (Mathers, 2006). Children with both of these disorders appear to have a much poorer prognosis than those with ADHD alone (Baker & Cantwell, 1992). One may surmise that the language skills of children with ADHD may be delayed because they do not practice or attend to their environment effectively. One may also think that these children exhibit ADHD symptoms because they lack efficient language skills necessary for behavioral self-control. Several researchers have addressed this issue and concluded that the symptoms of ADHD and language disability develop and are maintained independently (Cantwell & Baker, 1985, 1991). Nonetheless, children who tend to act quickly without thinking and also experience a language disorder are more likely to exhibit behavior problems (Berk & Landau, 1993).

Attention-Deficit/Hyperactivity Disorder and Learning Disabilities

Depending on the diagnostic criteria, approximately 20%–50% of children with ADHD also suffer from a concomitant, often language-based learning or reading disability

Self-Regulation

(for a review, see Barkley, 2005; Goldstein, 1997). Although ADHD may prevent a child from achieving his or her academic potential, the presence of LD may make a child appear more inattentive than others (McGee & Share, 1988). Students with ADHD often experience specific weaknesses within the Processing blocks that contribute to poor school performance. Both phonological and orthographic memory problems are common among these students, whereas weaknesses in motor memory are relatively rare (for a review, see Goldstein & Goldstein, 1998).

Although in the mid-1970s, children with ADHD were described as intellectually less competent than their peers, poor performance on intellectual tasks more likely results from the impact of impulsivity and inattention on test-taking behavior rather than on an innate lack of intelligence (Barkley, 1995; DuPaul & Stoner, 2003). In addition, because many children with ADHD also have LD, they often underperform or underachieve during the elementary years. By high school, at least 80% of these children fall behind in a basic academic subject requiring repetition and attention for competence, such as basic math knowledge, spelling, or written language (Barkley, 2005; Goldstein & Goldstein, 1998; Loney, Kramer, & Milich, 1981).

Attention-Deficit/Hyperactivity Disorder and Social Difficulties

Sociometric and play studies suggest that children with ADHD may be socially impaired (Andrade et al., 2014) and are not chosen as often by peers to be best friends or partners in activities (Pelham & Milich, 1984). An awareness of their difficulties can often precipitate lower self-esteem (Treuting & Hinshaw, 2001). Moreover, these children appear to experience either high-incidence/low-impact problems that result in poor social acceptance or low-incidence/high-impact problems that result in social rejection (Pelham & Milich, 1984). An example of a child with low-incidence/high-impact problems is the intermittently aggressive child on the playground. This child does not have to strike out at others more than once or twice per day to become unpopular with peers. Jeremy's pattern of performance fits this profile. One day on the way out to the playground, he pushed a flowerpot over a ledge, and the pot just missed landing on a child walking below.

In contrast, the shy, socially isolated child, seemingly incapable of grasping basic interactional skills, is an example of a child with high-incidence/low-impact problems. This child is often isolated and alone during free time in class or on the playground. Periodically, this child is observed interacting appropriately with other children, yet he or she seems hesitant, unsure, and uncomfortable doing so. Children with ADHD also have difficulty adapting their behavior to different situational demands (Barkley, 2005). The impulsive behavior patterns of children with ADHD can lead to social difficulties, making those with concomitant hyperactive-impulsive problems at an even greater risk of developing social difficulties (Pelham & Bender, 1982).

After just being diagnosed with ADHD, Ms. Hanson, Jeremy's mother, reflected about her early elementary years.

> I spent most of my sixth-grade year out in the hall. I remember watching through the little window of the door to see what they were doing. I felt so lonely and left out. I hated that teacher, and, by the way she treated me, I could tell she hated me, too. I was caught chewing gum once by the teacher, and she made me wear it on my nose all day. I remember holding it there because my tears had caused it to slide off. Everyone paraded by me as they went out to play, each one poking and hissing at me as they passed. I had to stay in, but that didn't matter because no one liked me anyway. Because the teacher picked on me,

so did everyone else. By that point, I hated school. I didn't have any friends, and my grades were poor. I had no idea what was wrong with me. I was just a "bad kid," and I had learned to accept it. I did not know at that time that, because of the way I was treated, these feelings would continue to haunt me later in life.

Attention-Deficit/Hyperactivity Disorder and Behavior Problems

For some individuals, the primary symptoms of ADHD may diminish in intensity by adolescence (Bagwell, Molina, Pelham, & Hoza, 2001; Faraone, Biederman, & Mick, 2006); however, most adolescents with ADHD continue to experience significant problems (for a review, see Goldstein, 1997; Srebnicki, Kolakowski, & Wolanczyk, 2013). At least 80% of adolescents with ADHD continue to manifest symptoms consistent with ADHD, and 60% develop at least one additional disruptive disorder (Barkley, Fischer, Edelbrock, & Smallish, 1990). Between 20% and 60% of adolescents with ADHD are involved in delinquent behavior, as compared with the typical occurrence of 3%–4% of adolescents without ADHD (Satterfield, Hoppe, & Schell, 1982). At least 50%–70% of these adolescents develop oppositional defiant disorder, often during younger years, and a significant number develop a conduct disorder (Barkley et al., 1990).

The high prevalence of delinquency issues for adolescents with ADHD most likely reflects the comorbidity of ADHD with other disruptive disorders, principally conduct disorder (Mordre, Groholt, Kjelsberg, Sandstad, & Myhre, 2011). The preponderance of the available data suggests that, although ADHD is clearly a risk factor for the development of adolescent antisocial problems, life experience (primarily factors within families) is the most powerful factor contributing to the onset and maintenance of delinquency, conduct disorder, and subsequent antisocial problems in adulthood (Barkley, 1997).

Many children and adolescents with ADHD are suspended from school at higher rates than their peers (Ackerman, Dykman, & Peters, 1977; DuPaul & Stoner, 2003), and adolescents with a history of ADHD are at greater risk of developing internalizing disorders, including depression and anxiety (Biederman, Faraone, Mick, & Lelon, 1995; Pliszka, 1992). The rates of comorbidity for ADHD and internalizing disorders have been estimated from 20% to 70% with a higher incidence being reported in children and adolescents also receiving a diagnosis of conduct disorder.

Adults diagnosed with ADHD during their childhood may not appear to be at significantly greater risk for developing serious legal and substance abuse problems in the absence of adolescent conduct disorder (for a review, see Barkley, 2005; Barkley, Murphy, & Fischer, 2010). Nevertheless, the high comorbidity of ADHD and conduct disorder raises serious concerns. Mannuzza and colleagues (1991) suggested that adults with ADHD appear at greater risk than others to receive diagnoses of antisocial and substance abuse problems. These authors found that in young adults with a history of ADHD, 43% still manifested the full symptoms of ADHD, 32% met the diagnostic criteria for antisocial personality disorder, and 10% were drug abusers. In addition, adults diagnosed with ADHD are at a greater risk for having internalizing mood, marital, and vocational problems (Barkley, 2005; Biederman et al., 1987).

Newer studies reinforce these findings that ADHD can contribute to negative outcomes in adults. In a 10-year follow up study, Biederman and colleagues (2006) compared more than 100 boys between the ages of 6 and 18 with ADHD to a control group without the disorder. By the age of 21, boys with ADHD had a much higher prevalence of antisocial, addictive, mood, and anxiety disorders, even though 93% of the boys had received treatment for the disorder at some point and 86% received

Self-Regulation

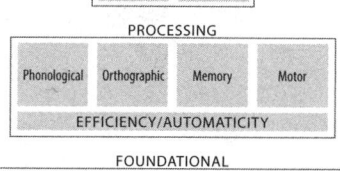

both medication and counseling. These longitudinal results suggest that ADHD is not just a childhood disorder and that follow-up treatment and counseling will be needed into adulthood.

Adults with ADHD may also experience problems similar to those they experienced in childhood when they reenter an educational environment. They may have trouble keeping up with class expectations and completing assignments in a timely manner. At any level, students with ADHD need caring and understanding instructors.

 Jeremy's mother, Ms. Hanson, described the following incident about returning to school:

> I started college at the age of 35. I had one professor who embarrassed me in front of the whole class. I raised my hand and asked a question, and she said that I needed to go back to first grade because I didn't understand the concept of something. All of a sudden, I was back in sixth grade, sitting out in the hall with gum on my nose. I hadn't thought much about that for a while, but the memories all came flooding back. I ran out of the class in tears. Twenty-six years later and it still affected me like that.

THE TEACHER'S ROLE IN THE EVALUATION OF ATTENTION, PLANNING, IMPULSE CONTROL, AND HYPERACTIVITY

Due to the pervasive nature of problems and the high comorbidity for additional problems, assessment for symptoms associated with ADHD involves a thorough emotional, neuropsychological, behavioral, and medical evaluation by a team of trained professionals. Rather than label or diagnose the behavior problem, teachers must describe the behaviors they observe. Factors required for children to succeed in a classroom become the basis of teachers' reports and concerns. Coming to class with a pencil, being able to see the blackboard, remaining in one's seat, participating, and so forth are all criteria that teachers can use to define the probability of success for students with ADHD.

Once a referral is made either to school personnel or to a parent and community professional, the teacher provides both qualitative and quantitative data. Qualitative data are often provided in terms of teacher reports, anecdotes, and work samples.

Part 2 of the Building Blocks Questionnaire can be used to consider symptoms consistent with the diagnosis of ADHD. Using a checklist like this can help organize a teacher's thoughts and concerns, allowing the teacher to provide a cohesive explanation to others concerning the child's attention problems.

Prior to the review of Jeremy's accommodation plan, Mr. Chavez, Jeremy's fifth-grade teacher, completed the Building Blocks Questionnaire for Jeremy, presented in Figure 4.3. The Hansons, Mr. Chavez, the principal, and the school psychologist met to discuss Jeremy's problems completing classroom tasks and to revise the accommodation plan. Each person's evaluation was similar to the first evaluation. Mr. Chavez felt that Jeremy was doing a better job of following directions but that he still had difficulty completing tasks.

Quantitative data are collected through the completion of standardized questionnaires that allow evaluators to compare the referred child to a general population. Examples of commonly used assessment measures to assess difficulties with attention include the *Behavior Assessment System for Children, Second Edition* (*BASC-2;* Reynolds & Kamphaus, 2004) or the *Conners' Rating Scales, Third Edition*

Self-Regulation	Rarely	Sometimes	Frequently
Appears restless and fidgety	☐	✓	☐
Shows inconsistencies in behavior depending on the type of task	☐	☐	✓
Has trouble staying seated	☐	☐	✓
Seems to act before thinking	☐	☐	✓
Fails to finish tasks	☐	☐	✓
Has trouble making transitions	☐	✓	☐
Has difficulty working independently on schoolwork or homework	☐	☐	✓
Has trouble persisting on routine tasks for extended periods of time	☐	☐	✓
Has difficulty listening to and following directions	☐	✓	☐
Interrupts others	☐	☐	✓

Figure 4.3. Building Blocks Questionnaire for Jeremy: Self-Regulation Foundational block.

(Conners, 2008). In some cases, the student is administered standardized tests to help rule out other conditions such as LD. Results from both qualitative and quantitative data are then evaluated by a pediatrician or psychologist to confirm the diagnosis of ADHD. Although the school provides invaluable information, medical personnel make the final diagnosis.

MEDICATION

Treatment of ADHD is multidisciplinary and maintained over a long period of time (Goldstein & Goldstein, 1998). By far, the most effective short-term interventions for ADHD are multimodal, reflecting the combined use of medical, behavioral, and environmental techniques. The use of medication reduces problems with impulsivity. Behavior management effectively deals with the consequences of symptoms, increasing the salience of behaving in a way consistent with classroom expectations. Environmental adjustments (e.g., making tasks more interesting and payoffs more valuable) reduce the risk of classroom problems. Regardless of the intervention, the basic underlying premise in managing problems of ADHD in the classroom involves increasing the child's capacity to reflect before acting.

The use of medication to treat ADHD has increased significantly since 1985 (Express Scripts Report, 2014; Jensen, 2000; Jensen et al., 1999; Safer et al., 1996). The use of ADHD medications among Americans rose 35.5% from 2008 to 2012, with boys ages 12 to 18 making up 9.3% of that population. While the number of girls on ADHD medications is half that of boys, women outnumber men in their use of drug therapies (Express Scripts Report, 2014). The CDC reported in 2014 that there has been an average 7% increase in medication use per year since 2007. They reported that 4.8 % of school-age children were being treated with stimulant medications in 2007, increasing to 6.1% in 2011. Spending on ADHD medication rose 14.2% in 2012, the greatest increase among any traditional drug category (Express Scripts Report, 2014).

Approximately 90% of children in the United States who take medication for ADHD receive stimulants, such as Ritalin (methylphenidate hydrochloride). Other stimulants such as dextroamphetamine sulfate (Adderall), pemoline (Cylert), and methamphetamine hydrochloride (Desoxyn), and the tricyclic antidepressants, such as imipramine (Tofranil), desipramine hydrochloride (Norpramin),

Self-Regulation

and nortriptyline hydrochloride (Pamelor), have also been reported as beneficial for ADHD symptoms. Pemoline (Cylert), however, is no longer recommended as a first-line treatment for ADHD due to associated liver problems. The antihypertensive medicines, clonidine (Catapres-TTS) and guanfacine hydrochloride (Tenex), have also been suggested as beneficial for treating ADHD. Atomoxetine (Strattera), a novel antidepressant, is also approved to treat ADHD. Unlike the stimulants, however, atomoxetine may take longer to adjust. In contrast, the selective serotonin reuptake inhibitors (SSRIs), such as fluoxetine hydrochloride (Prozac), paroxetine hydrochloride (Paxil), and sertraline hydrochloride (Zoloft), have not demonstrated an effectiveness rate much beyond placebo (Goldstein & Goldstein, 1998).

Effects of Medication

An extensive literature attests to the benefits of medicine, specifically stimulants, in reducing key symptoms of ADHD and thus improving daily functioning (for a review, see Barkley, 2005; Goldstein & Goldstein, 1998; Jenson & Cooper, 2004). Stimulants consistently have been reported to improve academic productivity and accuracy of class work (Douglas, Barr, O'Neil, & Britton, 1986), attention span, reading comprehension, and even complex problem solving (Balthazor, Wagner, & Pelham, 1991; Pelham, 1986). Related problems including peer interactions, peer status, and relationships with family members have been reported to improve with stimulants as well (Whalen & Henker, 1991).

Because the majority of children with ADHD receive stimulants, research has focused on this class of medication. The response of children with ADHD to the administration of stimulants is remarkably positive. Placebo-controlled, double-blind trials demonstrate that 75% to 80% of children with ADHD respond to stimulants, whereas only 30% to 40% respond to a placebo (Barkley, 1990; Greenhill & Osman, 1991). In classroom environments, trials have resulted in increased time on task, more work completed, and dramatic improvements in general conduct and behavior. Conflicts with classmates decline. Negative interactions between parents and children decline. The effect of stimulants on academic performance has been controversial, as the quality of work may improve, but the rate at which academic information is acquired may not increase dramatically. Researchers have demonstrated that for children with LD and ADHD, the degree to which the children responded to medication was a crucial factor in determining a child's response to and progress in a specialized reading program (Richardson, Kupietz, & Maitinsky, 1986).

DuPaul and Rapport (1993) examined 31 children with ADHD in a double-blind, placebo-controlled trial of four doses of stimulant medication. Ritalin exerted a significant positive effect on classroom measures of attention and academic efficiency to the point that these problems were no longer statistically deviant among those with ADHD. However, on individual examination, 25% of the children with ADHD failed to demonstrate normalized levels of classroom performance, suggesting that although stimulant medications are beneficial, a need for ancillary interventions remains.

Almost all children with ADHD who do not respond to one stimulant may benefit from another (Elia, Borcherding, Rapoport, & Keysor, 1991). The definition of a good response, however, is debatable. When a good response is defined as a reduction in the cardinal symptoms of ADHD and improvement in behavior and compliance at school, at least 80%–90% of children appropriately diagnosed with ADHD respond to medication. However, when a good response is defined by performance on a cognitive task in a laboratory setting, such as a paired associate learning task, a greater number of children with ADHD are unresponsive to stimulants (Swanson, Cantwell, Lerner, McBurnett, & Hanna, 1991).

The long-term effects of stimulants have been debated. Studies have demonstrated consistent short-term benefits but not robust long-term benefits into adulthood (Goldstein, 1999; for a review, see Barkley, 2005). When outlook is measured in terms of socioeconomic status, vocation, marriage, drug addiction, or criminal behavior, minimal long-term positive effects of stimulants are demonstrated. However, the immediate short-term benefits of stimulant medication far outweigh the liabilities and thus appear to justify the continued use of these medications in the treatment of ADHD.

Neurotransmitters

Medications used to treat ADHD affect brain chemistry, specifically chemicals known as neurotransmitters. These chemicals help the billions of brain cells to communicate effectively. Medicines used to treat ADHD appear to affect significantly the neurotransmitter called dopamine. The increased availability of dopamine allows more efficient and consistent cellular communication, particularly for messages involving self-control. This is not to suggest that ADHD results from a dopamine deficiency but rather that one link in the complex chain that leads to behaviors characteristic of ADHD may be the manner in which neurotransmitters operate. Researchers have also examined medications that affect other neurotransmitters, finding that some may yield benefits and also reduce ADHD symptoms. However, the majority of the research strongly points to dopamine as the primary neurotransmitter implicated in ADHD.

The medications used to treat ADHD have benefits as well as possible side effects. Psychostimulants such as Ritalin are often misunderstood. Take the quiz in Figure 4.4, adapted from Pancheri and Prater (1999), and then check your answers with the key at the bottom of the quiz.

Teachers play a critical role in monitoring the effects of medication on the behavior and schoolwork of children. An open line of communication is needed with parents and the prescribing physician. Teachers are not expected to be physicians or school nurses. When a child receiving medication for ADHD demonstrates any type of atypical behavior, physical complaints, or a change in school performance and work quality, the teacher should promptly inform the child's parents.

A CLASSROOM MODEL FOR MANAGING INATTENTION, IMPULSIVITY, POOR PLANNING, AND HYPERACTIVITY

The presence of knowledgeable, understanding teachers; the availability of appropriate support systems; and the opportunities for every student to engage successfully in a variety of classroom activities are imperative for children with these problems. Teachers, particularly those at an elementary level, play a critical role in helping children with these problems. These teachers focus on academic goals, carefully select instructional materials, structure and plan learning activities, involve students in the learning process, closely monitor student progress, and provide frequent feedback on progress and accomplishments (Goldstein & Goldstein, 1990). These opportunities build self-esteem and resilience, and they contribute to future successes. Yet as straightforward an issue as educational management appears to be, controversy follows ADHD regardless of the environment or situation in which

Self-Regulation

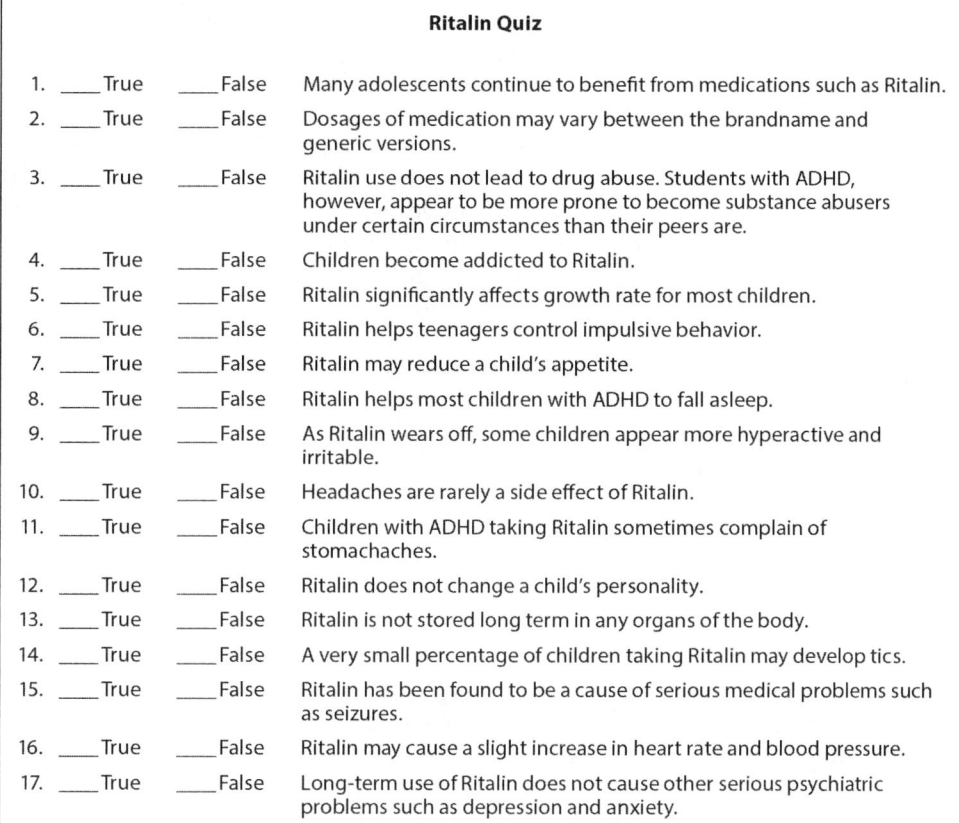

Ritalin Quiz

1. ___ True ___ False Many adolescents continue to benefit from medications such as Ritalin.
2. ___ True ___ False Dosages of medication may vary between the brandname and generic versions.
3. ___ True ___ False Ritalin use does not lead to drug abuse. Students with ADHD, however, appear to be more prone to become substance abusers under certain circumstances than their peers are.
4. ___ True ___ False Children become addicted to Ritalin.
5. ___ True ___ False Ritalin significantly affects growth rate for most children.
6. ___ True ___ False Ritalin helps teenagers control impulsive behavior.
7. ___ True ___ False Ritalin may reduce a child's appetite.
8. ___ True ___ False Ritalin helps most children with ADHD to fall asleep.
9. ___ True ___ False As Ritalin wears off, some children appear more hyperactive and irritable.
10. ___ True ___ False Headaches are rarely a side effect of Ritalin.
11. ___ True ___ False Children with ADHD taking Ritalin sometimes complain of stomachaches.
12. ___ True ___ False Ritalin does not change a child's personality.
13. ___ True ___ False Ritalin is not stored long term in any organs of the body.
14. ___ True ___ False A very small percentage of children taking Ritalin may develop tics.
15. ___ True ___ False Ritalin has been found to be a cause of serious medical problems such as seizures.
16. ___ True ___ False Ritalin may cause a slight increase in heart rate and blood pressure.
17. ___ True ___ False Long-term use of Ritalin does not cause other serious psychiatric problems such as depression and anxiety.

1. True; 2. False; 3. True; 4. False; 5. False; 6. True; 7. True; 8. False; 9. True; 10. False; 11. True; 12. True; 13. True; 14. True; 15. False; 16. True; 17. True

Figure 4.4. Ritalin quiz. (From Pancheri, C., & Prater, M.A. [1999]. What teachers and parents should know about ritalin. *Teaching Exceptional Children, 31*[4], 21. Copyright © 2001 by The Council for Exceptional Children. Reprinted by permission of SAGE Publications.)

it presents. Reid, Maag, and Vasa noted, "Not since the establishment of learning disability as a special education category has a condition so captivated both the professional community and the general public as has attention-deficit/hyperactivity disorder" (1994, p. 198). These authors questioned the validity of ADHD as a psychiatric disorder, the reliability of estimates used to justify the need for additional services, and the specificity of services offered to students with ADHD in school. Reid and colleagues (1994) concluded that all these factors preclude ADHD from being made a specific disability category and that new categories should not be added in the absence of solid, empirical knowledge. Others have argued that children's needs should be the primary means for determining whether they qualify for assistance rather than diagnosis (Stoner & Carey, 1992; Zirkel, 1992).

Despite the controversy, during the 1990s, ADHD became a widely used term in educational environments throughout the world. In 1992, the U.S. Department of Education set clear guidelines necessitating that schools identify and provide services for children with ADHD, and considerable literature has been directed at educators (Bowley & Walther, 1992; Buchoff, 1990; Burcham, Carlson, & Milich, 1993; Busch, 1993; Schwean, Parkinson, Francis, & Lee, 1993). Yet to this date, classroom teachers continue to receive minimal direction and instruction in how to work with these children.

Students' success may have different meanings for different teachers. For some, success for students with ADHD might mean reduced restlessness, fewer classroom disruptions, mastery of academic material, completion of assignments, increased understanding and execution of directions, and improved peer relations. The degree to which a teacher's definition of success is compatible with a student's capacity for change is critical. The teacher starts with a goal in mind, even if it is as simple as stating that he or she would like this child to function in a manner similar to the majority of children in the classroom. Historically, the majority of suggestions offered for the problems that children with ADHD experience have been directed toward specific challenging behaviors, such as those presented in Table 4.2. Although these solutions can be appropriate for a specific problem, in most instances a more comprehensive approach, such as the one described in the following section, is needed. This model includes a basic set of principles tied to the specific classroom problems of children with ADHD, offers a set of guidelines stemming logically from this model, and then addresses specific problems and suggestions to structure classrooms in order to facilitate success.

Classroom intervention strategies for ADHD may be categorized into two distinct sets (Goldstein & Goldstein, 1990). The first set is designed to change cognition, thoughts, and feelings with a goal of increasing skills and self-management. The second is designed to provide managed consequences and to manipulate environmental factors in order to increase the likelihood of the child's classroom success. Zentall (1995, 2006) emphasized that students with ADHD function better in classroom environments when they are allowed to move, channel activity appropriately, and talk and question actively and are provided with novel, interesting instruction.

Table 4.2. Attention-deficit/hyperactivity disorder (ADHD) characteristics and remedial strategies used by resource center teachers

Characteristic	Remedial strategy
Academic difficulties	Monitor progress, assist in planning and scheduling courses, maintain communication with other teachers
Cognitive fatigue	Provide prompts, cues, encouragement; teach metacognitive strategies
Fine motor dysfunction	Promote use of computers, calculators; modify assignments
Poor quality control	Encourage self-awareness and self-management
Disorganization	Support use of acquisition outlines, structured organizers, semantic maps
Time management problems	Foster use of daily notebook; assist in short and long-term planning
Performance inconsistency	Prompt student to use compensatory, self-help, self-monitoring skills
Problem understanding directions	Persuade student to request assistance, clarification; oversee implementation of standing instructional/test modifications
Difficulty sequencing information	Teach mnemonic devices
Poor working memory	Advocate the use of study skill techniques/test-taking strategies
Inconsistent attention patterns	Maintain close supervision; provide direct instruction
Difficulty expressing needs	Coach self-advocacy skill development through role play, verbal rehearsal
Social adjustment problems	Recommend and facilitate involvement in extracurricular activities

From Spinelli, C.G. (1997). Accommodating the adolescent with attention deficit disorder: The role of the resource center teacher. *Journal of Attention Disorders 1*(4), 213. Copyright © 1997 by SAGE Publications. Reprinted by permission of SAGE Publications.

Self-Regulation

Based in part on Zentall's suggestions, Goldstein (1995) defined three key goals for children with ADHD: to start, stop, and think in a manner similar to others. As a framework for educators, these goals focus intervention on increasing the child's ability to start when everyone else starts for both academic and nonacademic tasks, to stop when everyone else stops, and to think about what the teacher is saying. Providing a conceptual framework with an understanding of the importance of making tasks interesting, making payoffs valuable, and allowing opportunities for repeated trials are the key ingredients of successful educational intervention for children with ADHD.

In addition to the start/stop/think goals, a framework for implementation is suggested (Goldstein & Jones, 1998; Jones, 1989). This three-part framework focuses on the following:

1. *Brevity:* Children with ADHD begin most tasks with less effort than is necessary. The fact that they begin with less attentional effort results in their attention more quickly falling below a threshold necessary to remain on task. Thus, the axiom that attention in classroom environments is greatest during short activities is valid for children with ADHD. Frequent brief trials or lessons covering small chunks of information result in better classroom performance. Children with ADHD require more trials for success. The brevity concept suggests that these trials be of short duration. Furthermore, the actual pace at which tasks are presented has been found to be an instructional variable related to classroom challenging behaviors, as children respond more positively to increased opportunities to respond in the classroom (Lane, Menzies, Bruhn, & Crnobori, 2011). Data collected with special and general education students show that relatively fast pacing within the capacity of the student's ability to learn is associated with fewer complaints about classroom misbehavior.

2. *Variety:* Children with ADHD experience "flagging attention" (Douglas, 1983). As tasks are presented repeatedly, they perform with decreasing effort and motivation. Thus, children with ADHD may be quicker to perceive tasks as repetitive or uninteresting. If they require the need for repeated trials to develop the same level of competence as their peers, the challenge for the classroom teacher is to present the same material in slightly different ways or in different applications to maximize interest. Furthermore, the availability of choice as to what is to be learned is also an important variable. Choice increases task interest and results in greater effort and motivation. Children with ADHD function best when various materials to enhance visual, verbal, and tactile interactions are offered. The manipulation of materials makes the task more interesting and motivating.

3. *Routine:* A consistent routine and a structured environment enhanced by a highly organized format of activities are recommended for children with ADHD. Specific daily schedules, including well-planned experiences with managed transitions, are optimal. Specific rules, expectations, and consequences need to be clearly stated. A greater number of transitions within an educational day increase the likelihood that children with ADHD will struggle (Zentall, 2006). In addition, students with ADHD have particular difficulty with days that break the familiar routine (e.g., field trips, field days, assemblies). Adolescents with ADHD often have pronounced difficulties coping with the multiple transitions required during the school day.

Elementary students with ADHD often receive negative feedback in school for their inattentive behavior and inability to perform in accordance with the teacher's directions (Bender, 1997). Difficulty with listening may then cause the child to miss teachers' directions. This difficulty is exacerbated in stimulating situations, such as field trips or playground games.

When Jeremy was in fourth grade, his teacher wrote the note presented in Figure 4.5. Although one can understand and empathize with this teacher's frustration in this situation, it is important to understand that behaviors such as "not listening" compose part of the core symptomatology of this disability. Instead of

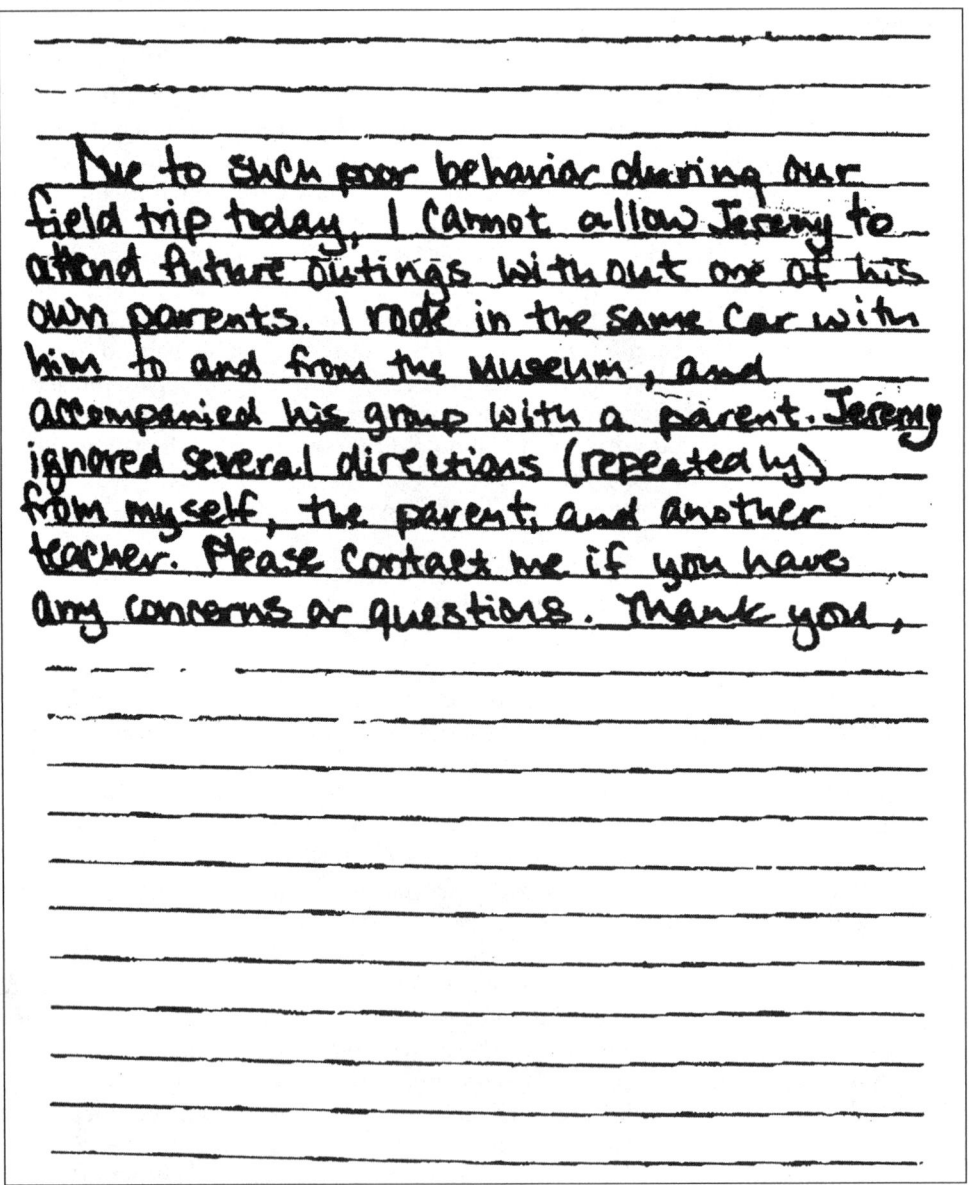

Figure 4.5. Teacher's note regarding what she perceived to be poor behavior from a child with attention-deficit/hyperactivity disorder.

Self-Regulation

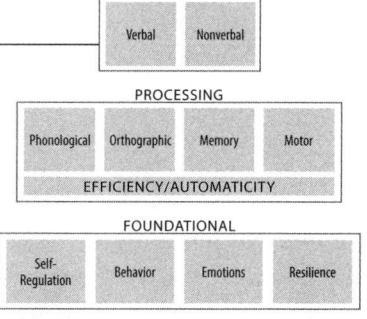

insisting on parental accompaniment, a more appropriate solution would have been to provide more support and monitoring during field trips. This may mean that one adult volunteers to supervise Jeremy for the day or that a responsible peer agrees to be a "field trip buddy." Jeremy understands the rules for behavior, but his impulsivity and inattention result in noncompliance that is unintentional. In other words, Jeremy is not in full control of his actions and behavior and should not be punished; his difficulty with following directions is fairly typical and expected of a child with this disorder.

Carefully planned daily schedules reflect strategic efforts to improve the classroom behavior and educational achievements of children with ADHD. Cooperative learning activities, such as those activities in which students work together during the learning process, can also be effective. Working with other students offers opportunities for students with ADHD to model more appropriate behaviors demonstrated by peers and to reinforce existing skills. Many students learn best through a combination of watching others and having the opportunity to practice and experiment with new behaviors. Figure 4.6 provides an overview of the classroom model.

Effectiveness of Interventions

The effectiveness of classroom-based interventions depends on three factors: 1) the characteristics of the child, 2) the components of the intervention, and 3) the interaction between the two. DuPaul and Stoner (2003) provide five guidelines for the design, implementation, and evaluation of interventions for learning and behavior problems. These are important considerations and appropriate to the development of effective interventions for students with ADHD.

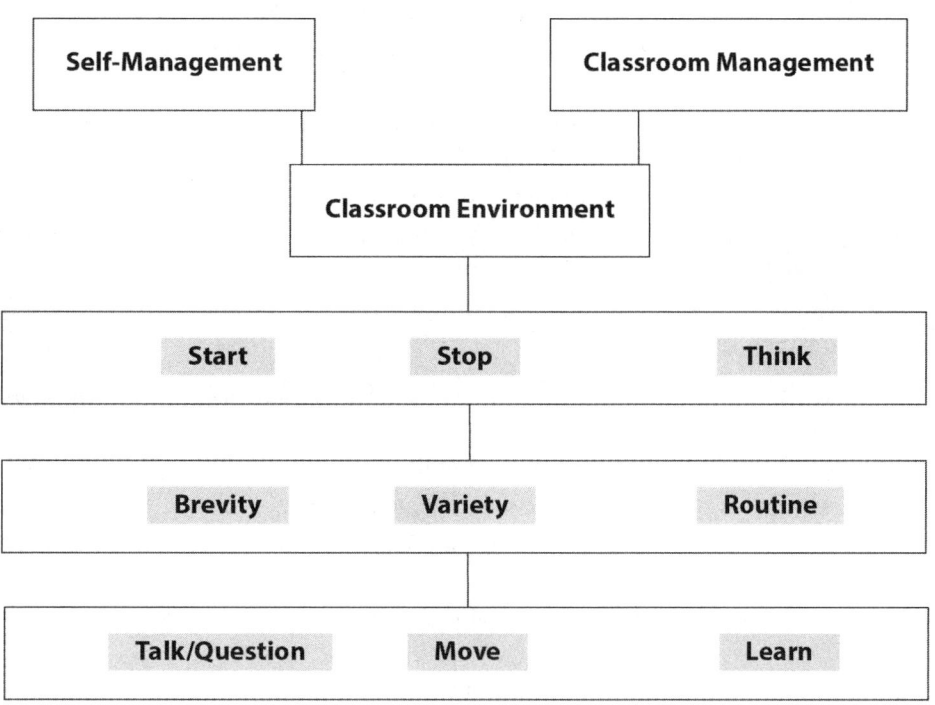

Figure 4.6. Overview of classroom model for educating children with attention-deficit/hyperactivity disorder.

1. Intervention development, evaluation, and revision are data-based activities.
2. Intervention development, evaluation, and revision are driven by what is best for the student and focused on attainment of clearly identified, defined, and socially valid student outcomes.
3. Intervention procedures should be thoroughly identified and defined, as well as implemented with inclusion by staff with clearly delineated roles.
4. Effective interventions lead to increased rates of appropriate behavior and/or learning, not solely decreases in undesirable or disturbing behavior.
5. Prior to implementation, an intervention's effects on the behaviors of the identified child, the teacher, and on the classroom are unknown.

Although a number of interventions are available, Rapport (1989) suggested that child characteristics include the following:

- Breadth and severity of behavior dysfunction
- Intelligence
- Presence or absence of LD
- Gender
- Presence of co-occurring classroom problems
- The time interval during which adequate intervention has not been administered (e.g., it may be more difficult to change the behavior of a sixth grader than a kindergartner)

Characteristics associated with behavioral interventions include the following:

- Using nonverbal feedback, such as placing a hand on a child's shoulder, to help the child focus on what he or she is supposed to be doing
- Limiting delays as much as possible between behavior and scheduled consequences
- Strengthening positive and productive behavior that is incompatible with nonproductive and inappropriate behavior
- Using a mixture of positive and negative consequences
- Incorporating a practical feedback system that does not require a disproportionate amount of teacher time

Children with ADHD appear to function better when the following issues are considered (Rapport, 1989):

- Limiting the number and types of distractors frequently printed in educational materials
- Planning short versus lengthy assignments
- Using stimulating assignments and materials whenever possible
- Minimizing repetitive drill exercises and, when necessary, breaking them into smaller chunks
- Making efforts to determine that a child understands assignments and prompts offered
- Using a highly sought behavior as reinforcement for a less desirable behavior (i.e., the Premack principle). More interesting assignments and other learning activities can serve as motivational incentives. For example, a child enjoying

Self-Regulation

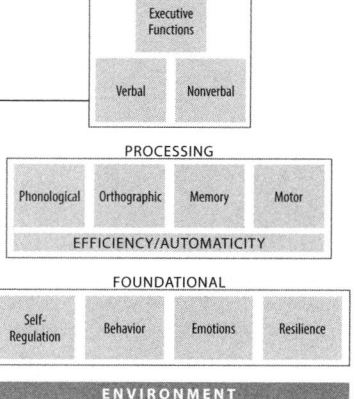

silent reading can be given the opportunity to have additional free time to read in school contingent on completing assigned math work.

The basic philosophy underlying these variables involves making tasks more interesting and rewards more valuable. Understanding and maintaining this framework can help teachers choose among possible classroom interventions.

Behavior Management Strategies

Numerous studies have documented the efficacy of a wide range of behavior-based classroom interventions for students with ADHD (Abramowitz & O'Leary, 1991; DuPaul, 1991; DuPaul & Stoner, 2003; DuPaul & Weyandt, 2006). These interventions either are contingency based (i.e., structured to provide consequences following the exhibition of desired or undesired behaviors) or address management of antecedent behaviors. The manipulation of consequences includes contingent teacher attention, both positive and negative, and classroom token economies, including reinforcement, response cost, and contingencies arranged between home and school. Teachers tend to manipulate consequences as a primary means of classroom intervention (Pfiffner & O'Leary, 1993) and use positive reinforcement along with mild forms of punishment. The management of consequences has become increasingly creative, ranging from the use of computers and related technology to the use of peers as tutors and consequence monitors (DuPaul & Weyandt, 2006; Raggi & Chronis, 2006). Peer tutoring may be a viable addition or alternative to teacher-mediated behavioral interventions for ADHD. Children may, however, promote challenging behaviors in their peers rather than encouraging displays of appropriate behaviors. Children with ADHD may find it particularly difficult to develop positive peer interactions due to a mismatch between their need for frequent and consistent reinforcement and the typical low rates of reinforcement that children provide to one another. The success of peer-mediated programs depends on the ability and motivation of children to learn and accurately implement them (O'Leary & O'Leary, 1977). The emphasis has shifted toward preventing and managing behavior through antecedent manipulations and environmental arrangements (Raggi & Chronis, 2006). In other words, the teacher attempts to predict which problems may occur so that these situations can be avoided. As an example, Jeremy's teacher would walk him each day to the bus stop. This eliminated negative confrontations with other students. A wide range of behavior management strategies are presented and reviewed in Chapter 5. The strategies are discussed from the perspective of ADHD, as well as the general management of classroom behaviors.

Planning Facilitation

Good planning skills help students achieve goals. Planning is therefore crucial to all activities that demand students to problem-solve. This includes self-monitoring and impulse control as well as the creation, assessment, and execution of a plan. The planning processes allow students to generate solutions, discriminate use of knowledge and skills, and manage other neuropsychological processes such as attention. Naglieri and Gottling (1995, 1997) designed a method to indirectly teach children to be more strategic and use planning in one-to-one tutoring sessions or in the classroom with the teacher. This training took place two to three times per week in half-hour blocks. Students were given first a 10-minute period for completing a mathematics page, then a 10-minute period for encouraging the use of strategies, and finally another 10-minute period for mathematics. Students were encouraged to recognize the need to plan new strategies when completing mathematics problems. The teacher provided probes that facilitated discussion and encouraged children to consider various ways to be more successful. When a student provided a response, this often became the starting point for discussion and further strategic development. This method is more fully described by Naglieri and Pickering (2003) and shown in Figure 4.7. Students exposed to this type of planning facilitation demonstrated a significant advancement in their ability to work independently and accurately. Additional information about teaching children to be more strategic is also provided by Ashman and Conway (1997) and Iseman (2005).

INTERACTIVE ISSUES

The following sections contain practical pointers and ideas to help students with ADHD in a variety of situations both in and out of the classroom. Teachers may find these suggestions helpful for students who have disruptive behavioral concerns in addition to ADHD.

Be Positive

Students with ADHD must be told what adults want to have happen rather than what they do not want to have happen. Although this is a simple concept, it is the

---

Planning Facilitation for Math Calculation

Math calculation involves recalling basic math facts, following procedures, working carefully, and checking one's work. Math calculation requires a careful—planful—approach to follow all the necessary steps.

Planning facilitation helps students develop useful strategies to carefully complete math problems through discussion and shared discovery. It encourages students to think about how they solve problems, rather than just think about whether their answer is correct. This helps them develop careful ways of doing math. Children who score low in planning are likely to improve the most from planning facilitation.

The following is an example of how parents and teachers might provide planning facilitation.

***Step 1:* Provide a math worksheet for a child to complete in 10 minutes.**

***Step 2:* Discuss with the child how he or she completed the worksheet and how he or she will go about completing problems in the future.** Probe rather than reinforce, using questions that encourage the child to consider whether his or her strategies worked. Facilitate planning by verbalizing ideas and explaining why some strategies work better than others.

Examples of probing questions include:

    How did you do the page?

    What do you notice about how this page was completed?

    Why did you do it that way? What did you expect to happen?

    How are you going to complete the page next time so you get more correct answers?

    What seemed to work well for you before, and what will you do next time?

    What are some reasons people make mistakes on problems like these?

    You say these are hard. Can you think of any ways to make them easier?

    There are many problems here. Can you figure out a way to do more?

    Do you think you will do anything differently next time?

It is important not to say things like, "Watch me. This is how to do it." "That's right. Good, now you're getting it!" "You made a mistake. Fix it now," or "Remember to use your favorite strategy."

***Step 3:* Give the child another math worksheet to complete in 10 minutes.**

Figure 4.7. Planning facilitation for math calculation. (From Naglieri, J.A., & Pickering, E.B. [2010]. *Helping children learn: Intervention handouts for use in school and at home* [2nd ed., p. 111]. Baltimore, MD: Paul H. Brookes Publishing Co.; adapted by permission.)

Self-Regulation

essence of being positive. For example, when Jeremy is exhibiting an undesirable behavior, instead of pointing out that behavior, Mr. Chavez would tell Jeremy what he wanted to see happening instead. The emphasis on what is to be done as opposed to what is to be stopped helps the student understand the task demands. This also avoids the frequent dilemma of the child following the teacher's direction to stop a particular behavior but then engaging in an alternate, nonproductive behavior. By telling students with ADHD specifically what should be happening and by making certain the child understands, the stage is set to punish noncompliance if the student doesn't follow through.

Give Clear Directions

Compliance and task completion increase when teachers provide simple, single directions and seek feedback. Often teachers are unaware of the complexity of instructions they provide in the classroom and issue a sequence of directions whenever guiding their students (Goldstein, 1995). For many students with ADHD, a teacher's simplification of instructions, followed by requiring the child to repeat directions, leads to increased compliance. When group instructions are given, a teacher may want to approach the child with ADHD and request the child to repeat the instruction to ensure comprehension.

State Rules

Compliance with instructions and classroom procedures increases when children are required to learn and follow a set of rules (Paine et al., 1983). On an intermittent basis, make certain that the child with ADHD understands the rules and behavioral expectations of specific environments. For example, before sending Jeremy out to recess, Mr. Chavez would quickly review with him behavioral expectations on the playground, highlighting rules that may be particularly difficult for Jeremy. Although this does not guarantee a reduction in impulsive behavior, it does set the stage to help the teacher understand that the child is aware of the rules even though he or she may be unable to consistently follow them.

Provide Cues

Providing the child with ADHD with external visual or auditory cues that do not directly involve teacher intervention can be beneficial in maintaining appropriate classroom behavior. External self-monitored cues help the child be an active participant in behavior change. An auditory or visual cue has been found to be as effective as direct teacher monitoring (Hayes & Nelson, 1983). Providing an auditory cue, such as running a tape on which an auditory stimulus such as a beep reminds the child to make sure that he or she is working, results in increased on-task behavior and academic performance (Blick & Test, 1987). A guideline of steps to follow to develop a self-monitoring program for improving task attention appears in Table 4.3. Figure 4.8 illustrates how to help a student begin a self-monitoring program.

The success of such a system requires the student to be motivated and cooperative. The intervention often works best with older students. Studies have suggested that students who were more accurate in recording their behaviors were more on task than the less accurate recorders (Hallahan & Sapona, 1983). The most promising self-management interventions for ADHD require students to not only monitor their behavior but also evaluate and reinforce their own performance (Barkley, 1990). These types of rewards move students away from reliance on external

Table 4.3. Self-monitoring program

1. Teacher explains to the class what on- and off-task attention/behavior is and also has class members model what it looks like to be on-task (either doing seat work, group work, or listening to teacher instruction) and off-task.
2. Teacher gives students a form for recording attention-to-task and models how the form is to be marked.
3. Teacher explains that students are to rate themselves as on- or off-task whenever they hear a tone on the audiotape the teacher will play at special times.
4. Have the students practice rating themselves for 5–10 minutes. Verbally reinforce appropriate rating behavior and verbally correct any inappropriate self-rating or behavior.
5. Show students a poster or handout that presents the standards for self-evaluation that the teacher has selected.
6. Have the children practice rating themselves for at least 20 intervals and then have them evaluate their own performance using the presented standards.
7. Explain how the children earn points, tokens, etc. for achieving the self-evaluation standards and explain how you would like them to keep track of those points, etc.
8. Explain how you will conduct honesty or accuracy checks and that, at first, children will earn bonus points for being accurate about their behavior, whether on- or off-task. Use several children to help you role-play an example of how a child can earn points for honestly rating himself on-task or off-task.
9. Conduct a trial run in which students self-monitor for 10–20 minutes, depending on their age, and then evaluate and reward their own behavior in which the teacher conducts accuracy checks.
10. After using the system in this way for a period of time, the teacher can slowly begin to raise the standards required, lengthen the period of self-monitoring, introduce point loss for students who rate themselves inaccurately, and so forth. It is recommended that one change be made at a time.

From Braswell, L., & Bloomquist, M.L. (1991). *Cognitive-behavioral therapy with ADHD children: Child, family and school interventions* (p. 210). New York, NY: Guilford Press; reprinted by permission.

rewards and toward improved self-monitoring and reflection of appropriate behaviors. This may be more acceptable for students at the secondary level.

Structure and Minimize Transitions

Children with ADHD appear to move easiest from formal to informal, focused to unfocused, or structured to unstructured environments. They are the last to begin work but the first to stop. If the teacher allows the child a few extra minutes in the morning to unwind and be off task, it will likely be more difficult to get the child to settle down and focus on task requirements. Even minor interruptions, such as someone entering the classroom, are often sufficient to take the child's attention away from a task. The child with ADHD may be the last child to settle down and return to work after a break such as recess and may have the most trouble with moving from one classroom to another efficiently. Keeping such informal transitions to a minimum, providing additional structure during transitional periods, providing positive reinforcement contingent on the child's abilities to successfully complete the transition, and helping the child with ADHD settle into a formal environment again can have a significant positive impact on overall classroom functioning.

The issue of transitions is even more important in secondary school environments, in which this problem is often among the most frequently reported by teachers. Attempt to minimize the number of transitions during the day as much as possible. In some instances, teachers may assign a peer to accompany the student from class to class. For some students, it is necessary to provide a second set of textbooks so that

Self-Regulation

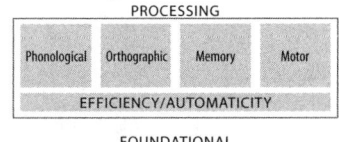
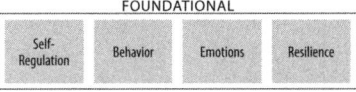

Training and Implementation of Self-Monitoring Program

The following script for a teacher's introduction of self-monitoring and the implementation scenario illustrate the application of the program with Jeremy.

TEACHER: Jeremy, you know how paying attention to your work has been a problem for you. You've heard teachers tell you, "Pay attention," "Get to work," "What are you supposed to be doing?" and things like that. Well, today we're going to start something that will help you help yourself pay attention better. First, we need to make sure that you know what paying attention means. This is what I mean by paying attention. [Teacher models immediate and sustained attention to task.] And this is what I mean by not paying attention. [Teacher models inattentive behaviors such as glancing around and playing with objects.] Now you tell me if I was paying attention. [Teacher models attentive and inattentive behaviors and requires the student to categorize them.] Okay, now let me show you what we're going to do. While you're working, this tape recorder will be turned on. Every once in awhile, you'll hear a little sound like this: [Teacher plays tone on tape.] And when you hear that sound, quietly ask yourself, "Was I paying attention?" If you answer "yes," put a check in this box on your green sheet. If you answer "no," put a check in the other box. Then go right back to work. When you hear the sound again, ask the question, answer it, mark your answer, and go back to work. Now, let me show you how it works. [Teacher models entire procedure.] Now, Jeremy, I bet you can do this. Tell me what you're going to do every time you hear a tone. Let's try it. I'll start the tape and you work on these papers. [Teacher observes Jeremy's implementation of the entire procedure, praises its correct use, and gradually withdraws.]

THE NEXT DAY

A classroom of students are engaged in various activities. The teacher is walking about the room, preparing for her next activity. Some students are sitting in a semicircle facing another teacher and answering questions she poses. Other students are sitting at their desks and writing on papers or workbooks. Jeremy is working at his own desk. The teacher picks up some work pages that have green strips of paper attached to their top.

TEACHER: [Walking up to Jeremy's desk]: Jeremy, here are your seat work pages for today. I'm going to start the tape, and I want you to self-record like you have been doing. What are you going to ask yourself when you hear the beep?

JEREMY: [Taking paper]: Was I paying attention?

TEACHER: Okay, that's it. [Turning away] Will, Balin, and Anne, it's time for spelling group. [Starts a tape recorder and walks toward front of room where three students are gathering.]

JEREMY: [Begins working on his assignments; he is continuing to work when a tone comes from the tape recorder. Jeremy's lips barely move as he almost inaudibly whispers.] Was I paying attention? Yes. [He marks on the green strip of paper and returns to work. Later, another tone comes from the tape recorder. Jeremy whispers.] Was I paying attention? Yes. [He marks on the green strip of paper and returns to work. Later as the students in one group laugh, Jeremy looks up and watches them. While he is looking up, a tone occurs.] Was I paying attention? No. [He marks the strip of paper and begins working again. He continues working, questioning himself when the tone occurs, and recording his answers.]

Figure 4.8. Training and implementation of a self-monitoring program. A premade cuing tape is available in Harvey Parker's program *Listen, look, and think: A self-regulation program for children* (ADD Warehouse, 1-800-233-9274, http://www.addwarehouse.com). (From Lloyd, J.W., Landrum, T.J., & Hallahan, D.P. [1991]. Self-monitoring applications for classroom intervention. In H.M. Walker, M.R. Shinn, & G. Stoner [Eds.], *Interventions for achievement and behavior problems* [pp. 310–311]. Silver Spring, MD: National Association of School Psychologists. Copyright 1991 by the National Association of School Psychologists, Bethesda, MD. Reprinted by permission of the publisher. www.nasponline.org)

the first set is left in each class and the second set is left at home (Jones, 1994). By doing this, children always have their books when and where they need them.

Provide a Consistent Routine

Children with ADHD appear to function significantly better in a consistent environment. Varying a sequence of daily activities may be confusing, may decrease attention to task, and may hamper work completion. The impulsive, spontaneous, and randomly organized teacher may match very well with a gifted, attentive child. The child with ADHD, however, experiences problems in a classroom lacking a planned routine. Those children tend to become less cognitively efficient as the day progresses, implying that more complex problem-solving tasks should be taught in the morning with less structured activities in the afternoon (Zagar & Bowers, 1983).

Keep Things Changing

Within the consistent routine, however, the child with ADHD functions significantly better when provided with multiple shortened work periods and opportunities for choice between work tasks. Children with ADHD respond to consequences, both positive and negative, in ways that are similar to other children; however, because of their inhibitory problems, they require more immediate, frequent, predictable, and meaningful reinforcers than other children. Reinforcement provided along this schedule does not constitute extortion or blackmail but rather better fits this child's temperament. See Chapter 5 for additional ideas on reinforcers for elementary and secondary students.

Allow Nondisruptive Movement

It is the impulsive, disorganized, subsequently inattentive style of the child with ADHD that primarily interferes with successful classroom performance. A teacher must prioritize classroom goals for the child with ADHD. Most teachers designate organization and work completion as priorities. The child with ADHD, even when taking medication and functioning successfully in the classroom, is likely during the course of the day to exhibit a greater degree of restless and overactive behavior than other children. This pattern of behavior needs not be seen as a detriment if the teacher is flexible and the child is completing work at a rate similar to other students.

Offer Feedback

Teachers frequently observe a direct relationship between the amount of one-to-one instruction that children with ADHD receive and their compliance and task completion. Children with ADHD function significantly better if they can be provided with immediate feedback and increased teacher attention. In some situations, moving a child's desk closer to the teacher is a positive rather than a negative way to facilitate the opportunity to provide functional feedback. In other situations, it is possible to employ adult aides, children from upper grades, or same-grade peers who serve as peer tutors during independent work periods. Peer tutoring has been shown to be effective in a variety of academic subjects for students with a diverse range of academic and cognitive abilities (Greenwood et al., 1979; Raggi & Chronis, 2006).

Pair an Undesirable Task with a Desirable Task

Often students with attentional difficulties increase their on-task behavior when a task that is repetitive and uninteresting is paired with a task that is motivating. For example, Jeremy's third-grade teacher knew that he loved to draw. After he completed several math word problems from his textbook, she encouraged him to draw a picture illustrating one of the problems. This mixture of an undesirable and desirable activity helped Jeremy to complete his work.

Build Success

Interactions with students with ADHD need to end successfully. Because of the pattern of negative reinforcement that students with ADHD frequently elicit from teachers and the multiple failures they frequently experience, they often end up being punished without being given the opportunity to succeed. Students with ADHD need opportunities to try again, succeed, and be praised. Many children with

Self-Regulation

ADHD develop a view of the world as a place in which they are unable to succeed and, over time, develop feelings of helplessness and hopelessness. A teacher must develop a system to provide frequent positive reinforcement for success no matter how minor it may be. A good rule of thumb is for teachers to note how often they reinforce all students in the classroom and then make an effort to reinforce the child with ADHD even more. The importance of success in predicting children's future life outcomes, especially those facing adversity, cannot be overstated (Werner, 2013).

Prepare for Changes

Unexpected or unexplained changes often precipitate significant behavior problems in children with ADHD because of their tendency to become overaroused easily and their difficulty in moving from one environment to another. Prepare the child with ADHD for changes by mentioning the amount of time remaining in a work period and by taking the child aside to explain any change in routine that might occur later in the day. Time countdowns and advance warnings help the child with ADHD anticipate changes and respond more appropriately.

Use Preventive Strategies

Anticipate potential problems and develop preventive rather than reactionary strategies. A thorough understanding of a child's skills and abilities facilitates the development of preventive intervention. A teacher may consider the task demands placed on the child with ADHD during a typical day and plan specific strategies for situations in which problems are anticipated. In a preventive model, the teacher intervenes by altering the demands placed on the child and by providing specific educational opportunities to increase competence. Although preventive strategies may not totally avoid problems, the old adage that an ounce of prevention is worth a pound of cure is particularly true with regard to children with ADHD. Planning ahead minimizes the severity of problems and reduces the development of secondary problems that result from repeated failures.

Use Class Time Effectively

With the increased need for structure and routine, planning for the effective use of class time is critical for students with ADHD. Unfortunately, teachers often spend a disproportionate amount of time planning for *what* to teach and insufficient time considering *how* they will teach. For example, elementary school teachers have been found to vary significantly in the actual time they use for instruction during the course of the day from 50% to 90% of the total school time available (for a review, see Goldstein, 1995). The following are some additional planning tips for teachers:

- Use an assignment notebook to be signed by the student and a parent to facilitate communication between home and school, as well as to teach students organization skills.
- When presenting a daily planner schedule to students, use both visual and verbal cues. Consider color-coding the list for easy recall and add verbal cues for additional support. Then select a student to come forward to orally go over the plan again for the class (Jones, 1994).
- As directions are written on the board, place them in boxes and use different colors to distinguish the work. Also, number information placed on the board and use highlighting or arrows to cue critical words (Jones, 1994).

- Teach students to highlight key directions on their own worksheet or test before they begin working so that the student with ADHD does not start before he or she clearly understands the task. When students with ADHD are required to remain on task for fixed amounts of time, they appear to manage their impulses more effectively (Jones, 1994).
- Arrange class schedules to allow specific times each day for calendar and homework recording. Encourage students to copy homework assignments together and to check on each other to make sure information has been recorded accurately (Goldstein & Goldstein, 1990).
- Provide students with advance schedules weekly of assignments, tests, and homework. Post a copy on the teacher's school web site and/or consider e-mailing it home in case a student needs to see a copy.

Based on an in-depth review of the available literature, Lerner and Lowenthal (1992) suggested that teachers consider the following 15 general guidelines, still relevant today, when working with students with ADHD:

1. Place the student in the least distracting location in the class. Ideally, this should be in the front of the class, away from doors, windows, air conditioners, heaters, and high-traffic areas.
2. Surround the student with good role models, preferably peers that the child views as significant. Encourage peer tutoring and cooperative learning.
3. Maintain a high teacher–student ratio whenever possible through the use of aides and volunteers.
4. Avoid unnecessary changes in schedules and monitor transitions. When unavoidable disruptions do occur, prepare the student as much as possible by explaining the situation and describing what behaviors are appropriate.
5. Maintain eye contact with the student when giving verbal instructions. Make directions clear, concise, and simple. Repeat instructions as needed in a calm voice.
6. Combine visual and tactile cues with verbal instructions because, generally, multiple instructional modalities are more effective in maintaining attention and increasing learning.
7. Make lists that help the student organize tasks. Have the student check off items when finished. Have students complete study guides when listening to presentations.
8. Adapt worksheets so that there is less material on each page.
9. Break assignments into small chunks. Provide immediate feedback on each assignment. Allow extra time if needed for the student to finish the assignment.
10. Ensure that the student has recorded homework assignments each day before leaving school. If necessary, set up a home–school program in which a parent helps the child organize and complete the homework.
11. If the child has difficulty staying in one place at school, alternate sitting with standing and activities that require moving around during the day.
12. Provide activities that require active participation, such as talking through problems or acting out the steps.
13. Use aides such as computers, calculators, tape recorders, and DVD players.
14. Provide the student with opportunities to demonstrate strengths at school.
15. Set up times in which the student can assist peers or tutor younger children.

Self-Regulation

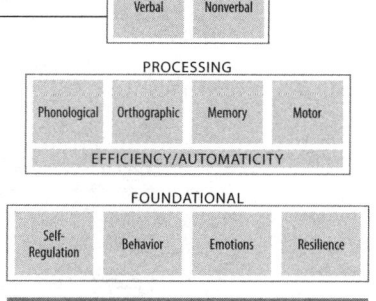

Adapt the Curriculum

Modifying a curriculum to improve behavior and increase classroom performance is a strategy that is based on an extensive research literature (Dunlap & Kern, 1996; Lane et al., 2011). Several chapters in this book provide specific suggestions for helping students with ADHD who also experience problems in school achievement. The following suggestions provide a limited, nonexhaustive list of practical ways to modify curriculum and materials that are particularly relevant to students with ADHD. These suggestions and many more can be found in several sources (e.g., DuPaul & Stoner, 2003; Goldstein & Jones, 1998; Jones, 1991, 1994; Mather & Jaffe, in press).

Reading

- Break classroom assignments into shorter assignments.
- Divide worksheets and workbooks into fragments or chunks. Encourage students to work on one chunk at a time.
- Have students listen to a reading selection on a tape or CD prior to class discussions.
- Consider having students read together in teams with one reading orally while the other listens. Students may switch roles every paragraph.
- Allow students to select high-interest material for independent reading reports and projects.
- Encourage students to orally discuss what they have read and use a tape recorder to record highlights.
- Use videotapes to present information.
- Use interactive software.

Mathematics

- Encourage students to use graph paper as a way to help with organization of columns.
- Use novel strategies such as a multiplication rap or song to increase interest in exerting the effort necessary to memorize math facts (see Additional Resources).
- Place visual models of lessons on the blackboard when students are required to work independently in class.
- Consider mnemonic strategies to help students remember math facts or multiple steps in math problems.
- Offer calculators as a means for checking the accuracy of work.
- Use interactive software for math review and drill.

Written language

- Teach students a simple system to work from a beginning idea and develop connecting thoughts to complete a structure for written projects.
- Offer untimed writing assignments. Break written assignments into parts with periodic checks to make certain that progress is being made.
- Provide a system to facilitate the organization of ideas when written assignments are required.

- Allow credit for hands-on projects and activities.
- Encourage the use of selected, high-interest software programs.
- Encourage the use of manipulatives when studying for spelling tests. Letter tiles or magnetic letters can be used to form words.
- Consider assigning two grades to written projects: one for content and one for spelling, grammar, and so forth (Jones, 1994).

Use Color-Coding

The effective use of color to draw attention to relevant, discriminative stimuli has been well documented (Zentall, 1989, 1995, 2006; Zentall & Kruczek, 1988). Children with ADHD attended more readily when color was added to relevant cues on a spelling task (Zentall, 1989). Zentall demonstrated that when children with ADHD practiced a spelling assignment with all black letters first and color was added, they outperformed other children in the study. Color should be used to enhance rather than distract from tasks. Color highlights key features in repetitive tasks, perhaps increasing interest and motivation. Color cues can also be added to written work, worksheets, and study sheets. In one study, the addition of color had an immediate effect on comprehension across testing assessments with boys who experience comprehension problems as well as ADHD (Belfiore, Grskovic, Murphy, & Zentall, 1996). Color highlighting was added to silent reading tasks. The first paragraph appeared in black and white with subsequent paragraphs each appearing in a different color. Teachers may find these additional tips regarding the use of color to be beneficial (Jones, 1994):

- Color-code material to improve associations. For example, many students with ADHD do not remember assignments and related materials. All materials can be color-coded. If the student's math book is coded in blue, a blue box can be provided in which math papers are to be placed. Students may also write their math homework with a blue pencil and place a blue dot on their daily calendars when a math test is scheduled.
- Divide weekly vocabulary lists into groups or categories (e.g., all words about animals can be placed in one group, all words that begin with *sh* in another, all words about cars in another). Each group can then be placed on its own color card.
- Color-code homework folders. Work going home goes in a green folder, work coming back goes in a red folder.
- When reading a literature book that may involve remembering characters and names, color-code characters as they are introduced in the book by placing a removable, colorful star or dot above the character's name.
- Color-code symbols when they change on worksheets. For example, make addition signs green and subtraction signs red.
- Alternate regular black markers with the use of colorful magic markers on a whiteboard to highlight specific letter patterns.
- Use color cues on word flashcards to identify patterns with spelling words.
- When studying for a content test such as history, color-code factual information. All dates to be remembered can be placed on one color card, important places on another color card, and so forth.
- When studying a foreign language and attempting to increase vocabulary recall, place all nouns on one color card, adjectives on another, and verbs on a third. Vocabulary cards can then be kept in a word box and reviewed often.

Self-Regulation

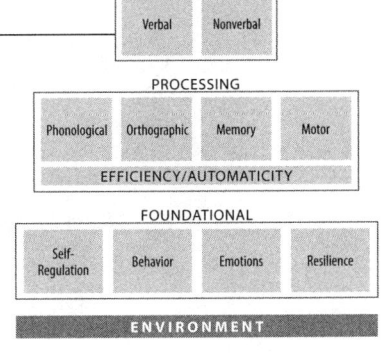

CONCLUSION

Teachers play a vital role in shaping the success of children with problems in planning, attention, impulsivity, and hyperactivity. Many but not all of these children qualify for a diagnosis of ADHD. Although the symptoms of ADHD can be significantly reduced with medication, the condition cannot be cured or eliminated. ADHD is a lifelong problem that must be managed. To be an effective manager, teachers must see the world through the eyes of the student with ADHD, attempt to understand the reasons that problems occur, know specific strategies for intervention, and know how to apply these strategies effectively in the classroom.

CHAPTER 5 OUTLINE

OPPOSITIONAL AND CONDUCT PROBLEMS

Causes of Oppositional and Conduct Problems
Classroom Interventions for Oppositional and Conduct Problems

PREVENTIVE APPROACHES TO DISCIPLINE AND BEHAVIOR

Classroom Expectations
Proactive Classroom Management Strategies
Addressing Classroom Conflicts
Building Parent Partnerships

BEHAVIOR MODIFICATION IN THE CLASSROOM

Classroom Observations
Reinforcement
Punishment

CONCLUSION

CHAPTER 5

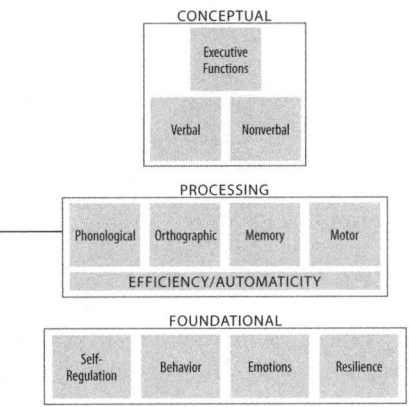

Understanding and Managing Challenging Behaviors

with Lauren Meyer

Children with disruptive behaviors present the most difficult challenges facing classroom teachers. A teacher's availability to other students is dramatically affected by verbal and physical aggression, tantrums, destruction of property, stealing, lying, and general noncompliance in the classroom. Disruptive students often demonstrate defiance toward authority figures and classroom rules. Some students struggle academically and may also demonstrate difficulties sustaining attention. Other students possess the ability to complete class assignments but fail to get along with peers and adults. These behaviors have been associated with long-term risk for school failure and later serious maladjustment (Bradley, Doolittle, & Bartolotta, 2008; Reinke, Herman, Petras, & Ialongo, 2008).

When he was in third grade, Samuel would steal items from the coats of other children. He would leave the school grounds during recess to go and steal candy from the nearby grocery store. In fact, each day when he left the school, Ms. Jones, his fourth-grade teacher, had to check his pockets to see what he had acquired during the day. By sixth grade, the stealing had lessened, but every day his sixth-grade teacher, Ms. Handler, felt that much of her time and energy was directed toward Samuel and his behavioral challenges. Samuel needed constant supervision. Ms. Handler completed the Behavior section of the Building Blocks Questionnaire, presented in Figure 5.1. Every column was checked with *Frequently* except for "Hurts self or others." Samuel was physically aggressive with his peers, but rarely did his aggression result in physical injury; more often, his actions resulted in arguments and hurt feelings.

OPPOSITIONAL AND CONDUCT PROBLEMS

Since 1980, researchers have identified a significant group of children, particularly boys beyond the preschool years, who exhibit two broad dimensions of disruptive behaviors. The first dimension, oppositionality, reflects a child's primary goal of guiding his or her own behavior, independent of adult rules and limits. The second dimension reflects this pattern to a more serious degree, combined with aggression in which the rights of other children, and in some cases teachers, are violated.

123

FOUNDATIONAL

BEHAVIOR	Rarely	Sometimes	Frequently
Has difficulty getting along with peers	☐	☐	✓
Is frequently in trouble at school	☐	☐	✓
Lacks engagement in classroom instruction	☐	☐	✓
Does not respond to discipline as expected	☐	☐	✓
Disturbs or distracts others	☐	☐	✓
Makes inappropriate physical contact with peers (e.g., shoving, pinching)	☐	☐	✓
Insults others verbally	☐	☐	✓
Refuses to comply when asked	☐	☐	✓
Seems argumentative	☐	☐	✓
Hurts self or others	☐	✓	☐

Figure 5.1. Building Blocks Questionnaire for Samuel: Behavior Foundational block.

Most researchers agree that oppositionality includes all but the most serious forms of physical aggression, which fall in the conduct realm (Connor & Doerfler, 2008; Goldstein & Rider, 2013). Some researchers have noted that children demonstrating oppositionality, particularly those who are spiteful, vindictive, and resentful in their actions, appear to have a significant risk of progressing to more serious aggressive acts (Loeber, Burke, Lahey, Winters, & Zera, 2000). Unlike problems of planning, attention, and self-regulation—conditions that link strongly to executive functioning constructs—problems with oppositionality and conduct appear to be powerfully affected by biological, functional, and psychosocial factors (Burke, Loeber, & Birmaher, 2002).

More often than not, when children demonstrate behavior problems at school, they also reveal similar behaviors at home. However, some children are much more likely to "let it all hang out" at home where they feel comfortable rather than at school where they fear a teacher may think poorly of them. When called by the school to discuss their child's academic problems, some parents come away with a distinct impression that the conference was about two entirely different children: the well-behaved, cooperative student whom the teacher sees in class each day and the defiant, angry, temperamental child whom the parents see at home. This is especially true for some anxious children who would never misbehave at school but then release their pent-up stress at home. Alternatively, it is quite possible the rigors of an academic environment will prompt a child to act out in the classroom. These students may demonstrate challenging behaviors as a coping mechanism to meet the difficulties of in-class assignments. Homework assignments, however, may lack the structure demanded in class and will therefore not trigger oppositional behaviors in the home.

The reasons are not clear why some children are much more willing to act out at school than others. Some children, in fact, may come into the world with the biological risk to be oppositional, with some evidence of genetic contributions (Eaves et al., 2000). As infants, they can be fussy or difficult to comfort. Every frustration as a toddler leads to a tantrum, which may illuminate general links to oppositional typologies as early as 18 months (Shaw, Owens, Giovannelli, & Winslow, 2001). As they grow older, these children continue to be quick to anger and do not appear to

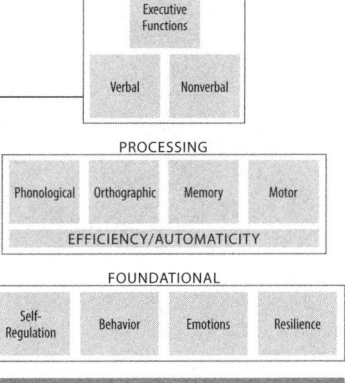

care about the feelings of others. When they are defiant at school, it is clear that they have brought their oppositionality with them to school. One day, for example, Samuel was particularly frustrated about a task at school and jumped on top of the table, yelling numerous obscenities at Ms. Handler. Unsure of what to do, Ms. Handler called the school psychologist, Ms. Kalamaros, for backup support. Ms. Kalamaros spent time talking with Samuel in a kind and rational voice before he agreed to step outside the classroom.

In contrast to Samuel, other children appear to be easygoing until they begin to experience problems at school. At that point, they may become angry, negative, and oppositional at home as well as at school. Many children who are struggling academically at school develop defiant patterns of behavior. Because their academic performance does not meet classroom expectations, they regularly receive huge doses of criticism from both teachers and peers. Eventually, this constant flow of negative feedback leads to frustration, and the child begins pushing back in retaliation. It is easy to appreciate how misconceptions regarding behavior occur when viewed at the beginning of a school year by a new teacher. This teacher may view the child's behaviors as simply disobedient when closer scrutiny would reveal that the behavior has followed, rather than preceded, poor school performance.

The essential characteristics of oppositional behaviors are negative, hostile, and defiant behaviors without more serious violations of the basic rights of others. Oppositional children are excessively argumentative with teachers; frequently lose their temper; and often appear angry, resentful, or easily annoyed with others. They tend to project the blame for their mistakes onto others. Many of the most significant and severe behaviors are often exhibited around the parent or teacher with whom they have the best relationship. Not surprisingly, such behaviors are rarely seen in brief interviews with school psychologists or counselors.

Problems with oppositionality usually begin in early adolescence. When the clinical diagnosis of oppositional defiant disorder is made, psychologists usually look for a pattern of negative, hostile, and defiant behavior that has lasted at least 6 months. The child is usually described as quickly losing his or her temper; being argumentative with adults; defying or refusing to comply with adults' requests or rules; deliberately doing things that annoy others; blaming others for mistakes or misbehavior; and being touchy, easily annoyed, angry and resentful, or spiteful and vindictive (American Psychiatric Association [APA], 2013). Furthermore, to meet diagnostic criteria, the disruptive behavior must cause significant problems at home, school, or work and must occur independently of other mental health concerns.

The more serious pattern of misbehaviors, referred to as conduct disorder, clinically refers to a persistent pattern of behavior in which the basic rights of others and major appropriate societal norms or rules are violated (APA, 2013). Conduct problems may include physical aggression, cruelty, destruction of property, theft, fire setting, confrontation with a victim, and even physical violence. Older children with serious conduct problems are often truant and experiment with drugs, alcohol, and sexual behavior. For the most part, Samuel's behaviors were not intended to hurt others, but he tended to hit, push, and shove other children far more frequently than did his other classmates.

Researchers report that the incidence of oppositional and conduct disorders among children is approximately 2.7% (Costello, Mustillo, Erkanli, Keeler, & Angold, 2003), whereas lifetime prevalence among adolescents has been recorded at 6.8% for conduct disorder and 12.6% for oppositional defiant disorder (Merikangas et al., 2010). Children with this pattern of disruptive behavior often have comorbid disorders of learning disabilities (LD), attention-deficit/hyperactivity disorder (ADHD), and emotional disorders. Oppositional defiant disorder can act as a strong predictor of both behavior and emotional disorders in later adult life (Loeber, Burke, & Pardini, 2009; Rowe, Costello, Angold, Copeland, & Maughan, 2010). For example, irritability in children is associated with emotional dysfunction, being headstrong is a characteristic highly correlated with ADHD, and hurtfulness is associated with callousness; all three constructs are correlated with symptoms predictive of conduct problems (Stringaris & Goodman, 2009). Oppositional defiant behaviors tend to decrease as children enter into adulthood, but conduct disorder symptoms, which may occur before preschool, increase in prevalence with age for both sexes (Costello et al., 2003; Loeber et al., 2000).

Classmates are often very sensitive to the aggressive behavior of their peers. Peer nomination has been found to correlate very well with teacher observations of aggressive children. In fact, teacher–peer agreement is even higher than teacher–parent ratings (Doll, Brehm, & Zucker, 2014). A number of systematic observation procedures are available that assess the behavioral, social, and emotional competence of students. Although individual student assessment data are often obtained for individual students of concern, classwide and schoolwide assessment tools are additional measures used to assess the functioning of a larger group of children. Four categories conceptualize these assessments, including 1) school and classroom climate surveys that ask students to describe their experience of learning and working in the classroom; 2) rating scales that ask students to rate characteristics of classmates; 3) tiered-rating multistep procedures that describe the nature and prevalence of problems within a classroom or school; and 4) analyzing archival data that describe learning conditions, behavior, and student achievement (Baker, 2008; Doll et al., 2014; Severson, Walker, Hope-Doolittle, Kratochwill, & Gresham, 2007). Peer reports can often provide a different lens through which to view the functioning of the classroom environment and may provide additional insights into which children need additional help and support.

Causes of Oppositional and Conduct Problems

The nature versus nurture issue concerning aggressive problems in children and adults is still unresolved, with discussions suggestive of an interplay between biology and environment. Parents may unwittingly train antisocial and inappropriate behavior at home because a child's coercive interactions and noncompliance feed parents' attempts to manage the child. In direct ways, this actually reinforces and strengthens rather than weakens the child's inappropriate behavior. The interactional styles of both parents and teachers, as well as the disciplinary techniques used and the consistency with which those techniques are administered, can significantly contribute to problems of oppositionality and conduct. The power of teachers' words, tone of voice, and actions are still being researched and increasingly understood. For example, one study found that typical children's attention and diligence in completing work varied depending on the style in which teachers provided instructions (Bugental, Lyon, Lin, McGrath, & Binbela, 1999). Student compliance rates were higher for teachers providing assertive, clear, and direct instructions compared with teachers whose style was deemed to be unassertive and less consistent.

Before children ever arrive in the classroom, they are significantly influenced by the home and community in which they were raised. Adolescent conduct problems have been linked to poor parental involvement and conflict management as

Understanding and Managing Challenging Behaviors

well as physical and/or sexual abuse in the home (Burke et al., 2002; Mallett, 2014). Maternal attitudes related to criticism, irritability, and coolness toward children are strongly related to the presence of behavior and conduct problems (Glasgow, Dornbusch, Troyer, Steinberg, & Ritter, 1997). Neighborhood influences have also been linked to the emergence of conduct problems. In 2000, Herrenkohl and colleagues found that other social factors, such as community disorganization, availability of drugs, and the presence of neighborhood adults involved in crime were predictive of later violence. According to McLoyd (1998), parenting behaviors appear to mediate the relationship between conduct disorder and socioeconomic status, as socioeconomic disadvantages influence parents' ability to manage problematic behavior. Research has also found that students who were given the opportunity to "bond with" their school reported positive perceptions of their academic experiences and achievement, with a documented decrease in delinquency and drug use (Ding & Hall, 2007). Clearly, identifying strategies to make students feel a part of their school environment and connected with adults at school can improve both student behavioral and academic functioning.

Classroom Interventions for Oppositional and Conduct Problems

Managing and modifying disruptive classroom behavior can at times overwhelm even the most experienced teachers. These patterns of behavior require a clear plan, an understanding of the rationale for certain interventions, the ability to apply interventions consistently, and the opportunity to troubleshoot and modify interventions as needed, often with the assistance of a classroom consultant, such as a school psychologist. Often, oppositional and conduct problems are managed rather than solved. Comprehensive approaches that emphasize behavioral and emotion regulation while promoting positive peer affiliation and social competence have demonstrated a significant, positive impact (Hektner, August, Bloomquist, Lee, & Klimes-Dougan, 2014). Furthermore, integrating parent and teacher trainings may be one way to increase the effectiveness of an intervention. In one study utilizing family systems methodology, a teacher-parent training demonstrated that increasing the effectiveness of parenting approaches can help motivate children to migrate from antisocial behaviors to more prosocial attitudes that become gradually internalized (Somech & Elizur, 2012). Positive daily school experiences also appear to be one of the best means of modifying and shaping this pattern of disturbing behavior. Facilitating ongoing dialogue among students, parents, and teachers can promote the concurrent management of challenging behaviors in the classroom and at home.

Models and techniques to manage disruptive behaviors in the classroom fall into three broad areas: 1) those that focus on prevention, 2) those that focus on correction and control of misbehavior, and 3) those that focus on intervention techniques. The first set of strategies focuses on procedures that reduce the likelihood of misbehavior. The second set of strategies focuses on the modification of behavior and strategies that provide teachers with ways to model more appropriate patterns of behavior. The third set of strategies may be implemented outside of classroom settings, such as counseling or family therapy, or inside the classroom using a more targeted approach. The remainder of this chapter provides prevention-oriented approaches as well as an overview of behavior modification techniques that can be used in the classroom. A few examples of these strategies appear in Table 5.1.

Table 5.1. General recommendations for preventing and correcting behavior problems

- Recognize that minor misbehavior is developmentally typical for children and adolescents. Hold high behavior expectations, but understand that such expectations will not always be met. Do not expect perfect behavior.
- Be patient. Understand that rarely do behaviors improve immediately and that the development of self-discipline takes a long time.
- Emphasize self-regulation and responsibility for one's own actions (i.e., self-discipline).
- Where appropriate, review and target functions of behavior and influencing factors. Reflect upon how the curriculum, instruction, expectations, and other classroom and school factors might be adapted to improve the student's behavior. Also consider various thoughts and emotions influencing behavior that might be targeted for intervention.
- Do not argue; speak calmly, firmly, and respectfully. Show disappointment in the student's misbehavior, but do not show anger. Do not model aggression, either verbally or nonverbally. If you are angry, wait until later before discussing the problem (or have someone else attend to it).
- Reinforce effort and achievement, not obedience per se.
- Make sure that the student understands what he or she did was wrong, why it was wrong, what should have been done differently, and what behavior should be exhibited in similar situations in the future.
- Avoid public humiliation. Where feasible, handle the correction privately.
- Make sure your expectations and standards for improvement are clear, reasonable, and realistic.
- Convey a sense of optimism and trust that the student's behavior will improve and will meet your expectations.
- Work to establish and maintain a positive teacher–student relationship. Convey your support. If the relationship is harmed due to the use of punishment, work quickly to restore the relationship by demonstrating warmth, caring, and support.
- Involve parents, especially when correction needs to be repeated. Establish a support system to help the student improve his or her behavior.

From BEAR, GEORGE G., DEVELOPING SELF-DISCIPLINE AND PREVENTING AND CORRECTING MISBEHAVIOR, 1st Ed., ©2005. Reprinted by permission of Pearson Education, Inc., New York, New York.

PREVENTIVE APPROACHES TO DISCIPLINE AND BEHAVIOR

Discipline is much more than a teacher's response to students' problems in the classroom. Discipline, or procedures for addressing behavioral concerns in the classroom, is a process by which teachers help students learn from mistakes as well as improve their behavior and academic performance. A preventive approach to classroom behavior works best. Such an approach reduces the occurrence of common disciplinary problems and helps a teacher deal much more effectively with them when they occur. As such, preventive approaches to behavior begin by putting into place a positive and effective learning environment, working to garner a better understanding of each and every student in the classroom, and developing a consistent means of communicating with parents. Such classrooms are places where all students can be successful academically, socially, and emotionally.

Classroom Expectations

Discipline can be referred to as a teacher's system of creating clearly stated expectations for behavior in the classroom, helping students understand those expectations, and using consequences and rewards. Employing good classroom management skills, an engaging and appropriate curriculum, and instructive approaches to resistant behaviors, teachers and other school support staff should only occasionally need to rely on reactive, consequence-based systems of discipline (Lane, Menzies, Bruhn, & Crnobori, 2011). Classroom expectations can be created to clearly communicate class- and schoolwide behavioral expectations. Classroom expectations should be brief and easy to understand, clearly conveying expected behavior rather

Understanding and Managing Challenging Behaviors

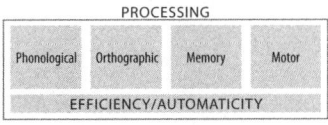

than restricted behavior. Not only can classroom teachers develop a few positively stated rules, but ideally the entire school staff should develop three to five positively stated schoolwide expectations. These are expectations each teacher can display, teach, and reinforce consistently. Select expectations that can cover a wide range of behaviors such as "Be respectful, be responsible, be safe" (see Figure 5.2). Such positively stated expectations clearly spell out for students what behaviors teachers desire to see in their students, versus those that they do not (e.g., "Don't run in the hall").

At the beginning of each school year, students quickly establish an understood set of norms and accepted classroom behaviors that are strongly influenced by the teacher's efforts and attention. Therefore, at the beginning of the school year, teachers should spend the greatest amount of time on defining classroom expectations and procedures, making them an automatic part of students' mind-sets. Classroom expectations and rules alone can have little effect on classroom behavior, whereas the combination of demonstrating approval for appropriate behavior and ignoring inappropriate behavior is most effective. Once students understand behavioral expectations, teachers and school staff will want to identify opportunities to positively reinforce students for following them. This could include verbal praise clearly describing the prosocial behavior the teacher is targeting. For example, "I like how Nathan is being safe by walking in the hallway" is much more powerful than reprimanding students for running in the hall. Focusing on the positive and supporting it with behavior-specific praise will shape student behavior more effectively than will reprimands. Prompts are an additional strategy teachers can use to help children more clearly understand behavioral expectations. For example, before Jeremy walks down the hall, a teacher could say, "Jeremy, please remember to walk down the hall quietly on your way to the lunch room."

Figure 5.2. Sample of schoolwide expectations: Elementary level. (Cheetah drawn by A. Mancillas, age 16.)

Proactive Classroom Management Strategies

A number of strategies can be implemented in the classroom that create opportunities for teachers and school staff to engage in positive interactions with students as well as avert problem situations before they take place (Walker, Ramsey, & Gresham, 2004). This includes basic strategies such as having teachers stand in close proximity to students in order to cue appropriate student behavior. Teachers are also encouraged to increase opportunities for students to respond to teacher prompts in order to more actively engage in the curriculum. This typically includes giving students approximately four to six opportunities to respond per minute, either verbally, written, individually, or in choral response. These can be effective strategies, as they help students avoid negative behaviors. Table 5.2 provides a number of prevention-oriented approaches that teachers can use in the classroom to promote positive teacher–student relationships. Other strategies include the physical arrangement of the classroom, student transitions, and student engagement, all of which are covered in more detail in Chapter 3.

The most important part of running an efficient and effective classroom must take place before the students arrive. Careful preparation and planning can ensure that all students successfully acquire knowledge and learn skills and that few disruptive or inappropriate behaviors occur. Students whose academic or social behavior is maladaptive present a special challenge. Six characteristics of classrooms where children can achieve academic and interpersonal success have been identified by

Table 5.2. Prevention-oriented strategies to promote positive student behaviors

Active supervision	Visually scan, move about, and interact with students while supervising a classroom or other designated area.
Proximity	Stand in close physical proximity in order to cue a student to appropriate behavior. Do not stand so close as to appear threatening.
Multitasking and attentiveness	Attend to more than one classroom event at a time and communicate to students, verbally or nonverbally, that you are monitoring all students' activities.
Pacing	Move through a lesson with appropriate momentum. Instruction should be smooth and focused and should eliminate common teacher behaviors that slow down the pace.
Appropriate use of praise	Use specific, appropriate, and contingent praise to provide feedback to a student on his or her behavior or work.
Opportunities to respond	Create frequent opportunities for students to respond to inquiries. Teachers should provide approximately four to six opportunities to respond per minute. The response can be individual, choral, verbal, written, or indicated through a gesture or signal.
Instructive feedback	Provide more effective learning for students by providing information about student responses. Once a student has responded, the teacher can present new or additional information or emphasize already learned concepts. The information is not necessarily corrective.
Choice and preferred activities	Offer students the opportunity to choose which instructional activity they would like to complete. This increases on-task behavior and decreases challenging behavior.
Token economies	Implement a classwide system to systematically reinforce students for positive behavior.
Formal teaching of prosocial behaviors	Teach specific social skills in either a small-group or whole-class format to address impairments in social skills. Teachers can purchase prepackaged curricula or develop their own.

From Lane, K.L., Menzies, H.M., Bruhn, A.L., & Crnobori, M. (2011). *Managing challenging behaviors in schools: Research-based strategies that work* (p. 76). New York, NY: Guilford Press; reprinted by permission from Guilford Press.

Understanding and Managing Challenging Behaviors

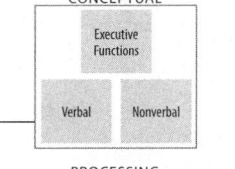
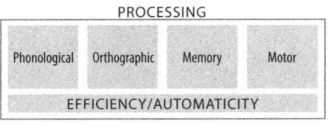
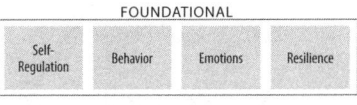

Doll and colleagues (2013). These classrooms are described in the following list and help to promote the positive student behaviors in parentheses:

1. Students believe they are competent and effective learners (academic efficacy).
2. Students set and work toward self-selected learning goals (academic self-determination).
3. Students behave appropriately and adaptively with a minimum of adult supervision (behavioral self-control).
4. Students have caring and authentic relationships with teachers (teacher–student relationships).
5. Students have ongoing and rewarding friendships with their classmates (peer relationships).
6. Families know about and strengthen the learning that occurs in the classroom (home–school relationships).

Teachers are encouraged to consider ways to integrate these proactive strategies into not only their instructional planning but also their daily interactions with students.

Addressing Classroom Conflicts

Preventive approaches to behavior also require that teachers do not view misconduct as a personal affront and that they avoid engaging in power struggles with students. No one wins a power struggle. When students attempt to engage teachers in a confrontation, teachers should not enter the battle. Instead, they should wait until a time when the interaction will be calmer and more positive.

Because of Samuel's disruptive behavior, his teacher, Ms. Handler, placed him on an hourly reinforcement system. Once, Ms. Handler was called to the office, so the student teacher was assigned the job of designating points on the point sheet located on Samuel's desk. Samuel had his baseball cap covering the point sheet. The student teacher moved the hat just a short distance. Samuel moved the hat back and said, "Don't touch my hat." The student teacher responded, "Samuel, you need to move your hat so I can give you your points for the day. Besides, hats are not allowed on desks during class time."

"Don't tell me what to do," Samuel responded.

"Samuel, you need to move your hat so I can give you your daily points."

"You're not the boss here, leave me alone," responded Samuel angrily.

"Samuel, you can either put your hat in the appropriate place or it will go on Ms. Handler's desk." Samuel then responded, "Don't touch my hat. Don't tell me what to do."

After waiting 30 seconds for Samuel to move his hat, the student teacher picked up the hat and moved it to Ms. Handler's desk. Unfortunately, the student teacher did not realize that Samuel was looking for a battle and had hoped that she would remove the hat. Samuel jumped up out of his chair and approached the student teacher with his hand clenched into a fist.

"I'm going to kick your ass," Samuel yelled, drawing everyone's attention. Samuel swung at the teacher with his right hand. Fortunately, his punch did not connect. The student teacher instructed Samuel to please leave the classroom. Samuel moved backward and fell over a chair. He threw the chair that he had tripped over toward the teacher. The student teacher, the only adult in the classroom, was uncertain of what to do. Again, she asked Samuel to leave the room, hoping that Ms. Handler would quickly return.

"I won't," said Samuel.

By this time, all the other students had stopped working and were watching Samuel and the student teacher. Samuel reached out for another chair and pushed it toward the teacher. At this time, Ms. Handler had just arrived back at the classroom and, hearing the altercation, called for the principal, a large but very gentle man. When the principal entered the room with Ms. Handler, he asked Samuel to please come out into the hallway. Samuel refused and appeared to be escalating out of control. The principal walked over to Samuel, placed his hand on Samuel's shoulder, and led Samuel into the hallway and down toward the school office.

The situation with Samuel may have been avoided if the student teacher had started by informing Samuel that he would not receive points and subsequently followed through with this consequence. Instead, the student teacher wound up in a power struggle, in which no one wins.

Becoming an effective classroom manager requires practice and knowledge of effective approaches. Effective preventive disciplinary approaches include the following:

1. *Use group examples as positive reinforcement.* Use subtle group prompts to enforce rules. This could include teacher comments such as, "I like how Nathan is working quietly at his desk." However, do not punish the entire class because of the misbehavior of one student.
2. *When it's over, move on.* Handle problems effectively as they occur. Once consequences are administered, do not carry a grudge or embarrass students at a later point by bringing up a past infraction.
3. *Learn students' histories.* Learn as much as possible about each student, particularly if a problem arises early on in the school year. If this happens with a student, make an effort to communicate further with the child's parents and previous teachers concerning his or her history. Often, past teachers can provide valuable insights and suggestions about strategies that worked well with the student. Keep notes of what strategies have been effective with individual students.
4. *Show respect.* Even during conflicts or difficult times, make an effort to maintain a sense of professionalism and respect for all students. When possible, try to provide constructive student feedback in a private, quiet setting. Embarrassing students in front of their peers can result in mistrust between teacher and student.
5. *Model desired behaviors.* Model self-discipline and courtesy and students will be more likely to engage in appropriate behavior as well. Students model behaviors they see demonstrated by important adults in their life.

Conflicts between students and teachers, as with Samuel and the student teacher, often develop from disagreements over whose concerns are more important in the classroom. Often, teachers' mind-sets are that students should do what they are told, when they are told to do it. Yet when teachers believe that they and their students can work together mutually to resolve problems, conflicts can be functional and serve useful purposes. Conflicts can be used as examples to teach conflict resolution, tolerance, and cooperation, as well as help a teacher modify ineffective classroom strategies. Conflict is dysfunctional when it establishes negative patterns of behavior among students, feeds intolerance, or results in aggression.

Class meetings can be an effective means of seeking solutions when conflicts involve multiple class members. In open meetings, students can express their feelings without retribution. In problem-solving meetings, the focus is on identifying the problem, reviewing alternatives, deciding on a solution, and implementing it. Finally, in decision-making meetings, the focus can be on choosing a future program or activities for the entire classroom. This latter type of meeting is effective when teachers desire input from the class when a set of choices presents themselves.

Understanding and Managing Challenging Behaviors

Teachers will also encounter conflicts between individual students. Effective strategies for dealing with these situations include cooling-off periods, mediation, reflective listening, cooperative time-outs, and role-playing or role reversal. When aggression breaks out between two students, the first step is to end the aggression and separate the participants until emotions have dissipated. Keep in mind that mediation strategies should be practiced and used with all students in non-confrontational situations. This increases the probability that mediation is applied effectively in conflict situations. The following three reflective listening steps can be used when conflicts between students occur:

1. Give each student the opportunity to tell his or her side without interruption.
2. If the problem is likely to recur, have participants develop some possible solutions and choose one to actively implement.
3. If the problem is unlikely to recur, have participants discuss more effective ways of coping with the problem should it ever happen again.

Reflective listening involves listening actively by paraphrasing and reflecting back what is heard. This can resolve conflict or at least define a problem so that everyone can agree on what to do next. Reflective phrases such as "sounds like," "in other words," "I hear you saying," and using "I" statements can be effective in helping each student communicate his or her feelings, as well as learn how to consider the other person's perspective.

Building Parent Partnerships

Results of developmental risk studies conducted over the last 70 years have identified risk and resiliency factors that can predict important long-term outcomes such as educational achievement, employment, and social adjustment (Masten, 2001; Werner, 2013). A significant finding is that the most powerful predictors were characteristics not of individual children but instead of the families, schools, and communities in which the children were raised. This suggests that when considering student well-being and resilience, a primary focus for prevention and interventions should include the impact that family, school, and community environments have on child and adolescent behaviors.

As mentioned previously, children with behavioral and emotional concerns often demonstrate difficulties in multiple environments. Finding strategies to integrate parents into the classroom as well as to promote open lines of communication between teacher and parents is integral to promoting positive student behaviors. At the beginning of the year, teachers should consider reaching out to parents through back-to-school night or an introductory letter home, introducing parents to classroom behavioral expectations as well as identifying preferred strategies for communication (e.g., e-mail, phone calls) when concerns arise. Teachers can also use proactive strategies to communicate with parents throughout the year, such as calling individual parents or sending home a note when a student experiences success in the classroom. Targeted outreach to parents when students are doing well can go a long way in establishing rapport with parents and students. If student behavior problems do arise, parents may then be more receptive to listening to a teacher's concerns.

Integrating parent feedback and input into behavior planning for students who are struggling at school is important, as parents can share essential information that may be unknown to the teacher. This includes interventions that have been successful in previous classrooms or educational settings as well as strategies parents have used to manage a child's misbehavior at home. Establishing a strong teacher–parent partnership is essential for managing student behavioral concerns in the classroom.

BEHAVIOR MODIFICATION IN THE CLASSROOM

Behavior modification assumes that observable and measurable negative behaviors are good targets for change. All behavior follows a set of consistent rules. Methods can be developed for defining, observing, and measuring behaviors as well as for designing effective interventions. Although behavior modification techniques can fail, it is usually due to the integrity of implementation, as plans can be implemented inefficiently or inconsistently. All behavior is maintained, changed, or shaped by the consequences of that behavior. Although there are certain limits—for example, temperamental or emotional influences related to disorders such as ADHD or depression—all children function more effectively under the right set of consequences.

A functional assessment of behavior typically includes a number of information-gathering strategies that are used to formulate a hypothesis about the function of an inappropriate behavior (Alberto & Troutman, 2013). A functional behavior assessment (FBA) is typically conducted by a school psychologist, social worker, or behavior analyst—in other words, a school professional with formal training in identifying, defining, observing, and measuring behaviors. The following multistep approach could also be used to manage behavior through consequences:

1. Define the problem, usually by count or description.
2. Design a way to change the behavior.
3. Identify an effective reinforcer.
4. Apply the reinforcer consistently to shape or change the behavior.

A number of strategies can be used to better understand a student's behavior. Such strategies are essential in defining the behavior of concern. Behavioral assessments are often needed to inform decisions about instruction and intervention.

Classroom Observations

Sometimes it is important to determine the approximate amount of time a student exhibits a particular behavior or to better understand in what contexts specific behaviors are occurring. Systematic direct observations (SDOs) are a type of classroom observation that allows an observer to take a snapshot of a student's behavior in his or her environment over some defined time period (Chafouleas, Riley-Tilman, & Sugai, 2007). Using a coding system, an observer collects data on predefined behaviors, often in multiple settings. Five characteristics have been identified by Salvia and Ysseldyke (2010) that highlight key features of SDOs: 1) the reason for observation is to measure specific behaviors, 2) these behaviors have been defined in operational terms, 3) the data are collected under standardized procedures that allow for a high level of objectivity, 4) the time and place for observations are specified and selected, and 5) data are scored and summarized in a standardized manner so they do not vary between observers. Although teachers can collect data on individual students in their classroom, using an outside observer such as the school psychologist or school counselor can be helpful in collecting baseline information or progress monitoring data to guide ongoing interventions. An SDO

SYSTEMATIC DIRECT OBSERVATION
Momentary Time Sampling for 10-minutes, 10-second intervals

OBSERVATION INSTRUCTIONS

Please complete the observation once a day. Across the 10-minute observation period, record the presence (+) or absence (–) of both **Disruptive Behavior** and **Academic Engagement** at the end of every 10-second interval.

Academic Engagement: Active or passive participation in the classroom activity. For example, writing, raising hand, answering a question, talking about a lesson, listening to the teacher, reading silently, or looking at instructional materials.

Disruptive Behavior: Any student action that interrupts regular school or classroom activity. For example, being out of seat, fidgeting, playing with objects, acting aggressively, talking/yelling about things that are unrelated to classroom instruction.

It is possible for both behaviors to be displayed at the same time. For instance, "Susie" may be actively writing on a worksheet as she talks to the student next to her. Her writing constitutes academic engagement, whereas her talking constitutes disruption.

Please remember to record the following information:

1. **Total %**: At the bottom of the form, provide the percentage of intervals in which each behavior was observed.
2. **Work Start Time**: Record the specific time at which the student began to work, down to the minute.
3. **Work End Time**: Record the specific time at which the student stopped working, down to the minute. This should correspond to the time at which the student either 1) finished the problem set, or 2) terminated the task (e.g., by walking away from the desk or ripping up the worksheet).
4. **Number of problems completed**: Record the total number of math problems completed by the student during the current work time.

SYSTEMATIC DIRECT OBSERVATION
Momentary Time Sampling for 10 minutes, with 10-second intervals

Student: _____ Date: _____

Observation Start Time: _____ Observation End Time: _____

Work Start Time: _____ Work End Time: _____

Disruptive Behavior: Any action that interrupts classroom activity. For example, being out of seat, fidgeting, playing with objects, acting aggressively, talking/yelling about things that are unrelated to classroom instruction.

Academic Engagement: Active or passive participation in the classroom activity. For example: writing, raising hand, answering a question, talking about a lesson, listening to the teacher, reading silently, or looking at instructional materials.

	0:10	0:20	0:30	0:40	0:50	1:00	1:10	1:20	1:30	1:40	1:50	2:00
DB												
AE												

	2:10	2:20	2:30	2:40	2:50	3:00	3:10	3:20	3:30	3:40	3:50	4:00
DB												
AE												

	4:10	4:20	4:30	4:40	4:50	5:00	5:10	5:20	5:30	5:40	5:50	6:00
DB												
AE												

	6:10	6:20	6:30	6:40	6:50	7:00	7:10	7:20	7:30	7:40	7:50	8:00
DB												
AE												

	8:10	8:20	8:30	8:40	8:50	9:00	9:10	9:20	9:30	9:40	9:50	10:00
DB												
AE												

Figure 5.3. Systematic direct observation sample form.

example is provided in Figure 5.3, with directions for use. Two specific behavior examples are provided (academic engagement and disruptive behavior); however, any operationally defined behavior could be substituted and used in this format of data collection.

Peer Comparison Observation Method

Emphasis on the problem as solely within an individual can miss important contributing indicators within the school context (Chafouleas et al., 2007). It can therefore be important to examine not only the individual but also the environment in which the student exists. This can be done by collecting both individual and comparison peer data. This format provides the observer an estimate of the group's behavior by observing and recording the behavior of not only the student of concern but also a peer comparison student during each interval. A round-robin format is used whereby a different peer is selected during each interval in order to ascertain a class average. For example, if completing 10-second interval recordings on academic engagement, the observer would mark a tally for the individual student of concern, as well as a different peer during each interval. The SDO form in Figure 5.3 could be used for this purpose by adding an additional peer comparison row for each targeted behavior of concern. At the end of the observation period, compute the percentage of academic engaged time for the student and the class. This may be accomplished using the formula provided in Figure 5.4.

When Jeremy was in third grade, a volunteer completed this type of observation for Jeremy and his classmates while they were engaged in a small-group activity. Jeremy had been on task for 34 of the 90 intervals. He had been off task for 56 of the 90 intervals. His total time on task was 34/90 × 100, or approximately 38% of the time. In contrast, Jeremy's classmates had been on task for 78 of the 90 intervals and had been off task for 12 of the intervals. His peers' total time on task was 78/90 × 100, or approximately 87% of the time.

As a general guideline, if a student is on task less than 60% of the time and the peer's average is 85% or more, the target student's attention to the task is problematic and should be the focus of intervention. If both students' on-task behavior is below 60%, the problem may be more related to classroom management (Rhode, Jenson, & Reavis, 1992). Whole-group intervention would be most appropriate in this case. When compared with his peers, Jeremy appears to be much more distractible and off task; therefore, the intervention could focus on ways to help Jeremy increase his attention to tasks in the classroom.

As a general rule, a student should be observed in at least two different settings or two different types of activities (Kazdin, 2012; Nock & Kurtz, 2005). Some students are only off task and distractible when presented with tasks they find uninteresting. Other students are distractible only during specific subjects, such as in a math class. Students' abilities to pay attention vary depending on the type of task, the difficulty of the material, the type of activity, the setting, the time of day, and the teacher's classroom management skills. Conducting a variety of classroom

$$\frac{\text{Number of on-task intervals}}{\text{Number of on-task + off-task intervals}} \times 100 = \text{Percentage of time spent on task}$$

Figure 5.4. Formula for the response discrepancy observation method.

Understanding and Managing Challenging Behaviors

observations can help differentiate in what areas the student is having difficulties and achieving success.

Observation forms can also be used to monitor student progress over time to determine the effectiveness of a given intervention. A number of observation forms are available that combine characteristics of systematic direct observation and behavior rating skills. These forms are designed to be used in a formative or repeated fashion to represent behavior that occurs over a specified period of time and under specific and similar conditions (Chafouleas et al., 2007). Examples include a daily behavior report card, home–school note, and Direct Behavior Ratings (DBRs). An example of a Direct Behavior Rating form that could be used with a student in the elementary grades is provided in Figure 5.5. This can be a quick and easy way for a classroom consultant, such as a school psychologist, to receive teacher feedback on a student's daily performance on defined behaviors of concern.

Reinforcement

Reinforcers are consequences that strengthen behavior. Punishments are consequences that weaken behavior. Students' behaviors are managed and changed by the consequences of classroom behavior. Consequences of behavior are directly related to the events that come either immediately before or after them. Table 5.3 provides examples of behavioral outcomes as they relate to various behavior modifications and events.

Reinforcement and punishment follow four basic principles: 1) reinforcement or punishment always follows behavior, 2) reinforcement or punishment follows the target behavior as soon as possible, 3) reinforcement or punishment fits the target behavior and must be meaningful to the child, and 4) multiple reinforcers or punishments are likely to be more effective than single reinforcers or punishments. For example, in Table 5.3, Lauren is positively reinforced whenever the teacher sees that she is working quietly at her desk. This includes positive teacher comments immediately after the desired behavior, such as, "Lauren, I like how you are working quietly at your desk and trying hard on each of your math problems." The teacher could also further reinforce Lauren's behavior by providing a second reinforcer, such as being given a mark or point toward a predetermined individual or classwide reward (e.g., extra recess time for elementary students, working toward a free homework coupon for secondary students).

Although reinforcement and punishment can be equally effective in reducing specific target behaviors in the classroom, reinforcement is by far more effective in helping children develop alternative, more functional behaviors. When Jeremy was in third grade, his teacher instituted a procedure in which he would receive a tally mark if she looked over and saw that he was tipping back in his chair. She placed four X's under each chair leg to remind him not to lean back. A more positive approach would be for the teacher to let Jeremy earn a tally mark each time she looked over and saw that all four legs of Jeremy's chair were on the floor. This would reinforce the desired behavior. Educators are encouraged to try a number of reinforcing strategies first before resorting to punishment as a means of reducing unwanted or aversive classroom behaviors.

Schedules

Schedules define and identify the amount of work required or the time that must elapse between reinforcers. Examples of schedules include continuous, fixed or

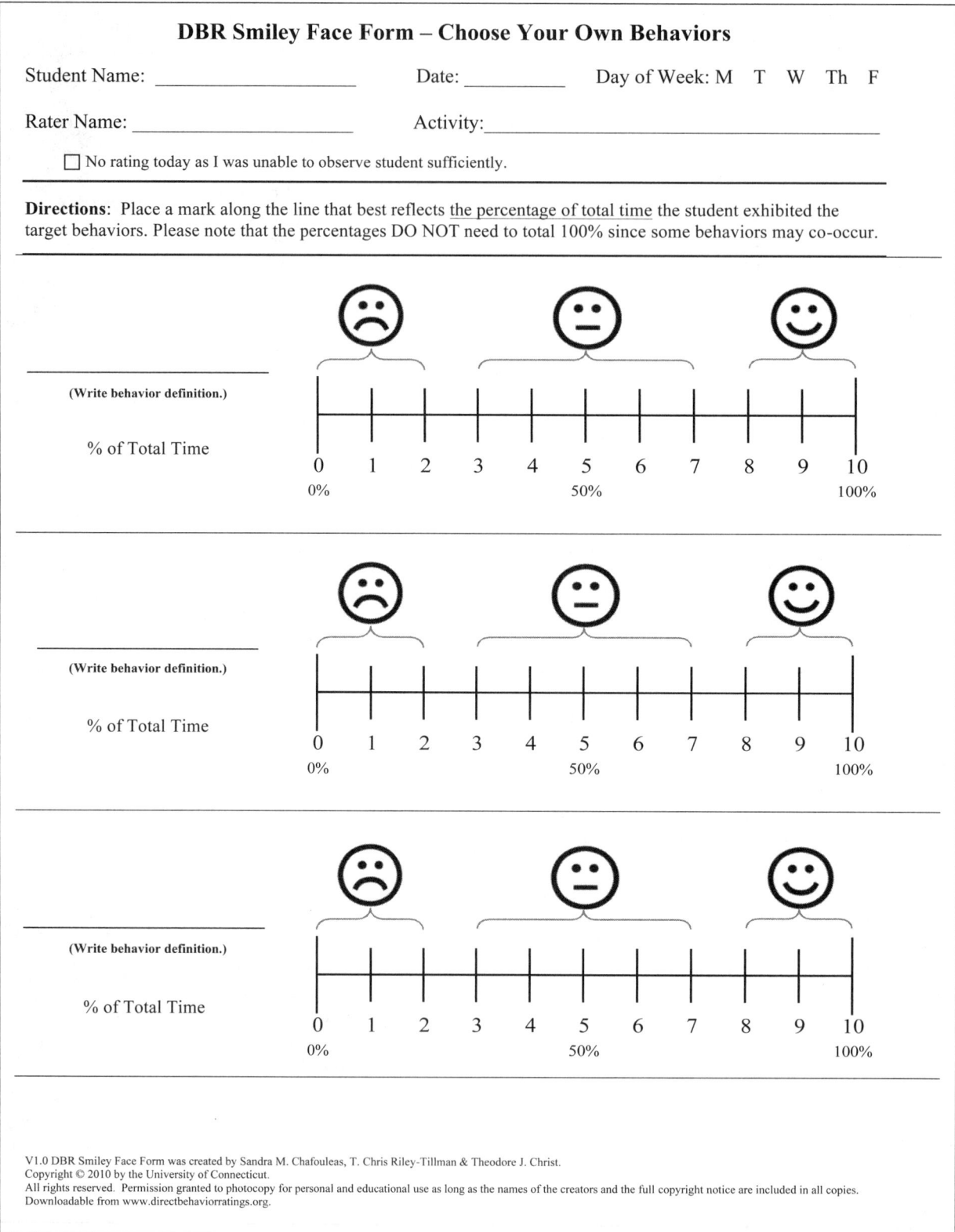

Figure 5.5. Direct Behavior Rating smiley face form. (From Chafouleas, S.M., Riley-Tillman, T.C., & Christ, T.J. [2010]. *Direct behavior ratings smiley face form.* Retrieved from www.directbehaviorratings.org)

Understanding and Managing Challenging Behaviors

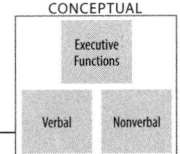

Table 5.3. Examples of behavioral outcomes resulting from various behavior modification classifications

Behavior modification	Behavior example	Consequences	Probable future effect on behavior
Positive reinforcement	Lauren works quietly at her desk.	The teacher praises and rewards Lauren.	Lauren will continue to work quietly at her desk.
Negative reinforcement	Nick complains his stomach hurts whenever it is time to go to math class.	Nick is allowed to go to the nurse's office without going to math class.	Nick will continue to complain his stomach hurts whenever it's time for math.
Extinction	Imelda teases Anna about her pink sweatshirt.	Imelda is ignored.	Imelda will stop teasing Anna.
Punishment	Isoken breaks all the crayons so that no one else can use them.	Isoken has to stay inside during recess.	Isoken will stop breaking the crayons.

variable interval (time-related), and fixed or variable ratio (related to how much work is completed). Continuous schedules of reinforcement (CRF) indicate that each time a student demonstrates a desired behavior, he or she will receive a reinforcer. CRF schedules are most useful when students are learning new behaviors (Alberto & Troutman, 2013). For example, a student may receive one reinforcer every time he or she raises a hand to ask a question. Once a student can achieve this behavior, say 80% of the time, the teacher may make the transition to a fixed-interval schedule. Now a student is reinforced only every other time he or she raises a hand. Fixed schedules result in higher rates of performance than continuous schedules over time. However, the drawback is that a student quickly learns that no reinforcement is going to be available until certain contingencies occur. There is less guesswork; therefore, there is likely to be a drop-off in the child's performance after earning a reward under a fixed schedule. The child works more diligently when getting closer to earning rewards and slows down after the reward is provided. In the classroom, a variable schedule that keeps a child guessing is likely to be more effective than a fixed schedule. The most successful plans start as a fixed schedule and move into a variable schedule of reinforcement.

In an effort to improve Samuel's classroom behavior, Ms. Handler set up a variable interval schedule. She told Samuel that he would earn points for appropriate behavior in the classroom. However, the number of points he earned and when he earned the points changed each day. Ms. Handler explained to Samuel that she would roll a die each day. The number on the die determined how many points Samuel obtained for good behavior. She then rolled the die a second time. That determined the number of times per day she would check on Samuel's behavior. If he had been behaving appropriately in the 15 minutes before being checked, then he received points that he could trade in at the end of the week for a reinforcing activity.

Keep in mind that variable schedules are not as good for shaping new behaviors but are excellent for maintaining well-learned behaviors.

Positive Reinforcement

The appropriate application of positive reinforcement has repeatedly been demonstrated to increase both on-task behavior and work completion (for reviews, see DuPaul & Stoner, 2003; Goldstein & Brooks, 2007; Zentall, 2006). In the early elementary school grades, teachers provide a significant degree of positive reinforcement when desired behaviors are exhibited; that is, when a desired behavior is exhibited, teachers frequently respond with a consequence that is likely to increase the recurrence of that behavior. Jeremy's first-grade teacher offered frequent praise when he was sitting quietly in his seat. Samuel's second-grade teacher complimented him whenever he returned from recess demonstrating appropriate behaviors on the playground.

By middle elementary school and through secondary school, however, teachers begin paying increasingly greater attention to undesirable behaviors and less attention to appropriate behaviors. Unfortunately, paying attention to undesirable behaviors causes them to cease in the short run but occur more frequently in the long run.

Children with poor self-control may often be more interested in tasks other than those on which the teacher is focusing. This leads to significantly more nonproductive activity and uneven, unpredictable classroom behavior. The overall rates of negative teacher–child interactions involving students whose behavior is typical, interestingly, are also higher in classrooms containing children with poor self-control. According to reports, teachers are more intense and controlling when interacting with children with poor self-control. Within school settings, children with ADHD appear to experience negative consequences because of their temperament and a performance history that often involves beginning but not completing tasks. Many teachers of students with ADHD unfortunately tend to focus on the student's misbehavior rather than on the reduction or termination of the behavior. Chapter 4 provides additional strategies and interventions for working with students with ADHD.

> Over the school year, Ms. Handler found that—in an effort to return Samuel to acceptable behavior—she paid attention to him when he was misbehaving. She realized that when he was not misbehaving (but rather behaving appropriately), she was failing to reinforce or provide him with positive feedback for good behavior. Though there were times when she had to intervene because Samuel was disrupting others, there were other times when Samuel's off-task or inappropriate behavior did not disturb or disrupt other students. Ms. Handler chose to ignore the nondisruptive behaviors and use her time instead to provide positive feedback to Samuel when he was behaving appropriately.

This naturally occurring pattern of teachers paying less attention to desirable behaviors and more attention to undesirable behaviors as children progress through school places children with disruptive behavior at a greater disadvantage than their classmates. In the first few grades, when teachers appear to be making a conscientious effort to positively reinforce their students, children with disruptive behaviors often do not receive their share of positive feedback. In the later grades, as teachers exhibit less positive reinforcement, perhaps because they feel that it is not needed, these children are placed at even greater risk.

Positive reinforcement programs should begin at the level at which children can succeed. All too often, a teacher will set up a wonderful behavior program but set the initial criteria for success too high. The disruptive child in this system rarely meets with success. Problem behavior must be defined operationally, and then a level of baseline occurrence must be obtained. At first, reinforcement should occur when the child is at or slightly better than baseline. For example, in first grade, Jeremy was out of his seat 10 times during a work period, so his teacher provided reinforcement when he was out of his seat no more than 8 times. As Jeremy became more

Understanding and Managing Challenging Behaviors

successful, the necessary criterion for reinforcement was gradually made stricter, allowing fewer out-of-seat behaviors during a given time period.

Positive reinforcement should follow immediately after a student demonstrates positive, prosocial behavior. The reinforcement should be specific and initially continuous, slowly moving to an intermittent schedule. There are different types of reinforcers. Material reinforcers provide the child with something tangible; even if material reinforcers are used, however, a kind word from the teacher should always accompany them. Social reinforcers are more versatile. As a general principle, it is easier to increase behavior than decrease it. Thus, when choosing a target behavior, it is preferable to focus on behaviors to be increased rather than on those to be decreased. Shea and Bauer (1987) described the following process to apply positive reinforcements effectively:

1. Select a target behavior to increase, define the behavior, and choose a reinforcer.
2. Observe the child and watch for the behavior.
3. Reinforce the target behavior every time it is exhibited.
4. Comment in a positive way about the behavior when providing reinforcement.
5. Be enthusiastic and interested.
6. Offer assistance.
7. Vary the reinforcer.

Select reinforcers that are age appropriate and not necessarily time limited, such as getting to participate in a popcorn party on Friday. Most important, do not deny students their basic rights (e.g., lunch, bathroom use, playground time) and then define these rights as positive reinforcers. At times, the use of a reinforcement list or menu can facilitate choosing a reinforcer that is meaningful to the child. The teacher can provide a list of enjoyable or free-time activities and ask the child to rank them by preference. The teacher can ask the child what he or she might do with free time; where he or she might like to sit; what he or she might like to learn about; and what kinds of activities make him or her feel needed, proud, and important in the classroom. Finally, one question a teacher may consider asking all students is, "What is the very best reward in this class that you could get for good work and behavior?"

Selection of Reinforcements

Some consequences that teachers provide for children are irrelevant and neither strengthen nor weaken the behavior they follow. Many teachers believe that placing stars on a chart as a reward or providing a prize are consequences that work with all children. Some children are motivated by these consequences, whereas others are not. Furthermore, children with poor self-control may find these consequences salient one day but lose interest in them quickly the next day. Therefore, the fact that certain consequences follow a child's behavior may neither strengthen nor weaken the chances for that behavior to recur. Teachers must evaluate whether chosen consequences are positively reinforcing or simply noise. A reinforcement menu or inventory completed jointly by the teacher and the child ensures that the former rather than the latter will occur. Additional time at recess, free time in class, material reinforcers, computer time, and class games may be most appropriate for elementary students. Secondary level students may favor activities that involve interaction with teachers, including acting as an assistant in grading papers, having lunch with the teacher, or playing a one-on-one game with an adult. Examples of positive reinforcement ideas based on the function of a student's behavior appear in Table 5.4.

Ms. Jones met with Jeremy when he was in her second-grade class to select a few reinforcers that would increase his time on task. Jeremy quickly offered several suggestions. He wanted time to look through books about dinosaurs, read some joke books, and play with blocks. He also wanted time for drawing and art projects. Ms. Jones explained that each morning, they would decide what assignments needed to be completed before break. When Jeremy completed the assignments, he could choose his reward. Ms. Jones also adapted the assignments so that he would be successful. For example, Jeremy was expected to write in his journal, but he could answer questions orally about his reading.

A teacher may develop a hierarchy of the behaviors that he or she would like to see a child exhibit. For example, in response to Jeremy's out-of-seat behavior, his teacher initiated a reinforcement system to increase in-seat behavior. Although Jeremy may earn multiple reinforcers for remaining in his seat, this does not guarantee that he will engage in constructive or appropriate behaviors while sitting. Often, multiple reinforcers and multiple levels of reinforcement must be initiated. For example, Jeremy was provided with one reinforcer for sitting and a second reinforcer for working while he was sitting. Do not make reinforcers time dependent (e.g., participating in a scheduled field trip). The student must have the opportunity to earn the reward. The variable element should be *when* Jeremy will receive the reward, not *if* he will earn it.

Token Economy

A token economy can be an individual or classwide intervention used to promote and increase specific student behaviors. When a student demonstrates a behavior previously identified by a teacher as appropriate, he or she can earn a token that can later be exchanged for a reward. The following procedure, adapted from DuPaul and Stoner (2003), may be used:

1. *Determine the behavior requiring intervention.* Using a variety of methods (e.g., teacher interviews, observations, situational rating scales), identify the student's behaviors that present the most serious challenges to learning. For example, Jeremy's teacher wanted him to start tasks promptly.

2. *Identify the situation in which the problematic behavior is most likely to occur.* For Jeremy, this was getting started on independent work in reading or writing.

3. *Take baseline data.* Before initiating the intervention, take baseline data on the frequency, severity, and/or intensity of the behaviors targeted for intervention and establish a system for monitoring progress. Some of the monitoring systems commonly used in schools include documenting the percentage of work completed, counting the number of times the behavior occurs in a given time period (e.g., 5 minutes), or counting the number of time periods during which the negative behavior does not occur. Jeremy typically did not begin a task until several minutes after instructions had been given.

4. *Select the primary and secondary reinforcers.* Token economies include primary reinforcers (i.e., the privileges, activities, and tangible items that the student is trying to earn) and secondary reinforcers (tokens that measure progress

Table 5.4. Reinforcer menu: Suggested reinforcers based on the function of the behavior

Function	Type	People		
		Students	Faculty and staff	Parents
Seeking positive reinforcement	Social attention	• Lunch with friend • Lunch with staff member of choice • Preferential seating • Reading time with adult • Meeting with the principal • Tutor/mentor younger class • Award given in front of class/school • Being featured in a positive behavior support video/skit • Praise postcard sent home	• Preferential parking spot • Award given during faculty meeting • Recognition during assembly • Being featured in a positive behavior support video/skit	• Student featured on school webpage • Student featured in newsletter or bulletin board • Phone call home from principal/teacher • Praise postcard sent home • Being featured in a positive behavior support video/skit
	Activity/task	• Lunch with a friend • Lunch with staff member of choice • Movie (on campus) • Preferential seating • Being class helper • Extra reading time • Participating in or attending positive behavior support assembly • Additional computer time • Additional recess time • Game of choice • Ticket to school event (e.g., sports, dance, play) • Extra basketball time • Feature spot in positive behavior support video	• Drawing winning positive behavior support ticket during assemblies • Ticket to school event (e.g., sports, play, dance) • Feature spot in positive behavior support video	• Ticket to school event (e.g., sports, dance, play) • Feature spot in positive behavior support video
	Tangible	• School supplies • Food coupon • School T-shirt or sweatshirt • Bike, radio, iPod • Candy, soft drinks • Gift cards (e.g., movies, stores, restaurants) • Discounted yearbook, dance ticket, sporting event	• Free yearbook • Gift certificate to local restaurant • Gift cards (e.g., movies, stores, restaurants) • Candy, soft drinks • School T-shirt or sweatshirt • School supplies • Car wash coupon	• Gift certificate (e.g., movies, stores, restaurants) • Postcard sent home regarding student's exemplary behavior • Bumper sticker for car • School T-shirt or sweatshirt
Avoiding negative reinforcement	Social attention	• Lunch in private area with peer and staff member of choosing • Extra computer time • Quiet time in the library • Get-out-of-class-participation pass • Get-out-of-physical-education pass • Preferential seating during school event	• Supervision at the positive behavior support assembly • Before/after school supervision • Hallway monitor	• Phone conference instead of on-campus conference • Get out of classroom support duty
	Activity/task	• Extra computer time (avoiding class time) • Homework pass • Front-of-the-lunch-line pass • Additional free time • Extra library time • Preferred parking (avoiding the long walk to class!)	• Extra planning period • Relief from bus duty • Relief from lunch duty	• Phone conference instead of on-campus conference • Get out of classroom support duty
	Tangible	• Certificate to drop lowest grade	• Certificate to avoid walkie-talkie duty in the hallway	• Certificate to avoid supervision duty at extracurricular activities

From UMBREIT, JOHN; FERRO, JOLENEA; LIAUPSIN, CARL J.; LANE, KATHLEEN L., FUNCTIONAL BEHAVIORAL ASSESSMENT AND FUNCTION-BASED INTERVENTION: AN EFFECTIVE, PRACTICAL APPROACH, 1st Ed., ©2007. Reprinted by permission of Pearson Education, Inc., New York, New York.

toward earning the desired reward, such as chips, check marks, or pennies). Jeremy and his teacher decided on drawing time for the primary reinforcer and tokens for the secondary reinforcer. Younger or less mature students usually require tangible items for the secondary reinforcer, whereas older students and adolescents often respond to check marks on a card. Students under the age of 5 generally do not understand the complexity of a two-tiered program and, consequently, need an immediate reward each time they produce the targeted positive behavior. Intangible and tangible reinforcers to be given on a frequent basis may include verbal praise specific to the behavior; a note to the parents; stickers on a card to bring home; or access to a grab bag of small, inexpensive items. Ensure that the rewards chosen are highly motivating to the student and are not easily available except within the behavior program.

5. *Assign point values to the behaviors.* Determine a point value for each demonstration of the target positive behavior or for refraining from the negative behavior. If you are targeting more than one behavior, determine and list the point value for each, assigning higher point values to more difficult tasks or behaviors. Break down complex tasks into parts, assigning a point value to each so that the student receives credit for those parts done well. Jeremy's teacher devised a plan where he would earn two tokens each time he started to work within 10 seconds.

6. *Develop a menu of privileges, activities, or tangible items for which the student can trade the tokens.* Assign a point value to each menu item according to its attraction for the student (e.g., 5 points for a toy from the "treasure box," 10 points for art supplies, 7 points to help deliver the school newspaper). Make sure that some rewards are valued low enough that a student could earn them in half a day or less. Initially, many students will not be able to delay gratification for more than a few hours, even with the intervening reinforcement of tokens.

7. *Explain to the student the relationship between the tokens and the primary reinforcers.* Depending on the developmental age of the student, this might include modeling the exchange of tokens for different objects. Activities and privileges on the menu can be represented by pictures and may be more appropriate reminders for younger children.

8. *Ensure immediate success.* Initially, set the behavioral criteria for earning tokens at a level the student is already capable of meeting (e.g., Jeremy will get a token when he starts his work within 30 seconds). The student must earn enough tokens to cash them in for a reward at least daily (often more frequently for a younger student) and should be encouraged to do so. Immediately, the system becomes real and the student experiences success. Remember that the tokens are only interim reinforcers. If they are not converted into rewards frequently and regularly, they will lose their effectiveness as motivators.

9. *Change rewards to maintain effectiveness and interest.* Monitor the effectiveness of the behavior program on an ongoing basis. Typically, rewards have to be changed periodically so that they maintain their novelty and motivational power. Criteria for rewards may need to be lowered or altered. When the student is maintaining the target behaviors at an improved level, gradually increase the criteria for earning the same number of tokens. When the student is maintaining the behavior at a lesser level of support, substitute

Understanding and Managing Challenging Behaviors

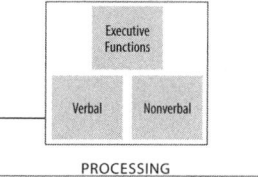
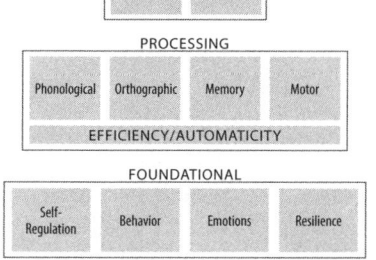

other problematic behaviors for intervention. Continue to reinforce previous behavior intermittently but with sufficient frequency that the student remains aware of the behavioral expectation and his or her ability to meet it.

10. *Promote generalization.* A student with behavior difficulties is unlikely to spontaneously generalize the positive behaviors developed in one situation to another situation. In all probability, the student will need guidance or direct training to do so, even in situations similar in structure and expectations. Typically, students have more difficulty maintaining behavior control in situations where the rules, structure, and supervision are unstructured or relaxed (e.g., school assemblies, lunch). Although behavioral interventions in such situations are more difficult to establish, they are usually necessary.

The most effective token economies are those that are implemented evenly and consistently. All adults who interact with a student throughout the day should be provided instruction on how to reinforce behaviors in multiple environments (e.g., art teacher, physical education teacher, adults in the cafeteria).

Negative Reinforcement

Negative reinforcement requires the child to work for the removal of an unpleasant consequence. The child's goal is to get rid of something that is unpleasant rather than to earn something that is desirable. In a negative reinforcement model, instead of working to earn a positive consequence, the child works to get away from an aversive consequence. Negative reinforcement is often used in the classroom to manage challenging behaviors. Teachers inadvertently pay attention to a child who may not be complying and withdraw their attention contingent on the child's compliance. Surprisingly, this strengthens rather than weakens the noncompliant behavior. The next time a similar situation occurs, the child again will not comply until confronted with the aversive consequence (i.e., the teacher's attention). Negative reinforcement is often seductive and coercive for teachers. It works in the short run, but in the long run, it is likely to strengthen rather than weaken the undesirable behavior.

Many of the same variables that affect positive reinforcement—immediacy, frequency, consistency—affect negative reinforcement. Behaviors that in and of themselves may not be negative become negative reinforcers when paired with certain events. For example, a teacher approaching a child who is not working quickly becomes a negative reinforcer, even though the action itself, the teacher walking up to the child, does not have a negative intention. Children with disruptive behavior often experience negative reinforcement because of their temperament, which makes it difficult for them to complete tasks; their consequent learning history reinforces them for beginning but rarely for finishing a task.

A number of simple, effective ways exist to deal with this problem. If a teacher uses negative reinforcement, he or she should pay attention to the student until the assignment is completed. Although this, too, is negative reinforcement, it teaches the child that the only way to get rid of the aversive consequence (i.e., the teacher's attention) is not just to start but also to complete the task at hand. As an example, the teacher may move the student's desk to a closer proximity until that particular piece of work is completed.

A second alternative involves the use of differential attention or ignoring. The term *differential attention* applies when ignoring is used as the negative consequence for exhibiting the undesirable behavior, and attention is used as a positive consequence for exhibiting the competing desirable behavior. This is an active process in which the teacher ignores the child engaged in an off-task activity but pays attention immediately when the child begins working. Many teachers avoid interaction with the child when he or she is on task for fear of interrupting the child's train of thought or good behavior. It is important, however, to reinforce the child when he or she is working so that a pattern of working to earn positive reinforcement is developed rather than working to avoid negative reinforcement.

Secondary school teachers may believe that if they ignore the adolescent exhibiting disruptive behavior, they may never have the opportunity to give positive attention because it won't be exhibited during an hour-long class. Waiting for the behavior to occur, however, even if it does not occur until the next day, is more effective in the long run than paying attention to off-task behavior that does not disturb other students. The teacher must distinguish between off-task behavior that disrupts and off-task behavior that does not disrupt. Differential attention works effectively for the latter. However, when a child is off task and disturbing others, a negative reinforcer holds an advantage in stemming the tide of an off-task behavior that involves other students as well. Many factors other than teacher attention maintain and influence student behavior.

Differential attention is a powerful intervention when used appropriately. Once the strategy of ignoring inappropriate behavior is employed, it must be continued despite a student's escalating behavior. If not, the teacher runs the risk of intermittently reinforcing the negative behavior, thereby strengthening its occurrence. For example, at first, Jeremy's teacher decided to use differential attention for his out-of-seat behavior, but she became sufficiently frustrated after he was out of his seat for 10 minutes. If she had responded by telling Jeremy to sit down, the behavior would have been reinforced rather than extinguished. The 10 minutes of ignoring would have been quickly lost in the one incident of negative attention. Jeremy would have received the desired attention of the teacher by persisting in a negative behavior.

Both children with poor self-control and children who are developing typically respond better to a continuous schedule of reinforcement than to a schedule in which the reinforcement is provided only sometimes. Praise is important for the development of other attributes in human beings, such as self-esteem, school attitude, and motivation toward academics (Redd, Morris, & Martin, 1975). In addition, the opposite is also true: A large amount of punishment can negatively affect emotional development and self-esteem.

Modeling

Through modeling, observation, and then imitation, children develop new behaviors. Modeling can be as simple as having a child watch another child sharpen a pencil. By watching the model, a child can learn a new behavior, inhibit a behavior, or strengthen a previously learned behavior (e.g., saying "thank you"). To use modeling effectively, a teacher must determine whether a child has the capacity to observe and then imitate the model. In classroom settings, a student's response to modeling is influenced by three factors: 1) the characteristics of the model (e.g., Is this a student whom the other students like and respect?); 2) the characteristics of the observer (e.g., Is this child capable of observing and imitating the behavior?); and 3) the positive or negative consequences associated with the behavior. Children are more likely to respond to teacher modeling when they view the teacher as competent, supportive, and nurturing. Moreover, learning is more important to students when their learning is important to a teacher they care about, and they

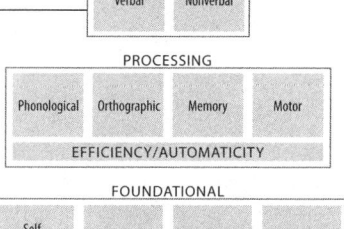

will work harder when they feel trusted and supported by their teacher (Frisby & Martin, 2010; Werner, 2013). Children are also more likely to imitate behaviors that result in positive consequences.

In 1970, Kaplan described a ripple effect in transactions between teachers and misbehaving students that affected not only those students but also the entire classroom. Teachers who were firm reduced the challenging behaviors both from the first child who misbehaved and from those students who saw the initial challenging behavior. When teachers enforced rules, the ripple effect worked in their favor. When they failed to follow through with rules, the ripple effect worked against them. Furthermore, the misbehaving student's social standing in the classroom was also an issue. When teachers successfully managed the behavior of high-status troublemakers, their control tended to benefit the entire classroom. Likewise, the ripple effect when high-status offenders were not managed effectively increased negative behaviors among other students.

Modeling is a powerful tool, often underused by teachers. When teachers are cheerful and enthusiastic, their attitudes are contagious. When they are respectful of students, students respect each other. When teachers are patient, fair, consistent, and optimistic, their students exhibit these traits as well. Teacher behavior sets the tone for the classroom environment. As Doll and colleagues wrote, "Of all the various school relationships that students are part of, teacher-student relationships are the most influential for students' academic success" (2009, p. 216).

A number of classroom routines and practices can be modeled that strengthen teacher–student relationships and help facilitate a "currency of caring" (Noblit, Rogers, & McCadden, 1995). Teachers can provide multiple opportunities for modeling appropriate behaviors by increasing the amount of time that they spend with their students (Hamre & Pianta, 2005). This could include engaging in ongoing, frequent conversations with students, where students see teachers listening to their concerns, showing an interest in their daily lives, and taking their concerns seriously. This type of modeling demonstrates positive, prosocial communications and behaviors where students not only feel a sense of comfort and security but also observe interpersonal skills they can emulate in their daily lives.

Peer modeling opportunities in the classroom are bountiful. Children often model someone they socially value and perceive as successful. Classroom practices can promote prosocial behaviors by encouraging students to work constructively together, share resources, and solve problems in a productive manner (Doll et al., 2014; Koplow, 2002). Prosocial behaviors emerge and conflicts decline in classes where there are open discussions of students' ongoing activities, problems, and celebrations (Doll & Brehm, 2010). Peers are important in shaping each other's enjoyment of school and learning, as well as reinforcing each other's commitment to being in school and doing well. Within natural classroom groups, higher achieving or more socially competent classmates can be taught to coach less skilled peers and engage them in strategic problem-solving behavior (Wentzel & Watkins, 2002). Across any strategy or intervention, the emphasis is placed on promoting and modeling positive interactions while ignoring or reducing negative interactions.

Shaping

Waiting for the appropriate target behavior or something close to that behavior to occur before reinforcing the behavior is referred to as shaping. Shaping can be used to establish behaviors that are not routinely exhibited. Shea and Bauer (2012) described the steps for effective shaping as the following:

1. Select a target behavior and define it.
2. Observe how often the behavior is exhibited.
3. Select reinforcers.
4. Decide on close approximations and reinforce successive approximations to the target behavior each time they occur.
5. Reinforce the newly established behavior on an every-time or continuous schedule as it occurs. The key to successful shaping is to reinforce closer approximations and not reinforce lesser approximations.

Any behavior that remotely resembles the target behavior should initially be reinforced. Prompts can be used and then faded. Shaping can be used for all kinds of behaviors in the classroom, including academics. Steps toward successive approximation, however, must be carefully thought out; otherwise, behaviors that are not working toward the desired goal may inadvertently be reinforced.

Punishment

Punishment weakens undesirable behavior but may not result in the elimination of a behavior (Miltenberger, 2012). In some cases, the cessation may be of short duration, and when the punishment is removed, the behavior may recur. Punishment can involve presentation of an aversive stimulus or the removal of a reinforcing stimulus following the occurrence of the undesirable behavior. Punishment is designed to reduce the probability that the behavior that precedes it will recur. Although punishment is an efficient way of changing behavior, it can become seductive and reinforcing for classroom teachers and can be overused. The greatest problem with punishment is that it does not provide an appropriate model of acceptable behavior. In other words, following the implementation of a punishment, a student may still lack an understanding of the desired behavior. Furthermore, in many classrooms, punishment is accompanied by an emotional response from the teacher. Although most teachers consider punishment to involve a reprimand, time-out, or loss of an activity such as recess, physical punishment is still used in 8.1% of classrooms in the United States (National Center for Education Statistics [NCES], 2010), even though it has a high emotional cost. However, punishment used alone—especially more severe punishments such as embarrassment or spanking—is becoming a less desirable form of behavior modification because these interventions are likely to erode self-esteem and further impair an already strained teacher–student relationship. When punishments are used, these guidelines should be followed:

1. All students are aware of which behaviors are punished and how they are punished.
2. Appropriate models for acceptable behavior are provided.
3. Punishments are offered immediately, consistently, and fairly.
4. Punishments are offered impersonally.
5. A natural or logical consequence should be used as often as possible.
6. The student being punished must understand the relationship between his or her behavior and the punishment with the potential incorporation of a debriefing activity.

Loss of the privilege during which the inappropriate behavior is exhibited is fair. Warning, nagging, threatening, and debating should be avoided. In other words,

Understanding and Managing Challenging Behaviors

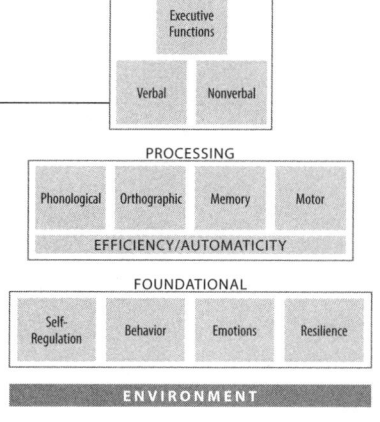

act, don't yak. Punishment can exert a complex, negative effect in the classroom and on teacher–student relationships. Furthermore, when less punishing interventions are combined with positive reinforcers, they tend to be effective in the long run. In 1946, Anderson and Brewer reported that teachers using dominating behaviors of force, threat, shame, and blame had higher rates of children displaying nonconforming behavior than teachers who were more positive and supportive. Personal hostility from teachers and punishments in an atmosphere containing minimal positive reinforcement and emotional warmth are unproductive. To be effective, punishment must be contingent on the behavior. It must be consistent, immediate, fair, and just; must be delivered impersonally; and must not involve the assignment of extra work that is unrelated to the act for which the student is being punished. Furthermore, the behavior and punishment should not be brought up later as a means to repunish the student for a previous behavior. Opportunities must also be offered for the student to exhibit and receive reinforcement for more appropriate behavior.

Teachers frequently tend to use reprimands in addition to contacting parents, taking away privileges, and time-out. Reprimands include a statement of appropriate alternative behavior. Students respond well to short reprimands followed by clear, directed statements that are explicit about the desired behavior. Effective reprimands are specific, do not humiliate the child, are provided immediately, and are given with a firm voice and controlled physical demeanor. They are often supported with a loss of privilege, including a statement encouraging more appropriate behavior. The teacher should attempt to describe the behavior rather than how he or she feels about the behavior. Instead of telling a student that he or she is rude for interrupting, a teacher could state, "You have interrupted me three times. I will answer your question as soon as I finish the explanation." This should be delivered calmly in a way that does not embarrass the child in the presence of others.

In fifth grade, Jeremy had complained to his mother that Mr. Chavez was always yelling at him to keep still or be quiet. Feeling particularly upset one afternoon, Jeremy wrote Mr. Chavez the letter presented in Figure 5.6. Fortunately, after reading this letter, Mr. Chavez understood that yelling was an ineffective way to manage Jeremy's behavior.

As evidenced by Jeremy's letter, a student's perception of a reprimand and reprimand style can influence its effectiveness. Sherman (1993) suggests that defiance is a result of strict discipline, which may result in the increase of misbehaviors. Way (2011) examined defiance more closely and found a significant interaction between punishment and authority. Students who believe noncompliance with rules and with teacher requests is acceptable demonstrated a greater level of disruption in schools with more severe punishments, in comparison to similar students enrolled in schools with more lenient punishment policies. Furthermore, students who reported more respect for school were attending a school whose punishment policy was not associated with classroom disruptions. The variation in student reports demonstrates the importance of magnifying the effects of disciplinary policies within the school environment.

Although it is important to be explicit about class expectations and what consequences will follow misbehavior, discussing the sequence of events is a valuable exercise for the student and teacher. "Think time" is a strategy used for providing emotional debriefing for older students after an incident has occurred (Nelson, Martella, & Marchand-Martella, 2002). Through this strategy, teachers are encouraged to catch the disruptive behavior early and to allow the student to

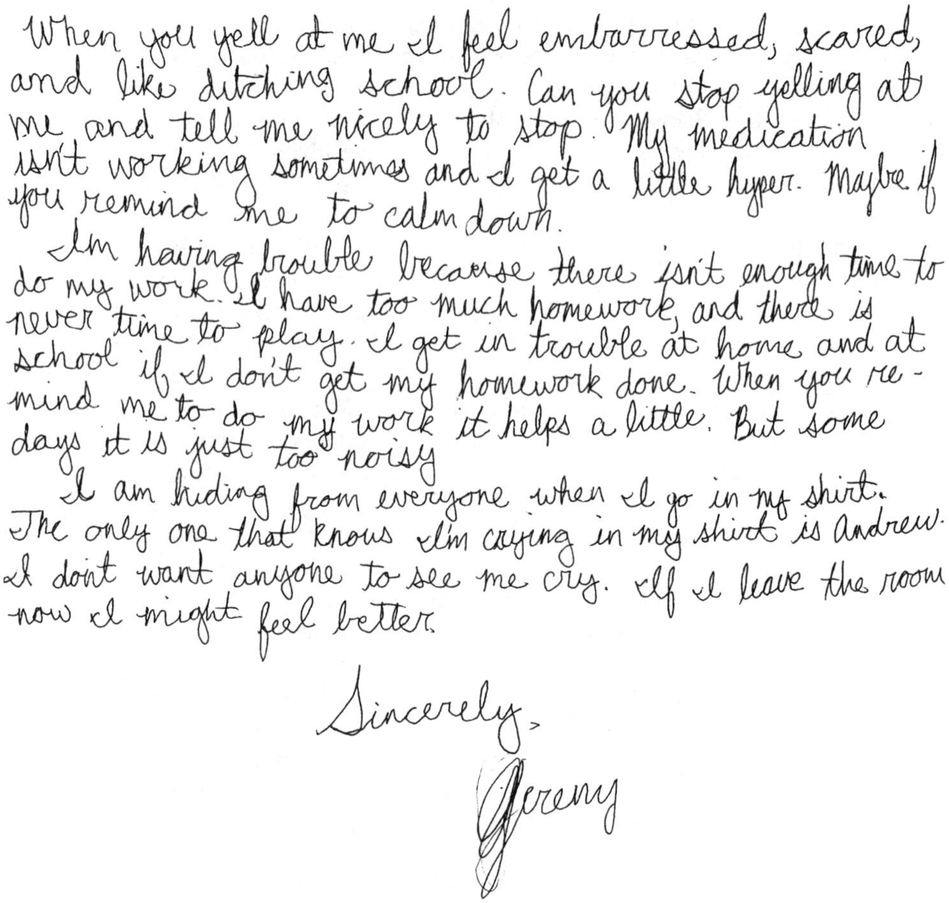

> When you yell at me I feel embarrassed, scared, and like ditching school. Can you stop yelling at me and tell me nicely to stop. My medication isn't working sometimes and I get a little hyper. Maybe if you remind me to calm down.
>
> I'm having trouble because there isn't enough time to do my work. I have too much homework, and there is never time to play. I get in trouble at home and at school if I don't get my homework done. When you remind me to do my work it helps a little. But some days it is just too noisy.
>
> I am hiding from everyone when I go in my shirt. The only one that knows I'm crying in my shirt is Andrew. I don't want anyone to see me cry. If I leave the room now I might feel better.
>
> Sincerely,
> Jeremy

Figure 5.6. Jeremy's letter to his teacher.

reflect on his or her behavior. Approximately 3–10 minutes following the misbehavior, after the student has regained emotional control, a teacher debriefs with the student. The student is asked to identify the challenging behavior, to describe his or her response in objective terms, to identify what the student was trying to accomplish, and to propose an appropriate punishment based on the given behavior. The student is also asked to fill out a debriefing form. When the form has been completed and the teacher and student have come to an agreement on the behavior of concern and resulting consequence, the student is asked to rejoin the class. This process allows the teacher and student to have a dialogue about acceptable in-class behaviors and to identify how the student can modify inappropriate behaviors.

Response Cost

Response cost is a punishing technique that involves the removal of a stimulus when a child engages in an undesirable behavior. Previously earned consequences are considered reinforcers. When they are lost, this is the response cost. The child's inappropriate behavior places in jeopardy what he or she has earned. In many situations, response cost in the form of a penalty or fine is combined with positive reinforcement. To be effective, more reinforcers must be earned than

Understanding and Managing Challenging Behaviors

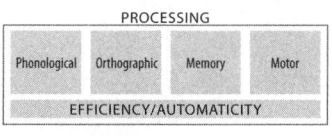
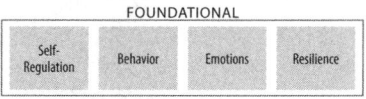

lost. If not, a child may lose reinforcers at a rate that leads to a negative value. Response cost is often used to reduce off-task behavior and improve compliance with directions.

Response cost is an effective method for managing consequences for children with ADHD or other disruptive behavior problems (Barkley, 2002). In a traditional model of response cost, many children with ADHD may immediately go bankrupt. Alternative systems have included adjusting the ratio of the number of reinforcers provided for each positive behavior versus those lost for negative behavior and increasing the number of opportunities to exhibit positive behavior and receive reinforcement. In the former case, six points might be provided for the appropriate behavior but only one point lost for the negative behavior. In the latter case, increased opportunities are provided, making it easier for a child to earn a greater number of points, thereby decreasing their chances of going bankrupt when they exhibit negative behavior.

A substantial body of research documents the effectiveness of response cost in the classroom (Nolan & Filter, 2012; Tanol, Johnson, McComas, & Cote, 2010). An earlier study (Rapport, Murphy, & Bailey, 1982) compared response cost and stimulant medication for task-related behavior in a group of boys with ADHD. The response cost procedure resulted in significant increases in on-task behavior and academic performance. Stimulant medication was notably less effective. Response cost has also been compared with a differential reinforcement paradigm, such as a token economy. Both conditions resulted in a decrease of disruptive behaviors. However, long-term response cost was the more effective intervention and has been indicated as a desirable method among teachers (Conyers et al., 2004; Mottram, Bray, Kehle, Broudy, & Jenson, 2002).

A response cost system can be as simple as chips in a cup, marks on a chart, or marbles in a jar. A more complex means of managing response cost includes electronic devices such as the Attention Training System (ATS), as described by Gordon and Davidson (1981) and Rapport (1987), which has shown utility in the classroom, as it operates as a manageable intervention for teachers to host (Dupaul, Guevremont, & Barkley, 1992; Gordon, Thomason, Cooper, & Ivers, 1991). The ATS is a remote-controlled counter that sits on a student's desk. This device provides the student with a digital readout showing the number of points he or she has earned. Using a remote-control device, points can be added or removed by the teacher from anywhere in the classroom, contingent on the child's on- and off-task behavior. By not having to move within physical proximity of the child, the teacher avoids becoming a negative reinforcer when the child is off task. DuPaul, Guevremont, and Barkley (1992) demonstrated the efficacy of response cost contingencies for managing classroom behavior and academic productivity using ATS. Response cost contingencies led to marked improvements on task-related attention and a reduction in ADHD symptoms during work time.

For response cost to be effective, a teacher must consider several factors (Miltenberger, 2012), including the following:

1. Which reinforcer will be removed? The teacher must have the ability to remove the reinforcer, and it must be contingent on the undesirable behavior.
2. Is the reinforcer immediate or delayed? In Samuel's case, a token may be removed immediately if he is talking out of turn; however, if a token economy has not been implemented, Samuel may lose the opportunity to participate in an activity occurring later in the day.

3. Is the response cost practical and acceptable? The teacher must be able to carry out the removal of the reinforcer but must not embarrass or stigmatize the student.

Like all methods of punishment, the procedure must be used consistently. The number of students in the program must be manageable, and highly motivating rewards must be provided. In addition, it is useful to partner with parents and guardians on the implementation of a response cost system, as parental involvement is widely acknowledged as a principal factor in skill building and attainment, as well as academic performance in children with ADHD (Barkley, 2000; Robin, 1998). The introduction of a school–home note allows the teacher to record daily behaviors and then inform the parent of in-school behavior patterns. Parents can follow up on consequences by providing powerful reinforcers that are unavailable in the school environment. Furthermore, by negotiating a daily note home or communication through a daily student planner, parents, teachers, and students are not only promoting communication but also accepting shared responsibility for academic success (Jurbergs, Palcic, & Kelley, 2007).

Response cost can be difficult to implement. Many teachers inadvertently become negative reinforcers when they approach the child to remove a consequence, thereby building failure into a potentially useful model. When students who become bankrupt quickly or who are oppositional from the start are placed in a group contingency situation with built-in failure (e.g., everyone must earn the reinforcer or no one has access to it), the result is often increased rather than decreased classroom problems.

Consequential versus Rule-Governed Behavior

Due to their inhibitory problems, children who are impulsive may function quite well under appropriate external or environmental consequences but struggle to develop the internal self-monitoring skills to govern their own behavior. Barkley (1981) referred to this latter issue as "problems following rule-governed behavior." Children who are impulsive may acquire behavior at a rate similar to others but take longer to learn to self-manage that behavior in the absence of external consequences and cues. Thus, even when appropriate reinforcers are earned, this child requires a greater number of successful trials to make the transition to self-management. In part, this speaks to the difference between behavior modification and behavior management. Teachers are repeatedly taught that if they provide consequences appropriately, within a reasonable period of time, children's behavior will change. Success is usually based on a child continuing to demonstrate the desired behavior when consequences are removed. When this model is applied to children who are impulsive, many potentially effective interventions are often deemed failures. For the child who is impulsive, demonstrating a behavior in the presence of consequences is not synonymous with having developed the self-management skills to independently and successfully demonstrate the behavior. For these children, it may be necessary for the teacher to shift his or her focus to behavior management; that is, the intervention may be deemed successful if the child's behavior is modified in the presence of consequences. As consequences are removed and the child's behavior regresses, this should not be interpreted as failure but rather as too quick of a change in the schedule of reinforcement. The child has yet to make the transition from consequentially managed behavior to rule-governed behavior for that particular task.

Understanding and Managing Challenging Behaviors

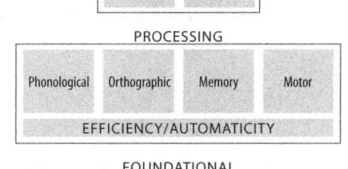

Three Keys to Using Punishment Effectively

Timing, intensity, and consistency are the three keys to using punishment effectively and appropriately in the classroom. The punishing procedures should be initiated as soon as possible after the aversive behavior is exhibited and should be as closely related to the misbehavior as possible. Furthermore, if punishments are too mild, they will not be effective and may slowly habituate the child to tolerate or adapt to more intensive or lengthy punishments. If too intense, however, punishments not only are abusive but likely will create other problems. Be conservative when using punishing techniques, but make certain their intensity is appropriate. To be effective, punishments must be consistent and predictable. Following punishment, the child should be allowed to return to the situation without being expected to exhibit overt guilt, and efforts should be made to reassure or reinforce the child. A consistent schedule of punishments should also be used. A continuous schedule of punishment for a specific targeted behavior is best. Finally, attempt to find out what drives the misbehavior and work toward managing the environment to minimize causative factors. As noted previously in this chapter, children with learning difficulties may misbehave out of frustration. This may also be the case for children who are experiencing symptoms of anxiety or depression. By identifying the child's goals and misbehavior, a teacher can present more appropriate opportunities and strategies to help a child achieve behavioral and academic success. When used appropriately, punishment can make a positive difference; however, punishing interventions should always follow efforts at using reinforcing interventions to model and shape appropriate classroom behavior.

CONCLUSION

The effective use of behavioral and cognitive strategies in the classroom may appear daunting even to experienced teachers. However, changing teacher behaviors and strategies is often the most efficient and effective means of improving all types of classroom behaviors, both disruptive and nondisruptive. Through practice comes proficiency. The Building Block of Behavior likely contains the largest and most challenging set of problems encountered in the classroom. By first understanding these problems and attempting to see the world through the eyes of students and by then developing and using a set of preventive approaches to discipline and intervention strategies regularly, problems of disruptive behavior can be effectively addressed and managed.

CHAPTER 6 OUTLINE

CHARACTERISTICS

Anxiety Disorders
Depressive Disorders
Trauma and Stress-Related Disorders
Comorbidity

ASSESSMENT

Informal
Formal

MANAGEMENT AND INTERVENTION

General Principles
Multi-tiered Systems of Support
Cognitive-Behavioral Therapy
Reinforced Practice and Participant Modeling
Trauma-Focused Cognitive-Behavioral Therapy

CONCLUSION

APPENDIX 6A: ANXIETY DISORDERS

APPENDIX 6B: DEPRESSIVE DISORDERS

APPENDIX 6C: DISORDERS OF TRAUMA AND STRESS

CHAPTER 6

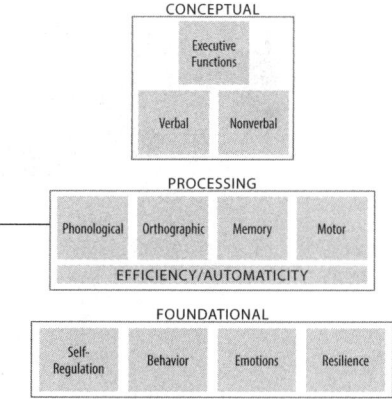

Emotions

Understanding and Managing Anxiety, Depression, Trauma, and Stress

with Gretchen Schoenfield and Jennifer M. White

This chapter provides an overview of anxiety, depression, trauma, and stress-related disorders in childhood. The intent is to help educators recognize the features of these conditions and manage symptoms in the classroom. Although educators should not attempt to diagnose psychiatric disorders in children, they may identify problematic behaviors in the classroom, assist students in managing these symptoms, and refer them to clinicians for additional assessment and treatment when needed.

CHARACTERISTICS

Disruptive (or externalizing) behaviors are usually more apparent to outside observers and therefore prompt teachers to seek out help and support more frequently than internalizing behaviors, such as anxiety or depression. Educators are in an optimal position to observe affective symptoms in children, assess the effects on interpersonal and academic functioning, and intervene. Common characteristics that may signify the need for further assessment and intervention include the following:

- Withdrawal
- Sad mood
- Emotional lability
- Anhedonia (loss of interest in usual activities)
- Poor frustration tolerance
- Social isolation / peer problems
- Somatic (physical) complaints
- Lethargy
- Inattention
- Avoidance

These disorders may cause significant distress to students and can be associated with impaired functioning. Functional impairments are wide ranging, with mild symptoms that may go unnoticed by others to more severe symptoms, including physical complaints, difficulties establishing and maintaining relationships with peers, and academic underperformance or failure. Affected individuals may be at greater risk for substance abuse problems and the development of additional mental health disorders in later adolescence and adulthood (O'Neil, Conner, & Kendall, 2011).

Anxiety Disorders

Anxiety disorders are characterized by feelings of anxiety, excessive fear, and behaviors, such as avoidance, that reflect these feelings. Fear may be understood as an emotional response to an immediate threat, real or imagined, whereas anxiety refers to a reaction to the expectation of a future threat. Normative fear and anxiety have overlapping as well as distinct features, with fear often resulting in a fight or flight response, whereas anxiety can often result in tension and avoidant behaviors.

Fear and anxiety are typical responses throughout an individual's life. Anxiety disorders differ from normative fear, worry, and anxiety in the severity and duration of symptoms, their proportion to a perceived or actual threat, their developmental appropriateness, and the degree to which they interfere with an individual's daily functioning. The *DSM-5* (American Psychiatric Association [APA], 2013) uses certain criteria to identify anxiety-related disorders; as summarized next, factors include the following:

- Persistent
- Reactions are excessive and disproportionate to the demands of a situation
- Causes distress of clinically significant proportions in significant functional areas
- Cannot be attributed to medicine, drugs, or other medical conditions or disorders

Appendix 6A describes specific anxiety disorders as identified in the *DSM-5* (APA, 2013).

Depressive Disorders

Sadness and grief in response to stress or losses are a typical part of the human experience. These emotions have varying durations, depending on the stressful event that precipitated them, but are generally expected to resolve or wane, particularly in terms of the effect they may have on an individual's daily functioning. They do not usually manifest in persistent self-critical or ruminative thought patterns associated with the depressive disorders. Symptoms that persist and manifest in significant distress and disruption in an individual's life may warrant clinical attention, as they may represent one of the depressive disorders, as conceptualized by the *DSM-5* (APA, 2013). Common to all the depressive disorders is a sad, empty, or irritable mood, along with somatic and cognitive symptoms that cause significant impairment in daily life.

The depressive disorders differ in terms of duration of symptoms, timing of onset, and the presumed causal attributions and include the following: disruptive mood dysregulation disorder, major depressive disorder, persistent depressive disorder

Emotions

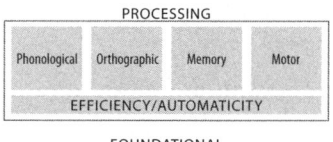
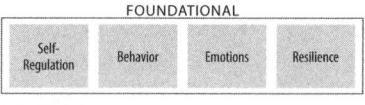

(dysthymia), premenstrual dysphoric disorder, substance/medication-induced depressive disorder, depressive disorder due to another medical condition, other specified depressive disorder, and unspecified depressive disorder. The latter two refer to conditions that do not meet full diagnostic criteria for one of the other depressive disorders and for situations in which a clinician chooses not to specify a disorder, such as cases in which there is insufficient information to make a more specific diagnosis.

Specifiers for all the depressive disorders, as they pertain to children and adolescents, include the presence of anxious distress, mixed features, melancholic features, atypical features, and psychotic features with seasonal pattern, with severity ranging from mild, to moderate, to severe (APA, 2013). To meet criteria for any of the depressive disorders, the symptoms must cause clinically significant distress or impairment in an individual's daily functioning and cannot be better explained by another psychiatric disorder. In addition, individuals with depressive disorders no longer meet diagnostic criteria for the family of disorders if they exhibit manic or hypomanic episodes, in which case their symptoms may be better explained by one of the bipolar disorders. Appendix 6B presents a summary of the most common depressive disorders.

Both anxiety and depression can lead to increased risk of suicide in students. Intentional suicide is rare in children younger than 12 years of age, which is thought to be due to limited access to means as well as stage of cognitive development (Freda, 2010). Suicide risk increases dramatically in adolescence. In fact, suicide is reportedly the third leading cause of death among individuals age 14 to 25 (Cash & Bridge, 2009). Males are generally at higher risk for completed suicide than females, though females are more likely to report suicidal thoughts and make nonlethal attempts. It is therefore critical for educators and school personnel to identify warning signs and be familiar with risk factors so youth who are at risk of self-harm may be promptly referred for services.

Risk factors for suicidality include a psychiatric disorder, depression being the most common, as well as conduct problems, substance (drug or alcohol) abuse, and access to means (Gould et al., 1998). Potential signs for suicidality may include the following:

- Communication of suicidal thoughts or thoughts about death or dying in the context of hopelessness, negativity, or sadness
- Note indicating suicidal thoughts
- Impulsive and aggressive behaviors
- A friend or family member having attempted or completed suicide
- Recent significant stressors or crises
- Unstable home environment
- Giving away possessions

Whereas some youth at risk of suicide may communicate suicidal thoughts directly or indirectly, others may not. If teachers, school personnel, or other students believe an individual is at risk for suicide, parents should be notified, and the school's crisis team must conduct a suicide risk assessment and help parents identify appropriate services. Most importantly, if a student is believed to be at risk of suicide, he or she should not be left unsupervised until a qualified mental health professional has determined that the risk of self-harm is no longer elevated.

Trauma and Stress-Related Disorders

Adverse experiences, loss, and major transitions are part of the human experience. The typical course of adjustment to these stressors may include fear, sadness, or anger. These symptoms may be expected to persist for longer duration and disrupt functioning to a greater degree in cases in which an individual has experienced a traumatic life event. A traumatic event is one that threatens injury, death, or the physical well-being of an individual and that typically causes feelings of horror, terror, or helplessness (La Greca et al., 2008). A traumatic event may include exposure to war, threatened or actual physical or sexual assault, developmentally inappropriate sexual experiences, being kidnapped or taken hostage, terrorist attacks, torture, being taken as a prisoner of war, natural or human-made disasters, severe accidents, catastrophic medical incidents, near-death injury, witnessing any of the aforementioned events, or indirect exposure through learning about a traumatic event that has happened to a close relative or friend (APA, 2013).

Reactions to trauma are highly variable and may be influenced by developmental level; cultural factors; trauma history; the environment in which the person is recovering; and variables such as temperament, preexisting anxiety or depressive disorders, and parental or family stress (Koenen et al., 2008). Nearly all children who have experienced a traumatic event demonstrate an affective or behavioral reaction in the early stages of recovery, with some responses representing adaptive strategies for coping with the traumatic events. Most individuals recover from single exposure to a trauma within several weeks or months. However, some individuals develop symptoms that persist and result in impairments in important areas of functioning, as is the case of trauma-related stressor disorders.

Trauma and stress are defined by psychological distress and clinical symptoms that develop after an individual has experienced a traumatic or stressful event. Clinical characteristics of the psychological distress are heterogeneous and may manifest as anxiety- or fear-based symptoms, externalizing or aggressive symptoms, dissociative symptoms, or some combination thereof. The *DSM-5* includes the following within the category of trauma- and stressor-related disorders: reactive attachment disorder, disinhibited social engagement disorder, posttraumatic stress disorder, acute stress disorder, the adjustment disorders, and other specified trauma- and stressor-related disorders (APA, 2013). As with the other disorders discussed in this chapter, *DSM-5* criteria for the disorders state that the symptoms must cause clinically significant impairment in an individual's functioning and not be attributable to the physiological effects of a substance or another medical condition. Appendix 6C describes specific trauma and stressor-related disorders.

Comorbidity

Comorbidity refers to the presence of two or more separate disorders occurring in one person at the same time (Klein & Risso, 1993). Anxiety and depression, for example, often co-occur (e.g., Garber & Weersing, 2010). In fact, studies suggest that co-occurring depression and anxiety are associated with a greater level of functional impairment than either disorder diagnosed alone (O'Neil, Podell, Benjamin, & Kendall, 2010). Numerous theoretical models have been discussed in the research literature to explain the nature of comorbid disorders that share similar characteristics. Some authors have proposed that high comorbidity estimates reflect flaws in the classification system, as many of the disorders have overlapping symptoms (Belzer & Schneier, 2004). Others have identified shared and multiple traits and factors

Emotions

that may predispose an individual to both conditions (for a review, see Cummings, Caporino, & Kendall, 2013). In school-age children, common disorders that also co-occur with anxiety and depressive disorders include attention-deficit/hyperactivity disorder (Schatz, 2006), learning disabilities or learning difficulties (Mammarella et al., 2014), and substance use disorders (Simon, 2009). With regard to comorbidity in trauma- and stress-related disorders, research suggests that the majority of people with posttraumatic stress also meet criteria for a range of co-occurring internalizing and externalizing disorders (Koenen et al., 2008; Scheeringa & Zeanah, 2008).

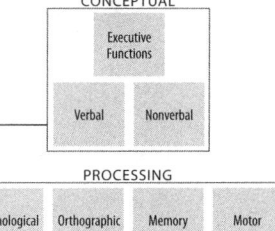

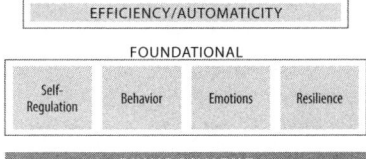

ASSESSMENT

The dynamics of interactions between teachers and students puts educators in an ideal position to identify warning signs of anxiety and depression. As behavioral indications of hopelessness and worry tend to be nondisruptive, particularly in their earliest stages, teachers and other school personnel need to be well informed about the symptoms of anxiety and depression.

Informal

Students with these types of problems present special challenges to teachers, as it is often difficult to figure out how to help.

Ms. Jones, Anthony's teacher, was concerned about his moods and behavior. Anthony appeared sad most days as well as irritable when teachers and other students attempted to engage him in group activities. This was especially noticeable on Fridays when his class participated in science centers. The class broke off into small groups and participated in engaging activities, such as games, role plays, and the building of earthworm habitats. Last week, Ms. Jones noticed Anthony hiding in the coatroom 15 minutes before the group activity began. Whereas most of the class would be excited and positive about these activities, Anthony did not demonstrate the same enthusiasm. On the playground, he was often seen lingering by himself. At the beginning of the year, his peers attempted to engage him, but what began with excuses about why he couldn't participate quickly turned into statements such as "Go away!" and "Leave me alone!" His peers stopped trying to include him in their activities. Ms. Jones often noticed Anthony yawning and putting his head down on his desk, as if he hadn't slept well the previous night. Anthony seemed to have less energy than his classmates. Ms. Jones often noticed that he looked toward the window during instructional time and later would appear not to understand what was required of him. Anthony was unable to persist on in-class assignments and often submitted unfinished work. Ms. Jones became concerned about Anthony's demeanor and started logging his behavior in a notebook. She discussed her concerns with the school psychologist and completed the Building Blocks Questionnaire presented in Figure 6.1.

Similarly, Ms. Perry had concerns about her student, Mark. Yesterday, she had pulled Mark aside before recess to let him know that she would not be returning to class that afternoon. The last time she had been absent, Mark had burst into tears and refused to work for the substitute teacher. Mark had a difficult time adapting to unexpected changes to his schedule. For example, Mark's class had library time every Wednesday. However, when a schoolwide assembly was scheduled during library time, Mark was fearful of getting into trouble for not returning his library book. For the rest of the afternoon, he had difficulty concentrating on his work and seemed restless, irritable, and later fatigued. Mark tended to avoid challenges or taking risks. He refused to answer questions unless he was certain he was correct. Mark often appeared tense and would easily startle with sudden noises or physical touch. He often complained of stomachaches. Ms. Perry also noticed that he avoided using the group restroom and instead would walk across campus to use the one private restroom available to students. Ms. Perry established good rapport with Mark but had concerns about his ability to trust others. She completed the Building Blocks Questionnaire, presented in Figure 6.2, in an effort to gain a greater understanding of his needs.

Foundational Blocks

Emotions	Rarely	Sometimes	Frequently
Appears sad	☐	☐	✓
Changes mood quickly	☐	✓	☐
Worries excessively	☐	✓	☐
Complains or presents with physical ailments (e.g., nausea, fatigue, headache)	✓	☐	☐
Appears tense and anxious	☐	✓	☐
Cries	✓	☐	☐
Isolates self from others / has poor peer relationships	☐	☐	✓
Has difficulty listening to and following directions	☐	☐	✓
Seems bored or disinterested	☐	☐	✓
Puts forth little effort	☐	✓	☐

Figure 6.1. Building Blocks Questionnaire as completed by Anthony's teacher, Ms. Jones.

If a teacher notices such symptoms, an important first step is to record observational data about the student. Anecdotal notes, or even a daily log completed over a 1- or 2-week period, can be helpful in identifying concerning behaviors.

As Figure 6.3 demonstrates, Ms. Jones focused on the facts and observations of Anthony's behavior rather than conclusions about the nature of his difficulties. Information such as a description of the symptoms, time of day, frequency, circumstances surrounding the symptoms, and if any classroom strategies lessened or increased the symptoms should be included. Such pertinent information can later be shared with a school counselor, administrator, or psychologist to assist with identifying interventions and support for the student.

Formal

Once a student is working directly with a school- or community-employed psychologist or social worker, it is common for a specialist to enlist the teacher to complete

Emotions	Rarely	Sometimes	Frequently
Appears sad	☐	✓	☐
Changes mood quickly	☐	✓	☐
Worries excessively	☐	☐	✓
Complains or presents with physical ailments (e.g., nausea, fatigue, headache)	☐	☐	✓
Appears tense and anxious	☐	☐	✓
Cries	☐	✓	☐
Isolates self from others / has poor peer relationships	✓	☐	☐
Has difficulty listening to and following directions	☐	✓	☐
Seems bored or disinterested	✓	☐	☐
Puts forth little effort	✓	☐	☐

Figure 6.2. Building Blocks Questionnaire as completed by Mark's teacher, Ms. Perry.

Emotions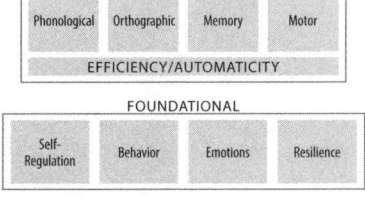

MONDAY, OCTOBER 8TH, 8:30 A.M.

Anthony came into school this morning and seemed unhappy and quiet. He worked for a period of time and then put his head on his desk. I had a difficult time motivating him to work. I asked him why he wasn't doing his work and he became agitated and said he was just too tired.

12:45 P.M.

I noticed that at recess, Anthony walked alone and didn't play with his peers at lunch.

TUESDAY, OCTOBER 9TH, 3:00 P.M.

We had a new student, Ana, from Guatemala join the class today and Anthony made a great effort to welcome and comfort her. She seemed sad and unsure of herself, with limited knowledge of the English language. Anthony sat next to her at lunch and showed her the cafeteria procedures. Overall, Anthony had a great day!

WEDNESDAY, OCTOBER 10TH, 10:00 A.M.

Anthony had a difficult time paying attention to and completing the math lesson on estimation today. It was a fun activity for most of the students, guessing the number of gumballs in a jar and then finding the median, mean, and mode of the estimated numbers. However, several times, Anthony was caught staring out the window, and I had to remind him to stay focused on his work. While he is typically quick to catch on to math concepts, he did not seem to understand what to do and did not finish the assignment. I think I will move his desk so that he is closer to me and away from the distractions outside.

THURSDAY, OCTOBER 10TH, 2:15 P.M.

Anthony sat by himself during free time. Ana, the new student, seems to be choosing to spend her time with another little girl in the class. Anthony acts as if this does not bother him, but he seems hurt and sad. I asked him to help me arrange the books on the library shelf. He worked diligently on this task.

FRIDAY, OCTOBER 11TH, 3:30 P.M.

We have science centers each Friday, and last week, Anthony was found hiding in the coat closet. Today, he did not hide but would not participate in the activities. He moved from center to center without completing the tasks and looked sad all day. I asked him if he was worried about something, and he said he wasn't. I am going to consult with the school psychologist and try to set up a meeting with Anthony's mother. I must find some ways to help Anthony feel better in school.

Figure 6.3. Behavior log: Anthony.

behavior rating scales and/or checklists to gain further insight into a child's needs. Although symptoms may be assessed and identified by teachers using informal recording approaches, such as brief checklists and logs, there are times in which formal assessment is an appropriate next step. One such example may be if a student continues to exhibit fearfulness, avoidance, or marked sadness and withdrawal that universal or targeted interventions have not adequately addressed. In such a case, information regarding the severity of the symptoms will be helpful in guiding intervention. In most school settings, school psychologists or social workers can administer and interpret formal questionnaires assessing behavioral and socioemotional functioning.

A multitude of rating scales have been published over the years to assess childhood behaviors and socioemotional functioning. Assessment approaches may differ depending on the district and the practitioners, but a common method is to first administer multitrait, multi-informant methods that draw on the expertise of school staff, parents, and student self-reports (when appropriate). These assessments are intended to assess behavior across multiple settings, including formal and informal school and home environments. Depending on the results of these omnibus measures, practitioners may choose to administer narrow-construct measures to more precisely identify the nature of the symptoms, which may be useful in guiding more intensive interventions.

In conjunction with administering any formal questionnaires, school mental health personnel should conduct a clinical interview with the child's parents to obtain additional information and context. The clinician may or may not choose to conduct the interview with the child present. Structured developmental history questionnaires can also be administered at this time, as they may reveal information regarding a child's developmental, medical, behavioral, and family history, which can provide context for interpreting results of formal assessment data. Results of the omnibus questionnaires may alert practitioners to elevated behaviors or concerns that may be the focus of additional assessment and, ultimately, treatment. Additional assessment can occur with narrow-construct instruments, which may form the basis of a diagnostic conceptualization. Administering narrow-construct assessments may help the practitioner identify treatment goals as well as signify the potential need for a referral for outpatient treatment with a psychiatrist or psychologist. See Figure 6.4 for a list of commonly used measures.

MANAGEMENT AND INTERVENTION

Classroom teachers are not responsible for labeling the cause or making a diagnosis of a disorder. A teacher's role is to describe what he or she observes and organize

Broad-construct measures	Domains assessed	Age range
Behavior Assessment System for Children, Second Edition (BASC-2), parent and teacher report (Reynolds & Kamphaus, 2004)	Internalizing disorders, externalizing disorders, behavioral symptoms, adaptive functioning	2–21 (college version, 18–25)
Achenbach Child Behavior Checklist (CBCL), youth self-report, teacher report form	Socioemotional, behavior, language	1½ to 90+
Narrow-construct measures		
Beck Youth Inventories, self-report (Beck, Beck, & Jolly, 2005)	Anxiety, depression	7–18
State-Trait Anxiety Inventory for Children (STAIC), self-report (Spielberger, 1973)	Anxiety	6–14
Revised Children's Manifest Anxiety Scales (RCMAS), self-report (Reynolds & Richmond, 1985)	Anxiety	6–19
Children's Depression Inventory 2 (CDI 2), self-report (Kovacs, 2010)	Depression	7–17
Child PTSD Symptom Scale (CPSS), self-report (Foa, Johnson, Feeny, & Treadwell, 2001)	Posttraumatic stress disorder	8–18
Children's PTSD Inventory, self-report (Saigh, 2003)	Posttraumatic stress disorder	6–18
Trauma Symptom Checklist for Children, self-report (Briere, 1996)	Posttraumatic stress disorder	8–16

Figure 6.4. Commonly used formal assessments of behavior and affective functioning.

Emotions

that information to present to school consultants and parents. Most schools have a specific referral process for teachers to follow that designates the school-based practitioners and/or administrators to refer to when a student presents signs of depression and anxiety. Teachers should familiarize themselves with this protocol and share the observational data they collect with these individuals. Moreover, school-based practitioners should guide educators in effective data observation and collection procedures that can assist with identification and treatment. Teachers should view themselves as allies in detecting problems and concerns as well as in helping to identify solutions that can help students feel supported.

General Principles

Although teachers should seek input from psychologists, social workers, and administrators for guidance in appropriate modifications and accommodations for students displaying anxiety, depression, trauma, and stress in the classroom, teachers can employ general principles to create a more conducive learning environment. It is critical for all school personnel to maintain compassion and empathy when making decisions and developing programs for struggling students. Teachers have the ability to create a classroom that could potentially lessen the difficulties students with depression and anxiety experience daily. Although more specific interventions will be discussed later in the chapter, Table 6.1 presents a list of strategies that, when implemented by educators, can help students cope with anxiety and depression.

Both Anthony and Mark may have mental health conditions that warrant further evaluation and treatment. However, by implementing some of the aforementioned strategies in the classroom, their teachers may be able to promote an optimal environment for their success.

In Anthony's case, Ms. Jones felt that his tendency to hide in the coat closet was an important behavior to target, as he was missing critical instruction time. She first had a private conversation with Anthony about his feelings and needs. During this conversation, she discovered that Anthony needed a safe cooldown area when he felt upset or overwhelmed. Together, they decided that the large beanbag in the corner of the room was a place where Anthony felt comfortable but could still access teacher instruction. Ms. Jones felt it was important for Anthony to communicate when he needed to retreat to the cooldown area, so together they identified a nonverbal signal to convey this. They agreed that when Anthony would place his pencil box in the top left corner of his desk, Ms. Jones would know he needed access to private time in the corner of the classroom on the beanbag. Ms. Jones was willing to implement this strategy as a first step in increasing the time Anthony was involved in teacher instruction and classroom activities.

In Mark's case, rather than targeting a specific behavior, Ms. Perry attempted to create a structured environment with a predictable routine, realizing that fair warning and strategies to manage any distress associated with a routine change would be important. One classwide strategy that Ms. Perry uses is progressive muscle relaxation (PMR; see Figure 6.5). She leads the entire class through this relaxation exercise routinely, and when she anticipates potentially anxiety-provoking situations for either the class or an individual student, such as prior to an exam or an unexpected change in routine, Ms. Perry implements this activity not only to provide support to Mark without singling him out but also to benefit the entire class. As Ms. Jones had done for Anthony, Ms. Perry maintained a behavior log for Mark and discussed her concerns with the school psychologist.

Multi-tiered Systems of Support

As with academic interventions, a three-tiered system of interventions is often used as a framework for servicing students with mental health needs, including anxiety

Table 6.1. General principles to ease anxiety and depression

General classroom	Provide a consistent, structured routine.
	Keep a daily schedule posted where it can be easily viewed by students.
	Discuss classroom rules and expectations and visibly post for students.
	Warn students of upcoming transitions or changes in schedule.
	Provide consistent response to behavior and academic difficulties (e.g., If I don't turn in my homework, _____ will happen).
	Explicitly teach each step of time management and study skills so students learn how to prepare for projects, presentations, and tests.
	Implement daily or weekly mindfulness techniques such as progressive muscle relaxation (see Figure 6.5).
	Consider how lighting, noise, music, sound, and activity can affect anxiety and mood.
	Allow transition time when schedule or learning is interrupted (e.g., coming in from recess or physical education).
	Model self-talk when feeling stressed. "I notice that when I am stressed, my body does _____. I notice that by (breathing, walking, taking a drink of water), my body becomes more calm."
	Have students role-play ways to handle stress and anxiety.
Individual students	Discuss privately with the student what he or she feels and needs; brainstorm together what interventions the student feels would be helpful. Giving the student choices and control when possible may assist with the anxiety.
	Create a nonverbal signal or cue that students can display when they need assistance with anxiety.
	Allow periodic breaks and extra time to complete assignments.
	Provide a "cool-down place" or "private office"—an area away from the regular instruction of the class where the student can have some privacy to manage his or her anxiety.
	For students who struggle with test anxiety, a star can be written periodically throughout the test; when the student gets to the star, it can be a reminder to take a minute to breathe, relax, or implement techniques to decrease anxiety.

and depression (Macklem, 2011). According to *Depression in Children and Adolescents: Guidelines for School Practice* in 2013, key components of a tertiary system of intervention include levels of support that increase in intensity and focus, use of research-based training programs, and consideration of a student's response to intervention (RTI) when determining movement within the tiers (Vaillancourt, Cowan, & Kalamaros Skalski, n.d.).

Interventions within Tier I are provided to the entire population and focus upon instruction of social emotion regulation skills to prevent problematic behaviors. Tier II intervention targets a smaller population of students who did not show adequate response to Tier I instruction and require more explicit, concentrated support. Tier III instruction is often individualized to a specific student's needs, and the level of intensity and specificity increases from Tier II interventions. Such a system allows service providers to more accurately target the needs of students and more appropriately differentiate the interventions utilized. The tiered approach is intended to be collaborative with classroom teachers, school psychologists, counselors, family members, and outside specialists to accurately and effectively support students.

Tier I instruction is universal, provided to the whole group, and typically facilitated by the classroom teacher. Tier I interventions are preventive in nature and focus upon developing social and emotional health through education and skill

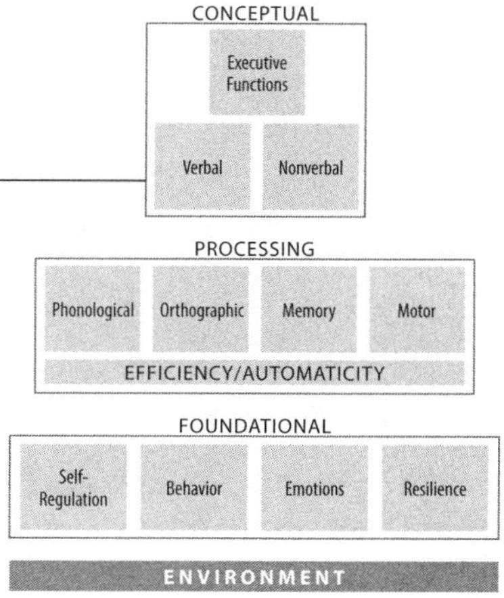

Emotions

INTRODUCTION

Today we're going to practice some special kinds of exercises called relaxation exercises. These exercises help you to learn how to relax when you're feeling uptight and help you get rid of those butterflies-in-your-stomach feelings. They're also neat because you can learn how to do some of them without anyone really noticing.

In order for you to get the best feelings from these exercises, there are some rules you must follow. First, you must do exactly what I say, even if it seems silly. Second, you must try hard to do what I say. Third, you must pay attention to your body. Throughout these exercises, pay attention to how your muscles feel when they are tight and when they are loose and relaxed. And fourth, you must practice. The more you practice, the more relaxed you can get. Do you have any questions?

ARE YOU READY TO BEGIN?

Okay, first, get as comfortable as you can in your chair. Sit back, get both feet on the floor, and just let your arms hang loose. That's fine. Now close your eyes and don't open them until I say to. Remember to follow my instructions very carefully, try hard, and pay attention to your body. Here we go!

HANDS AND ARMS

Pretend you have a whole lemon in your left hand. Now squeeze it hard. Try to squeeze all the juice out. Feel the tightness in your hand and arm as you squeeze. Now drop the lemon. Notice how your muscles feel when they are relaxed. Take another lemon and squeeze. Try to squeeze this one harder than you did the first one. That's right. Real hard. Now drop the lemon and relax. See how much better your hand and arm feel when they are relaxed. Once again, take a lemon in your left hand and squeeze all the juice out. Don't leave a single drop. Squeeze hard. Good. Now relax and let the lemon fall from your hand.

(Repeat the process for the right hand and arm.)

ARMS AND SHOULDERS

Pretend you are a furry, lazy cat. You want to stretch. Stretch your arms out in front of you. Raise them up high over your head. Way back. Feel the pull in your shoulders. Stretch higher. Now just let your arms drop back to your side. Okay, kitten, let's stretch again. Stretch your arms out in front of you. Raise them over your head. Pull them back, way back. Pull hard. Now let them drop quickly. Good. Notice how your shoulders feel more relaxed. This time, let's have a great big stretch. Try to touch the ceiling. Stretch your arms way out in front of you. Raise them way up high over your head. Push them way, way back. Notice the tension and pull in your arms and shoulders. Hold tight, now. Great. Let them drop very quickly and feel how good it is to be relaxed. It feels good and warm and lazy.

JAW

You have a giant jawbreaker bubble gum in your mouth. It's very hard to chew. Bite down on it. Hard! Let your neck muscles help you. Now relax. Just let your jaw hang loose. Notice how good it feels just to let your jaw drop. Okay, let's tackle that jawbreaker again now. Bite down. Hard! Try to squeeze it out between your teeth. That's good. You're really tearing that gum up. Now relax again. Just let your jaw drop off your face. It feels good just to let go and not have to fight that bubble gum. Okay, one more time. We're really going to tear it up this time. Bite down. Hard as you can. Harder. Oh, you're really working hard. Good. Now relax. Try to relax your whole body. You've beaten that bubble gum. Let yourself go as loose as you can.

FACE AND NOSE

Here comes a pesky old fly. He has landed on your nose. Try to get him off without using your hands. That's right, wrinkle up your nose. Make as many wrinkles in your nose as you can. Scrunch your nose up real hard. Good. You've chased him away. Now you can relax your nose. Oops, here he comes back again. Right back in the middle of your nose. Wrinkle up your nose again. Shoo him off. Wrinkle it up hard. Hold it just as tight as you can. Okay, he flew away. You can relax your face. Notice that when you scrunch up your nose, your cheeks and your mouth and your forehead and your eyes all help you, and they get tight too. So when you relax your nose, your whole body relaxes too, and that feels good. Uh-oh. This time that old fly has come back, but this time he's on your forehead. Make lots of wrinkles. Try to catch him between all those wrinkles. Hold it tight, now. Okay, you can let go. He's gone for good. Now you can just relax. Let your face go smooth, no wrinkles anywhere. Your face feels nice and smooth and relaxed.

Figure 6.5. Progressive muscle relaxation for children. (From Koeppen, A.S. [1974]. Relaxation training for children. *Elementary School Guidance and Counseling, 9,* 14–21. Elementary school guidance & counseling by AMERICAN SCHOOL COUNSELOR ASSOCIATION Reproduced with permission of AMERICAN SCHOOL COUNSELOR ASSOCIATION in the format Republish in a book via Copyright Clearance Center.)

(continued)

Figure 6.5. *(continued)*

STOMACH

Hey! Here comes a cute baby elephant. But he's not watching where he's going. He doesn't see you lying in the grass, and he's about to step on your stomach. Don't move. You don't have time to get out of the way. Just get ready for him. Make your stomach very hard. Tighten up your stomach muscles real tight. Hold it. It looks like he is going the other way. You can relax now. Let your stomach go soft. Let it be as relaxed as you can. That feels so much better. Oops, he's coming this way again. Get ready. Tighten up your stomach. Real hard. If he steps on you when your stomach is hard, it won't hurt. Make your stomach into a rock. Okay, he's moving away again. You can relax now. Kind of settle down, get comfortable, and relax. Notice the difference between a tight stomach and a relaxed one. That's how we want to feel—nice and loose and relaxed. You won't believe this, but this time he's coming your way and no turning around. He's headed straight for you. Tighten up. Tighten hard. Here he comes. This is really it. You've got to hold on tight. He's stepping on you. He's stepped over you. Now he's gone for good. You can relax completely. You're safe. Everything is okay, and you can feel nice and relaxed.

This time imagine that you want to squeeze through a narrow fence and the boards have splinters on them. You'll have to make yourself very skinny if you're going to make it through. Suck your stomach in. Try to squeeze it up against your backbone. Try to be skinny as you can. You've got to be skinny now. Just relax and feel your stomach being warm and loose. Okay, let's try to get through that fence now. Squeeze up your stomach. Make it touch your backbone. Get it real small and tight. Get it as skinny as you can. Hold tight, now. You've got to squeeze through. You got through that narrow little fence and no splinters! You can relax now. Settle back and let your stomach come back out where it belongs. You can feel really good now. You've done fine.

LEGS AND FEET

Now pretend that you are standing barefoot in a big, fat mud puddle. Squish your toes down deep into the mud. Try to get your feet down to the bottom of the mud puddle. You'll probably need your legs to help you push. Push down, spread your toes apart, feel the mud squish up between your toes. Now step out of the mud puddle. Relax your feet. Let your toes go loose and feel how nice that it feels to be relaxed. Back into the mud puddle. Squish your toes down. Let your leg muscles help push your feet down. Push your feet. Hard. Try to squeeze that puddle dry. Okay. Come back out now. Relax your feet, relax your legs, relax your toes. It feels so good to be relaxed. No tenseness anywhere. You feel kind of warm and tingly.

CONCLUSION

Stay as relaxed as you can. Let your whole body go limp and feel all your muscles relaxed. In a few minutes, I will ask you to open your eyes, and that will be the end of this practice session. As you go through the day, remember how good it feels to be relaxed. Sometimes you have to make yourself tighter before you can be relaxed, just as we did in these exercises. Practice these exercises every day to get more and more relaxed. A good time to practice is at night, after you have gone to bed and the lights are out and you won't be disturbed. It will help you get to sleep. Then, when you are really a good relaxer, you can help yourself relax at school. Just remember the elephant, or the jawbreaker, or the mud puddle, and you can do our exercises and nobody will know.

Today is a good day, and you are ready to feel very relaxed. You've worked hard and it feels good to work hard. Very slowly, now, open your eyes and wiggle your muscles around a little. Very good. You've done a good job. You're going to be a super relaxer.

---

building (Barrett, Eber, & Weist, 2012). Interventions at this level are intended to be successful for 80%–90% of the population and address basic social-emotional skills (Barrett et al., 2012). Programs adopted by schools and classrooms to provide Tier I interventions should be evidence based, relevant to the school population, and involve the entire school community, including parents. Many research-based, Tier I mental health intervention programs exist, and school professionals should determine which program will most benefit their school community. CASEL (Collaborative for Academic, Social, and Emotional Learning) is an organization whose goal is to integrate social and emotional learning into schools. CASEL released a report in 2007 of social and emotional learning (SEL) reviewing more than 700 programs (Macklem, 2011). CASEL also provides a scoring rubric for evaluating the effectiveness of programs that can be used at the classroom or school-wide level.

Emotions

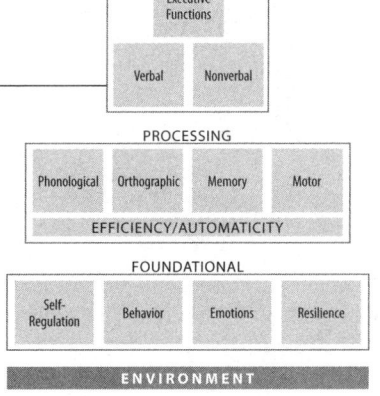

For those students who continue to show signs of anxiety, depression, and other mental health concerns or may be at a greater risk for developing problematic behaviors, Tier II intervention may be provided. At this level, the support is an extension of Tier I intervention but is more concentrated than Tier I instruction and may even provide more time or frequency to the support. However, this instruction is still generalized to the group, and not all participants may have the same diagnosis or specific difficulties. For instance, a social-emotional group focusing on communication skills may be provided to a small group of students identified with depression, anger outbursts, PTSD, and so forth. Regardless of the specific nature of the difficulty, appropriate Tier II interventions are designed to keep problematic behaviors from escalating and allow students some support with their symptoms. At this level, a specialist may or may not be providing the intervention, but it is typically separate from students' classroom environment and teacher. Again, intervention should be evidence based, and the students' progress should be monitored. Cognitive-behavioral therapy (CBT), which is discussed in the next section, is an example of a Tier I and II intervention that may be implemented if a specialist or trained teacher provides the treatment. A student who does not show adequate success from Tier II support is then typically referred to Tier III interventions.

Tier III interventions are typically for those students with the most severe, recurring, and pervasive needs, which encompass roughly 5% of the school-age population (Barrett et al., 2012). Students at this level may or may not have a diagnosis, and referral for identification is often made at this level. A school psychologist, counselor, or other trained specialist may provide evidence-based therapeutic interventions at the most intense level. The support is specific to an individual student, concentrating more intently on certain needs and skills. Supports at this level often involve functional plans that address behaviors both at school and at home and comprehensive supports that include community specialists to assist with addressing the student's needs.

Cognitive-Behavioral Therapy

As discussed previously, anxiety, depression, and stress-related disorders reflect an overlapping triad of affected cognitions, behaviors, and emotions. Strategies to address these symptoms therefore have similar roots. Cognitive-behavioral therapy (CBT) demonstrates strong empirical support for decreasing internalizing symptoms in youth.

CBT is used to address a range of behavioral and emotional symptoms in children and adolescents (e.g., Barrett, 2004; Beidel & Turner, 2005; Kendall & Hedtke, 2006). The focus of CBT is on the relationship among thoughts, emotions, and behaviors. The core principle of CBT is that cognitions (thoughts, beliefs, and interpretations) strongly influence emotions and behaviors. Cognitions are viewed as mechanisms by which internalizing symptoms develop. As such, managing these cognitions involves replacing them with more adaptive, realistic thoughts. CBT practitioners help individuals challenge irrational thoughts, develop self-awareness, begin to self-monitor, and develop coping skills that can generalize to other aspects of life.

For example, social anxiety is one of the most common anxiety disorders in adolescence. When an individual fears negative evaluation from others (e.g., "They will think I'm stupid"), this may lead to avoidance of anxiety-provoking situations, such as raising one's hand to ask or answer a question in class. The consequences of these actions may include an incomplete understanding of lecture material or lower grades for failure to participate in class. Broadly defined, a CBT intervention may include the following steps:

- Recognize negative automatic thoughts ("They will think I'm stupid").
- Use distraction to stop negative automatic thoughts (NATs).
- Turn a NAT into a neutral self-statement ("I feel worried about what they will think").
- Use relaxation training to address physiological arousal (deep breathing, progressive muscle tensing, visualization).
- Expose yourself to anxiety-provoking situations to habituate to the NAT.
- Modify distorted thoughts and replace the NAT with rational, helpful beliefs.

Several CBT interventions have been translated into structured programs that can be implemented in a variety of settings, including schools (Barrett & Turner, 2001; Owens & Murphy, 2004; Warner, Fisher, Shrout, Rathor, & Klein, 2007). CBT techniques can be applied at an individual or group level. With appropriate training, teachers, counselors, and other school personnel can implement such programs to manage internalizing symptoms in children. An example of a CBT program that has been implemented successfully in the school setting, with teachers as the primary facilitators, is the FRIENDS program (Barrett, 2004). FRIENDS is designed for children from 8 to 12 years of age, but the program has been adapted to include adolescents. The program teaches individuals to recognize signs and symptoms of their anxiety and use coping strategies to reduce their symptoms. Techniques include relaxation, cognitive restructuring, attention training, exposure, and family and peer support. The program involves 10 weekly sessions and 2 booster sessions that occur 1 and 3 months after the final session. The program also includes sessions for parents, which include education on the program, parent training, and the use of reinforcement strategies at home.

The ACTION program is a group-based CBT intervention originally designed to ameliorate depressive symptoms in females between the ages of 9 and 13, but it can be modified for males, adolescents, and individual treatment (Stark, Krumholz, Ridley, & Hamilton, 2009). The intervention is conducted over 20 sessions with children and also includes 8 parent sessions. Similar to the FRIENDS program, the focus of the intervention includes psychoeducation, goal setting, coping skills training, problem solving, and cognitive restructuring, as well as activities that help students build a positive self-image.

A team meeting took place to discuss concerns regarding Anthony's behavior and emotional functioning. In attendance was Anthony's father, Ms. Jones, the school psychologist, and the principal. Based on results of the logs that Ms. Jones maintained and formal questionnaires completed by Ms. Jones and Anthony's father, it was determined that Anthony would benefit from a group therapy program that took place at the community center after school. Over time, Ms. Jones began to notice changes in how Anthony managed his sad feelings. He described his feelings more often, began to join peer groups, and showed fewer anger outbursts when he felt like being alone.

Reinforced Practice and Participant Modeling

The treatment of specific phobias in children has a rich literature base, with two approaches meeting rigorous standards for being considered well established. The first approach is participant modeling, which is based on the theory of observational

Emotions

learning (Bandura, 1969). Observational learning is a process by which an individual adopts behaviors or response patterns that are modeled by another person. Participant modeling, as a treatment approach for reducing fear of a specific stimulus, involves a child approaching the anxiety-provoking stimulus in a series of graduated steps after first observing a peer do the same. Participant modeling may be easily implemented in the classroom environment, given multiple familiar peers who can serve as models.

> Mark was afraid to speak in front of his class and would therefore avoid volunteering to read aloud. Ms. Perry sat Mark next to Jack, a well-liked classmate who read aloud confidently. She paired the two to read aloud to one another during small group exercises. She gradually increased the size of the group while encouraging Mark to read silently, moving his lips along with another student.

Reinforced practice is a second approach based on the principles of behavior modification that uses positive reinforcement and gradual exposure to change behaviors toward a range of feared situations or stimuli. Positive reinforcement may be understood as an event, object, or activity that follows a behavior and ultimately increases the occurrence of that behavior (Kazdin, 2012). A reinforcer (e.g., praise, a tangible reward, involvement in a desirable activity) in the context of a therapeutic intervention for specific fears or phobias may be given as the child practices approaching the feared stimulus in a series of graduated steps. The reinforcer is then faded and eventually withdrawn once the child has successfully approached the stimulus without exhibiting a fear response.

Trauma-Focused Cognitive-Behavioral Therapy

Trauma-focused cognitive-behavioral therapy (TF-CBT) is a treatment modality based on the principles of cognitive-behavioral therapy developed to ameliorate symptoms of PTSD (Cohen, Mannario, & Deblinger, 2006). Elements of TF-CBT include psychoeducation, coping skills, gradual exposure to trauma-related stimuli, cognitive processing of trauma-related thoughts and beliefs, and parent or caregiver involvement. Goals of TF-CBT are for individuals who have experienced trauma and who have trauma-related symptoms to become educated about their symptoms, learn strategies to cope with stress and regulate emotions, learn to reduce emotional-cognitive-behavioral responses to trauma-related stimuli, process the traumatic experience, reestablish a sense of security, and gain adaptive interpersonal skills (Deblinger, Cohen, & Mannarino, 2003).

The status of the research on TF-CBT suggests that the intervention may be effective in treating trauma-related symptoms in school-age children and adolescents when compared with other treatment modalities. However, there is inconsistent evidence to support its use in treating secondary disorders and behavior problems that commonly emerge after the onset of posttraumatic stress disorder (Ramirez de Arellano et al., 2014).

Research support for school-based TF-CBT interventions is limited, but results of a few recent studies are promising (e.g., Kataoka et al., 2003; Morsette et al., 2009; Stein et al., 2003). Cognitive Behavioral Intervention for Trauma in Schools (CBITS) is a school-based intervention designed for students ages 8 through 15. This program is designed for children and youth who have been exposed to traumatic events, such as community and school violence, accidents, physical abuse, and domestic violence, and present with symptoms of posttraumatic stress. The recommended format includes group-based weekly sessions, 1 to 3 individual sessions, and 2 parent sessions conducted over 10 weeks. Key components of CBITS include psychoeducation, relaxation, social problem solving, cognitive restructuring, imaginal exposure, exposure to reminders (trauma-related stimuli), and development of a trauma narrative.

After a few sessions with the school psychologist involving Mark, his mother, and his stepfather, it was decided that he would benefit from an intervention targeted for children who have been the victim of abuse and who have also witnessed domestic violence. The school psychologist recommended TF-CBT with an individual and family focus due to Mark's difficulty trusting others, which interfered with his ability to establish a relationship with his stepfather, as well as his stepsiblings and peers at school. The school psychologist explained to Mark's parents that, ideally, therapy would help Mark learn to trust others, to process his emotions surrounding traumatic events that he experienced, to gain awareness of how his reactions were often out of proportion to that particular situation, and to identify new ways of coping with anxiousness and distress.

CONCLUSION

The two students described in this chapter, Mark and Anthony, have symptoms that appear severe enough to warrant clinical attention. Anthony presents with depressive symptoms that persist and interfere with academic and interpersonal functioning. Mark exhibits very elevated anxiety levels, as well as a history that raises questions regarding possible posttraumatic stress. In both cases, a formal referral to the school psychologist was appropriate for additional assessment. Based on results of a formal assessment, the school psychologist was in a better position to identify and refer the student to appropriate services.

Students who experience anxiety, depression, trauma, or stress may be at risk for a variety of potential problems, ranging from academic underperformance, low self-esteem, difficulty with interpersonal relationships, substance abuse, suicidal ideation, and affective disorders in adulthood. As such, there is a critical need to implement school-based interventions for students who demonstrate these difficulties. Given that students spend a significant amount of time in school, teachers are valuable resources in the referral and evaluation of at-risk students. Teachers and other school personnel can also implement effective interventions in the classroom to support at-risk students.

Classroom teachers should observe, document, and communicate their observations of students of concern to relevant parties such as parents, administrators, school psychologists, and outside specialists, as appropriate. Although not all students who present with anxiety, depression, or stress-related symptoms meet diagnostic criteria for a psychiatric disorder, many students will benefit from gaining coping skills and problem-solving skills to manage their symptoms. In addition, teachers and other school personnel should be familiar with mental health disorders and symptoms and common assessment and intervention approaches so that they may successfully create a supportive learning environment.

APPENDIX 6A

Anxiety Disorders

SEPARATION ANXIETY DISORDER

Separation anxiety disorder manifests in a minimum of three of the following ways (APA, 2013):

- Experiencing recurring and excessive stress upon anticipation of, or the actual experience of, separation
- Worrying persistently and excessively about unexpected events that might result in separation
- Not wanting to be away from home for fear of being separated
- Not wanting to be alone or away from attachment figure
- Wanting to sleep near a significant attachment figure
- Experiencing recurring nightmares about separation
- Recurring complaints about physical ailments upon real or expected separation

The fear, anxiety, or avoidance is persistent, lasting at least 4 weeks in children or adolescents under 18 years of age and specified as causing significant impairment and not better explained by another disorder.

In children and adolescents, 6- to 12-month prevalence is estimated to be approximately 4%–5% (Masi, Mucci, & Millepiedi, 2001). It is the most prevalent anxiety disorder in children younger than 12 years of age (APA, 2013). The onset of separation anxiety disorder may occur during the preschool years, and the prevalence of separation anxiety disorder decreases throughout childhood and adolescence.

SELECTIVE MUTISM

Selective mutism is a consistent failure to speak in specific social situations in which there is an expectation for speaking—with a preservation of speech in other situations—that interferes with achievement or social communication and lasts at least 1 month. The difficulty is not related to a lack of knowledge or comfort with the language or better explained by a communication disorder or other mental health disorder. Such individuals may not initiate or reciprocate in social conversations and may not speak when called upon in school to answer questions or perform choral reading.

Selective mutism is relatively rare, compared with other anxiety disorders in childhood, with prevalence estimates ranging from 0.03% to 1% in clinical, school-based, and community samples (APA, 2013; Bergman, Piacentini, & McCracken,

2002). The disorder occurs more commonly in younger children, with onset usually occurring before 5 years of age. Children presenting with selective mutism may exhibit oppositional behaviors, but these are generally limited to situations requiring speech.

SPECIFIC PHOBIA

Specific phobia is defined as marked fear or anxiety about a specific object or situation that almost always emerges when the individual is confronted by the feared stimulus. In children, these behaviors may include crying, tantrums, freezing, or clinging. Specified phobias may include fear of animals, fear of the natural environment, fear of blood-injection injury (blood, injury, and/or injection/needles), situational fears, and/or other fears (e.g., costumed characters, ghosts, choking). Children with specific phobia typically experience elevated physiological arousal either when anticipating or confronting the feared stimulus. This may include elevated heart rate, swift blood pressure changes, perspiration, or, in some cases, fainting or near fainting episodes. The fear, anxiety, or avoidance is persistent, usually lasts for 6 months or longer, and is not better explained by another disorder.

Specific phobias may develop in the context of exposure or witness to an actual traumatic event, hearing a traumatic event recalled during conversation or media coverage, or for no apparent reason. Specific phobias may develop during early childhood, with most cases presenting prior to 10 years old. Prevalence of specific phobias in childhood in U.S. community samples range from 5% in children to 16% in adolescents, with females outnumbering males by approximately 2:1 (APA, 2013).

SOCIAL ANXIETY DISORDER

Social anxiety disorder is one of the most common anxiety disorders in childhood and adolescence. It is characterized by self-consciousness that exceeds typical shyness and/or intense fear and anxiety in situations in which the individual may be subject to scrutiny or negative evaluation. Further, the individual may be fearful of exhibiting obvious symptoms of anxiety, such as blushing, trembling, perspiration, difficulty with speech, and staring, with the reaction negatively evaluated by others. Fear of offending others or being rejected often accompanies these symptoms, as the affected individuals may avoid feared situations or demonstrate intense fear or anxiety of these situations. The duration of the anxiety must be more than 6 months in order to meet diagnostic criteria. Prevalence estimates in children and adolescents are approximately 7% and tend to decrease into adulthood (APA, 2013).

PANIC DISORDER

Panic disorder is uncommon in children, with prevalence estimates in people younger than 14 years of age less than 0.4% (Beesdo, Knappe, & Pine, 2009). However, the occurrence of "fearful spells" in childhood may be observed, often retrospectively in individuals who develop panic disorder in adolescence or adulthood. A panic attack is defined as a sudden feeling of intense fear or discomfort that peaks within minutes, during which time at least four of the following symptoms occur: palpitations, sweating, trembling, shortness of breath, feelings of choking, chest pain or discomfort, nausea or stomach discomfort, chills or heat sensation, dizziness or light-headedness, numbness or tingling sensations, fear of losing control, or fear of dying (APA, 2013). Panic disorder refers to recurrent unexpected panic attacks.

Emotions

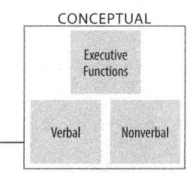
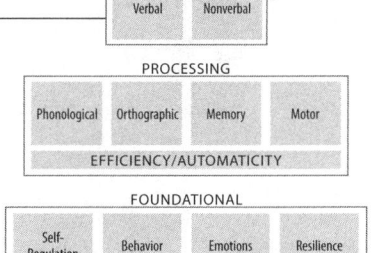

AGORAPHOBIA

Agoraphobia may have an onset in childhood, but it is very uncommon, as incidence peaks in late adolescence and young adulthood (Copeland, Angold, Shanahan, & Costello, 2014). Agoraphobia is characterized by marked fear or anxiety about two or more of the following: using public transportation, being in open spaces, being in enclosed spaces, standing in line or being in a crowd, or being outside of the home alone. The affected individual actively avoids these situations due to thoughts that he or she may not be able to escape or will not have access to help in case he or she develops panic symptoms. To meet diagnostic criteria, the fear, anxiety, or avoidance must be persistent, lasting for at least 6 months.

GENERALIZED ANXIETY DISORDER

Generalized anxiety disorder is characterized by excessive and uncontrollable worry about a broad array of situations and events, manifesting in one of the following in children or three of the following in adolescents and adults: restlessness; fatigue; reduced concentration; irritability; tension; or physical symptoms such as headaches, tension, or sleep disturbance. The anxiety and worry must occur more days than not for at least 6 months about several situations or activities in order to meet diagnostic criteria. Generalized anxiety disorder occurs in more than 10% of children and adolescents, with females twice as likely to meet criteria for the disorder (APA, 2013).

SUBSTANCE/MEDICATION-INDUCED ANXIETY DISORDER AND ANXIETY DISORDER DUE TO ANOTHER MEDICAL CONDITION

In substance/medication-induced anxiety disorder and anxiety disorder due to another medical condition, the primary feature is panic attack or anxiety with evidence from history, physical examination, or laboratory findings that associate the onset with a substance/medication or medical condition. In other words, the panic or the anxiety response is thought to be a result of the medication or the medical condition. In some cases, once the medication is withdrawn or the medical condition has resolved or is properly managed, the panic and anxiety responses abate.

APPENDIX 6B

Depressive Disorders

DISRUPTIVE MOOD DYSREGULATION DISORDER

Disruptive mood dysregulation disorder was added to the *DSM-5* to address contention regarding the possible overidentification of bipolar disorder in children and refers to persistent irritability and marked episodes of behavioral dyscontrol in children who are 12 years old or younger, usually in response to frustration or stressful situations. Although the presentation appears consistent with an externalizing disorder, it is included within the family of depressive disorders in order to distinguish it from the bipolar disorders as well as in consideration of the more typical longitudinal pattern of developing into a unipolar depression in adolescence and adulthood. Disruptive mood dysregulation disorder is characterized by severe recurrent temper outbursts manifesting in either verbal rages, physical aggression toward people or property, or both that are inconsistent with the individual's developmental level. The temper outbursts occur three or more times per week and are present for at least 12 months, during which the individual has not had a period lasting more than 3 months in which the outbursts did not occur. The individual's persistent mood status between the temper outbursts appears irritable and angry and is observable by others. The persistent mood status and the temper outbursts occur in at least two or three settings. The age of initial diagnosis must be between 6 and 18 years. To meet criteria, the behaviors do not occur exclusively during an episode of a major depressive disorder and cannot be better explained by another mental health disorder, such as one of the other depressive disorders, trauma- or stressor-related disorders, anxiety disorders, or an autism spectrum disorder. However, disruptive mood dysregulation disorder can be comorbid with any of the aforementioned disorders. The diagnosis cannot co-occur with oppositional defiant disorder, intermittent explosive disorder, or bipolar disorder, though it can coexist with attention-deficit/hyperactivity disorder, conduct disorder, and substance use disorders.

The onset of the disorder must precede 10 years of age, and validity has only been established in individuals ages 7–18 years. Prevalence of disruptive mood dysregulation disorder has not yet been identified, as the diagnosis is new. However, community referrals for chronic and severe persistent irritability are estimated to fall in the 2%–5% range, with higher incidence of referral in males and school-age children versus adolescence (APA, 2013).

MAJOR DEPRESSIVE DISORDER

Major depressive disorder is characterized by episodes lasting for at least 2 weeks in which five or more symptoms must be present, two of which must include the

Emotions

following: 1) persistently depressed mood, which includes feeling sad or empty, hopelessness, tearfulness, or irritable mood, which is more common in children and adolescents; or 2) loss of interest or pleasure. The remaining criteria include significant weight loss or weight gain; insomnia or hypersomnia; restlessness or psychomotor slowing; fatigue and loss of energy; feelings of worthlessness or excessive or inappropriate guilt; poor concentration or indecisiveness; or recurrent thoughts of death, suicidal ideation with or without intent or plan, or suicide attempt. The prevalence of major depressive disorder in childhood is estimated at 2% (Kessler et al., 2010), increasing to between 5% and 8% in adolescence and adulthood (Costello, Erkanli, & Angold, 2006) with increased risk beginning in adolescence.

PERSISTENT DEPRESSIVE DISORDER (DYSTHYMIA)

Persistent depressive disorder (dysthymia) is characterized by a depressed mood that is present for most of the day for more days than not that persists for 2 years in adults and for 1 year in children and adolescents. During the 1- or 2-year period in which the symptoms are experienced, the individual must not have been symptom free for more than 2 months. Criteria for a major depressive disorder may be present as well, the symptoms cause clinically significant impairment in one or more important areas of functioning, and the symptoms are not better explained by another disorder or the effects of a medication or another medical condition. As summarized next, at least two of the following symptoms must be present (APA, 2013):

- Appetite changes (decreased or increased)
- Difficulty sleeping or excessive sleeping
- Fatigue
- Decreased self-esteem
- Trouble concentrating or making decisions
- Feeling hopeless

The conceptualization of persistent depressive disorder (dysthymia) is new to the *DSM-5* and represents a combination of *DSM-IV* dysthymic disorder and chronic major depressive disorder. Twelve-month prevalence estimates for persistent depressive disorder (dysthymia) is 0.5% throughout the lifespan (APA, 2013). Research investigating the prevalence of persistent depressive disorder in children and adolescents is limited. A few early studies report estimates ranging from 0.6% to 1.7% in children and 1.6% to 8.0% in adolescents (for a review, see Turgay, 2005).

PREMENSTRUAL DYSPHORIC DISORDER

Premenstrual dysphoric disorder generally manifests as mood lability, irritability, depressed mood, or anxiety symptoms that occur during the premenstrual phase of a menstrual cycle and abate at or shortly after the onset of menses. Physical symptoms, such as poor concentration, lethargy, change in appetite and sleep patterns, feelings of being overwhelmed, and pain or swelling in the breasts or muscles with bloating or weight gain are often present. The symptoms must cause clinically significant distress or impairment in daily functions, must not be an exacerbation or extension of another affective or personality disorder, and must have occurred during most menstrual cycles during the past year.

SUBSTANCE/MEDICATION-INDUCED DEPRESSIVE DISORDER AND DEPRESSIVE DISORDER DUE TO ANOTHER MEDICAL CONDITION

In substance/medication-induced depressive disorder and depressive disorder due to another medical condition, the primary feature is depressed mood or anhedonia and diminished interest in activities, with evidence from history, physical examination, or laboratory findings that associate the onset with a substance/medication or medical condition. In other words, the depressed mood or anhedonia is thought to be a result of the medication or the medical condition. In some cases, once the medication is withdrawn or the medical condition has resolved or is properly managed, the mood symptoms dissipate.

APPENDIX 6C

Disorders of Trauma and Stress

POSTTRAUMATIC STRESS DISORDER

Posttraumatic stress disorder (PTSD) may develop after direct exposure to one or more traumatic events. The trauma is reexperienced in several ways, which may include recurrent, involuntary, and intrusive memories and/or distressing dreams, with accompanying sensory, emotional, or physiological behavior features. The individual may experience dissociative episodes that can last for a few seconds, hours, or days and range from a brief sensory intrusion about part of the traumatic event to complete loss of awareness and orientation to time and place. Dissociative symptoms may include depersonalization, defined as persistent experiences of detachment from one's body or mental processes or derealization in which one experiences a sense of unreality of his or her surroundings. Thoughts or stimuli that resemble or serve to remind one of the traumatic event may trigger distress, and such stimuli are generally avoided. Changes in cognition or mood may occur in which an individual may have loss of recall for the traumatic event, have distorted cognitions or beliefs about the event, have a persistent emotional state, have diminished interest in activities, experience feelings of detachment from others, and experience an inability to experience positive emotions. Arousal and reactivity symptoms may include irritability and anger outbursts, hypervigilance, exaggerated startle response, concentration difficulty, sleep disturbance, and reckless or self-destructive behavior. Symptoms must persist for more than 1 month.

Diagnostic criteria for posttraumatic stress disorder in children 6 years and younger differ slightly. Specifically omitted from criteria are 1) experiencing repeated or extreme exposure to aversive details of a traumatic event, such as first responders to a disaster and law enforcement officials repeatedly exposed to trauma while at work; 2) persistent avoidance of stimuli that do not include avoiding memories, thoughts, or feelings about the traumatic event; and 3) alterations in arousal and reactivity associated with the traumatic event that do not include reckless or self-destructive behavior. Negative alterations in cognition include substantially increased frequency of negative emotional states, socially withdrawn behavior, and persistent reduction in the display of positive emotions. In addition, *DSM-5* criteria for children age 6 and younger include repetitive play in which themes or aspects of the traumatic event are evident and/or content related to the traumatic event is reenacted. In addition, the child may experience distressing dreams in which the content is not specifically recognizable or related to the trauma. Developmental regression affecting language, behavior, play, and toileting habits may also be present.

PTSD may occur in individuals older than 12 months of age. Symptoms usually appear within the first 3 months of the traumatic event but may not emerge for several months or even years. The lifetime prevalence of posttraumatic stress disorder in children is estimated to be 5% (Merikangas et al., 2010).

ACUTE STRESS DISORDER

Acute stress disorder is characterized by the development of specific symptoms that last from 3 days to 1 month following exposure to trauma. The traumatic event may be experienced directly or indirectly and may include exposure to actual or threated death, serious injury, sexual violation directly experienced or witnessed, or learning a close family member or friend was the victim of the trauma. Nine or more symptoms must be present from the following categories: intrusion symptoms, negative mood, dissociative symptoms, avoidance symptoms, and arousal symptoms that are similar to the diagnostic criteria for posttraumatic stress disorder. The affected individual typically presents with an anxiety response that includes reexperiencing the traumatic event or reaction to it. Some experience a sense of detachment or dissociation. Irritability and anger may be a clinical picture for some.

The primary difference between acute stress disorder and posttraumatic stress disorder is duration of symptoms, which cannot exceed 1 month in order to meet symptom criteria for acute stress disorder. Prevalence estimates of acute stress disorder vary depending on the type of trauma experienced or witnessed, with the lowest rates occurring for work-related accidents (6%–12%) and the highest rates (20%–50%) reported in individuals who have experienced interpersonal trauma such as assault or rape (APA, 2013).

ADJUSTMENT DISORDERS

The adjustment disorders are characterized by the presence of emotional or behavioral symptoms that develop in response to one or more significant stressors. Common examples of significant stressors include divorce, relocation, a medical condition, sudden change in financial status, or loss of a home. Symptoms are generally thought to be less impairing than acute stress or posttraumatic stress symptoms. Symptoms develop within 3 months of a stressor and last no longer than 6 months after the stressor is no longer present. An adjustment disorder may continue to be diagnosed after a 6-month period if the consequences endure. The emotional or behavioral symptoms cause distress that is out of proportion to the severity or intensity of the stressor and cause significant impairment in social, academic, occupational, or other important areas of functioning. The symptoms must be distinguished from an exacerbation or manifestation of a preexisting mental disorder. As summarized next, indicators of an adjustment disorder include the following (APA, 2013):

- Feeling hopeless, depressed, despondent
- Being anxious, nervous, or fearful of separation
- Being both anxious and depressed
- Displaying noncompliant and oppositional behavior
- Being both depressed and anxious and exhibiting disturbed conduct

Adjustment disorders are common, with prevalence estimates ranging from 5% to 20% in clinical settings. *DSM-5* diagnostic criteria allow for delayed presentations

Emotions

as well as presentations in which symptoms manifest for more than 6 months without experiencing direct and persistent consequences of the stressor. These presentations may be diagnosed under the category of other specified trauma- and stressor-related disorder, which also includes cultural syndromes and persistent complex bereavement. Unspecified trauma- and stressor-related disorder is used when the clinician chooses not to specify the reason criteria are not met for another trauma- and stressor-related disorder, such as cases in which there is insufficient information to do so.

REACTIVE ATTACHMENT DISORDER

Reactive attachment disorder may occur in infancy and early childhood and is defined by a pattern of disturbed and developmentally inappropriate attachment behaviors, in which a child minimally seeks or responds to an attachment figure for comfort, support, protection, or nurturing. A persistent or social and emotional disturbance must be present and includes minimal social and emotional responsiveness to others; limited positive affect; or episodes of sudden or unexplained irritability, sadness, or fearfulness during interactions with adult caregivers. The disorder is thought to be due to an absent or underdeveloped attachment between the child and his or her adult caregivers, caused by social neglect or deprivation of basic emotional needs, repeated changes of primary caregivers, and/or rearing in settings that limit opportunities to form selective attachments, such as institutions with very high child-to-caregiver ratios. Age of onset is no earlier than 9 months, and symptoms must be evident by 5 years of age.

DISINHIBITED SOCIAL ENGAGEMENT DISORDER

Disinhibited social engagement disorder essentially refers to the absence of typical reticence when interacting with strangers, generally in the context of a history of grossly pathogenic care and/or not having formed a selective attachment to a particular caregiver. In order to meet *DSM-5* diagnostic criteria, the child has to have experienced extremely insufficient care, which may include persistent lack of having basic emotional needs met, repeated changes of primary caregivers, and being raised in situations that severely limit opportunities to form selective attachments. The overly familiar behaviors are generally considered inappropriate, given the individual's sociocultural context. The diagnosis can be made in a child who is at least 9 months old. The behaviors manifest in minimal hesitation in approaching unfamiliar adults; verbal and physical behavior that is overly familiar; minimal checking in with a caregiver when parting from him or her to engage in another activity, even in an unfamiliar environment; and little or no reluctance in following and being under the care of an unfamiliar adult. *DSM-5* diagnostic criteria state explicitly that the behaviors cannot be due exclusively to impulsivity. Prevalence estimates of disinhibited social engagement disorder in the general population are presently unknown. However, in high-risk populations, the disorder is estimated to occur in up to 20% of the population.

CHAPTER 7 OUTLINE

COMPONENTS OF THE MIND-SETS OF EFFECTIVE EDUCATORS

Attribution Theory
Students' Basic Needs
Islands of Competence

STRATEGIES FOR FOSTERING SELF-ESTEEM, MOTIVATION, HOPE, AND RESILIENCE

The Orientation Period
Accepting Students for Who They Are
Helping Students Develop a Sense of Responsibility
Increasing Students' Sense of Ownership
Helping Students Establish Self-Discipline
Promoting Self-Advocacy Skills
Providing Positive Feedback and Encouragement
Teaching Students to Cope with Mistakes and Failure

CONCLUSION

CHAPTER 7

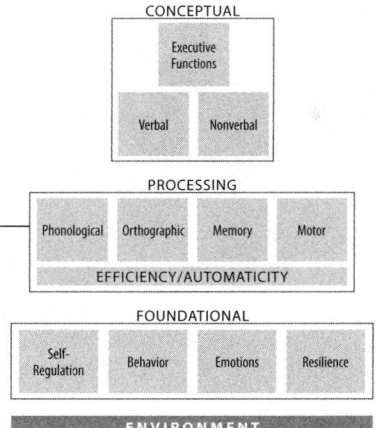

Strategies to Promote Resilience

with Robert Brooks

Jeremy often had difficulty sitting still and completing his schoolwork, but it was his tendency to speak without thinking that caused frequent and sometimes amusing problems in Mr. Chavez's fifth-grade class. Jeremy and six of his classmates were supposed to be working independently on a series of math sheets. Mr. Chavez was supervising their work and providing assistance as needed. However, Jeremy was experiencing great difficulty keeping his mind focused on his work instead of talking to his neighbors. After multiple reminders to stay focused and quiet, out of exasperation, Mr. Chavez asked Jeremy to come to the front of the room. He then explained to the other students that it was clear that Jeremy knew exactly how to complete his math assignment because he was choosing to talk rather than do his work. Then he asked Jeremy to teach the remainder of the class. Jeremy at first looked perplexed and then anxious as he realized that Mr. Chavez was serious.

Mr. Chavez encouraged Jeremy to teach the class. First, Jeremy said he could not do it. Mr. Chavez at this point informed Jeremy that he must. Out of frustration, Mr. Chavez had placed Jeremy in an untenable position. His unspoken intent was to embarrass Jeremy, hoping that he would then focus on his work for the remainder of the class.

Jeremy stood frozen for a few seconds. The other students in the class were clearly anxious yet relieved that they were not in the hot seat. Then Jeremy's eyes lit up. He looked around the room. A smile came to his face. Before Mr. Chavez could say anything, Jeremy announced, "Recess!" Everyone laughed, even Mr. Chavez. Although many children in this situation might have broken down and cried or stood frozen with anxiety, Jeremy demonstrated a certain resiliency, a quality that allowed him to work through a stressful situation.

Mr. Chavez's beliefs about why Jeremy acted the way he did influenced the strategy he used in an attempt to lessen Jeremy's seemingly disruptive behavior. He basically viewed this behavior as something Jeremy could control if he wanted to do so, prompting him to initiate a consequence tinged with the possibility of humiliation. In daily life, people possess certain assumptions about themselves, their children, and other people that influence their actions and interpersonal relationships. Often, they are unaware of these assumptions, although the assumptions constantly operate, directing people's behavior. These assumptions may be seen as part of their mind-set, affecting the ways in which they perceive and respond to people and events.

This chapter examines the components of the mind-set of effective educators. These educators touch the hearts and minds of students; they appreciate the forces that truly motivate students; and they recognize that what they do each day in class contributes to students' self-esteem, resilience, sense of competence, and optimism. The more teachers can articulate these components and make them conscious guides, the more effectively they can develop and implement strategies that foster learning.

COMPONENTS OF THE MIND-SETS OF EFFECTIVE EDUCATORS

Effective educators focus equally on academic subjects and on the self-esteem, dignity, and social-emotional lives of students. A high school science teacher raised the following question at a workshop:

> I am a science teacher. I know how to convey science facts to my students. Why should I spend time thinking about the emotional and social lives of students or about their self-esteem? With all the material I have to cover, I don't have time to focus on other issues. If anything, this would just distract me from teaching science.

Although most educators would take issue with the views expressed by this teacher, a number may concur, especially in today's educational climate of high-stakes testing and meeting the Common Core State Standards.

Nurturing a student's emotional and social well-being is not mutually exclusive from teaching academic skills and content. Strengthening a student's self-worth is an essential part of all education. If anything, a student's feelings of belonging, security, and self-esteem in the classroom serve as the foundation for increased learning, motivation, self-discipline, responsibility, and the capacity to deal more comfortably with mistakes (Brooks, Brooks, & Goldstein, 2012; Cohen, 2006). What may have contributed to this dichotomy are different perceptions of what is meant by self-esteem. Although some educators view a student's self-esteem as an integral part of the learning process, others argue that those who focus on fostering self-esteem are doing so at the expense of teaching students self-discipline, accountability, and responsibility; the latter group perceives self-esteem strategies as giving in to students and not holding them accountable for their actions (Brooks, 1999a).

One basis for the existence of the varying perspectives about the concept of self-esteem may reside in the confusion between what Lerner referred to as "feel-good-now self-esteem" and "earned self-esteem":

> Earned self-esteem is based on success in meeting the tests of reality—measuring up to standards at home and at school. It is necessarily hard-won and develops slowly, but it is stable and long lasting, and provides a secure foundation for further growth and development. (1996, p. 12)

In striking contrast, feel-good-now self-esteem is an approach to self-esteem that does not challenge children, set realistic expectations and goals, or teach them how to deal with frustration and mistakes.

The concept of self-esteem used in this chapter may be understood as including the feelings and thoughts that students have about their competence and worth and about their abilities to make a difference, to have control over their lives, to develop self-discipline, to confront rather than retreat from challenges, to learn from both

Strategies to Promote Resilience

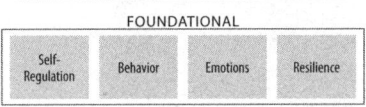

success and failure, and to treat themselves and others with dignity and respect. Self-esteem guides and motivates one's actions, and, in turn, the outcome of these actions influences one's self-esteem so that a dynamic, reciprocal process is constantly in force (Brooks, 1999b).

The time has come to expend less energy debating whether educators should also focus on strengthening the self-esteem and social-emotional needs of students and spend more energy attempting to answer how to best address these needs in the classroom (Goldstein & Brooks, 2007). Effective educators recognize that students learn more comfortably in an atmosphere in which they feel safe and secure, in which they are not haunted by fears of being ridiculed or humiliated, in which they feel challenged to develop and meet realistic goals, in which they sense that teachers genuinely care about them and respect their individuality, and in which learning is experienced as exciting. It is within such an atmosphere that self-esteem, motivation, hope, and resilience are nurtured.

The journal entry in Figure 7.1 was written by an 18-year-old student. This entry depicts how much pain and sadness can be experienced by students who

> Today I was so emarsit in englsh that I never want to go to englsh class agin. When you said you were going to pass out the paper back out I know it was going to be bad. I cant furguit out but the louds kid in the class allways get my paper! She make fun of my spelling and calls my name out in front of the hole class. Then she keeps pointing out my miss spelled words and all the kid around her laugf and look at me. This is not frist time I have ben im basrst in class. I hate pop corn reading. and I just sit there and freek out and cant lisin to the story, and then a kid calls on me and I have to say pass or just trarn Red in my faces. I hate english and hate thinking about it. These jonals dont halpe me and I hate doing them! Im not go to be a writer as me job so there no point in it. Spelling and Read are my disabiltes and I get No help to get eney beter in it. The school doesnt help me and that why I hate school and all the kid who laugh at me!
> School Just Herts Me.

Figure 7.1. "School just hurts me."

struggle to learn to read and spell. Not only does he feel that he does not receive any help for his problems; he also feels ridiculed by his peers because of his disabilities. All educators would agree that school experiences should not hurt children, but for children who struggle, negative school experiences can harm self-esteem. In discussing the inclusion of students with learning disabilities (LD) in general education classrooms, Herr and Bateman stated,

> We firmly believe that it does students with LD little good to be included and socialized in general education classrooms for 12 years if the result is that these students leave high-school reading at a second- or third-grade level and with serious self-esteem issues. (2013, p. 66)

Effective educators recognize that a teacher has a lifelong impact on a student's capacity to be resilient (Brooks, 2004). Since the early 1980s, increased efforts have been directed to understanding not only the risk factors that contribute to the emergence and maintenance of learning, emotional, and behavior disorders but also the protective factors that serve to buttress the resources of children to help them become more resilient (Brooks, 1999b; Katz, 1997; Rutter, 1987; Werner & Smith, 1992). Different variables have been delineated that contribute to resilience, including a child's inborn temperament; self-confidence; problem-solving and coping skills; self-esteem; character; and close connections to family, friends, and the community (Ginsburg, 2011).

In terms of support from outside the family, schools have been spotlighted as environments that can provide children with experiences that enhance their self-esteem and competence, thereby reinforcing resilience (Ginsburg, 2011; Goldstein & Brooks, 2007; Thomsen, 2002). For example, Ginsburg noted,

> Children who are well connected to their schools are more likely to thrive educationally, emotionally, and socially. If they view school as a safe, protected place and understand that the adults at school care about their well-being, children are more likely to soak up knowledge and absorb the invaluable life lesson that learning is pleasurable and rewarding. (2011, pp. 152–153)

The late psychologist Julius Segal wrote about resilient children:

> From studies conducted around the world, researchers have distilled a number of factors that enable such children of misfortune to beat the heavy odds against them. One factor turns out to be the presence in their lives of a charismatic adult—a person with whom they can identify and from whom they gather strength. And in a surprising number of cases, that person turns out to be a teacher. (1988, p. 2)

Effective educators understand the mind-set of resilient students. They possess a sense of how resilient students perceive themselves and their world, especially in comparison with students who are not resilient. Obviously, if educators are to nurture resilience in students, they must understand the characteristics of the mind-set of resilient children so that these characteristics can be reinforced in the classroom. In addition to having high self-esteem, resilient children possess good self-discipline (Goldstein & Brooks, 2007). They are hopeful and optimistic, feel appreciated, and have learned to establish realistic goals and expectations for themselves. They have developed the capacity to solve problems and make decisions and thus are more likely to perceive mistakes and obstacles as challenges to confront rather than as stressors to avoid. They rely on coping strategies that are growth fostering rather than self-defeating. They do not deny their vulnerabilities but are cognizant of their talents. Their self-concept is filled with images of strength and competence. They have developed effective interpersonal skills with peers and adults alike and are able to seek out assistance in a comfortable, appropriate manner from adults who can provide the support they require (Brooks & Goldstein, 2001).

Strategies to Promote Resilience

Effective educators are not misled by the overt negative behaviors of their students. They are aware that the wide varieties of problematic behaviors displayed by students are signals of low self-esteem and feelings of vulnerability. The indications of low self-esteem may vary considerably from one student to the next. In general, children experience low self-esteem in situations in which they do not feel successful but not in those situations in which they feel more competent. For instance, a child with a specific learning disability may feel inadequate in the classroom but may engage in certain sports with self-confidence. Unfortunately, some children have such low self-esteem that they feel confident in few, if any, areas.

Some children openly convey feelings of despair, a lack of confidence, and a loss of hope with such statements as "I'm stupid," "I always do things wrong," or "I was born with half a brain." Other students do not express their low self-esteem directly. Instead, it can be inferred from the coping strategies they use to manage stress, frustration, and failure. Students with high self-esteem display strategies for coping that are adaptive and that nurture growth. A child struggling with math will ask for additional help and then spend more time practicing the new information.

Although Maria struggled with self-esteem because of her difficulties with reading and writing, she felt comfortable approaching her teachers when she had trouble understanding or completing an assignment. She knew that they would provide additional help and explanation. She also found that asking for clarifications on tests reduced the likelihood that she would make unintended errors. Maria knew that it took her longer to complete tasks than other students, so she always planned enough time for studying.

In marked contrast to Maria, students with low self-esteem, such as Samuel, frequently rely on counterproductive coping behaviors that actually intensify their difficulties.

Although sixth-grader Samuel swaggered around the classroom and on the playground as if he possessed good self-esteem, his self-esteem appeared to be based on taking pride in doing exactly the opposite of what his teachers, classmates, and even parents wanted him to do. Samuel's struggles in life had led him to develop a set of coping strategies that created the very antithesis of the kind of self-esteem discussed in this chapter. Samuel's strong negative feelings about himself were deeply cloaked in a pattern of disrespectful, aggressive, and defiant behavior. Ms. Handler, Samuel's teacher, felt challenged to identify strategies and activities that might help him develop a resilient mind-set. With Samuel in mind, Ms. Handler completed the items from the Resilience section of the Building Blocks Questionnaire. Her responses appear in Figure 7.2.

The behaviors that follow are frequently used by children like Samuel with low self-esteem to cope with the reality or the perceived possibility of failure. Although all children display some of these self-defeating behaviors at times, low self-esteem is strongly suggested when these behaviors appear with regularity. Self-defeating behaviors include the following:

- *Quitting and avoiding:* Some students may stop trying, often offering excuses such as the work was irrelevant or stupid, when they become frustrated because they cannot succeed at a task or assignment. Students would rather avoid a task or refuse to try rather than have anyone believe they are incapable or stupid; these children seem to prefer to have the adults around them focus on their unwillingness to comply.

Foundational Blocks

Resilience	Rarely	Sometimes	Frequently
Seems disinterested in academic tasks	☐	☐	☑
Complains about not being smart	☐	☐	☑
Complains that academic tasks are too difficult	☐	☐	☑
Has limited interactions with classmates	☑	☐	☐
Complains about not being liked	☐	☑	☐
Makes negative comments about self	☐	☐	☑
Gives up easily on tasks and assignments	☐	☐	☑
Seems overly sensitive to criticism	☐	☐	☑
Has trouble with stressful situations	☐	☐	☑
Seems to lack self-confidence	☐	☐	☑

Figure 7.2. Building Blocks Questionnaire as completed by Samuel's teacher, Ms. Handler.

- *Cheating:* Students who believe that they cannot master a learning task or do well on a test are vulnerable to copying answers from others, plagiarizing materials from books or the Internet, or handing in someone else's paper.
- *Rationalizing:* Students who do not believe they are capable of succeeding frequently offer excuses for failure rather than accepting responsibility for their actions.
- *Clowning and regressing:* Some students who lack confidence consistently act silly, clown around, or behave younger than they are. They resort to these ways of coping to minimize the significance of failing in certain situations, but this strategy often backfires, leading to ridicule from peers or disciplinary actions from their teachers.
- *Controlling:* Many children with low self-esteem believe they possess little control over what transpires in their lives, which contributes to a sense of helplessness. In what appears to be paradoxical, they may attempt to avoid these uncomfortable feelings by pushing around others.
- *Aggressiveness and bullying:* Teasing and put-downs are common counterproductive ways of managing frustration and low self-esteem.
- *Using passive-aggressive behavior:* Some students with low self-esteem attempt to exert control by promising to meet particular responsibilities and then not meeting them. Such children are likely to be labeled oppositional.
- *Denying:* Children with low self-esteem commonly use denial as a strategy for dealing with the pain that might result if they were to acknowledge their limitations and vulnerabilities.
- *Complaining of boredom:* When frustrated, students may complain that the work they are being asked to complete is boring, uninteresting, or irrelevant. They may yawn, look tired, or put their head down on the desk to demonstrate to the teacher how uninvolved they are, when, in reality, they actually feel that the task is beyond their ability to complete.
- *Rushing:* Students with low self-esteem may rush through work as a means of contending with their difficulties. For these children, rapid completion is a higher priority than accuracy.

Strategies to Promote Resilience

The common thread that runs through all of these is self-defeating coping strategies. Their use reflects the child's vulnerable feelings, wishes to avoid feeling humiliated, and, in many respects, desperate attempts to maintain a sense of self-esteem and dignity. The reliance on these kinds of coping strategies exacerbates an already troubled situation. Effective educators recognize the roots of these counterproductive behaviors and ask, "What can I do to lessen this student's anxiety and vulnerability and increase his or her self-esteem and confidence?" This question prompts educators to look for frameworks for understanding the components of self-esteem and the strategies that follow from these frameworks. Two frameworks have been proven to be particularly helpful to educators in guiding their interactions with students.

Attribution Theory

One influential framework for examining the dimensions of self-esteem and optimism is attribution theory, which was initially proposed by Weiner (1974) and applied by many clinicians and researchers (e.g., Brooks, 1991; Brooks & Goldstein, 2001; Eccles & Wigfield, 2002). The appeal of this theory is that its basic premises are applicable to real-life situations, providing guideposts for interventions that foster self-esteem, motivation, and resilience. Children encounter many pressures and challenges as they develop, some of which lead to success, others that lead to failure. Attribution theory examines the explanations that people offer for why they think they succeeded or failed at a task or situation—explanations that are directly linked to self-esteem and a sense of hope.

Children with high self-esteem typically perceive their successes as based in a large part on their own efforts, resources, and abilities. These children assume realistic ownership for their accomplishments and feel a sense of personal control over what transpires in their lives. Although they will acknowledge the importance of supportive adults in their lives who helped them to learn and succeed, they recognize that without their own effort and persistence, such success would not have occurred.

Although Mark had little home support, he recognized that his efforts could influence results. On his social studies test, he wrote "I don't know" for most of the questions. He was asked to choose three explorers from a list and then describe one important thing that each did. His answers and his note to Mrs. Perry are presented in Figure 7.3. Mark freely admitted that he did not study. Even though he took responsibility for his behavior, Mark now needs to learn how to be better prepared for tests.

In contrast, children with low self-esteem lacking in qualities of resilience often believe that their successes are a result of factors outside their control, such as luck or chance. Such children are quick to minimize or dismiss a high test grade with comments such as "The teacher made the test easy" or "I was lucky." Not surprisingly, this type of self-perception lessens confidence about future successes.

In terms of mistakes and failures, children with high self-esteem are prone to believe that mistakes are experiences to learn from rather than to feel defeated by. Mistakes result from factors that can be changed, such as a lack of adequate effort when engaged in reaching a realistically attainable goal or the use of ineffective strategies when studying for a test. Children with low self-esteem, when faced with mistakes and failure, are susceptible to believing that they cannot correct the situation. They view mistakes as resulting from factors that cannot be modified, such as

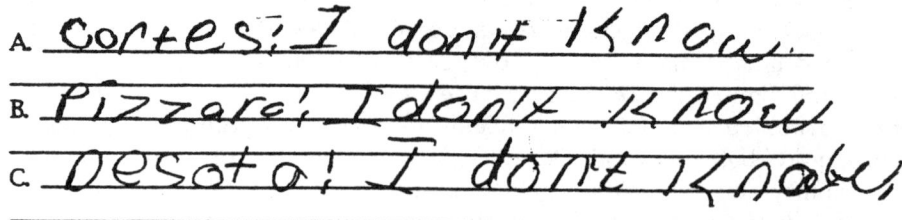

Figure 7.3. Mark's social studies test.

a lack of ability or intelligence. This belief elicits a feeling of helplessness and hopelessness. Intensifying this negative scenario is that future success becomes less probable because these children expect to fail, and, in response, they retreat from age-expected demands and resort to self-defeating coping strategies that worsen their situation. The mind-set of effective educators recognizes that the tenets of attribution theory contain significant implications for teaching and responding to students in ways that foster their self-esteem, resilience, and motivation. It provides a blueprint for asking the following questions:

> How do we create a school environment to reinforce the probability that students not only succeed but also experience their achievements as based in large part on their own abilities and efforts and not on luck or fate? Stated somewhat differently, how do we empower and reinforce a sense of personal control in children and adolescents so that they assume an increasing feeling of ownership and responsibility for their own lives? (Brooks, 1999b)

The importance of personal control and empowerment as the basic scaffolding of self-esteem, motivation, and resilience has been highlighted by a number of clinicians and researchers (e.g., Brooks & Goldstein, 2001; Glasser, 1997; Miller & Daniel, 2007).

How do we create an environment that reinforces the belief in students that mistakes and failure can serve as the basis for learning and are not only accepted but also expected? How do we instill in all students the conviction that their failures need not represent an albatross around their necks but rather that they can learn and succeed? How do we create safe and comfortable classroom environments that lessen or even eradicate fears of being humiliated and embarrassed for making a mistake or not understanding something the first time?

Students' Basic Needs

A second framework for examining self-esteem as well as motivation is based on the work of psychologist Edward Deci and his colleagues, who have examined self-esteem and motivation by examining students' basic needs (Deci & Flaste, 1995). His model, which has many similarities to Glasser's (1997) choice theory (formerly called control theory) and Brendtro, Brokenleg, and Van Bockern's (1990) circle of caring philosophy, suggests that students are more willing to confront and persevere

Strategies to Promote Resilience

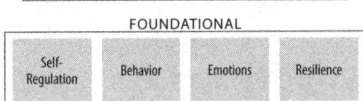

at learning tasks when educators have created a school environment in which their basic needs are satisfied. Deci and Flaste (1995) highlighted that effective educators recognize three factors that foster self-esteem and resilience in children and adolescents: to feel connected, autonomous, and competent.

Feeling Connected

Students are more likely to thrive in school when they feel they belong and feel welcome in the school setting. When we asked students of all ages what a teacher could do each day to help them feel welcome in school, the two most frequent responses were 1) greet students warmly and use their name and 2) smile at the student. Obviously, small gestures can go a long way toward helping students to feel they belong.

Feeling Autonomous

At the core of many theories of self-esteem, motivation, and resilience, including attribution theory, is the concept of ownership and self-determination. Motivation and resilience are increased when students feel their voice and opinions are being heard and respected and when they believe they have some control over what occurs in their lives. If children and adolescents feel that they are constantly being told what to do and that their lives are being dictated by others, they are less likely to be enthusiastic about involving themselves in tasks that they feel are being imposed on them. If anything, their primary motivation may be to avoid or oppose what others wish them to do, and a power struggle is likely to ensue. The mind-set of effective educators appreciates that if students are to feel a sense of self-determination and ownership, they must be taught how to 1) set realistic short- and long-term goals, 2) solve problems, 3) make wise choices and decisions to achieve their goals (this can involve academic content as well as social or interpersonal issues in a classroom such as bullying), and 4) establish new goals when indicated.

Feeling Competent

All children wish to feel successful and want to have areas in their lives in which they feel competent and accomplished—areas that elicit satisfaction and pride. As apparent in the journal entry in Figure 7.1, some students view school as the place in which their impairments rather than their strengths are highlighted. These feelings of incompetence may prompt students to retreat from challenges and engage in self-defeating coping strategies that serve to intensify an already problematic situation. In recognizing their students' need to feel competent, effective teachers understand the importance of positive feedback and encouragement. In addition, they are aware that a focus on encouragement is not the same as giving false praise or inflated grades; students are very perceptive in knowing when they are receiving undeserved positive evaluations. Positive feedback must always be predicated on actual accomplishment and success.

Islands of Competence

Many individualized educational plans focus only on a student's weaknesses with strategies for fixing or addressing these weaknesses. Even when strengths are listed, little attention is directed to the ways in which these strengths might be used or nourished in the student's educational program. Effective educators appreciate the importance of identifying, reinforcing, and displaying each student's unique talents or islands of competence. All students have particular strengths, although not necessarily in the academic arena. Many students are confident while playing football or baseball but are uneasy while taking a test in school or conversing with peers. Other students are self-assured in the classroom but very self-conscious while engaged in sports. Still others approach the task of fixing a car, playing the piano, or painting a picture with great confidence but are terrified by the thought of writing an essay. For example, Ben loved to play tennis; Andy loved to draw; and Maria spent each afternoon at the stables riding her horse. The effective educator discovers the strengths of each student in the classroom.

Unfortunately, some students experience self-doubt and failure in many situations. If they judge these situations to be important to significant others in their life, their overall sense of competence suffers markedly. Given their low self-esteem, many children who are at risk seem to perceive that they are swimming or drowning in an ocean of inadequacy. To counteract this image of despair, effective teachers realize that every student possesses islands of competence, areas that are (or have the potential to be) sources of pride and accomplishment. If educators want to be charismatic adults in the lives of these students, they must assume the responsibility for identifying and reinforcing these islands of competence; in so doing, they may create a ripple effect that provides children with the courage, strength, and motivation to venture forth and confront difficult tasks.

Researchers and clinicians have emphasized the importance of calling on selected islands of competence in building self-confidence. For instance, Rutter, when discussing resilient children, observed, "Experience of success in one arena of life led to enhanced self-esteem and a feeling of self-efficacy, enabling them to cope more successfully with subsequent life challenges and adaptations" (1985, p. 604). Katz observed, "Being able to showcase our talents, and to have them valued by important people in our lives, helps us define our identities around that which we do best" (1994, p. 10). Werner, describing a group of children who were at risk, wrote, "Most of the resilient children in our high-risk group were not unusually talented, but they took great pleasure in hobbies that brought them solace when things fell apart in their homes" (1993, p. 511).

STRATEGIES FOR FOSTERING SELF-ESTEEM, MOTIVATION, HOPE, AND RESILIENCE

Effective educators develop and implement strategies for reinforcing self-esteem, motivation, hope, and resilience in students. Effective teachers recognize that a number of interventions can be used to create a positive school climate in which students' social and emotional growth is enhanced and in which students are genuinely excited and motivated about learning. If these strategies are to be effective, teachers must maintain a positive mind-set—one that avoids blaming students, that focuses on and reinforces the unique gifts of each student, and that recognizes that student success has as much to do with the classroom environment as it has to do with the attitudes that students initially bring into this setting.

The Orientation Period

At the beginning of the school year, an orienting period may be used to enhance this mind-set, although it may also be implemented later in the year as well. Ideally, the orientation period is divided into two parts. The first part takes place a day or so before students arrive for the new school year. During this period, teachers

Strategies to Promote Resilience

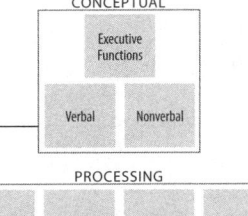
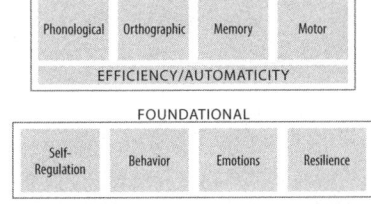

and school administrators as a staff reflect on and discuss why they became educators, what they perceive as their essential roles, what factors they believe are most important in creating a positive school climate, how they would describe a favorite and not-so-favorite teacher when they were students, and how they would like their students to describe them. They also consider the kinds of support they require from each other during the year to minimize cynicism and burnout.

These exercises promote staff cohesion and support and help teachers to keep in the forefront the belief that they have a lifelong effect on students. When educators are asked to recall one of their most positive and one of their most negative memories of school involving a teacher, they can be encouraged to think about how they can use their own memories of school to guide what they do with their students today. These exercises remind teachers of their powerful influence not only on the academic life of students but on their social and emotional life as well.

The second part of the orientation period occurs during the first 2 or 3 days of school, with the main focus on helping each student feel safe and secure in the school environment. During this time, teachers should not feel compelled to take out books or review academic content but instead concentrate on creating a classroom climate in which meeting the needs of students is directly assessed (Deci & Flaste, 1995). If a teacher attempts to engage children in academic tasks too quickly, it is often at the expense of getting to know students, lessening their anxiety (especially students with special needs), or helping them to feel a sense of belonging in the classroom and ownership for their education.

Although some might argue that this orientation period is a waste of a few days of classroom teaching, using the first few days to meet the needs of students can result in students becoming more motivated to learn, involved in their own education, involved as class members, capable of dealing with frustration and mistakes, self-disciplined, and respectful. This process can best be described by reviewing several selected strategies for fostering self-esteem, motivation, hope, and resilience.

Accepting Students for Who They Are

Extensive research documents the significant differences in children from birth, such as in their temperaments, learning styles, and development of language and motor abilities (Keogh, 2003; Levine, 2002). Unfortunately, people often give lip service to these differences and fail to truly accept children for who they are. Teachers may respond to students as if they were a homogeneous group and fail to establish realistic expectations, goals, and appropriate accommodations on the basis of the unique qualities of each child. One result of this mismatch between expectations and reality is that students begin to feel that they are not welcome or accepted and, in many instances, believe that they are disappointing the adults in their lives.

Some teachers still question the fairness of making accommodations for children, arguing that other students would be offended and upset by a situation that they perceive to be unfair. Although one can understand this concern, if children are different from birth, the least fair thing we can do is treat all children the same at school or at home. Someone once said, "There is nothing as unequal as the equal treatment of unequals." Fairness should always be predicated on knowledge of the unique makeup of each child; if it is not, many children with disabilities or difficulties in the classroom will feel that they are always being criticized for things they are not capable of doing. In fifth grade Katy could remember how to spell the words assigned for the spelling test, but she had trouble composing sentences. Maria wrote detailed sentences but had trouble spelling the words. Andy's writing was barely legible.

One of the most effective ways to address the issue of fairness is to discuss it openly with students so that the other children do not resent those who are receiving modifications. This can be done during the second part of the orientation period. For example, to lessen the possibility of students perceiving a teacher as being unfair because of different expectations for different students, a teacher could discuss with students on the first day of school how each one of them is different and unique, how some students can run more quickly than others, how some can read more rapidly, and how some can solve math problems more efficiently. The teacher can then say that in light of these differences, there will be different expectations for the amount and kind of work that is done by each student. The teacher should then add, "One of my concerns is that because of different expectations, some of you may begin to feel that I am not being fair. If any of you begin to feel that way, please let me know so we can discuss it. This is very important because if students believe that things are not fair in a classroom, it can interfere with learning."

Feedback indicates that when a teacher introduces the issue of fairness before it becomes a problem, it basically remains a nonissue and permits a teacher to accommodate each student's unique needs without triggering negative feelings in other students. In addition, it educates students about individual differences, resulting in an atmosphere of greater tolerance and acceptance. Teachers should also share this message about fairness with parents so that they are kept informed of how and why accommodations are implemented in the classroom. Family meetings at home can be used in a similar way to discuss realistic expectations for each of the children so as to lessen sibling rivalry or jealousy.

Many accommodations do not require major modifications in a student's program, nor do they demand vastly different educational plans for each student. There is a great deal of overlap in the educational needs of children. All parties—students, parents, teachers, therapists—need to appreciate a child's strengths and weaknesses, develop and share common expectations and goals, and implement realistic strategies to reach these goals.

Teachers must help students understand their strengths, their vulnerabilities, and the accommodations that will assist them to learn and achieve. This task is often more difficult for children who have the so-called hidden disabilities such as SLD or ADHD. When done successfully, these children feel increasingly welcome in the environment, an important factor in improving self-esteem and resilience. Examples of frequently used accommodations follow.

Many children with learning or attention problems expend a great deal of energy attempting to focus and learn in school. Then they are required to complete homework, which, given their learning problems, may take two or three times as long as their peers. Often they are unable to complete entire assignments. Not surprisingly, by bedtime, they are frustrated and exhausted, as are their parents. Andy remarked one night while doing math homework, "What are they trying to do? Turn me into a zombie?" Clearly, the homework involved too many problems. Katy said one evening to her mother, "I feel like they make me climb a big mountain all day long and then do it over again at night." Just as during the school day, homework assignments were often too difficult for Katy to complete without assistance.

Rather than continuing to engage in practices that make the learning process aversive, a more reasonable approach is to set a time limit for doing homework, regardless of how much work the child has actually accomplished. For example, if most students can complete their math homework in an hour, that should be the

Strategies to Promote Resilience

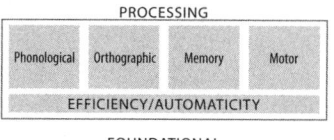
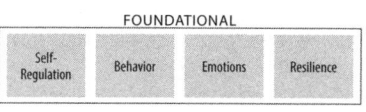

limit for all children, even if they complete only half of the math problems. Parents can verify that their child indeed spent a certain amount of time on homework.

Some may contend that these adjustments are unfair and represent a watering down of expectations for certain students. Continuing to provide students with the necessary assistance enables them to accomplish more and be more successful. To ask students who struggle to spend several more hours each evening on schoolwork than others typically proves counterproductive and may turn them off to school.

In addition to taking longer to finish homework, a number of students take longer than their peers to finish tests. The logical strategy is to permit them to take untimed tests, which is becoming an increasingly common practice. This strategy worked exceptionally well for Ben in his eighth-grade English class.

Ms. Roberts took Ben aside and empathized with how hard he worked but how difficult it was for him to quickly put his ideas on paper. She offered Ben the opportunity to return at the end of the school day and use additional time to complete his English test. Ben earned a B+ on this test, an appreciable jump from previous C and D grades he had received. Without the pressure of time, Ben was relaxed and could think more clearly. Ben asked Ms. Roberts, "Who was the person who developed timed tests and why did that person develop them?" This is an interesting question to ponder because in the larger world, although everyone confronts deadlines, adults typically possess more flexibility in getting work done than is afforded to students on tests in school.

Some students have difficulty copying homework assignments from the blackboard. Providing these students with a monthly syllabus of assignments can help to offset the possibility of assignments being copied incorrectly. College professors typically distribute a syllabus of homework and readings for the entire semester during the first class—might not the same practice be effective for students in elementary, middle, or high schools? Another possible accommodation is to assign a buddy to a student to ensure that homework assignments and due dates are accurate. Katy called her study buddy several times a week to clarify homework assignments.

Some students require more physical activity than other students or they become restless and unfocused, perhaps getting into trouble. These children can be provided with regular opportunities to bring messages to the office or to move around the classroom more frequently. Someone once said that an effective strategy for a student like Jeremy is to assign him two seats. That way when he is up and moving around, he is on his way to his other chair.

Although accommodations such as these communicate a sense of acceptance to children with exceptional needs, other ways exist for helping these children feel they belong and are welcome, especially in the school environment. A positive telephone call home or a note from a teacher can serve as a powerful sign of acceptance. The good news postcard (Figure 7.4) that Ben's parents received made Ben's progress and efforts feel valued.

Helping Students Develop a Sense of Responsibility

If children are to develop a sense of ownership and pride, they need ample opportunities for assuming responsibility, especially opportunities that help them feel they are making a contribution to their home, school, and community. For example, children feel a more positive attachment to school and are more motivated to learn if they are encouraged to contribute to the school milieu, an especially important tactic for students who feel alienated. The experience of making a positive difference in the lives of others builds self-respect, self-control, hopefulness, and resilience and

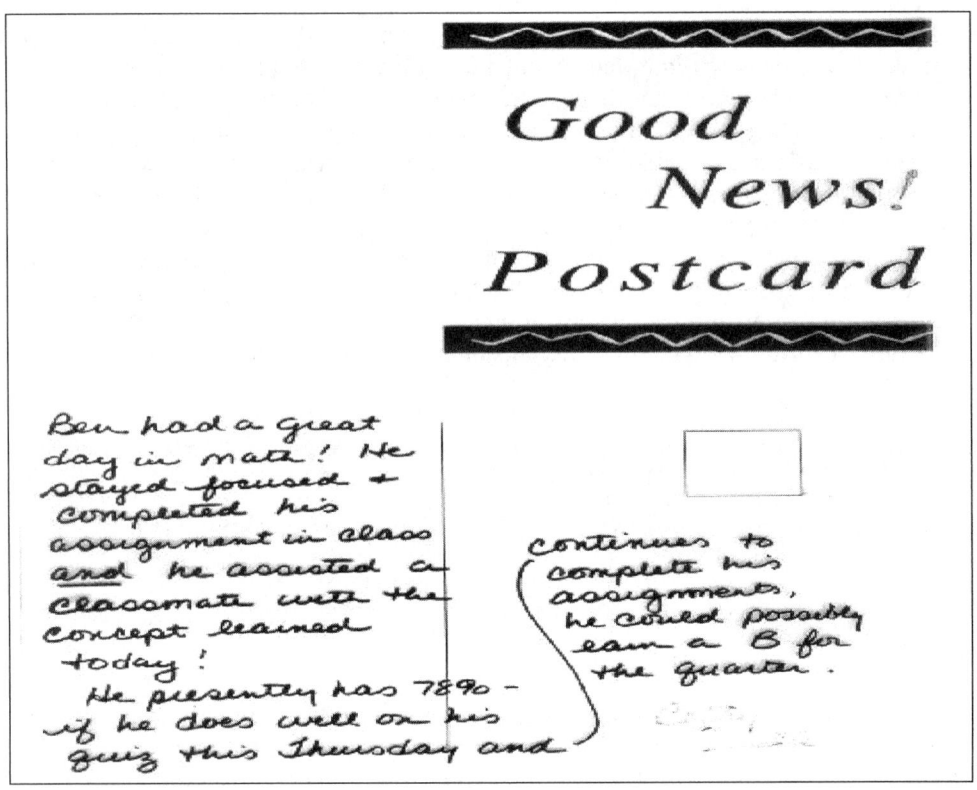

Figure 7.4. Ben's good news postcard.

serves as a powerful antidote to feelings of defeatism and despair (Brooks & Goldstein, 2001). Several examples of this strategy follow.

Stephanie, a fourth grader, was socially isolated, and her struggle with memorization in the classroom began to take its toll on her self-esteem and resilience. Stephanie began waking up each morning with a stomachache and resisted attending school. Stephanie's parents and teacher understood the stress she was experiencing socially and academically. They decided to turn to one of Stephanie's strengths as a means of helping her gain a sense of competence at school. Stephanie spent many hours training and taking care of her dog. Stephanie's teacher recruited her as the pet monitor of the class, a position that involved taking care of the classroom fish and gerbils. On a visit to the classroom, the principal commented that the pets in this classroom seemed to be very well taken care of. He asked Stephanie if she would be willing to train other pet monitors in other classrooms. Eventually, with the help of her teacher, Stephanie wrote a brief manual about pet care that the principal placed in the school library. Although Stephanie continued to struggle socially and academically, she was no longer sick before going to school and seemed to gather strength from her job, enabling her to persevere academically and become more accepted in the classroom.

Ms. McGrew was increasingly worried about Katy, one of her fifth-grade students. Katy was struggling to learn new concepts in the classroom. Ms. McGrew watched as Katy's academic confidence and self-esteem declined as the school year progressed. She decided to offer Katy the opportunity to teach others, recognizing that this activity often serves to boost self-confidence. Katy was asked to tutor first-grade students who were struggling with learning how to read. Learning to read had been relatively easy for Katy. The tutoring activity was so helpful that Ms. McGrew established a partnership between her class and a first-grade class so that all students could benefit from this strategy. A noticeable feeling of community began to develop. Katy approached her schoolwork diligently and with renewed effort for the remainder of the school year.

Strategies to Promote Resilience

By the time Jeremy was in high school, the teachers referred to him as a "roamer." They used this term because instead of coming to his homeroom, he usually roamed the halls. In a consultation meeting with the teachers, the school psychologist asked what interventions had been attempted. The teachers listed a number of them, including a behavior contract system. They noted that none of these interventions seemed to help. Half kidding, the school psychologist asked if perhaps Jeremy had a need to roam. At first, the teachers looked bewildered, but then they agreed and said that given his hyperactivity, perhaps he did need physical activity at the beginning of the day to become settled. They came up with the idea of implementing a physical activity that would also make him feel he was helping out. Jeremy was offered the job of attendance monitor of the school, which required him to walk through the halls during homeroom period to check that a teacher was present in each classroom and then to report back to the principal's office. With this new responsibility, his behavior and the teachers' attitudes toward him improved significantly.

These kinds of contributory activities provide concrete evidence to students that they can be successful, that they are capable, and that they can earn respect—feelings that nurture their self-esteem and resilience. When describing the value of students helping others, Werner wrote,

> Self-esteem and self-efficacy also grew when children took on a responsible position commensurate with their ability, whether it was part-time paid work, managing the household when a parent was incapacitated, or, most often, caring for younger siblings. At some point in their young lives, usually in middle childhood and adolescence, the children who grew into resilient adults were required to carry out some socially desirable task to prevent others in their family, neighborhood, or community from experiencing distress or discomfort. (1993, p. 511)

Increasing Students' Sense of Ownership

An essential ingredient of high self-esteem and resilience is the belief that one has some control over what is occurring in one's life. To reinforce this belief in students, teachers must provide them with opportunities to learn the skills necessary for making sound decisions and solving problems and to apply and refine these skills (Brooks et al., 2012). Several examples of teaching decision making and problem solving in school follow.

Mr. Chavez recruited a group of students with special needs to conduct research about existing charities. On the basis of their research, they decided which charity to support and then decided upon the most effective ways of raising money. These activities enhanced their self-esteem and reinforced the academic skills involved in the project.

Teachers can provide their students with a choice of which homework problems to do. For instance, if there are eight problems on a page, students can be permitted to choose for themselves six to complete. In feedback we have received from teachers, they report receiving more homework regularly when providing students with some choice.

Too often we attempt to solve students' problems by telling them what to do, thereby robbing them of an opportunity to learn how to solve problems by themselves. Allowing children and adolescents to solve problems on their own does not mean that teachers are not involved to provide guidance or that they should not respond to a crisis. Most problems are not crises, so teachers can allow children to derive their own solutions to problems they face.

Several steps are involved to strengthen problem-solving skills in students. A first step is for all parties to agree that a problem exists. This typically requires the students to actively consider the perspective of others. For example, Ms. Roberts, a middle school teacher, reported an ongoing problem with students making fun of each other. This had occurred for months, even though she constantly reminded them not to engage in this behavior. A more effective approach than a verbal reminder would be to 1) ask the students if they thought the teasing that was occurring in the class was a problem (if the students said that it was not a problem, Ms. Roberts could use their response to discuss why and how making fun of others interferes with a positive learning environment); 2) ask the students to consider possible solutions to the problem; and 3) attempt the solution that seems most probable to be effective. Solutions that arise from children (with the necessary input of adults) are more likely to be successful than those that are handed down by adults. The active involvement of students helps them to feel in control and reinforces their sense of ownership and empowerment—important ingredients in strengthening resilience and altering undesirable behaviors.

Helping Students Establish Self-Discipline

It is difficult to conceive of children developing high self-esteem and resilience if they do not possess self-discipline, or a realistic ability to stop, judge, reason, and reflect on one's behavior and its effect on others. Children are often labeled as difficult when they encounter problems in developing self-discipline. Adults describe such children as acting before they think. Unfortunately, these children, who are most in need of limits and structure, are quick to experience such limits as unfair impositions on their life. It is often a Herculean task to establish rules in a manner that is not immediately rejected by children who feel that the rules have been proposed arbitrarily.

A major goal of discipline—in addition to establishing a safe and secure environment—is to help students develop self-discipline (Fay, Cline, & Sornson, 2005; Ginsburg, 2011). If children are to assume ownership for their actions and not view rules as being unfairly set, they must understand the purpose of rules and contribute within reason to the formation of rules, guidelines, and consequences. Teachers and parents walk a tightrope where discipline is concerned, maintaining a delicate balance between rigidity and flexibility; striving to blend warmth, nurturance, acceptance, and humor with realistic expectations; and providing clear-cut guidelines and logical, natural consequences. If a child constantly challenges rules in school, teachers must strive to understand why this occurs and ask if what is being required is appropriate for this particular child. The development of resilience and self-discipline comes with relinquishing tight control in favor of guidance, attention, and support so that children have the opportunities to test their inner control (Ginsburg, 2011).

Also, teachers should focus on ways to prevent the emergence of misbehavior rather than expending all their time and energy struggling with what action to take and what form of discipline to use once the misbehavior has occurred. Educators should anticipate situations that are likely to prove problematic for children and result in disruptive behaviors. Although it is often a difficult task, teachers should help students to avoid these situations until they are better able to manage problems and develop realistic alternative behaviors.

During the orientation period described earlier, teachers may ask students 1) what rules they think are necessary for both students and teachers to follow for the class to run smoothly; 2) what the best ways are to remember these rules so that adults are not constantly reminding them (i.e., nagging them) and so they are not constantly reminding the teachers; and 3) what the consequences should be if someone (including the teacher) forgets a rule. Obviously, some rules related to safety are

Strategies to Promote Resilience

not negotiable. Students are more likely to remember and adhere to rules that they have helped to create. Skillfully involving students in this process does not result in anarchy; rather, it increases understanding of the necessity for rules and increases motivation to follow the rules.

One assistant principal of a middle school asked students to write or dictate a brief essay while they were serving detention. He was trying to encourage the students to reflect on their behaviors and to consider alternative ways of coping with difficulties. If they did not feel like writing, they were allowed to dictate their thoughts into a recorder. They were given a choice of more than 30 topics, including what they would do if they ran the school, what they could do in the future to avoid detention, and what dreams they had about their future. Many of the students were able to reflect on their lives and their behaviors and think about alternative ways of behaving in the future.

Promoting Self-Advocacy Skills

Many students who are at risk for or are experiencing learning or behavioral challenges may struggle with self-advocacy skills, sometimes lacking the skill set to plan ahead and successfully negotiate teacher and student relationships. Just as students with disabilities require direct instruction to develop effective learning strategies, they also need instruction and modeling in self-advocacy (Carter, Lane, Pierson, & Glaeser, 2006; Izzo & Lamb, 2002). Research reveals that students who have identified strategies for explaining their learning and behavioral needs demonstrate an increased ability to approach teachers about needed accommodations as well as achieve greater attainment of their own personal goals (Brewer, Fowler, Test, & Wood, 2005; Brinckerhoff, 1993; Phillips, 1990). Further, children who have received self-advocacy instruction have been found to have improved interpersonal skills by demonstrating more self-confidence as well as becoming more self-reflective about their strengths and educational needs (Eisenman, Chamberlin, & McGahee-Kovac, 2005). Increasing students' ability to communicate with their teachers and advocate for their needs can result in positive short- and long-term gains.

Multiple strategies can be used to teach these skills, including prompting, role-playing, and using published curricula or lesson plans. As knowledge of self and communication skills appear to be some of the most critical components of learning how to advocate for one's self (Brewer et al., 2005; Eisenman & Tascione, 2002), teachers and school practitioners may consider targeting these two areas when working directly with students. An initial step in promoting self-advocacy skills may include having a teacher or school mental health professional talk individually with a student about his or her learning needs in order to increase awareness of that student's strengths and weaknesses. Step two may include identifying strategies or ways in which students should approach their teacher or other school staff to communicate their individual needs. This may include writing a sample script of what a student might say, making a written list of steps that walk the student through the process, and/or having a student practice verbalizing what could be said to a teacher. Problem-solving the most appropriate setting, timing, and expected teacher responses for these conversations is important to ensure a student's comfort level. It is also necessary to provide follow-up sessions where a student can report back on the results of his or her initial attempts at communication.

For example, take Jeremy, the fifth-grade student introduced in Chapter 1. Mr. Chavez, Jeremy's teacher, described him as a "moving target who can't control his movements." Although Jeremy had been diagnosed with ADHD and was receiving medical treatment and counseling, he still had trouble following directions and completing tasks. One day, after blurting out a response in class, Jeremy explained, "I just can't keep the words in my mouth." By working individually with Jeremy, Mr. Chavez could begin to help Jeremy problem-solve strategies for how to appropriately participate in classroom discussions. This could include writing down any questions he had instead of blurting them out, counting to five silently in his head before raising his hand, and/or quietly asking a peer for help or assistance instead of always relying on Mr. Chavez. Mr. Chavez could also role-play these scenarios with Jeremy to help him visualize what it may look like in the classroom setting. Holding an individual 10- to 15-minute meeting with Jeremy sends the message that Mr. Chavez cares about Jeremy's well-being and wants to help identify solutions that will assist Jeremy in being successful in the classroom.

Teachers can instill self-advocacy skills at a broader classroom level by offering students choices in what assignment to complete first and in the format of instruction (e.g., independent seat work, online computer programs, cooperative learning groups, peer tutoring; Fiedler & Danneker, 2007). These types of choices provide students with opportunities for daily practice in making choices, problem solving, and independence. As discussed previously, promoting self-determination and ownership over learning is an essential ingredient of high self-esteem and resilience. Price, Wolensky, and Mulligan (2002) offer a number of instructional practices that can enhance self-determination skills in the classroom:

- Encourage mutual responsibility and goal setting between teacher and students.
- Assist students in identifying their strengths and support needs.
- Incorporate students' life experiences into learning activities.
- Structure teaching and learning to be more problem oriented.
- Infuse student choice throughout the school day.
- Anticipate future adult roles and responsibilities of students and incorporate the information into learning activities.

These examples demonstrate that students can be supported in using self-advocacy skills with a minimal investment of time and resources. The disposition of teachers and school staff plays an important role in empowering students to take on an active role in advocating for their own learning and behavioral needs. Figure 7.5 is a letter written by Travis Frank after he graduated from high school in which he describes the importance of self-advocacy.

Providing Positive Feedback and Encouragement

Positive feedback and encouragement fall under the umbrella of discipline, but they are listed separately to emphasize their importance. Self-esteem and resilience are nurtured when teachers and parents communicate realistic appreciation and encouragement to children and adolescents; however, this positive communication is often limited or absent, especially when too prominent a focus is placed on a student's negative behaviors. Words and actions that help students to feel genuinely special are energizing and demonstrate to children that adults accept and believe in them. Even a small gesture of appreciation can create a lifelong impact.

John's history teacher, Dr. Mantell, had more than 150 students in her classes. She informed the students at the beginning of the year that she planned to call each of them at least twice at home

Strategies to Promote Resilience

> Dear Reader:
>
> Self-advocacy is one of the biggest transitions teenagers *need to* make. This is the point where they make decisions about what they need and how they plan to get it: the point where Mom and Dad are their last line of defense and they start to learn what really matters. I found this out firsthand when in 7th grade. I had a pretty inactive advocate, so I took charge and started talking to my teachers about how they could help me do better. This was sometimes ineffective, so I did the next best thing: I started carrying a copy of my IEP. This proved somewhat effective; though this was only a taste of what true self-advocacy was, it got me ready for what was to come in high school. My advocate, who was the head of the Special Ed. Department, had tried this method of planning with only one other and had success. There was paper after paper showing my strengths and weaknesses, as well as my goals. This program showed me where I wanted to be and made me think of how I could get there. The next step was to help me plan my own meeting in which I would have control of the whole meeting. I would start, introduce, and conduct the meeting; this was not as hard to plan as it sounds, but it does take an ability to control adults when they argue. The best thing I have ever done was taking charge: I now have full power over my school life, I see my advocate when I feel that there is a need for a change in my IEP, and I don't rely on him for simple things like more time for homework. I have been able to spread my wings, so to speak—and to think that 10 years ago I couldn't read, 7 years ago they didn't even think I could make it to grade level, 3 years ago I met grade level, and now my teachers say that my reading and writing skills may be near honors level. When you take charge of your life, you find that no wall is too big to jump, no wall is too strong to break down, and no wall will ever stand in your way. I can't count the ways self-advocacy has helped me or what the best part really is. Instead, I leave you with this: I was at least 3 grades behind at the start of 6th grade, meaning I only had the reading skills of an 8 year old, and yet I sit here speaking on behalf of all Special Ed. kids who have been told, "You'll never do anything" or "You're not smart enough." Yes you can, and yes you are. The only way you fail is when you stop fighting, when you give up and stop trying; you need to show that teen spirit of never knowing when to quit and say, "Help me or get out of my way." To the parents, teachers, and everyone else trying to help these kids, you too must never give up, and you must keep watch over the kids' progress, being ready to stop anyone trying to hurt that progress. If you fight, then we will help, and in doing so, we will one day shine through, leaving all who said, "No you can't" in our wake.
>
> Sincerely,
> Travis Frank
>
> P.S. I'd like to thank all those who have helped me, my parents, and my teachers. To all the others who believed in me and helped me get this far, thank you to all of you. We had good days and bad days, but through it all, I succeeded, and now I will help force open the doors for others to succeed as well.

Figure 7.5. Travis's letter.

during the year to find out how they were doing. On average, she spent about 7–8 minutes each evening on the telephone. Her calls had positive results. Students were more respectful and more disciplined in class and turned in assignments on a more regular basis. Dr. Mantell knew how to help students feel welcome and appreciated.

When students have at least one adult in school who cares about and advocates for them, they are less likely to drop out and more likely to attend school. A brief note of encouragement written by a teacher on a child's paper can be a source of positive motivation. This is especially important for students who are at risk and may feel discouraged by their slow progress. The emotional support and encouragement offered by significant adults in a child's life are crucial for promoting self-worth and resilience. When Ben was in third grade, his teacher realized the value of positive comments, even though Ben's writing ability was below many of the other students in the class. Figure 7.6 illustrates a comment by his teacher, Ms. Chandler.

Teaching Students to Cope with Mistakes and Failure

All students worry about making mistakes and appearing foolish. Given the many struggles that children with learning and attentional problems face, they are

Foundational Blocks

Figure 7.6. Teacher's comment on Ben's paper.

typically more anxious about making mistakes than their classmates; consequently, they retreat from challenging tasks rather than risking possible failure and humiliation. The coping strategies they employ to avoid learning tasks that they feel are beyond their skills typically prove self-defeating.

Samuel frequently gave up on classroom tasks. One day, he became frustrated with a particular math assignment that he did not understand how to do. As he was going out to recess, he turned in his paper with the note presented in Figure 7.7. Samuel had decided his efforts did not pay off.

As attribution theory highlights, the development of high self-esteem and resilience is intimately linked to a child's experience with and perception of failure.

Strategies to Promote Resilience

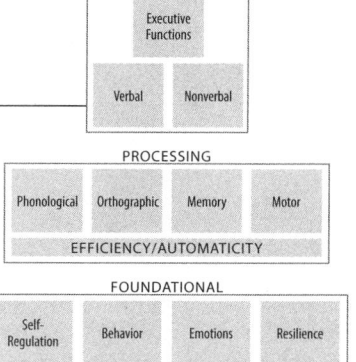

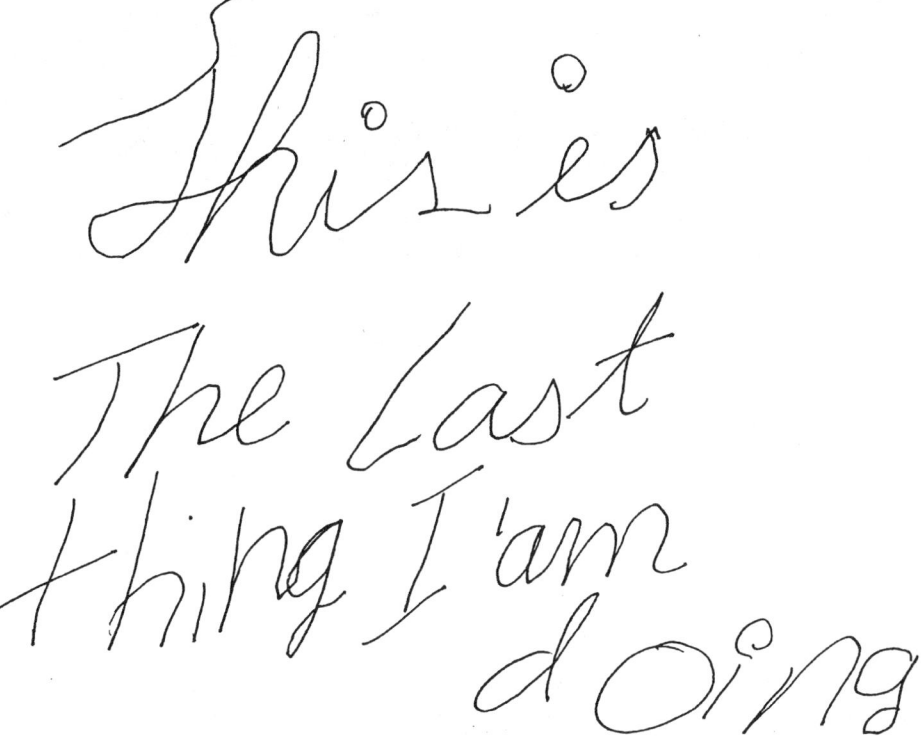

Figure 7.7. Samuel's note.

Consequently, efforts must be made to help students like Samuel realize that mistakes are an important ingredient in the process of learning. Mistakes represent teachable moments.

Teachers must examine how they respond to a student's mistakes. They must have realistic expectations for students and not overreact to their mistakes. All teachers become frustrated, at times, with the behavior of children, but disparaging remarks such as "How often do I have to repeat myself?" or "Were you listening carefully in the first place?" or "You would do okay if you only tried harder" are counterproductive. For example, if a student is having difficulty listening carefully, it is far more helpful if a teacher says, "I can see that those directions might have been too long and too confusing. Let's try to figure out what each of us can do that will help." Such a statement is not accusatory and also enlists the student's assistance in addressing the problem.

Teachers must also be careful of the types of comments that they write on students' papers. It is important to provide positive, encouraging remarks and to keep in mind that many students are doing the best that they can do. At the beginning of second grade, Ms. Abram would write comments such as "Can't read," "Please try harder," and "Work more carefully, please." Figure 7.8 provides a sample of one response to Andy's paper: "I had a spider in my mom's bedroom and I put him outside." Andy has severe weaknesses in motor development, and these types of comments are only discouraging.

If a student does not know an answer immediately, some teachers call on other students until the correct answer is obtained. What this practice communicates to students is that the teacher is more interested in the correct answer than in the

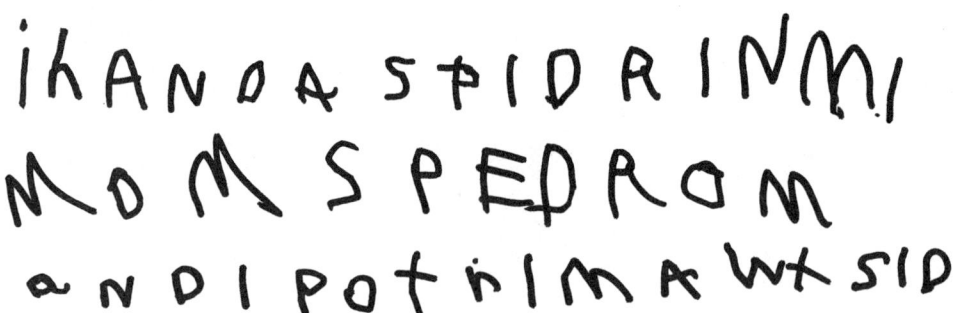

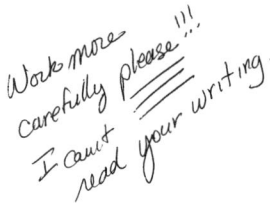

Figure 7.8. Teacher's comment on Andy's writing.

process of solving the problem. If a child does not know the correct answer, it is far more effective for a teacher to say, "Let's review how to solve that problem." By doing so, the teacher is using the child's lack of knowledge as a teachable moment and reinforcing the message that people learn from mistakes. Such a teacher recognizes two important facts: First, if one student does not know an answer, there are probably other students who also do not understand the material. Second, if a student does not know how to solve a problem, just hearing the correct answer from another student is not helpful. Of course, additional assistance, practice, feedback, and instruction may be necessary for students who have repeated difficulties grasping material.

Because the fear of failure is such a powerful force, it should be addressed in the classroom before students make a mistake. This can be accomplished during the orientation period at the beginning of the school year. A teacher can ask, "Who feels that they are going to make a mistake or not understand something in class this year?" Before any of the students can respond, the teacher can raise his or her hand and begin a discussion of how the fear of making mistakes affects learning. The teacher can then involve the class in problem solving by asking what he or she can do as their teacher and what they can do as class members to minimize the fear of failing and looking foolish. Openly acknowledging the fear of failure renders it less potent and less destructive. Teachers can show students that not comprehending material is to be expected and that the teacher's role is to help them to learn. As attribution theory has taught us, students have higher self-esteem and are more resilient when they perceive mistakes as experiences from which to learn.

CONCLUSION

A basic characteristic of resilient children is that their self-esteem and sense of academic competence either have been maintained or, if damaged, have been repaired. Resilient children possess a feeling of hope, optimism, ownership, and personal control. This feeling is nurtured by charismatic adults who provide experiences that reinforce students' islands of competence and enhance children's feelings of

Strategies to Promote Resilience

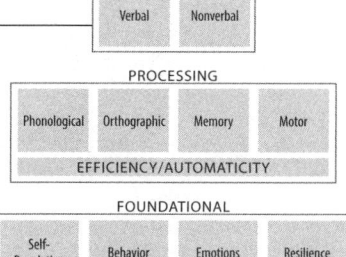

self-worth. If goals for these children are to develop self-esteem, self-respect, self-discipline, and compassion, educators must work diligently to become charismatic adults. The school environment is a prime location for resilience to be nurtured. Effective educators possess a mind-set enabling them to recognize the lifelong effect they have on their students.

SECTION III
Processing Blocks

CHAPTER 8 OUTLINE

DEFINITIONS

- Evolution of the Definitions of Learning Disability
- Legal Definitions
- Individuals with Disabilities Education Improvement Act of 2004
- Aptitude–Achievement Discrepancy
- Response to Intervention
- Alternative Research-Based Methods: A Pattern of Strengths and Weaknesses

THE PROCESSING BLOCKS

PHONOLOGICAL PROCESSING BLOCK

- Phonological Processing Block Questionnaire
- Phonological Awareness Terminology
- Phonological Dyslexia
- International Dyslexia Association Definition of Dyslexia
- Brief Historical Review
- Developmental Sequence
- Assessment and Instructional Activities
- Segmentation and Blending

ORTHOGRAPHIC PROCESSING BLOCK

- Definition of Orthographic Awareness
- Characteristics of Poor Orthographic Awareness
- Orthographic Processing Block Questionnaire
- Brief Historical Review of Orthographic Dyslexia
- Research on Orthographic Dyslexia
- Implications for Intervention

MEMORY BLOCK

- Short-Term Memory
- Working Memory
- Memory Block Questionnaire

MOTOR BLOCK

- Motor Block Questionnaire
- Fine Motor Development

EFFICIENCY/AUTOMATICITY BLOCK

- Efficiency/Automaticity Block Questionnaire
- Rapid Automatized Naming
- Processing Speed

CLASSROOM ACCOMMODATIONS

- Copying
- Timed Tests
- Following Directions
- Assignments

CONCLUSION

APPENDIX 8A: PHONOLOGICAL AWARENESS SKILLS SCREENER

APPENDIX 8B: THE RELATIONSHIP BETWEEN SPEECH SOUNDS AND SPELLING DEVELOPMENT

CHAPTER 8

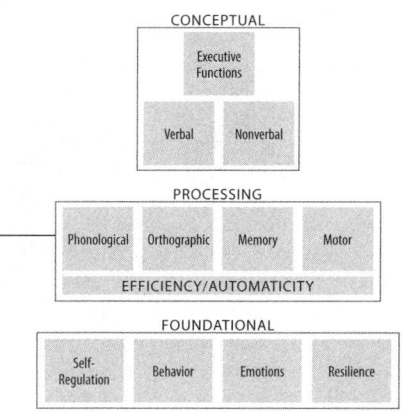

Specific Learning Disabilities and the Processing Blocks

with Deborah A. Schneider

Although the Building Blocks model can help a teacher understand both learning and behavior problems, this type of model is not used in schools to identify students as having specific learning disabilities (SLD). Within school settings, the category of SLD has traditionally been reserved for children who do not learn even though they possess a general capacity for learning (Ingersoll & Goldstein, 1993). Professionals in the field have not, however, arrived at a consensus regarding exactly how SLD should be defined or identified. Before discussing the abilities in the Processing blocks, we present a brief historical overview of the underpinnings and evolution of the terminology in the field of SLD.

DEFINITIONS

Despite continuing efforts at clarification, the definitions and diagnostic criteria for SLD vary widely within academic, community, and even vocational settings. Some believe that the characteristics described by the term *learning disability* are so heterogeneous that the creation of a precise, clear working definition is impossible (Rutter, 1978). Some suggest that SLD should be defined as the existence of unexpected patterns of strengths and weaknesses within academic skills or significant "variation in achievement markers" among academic domains (Fletcher, Lyon, Fuchs, & Barnes, 2007, p. 4). Others stress the importance of significant intraindividual variation across cognitive, linguistic, and academic abilities in defining SLD (Mather & Gregg, 2006). Historically, SLD has been linked to the concept of "unexpected" underachievement, where some aspects of an individual's academic achievement are far lower than would be predicted by his or her performance in other academic or cognitive domains. This concept of unexpected underachievement can be traced back to the late 19th and early 20th centuries, when physicians documented children and adults with "word blindness," individuals who could not read well, despite those individuals having average or above-average intelligence.

Evolution of the Definitions of Learning Disability

Beginning in the late 1880s, the concept and subsequent definitions of learning disability developed parallel with—but relatively independently from—the fields of neurology, psychology, and education. Broca (1861) identified a neurobiological origin for language impairments in some individuals of otherwise typical cognitive ability. In 1922, Hohman described a group of children with behavior problems, hyperactivity, and learning difficulties resulting from encephalitis. Subsequent research and labels for these children with impaired achievement reflected a belief that this disability was the result of some brain-based dysfunction. Strauss and Lehtinen (1947) introduced the term *minimal brain damage* to describe characteristics consistent with learning disability. Since that time, a variety of other terms have also been used to describe this population of children (see Table 8.1).

In 1962 and 1963, Kirk and Bateman initiated an effort to define learning disability on the basis of objective data. The term *learning disability* was intended to describe an impairment in learning capacity that was not the result of an intellectual disability. They explained this term as follows:

> A learning disability refers to a retardation, disorder, or delayed development in one or more of the processes of speech, language, reading, writing, arithmetic, or other school subjects resulting from a psychological handicap caused by possible cerebral dysfunction and/or emotional or behavioral disturbances. It is not the result of mental retardation, sensory deprivation, or cultural or instructional factors. (p. 73)

These concepts were incorporated into the definition of learning disability presented to Congress by the National Advisory Committee on Handicapped Children:

> Those children who have a disorder in one or more of the basic psychological processes involved in understanding or using language, spoken or written, which disorder may manifest itself in imperfect ability to listen, think, speak, read, write, spell or do mathematical calculations. Such disorders include conditions such as perceptual handicaps, brain injury, minimal brain dysfunction, dyslexia and developmental aphasia. This term does not include learning problems that are primarily the result of visual, hearing or motor handicaps, of mental retardation, of emotional disturbances or of environmental, cultural or economic disadvantage. (1968, p. 82)

This definition acknowledged that a variety of developmental and environmental factors might contribute to learning difficulties. The definition also specified that children whose faulty school performance was primarily the result of environmental influences, foundational skill impairments, emotional or behavior disorders, or physical or sensory disabilities should not be characterized as having an SLD.

Legal Definitions

An adapted version of this basic definition was incorporated into the Education for All Handicapped Children Act of 1975 (PL 94-142), which guaranteed specialized services for children with disabilities, including SLD. This federal law mandating education for all children with disabilities ruled out emotional and behavioral factors as causes of SLD, placing emotional and behavior disorders in a separate service category.

In 1981, six professional organizations met and reached a consensus definition for learning disability. This definition reinforced the original concept of learning disability as an inclusive term used to provide a general description of children failing to learn despite apparently adequate cognitive capacity:

Specific Learning Disabilities and the Processing Blocks

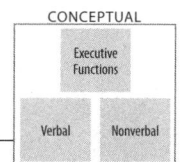

Table 8.1. Examples of historical definitions of learning/reading disorders

Year	Term
1877	Word blindness (Kussmaul, 1877b)
1884	Dyslexia (Berlin, 1884)
1895	Word blindness (Hinshelwood, 1895)
1925	*Strephosymbolia* ("twisted symbols"; Orton, 1925)
1937	Word deafness (Orton, 1937)
1947	Brain-injured or brain-damaged (Strauss & Lehtinen, 1947)
1962	Minimal brain dysfunction (Clements & Peters, 1962)
1962/1963	Learning disabilities (Kirk & Bateman, 1962/1963)
1964	Developmental dyslexia (Critchley, 1964)
1967–1968	Specific learning disabilities (National Advisory Committee on Handicapped Children, 1968)
1970	Specific learning disabilities (Elementary and Secondary Education Act Amendments of 1969: Title VI, Education of the Handicapped Act of 1970 [PL 91-230])
1971	Psycholinguistic learning disabilities (Kirk & Kirk, 1971)
1975	Learning disabilities (Education for All Handicapped Children Act of 1975 [PL 94-142])
1980	Specific developmental disorders (American Psychiatric Association, 1980)
1994	Learning disorders (American Psychiatric Association, 1994)
2013	Specific learning disorders (American Psychiatric Association, 2013)

From Silver, A. A., & Hagin, R. A. (1990). *Disorders of learning in childhood* (p. 51). New York, NY: John Wiley & Sons, Inc.; adapted by permission. Copyright © 1990 John Wiley & Sons. Reproduced with permission of John Wiley & Sons, Inc.

Learning disabilities is a generic term that refers to a heterogeneous group of disorders manifested by significant difficulties in the acquisition and use of listening, speaking, writing, reasoning or mathematical abilities. These disorders are intrinsic to the individual and presumed to be due to central nervous system dysfunction. Even though a learning disability may occur concomitantly with other handicapping conditions (such as sensory impairment, mental retardation), social and emotional disturbances or environmental influences (such as cultural differences, insufficient or inappropriate instruction, psychogenic factors), it is not the direct result of those conditions or influences. (Hammill, Leigh, McNutt, & Larsen, 1981, p. 336)

In 1987, the Interagency Committee on Learning Disabilities maintained this basic definition and added language acknowledging the potential role of SLD in creating or worsening problems in social skills. This was the first step in recognizing that the underlying skill impairments that contribute to faulty achievement can also play a role in the development, or lack thereof, of important interpersonal and behavior skills.

Each of these definitions of the term *learning disability* focused on performance rather than etiology, except as an exclusionary criterion, reflecting the perception that a person with SLD may struggle to accomplish academic tasks that others accomplish with ease. Although the definitions explained that these difficulties could not be attributed to poor teaching, environmental deprivation, or limited experience, they did not identify the factors responsible for underperformance other than providing allusions to the presumed role of neurological and biological processes (Kavanagh, 1988). Although their focus on performance facilitated the process of diagnosis, it did little to clarify the etiology of various learning disabilities or promote the selection of appropriate treatments—that is, the modification of the educational environment and the selection of teaching strategies to improve and accelerate achievement. In other words, this focus on labels (e.g., reading disability) may have encouraged practitioners and educators to overlook the cause of the SLD (e.g., poor phonological or orthographic processing) and therefore not consider the reasons for the difficulties when designing an appropriate intervention plan. As an example, few students receive instructional interventions that are designed to address these impairments, despite the well-established importance of phonological, orthographic, and morphological processes to accurate and fluent reading (Berninger & Abbott, 1994). Furthermore, 90% of educators report feeling unprepared by their formal education to work with students with dyslexia (Wadlington & Wadlington, 2005).

Individuals with Disabilities Education Improvement Act of 2004

The recommended procedures for identifying SLD were revised with the ratification of the Individuals with Disabilities Education Improvement Act (IDEA) of 2004 (PL 108-446). IDEA 2004 was signed into law on December 3, 2004, by President George W. Bush; the provisions of the act became effective on July 1, 2005; and the final regulations were published on August 14, 2006. In the reauthorization, the definition of SLD was maintained as "a disorder in one or more of the basic psychological processes involved in understanding or in using language, spoken or written, which . . . may manifest itself in the imperfect ability to listen, think, speak, read well, or do mathematical calculations" (20 U.S.C. §1401 [30]); however, IDEA 2004 included language specifically prohibiting the use of any single assessment instrument or procedure as the sole criterion for the identification of a disability. Furthermore, the reauthorization provided for the use of a response to intervention (RTI) approach to the documentation of SLD. Detailed information on IDEA 2004 and the implementation of RTI, described later in this chapter, can be found on the National Research Center on Learning Disabilities web site (http://www.nrcld.org), the federal web site dedicated to IDEA 2004 (http://idea.ed.gov), and LD Online (http://www.ldonline.org/article/11202).

Some of the notable provisions of IDEA 2004 regarding the identification of SLD and the provision of related services include the following:

> The group described in 34 CFR 300.306 may determine that a child has a specific learning disability, as defined in 34 CFR 300.8(c)(10), if:
>
> - The child does not achieve adequately for the child's age or to meet State-approved grade-level standards in one or more of the following areas, when provided with learning experiences and instruction appropriate for the child's age or State-approved grade-level standards:
>   - Oral expression
>   - Listening comprehension
>   - Written expression
>   - Basic reading skills
>   - Reading fluency skills
>   - Reading comprehension
>   - Mathematics calculation
>   - Mathematics problem solving
> - The child does not make sufficient progress to meet age or State-approved grade-level standards in one or more of the areas identified in 34 CFR 300.309(a)(1) when using a

Specific Learning Disabilities and the Processing Blocks

process based on the child's response to scientific, research-based intervention; or the child exhibits a pattern of strengths and weaknesses in performance, achievement, or both, relative to age, State-approved grade-level standards, or intellectual development, that is determined by the group to be relevant to the identification of a specific learning disability, using appropriate assessments, consistent with 34 CFR 300.304 and 300.305; and the group determines that its findings under 34 CFR 300.309(a)(1) and (2) are not primarily the result of:

- A visual, hearing, or motor disability;
- Mental retardation;
- Emotional disturbance;
- Cultural factors;
- Environmental or economic disadvantage; or
- Limited English proficiency.

To ensure that underachievement in a child suspected of having a specific learning disability is not due to lack of appropriate instruction in reading or math, the group must consider, as part of the evaluation described in 34 CFR 300.304 through 300.306:

- Data that demonstrate that prior to, or as a part of, the referral process, the child was provided appropriate instruction in regular education settings, delivered by qualified personnel; and
- Data-based documentation of repeated assessments of achievement at reasonable intervals, reflecting formal assessment of student progress during instruction, which was provided to the child's parents.

The central changes in the law reflect an acknowledgement that comprehensive information, such as classroom performance, information-processing abilities, intellectual capacity, and qualitative information from parents and teachers, must be gathered to refute or support a diagnosis of SLD. Moreover, the policies and procedures for identifying students with SLD have been modified such that an aptitude–achievement discrepancy is no longer a requirement for diagnosis. The IDEA regulations specify that each state must adopt, consistent with 34 CFR 300.309, criteria for determining whether a child has a specific learning disability as defined in 34 CFR 300.8(c)(10). In addition, the criteria adopted by the state 1) must not require the use of a severe discrepancy between intellectual ability and achievement for determining whether a child has a specific learning disability, as defined in 34 CFR 300.8(c)(10); 2) must permit the use of a process based on the child's response to scientific, research-based intervention; and 3) may permit the use of other alternative research-based procedures for determining whether a child has a specific learning disability, as defined in 34 CFR 300.8(c)(10). Thus, under IDEA 2004, school districts may use 1) an aptitude–achievement discrepancy, 2) a process based on response to research-based interventions, or 3) alternative research-based procedures as part of the identification process.

Aptitude–Achievement Discrepancy

Because some school districts are still using an aptitude–achievement discrepancy as the major criterion for the identification of SLD, it is important to understand how the use of this criterion came about and some of the problems and concerns as well as the utility of discrepancy formulae. In the discrepancy model, a student's actual achievement (based on measures of oral expression, listening comprehension, written expression, basic reading, reading fluency, reading comprehension, and mathematical calculation or mathematical problem solving) was compared with his or her predicted achievement (based on measures of intellectual functioning). This discrepancy model became the method for determining which students would receive special education services and how much funding should be directed to those services.

Owing to legal mandates and the definition of learning disabilities provided in the Education for All Handicapped Children Act of 1975 (PL 94-142), as well as the subsequent revisions and reauthorizations, an aptitude–achievement discrepancy model was routinely used for SLD identification in the past. As noted, some school districts still use the discrepancy criteria as one component of a special education evaluation; however, under IDEA 2004, states may no longer mandate its use. Furthermore, sole reliance on this procedure for SLD identification has decreased because of not only legal mandates but also problems associated with using this model as the sole basis for identifying SLD.

Problems with the Aptitude–Achievement Discrepancy Model

Since the 1980s, the use of an aptitude–achievement discrepancy model as the sole or determining criterion for the diagnosis of dyslexia and SLD has been questioned and criticized (Stanovich, 1994; Stanovich, 2005). The problems in using a formula to identify children are many, serious, and too often disregarded (Bateman, 1992). Although this formula was used widely in schools, it was described as being both unnecessary (Mather & Healey, 1990) and invalid (Lyon, 1995). Simpson and Buckhalt observed,

> Though the formula method may have some appeal because it requires less clinical competence and judgment, the fact remains that reducing an important diagnostic decision to a mathematical equation gives a false sense of objectivity to a contrived procedure that is still essentially subjective. (1990, p. 274)

Despite a plethora of criticisms and concerns, state and district identification guidelines continued to demonstrate increased reliance on formulae (Frankenberger & Fronzaglio, 1991). To further complicate matters, state and school district guidelines varied with regard to the specific method used to define a discrepancy and the magnitude of the discrepancy required in order for a child to be deemed eligible for services. Therefore, a child could be identified as having SLD in one district and then denied services in another. Nonetheless, in both public school and vocational education settings, the most widely accepted criterion for determination of SLD remained a significant difference between standard scores on intelligence and achievement tests, typically 1.5 standard deviations or more. Describing use of the discrepancy model, Berninger explained, "The criterion set for the size of discrepancy that counts as a reading or writing disability is always arbitrary and varies widely among states and among schools within states" (1996, pp. 158–159). She further observed, "Whether a child is or is not diagnosed as learning disabled depends on the state and the local criteria in which a child lives or on the personal philosophy of an independent evaluator who assesses the child" (p. 164). Such criticisms should not be construed to undermine the existence of SLD—only the validity of the ability–achievement discrepancy procedure as the sole criterion for its diagnosis. According to Stanovich, the

> critics of discrepancy definitions are [not] denying the existence of severe reading disability *per se* or the importance of remedial help. Instead, they are questioning the rationale of differential treatment and resources being allocated on the basis of IQ-achievement discrepancy. (1999, p. 355)

Specific Learning Disabilities and the Processing Blocks

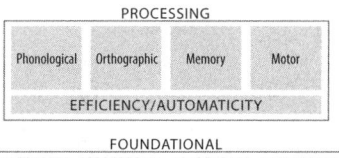

Preschool Through Second Grade

For children in preschool through second grade, the diagnosis of an aptitude–achievement discrepancy was predicated on failure. Children needed to fall behind their predicted level of performance to be deemed technically eligible for diagnosis and services. This often resulted in services being delayed until well into third grade or beyond. In fact, some school districts would not evaluate children for eligibility for services under the SLD category until the second grade. Thus, children were forced to cross a threshold of severe academic failure prior to receiving help. In the interim, the children made minimal progress, and once identified, students who were struggling to keep up then faced the arduous task of catching up and keeping up simultaneously. After attending a staffing in which a struggling student did not qualify for help, one frustrated second-grade teacher lamented,

> You have to be careful of what early intervention you do for your children because it can backfire. You provide a child with help in first and second grade and then they don't have a big enough gap between scores to qualify for services.

Fletcher and colleagues described how rigid discrepancy models can prevent early intervention:

> The treatment implications of discrepancy models are perhaps the most serious limitations. The average age of identification of children with LD is about 10 years of age. This is partly an effect of the need for children who are struggling with academic skills to stay at the floor of the achievement tests as they fail to master skills to obtain a sufficiently low score to obtain a discrepancy. The use of discrepancy clearly moves the identification and intervention component to the later part of elementary school. Unfortunately, it is also clear that severe RD [reading disabilities] identified after age 8 may be more refractory to intervention, reflecting observations made many years ago. (1998, p. 197)

Third Grade and Beyond

Students who are not diagnosed with SLD until third grade or beyond more often suffer from concomitant social, behavior, and emotional problems in the Foundational blocks. Their poor school performance contributes to lowered self-image and self-esteem. Attitude and motivation may become as much of a barrier to learning as the SLD itself. As students progress through school, the magnitude of the discrepancy between predicted performance (based on the results of an intelligence test) and actual performance (based on the results of achievement tests) may decrease. As a result, using the discrepancy model, a student with a real SLD may become excluded from services and legal protections.

One reason for the decrease in the ability–achievement gap among older students is that effective interventions may have resulted in improved academic performance or that the person has learned compensatory strategies to circumvent difficulties. With regard to reading, such individuals have been described as "compensated dyslexics." Difficulties in learning could also result in artificially low performance on the intelligence or aptitude measure. In other words, because of limited reading experiences, the student has reduced exposure to vocabulary and knowledge that is subsequently reflected by lowered aptitude scores. A further consideration is that selected tests may be inadequate for the purpose. For example, the student who initially struggled to learn to decode may now be able to read a list of words with accurate pronunciation, thereby attaining an average score on a measure of word identification. The student's poor performance in reading, however, is now due to limitations in speed and fluency (reading abilities that were not tested) rather than poor word identification skill. Furthermore, problems related to impairments in attention or memory might not qualify a child for services unless a significant aptitude–achievement discrepancy could be demonstrated. Similarly, children with other cognitive impairments that may affect their daily classroom performance, such as a slow speed of processing, would not qualify for special services unless they obtained sufficiently low scores on standardized achievement tests as well (Goldstein & Goldstein, 1998).

Strengths of the Aptitude–Achievement Discrepancy Model

Some aspects of an ability–achievement discrepancy model do, however, make sense as a part of an evaluation procedure to document SLD. Recent empirical evidence indicates that differential relationships exist between intelligence test scores and reading in typical readers versus those scores in readers with specific reading disabilities (Ferrer, Shaywitz, Holahan, Marchione, & Shaywitz, 2010). Ferrer and colleagues found that intelligence and reading test scores were highly related in good readers, but they were not in readers with dyslexia. These children may appear to be reading at a level consistent with their peers, but they are underachieving in relation to their academic potential and intelligence. Thus, for individuals with high intelligence, an ability–achievement discrepancy actually operationalizes the concept of unexpected underachievement.

In certain situations, an ability–achievement discrepancy can provide important diagnostic information. An ability–achievement discrepancy is particularly useful with individuals who are gifted but also have SLD; these students are often referred to as being twice exceptional. For example, some people of high ability have decoding skills that are significantly weaker than expected and would only qualify for services if an ability–achievement discrepancy criterion is used; these individuals should be identified and receive interventions (Peterson & Pennington, 2012). Although these students often achieve at age or grade expectations, their performance is often far below estimates of their learning potential. Their superior intellects may mask their SLD, making them less likely to be identified as having either exceptionality (Crepeau-Hobson & Bianco, 2011).

An ability–achievement discrepancy can also be useful for documenting the need for specific accommodations, such as audio-recorded books or the use of voice recognition software. When a large discrepancy exists between an individual's verbal ability and reading and written language performance, specific accommodations are often required to ensure an accurate assessment of knowledge. Despite the utility of an ability–achievement discrepancy procedure in some cases, sole reliance on this type of discrepancy alone is too narrow, rarely leads to instructional recommendations, and obscures the cognitive abilities underlying academic achievement (Mather & Gregg, 2006; Semrud-Clikeman, 2005). Thus, a major criticism associated with use of the ability–achievement discrepancy is the focus upon various formulae as the key to eligibility but not the construct itself (Mather, Shaywitz, & Shaywitz, 2013).

Response to Intervention

As noted, states are no longer allowed to require the documentation of a significant aptitude–achievement discrepancy to identify SLD (IDEA 2004, 34 CFR 300.8[c][10]), and states must permit other alternative research-based procedures for diagnosing SLD (34 CFR 300.8[c][10]). In addition, the language in IDEA 2004 specifies that a local educational agency may use a process that determines whether a child

Specific Learning Disabilities and the Processing Blocks

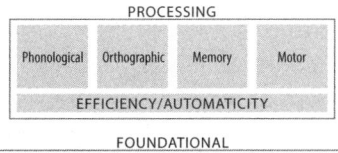

responds to scientific research-based intervention as *part* of the evaluation process (Sec. 614[b][6B]). Within schools, this process is often referred to as RTI. As with the use of the discrepancy model, RTI is not mandated.

RTI is perhaps most accurately described as an early intervention and prevention treatment model that incorporates systematic, schoolwide reform and intervention efforts to help all students. The advantages of RTI are that it places value on early intervention for the prevention of difficulties and can identify a wide range of students who are struggling learners, not just those with disabilities or special education needs (Berninger & May, 2011). Presently, many states have implemented or are planning to implement some form of RTI with the hopes of 1) reducing the number of students referred for evaluations; 2) providing early intervention to all children in a more timely fashion; 3) providing more specific, intensive interventions to the children who need the most help; 4) increasing the validity of actual special education placement decisions; and 5) monitoring the progress of all students. Considerable heterogeneity exists, however, in the methods and procedures used within RTI models (Decker, 2012).

Although the use of RTI can document the presence of low achievement or identify a pool of at-risk students, it does not diagnose SLD, identify the etiology of students' difficulties, and may not address how the teacher should alter instruction to ensure the student responds (Berninger & May, 2011; Kavale, 2005; Kavale, Kaufman, Naglieri, & Hale, 2005; Mather & Kaufman, 2006; National Joint Committee on Learning Disabilities [NJCLD], 2005). Furthermore, RTI does not take into account the various linguistic and neuropsychological functions that underlie academic performance, and may not provide a clear rationale for selecting alternative types of instruction or service delivery that may be more effective for an individual student. Other problems with RTI include the use of widely varying instruments and assessment procedures, creating the potential for measurement error, invalid results, and inaccurate identification (McKenzie, 2009). Most of the work on the implementation of RTI has focused on the early elementary years, and little empirical evidence exists that these models can be implemented effectively with children in the upper grades (Semrud-Clikeman, 2005).

RTI models use brief, curriculum-based probes to track each student's growth and document individual performance relative to grade-level norms. In nearly all RTI models, repeated curriculum-based measurements are used to document the outcomes of instruction; students with the poorest response to instruction receive increased educational assistance. The goals of the assessments are to compare individual performance to that of grade-level peers and determine whether students are achieving expected rates of growth. Students who consistently fail to meet achievement targets are provided with increasingly intensive and individualized educational services and supports. The NJCLD (2005) specified the following core concepts of RTI: 1) use of scientific, research-based interventions in general education; 2) measurement of student response to the interventions; and 3) use of the response data to alter or increase the intensity of the interventions.

Although RTI approaches vary considerably among schools and districts, most employ a three- or four-tiered data-based model of intervention that delineates a continuum of services. The primary tier (Tier I) is general education inclusive of core curricula and instructional methods; the secondary tier (Tier II) provides more specialized intervention and small-group instruction; and the tertiary tier (Tier III) provides more individualized and intensive services and may result in a comprehensive evaluation and consideration for special education eligibility.

The advantages of an RTI approach are clear. Prereferral interventions provide a direct focus on student learning and outcomes and increase accountability for all students regardless of whether they are eventually referred for special education (NJCLD, 2005). In many cases, RTI can also result in earlier identification and intervention (Fuchs, Mock, Morgan, & Young, 2003; Fuchs & Vaughn, 2005) than can an ability–achievement discrepancy procedure. Clearly, implementation of RTI in the general education curriculum adds an important dimension to the screening equation for areas of basic academic skills (e.g., reading, decoding, spelling, math computation; Speece, 2005).

Much remains to be known about how RTI models will be implemented in schools. Fuchs and Deshler (2007) discussed the unknowns of RTI implementation, including 1) identifying the purpose of RTI (early intervention or disability identification); 2) identifying the conditions of successful implementation; 3) determining the nature of instruction in Tier I; 4) determining how to use problem solving to promote the academic achievement among at-risk children as well as children with severe learning problems; 5) deciding how to evaluate nonresponsiveness and identify the nonresponders; 6) determining the relevance for middle and high school students; 7) deciding how to apply RTI principles to other areas besides early reading; and 8) determining whether RTI implementation is successful.

The data collected in one-stage RTI models appear insufficient, however, for the early, accurate identification of struggling readers. Recent research has suggested that the one-stage screening procedures that are often employed in many RTI models result in unacceptably high rates of false positives (Fuchs, Fuchs, & Compton, 2012). Instead, the use of a two-stage screen that includes additional cognitive and academic measures has been found to greatly improve classification accuracy (Fuchs et al., 2012). As a result, more refined and in-depth assessments are needed to help identify students whose failure to respond to secondary interventions can be predicted and so that more intensive interventions are provided in a more timely fashion (Fuchs et al., 2012).

The mandated procedures for identifying children with SLD in public schools still focus on academic performance impairments rather than on the underlying correlates and causes of the difficulties. As with the aptitude–achievement discrepancy model, children are unlikely to be identified until after they have failed to make adequate progress; in addition, the use of the model may lead to a denial of services to some children who are at risk for SLD (Semrud-Clikeman, 2005), especially those who have developed strong compensatory strategies or twice exceptional students—those with both SLD and areas of giftedness.

Rather than wait for a child to demonstrate poor performance, attempts should be made to examine the factors and the underlying abilities related to school difficulties. As Scarborough explained,

> Instead of casting the preschool characteristics of dyslexic children as "precursors" and the reading problems of these children as "outcomes", it might be more helpful to view both as successive, observable symptoms of the same condition. . . . Therefore, while the education goal may be to explain reading disability for its own sake, the neuropsychological goal is to define the nature of the fundamental difficulty that manifests itself most evidently, but not solely, as underachievement in reading. (1991, pp. 38–39)

Like the discrepancy model, RTI may not differentiate among learners with varying learning needs (Semrud-Clikeman, 2005) or help answer the question of why a certain student is struggling. Many potential extrinsic and intrinsic factors could explain why a student might not respond to a particular intervention. Students with a variety of conditions (e.g., attention-deficit/hyperactivity disorder, behavior

Specific Learning Disabilities and the Processing Blocks

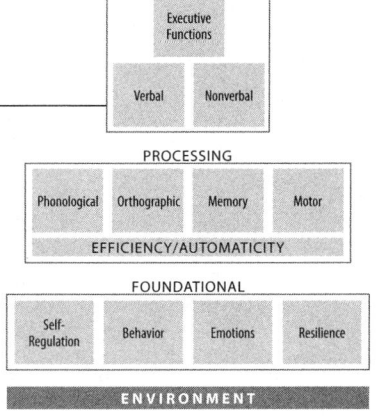

disorders, language impairments, English language learners [ELLs]) may show low responsiveness to intervention and be misidentified as having SLD. Furthermore, high-ability students with SLD would not be identified for services because they would partially compensate for their difficulties through the use of their strengths in language and reasoning. Thus, they would be denied the individualized instruction that would enable them to make progress consistent with their high abilities (NJCLD, 2005). As Martin observed, the "evaluation for a learning disability is not triggered only by failure. It is designed to determine if the student has a learning disability no matter how well the student is currently performing" (2005, p. 145). Highly intelligent people can have SLD, and the sole use of RTI will result in these individuals being overlooked and denied needed services and accommodations. The reason or reasons *why* a student is not learning matters (Mather & Kaufman, 2006).

As a final point, clinical judgment is needed for accurate identification. Trained educational personnel make good decisions, and accurate diagnoses and placement decisions are made by people—not test scores or formulae. As Bateman stated,

> The key to preventing further overidentification and misidentification is to exercise trained professional judgment. Our widespread reluctance to use this essential professional judgment in determining eligibility has been due not only to the eligibility teams' lack of experience but also to a fear that courts expect objective quantification as the sole or major basis for decision making. Nothing could be further from the truth. The courts show the highest respect for professional judgment, originally of medical doctors and now of most other qualified experts, too.... First, if not foremost, it is a violation of law to rely on anything other than professional judgment. (1992, pp. 29, 32)

Learning disabilities cannot be validly identified through the exclusive use of aptitude–achievement discrepancy procedures or sole reliance on an RTI model. Skilled professionals must review a variety of factors including a student's school records, family history, performance on standardized tests, response to classroom instruction, and rate of progress. The emphasis is placed on understanding a student's unique learning abilities as well as any learning disabilities.

The NJCLD reiterated the federal guidelines that RTI can be one component of the identification process but noted that the "RTI process does not replace the need for a comprehensive evaluation" (2010, p. 7). A recent policy memo from the Office of Special Education and Rehabilitative Services (January 21, 2011) specified that participation in an RTI process cannot be used as a reason to delay or deny initial evaluations for children suspected of having a disability. Thus, as components of the evaluation process, both ability–achievement discrepancy and RTI have potential benefits but also serious flaws (Decker, 2012). Furthermore, because regulations differ from state to state and local policies within states often vary dramatically, both models also face the issue of interstate and intrastate variability in the determination of exactly which students will be identified as having SLD (Lindstrom & Sayeski, 2013).

Alternative Research-Based Methods: A Pattern of Strengths and Weaknesses

In addition to ability–achievement and RTI approaches, a third option is available to schools for SLD identification. IDEA regulation § 300.309(a)(2)(ii) permits consideration of whether or not a child exhibits a significant pattern of strengths and weaknesses in performance, achievement, or both as part of the identification process. Such patterns of strengths and weaknesses are evaluated by the team relative to the child's overall intellectual development and his or her particular learning challenges in order to determine their relevance. In addition, the team must determine that the underachievement is not primarily the result of a visual, hearing, or motor disability; an intellectual disability; an emotional disturbance; cultural factors; an environmental or economic disadvantage; or limited English proficiency (IDEA regulation § 300.309[a][3]). A few states (e.g., Idaho, West Virginia) and school districts within states (e.g., Wayne County, Michigan; Portland, Oregon) have elected to use such an alternative, research-based approach, which is most often described as a pattern of strengths and weaknesses (PSW) approach.

In most instances, a PSW approach is combined with an RTI model for prevention so that evaluators can consider both a student's level of responsiveness to evidence-based interventions and his or her unique profile of strengths and weaknesses. One major benefit of the PSW approach is that it aligns the definition of SLD, an impairment in basic cognitive processing, with the procedures to be used for operationalizing identification. Kavale, Kauffman, Bachmeier, and Lefever explained, "Cognitive processing assessment aligns diagnostic procedures with a clearly articulated SLD definitional component: a disorder in one or more of the basic psychological processes" (2008, p. 144). Both discrepancy and RTI approaches measure possible secondary symptoms of a learning disability rather than the cognitive impairments that underlie SLD (Callinan et al., 2013). Findings from both the neuroimaging and neuropsychological fields indicate that students with SLD often have deficient performance on measures of working memory, processing speed, auditory processing ability, and executive functions; thus, evaluation of these abilities is necessary to determine the most appropriate program (Semrud-Clikeman, 2005). Although these patterns are but one piece of a complex puzzle, they are essential for making an accurate diagnosis and determining the necessary accommodations and interventions.

A PSW approach involves three steps: 1) identifying processing strengths and weaknesses, 2) determining if areas of cognitive weakness have a research-based link to academic performance, and 3) analyzing the results to see if the pattern is consistent with a profile of SLD (Fiorello, Flanagan, & Hale, 2014; Schultz, Simpson, & Lynch, 2012). The PSW approach is tantamount not to merely listing an individual's unique strengths and weaknesses to determine the existence of an SLD but rather to determining whether or not the particular PSW is consistent with the suspected SLD. This may include a child with suspected dyslexia who has weaknesses in orthographic processing but strengths in listening comprehension and reasoning or a child with a suspected specific mathematics disability who has weaknesses in nonverbal reasoning or working memory but a strength in oral language.

Often, a student's strengths can be used to justify the selection of accommodations. For example, a student with advanced oral language abilities but relatively poor reading and writing skills would benefit from oral examinations as well as the use of assistive technology. In addition, identification of an individual's overall pattern of cognitive strengths and weaknesses can increase self-understanding and can be, in itself, therapeutic (Suhr, 2008). The ultimate goal of a PSW approach is to document a student's pattern of strengths and weaknesses so as to provide better services and more targeted interventions (Hooper, 1996; NJCLD, 2011; Norton & Wolf, 2012). The diagnosis of SLD using a PSW approach results in the identification of the specific subtype of SLD and can have implications for both instruction and prognosis. The best method for identifying students with SLD is to assess cognitive processing, as impairments in cognitive processing may lead to eventual achievement difficulties (Callinan et al., 2013). This type of approach also includes consideration of history, past interventions, and exclusionary factors (Fiorello et al., 2014).

Specific Learning Disabilities and the Processing Blocks

Many children and adults with SLD in reading and/or mathematics do have identifiable cognitive difficulties (Swanson, 2013). Ironically, in an era when educational practitioners are encouraged to use evidence-based instructional practices, they are not always encouraged to use evidence-based differential diagnoses of SLD (Berninger & May, 2011). However, the inclusion of RTI data with comprehensive cognitive assessment, addressing both processing strengths and weaknesses, would ground the identification process in a strong evidence base and ensure that any student classified as SLD meets IDEA 2004 statutory and regulatory requirements (Lindstrom & Sayeski, 2013). Although concerns have also been raised about how to operationalize a PSW approach (e.g., Miciak, Fletcher, Steubing, Vaughn, & Tolar, 2014), the concept of this approach is most in line with the understanding of a pattern of strengths and weaknesses in the Building Blocks model.

THE PROCESSING BLOCKS

The Building Blocks model provides a framework for thinking about and understanding a child's intraindividual strengths and weaknesses in performance, which is the essential consideration in determining whether or not an individual has a specific learning disability. As described in Chapter 2, the abilities in the Processing blocks help children to acquire, produce, recall, and retrieve information. For example, three areas of impairment that could be highlighted as marker variables for SLD are 1) phonological processing, 2) rapid automatized naming, and 3) verbal working memory (Callinan, Cunningham, & Theiler, 2013; Swanson, 2013). These cognitive abilities help children to master many of the symbolic aspects of language (i.e., word identification, spelling, calculating, and handwriting). Skill in recognizing processing problems in these areas can help educators identify a student's specific problems and then select and implement appropriate accommodations and effective interventions.

This part of the chapter provides a review of the difficulties that children experience when they have weaknesses in the Phonological, Orthographic, Memory, Motor, and/or Efficiency/Automaticity Processing blocks as well as several informal assessments and interventions that can be used. The major focus of the chapter is on word identification abilities because dyslexia, typified by poor decoding ability, is the most common learning disability affecting children (Shaywitz, 2003; Shaywitz & Shaywitz, 2003).

PHONOLOGICAL PROCESSING BLOCK

Phonological processing ability—in particular, phonological awareness and its relationship to the acquisition of reading skills (Mesmer & Griffith, 2005)—has been a major focus of reading research for decades (Chard & Dickson, 1999). As students learn an alphabetically encoded language such as English, a critical first step is becoming aware that speech can be divided or sequenced into a series of discrete sounds, words, syllables, and phonemes. Impairments in phonological skills and their metacognitive components are among the most frequently cited impairments in individuals with reading-related disabilities (Felton, 1993; Perfetti, 1992; Torgesen, 2005; Wagner & Torgesen, 1987).

Phonological Processing Block Questionnaire

Preschool was the first time that Maria's mother noted her difficulties with sounds. Maria would talk about the "aminals" and her favorite food, "psaghetti." Although confusions in articulation were resolved by the end of first grade, difficulties with reading and spelling persisted. In sixth grade, when she was reading a story about a bicycle race, Maria came to the sentence "A foul had been made." She misread the sentence as "The fool had been mad." With a puzzled expression, she asked, "A fool?" Maria monitored her reading for understanding, but she had such difficulty identifying words accurately that her comprehension was affected.

Because he was knowledgeable about Maria's reading and writing skills, Mr. Arnold, Maria's sixth-grade teacher, completed the Phonological Processing section of the Building Blocks Questionnaire with the help of Maria's mother, who could recall Maria's development in first and second grade. Many of the statements were marked with a check in the *Frequently* column (see Figure 8.1).

This section presents a description of terminology, provides an explanation of phonological dyslexia, describes specific instructional activities for helping students learn to perceive and manipulate sounds, and explains the relationships between speech sounds and print. Chapter 9 presents specific strategies for helping students move from an understanding of speech sounds to print as well as examples of specific strategies for helping students improve decoding and encoding abilities.

Phonological Awareness Terminology

Phonological awareness is an oral language ability that includes the ability to attend to various aspects of the phonology, or sound structure, of speech. Phonology refers to the relationships among speech sounds that form the basis for human language. Metacognitive components of this ability include the understanding that spoken language is made up of a series of sounds that are arranged in a particular order (Clark & Uhry, 1995; Ryder, Tunmer, & Greaney, 2008). English words can be divided into three main levels of analysis: 1) syllables, 2) onsets and rimes, and 3) phonemes. In the English language, syllables are formed by single vowels or vowels with combinations of consonants. The onset refers to the initial part of the syllable (i.e., one or more consonants) that precedes the vowel in a monosyllabic word, and the rime is the ending unit. In English, every syllable has a rime but not necessarily an onset. For example, in the word *open*, the first syllable /ō/ is considered to be a rime, but the second syllable /pĕn/ contains both the onset /p/ and the rime /ĕn/. Phonemes are the smallest perceptually distinct units of speech. Phonemic awareness is the ability to recognize that words are composed of discrete segments of speech sounds.

Phonological	Rarely	Sometimes	Frequently
Has trouble rhyming words	✓	☐	☐
Has difficulty producing or pronouncing certain sounds	☐	☐	✓
Has trouble putting sounds together to pronounce words (blending) when reading	☐	☐	✓
Has difficulty breaking sounds apart in words (segmenting) when spelling	☐	☐	✓
Has trouble manipulating sounds (e.g., substitution, deletion)	☐	☐	✓
Has trouble distinguishing letters with similar sounds (e.g., /b/ and /p/, /f/, and /v/) in speech and when spelling	☐	☐	✓
Has difficulty sounding out words	☐	☐	✓
Has trouble ordering sounds in a correct sequence when spelling	☐	☐	✓
Has trouble pronouncing multisyllabic words	☐	☐	✓
Confuses words that sound alike	☐	☐	✓

Figure 8.1. Building Blocks Questionnaire for Maria: Phonological Processing block.

Specific Learning Disabilities and the Processing Blocks

This awareness allows students to perceive and manipulate language sounds. The number of sounds in a word is not necessarily the same as the number of letters. For example, the word *soap* has three sounds: /s/, /ō/, /p/, whereas the word *fox* has four sounds: /f/, /ŏ/, /k/, and /s/. When children are first learning to write, they listen carefully to words and attempt to record the sounds that they hear. When Ben was in second grade, he posted the note displayed in Figure 8.2 on his bedroom door. Notice that he has attempted to capture the sounds of the letters *qu* by using *cw*.

Phonological Dyslexia

A substantial body of research supports the link between phonological processing abilities and the subsequent development of reading skill (e.g., Ehri & Roberts, 2006; Hogan, Catts, & Little, 2005; Lyon, 1995; Perfetti, 1992; Scarborough, 2009; Torgesen, 1992, 1993; Wagner & Torgesen, 1987). Phonological dyslexia refers to a problem with the acquisition of decoding or encoding skills that is caused by difficulty with manipulating and integrating the sounds of a language effectively (Heim et al., 2008; Newby, Recht, & Caldwell, 1993; Richardson, 1992; Westman, 1996). In other words, the poor phonological awareness characteristic of phonological dyslexia impairs the ability to segment, analyze, and synthesize speech sounds (Stanovich, 1982a, 1982b). These impairments make up the most common cognitive characteristics of individuals with dyslexia (Felton, 1993; Perfetti, 1992; Torgesen, 2005; Wagner & Torgesen, 1987). Students with phonologically based reading impairments perform poorly on measures of phonological awareness as well as measures involving the application of speech sounds to letters, such as reading and spelling nonsense words that conform to regular English spelling patterns (Stanovich, Siegel, & Gottardo, 1997; Torgesen, 2005).

Phonological processes are also critical to the development of encoding or spelling skills (Bailet, 1991; Caravolas, Volín, & Hulme, 2005) because spelling requires an awareness of the internal structure of words (Blachman, 1994). Phonological abilities are related significantly to spelling performance through high school (Calfee, Lindamood, & Lindamood, 1973). Even spelling problems in adults often reflect

Figure 8.2. "Be Quiet" note by Ben.

specific impairments in the phonological aspects of language (Maughan et al., 2009; Moats, 1991). For example, Bruck (1993) found that although college students with a childhood diagnosis of dyslexia attempted to preserve the phonological structure of words, their knowledge of sound–symbol associations was limited. Throughout their school careers, individuals with phonological dyslexia are often identifiable by their phonetically inaccurate misspellings (Boder, 1973; Johnson, 1995; Mather, Wendling, & Roberts, 2009).

The following list summarizes several characteristics that are symptomatic of phonological dyslexia.

Early speech/language difficulties
- Articulation errors
- Mispronunciations of multisyllabic words

Word identification (decoding)
- Trouble remembering sound–symbol relationships
- Confusion between similar sounds (e.g., /b/, /p/)
- Overreliance on whole-word and context cues
- Difficulty sequencing sounds in words
- Trouble reading multisyllabic words
- Trouble reading phonically regular nonsense words
- Difficulty applying phonics to pronounce unfamiliar words
- Slow reading rate

Spelling (encoding)
- Confusion between similar sounds (e.g., vowels, voiced and unvoiced consonant pairs)
- Difficulty sequencing sounds
- Tendency to omit some sounds
- Tendency to include a few unnecessary sounds
- Difficulty representing each syllable
- Tendency to rely on the visual appearance of words rather than on the letter–sound relationships

International Dyslexia Association Definition of Dyslexia

In April 1994, the International Dyslexia Association (IDA; formerly called the Orton Dyslexia Society) Research Committee, a group comprising investigators and representatives from advocacy groups, and the National Institute of Child Health and Human Development (NICHD) proposed a revised definition of dyslexia (Lyon, 1995). This definition states,

> Dyslexia is one of several distinct learning disabilities. It is a specific language-based disorder of constitutional origin characterized by difficulties in single word decoding, usually reflecting insufficient phonological processing abilities. These difficulties in single word decoding are often unexpected in relation to age and other cognitive and academic abilities; they are not the result of generalized developmental delay or sensory impairment. Dyslexia is manifested by variable difficulty with different forms of language, often including, in addition to problems reading, a conspicuous problem with acquiring proficiency in writing and spelling. (p. 9)

Specific Learning Disabilities and the Processing Blocks

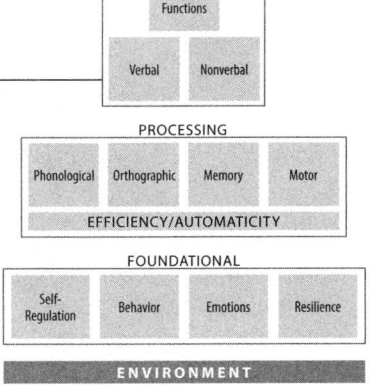

More recently, members of the working group of IDA expanded and updated this working definition (Lyon, Shaywitz, & Shaywitz, 2003). This revised definition states,

> Dyslexia is a specific learning disability that is neurobiological in origin. It is characterized by difficulties with accurate and/or fluent word recognition and by poor spelling and decoding abilities. These difficulties typically result from a deficit in the phonological component of language that is often unexpected in relation to other cognitive abilities and the provision of effective classroom instruction. Secondary consequences may include problems in reading comprehension and reduced reading experience that can impede growth of vocabulary and background knowledge. (Lyon et al., 2003, p. 2)

This definition explains that dyslexia is not a problem in reading comprehension, although it can affect the development of vocabulary and background knowledge.

Brief Historical Review

Several decades after descriptions were written about the condition called word blindness, another type of reading disability was recognized. Orton (1937), one of the pioneer investigators of the developmental language disability that characterized word deafness, noted that although children with this condition had adequate hearing, they had difficulties with recalling the auditory patterns of spoken words. Likewise, Monroe and Backus (1937) discussed the children who lacked proper discrimination of sounds. They noted that these children, who would now be described as having phonological dyslexia, exhibited some of the following characteristics in reading: errors in the vowel and consonant sounds of words, additions and omissions of sounds, confusion of words that sound alike, and poor understanding of oral directions.

In the 1970s, Bakker (1972) proposed that dyslexia may be caused by deficient word perception and verbal sequential memory. His work revived interest in phonology and helped clarify the distinction between auditory or phonological dyslexia and generalized language disorders (Vellutino, 1979). Many research studies were conducted during the early 1970s providing support for the existence of phonological dyslexia (e.g., Bannatyne, 1971; Corkin, 1974; Downing, 1973; Elkonin, 1973; Liberman, 1973). Two researchers, Downing (1973) and Elkonin (1973), simultaneously but independently explained the intrinsic relationship between reading disorders and poor phonemic awareness. Phonological skill impairments are often the underlying cause of severe word identification and spelling problems (DeFries, Olson, Pennington, & Smith, 1991; Ehri, 1994; Felton & Wood, 1989; Liberman & Shankweiler, 1985; Stanovich, 1991; Vellutino & Scanlon, 1987).

Symptoms consistent with a description of phonological dyslexia have been described in the literature for more than 85 years (e.g., Geschwind, 1982; Monroe, 1932; Orton, 1925, 1937; Vellutino, 1979). This type of dyslexia has been variously referred to as *dysphonetic* (Boder, 1973), P-type (Bakker, 1972, 1992), and *accuracy disabled* (Lovett, 1987). Although the terminology used to describe phonological dyslexia has varied, descriptions of its major characteristics have remained remarkably consistent. As Richardson (1992) observed, "Much in our medical and psycholinguistic history substantiates the proposition that developmental dyslexia is a specific developmental language disorder involving some phonological processing deficits" (p. 46).

Developmental Sequence

Efficient phonological processing abilities are needed to learn to read and spell successfully (Hogan, Catts, & Little, 2005). For most children, phonological awareness and knowledge of phoneme–grapheme correspondences develop naturally over the preschool and early elementary years, progressing from the skill of rhyming words to the ability to hear and manipulate individual sounds within words. In general, many children in preschool and most students in kindergarten are able to rhyme words. The majority of first-grade students can count syllables, delete part of a compound word, and count and blend syllables (Moats & Tolman, 2009). By second grade, most children can perform all types of tasks involving phonemic manipulations, such as deleting a sound from the front, middle, or end of a word. Anthony and Francis (2005) described the two overlapping patterns of development: 1) children increase sensitivity to smaller parts of words as they grow older; and 2) children can first detect and manipulate syllables in words, then onsets and rimes, and finally phonemes.

Most children do not start school understanding the relationships between spoken and written words and their sounds and letters. Fortunately, when young children lack grapheme–phoneme awareness, they may be taught these relationships directly prior to school entry or within the kindergarten or first-grade year. If students continue to have trouble with these tasks following direct instruction, they need to spend time with activities that help them discover these relationships. For some children, awareness of language sounds does not come naturally or easily. As a general principle, children must move from easier tasks, such as rhyming, to more complex tasks, such as blending, segmenting, and manipulating phonemes (Anthony & Francis, 2005; Ehri & Roberts, 2006). Unlike verbal short-term memory, phonological awareness skills can be taught. Similar tasks may be used for informal assessment and instruction in these skills.

Assessment and Instructional Activities

Students who are in kindergarten through second grade and older students having trouble learning to decode or encode need to develop knowledge of the sound structure of language. The purposes of assessing phonological abilities are twofold: 1) to identify students who are at risk for reading failure (Hogan et al., 2005) and 2) to monitor the progress of students who are receiving instruction (Chard & Dickson, 1999).

Student knowledge can be assessed using several types of tasks. Appendix 8A includes instructions for administration of the Phonological Awareness Skills Screener (PASS). Administration time for the PASS is approximately 15 minutes. This assessment has been extensively field tested and includes 10 measures of phonological awareness. Local norms can be developed by administering the test to 100 students at kindergarten, first-grade, and second-grade levels. Results should be expected to differ depending on whether the instrument is administered at the beginning or end of the school year. The most important information obtained from the PASS is not quantitative but a determination of what types of tasks a student can and cannot do. (Figure 8A.1 and Figure 8A.2 are also available as downloads.)

Phonological abilities can also be assessed in a less formal way. The following are some examples of tasks, presented from easiest to most difficult, that students can be asked to do to demonstrate their phonological abilities. If a student is unable to perform a task, instruction can be designed to teach that specific skill.

Rhyme recognition:

"Tell me the two words that rhyme."
1. *cat, dog, hat*
2. *tree, bee, house*

Specific Learning Disabilities and the Processing Blocks

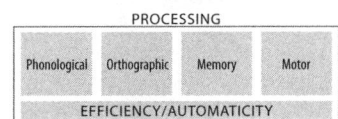
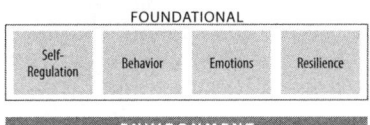

   3. *top, star, hop*
   4. *stop, man, fan*
   5. *wall, car, fall*

Rhyme production:

"Tell me all the words you can think of that rhyme with the following:"
   1. *cat*
   2. *see*
   3. *log*
   4. *shoe*
   5. *pig*

Phoneme matching:

"Tell me the word that starts with a different sound."
   1. *ball, bat, tree*
   2. *step, dog, star*
   3. *boy, clock, clown*
   4. *milk, man, shoe*
   5. *apple, car, ax*

Word counting:

"Clap or tap out the number of words you hear in each sentence."
   1. Jim runs.
   2. Pat drives a car.
   3. Bill went to school.
   4. Jane had a big lunch.
   5. Tom likes to ride his bike.

Syllable counting:

"Clap or tap out the number of syllables you hear in each word."
   1. *maybe* (2)
   2. *turtle* (2)
   3. *exercise* (3)
   4. *carpenter* (3)
   5. *basketball* (3)

Compound word deletion:

"Say the word."
   1. *cowboy* without *cow*
   2. *cupcake* without *cup*
   3. *birthday* without *birth*
   4. *rainbow* without *rain*
   5. *sunshine* without *shine*

Syllable blending:

"Tell me the word I am trying to say." [Pause for about 1 second between syllables.]
   1. tur•tle
   2. hap•py
   3. pen•cil
   4. com•pu•ter
   5. car•pen•ter

Sound blending:

"Tell me the word I am trying to say." [Make the sounds of the letters as they are usually pronounced, and pause for about 1 second between parts.]
1. c•at
2. sh•oe
3. b•ir•d
4. t•a•b•le
5. h•a•m•b•ur•g•er

Sound counting:

"How many sounds do you hear in the word?"
1. *toy* (2)
2. *girl* (3)
3. *box* (4)
4. *eight* (2)
5. *rabbit* (5)

Although the word *box* is composed of three letters, there are four separate phonemes (i.e., /b/, /ŏ/, /k/, /s/). If the student is not ready to count the number of sounds, have him or her push forward a poker chip for each sound as you pronounce the word slowly.

Phoneme deletion: Say the following:
1. *hat* without the /h/ sound
2. *ran* without the /r/ sound
3. *sold* without the /s/ sound
4. *gate* without the /g/ sound
5. *cart* without the /t/ sound

Phoneme substitution:
1. Change the /t/ in *tip* to /r/.
2. Change the /n/ in *can* to /t/.
3. Change the /ă/ in *hat* to /ĭ/.
4. Change the /s/ in *slip* to a /f/.
5. Change the /m/ in *smart* to a /t/.

Classroom activities for promoting phonological awareness are most successful when they are interactive and game-like, involving singing, rhyming, clapping, and movement. The goals of these activities are to draw students' attention to the elements of spoken speech and increase their ability to analyze speech sounds. Several carefully developed commercial programs and compilations of classroom activities are available for promoting phonological awareness (e.g., Adams, Foorman, Lundberg, & Beeler, 1998; Blachman, Ball, Black, & Tangel, 2000; see Additional Resources).

Students benefit from performing activities involving rhyming words; clapping out and counting the number of syllables in words; and pronouncing words slowly by syllables and phonemes. Activities such as reading nursery rhymes or poems or singing songs can be included in storytime. Many books are available that emphasize rhyming words, and familiar songs can be adapted to introduce letter names and their corresponding sounds.

A simple way to introduce letter sounds is to adapt a children's song for phonics instruction (Edelen-Smith, 1997).

Specific Learning Disabilities and the Processing Blocks

Ms. Janus, a kindergarten teacher, would sing the following song to the tune of "Old MacDonald Had a Farm": "What is the sound that starts these words: *book* and *box* and *bear*? What is the sound that starts these words: *book* and *box* and *bear*?" She would then pause for the children to respond and then continue, "/B/ is the sound that starts these words: *book* and *box* and *bear*. /B/ is the sound that starts these words: *book* and *box* and *bear*. With a /b/ /b/ here and a /b/ /b/ there . . ."

Segmentation and Blending

The two most important phonological awareness abilities for word reading and spelling are blending (synthesizing sounds) and segmentation (analyzing sounds; Ehri, 2006). For blending, children are presented with a series of sounds and then asked to push the sounds together to form a word. For segmentation, children are presented with a word and then asked to break the word apart into the individual sounds. Some students have trouble learning how to segment and then blend sounds. When Maria was first learning to blend, she would sound out the word, but she was not able to put it back together again. Gradually, she learned how to pronounce the word aloud, but she still had trouble with silent reading.

Both segmentation and blending can be taught using a variety of manipulatives, including plastic markers, poker chips, colored tiles, magnetic letters, and scrabble tiles. Different-colored chips can be used to represent the consonant and vowel sounds (e.g., consonant sounds are blue and vowel sounds are red). Using letters, the teacher can demonstrate how to pull the sounds of a word apart and then push the sounds back together again to form a word. Without appropriate intervention and explicit instruction in important phonological skills such as blending and segmentation, the reading development of children with poor phonological processing skills will be impeded (Lipka, Lesaux, & Siegel, 2006).

Teaching Segmentation

The following sequence may be used to assess or teach segmentation. Begin with tasks that require students to segment compound words (e.g., *raincoat*) and then progress to syllables. An easy way to help students learn to count the number of syllables is to have them place their hand under their chin and then say the word aloud. The number of syllables is equal to the number of times the chin drops. When students have learned to break words into syllables, teach them how to segment short words into onsets and rimes (e.g., c-at) and then into individual phonemes.

Blending Words

The purpose of teaching blending is to help young children combine letter sounds to be able to pronounce or decode words (Ehri, 2006). Chard and Osborn (1999a) recommended a three-step procedure for helping students like Maria learn to blend sounds together to pronounce words more easily:

1. Encourage students to blend sounds together as quickly as possible rather than stopping between the sounds.
2. Ask students to follow the sounding out of the word with a fast pronunciation of the word.
3. Have students move from sounding out words aloud to sounding out words in their heads.

Gradually, as skill progresses, word reading changes from an overt activity to a covert activity. At this stage, the teacher may need to model for students by mouthing the pronunciation of words, showing them how words can be sounded out silently.

The difficulty level of a blending task is affected by both the length of the pause between the sounds as well as the number of sounds that are presented in the sequence. A word that is sounded with a short pause between the sounds is much easier to blend than a word that is presented with a one-second interval between the sounds. Instruction then begins with words with two sounds (/sh/oe/), then three sounds (/c/a/t/), and finally four sounds (/s/a/n/d/; Kirk, Kirk, Minskoff, Mather, & Roberts, 2007). In addition, speech sounds that can be prolonged and sustained (e.g., /s/, /f/, /m/, /l/, /n/, /r/, /v/, /z/) are easier to blend than those that cannot (e.g., /b/, /t/; Carnine, Silbert, Kame'enui, & Tarver, 2010). Carnine and colleagues described a similar procedure called telescoping sounds in which a student transforms a series of blended sounds pronounced quickly in succession (/i/ /i/ /i/ /t/ /t/ /t/) into a word (*it*) said at a typical rate.

Chapter 9 describes several techniques for helping a student move from understanding individual speech sounds to pairing those sounds with printed letters. A teacher can informally assess a student's grasp of the alphabetic principle and knowledge of phoneme–grapheme relationships by analyzing his or her attempted spellings. An understanding of how specific speech sounds relate to written language development can help the teacher pinpoint specific student difficulties and select appropriate interventions. In her book *Speech to Print: Language Essentials for Teachers,* Moats (2010) provided a comprehensive guide to help teachers understand language structure and exactly how the phonological, or speech–sound processing, system relates to print. The Florida Center for Reading Research webpage (http://www.fcrr.org) also provides a video podcast for teachers on how to pronounce the sounds of standard English.

Figure 8.3 presents a writing sample from Maria's journal when she was in fifth grade. Write down all the misspelled words and then attempt to identify why Maria has spelled the words in these ways. Next, review the information in Appendix 8B and then review the spellings again.

ORTHOGRAPHIC PROCESSING BLOCK

Orthography refers to the spelling system of a language. Orthographic processing or awareness refers to the ability to form a mental image of words and specific letter sequences. This section provides a description of orthographic awareness, a review of characteristics associated with weaknesses in this ability, a brief historic account, a review of related research, and a discussion of implications for intervention.

Definition of Orthographic Awareness

Orthographic awareness is the ability to perceive and recall letters, letter strings, and words. This ability helps students to establish detailed visual or mental representations of letter strings and words and to have rapid, fluent access to these representations. Successful word identification involves the abilities to 1) identify letters in written words, word strings, or nonwords; 2) remember the position of each letter in the word; and 3) recall in sequence the letters that belong together. Vellutino, Scanlon, and Tanzman (1994) defined this process of orthographic coding as "the ability to represent the unique array of letters that defines a printed word, as well as general attributes of the writing system such as sequential dependencies,

Specific Learning Disabilities and the Processing Blocks

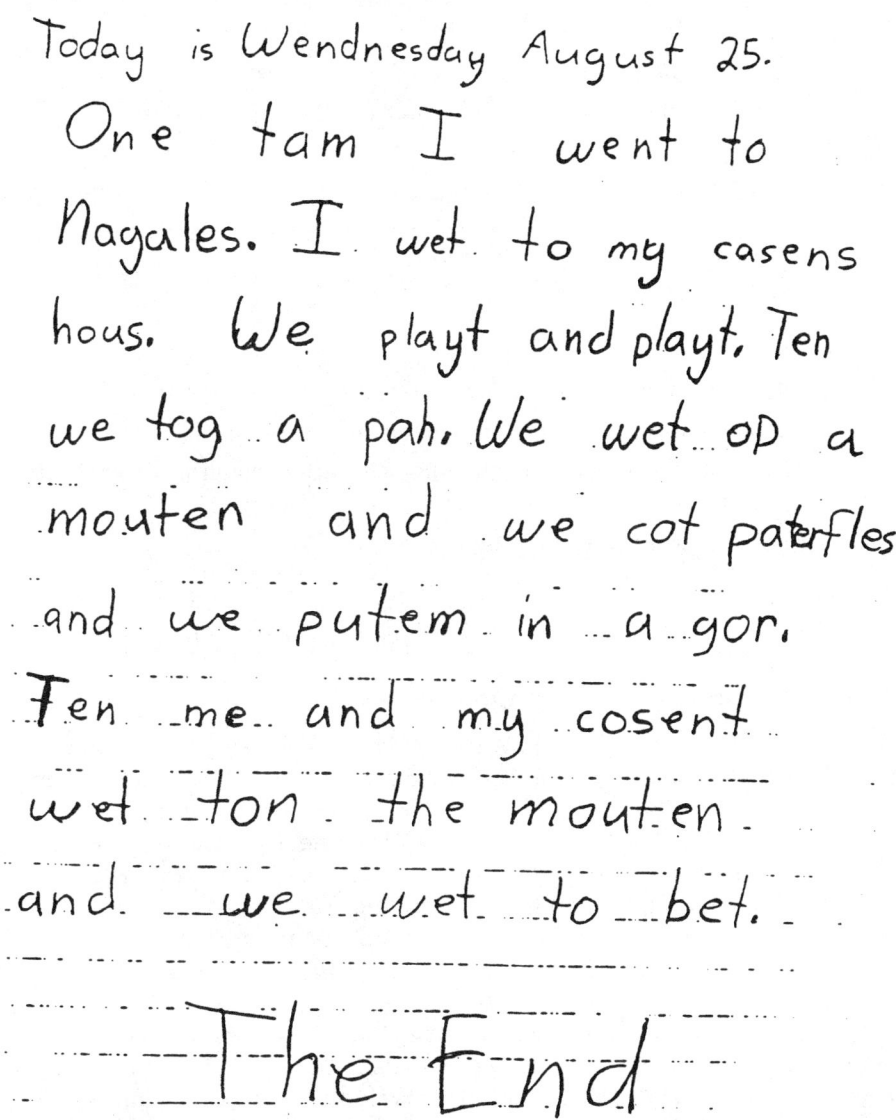

Figure 8.3. Writing sample from Maria's journal.

structural redundancies, and letter position frequencies" (p. 314). This knowledge refers specifically to print (Corcos & Willows, 1993). The term *orthographic dyslexia* is used to describe students whose reading and spelling problems are characterized by poor memory of letterforms and letter strings (Mather et al., 2009).

The following list, adapted from Mather et al. (2009) and Willows and Terepocki (1993), summarizes several characteristics of individuals with orthographic dyslexia.

Symbol recognition and recall difficulties
- Difficulty learning how to form symbols
- Confusion of symbols similar in appearance (e.g., *b* and *d*, *n* and *u*, *2* and *5*)
- Trouble with near-point and far-point copying tasks
- Tendency to reverse letters or numbers past the age of 7

Word identification (decoding)
- Trouble with accurate and rapid word recognition
- Trouble reading exception or irregular words
- Trouble remembering how words look
- Trouble remembering letter sequences
- Overreliance on phonological and contextual strategies as aids in word identification
- Slow reading speed

Spelling (encoding)
- Tendency to reverse and transpose letters (e.g., *grils* for *girls*)
- Tendency to use different spellings for the same word (e.g., *Pual* and *Paul*)
- Tendency to overrely on the phonological rather than the visual features of words
- Tendency to omit word endings

Calculating
- Tendency to reverse or transpose digits (e.g., *12* for *21*)

Characteristics of Poor Orthographic Awareness

Students with poor orthographic awareness often have symbol recognition and recall difficulties from a young age and make errors in letter or number formation. For example, by the time Ben had finished kindergarten, he recognized only two letters of the alphabet: the letters *b* and *n* in his name. As Ben progressed through school, he continued to struggle. At the age of 7, he made frequent errors in letter and number orientation. He had trouble copying from both textbooks and chalkboards because of his difficulty maintaining and sustaining a mental image of letter strings. As his eyes moved from one surface to another, he would lose his place. These difficulties followed Ben into adulthood.

With regard to reading performance, Ben was slow to recognize high-frequency words, exception words (e.g., words with irregular spelling patterns), and syllable units. Because he tended to overrely on phonics and contextual strategies to compensate, he frequently confused similar-looking letters or words and sometimes had more difficulty recognizing short, common words, such as *were*, *how*, and *said*, than longer, more meaningful words, such as *dinosaur* or *elevator*. Ben lost his place easily when reading and needed to use his finger to track lines of print. Even after he was taught to decode, Ben demonstrated a compromised, slow reading rate and tended to confuse words with similar appearance (e.g., *feather* and *father*).

Spelling causes students like Ben the most difficulty because successful performance depends on recall of letter–sound sequences and patterns. In eighth grade, after Ben had read *Tom Sawyer*, he spelled the name *Becky* six different ways in the first draft of his book report (*Becy, Beacey, Becky, Beacky, Beke, Beckey*). These inconsistencies, coupled with his misspellings of simple high-frequency words such as *they*, *was*, and *were*, illustrated that Ben did not recall spellings easily. In addition, when Ben attempted to spell a word, the spellings were reasonable in terms of the sequence of sounds but impossible in terms of English regularities and spelling rules (e.g., *egz* for *eggs*). On one paper, Ben spelled the word *exact* as *egzakt*. In most

Specific Learning Disabilities and the Processing Blocks

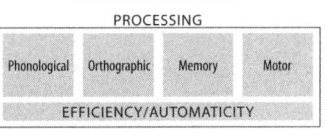
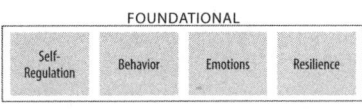

instances, the obvious symptom of this problem in later years is spelling that is phonetically accurate but violates the rules of English spelling.

Some students with poor orthographic awareness do not have problems learning to read but do experience problems in learning to spell. In a synthesis of Samuel Orton's work, June Orton (1966) explained that for these students, visual memory of words is sufficient enough to recognize the printed word in reading but not strong enough to recall the image of the word to reconstruct it for spelling. In other words, for reading, one has to identify the word; for spelling, one has to produce the entire pattern.

These types of symbolic confusions can also affect performance in computation, and students with orthographic dyslexia often have trouble memorizing math facts. One day, as Ben was attempting to solve some multiplication problems, he remarked, "Ugh, multiplication—this feels just like spelling. What is this doing to me?" Even in fifth grade, Ben still reversed the number 5 and transposed numbers when working at his desk or when copying a problem from the board. By the time Ben had copied the problems from the board, he was so far behind that the teacher had already transitioned to a new topic.

Students like Ben are likely to work slowly and lose their place often. They may confuse operation symbols (e.g., addition and multiplication signs), have trouble retaining basic facts, and reverse or transpose digits. As they progress in school, they may have difficulty learning multistep computations, such as the sequence of steps required in long division, and filling out tests with bubble or Scantron sheets.

Orthographic Processing Block Questionnaire

As Ben's eighth-grade English teacher, Ms. Roberts, was knowledgeable about Ben's reading and writing skills, she completed the Orthographic Processing block items on the Building Blocks Questionnaire (see Figure 8.4). If this checklist had been completed for Ben in first or second grade, all the statements would have received a check in the *Frequently* column.

Figure 8.5 presents an excerpt from a story Ben was creating for Ms. Roberts's English class. Notice the different spellings of the word *people,* the transpositions (e.g., *tow bays* for *two days*), and the reliance on sounds for spelling rather than on the visual appearance of the word (e.g., *howssis* for *houses*). Ben's weakness in forming and recalling visual images needed for accurate word pronunciation and spelling is apparent. He seems to lack sensitivity to orthographic redundancies or common English spelling patterns. Despite repeated exposures to words, mental images of common words are only partially retained. As students such as Ben progress through school, limited retention of letter strings and spelling patterns usually has a pronounced effect on the students' word identification and spelling development. These orthographic processing skills predict differences in word recognition independent of phonological factors (Cunningham & Stanovich, 1998).

Brief Historical Review of Orthographic Dyslexia

Although the characteristics described tend to vary slightly, early case studies of visually based reading problems, now termed orthographic dyslexia, are described in several sources (e.g., Fernald, 1943; Hinshelwood, 1917; Morgan, 1896; Orton, 1925, 1937). Names to describe the common symptoms of orthographic dyslexia include *word blindness* (Hinshelwood, 1902; Orton, 1925), *visual dyslexia* (Johnson & Myklebust, 1971), *dyseidetic dyslexia* (Boder, 1973), *L-type dyslexia* (Bakker, 1980,

PROCESSING

Orthographic	Rarely	Sometimes	Frequently
Forgets how letters look	✓		
Confuses letters with similar appearance (e.g., *n* for *h*)			✓
Misreads little words in text (e.g., *were* for *where*)			✓
Reverses letters when spelling (e.g., *b* instead of *d*)		✓	
Transposes letters when reading or writing (e.g., *on* instead of *no*)		✓	
Has trouble remembering irregular words for reading and spelling		✓	
Has difficulty copying from a book or board to paper			✓
Spells the same word in different ways			✓
Spells words the way they sound rather than the way they look			✓
Reads at a slow rate			✓

Figure 8.4. Building Blocks Questionnaire for Ben: Orthographic Processing block.

1992), *rate-disabled dyslexia* (Lovett, 1987), *visual-perceptual impairment* (Lyon & Watson, 1981), *visual-spatial impairment* (Morris, Blashfield, & Satz, 1986), *surface dyslexia* (Castles & Coltheart, 1993; Marshall & Newcombe, 1978), and *logographic dyslexia* (Seymour & Evans, 1999).

Discussion of orthographic dyslexia can be traced back to the late 1800s. In 1872, Sir William Broadbent described cortical damage present in an autopsy of an individual who had had reading disabilities (Critchley, 1964; Richardson, 1992). Five years later, Kussmaul (1877b) noted that "a complete text blindness may exist although the power of sight, the intellect, and the powers of speech are intact" (p. 595). In other words, the problem does not affect the development of abilities within the Conceptual blocks. In 1887, Berlin used the term *dyslexia* to describe a condition acquired through cerebral disease (cited in Richardson, 1992). It appears that the term *word blindness* was first applied to individuals with aphasia who had lost the ability to read (Kussmaul, 1877a). In 1896, Morgan described a reading difficulty that he referred to as congenital word blindness. In 1895, Hinshelwood, a surgeon at the Glasgow Eye Infirmary, wrote an article that described acquired word blindness. The following year, two accounts of congenital word blindness were published.

The first account was written by James Kerr, a health officer, who described a boy of average or above-average intelligence who suffered from word blindness despite being able to identify the letters in words (cited in Critchley, 1964). The second article, written by Morgan, described the characteristics of an intelligent 14-year-old boy who excelled in arithmetic but could not read:

> His greatest difficulty has been—and is now—his inability to learn to read. This inability is so remarkable, and so pronounced, that I have no doubt it is due to some congenital defect.... The following is the result of an examination I made a short time since. He knows all his letters and can write them and read them. In writing from dictation, he comes to grief over any but the simplest words. For instance, I dictated the following sentence: "Now, you watch me while I spin it." He wrote, "Now you word me wale I spin it" and again, "Carefully winding the string round the peg" was written "culfuly winder the sturng rond the pag." In writing his own name, he made a mistake, putting "Precy" for "Percy," and he did not notice the mistake until his attention was called to it more than once.... I then asked him to read me a sentence out of an easy child's book without spelling the words. The result was curious. He did not read a single

Specific Learning Disabilities and the Processing Blocks

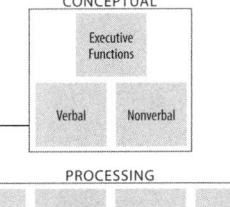

> thay had a scledbashins for too thay that was the murder tow bays later a nother merder acherd. pepe were so skard that thay cent of own pepol wer fed op pepol we starting to think ther was a gost in the town. nothing like this has haping cant so mouth hapin to an smoll comudity werz efry one nose evry one for one holl whek every thieg was flneintell a nother merder ocurd pepoll started to Loke there howssls up wach thay have never done befor

Figure 8.5. Excerpt from a story by Ben.

word correctly, with the exception of "and," "the," "of," "that," etc.; the other words seemed to be quite unknown to him, and he could not even make an attempt to pronounce them.... He seems to have no power of preserving and storing up the visual impression produced by words—hence the words, though seen, have no significance for him. His visual memory for words is defective or absent, which is equivalent to saying that he is what Kussmaul has termed "word blind." I may add that the boy is bright and of average intelligence in conversation . . . his eyesight is good. The schoolmaster who has taught him for some years says that he would be the smartest lad in the school if the instruction were entirely oral. (1896, p. 94)

In 1902, Hinshelwood described in detail two cases of congenital word blindness in which the reading problem was attributed to a defect in the visual memory of letters and words. He reached the following conclusions, which remain pertinent today: 1) Particular areas of the brain appear to be involved; 2) the children often have average or above-average intelligence and good memory in other respects; 3) the problem with reading is localized, not generalized to all areas of performance; 4) the children do not learn to read with the same rapidity as other children; 5) the earlier the problem is identified, the better, so as not to waste valuable time; 6) the children must be taught by special methods adapted to help them overcome their difficulties; 7) the sense of touch can help children retain visual impressions;

and 8) persistent and persevering attempts will often help children improve their reading. He further noted that the diagnosis itself is easy to make because the features of the disorder are so distinct and easily understood. More than a century later, Shaywitz reiterated that "the diagnosis of dyslexia is as precise and scientifically informed as almost any diagnosis in medicine" (2003, p. 165).

In 1917, Hinshelwood reviewed the articles by Kerr and Morgan in his seminal monograph titled *Congenital Word-Blindness*. Within this monograph, Hinshelwood attempted to clarify the distinction between word blindness and more generalized developmental delays:

> When I see it stated that congenital word-blindness may be combined with any amount of other mental defects from mere dullness to low-grade mental defects, imbecility, or idiocy, I can understand how confusion has arisen from the loose application of the term *congenital word-blindness* to all conditions in which there is defective development of the visual memory center, quite independently of any consideration as to whether it is a strict local defect or only a symptom of a general cerebral degeneration. It is a great injustice to the children affected with the pure type of congenital word-blindness, a strict local affection [sic], to be placed in the same category as others suffering from generalized cerebral defects, as the former can be successfully dealt with, while the latter are practically irremediable. (pp. 93–94)

The first report on word blindness to appear in the American medical literature was written by Samuel Orton (1925). Orton agreed with Hinshelwood that word blindness 1) was not related to intellectual disability, 2) ranged from mild to severe, and 3) was caused by physiological impairments in the brain. One specific characteristic that Orton observed in the children he studied was the instability and poor recall of both the orientation and order of letters. He identified this intrinsic disability as strephosymbolia, which literally means "twisted symbols" (S.T. Orton, 1925, 1937; J. Orton, 1966). Monroe and Backus (1937) also noted that children with visual defects affecting reading tended to show the following characteristics: 1) excessive reversals, 2) line and word skipping, 3) slow reading rate, 4) errors on words with similar spelling configurations (e.g., *bread* and *beard*), and 5) complaints of eyestrain when reading.

Research on Orthographic Dyslexia

The central difficulties associated with orthographic dyslexia are problems with sight word retention, reading and spelling irregular letter strings, and rapid word identification. A common characteristic of individuals with orthographic dyslexia is that they have difficulty storing mental representations of irregular words (Boder, 1973; Newby et al., 1993; Siegel, 2007; Thomson, Richardson, & Goswami, 2005; Westman, 1996; Willows, Kruk, & Corcos, 1993). As a result, their performance reading exception words (i.e., words with irregular spelling patterns, such as *yacht*) is typically lower than their performance reading phonically regular nonsense words (e.g., *pab*).

Despite sufficient phonological awareness, students with orthographic dyslexia typically have difficulty with tasks that involve the application of phonological skills, such as pronouncing phonically regular nonsense words. This is because a task like the reading of nonsense words involves both phonological abilities (i.e., application of speech sounds to print) and orthographic abilities (i.e., rapid recognition of the common letter patterns).

When Ben was in fourth grade, he scored in the superior range on several tasks measuring phonological awareness, such as the ability to blend and segment sounds. On a test of nonword reading, however, Ben scored in the low average range. Presumably, in Ben's case, his difficulties with reading nonwords stemmed from poor

Specific Learning Disabilities and the Processing Blocks

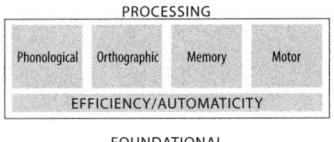
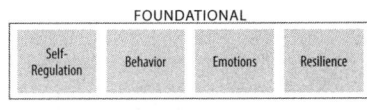

recall of orthographic representations or spelling–sound (grapheme–phoneme) correspondences rather than poor phonological awareness. In other words, a failure to internalize grapheme–phoneme correspondences affects learning to read and spell all types of letter strings, but exception words are the most difficult and vulnerable (Manis, Seidenberg, Doi, McBride-Chang, & Petersen, 1996).

Manis and colleagues (1996) suggested that phonological and orthographic subtypes may be differentiated by comparing performance on tasks that involve orthographic abilities (e.g., identifying the correct spelling of a word from several possible phonically regular spellings, such as *rain* or *rane*) with tasks that involve phonological skills (e.g., reading or spelling phonically regular nonsense words). Students with orthographic dyslexia will have low levels of orthographic knowledge relative to their phonological skill, whereas students with phonological dyslexia will be more impaired in phonological skills.

In addition, one has to consider reading development in the context of a specific language (e.g., Spanish has more regular grapheme–phoneme correspondence than English). Children learning more consistent orthographies (e.g., Finnish or Spanish) learn to read more quickly than those learning to read and spell less consistent orthographies (e.g., English or French). It appears that basic processes of phonological development may be universal across alphabetic languages, whereas the relative phoneme–grapheme relationships are language specific (i.e., languages may use different symbols to represent the same sound). Furthermore, orthographic depth (i.e., the consistency of phoneme–grapheme relationships across words in a language) varies from language to language, making some languages easier to read and spell than others (Goswami, 2006). These differences in orthographies should be considered when helping ELLs. In addition, the nature of orthography of the native language will influence how children attempt to spell the English words that they are learning (Joshi, Hoien, Feng, Chengappa, & Boulware-Gooden, 2006).

Table 8.2 presents two lists of words that can be used for an informal assessment. The first list consists of phonically regular nonwords that are spelled as if they were real English words. The second list contains examples of exception words that have irregular elements. Students may read or attempt to spell these words. Analysis of performance on these two tasks may provide some insight into the factors contributing to a student's reading or spelling difficulties.

Students who have trouble reading exception words will also have trouble spelling the irregular parts of words. Review the sample of Ben's writing presented in Figure 8.5. Notice that even simple high-frequency words such as *they* are misspelled. Although there are a few misspellings indicative of phonological confusions (e.g., *evry* and *efry* for *every*), clearly his difficulties with spelling are more attributed to the poor recall of letter strings than to weaknesses in phonology.

Misspellings by students with this difficulty often have good phonemic resemblance to the target words (Freebody & Byrne, 1988; Johnson, 1995; Westman, 1996; Willows et al., 1993). Freebody and Byrne suggested that the existence of phonetically accurate spellings in these individuals confirms that their literacy development is hindered by something other than poor phonological processing.

This type of problem persists into adulthood. Figure 8.6 depicts several sample spellings (*shout, correct, believe, suggestion, equipment, literature, precious, executive, physician*) by Ryan when he was a senior in high school. Note that Ryan was able to sequence sounds correctly but produced improbable spelling patterns and still had not mastered common English spelling patterns, such as the *-tion* in the word *suggestion*. He also had not mastered basic English spelling rules, such as knowing that English words do not end with the letter *v*.

Table 8.2. List of regular nonwords and exception words

Regular nonwords	Exception words
barches	once
tranning	sure
straking	who
quib	laugh
smuff	island
meck	comb
widge	does
crusp	echo
gruzz	machine
bungic	tough

To quickly determine whether a student forms orthographic images with ease, show him or her a novel word and then cover it up and ask him or her to write the word from memory. When Ben was in fourth grade, Mr. Steen wrote the word *game* at the top of a page. He instructed Ben to look at the word and then covered the word and asked Ben to write it without looking. Ben's attempts are presented in Figure 8.7. On the sixth trial, Ben finally wrote the word correctly.

A popular oversimplification of orthographic dyslexia is that it causes people to see images or words backward (Richardson & DiBenedetto, 1996). It is not this simple. In extreme cases, however, students with this type of difficulty do reverse many letters and sometimes even produce mirror writing. Figure 8.8 depicts the spelling test of a third-grade girl, Sara. Notice that even though many of her letters are reversed, several of the words are spelled accurately. She had practiced the words orally with her father the prior evening.

This type of mirror writing can even persist into adulthood. Figure 8.9 presents a brief sample from Esther, a young woman enrolled in a university program for students with SLD. She produced this text by writing with both hands simultaneously. Although she has learned how to write conventionally, she reports that it takes her twice as long to write if she has to proceed from left to right. When she takes notes in classes, she often writes them from right to left.

Goulandris and Snowling (1991) described an undergraduate student with developmental dyslexia. Although her earlier reading difficulties were resolved by this time and her phonological reading strategies were within the normal range, she experienced serious difficulties with spelling. Her difficulties were most pronounced when she was asked to spell irregular words and homophones, words with the same sound but different spellings (e.g., *blue* and *blew*). Goulandris and Snowling suggested that this young woman's difficulties appeared to be related to a problem with constructing detailed orthographic representations of words for spelling. This failure to establish images may contribute to a compromised reading rate as well. As observed by Reitsma, "The ability to store the orthographic form of words in memory may be fundamental to attaining fluency in reading" (1989, p. 65).

Implications for Intervention

Unlike phonological awareness, little is known about how to improve the abilities related to orthographic coding. For students with weaknesses in the recall of

Specific Learning Disabilities and the Processing Blocks

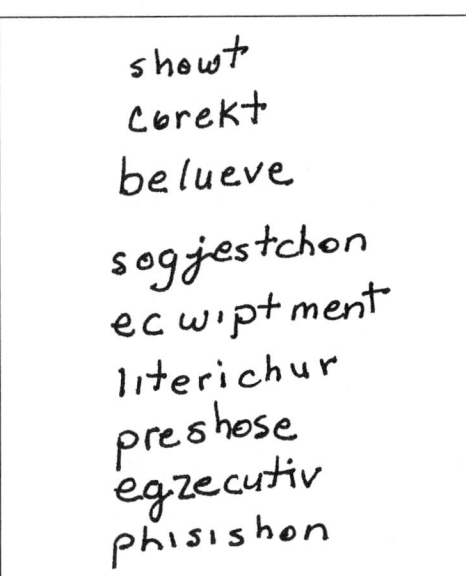

Figure 8.6. Ryan's spellings.

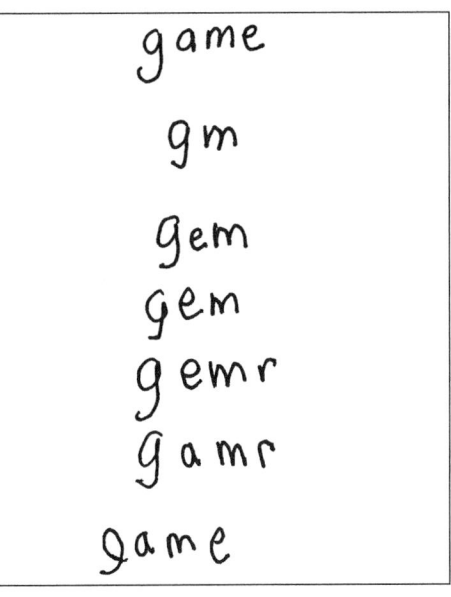

Figure 8.7. Ben's spelling of *game*.

symbols, multisensory procedures seem most promising. Multisensory procedures can be used to teach word identification, spelling, and math facts and enhance memory (e.g., Birsh, 2005). Tracing activities, for example, appear to 1) provide a memory trace that improves retention of letters, words, and numbers; 2) improve visual discrimination; 3) direct attention to word learning; 4) increase visual memory of words; and 5) help develop associations between spoken and written words (Hulme, 1981).

As an example, training in the spelling of irregular words has been found to improve the quality of stored orthographic representations (Brunsdon, Coltheart, & Nickels, 2005). In this procedure, irregular words were written on flashcards with the correct spelling. The word was read aloud, and the student was asked to copy the word. The word was then removed from view, and the student was asked to write the word after a 10-second delay. If incorrect, the student was shown the flashcard again for 5 seconds and then asked again to write the word from memory. If the response was correct, he was then asked to write the word from dictation. This procedure resulted in increased reliance on orthography for spelling as opposed to an overreliance on phoneme-to-grapheme conversions. These and other multisensory approaches to learning the spellings of irregular words are discussed more thoroughly in Chapter 9. Instructional techniques directed toward building rate and fluency within specific academic domains (e.g., reading fluency methods, timed writings, math fact flashcards) can also help students who have difficulty recalling symbols.

Students who experience difficulty with learning to read often have slow reading rates into adulthood. Chapter 9 reviews specific techniques for assessing and improving reading speed. In first and second grade, Ryan, Maria, and Ben all had difficulty learning to pronounce words because of weaknesses within the Processing blocks. Although Maria's problems were related to phonology, Ben's difficulties were related to orthography, and Ryan had weaknesses in both areas, they all had trouble reading rapidly and using reading to learn. Unfortunately, a weakness in the Processing blocks can go on to affect performance in the Conceptual blocks unless certain accommodations, such as listening to recorded books, are made.

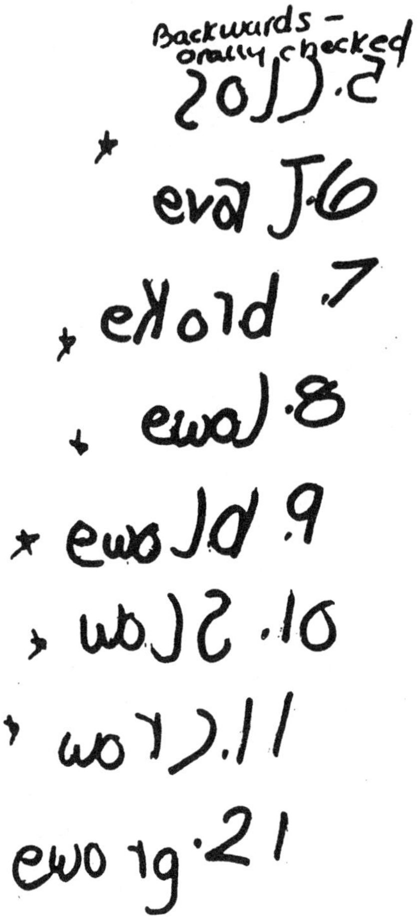

Figure 8.8. Items from Sara's spelling test with a teacher's note.

MEMORY BLOCK

The Memory block includes various types of memory processes: short-term memory, working memory, and attentional control. Short-term memory, sometimes called memory span, refers to the ability to hold information in mind and then reproduce it in the same manner in which it was represented. For example, repeating a string of numbers, such as a telephone number, is an example of a short-term memory task. In contrast, working memory involves both the capacity to hold information in the mind and the ability to manipulate or transform that information, thus increasing the demands of controlled attention. An example would be asking a person to listen to a series of letters and then repeat the letters in a reversed order. More contextual examples of working memory include the type of mental juggling involved when one is asked to solve a long division problem or a multistep math word problem. Students with reading disabilities often have impairments in both short-term memory and working memory; consequently, they have trouble accessing speech-based information and monitoring attentional processes (Swanson et al., 2009). Students with weaknesses in working memory can have difficulties that extend into both reading and mathematics (Gathercole & Holmes, 2014).

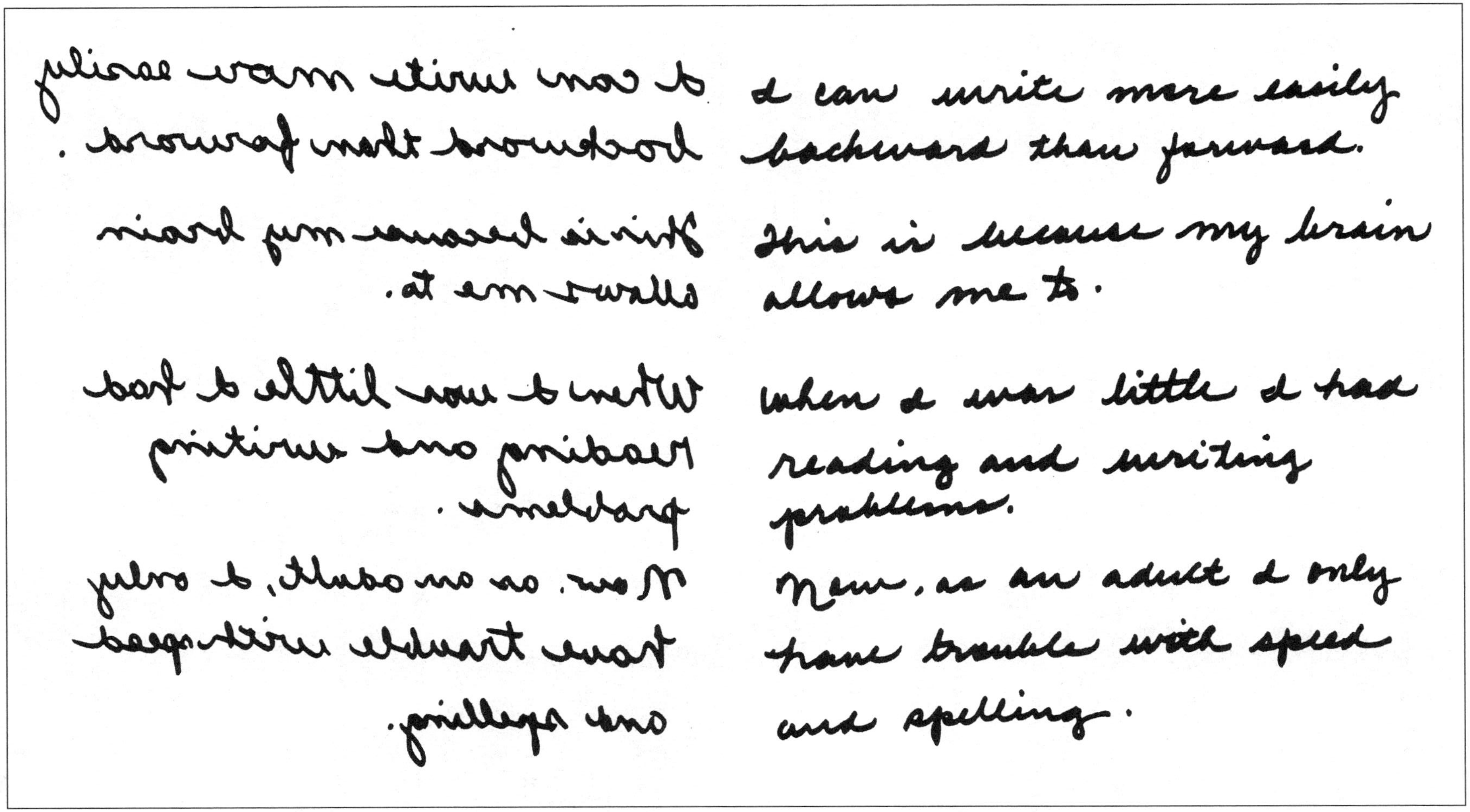

Figure 8.9. Esther's backward and forward writing.

Short-Term Memory

Short-term memory involves the ability to hold information in mind and at the ready for brief periods of time. Unlike long-term memory, whose capacity is theoretically limitless, short-term memory appears to have a considerably limited capacity (Ericsson & Kintsch, 1995), usually in the range of five to nine chunks or elements of information. Weakness in memory span—in particular, verbal short-term memory—is one of the most frequently reported cognitive characteristics of individuals with reading disabilities (Morris et al., 1998; Swanson, Zheng, & Jerman, 2009; Thomson et al., 2005; Torgesen & Burgess, 1998). Verbal short-term memory involves the ability to hold verbal information in mind for brief periods of time and reproduce it exactly as presented. Tasks that assess performance in this area, such as repeating a series of digits in sequence or saying the months in order, require processing the phonological features of language. Students with poor verbal short-term memory may struggle to follow directions, memorize math facts or counting patterns, or keep pace with oral directions in the classroom.

Working Memory

Although sometimes considered to include short-term memory, working memory is more complex, as it taps into abilities that are found in other blocks, including self-regulation and executive functions. Working memory involves the capacity to hold information in mind and simultaneously manipulate or transform that information in some meaningful way. The term *working memory* was in use as early as 1960 (Baddeley, 2003; Cowan, 2014), having derived from models of cognition in which the brain was compared with a computer, with several related, but distinct, memory systems. Among these were long-term memory, in which information was stored; short-term memory, in which information was briefly held in mind; and working memory, sometimes described as a subset of short-term memory (Baddeley, 2000), in which information was both briefly held in mind and manipulated. In 1974, Baddeley and Hitch proposed a multifaceted model of working memory, in which several brain systems worked together to maintain attention to salient information, hold that information in mind, and direct cognitive processes to the manipulation of that information. The most recent revision of the model includes a central executive, whose role is to supervise and direct working memory processes and control three major subordinate systems: the phonological loop, which, in coordination with two main subsystems, holds and continually rehearses auditory and phonological information; the visuo-spatial scratchpad, which, also in coordination with two major subsystems, holds and manipulates visual and spatial information; and the episodic buffer, which holds and integrates both visual and spatial information (Baddeley, 2000).

By contrast, Cowan (2014) described a less compartmentalized model of working memory, in which working memory processes are the product of incoming sensory memory, the activation of representations stored in long-term memory, and the focus of attention directed toward the most relevant of those representations. Likewise, Ericsson and Kintsch (1995) argued that long-term memory played an important role in the synthesis and manipulation of newly acquired information. According to Ericsson and Kintsch (1995), only a small amount of conceptual information is stored in short-term working memory. That conceptual information, however, activates retrieval structures, which, in turn, draw upon relevant

Specific Learning Disabilities and the Processing Blocks

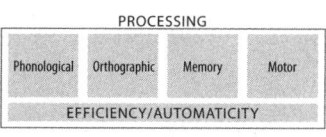
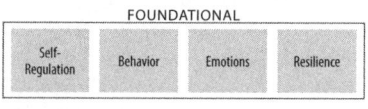

representations in long-term working memory, allowing the individual to synthesize and manipulate large amounts of information (Ericsson & Kintsch, 1995).

Poor working memory is a common problem for both children and adults with SLD (Swanson et al., 2009). In a meta-analysis of the results of 43 studies conducted between 1963 and 2006, Swanson and colleagues (2009) found that children with reading disabilities performed poorly on tests of working memory, including nonword repetition, letter recall, number recall, and word string recall. Likewise, in a summary of the working memory difficulties typical of children and adults with learning disabilities, Swanson and Zheng (2013) concluded that weaknesses in working memory can affect performance on lower order tasks, such as simple arithmetic computation, as well as on higher order cognitively demanding processes, such as reading comprehension, written expression, and math problem solving. Although it appears that working memory performance can be improved through training, few studies have shown that this training directly affects performance on academic measures (Gathercole & Holmes, 2014; Swanson & Zheng, 2013). Gathercole and Holmes suggest that the best way to help students with working memory problems is to provide intensive training, practice using mnemonic strategies, and modulate the classroom environment to avoid an overload on working memory.

Students with weaknesses in short-term and working memory often also have difficulty following lengthy discussions or directions and thus require specific classroom accommodations and compensations as they progress through school. Some students have weaknesses in both short-term memory and phonological awareness. Others, like Maria, only have difficulty with the phonological aspects of language. Although specific strategies and accommodations can be used to enhance memory performance, memory is a capacity that is more innate and difficult to alter. Examples of common classroom accommodations are provided in the "Classroom Accommodations" section.

 Memory Block Questionnaire

Mr. Steen, Ryan's fourth-grade teacher, was knowledgeable about Ryan's academic skills and completed the Memory Processing block items on the Building Blocks Questionnaire (see Figure 8.10). Mr. Steen felt that Ryan was sometimes confused by multistep problems and would forget previously learned materials. Ryan's problems appeared to be primarily related to memorizing information, such as number sequences and math facts, as well as difficulty repeating information, following directions, and retaining information that he had studied for tests.

MOTOR BLOCK

Andy's second-grade teacher, Ms. Abram, expressed her concerns about Andy's handwriting to the special education teacher. She described his writing in this way:

> His letters are big and different sizes. Even when copying from the board or a paper right next to him, I cannot always figure out the letters. His letters are often reversed and they are never on the line. The letters tend to drift off above and to the right of the first letter of the words so that the words seem to float on the page. In fact, his papers tend to resemble a bowl of alphabet soup.

Andy had the poorest fine motor skills of any child she had ever taught. Even though Andy wrote daily, his handwriting did not seem to be improving. During school, he often sat at his desk with his arms wrapped around his paper so that no one could see his writing. In fact, Andy's handwriting difficulties were beginning to affect the Foundational blocks of Behavior, Emotions, and Resilience. Ms. Abram placed comments on his papers, such as "Work carefully, please" or "Please form letters neatly," but this feedback did not seem to help. His most recent paper was returned with the comment

PROCESSING

Memory	Rarely	Sometimes	Frequently
Has trouble following multistep directions	☐	☐	☑
Has trouble learning the days of the week and months of the year in sequence	☐	☐	☑
Has trouble repeating sentences accurately	☐	☐	☑
Has trouble skip counting in math (e.g., 2, 4, 6 . . .)	☐	☐	☑
Gets confused when solving multistep problems	☐	☑	☐
Has trouble memorizing math facts	☐	☐	☑
Forgets previously learned information	☐	☑	☐
Forgets studied information for tests	☐	☐	☑
Forgets materials, due dates, and/or required assignments	☐	☐	☑
Has trouble with mental math	☐	☐	☑

Figure 8.10. Building Blocks Questionnaire for Ryan: Memory Processing block.

"Can't read!" Although one can empathize with her frustration, it is tempting to write back, "Can't write." Andy attempted to work carefully, but he had trouble with performing the motor movements needed for letter formation. A sample of his writing and a picture are presented in Figure 8.11. The sentence reads, "Me and Sean built a fort."

Andy's school performance was becoming increasingly influenced by his difficulty with writing legibly. These difficulties stemmed from a severe weakness in the Motor block—they were not the result of a poor attitude or lack of effort. Handwriting involves integration of skills within the Orthographic and Motor blocks. As illustrated in Figure 8.12, writing requires the student to retrieve a mental image of the letterform and then to produce that image on paper.

Andy had difficulty with any task involving fine motor skills. By the time he had completed kindergarten, he still could not write his name legibly or cut with scissors. His attempts at drawing in a coloring book consisted of scribbles and a few straight lines drawn through the pictures. He only engaged in these types of activities when required to do so by his teachers or parents. Because writing was so difficult for him, he did not practice as often as the other students. These types of difficulties lead students to avoid writing, which further arrests writing development (Berninger, Mizokawa, & Bragg, 1991; Christensen, 2005). Thus, skill development is affected by both the weaknesses in motor skills and avoidance of tasks that would actually improve skill.

In contrast to his motor skills, Andy's oral language skills were well developed. He expressed himself clearly and was quite imaginative. He loved reading books and telling stories. His strengths within the Conceptual block of language were as readily apparent as his weaknesses within the Motor block. In fact, Andy's oral language had always seemed advanced for his age. His parents reported that, before entering school, he would talk excessively, regardless of whether anyone was around to listen.

Andy was referred to the school occupational therapist in first grade and identified as having a sensory-motor integration impairment. In her evaluation, the school occupational therapist noted that he was well below his age level on tasks involving both visual and motor skills. His printing of uppercase letters was characterized by numerous reversals (9 out of 26, or 34%), as was his printing of the numbers 1–10. She noted that on all tasks involving fine motor skills, he had a slow response speed. He was unable to stay within ¼" of graded curved and angled lines or to color within a small given area. His grip was described as an overlapping thumb grasp and was contributing to lack of control. In contrast, on tasks involving non–motor-visual-perceptual skills, Andy scored within the average range.

Delays were also noted in gross motor tasks. He still had difficulty with buttoning his shirt and tying his shoes. In second grade, his parents reported that if he was not awakened midway through the night, he would still wet the bed. He walked on his toes, and, when standing, his feet seemed to be splayed in opposite directions. He often tripped when running down the hallway or coming down stairs. He seemed to lose his balance easily. Although Andy was almost 9 years old, he had not learned how to ride a bike. These are all characteristics of a medical condition referred to as a developmental motor coordination disorder.

Specific Learning Disabilities and the Processing Blocks

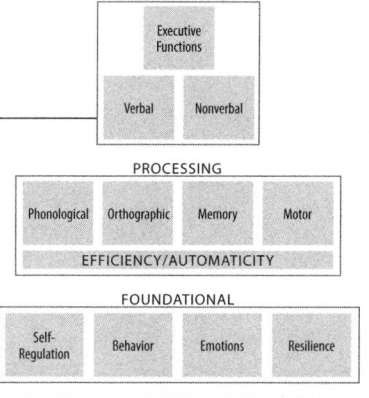

Figure 8.11. Writing sample for Andy: "Me and Sean built a fort."

Because of these developmental delays, the first-grade teacher had wondered if Andy should repeat first grade. He seemed uninterested in learning to write. Mr. and Mrs. Parson, Andy's parents, struggled with the decision. Andy's motor skills were delayed, but they wondered if eventually he would just catch up. They finally decided against retention because of Andy's strengths in the Conceptual block of verbal abilities. His good oral language abilities would enable him to keep up with peers on certain activities, although he would continue to struggle with activities involving gross motor skills, such as sports, and fine motor skills, such as handwriting. The occupational therapist summarized, "As the academic demands increase, Andy's weakness in fine motor, gross motor, and motor planning will affect his classroom and playground performance. Occupational therapy is recommended to focus on improving these skills."

Motor Block Questionnaire

Ms. Abram had contacted the school's occupational therapist to discuss ways in which she could help Andy in the classroom. Prior to the meeting, Ms. Abram completed the Motor section of the Building Blocks Questionnaire. Her responses

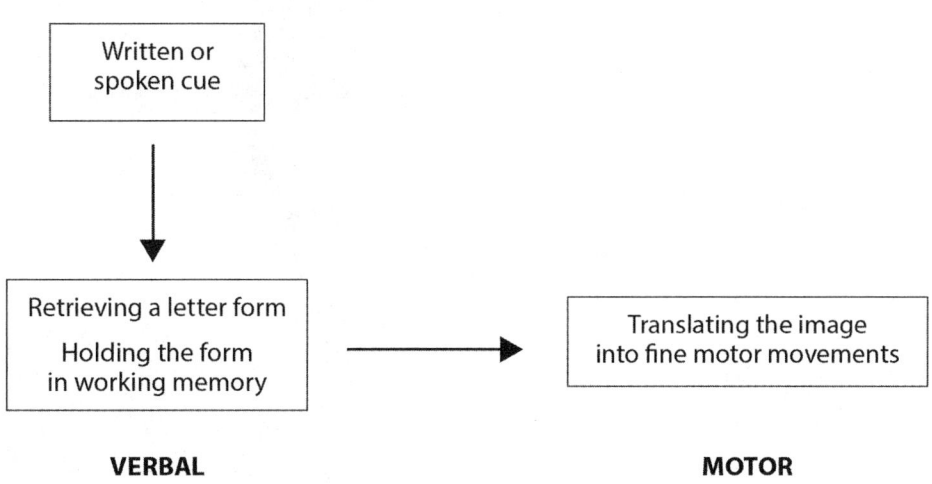

Figure 8.12. Visual and motor skills for handwriting.

are shown in Figure 8.13. Andy was just beginning to learn cursive writing, so she left that statement blank. She checked *Frequently* for the question about seeming disinterested in writing; Andy loved to draw, but he didn't like to write.

Although delayed development in either gross or fine motor skills can affect a child's school performance, weaknesses in fine motor skills pose a greater barrier to academic success. For this reason, the focus in this book is on helping a student develop fine motor skills, or what are sometimes referred to as visual-motor skills. As depicted in Figure 8.11, handwriting primarily involves the integration of both visual and motor skills. Chapter 9 provides specific suggestions for helping students with poor handwriting.

Fine Motor Development

Preschool children engage in many fine motor activities as they learn to build with blocks, draw, and turn the pages in a book. For most children, these skills develop naturally because children enjoy activities involving coloring, painting, cutting, drawing, and writing. Gradually, as a child progresses in school, drawing and coloring are viewed as supplementary or optional activities, whereas writing becomes increasingly required. Some children continue to struggle to draw a straight line or a circle.

Just as with reading, some children have difficulty with producing acceptable writing, even though they have practiced and have had adequate instruction (Hamstra-Bletz & Blote, 1993; Christensen, 2005). For these writers, so much energy is expended in trying to produce motor patterns that the quality and quantity of writing are often lacking. These difficulties appear in first grade and continue into higher grades. Figure 8.14 displays Andy's attempt to write the alphabet at the end of second grade. His class had spent time each day practicing writing skills, but Andy was still struggling with letter formation.

The next section presents several strategies for informally evaluating handwriting ability, specifically considering the types of errors the child is making, as

PROCESSING

Motor	Rarely	Sometimes	Frequently
Draws pictures that seem immature for age	☐	☐	☑
Has difficulties with tasks involving fine motor coordination (e.g., tying shoes)	☐	☐	☑
Seems disinterested in learning to write	☐	☐	☑
Has trouble holding a pencil or pen correctly	☐	☐	☑
Forms letters in odd ways (e.g., starts from the bottom rather than the top)	☐	☐	☑
Has poor spacing between letters and words	☐	☐	☑
Has papers that appear messy	☐	☐	☑
Has unusual letter formations	☐	☐	☑
Has difficulty learning cursive writing	☐	☐	☐
Has a slow rate of writing	☐	☐	☑

Figure 8.13. Building Blocks Questionnaire for Andy: Motor Processing block.

Specific Learning Disabilities and the Processing Blocks

well as his or her speed of writing. Specific instructional strategies for improving handwriting are presented in Chapter 9.

Legibility

Figure 8.15 provides an example of a simple form to use for the evaluation of handwriting. By observing the student, one can ascertain quickly which aspects of handwriting need improvement.

Handwriting Rate

One characteristic of students with difficulties in motor development is slow handwriting speed. Some students do not have the expected writing speed for their grade and thus are often slow when completing writing assignments. Although writing speed increases each year, when compared with their classmates, students with SLD demonstrate a relatively slower rate (Weintraub & Graham, 1998). These students may be diagnosed with dysgraphia, which is discussed more in Chapter 9. Individuals who exhibit the greatest neurological dysfunction associated with dysgraphia tend to have the most severely affected writing speed (Van Hoorn, Maathuis, & Hadders-Algra, 2013). As a consequence, these students often have trouble keeping up when taking notes, are slow copying off boards or from books, and take longer to complete writing assignments. On the basis of handwriting alone, students with poor handwriting may accomplish in 50 minutes what peers with average achievement can do in 30 minutes (Weintraub & Graham, 1998). Figure 8.16 presents the handwriting of Alex, a student in college who was enrolled in an introductory course about SLD. Note that he is defining the term *dysgraphia,* an inability to produce the motor patterns necessary for writing. His handwriting is so slow and difficult to read that he either has to have a scribe when taking examinations or has to write his responses on a computer.

One can easily determine if a student has the expected writing speed for his or her grade by using the Zaner-Bloser scale of handwriting proficiency (Barbe, Lucas, Wasylyk, Hackney, & Braun, 1987). To do a simple evaluation, ask the student to copy a sentence that contains most or all the letters of the alphabet, such as "The quick brown fox jumps over the lazy dog." Have the student practice the sentence one time, and then ask him or her to copy the sentence as many times as possible in 3 minutes. Count the total number of letters that the child has written in the 3-minute period, and then divide this number by 3 to get the total letters per minute (lpm). The student's proficiency level can be compared with the following scale:

Grade 1: 25 lpm

Grade 2: 30 lpm

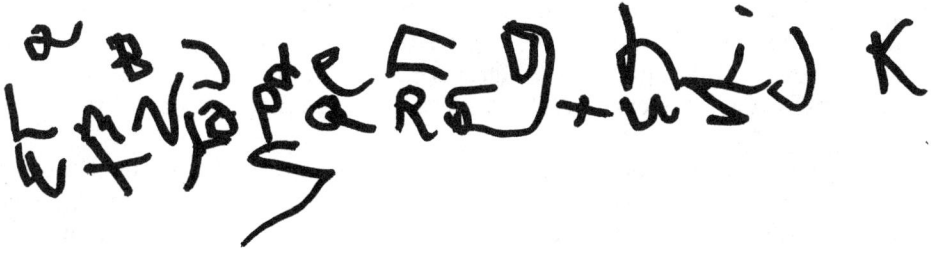

Figure 8.14. Andy's written alphabet.

Handwriting Evaluation Scale

Student _____ Date _____
Teacher _____ Grade _____

	Satisfactory	Needs Improvement
Pencil grip	☐	☐
Letter formation	☐	☐
Word formation	☐	☐
Size	☐	☐
Spacing	☐	☐
Alignment	☐	☐
Slant	☐	☐
Rate	☐	☐
Neatness	☐	☐

Specific concerns: _____
_____
_____

Figure 8.15. Handwriting evaluation scale.

Grade 3: 38 lpm

Grade 4: 45 lpm

Grade 5: 60 lpm

Grade 6: 67 lpm

Grade 7: 74 lpm

Ms. Abram asked Andy to copy the sentence "The quick brown fox jumped over the lazy dog" in his best handwriting. She then asked Andy to write the sentence as many times as he could in 3 minutes. The results of this informal evaluation are presented in Figure 8.17. Andy wrote approximately 78 letters within the 3-minute period, so his average was 26 lpm. His speed is lower than most of his classmates, and his legibility is very poor.

Graham, Berninger, Weintraub, and Shafer (1997) provided normative data on handwriting speed for both girls and boys in Grades 1–9. In a study investigating the speed and legibility of 900 children in Grades 1–9, they found that 1) girls' handwriting was more legible than boys' handwriting; 2) although girls tend to write faster than boys overall, significant differences were noted in Grades 1, 6, and 7; and 3) right-handers were faster than left-handers, although there was no difference in legibility.

For this procedure, children were asked to copy a paragraph as quickly as possible without making any mistakes for 1.5 minutes (see Table 8.3). In general, these reported speeds are somewhat faster than the Zaner-Bloser scale. This may be because students wrote only 1.5 minutes as opposed to 3 minutes, and handwriting speed is likely to slow down with increased time.

Specific Learning Disabilities and the Processing Blocks

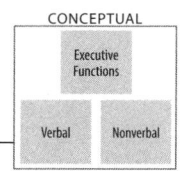

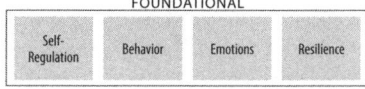

Figure 8.16. Alex's handwriting: "*Dysgraphia:* Inability to produce the motor patterns necessary for writing."

Graham and colleagues observed that considerable variability existed in children's handwriting speeds at each grade level tested. For example, in Grade 5, speed ranged from 43 lpm to 125 lpm. As a general principle in working with students like Andy, emphasis should be placed on legibility rather than speed (Hamstra-Bletz & Blote, 1993). Andy also had difficulty forming numbers and, as a consequence, worked slowly on the timed math problems he was asked to solve in the classroom. Students with developmental delays in visual-motor skill often require classroom accommodations throughout their school careers. The occupational therapist suggested that Ms. Abram provide the following accommodations for Andy:

1. Eliminate copying from the chalkboard or the textbook. Instead, provide Andy with prewritten notes and assignments.
2. Provide extended time on tasks involving writing.
3. Shorten writing assignments, and encourage Andy to supplement his work with illustrations, clip art, and verbal explanations.
4. Introduce keyboarding skills. As Andy's skills develop, provide him with the option of using a word processor at his desk rather than paper and pencil.
5. Use graph paper for place value or when adding and subtracting two-digit numbers.

As students progress in school, they may need additional adjustments, such as photocopying notes of another student or being permitted to answer questions

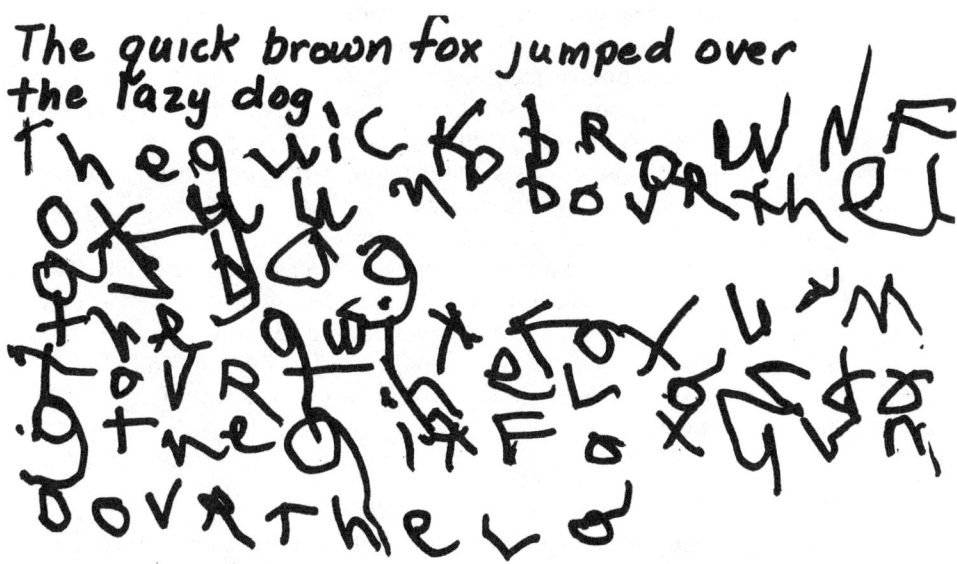

Figure 8.17. Andy's writing speed test with his teacher's writing at the top.

Table 8.3. The mean handwriting speeds for girls and boys in Grades 1–9 as measured in letters per minute (lpm)

Grade	Girls	Boys
1	21	17
2	36	32
3	50	45
4	66	61
5	75	71
6	91	78
7	109	91
8	118	112
9	121	114

Copyright 1999 from *The development of handwriting speed and legibility in grades 1 through 9* by Graham, S., Berninger, V., Weintraub, N., & Schafer, W. Adapted by permission of Taylor & Francis, LLC (http://www.tandfonline.com).

orally. The last section of this chapter and Chapter 9 provide additional information about the types of classroom accommodations that students with weaknesses in the Processing blocks often require.

EFFICIENCY/AUTOMATICITY BLOCK

The Efficiency/Automaticity block involves the speed and ease with which a student reads, writes, and calculates. Although efficiency and automaticity are governed and delimited by underlying cognitive processing abilities, speed and ease are gained through repeated practice. Once automaticity has been accomplished, a task can be completed with little effort.

Efficiency/Automaticity Block Questionnaire

Because he was knowledgeable about Ryan's academic skills, Mr. Steen, Ryan's fourth-grade teacher, also completed the Efficiency/Automaticity block items on the Building Blocks Questionnaire (see Figure 8.18). He thought that Ryan was sometimes slow completing routine tasks, retrieving information, and performing step-by-step problems. Ryan's reading, writing, and math computation rates, however, were significantly slow compared with his peers. Mr. Steen had noticed that on timed math facts tests, Ryan only got halfway down the page, whereas most of his peers had nearly finished the sheet in the allotted time.

Among the cognitive abilities and processes most essential to efficiency and automaticity with academic tasks are rapid automatized naming (RAN) ability, or the capacity to rapidly and fluently identify, retrieve, and name simple symbolic information, and processing speed, or the rapidity with which an individual can accurately complete cognitive tasks. In addition, fine motor ability and speed can affect writing-related tasks.

Rapid Automatized Naming

Another ability that may be particularly relevant to the Efficiency/Automaticity block is RAN ability. RAN ability involves the fluent retrieval of symbolic information. Tests of RAN measure the rapid retrieval of continuously presented, highly

Specific Learning Disabilities and the Processing Blocks

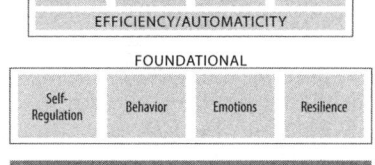

familiar symbols of a single type (e.g., objects, colors, letters, or numbers; Norton & Wolf, 2012). On tasks that assess RAN ability, a student is typically shown an array of objects, colors, letters, or digits that repeat in pattern (6–8 in a row, with a total of 30–50) and asked to name the symbols as quickly as possible. Several RAN tests are available commercially, including the *Rapid Automatized Naming and Rapid Alternating Stimulus Tests* (Wolf & Denckla, 2006). Although the relationship between RAN ability and reading is not yet well understood, poor RAN ability is associated with reading-related difficulties (Badian, 2005; Korhonen, 1991), and individuals with impairments in both RAN ability and phonological awareness tend to be most severely affected (Badian, 1998, 2005; Bowers, Sunseth, & Golden, 1999; Wagner et al., 1993; Wolf & Bowers, 1999).

Brief History of Rapid Automatized Naming

The first documented test of RAN was developed by Geschwind and Fusillo (1966), who created a novel color naming instrument to examine the cognitive capacities of stroke patients with alexia whose spelling abilities remained intact. Geschwind and Fusillo (1966) discovered that these patients were able to match color swatches but were unable to name colors when presented with a RAN task. Intrigued by the unique pattern of cognitive impairments reported in Geschwind and Fusillo's (1966) research, Denckla sought out research participants who displayed a similar apparent decoupling of visual and auditory processing (as cited in Denckla & Cutting, 1999). In her subsequent research, Denckla (1972b) found that among young boys with dyslexia, serial color naming was often slow and laborious. The potential for these tasks to predict and diagnose reading-related difficulties was seized upon by Denckla and Rudel, who developed and evaluated several RAN instruments, including tests of color, letter, numeral, and symbol naming (1974, 1976).

Rapid Automatized Naming as a Predictor

In their research, Denckla and Rudel (1974, 1976) found that latency in RAN, or pause time, as opposed to rate of error, was a more robust predictor of reading-related

PROCESSING

Efficiency/Automaticity	Rarely	Sometimes	Frequently
Requires more time to complete tasks	☐	☐	✓
Has difficulty naming things rapidly	☐	☐	✓
Requires more time on tests	☐	☐	✓
Has a slow speed completing routine tasks	☐	✓	☐
Retrieves information slowly	☐	✓	☐
Performs step-by-step processes slowly	☐	✓	☐
Completes detailed assignments slowly	☐	☐	✓
Has a slow rate of reading	☐	☐	✓
Has a slow rate of writing	☐	☐	✓
Has a slow rate of completing math computations	☐	☐	✓

Figure 8.18. Building Blocks Questionnaire for Ryan: Efficiency/Automaticity Processing block.

difficulties. Similar results have since been reported by other researchers (e.g., Boets et al., 2010; Brizzolara et al., 2006; Georgiou, Parrila, & Kirby, 2006; Katzir et al., 2006; Wolf et al., 2002). Moreover, RAN tasks have been shown to reliably predict future reading ability in preliterate children (Furnes & Samuelsson, 2011; Lervåg & Hulme, 2009), making RAN a useful screening tool for the early identification of specific reading disability.

What Rapid Automatized Naming Measures

Although it is widely agreed that performance on RAN tasks is highly correlated with reading ability (Powell, Stainthorp, Stuart, Garwood, & Quinlan, 2007; Savage & Frederickson, 2005; Wolf & Bowers, 1999), and poor RAN performance is a cognitive marker for specific reading disability (Georgiou & Parrila, 2013), a lack of consensus exists in regard to exactly which mental operations are involved in RAN. Some have argued that performance on RAN tasks captures a distinct cognitive ability that provides a unique contribution to reading achievement (Powell et al., 2007; Wolf, Bowers, & Biddle, 2000), whereas others have maintained that RAN performance does not capture an independent cognitive ability but is a subtype of phonological processing (Swanson, Trainin, Necoechea, & Hammill, 2003; Torgesen & Burgess, 1998). For example, Torgesen and Burgess (1998) proposed that RAN tasks drew on aspects of phonological processing skill and cited three reasons for this belief: 1) performance on RAN tasks is highly correlated with phonological skills; 2) as with phonological skills, RAN ability shows a unique relationship to the development of early literacy skills; and 3) no evidence exists to support the assertion that RAN ability contributes uniquely to the development of orthographic representations of words. Likewise, Schatschneider, Carlson, Francis, Foorman, and Fletcher (2002) asserted that RAN tasks require the interplay of numerous cognitive abilities and that conflating those abilities into a single construct served to obscure the complex nature of the cognitive processes underlying RAN performance. This position has been supported by other researchers, who have identified processing speed (Decker, Roberts, & Englund, 2013; Kail & Hall, 1994; Kail, Hall, & Caskey, 1999), aspects of long-term storage and retrieval (Decker et al., 2013), and aspects of auditory processing (Decker et al., 2013) as significant predictors of RAN ability.

Others have suggested that RAN tasks measure aspects of visual processing and processing speed that are particularly important to the development of internal orthographic representations and fluent reading (Badian, 1997, 1998; Wolf & Bowers, 1999). Bowers and Wolf (1993) hypothesized that slow RAN speed signified disruption of the automatic processes that result in quick word recognition. They noted that RAN speed is determined by a complex ensemble of attentional, memory, cognitive, perceptual, motor, and linguistic processes that need to work in concert. Individuals who have difficulty rapidly retrieving and labeling visual symbols tend to perform poorly on these measures. Conceivably, their lack of automaticity affects processing speed (i.e., the ability to scan symbols rapidly) and efficiency. Morris and colleagues (1998) referred to this specific subtype as a rate impairment. Students with rate impairments were impaired on tasks requiring RAN but not on measures of phonological awareness.

A similar explanation is that rapid sequential processing is common to naming speed, processing speed, and reading tasks and that slow RAN reflects a global impairment in the rapid execution of a variety of cognitive processes (Kail et al.,

Specific Learning Disabilities and the Processing Blocks

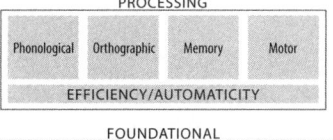
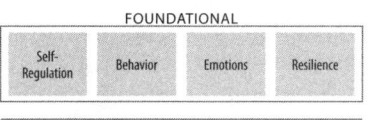

1999). It appears that whatever RAN represents, it is partially subsumed under the rubric of processing speed (Denckla & Cutting, 1999).

Meyer, Wood, Hart, and Felton (1998) found that performance on RAN tasks had predictive power for only poor readers. They suggested that this predictive power comes from the automaticity of retrieval. For a few students, slow performance on RAN tasks may be more likely linked to a slow speed of word retrieval (probably more related to the Verbal block), whereas for others, RAN tasks appear to be tapping processes within the visual domain, primarily orthographic processing skills. If common letter patterns are not recognized easily and quickly, orthographic pattern knowledge is slow to develop (Bowers & Wolf, 1993).

Although some inconsistencies exist among research findings, Georgiou and Parrila (2013) summarized what the existing research suggests about RAN:

1. Letter and digit naming are more powerful predictors of reading than color and object naming.
2. RAN is more strongly related to word reading fluency than to word reading accuracy.
3. The relationship between RAN and reading fluency increases in later grades.
4. RAN is a cognitive marker of developmental dyslexia.
5. Pause time reliably differentiates children with dyslexia from typical developing readers.
6. RAN predicts reading across a wide range of languages.
7. Although RAN appears related to phonological processing, orthographic processing, and processing speed, it adds unique variance to the prediction of reading.

In general, students with RAN impairments have less knowledge of orthographic patterns and are slower readers than students with poor phonemic awareness alone. In addition, orthographic pattern knowledge depends in part on the processes tapped by naming speed (Bowers et al., 1999). Although a consensus regarding how RAN ability affects reading development has yet to be reached, one fact appears to be clear: Students with weaknesses in both phonological awareness and RAN abilities have the most pronounced reading impairments and are the most resistant to intervention (Badian, 1998, 2005; Bowers et al., 1999; Wagner, Torgesen, Laughon, Simmons, & Rashotte, 1993; Wolf & Bowers, 1999). Bowers and colleagues (1999) noted that these children with double impairments are clearly impaired on all reading measures. Although future research will be required to confirm the cognitive processes underlying RAN performance, students with naming impairments appear to have a poorer prognosis for reading success than do students in other subgroups (Badian, 2005; Korhonen, 1991). Denckla (1979) described these students as a "hard-to-learn group." Clearly, these students require intensive interventions that focus on the development of both phonemic awareness and reading fluency. These factors continue to play a role in adult reading achievement; research has shown that adults with weaknesses in both phonological awareness and RAN have significantly lower reading achievement than adults with no impairment or a single impairment (Miller et al., 2006).

As observed by Monroe (1932), a broad constellation of factors may affect reading and writing development. Reading difficulties are most often caused by a multiplicity of factors rather than a double or even a triple impairment (Wolf, 1999). For example, in fourth grade, Ryan showed weaknesses in phonological processing, orthographic processing, and memory. He also had low scores on tests of RAN and processing speed. Although his reading had improved as the result of a structured reading program, his rate of word recognition was still severely compromised.

Processing Speed

Much research has focused on RAN as a correlate of reading disability; however, individuals with dyslexia may also demonstrate other speed-related impairments—in particular, impairments in processing speed (Shanahan et al., 2006). Processing speed refers to the speed with which an individual is able to complete a cognitive task with a reasonable degree of accuracy (Jacobson et al., 2011). It is a complex cognitive ability that involves speed of input or perception; speed of output; and the speed of integrating perceptual, cognitive, and output processes. An individual's speed of processing affects fluency and automaticity with cognitive tasks. Kail (1991) observed, "In the face of limited processing resources, the speed of processing is critical because it determines in part how rapidly limited resources can be reallocated to other cognitive tasks" (p. 152). As an example, how quickly a reader can recognize or decode a word affects comprehension. If the reader's cognitive resources are focused on decoding a word, there will be limited resources available for comprehension. Similarly, how quickly a student can solve a computation or write a sentence will affect production.

Processing speed underlies the rapid and efficient completion of academic tasks and therefore may be one of the foundational cognitive abilities required for fluent reading and writing (Mahone, 2011). Because processing speed is contingent on a variety of cognitive processes, individuals with reading or computational difficulties may have impairments in one or more aspects of processing speed. Standardized tests of processing speed are always timed and are clerical in nature. They involve tasks such as circling the matching pictures, digits, or letters in a row or identifying if symbols are the same or different.

Processing speed is an important correlate of both reading and computational impairments and appears to be a shared cognitive correlate of both reading disabilities and attention-deficit/hyperactivity disorder (ADHD; Shanahan et al., 2006). Reading disabilities and ADHD have a high degree of comorbidity, and impairments in processing speed may partially explain the overlap in the disorders (Shanahan et al., 2006). Furthermore, research suggests that impairments in working memory, another cognitive process in which individuals with SLD (Semrud-Clikeman, 2005) and ADHD (Jacobson et al., 2011) often exhibit difficulty, may play an important role in both processing speed impairments and fluency-related reading difficulties in individuals with ADHD (Jacobson et al., 2011).

Evidence of processing speed impairments has been noted on both linguistic and nonlinguistic tasks for individuals with reading disabilities (Shanahan et al., 2006). Some students may process linguistic information slowly, whereas others process symbolic information slowly (more common in dyslexia). Kail and Hall (1994) found that a general impairment in processing speed explained the observed link between RAN and reading. Because processing speed underlies performance in many areas and is not specific to one area or one type of disability, it is sometimes referred to as a domain-general impairment rather than an impairment specific to just one area or disability. For example, individuals with dyslexia, as well as

Specific Learning Disabilities and the Processing Blocks

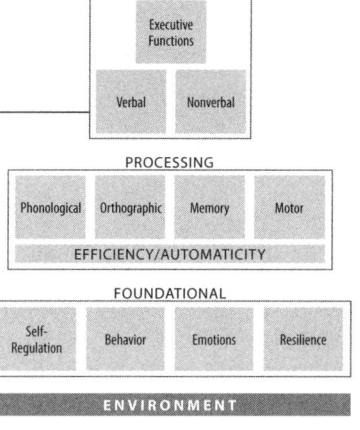

individuals with ADHD, often have slow processing speed (Eden & Vaidya, 2008), although children with dyslexia demonstrate greater impairments than do children with ADHD (Shanahan et al., 2006).

In addition to reading fluency, slow processing speed also appears to be related to computational difficulties (Fuchs et al., 2008). In examining the performance of 924 third-grade students, Fuchs and colleagues found that specific computational difficulty was associated with a strength in language and weaknesses in attentive behavior and processing speed, whereas problem-solving difficulty was associated with deficient language, as well as race and poverty. Hecht, Torgesen, Wagner, and Rashotte (2001) also found that processing speed was an important correlate of computational skill while controlling for vocabulary knowledge. These findings suggest that students' cognitive characteristics differ as a function of the type of math: computation or problem solving.

CLASSROOM ACCOMMODATIONS

Children with weaknesses in the abilities of the Processing blocks often require accommodations or adjustments in the classroom so that they can be successful. They may require oral examinations, less material presented on a page, or special pencils or pencil grips. For accommodations to be effective, they must be fully supported by the student and the general education teacher. Ensuring this acceptance often requires discussion and adaptations. Children do not like to appear or feel different from other children. If an accommodation singles them out as different, students are unlikely to comply.

When Ryan was in fifth grade, he obtained low scores on the weekly spelling tests. His teacher suggested that Ryan only take the first 5 words; Ryan refused and said he wanted to do all 20 words, just like everyone else. His teacher then suggested that he take all 20 words, but they would have a silent pact regarding which 5 words she would grade. Ryan agreed that this would be a good accommodation.

Examples of the most common accommodations for students with weaknesses in the Processing blocks are described in the following section. Chapter 9 provides additional ideas for students who are particularly low in one subject area, such as spelling or calculating.

Copying

Students with weaknesses in the memory of forms and symbols often have difficulty copying information from chalkboards or from a textbook to a piece of paper. To circumvent this difficulty, students can be provided ahead of time with lecture notes or problems to be copied from a textbook or the chalkboard. These students are also likely to have trouble filling out bubble sheets. When Ben was in fifth grade, his teacher sent home the note in Figure 8.19. To reduce frustration for students like Ben, provide an enlarged bubble sheet or let the student mark the answers directly on the test book.

Timed Tests

Students who have had trouble with language sounds, retention of letter strings, or production of symbols often have compromised decoding and encoding rates and are likely to require extended time on reading, writing, and math assignments and examinations. As students with dyslexia proceed through school, they may become more accurate but still read slowly; thus, they may require the accommodation of extended time on examinations (Shaywitz & Shaywitz, 2003).

If an examination is timed, estimate the appropriate amount of time the student needs to have equal access to the test questions. If the examination is not timed, the student should have as much time as he or she needs in order to complete the test. In fact, if the purpose of an examination is to test knowledge, all students should have as much time as needed. If speed is judged to be a necessary factor for performance, then a time limit must be set. As noted by Stanovich, "In those (probably very few) cases where speed is judged to be a genuine academic virtue, no time accommodation should be given to anyone" (1999, p. 358).

Following Directions

Students with weaknesses in verbal short-term memory may have difficulty following lengthy directions. For this type of student, the teacher may need to ask him or her to repeat instructions to ensure understanding; repeat and simplify instructions; and supplement oral instructions with visual instructions and demonstrations. Peer tutors can be enlisted to clarify assignments or in-class instructions.

Assignments

Because of the slow processing of symbols, some students need to have the amount of work they are assigned adjusted. Instead of assigning a specific amount of homework, advise students to accomplish as much as they can within a certain time frame. For example, Ms. Abram advised Andy that he should spend no more than 30 minutes on his nightly homework. Within the classroom, ask the student to complete as many problems as he or she can within a 15-minute period rather than assigning a specific number of problems.

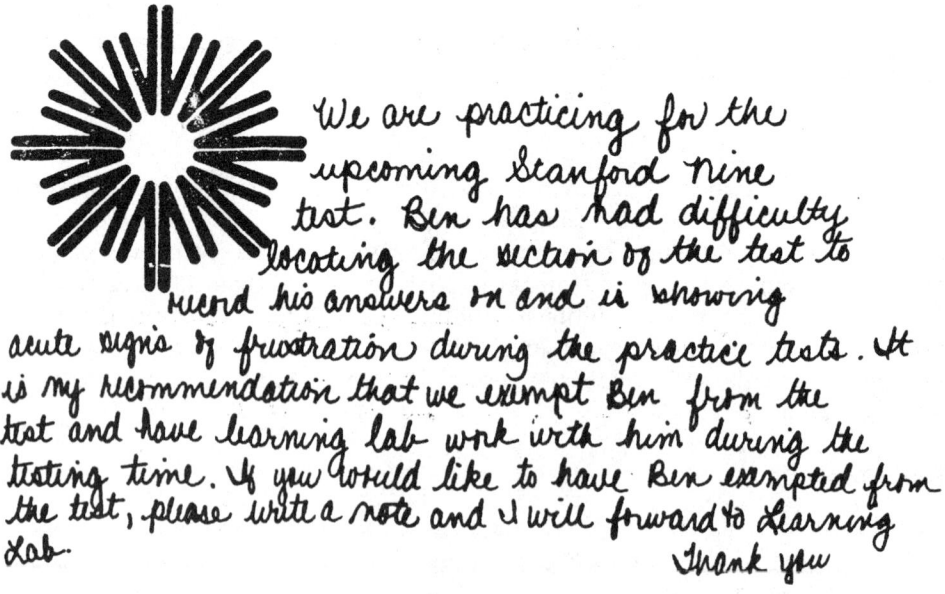

Figure 8.19. Ben's teacher's note.

Specific Learning Disabilities and the Processing Blocks

CONCLUSION

Children who experience these difficulties in learning are heterogeneous in diagnosis and prognosis (Korhonen, 1991). For example, some students with reading impairments have phonological disorders, whereas others have specific orthographic impairments and are slow to recognize words and spelling patterns. Some students with math difficulties have problems with attention, whereas others have weaknesses in working memory. Understanding the various types of abilities that can affect learning can enhance a teacher's ability to diagnose the problem accurately and develop systematic interventions (Lyon, 1995; Semrud-Clikeman, 1996).

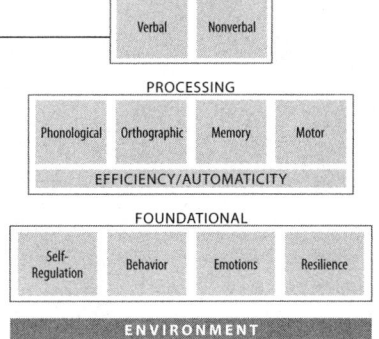

APPENDIX **8A**

Phonological Awareness Skills Screener

The Phonological Awareness Skills Screener (PASS) is designed for students in kindergarten through second grade, although it may also be used with older students who are experiencing difficulty developing phonological awareness. The primary purpose of this informal assessment is to identify students who are at risk for reading and spelling difficulties. It is designed to detect specific areas of weakness and help teachers determine what type of instruction would best support the development of phonological awareness skills.

ADMINISTRATION INSTRUCTIONS

Materials

To administer this test, you will need a set of 10 colored blocks, chips, or tiles (all the same color); a test record form (see Figure 8A.1); and the following directions. The PASS includes 10 brief sections, each of which will require about 1–3 minutes to complete:

1. Word discrimination
2. Rhyme recognition
3. Rhyme production
4. Syllable blending
5. Syllable segmentation
6. Syllable deletion
7. Phoneme recognition
8. Phoneme blending
9. Phoneme segmentation
10. Phoneme deletion

Instructions

Each section contains instructions and a script for the teacher that provides student directions. You may rephrase the directions as needed to ensure that the student understands the task. Begin each section only when you are satisfied the student understands the task. If the student does understand what is required for a task, do not administer that section. Do not penalize for articulation or sound production errors. If needed, you may repeat any item. Be sure to provide enough time for the student to respond.

Specific Learning Disabilities and the Processing Blocks

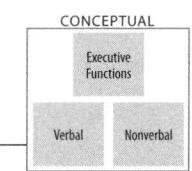

- *Stopping points:* For each section, discontinue administration if the student cannot perform any of the sample items or misses three items in a row.
- *Scoring:* Score correct responses 1; incorrect responses 0. Write in errors next to each incorrect item.

1. **Word Discrimination**

Before administering any item in this section, place a flat hand a few inches from your mouth to obscure the manner of articulation of each word. Be sure that the student cannot see the movement of your lips or tongue. Say, "I'm going to say two words, and I want you to tell me whether they are the same or different. For example, if I say, 'Car, car,' you would say, 'Same.' If I say, 'Horse, house,' you would say, 'Different.' Now you try one: *frog, frog*." If the student provides the correct response, say, "That's right. They are the same." If the student provides an incorrect response or does not respond, say, "*Frog* and *frog* are the same. Here's another: *plane, bike*." If the student provides the correct response, say, "That's right. They are different. Here are some more." Pause about 1 second between words. If the student does not seem to understand the task, practice with two or three additional examples (e.g., *blue, blue; dog, sock*).

2. **Rhyme Recognition**

When administering items in this section, pause briefly after each word. Say, "I am going to say three words, and I want you to tell me the two words that end with the same sounds or rhyme. If I say, 'What ends the same or rhymes with *cat? Hat* or *sun?*' you would say *hat* because *cat* and *hat* both end the same or rhyme. Now you do one. What rhymes with *sun? Cat* or *run?* What rhymes with *moon? Car* or *spoon?*" If the student does not seem to understand, practice with two or three additional examples (e.g., "What ends the same or rhymes with *blue? New* or *tree?* What ends the same or rhymes with *ten? Step* or *men?*") Begin each item with "What ends the same or rhymes with ____?"

3. **Rhyme Production**

Say, "I'm going to say some words that end the same or rhyme. *Cat* rhymes with *hat,* and *boat* rhymes with *coat.* Now you do one. Tell me a word that ends the same or rhymes with *tree.*" If the student does not seem to understand, practice with two or three additional examples (e.g., "What rhymes with *wall?*" "What rhymes with *ten?*"). Accept rhyming nonsense words as correct. Begin each item by saying, "What rhymes with ____?"

4. **Syllable Blending**

When administering items in this section, pause for about a half second between word parts. Say, "I am going to say the parts of a word and then put them together to say the whole word. If I say, cup•cake, the whole word would be *cupcake.* Rain•coat would be *raincoat.* Now you do one. What is sail•boat?" Pause for the student to respond. If the student does not seem to understand, give another example (e.g., horse•shoe, sun•shine).

Say, "Here is a different one. If I say tur•tle, the whole word would be *turtle.* What is pen•cil?" If the student does not seem to understand, practice with two or three additional examples (e.g., han•dle, tall•er). Begin each item with "What is ____?"

257

5. Syllable Segmentation

Say, "I'm going to use these blocks to break a word into parts. *Cupcake* has two parts." Push forward one block for each part as you say it. Then point to each block and say, "This block is *cup*, and this one is *cake*." After each item, push the blocks back into a group. Push the blocks in front of the student and say, "Now you do one. Use the blocks (chips, tiles) to tell and show me the two parts of *football*." If the student does not understand, practice with two or three additional examples (e.g., *raindrop, popcorn, toothbrush*). If the student provides an incorrect response or does not respond, discontinue this section.

Say, "Here is a different one. The word *doctor* has two parts." Push forward one block as you say each part. "This first block is /doc/ and this next one is /tor/. Now you do one. Use the blocks to tell and show me the word *paper*." If the student does not understand, practice with two or three additional examples (e.g., *flying, happy, running*). Say, "Here's another one. The word *somersault* has three parts." Push forward one block as you say each part. "Now you do it. Use the blocks to tell and show me the word *somersault*." For an item to be scored correct, the student must accurately break the words into syllables orally, but the student is not required to identify the correct number of blocks. Begin each item with, "Tell and show me the parts of ___."

6. Syllable Deletion

Say, "I'm going to say a word and leave off one part. If I say *raincoat* but don't say *rain*, it would be *coat*. Now you do one. Say the word *goldfish*." Pause for a response. "Now say the word *goldfish* but don't say *fish*." If the student does not seem to understand, practice with two or three additional examples (e.g., *raindrop, popcorn, toothbrush*).

Say, "Here is a different one. The word *turkey* has two parts. The first part is /tur/ and the second part is /key/. If I say *turkey* but don't say /tur/, it would be /key/. Now you do one. Say the word *candle*. Now say the word *candle* but don't say /dle/." If the student does not understand, practice with two or three additional examples (e.g., *flying, candy, funny*). For a correct response, the student needs to delete the syllable. Begin each item with, "Say the word ___ but don't say ___."

7. Phoneme Recognition

Say, "I'm going to say a word and then ask you to tell me another word that starts with the same sound. If I say, 'What starts with the same sound as the word *bat*?' you could say *boy, bike,* or *boat*. Tell me a word that starts with the same sound as the word *cat*." If the student provides the correct response, say, "That's right. The word ___ starts with the same sound as *cat*." If the child says a rhyming word on any of the samples or items, say, "That word rhymes. Tell me a word that starts with the same sound as ___." If the student provides an incorrect response or does not respond, say, "You could say *car* or *cake*." Say, "Let's try another. What starts with the same sound as the word *mother*?" If the student provides the correct response, say, "That's right. The word ___ starts with the same sound as *mother*." If the student does not seem to understand, practice with two or three additional examples (e.g., *girl, fan, run*). Begin each item with, "Tell me a word that starts with the same sound as ___."

If the student responds incorrectly or does not respond, say, "Does ___ start with the same sound as ___?" Provide three samples (e.g., *girl, gate; dog, dad; hot, hid*). If the student still does not seem to understand, discontinue this section.

Specific Learning Disabilities and the Processing Blocks

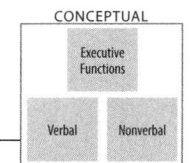
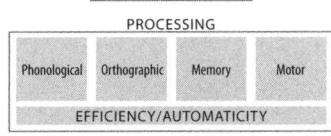

8. **Phoneme Blending**

Say, "Now I'm going to say the sounds of a word slowly and then say the whole word." Pronounce each phoneme as it sounds in the word and pause about one second between sounds. "Listen . . . /s/•/oa/•/p/ is *soap.* Now you do one. What is /b/•/e/?" If the student does not seem to understand, practice with two or three additional items (e.g., /s/•/o/, /b/•/i/•/ke/). Begin each item with "What is ____?"

9. **Phoneme Segmentation**

Say, "I'm going to use the blocks to show you all the sounds in a word. The word *time* has the sounds /t/ /i/ /m/." Push a block forward as you say each sound. Push the blocks back together and say, "The word *play* has the sounds /p/ /l/ /ay/." Place the blocks in front of the student. "Now you do one. Tell and show me the sounds in the word *toe.*" If the student does not seem to understand, provide two or three additional examples (e.g., *row, make, boat*). After each item, push the blocks back into a group. For an item to be scored correct, the student must segment the sounds correctly, but the student is not required to identify the correct number of blocks. Begin each item with "Tell and show me the sounds in ____."

10. **Phoneme Deletion**

Say, "I'm going to say a word and leave off one sound. If I say *seat* but don't say /s/, it would be *eat.* If I say *past* but don't say /t/, it would be *pass.* Now you do one. If I say, *sat* but don't say /s/, it would be ____?" If the student does not seem to understand, practice with two or three additional items (e.g., "If I say *pan* but don't say /p/, it would be ____?"; "If I say *rat* but don't say /r/, it would be ____?"). Begin each item with "If I say ____ but don't say (the sound), it would be ____?"

This assessment tool was originally developed by Mather in collaboration with Podhajski, Rhein, and Babur. The first version was titled *Screening of Early Reading Processes* and was published in Mather and Goldstein (2001). The phonological segmentation tasks were adapted from Sawyer's (1987) *Test of Awareness of Language Segments.* The most recent edition, PASS, was revised by Mather, Sammons, Podhajski, Kroese, and Varricchio (2000).

OPTIONAL LETTER–SOUND IDENTIFICATION SECTION

Figure 8A.2 includes two other letter–sound identification charts and recording sheets, one for uppercase letters and one for lowercase letters. A checklist for each is included for recording purposes. Score 1 for correct and 0 for incorrect. You may ask the student to identify the letter names, the letter sounds, or both.

Say, "I want you to tell me the names [or sounds] of these letters. Start here [Point to the first letter in the upper left corner] and end here [Point to the last letter in the lower right corner]." If the student does not read across the rows, point to each letter.

Record the total number correct. If desired, record errors on specific letters on the blank next to the letter. For example, if a student identified the letter *b* as *d,* you would write a *d* next to the *b.*

Note: For the vowel sounds, if a student says the long sound or the letter name, say, "Tell me another sound for that letter." When asking for the sounds of letters *c* and *g,* if the student says the soft sound, /s/ or /j/, say, "Tell me another sound for that letter."

PASS Test Record

Name _____ Grade _____ Age _____ Test Date _____ Total Score _____

1: Word discrimination
Samples: frog/frog: same; plane/bike: different

___ 1. bye / pie
___ 2. back / bag
___ 3. gum / gum
___ 4. bass / bass
___ 5. cub / cup
___ 6. fly / fly
___ 7. comb / cone
___ 8. teeth / teethe
___ 9. pull / pull
___ 10. with / whiff
Total ___

2: Rhyme recognition
Samples: sun: cat, run? moon: car, spoon?

___ 1. rat: hat, car?
___ 2. man: dog, fan?
___ 3. back: sack, trip?
___ 4. night: fan, light?
___ 5. hole: pole, clock?
___ 6. street: nap, meet?
___ 7. show: toe, plane?
___ 8. fast: race, last?
___ 9. shark: dark, pork?
___ 10. mouth: north, south?
Total ___

3: Rhyme production
Sample: tree

___ 1. bat
___ 2. hop
___ 3. rag
___ 4. fun
___ 5. seat
___ 6. tail
___ 7. night
___ 8. ringing
___ 9. money
___ 10. stamp
Total ___

4: Syllable blending
Samples: sail•boat, pen•cil

___ 1. snow•man
___ 2. sun•set
___ 3. jump•ing
___ 4. can•dle
___ 5. ho•tel
___ 6. bas•ket•ball
___ 7. po•lice•man
___ 8. kin•der•gar•ten
___ 9. hel•i•cop•ter
___ 10. hip•po•pot•a•mus
Total ___

5: Syllable segmentation
Samples: foot•ball, pa•per, so•mer•sault

___ 1. hotdog (hot•dog)
___ 2. baseball (base•ball)
___ 3. doorbell (door•bell)
___ 4. funny (fun•ny)
___ 5. camping (camp•ing)
___ 6. elbow (el•bow)
___ 7. computer (com•pu•ter)
___ 8. radio (ra•di•o)
___ 9. transportation (trans•por•ta•tion)
___ 10. vacationing (va•ca•tion•ing)
Total ___

6: Syllable deletion
Samples: goldfish / fish (gold), candle / "dle" (can)

___ 1. pancake but don't say cake
___ 2. starfish but don't say fish
___ 3. haircut but don't say hair
___ 4. rainbow but don't say rain
___ 5. teacher but don't say /er/
___ 6. slowly but don't say /ly/
___ 7. walnut but don't say wall
___ 8. enjoy but don't say /en/
___ 9. paperback but don't say back
___ 10. outstanding but don't say out
Total ___

7: Phoneme recognition
Samples: cat; mother

___ 1. boy
___ 2. sun
___ 3. car
___ 4. fish
___ 5. horse
___ 6. nest
___ 7. apple
___ 8. jump
___ 9. shoe
___ 10. chop
Total ___

8: Phoneme blending
Sample: /b/ /e/ /(be)

___ 1. /sh/ /e/ /(she)
___ 2. /n/ /o/ /(no)
___ 3. /s/ /a/ /t/ /(sat)
___ 4. /t/ /e/ /n/ /(ten)
___ 5. /b/ /a/ /ke/ /(bake)
___ 6. /s/ /p/ /o/ /t/ /(spot)
___ 7. /f/ /i/ /n/ /d/ /(find)
___ 8. /l/ /e/ /tt/ /er/ /(letter)
___ 9. /w/ /i/ /n/ /d/ /ow/ /(window)
___ 10. /b/ /a/ /s/ /k/ /e/ /t/ /(basket)
Total ___

9: Phoneme segmentation
Sample: toe /t/ /oe/ (2)

___ 1. me /m/ /e/ (2)
___ 2. go /g/ /o/ (2)
___ 3. bit /b/ /i/ /t/ (3)
___ 4. red /r/ /e/ /d/ (3)
___ 5. food /f/ /oo/ /d/ (3)
___ 6. skate /s/ /k/ /a/ /te/ (4)
___ 7. rust /r/ /u/ /s/ /t/ (4)
___ 8. grasp /g/ /r/ /a/ /s/ /p/ (5)
___ 9. friend /f/ /r/ /ie/ /n/ /d/ (5)
___ 10. splash /s/ /p/ /l/ /a/ /sh/ (5)
Total ___

10: Phoneme deletion
Sample: sat but don't say /s/ (at)

___ 1. ran but don't say /r/ (an)
___ 2. beat but don't say /b/ (eat)
___ 3. make but don't say /k/ (may)
___ 4. shown but don't say /n/ (show)
___ 5. blame but don't say /b/ (lame)
___ 6. hold but don't say /d/ (hole)
___ 7. cart but don't say /t/ (car)
___ 8. sting but don't say /t/ (sing)
___ 9. frame but don't say /r/ (fame)
___ 10. splint but don't say /n/ (split)
Total ___

Rhyming score (2 and 3) ___ Blending score (4 and 8) ___ Segmenting score (5 and 9) ___ Deleting score (6 and 10) ___ Phoneme discrimination score (1 and 7) ___

Figure 8A.1. The Phonological Awareness Skills Screener (PASS) test record form.

Learning Disabilities and Challenging Behaviors: Using the Building Blocks Model to Guide Intervention and Classroom Management, Third Edition, by Nancy Mather, Sam Goldstein, and Katie Eklund.
Copyright © 2015 Paul H. Brookes Publishing Co. All rights reserved.

F	Z	U	V	N	R	S
D	K	X	T	B	Y	I
M	O	J	G	W	P	
C	A	E	L	H	Q	

d	k	u	o	r	v	q
n	t	s	x	z	y	i
m	g	e	b	j	p	
a	c	w	f	l	h	

Figure 8A.2. Letter–Sound Identification charts and recording sheets. (*Key:* 1 = Correct response; 0 = Incorrect response. Correct responses = short vowel sounds for vowels [*a, e, i, o, u*] and hard sounds for *c* and *g* [e.g., *cat, gate*].)

(continued)

Figure 8A.2. (continued)

LETTER–SOUND IDENTIFICATION
Uppercase

Name _____

	Date		Date		Date		Date	
	Name	Sound	Name	Sound	Name	Sound	Name	Sound
F								
Z								
U								
V								
N								
R								
S								
D								
K								
X								
T								
B								
Y								
I								
M								
O								
J								
G								
W								
P								
C								
A								
E								
L								
H								
Q								
Totals								

Learning Disabilities and Challenging Behaviors: Using the Building Blocks Model to Guide Intervention and Classroom Management, Third Edition, by Nancy Mather, Sam Goldstein, and Katie Eklund.
Copyright © 2015 Paul H. Brookes Publishing Co. All rights reserved.

Figure 8A.2. *(continued)*

LETTER–SOUND IDENTIFICATION
Lowercase

Name _____

	Date		Date		Date		Date	
	Name	Sound	Name	Sound	Name	Sound	Name	Sound
d								
k								
u								
o								
r								
v								
q								
n								
t								
s								
x								
z								
y								
i								
m								
g								
e								
b								
j								
p								
a								
c								
w								
f								
l								
h								
Totals								

Learning Disabilities and Challenging Behaviors: Using the Building Blocks Model to Guide Intervention and Classroom Management, Third Edition, by Nancy Mather, Sam Goldstein, and Katie Eklund.
Copyright © 2015 Paul H. Brookes Publishing Co. All rights reserved.

APPENDIX 8B

The Relationship Between Speech Sounds and Spelling Development

Children's ability to spell develops through gradual refinement of their phonological and orthographic knowledge. Because young children have little knowledge of how spellings are influenced by word derivations, inflections, and lexical forms (e.g., *please* and *pleasant*), they typically spell what they hear. Developing writers have an unconscious knowledge of aspects of the English sound system, and their misspellings often reflect their developing linguistic knowledge (Treiman, 1998).

The information in this section has been synthesized and adapted from four sources (Moats, 1995, 2010; Read, 1971; Wilde, 1997). Although this information is somewhat technical, an understanding of the English sound system can help educators understand the reasons why younger students spell words the way they do as well as recognize linguistic difficulties with older students.

Phonemes are the smallest units of sound in a spoken language, and in an alphabetic language, phonemes are represented by graphemes (i.e., letters or groups of letters that represent a single sound). Most dialects of English have between 40 and 44 phonemes, but there are approximately 250 graphemes (i.e., letters or groups of letters) used to represent those phonemes. For example, consider the phoneme /f/. This sound can be spelled with several different graphemes: *f, ff, ph, lf,* or *gh.* Because there are several alternative spelling possibilities for most sounds of English, the process of spelling words is often much more difficult than the process of reading words. Rules regarding the allowable positions of letters within words underlie the spelling system; however, these rules are derived from many different sources and can be different from word to word, depending on the word's origin. Nevertheless, some rules remain consistent regardless of word origin. For example, an English word cannot begin with the letters *ff,* and standard English words almost never end in the letter *v.*

CONSONANTS AND VOWELS

Sounds of English fall under two main categories depending on the manner in which they are produced: consonants and vowels. For consonant sounds, air flow is obstructed or cut off partially or incompletely. For vowel sounds, air flow remains unobstructed. Sometimes consonants are called closed sounds and vowels are called open sounds.

Specific Learning Disabilities and the Processing Blocks

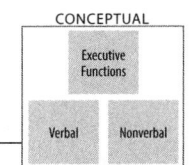
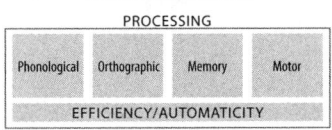
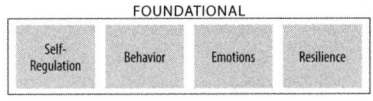

Consonants

Single consonant sounds (phonemes) can be represented by single graphemes, digraphs, or trigraphs. Multiple consonant sounds can be combined into blends, which are usually represented by multiple graphemes. Blends are two or more consonant sounds occurring in sequence that retain their identity (e.g., *bl* or *fr*). Digraphs and trigraphs refer to two or three adjacent letters that represent one phoneme not represented by either letter alone (e.g., *sh, gh,* or *tch*). Digraphs and trigraphs are particularly hard for children to learn to spell because they contain letters that are associated with different phonemes when they occur on their own. Therefore, children may leave out one letter in a digraph, spelling *ch,* for example, with the letter *c* or *h* or *ck* with the letter *c* or *k*.

Consonants are classified by the place of articulation (where the sound is made), manner of articulation (how the sound is made), and voicing (use of the vocal cords in sound production). The prescribed spelling of consonant sounds varies based on word origin; however, children's orthographic substitutions are often reasonable and may more accurately represent the phonemes of a word than does the word's actual spelling.

Voicing

Consonant sounds may be voiced or unvoiced. When voiced sounds (e.g., /b/ or /g/) are produced, the vocal cords vibrate, but when unvoiced sounds (e.g., /p/ or /k/) are produced, the vocal cords do not vibrate. The English language has eight pairs of consonant phonemes that differ only in voicing. Table 8B.1 lists the eight pairs of voiced and unvoiced consonants. The LiPS program (Lindamood & Lindamood, 1998) has child-friendly terminology for introducing these sounds, such as referring to /p/ and /b/ as "lip poppers" and /t/ and /d/ as "tip tappers." In the program, unvoiced sounds are referred to as "quiet sounds," whereas the voiced sounds are called "noisy sounds."

Place of Articulation

Place of articulation refers to where the sound is made in the mouth. Different sounds are pronounced using these different parts of the mouth:

1. Lips (bilabial): sounds made by bringing the lips together (e.g., /b/, /p/)
2. Lips and teeth (labiodental): sounds made with lips and teeth (e.g., /f/, /v/)

Table 8B.1. Voiced and unvoiced consonant pairs

Voiced	Unvoiced
/b/	/p/
/d/	/t/
/g/	/k/
/v/	/f/
/th/	/th/
/z/	/s/
/zh/	/sh/
/j/	/ch/

3. Tongue between the teeth (interdental): sounds made with the tongue between the teeth (e.g., /th/)
4. Tongue behind the teeth (alveolar): sounds made that use the ridge behind the teeth (e.g., /t/, /d/)
5. Roof of the mouth (palatal): sounds made that use the roof of the mouth (e.g., /j/)
6. Back of the mouth (velar): sounds made that use the soft palate at the back of the mouth cavity (e.g., /k/, /j/)
7. Throat (glottal): sound made at the vocal folds (e.g., /h/)

Manner of Articulation

Consonants are divided into the following five groups based on how the sound is obstructed as it travels through the mouth or nose: 1) stops (e.g., /b/ /p/), 2) nasals (e.g., /m/, /n/), 3) fricatives (e.g., /f/, /v/), 4) affricates (e.g., /j/), 5) glides (e.g., /w/), and 6) liquids (e.g., /l/, /r/). As noted, some of these are voiced (i.e., vocal cords vibrate), whereas others are unvoiced (i.e., vocal cords do not vibrate).

Stops

Stops are formed by closing off the stream of the breath completely (see Table 8B.2). These sounds last only a short time. In English, /t/ and /d/ are often reduced to a tongue flap between vowel sounds and are therefore indistinguishable in certain words (e.g., ladder and latter). Consequently, a child may spell *lidl* for *little* or *spitr* for *spider*.

Nasals

In English, nasals are formed by lowering the soft palate to allow air to escape through the nose (see Table 8B.3). These consonant sounds are acquired later in development than are most other consonant sounds. When a nasal (or liquid) occurs before a voiceless stop (e.g., /t/, /p/, /k/), children often omit the letter corresponding to the nasal sound in the written word because the nasal sound is not pronounced as strongly (e.g., wet for went). Omissions of nasals from written consonant blends account for a large proportion of the spelling errors children make through sixth grade. Children can learn how to detect nasals in words by holding their nose while pronouncing the words (e.g., wet and went). When a word contains a nasal sound, the air is trapped and makes a "nosy" sound. Children may overgeneralize the most common spelling of the /ng/ sound (e.g., *thingk* for *think*), or they may use the letter *g* to represent the /ng/ sound, such as in spelling the word *finger* as *fegr*. They also tend to spell *-ing* endings as *-eg* or *-ig*.

Table 8B.2. Examples of stops

	Voiced	Unvoiced
Lips (bilabial)	/b/ big	/p/ pig
Front of mouth (alveolar)	/d/ dip	/t/ tip
Back of mouth (velar)	/g/ got	/k/ cot

Specific Learning Disabilities and the Processing Blocks

Table 8B.3. Examples of nasals

Lips (bilabial)	/m/ mice
Front of mouth (alveolar)	/n/ nice
Back of mouth (velar)	/ng/ sing, sink

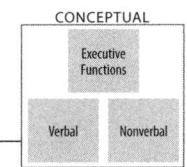
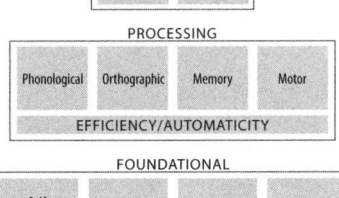

Fricatives

Fricatives are created by forcing air through a narrow channel between two articulators (see Table 8B.4). The vibrating airflow that is created is called frication. Some fricatives have a hissing (e.g., /s/, /z/) or hushing (e.g., /sh/, /zh/) sound; these fricatives are called sibilants. All the fricatives can be produced continuously, which means you can sustain the sound as long as you have breath. Because the voicing of fricatives is highly dependent on the phonemic environment in English, children may have difficulty identifying the correct grapheme or digraph to represent a fricative sound.

Affricates

Affricates are phonemes that are initially articulated as stops but released as fricatives (Table 8B.5). In English, the /ch/ and /j/ sounds are affricates. Examples include *chill, chip,* and *gypsy.* In certain dialects of English, /t/ and /d/ are affricated when they immediately precede an /r/ sound. Examples include saying *chrain* for train or *jress* for dress. The affrication of stops before an /r/ is common in the speech of some young children. Children may spell the /t/ sound as /ch/ and the /d/ sound as /j/, particularly before the letter *r.* They then produce the following types of spellings: *chrap* for trap or *jragn* or *jragin* for dragon. Children may continue to make such orthographic substitutions until they are taught to use the conventional spellings of these sounds.

Glides

Glides are considered semivowels (see Table 8B.6). These sounds are articulated like vowels, but they function like consonants in spoken language (i.e., they act as syllable boundaries). In spoken English, glides always occur right before vowel sounds and are never followed by another consonant sound. Diphthongs (two adjacent vowel sounds that occur within the same syllable) are glided, so children may attempt to spell the entire diphthong using only the grapheme that best represents the glide (e.g., *flwr* for flower).

Table 8B.4. Examples of fricatives

	Voiced	Unvoiced
Lips/teeth (labiodental)	/v/ vine	/f/ fine
Teeth (dental)	/th/ thy	/th/ thigh
Front of mouth (alveolar)	/z/ zip	/s/ sip
Roof of mouth (palatal)	/zh/ genre	/sh/ ship

Table 8B.5. Examples of affricates

	Voiced	Unvoiced
Roof of mouth (palatal)	/j/ jar	/ch/ char

Liquids

Liquids are a class of consonants in which the tongue partially obstructs the mouth, leaving the air to flow relatively freely through the unobstructed portion of the mouth (see Table 8B.7). In English, liquids tend to have a more sonorous and resonant quality than other consonants, and they can behave like vowels in some phonemic environments and like consonants in others. For example, the /l/ in *riddle* behaves much like a vowel, but the /l/ in *lid* behaves more like a consonant. Because liquids can behave like vowels, children may have difficulty distinguishing liquid sounds from vowel sounds when these sounds are adjacent. Thus, when writing, children often omit vowels when they are in close proximity to liquids. When vowels and liquids occur at the end of a word, the vowel sound is usually written as an *e*; however, children rarely represent such vowels in early writing, writing *tigr* for tiger or *tabl* for table. This omission of vowels next to liquids also occurs when the liquids occupy a medial position in words (e.g., *hrd* for heard, *grl* for girl).

Vowels

Depending on the dialect, English has about a dozen single phoneme vowel sounds (i.e., not including diphthongs) but phonics instruction tends to focus mostly on the long (tense) and short (lax) sounds. The number and type of vowel sounds vary from dialect to dialect, and some words that have the same vowel sound in one dialect may have different vowel sounds in another (e.g., *pin* and *pen* tend to have the same pronunciation in many parts of the Southern United States).

Vowels are a class of speech sounds that are made with an open vocal tract so that the sound is unobstructed. All English vowels are voiced, meaning that the vocal cords vibrate when vowel sound are produced. As with consonant sounds, vowel sounds are characterized by their articulatory properties. The sound of a vowel is determined by where it occurs in the mouth. Vowels are described in terms of the position of the tongue during articulation: front or back; and high, mid, or low.

Look at your mouth in a mirror and pronounce the following sequence of words while exaggerating the vowel sound: *beet, bit, bet, bat, but, good, boot, bought, hot.* Notice how your mouth moves from a more closed, smiley position to a more rounded open position. When children are spelling, vowel substitutions tend to be made with vowels that are adjacent in articulation, particularly the short (lax) /e/ and /i/ sounds. Most children do not master vowel spellings until fourth grade.

Table 8B.6. Examples of glides

Mouth moves from one vowel-like position to another	/w/ wet
	/y/ yet

Table 8B.7. Examples of liquids

Tip of tongue curls up	/r/ rap
Sides of tongue curl in	/l/ lap

Specific Learning Disabilities and the Processing Blocks

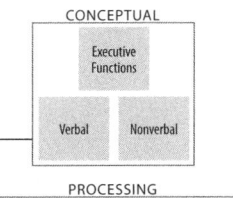
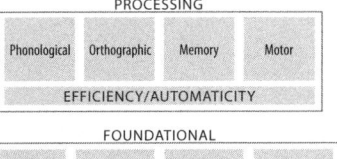

Short and Long Vowel Sounds

Although the terms *short vowel* and *long vowel* are used in phonics instruction, linguists use the terms *lax* for short vowels and *tense* for long vowels (Moats, 2010). The terms *long* and *short* are derived from a perception that tense vowels are held longer than lax vowels. In fact, in English, tense vowels are highly variable in length of articulation in comparison to lax vowels, which tend to be only briefly articulated. Another feature that distinguishes tense vowels from long vowels is the likelihood that the vowel is checked (i.e., followed by a consonant sound) within a syllable. In English, lax vowels are almost always checked in a stressed syllable, but tense vowels often are not.

Long (or tense) vowel sounds often sound like the names of the letters that are most commonly used to represent them (e.g., the /ee/ sound in *keep* sounds like the name of the letter *E*). Therefore, it is not uncommon for a child to write *ke* for key or *lade* for lady. Likewise, a child may spell a word such as igloo as *egloo* because the initial sound sounds like a long /e/ sound. Vowel sounds are often distorted when followed by an /r/, making words with vowels followed by /r/ harder to spell than other words.

Diphthongs

Diphthongs are not single sounds such as simple lax or tense vowels but are created when the tongue glides from one vowel position to another in the same syllable (e.g., /oi/, /ow/). Depending on the dialect, English has at least eight diphthongs, but most phonics programs tend to focus on just two: /oi/ and /ow/. The most common letters used to represent these sounds are *oi, oy, ow,* and *ou.*

Many of the spoken diphthongs of English, especially those beginning with long vowel sounds, are represented by single "long vowel" graphemes; examples include words such as *lure, pane,* and *hide*. Because children can hear the gliding sounds in these words, they may attempt to spell them using vowel digraphs, especially in words in which the vowel is followed by a voiced consonant such as /d/ (e.g., writing *raed* or *riyd* for ride or spelling the word fly as *fliy* and try as *triy*). It is therefore necessary to teach these vowel sounds as simple "long vowels" rather than diphthongs.

Digraph

A digraph is one consonant or vowel sound represented by two graphemes. Consonant digraphs for sounds that do not have single-letter equivalents, including *th, ch, sh,* and *ng,* must be taught explicitly, as must consonant digraphs for phonemes that have single letter equivalents (e.g., *wh* and *w* or *ph* and *f*). Vowel digraphs can be particularly challenging; children often omit one vowel grapheme from a vowel digraph, writing only the grapheme that best corresponds to the vowel sound (e.g., *fet* for feet, *bot* for boat).

Schwa

A schwa sound is a weak midcentral vowel sound that occurs in unstressed syllables (e.g., the first syllable in *about* and *upon*). This sound is represented by an upside-down lowercase e (ə). The schwa sound is the most likely vowel sound to be misspelled because the schwa can replace any vowel in an unstressed syllable, making it hard for the listener to determine what vowel was replaced. The spelling of the unstressed schwa sound becomes particularly problematic in third grade and beyond.

As children practice applying their knowledge of phonology to their temporary spellings, their proficiency increases. Through repeated exposures to phonological, orthographic, and morphological patterns, most children gradually come to master conventional spellings. Children with weaknesses in phonology, however, often continue to make these types of errors. After reading this appendix, reanalyze Maria's spelling in Figure 8.3. Try to identify all the errors that Maria makes on vowel sounds, nasals, and voiced and unvoiced consonant pairs.

CHAPTER 9 OUTLINE

DECODING AND ENCODING

- Skill Development in Decoding and Encoding
- Ehri's Phase Theory for Decoding and Encoding
- Stage Theories and the Strategy Approach for Spelling
- Spelling Assessment and Instruction
- Phonological Awareness to Print

PHONICS

- Synthetic Phonics
- Analytic Phonics

TYPE OF TEXT

- Instructional Level
- Decodable Text
- High-Frequency Words
- Multisensory Procedures for Reading and Writing

READING FLUENCY

- Determining a Student's Reading Rate
- Curriculum-Based Measurement for Reading
- Adjusting Reading Rate
- Instructional Activities for Increasing Reading Rate

CALCULATING

- Early Concepts
- Calculation Assessment
- Dyscalculia
- Multisensory Procedures for Calculation
- Calculators
- Error Analysis
- Modeling

HANDWRITING

- Readiness
- Fundamentals
- Developmental Stages
- General Principles
- Choosing a Writing Style
- Letter Formation
- Strategies to Build Writing Speed
- Computers
- Dysgraphia

CONCLUSION

APPENDIX 9A: FRY'S 600 INSTANT WORDS

CHAPTER 9

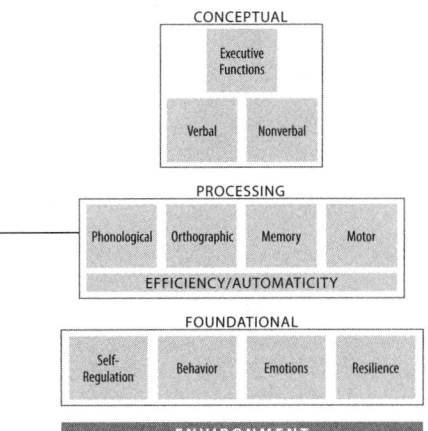

Instruction for the Processing Blocks

Decoding and Encoding, Reading Fluency, Calculating, and Handwriting

with Breanna Sherrow

Failure to learn to read as others do is a major catastrophe in a child's life.

—Dolch, 1939, p. 1

Students who have weaknesses in the Processing blocks and symbolic learning, such as Andy, Maria, Ryan, and Ben, require more repetition, more practice, and more review to acquire basic skills than children without these weaknesses. In general, instruction needs to be highly systematic and carefully designed, aimed at improving the overall level of skill and efficiency of the learner. In fact, when the results of intervention studies are compared, the type of the program is less important than its comprehensiveness and intensity (Fletcher et al., 2007). For basic skills instruction, effective strategies include the following components: 1) drills and probes, 2) provision of immediate feedback, 3) rapid pacing of instruction, and 4) carefully sequenced instruction (Swanson & Hoskyn, 1998). In addition, instruction needs to be adapted to the level of skill development. In this chapter, we discuss strategies for improving students' skills in decoding and encoding, reading fluency, calculating, and handwriting.

DECODING AND ENCODING

Decoding involves translating written print into speech by matching graphemes (a letter or combination of letters) to their phonemes (sounds). Encoding or spelling involves the reverse process, matching the sounds of the word to the correct letters they represent. Even though decoding mainly applies to reading and encoding mainly applies to spelling, both use similar processes such as sound–letter relationships (phoneme–grapheme) and the ability to recall letter strings and words. Even though learning to read and learning to spell involve almost identical processes, spelling is much more difficult (Ehri, 1997).

In order to identify a printed word on a page, a student needs to be able to break the sounds apart and then blend the sounds backs together to make the word—this is all a part of decoding. For example, if the student sees the word *boat,* the student needs to be able to break apart the sounds into /b/ /o/ /a/ /t/ and then be able to put the letters back together and blend to make the word *boat* again. When spelling a word, a student needs to be able to break pronunciations into the component sounds.

As noted in Chapter 8, dyslexia causes a breakdown in the acquisition and application of alphabet knowledge (i.e., phonology, orthography, or both), which results in slow, labored reading development; delayed automaticity; and poor spelling. Intervention requires direct, intensive instruction in the alphabetic system, followed by methods to build rate and fluency. Dyslexia, a neurobiological reading disorder, is the most common form of specific learning disability (SLD) with primary academic skill impairments in word reading and spelling (Fletcher et al., 2007). Children with dyslexia require substantially more practice to learn to read and spell. Moats (1995) indicated that before children with dyslexia can memorize a word, they require as many as 40 opportunities to write it correctly. Thus, students with dyslexia need direct, systematic instruction in both decoding and encoding. Students with reading disabilities need highly intensive reading interventions delivered by highly trained reading teachers that occur in small groups for 45 minutes or more per day; this type of intervention may be needed for several years (Vaughn & Wanzek, 2014).

As teachers work with students who are struggling to decode, they should also concentrate on helping students improve their spelling skills, as spelling is linked to reading (Mehta, Foorman, Branum-Martin, & Taylor, 2005). Students with word recognition and spelling problems require explicit instruction and practice in reading and spelling single words (Berninger et al., 2000). A meta-analysis conducted by Graham and Hebert (2010) summarized key elements of the impact of writing on reading outcomes and found that teaching spelling among students in Grades 1 to 7 had a significant impact on reading fluency, and teaching spelling skills in Grades 1 to 5 had a moderate impact on improving students' word reading skills (Graham & Hebert, 2010). The many aspects of reading and writing intertwine together into a braid that makes all the parts stronger (Bear, Invernizzi, Templeton, & Johnson, 2011).

Both decoding and encoding involve the language systems of phonology, orthography, and morphology. An individual may attempt to sound out a word by breaking it into its constituent elements or may recognize a word by sight. He or she may break the word apart into syllable units or by the prefix and the root word. With encoding, the writer must begin with sounds and images and then represent these patterns in writing. Thus, learning to encode is far more difficult than learning to decode, because to decode, one must produce single pronunciations and meanings for written words, whereas to encode, one must produce multiple letters in correct sequence (Ehri, 2000).

Figure 9.1 illustrates the relationship among decoding and encoding and phonological, orthographic, and motor abilities. As described by Berninger and colleagues, "Learning to spell requires that the mind's eye, ear, mouth, and hand learn to communicate in processing and producing spoken words" (2000, p. 118).

Results from a recent meta-analysis summarizing the effectiveness of treatment approaches for children and adolescents with reading disabilities suggested that interventions delivered by peers can be effective in improving reading performance (Galuschka, Ise, Krick, & Schulte-Köme, 2014). One type of student-led intervention practice is peer tutoring. Although peer tutoring typically involves pairing two students (one to act as the tutor and one to act as the tutee), peer tutoring can involve a variety of configurations. Different arrangements for peer

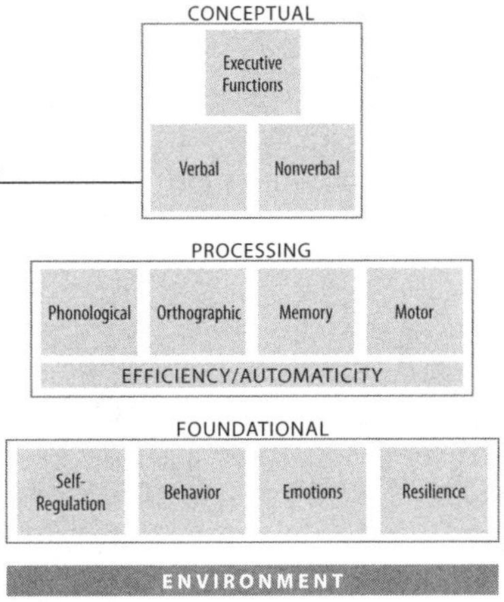

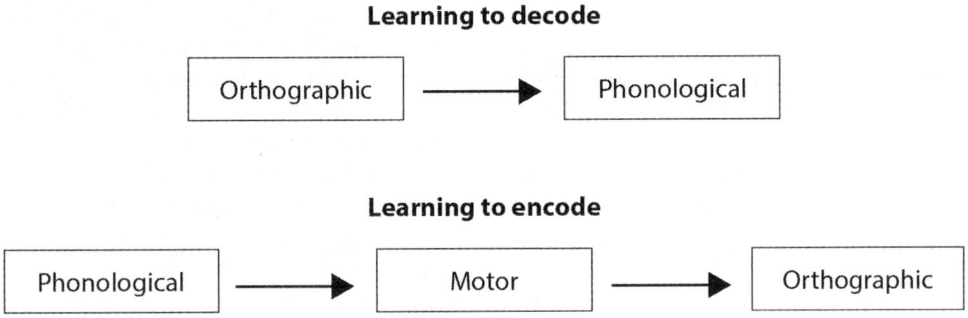

Instruction for the Processing Blocks

Learning to decode

Orthographic → Phonological

Learning to encode

Phonological → Motor → Orthographic

Figure 9.1. Relationship between decoding and encoding.

tutoring include total class peer tutoring or classwide peer tutoring, mixed ability peer tutoring, and cross-age tutoring. One study investigated the impact of a peer-tutoring intervention on middle school students with and without disabilities across cotaught and non-cotaught science classroom settings. The term *cotaught* describes a classroom where two teachers teach in conjunction with one another. Often a general education teacher will teach alongside a special education teacher so that the needs of students with and without disabilities can be addressed at the same time. Overall, students in the cotaught classrooms outperformed students in the control groups on both unit tests and cumulative posttests (McDuffie, Mastropieri, & Scruggs, 2009).

Skill Development in Decoding and Encoding

As students learn to read, they progress naturally through various stages or phases. As noted in Chapter 8, phonological and orthographic awareness provide support for both decoding and encoding development. When young children are first introduced to reading, they often memorize words as whole units. With more exposure to print, they develop the knowledge that, in an alphabetic language such as English, printed letters represent speech sounds (i.e., the alphabetic principle). Students start observing the details and differences among words. They then begin to notice that words are formed of common parts and units. Soon their attempts to decode new words are based on letter groupings and orthographic patterns as opposed to single letters and sounds. The more they engage in reading, the more rapidly they recognize words and the more fluent their reading becomes. Skilled word identification then provides the reader with the opportunity to comprehend. As we discuss in Chapters 10 and 11, as long as a student has developed skilled word identification, comprehension of text is related to the abilities in the Conceptual blocks, including verbal abilities and executive functioning.

For many students, learning to read follows a natural progression, but for children with severe weaknesses in symbolic learning, it does not. Spear-Swerling and Sternberg (1996) discussed what happens when poor readers go "off track" on the road to reading success or fail to progress typically in skill acquisition. In addition to struggling with reading, they descend to the "swamp of reading disability" (Spear-Swerling & Sternberg, 1996, p. 134). This swamp is characterized by lowered expectations from teachers, lowered levels of practice, and lowered levels of motivation. Once a student is entangled in the swamp, it is difficult to get back on track. For example, even as late as middle school, neither Ryan nor Ben spent time reading unless an adult sat and read along with them.

Some students are not able to decode words in a complete and accurate manner even in middle school and secondary school. When Ben's reading and spelling development were reviewed in eighth grade, it became apparent that he went off track in second grade. In second grade, Ben had trouble memorizing words and building a sight vocabulary. He hesitated before pronouncing common words such as *of.* His oral reading was characterized by numerous pauses and repetitions. He also did not analyze words carefully when trying to pronounce them. When reading a short passage from an informal reading inventory in third grade, he identified the word *penny* as *party,* and then in the next line, he read it as *pretty.* In spelling, he had difficulty with producing letter sequences and spelling irregular words. Ben made many reading and spelling errors and tended to misread words that were similar in appearance. For example, he misread the word *experiment* as *experience.* This weakness appears to be most related to insufficient formation of orthographic images in memory and failure to note all the features in the word.

Students with weaknesses in symbolic learning often experience difficulty during a stage of reading development or when developing strategies for word identification. Ehri (1998) explained that skilled readers can identify different words when reading in at least five different ways:

1. By blending the sounds of letters into words
2. By pronouncing and blending spelling patterns
3. By retrieving sight words from memory
4. By making analogies to words already known by sight
5. By using context clues to predict words

A central goal of instruction is to ensure that students can use all the strategies for word identification and that they do not have to rely on one strategy, such as guessing at the words solely on the basis of context. As Ehri noted, skilled reading is based on retrieving sight words rapidly and easily from memory because all the other cuing systems require attention and disrupt the reading process. Thus, the Efficiency/Automaticity block underlies and promotes skilled reading performance.

When Maria was in first grade, her teacher observed that she seemed to rely primarily on context clues. She would look at the picture, think of words that made sense, and make up the text. She showed limited ability to use phoneme–grapheme (i.e., sound–letter) clues to check her word predictions. She also seemed unaware of where word breaks were in the text and how these breaks might relate to the space breaks on the page. For example, where the text said, "The hand," Maria ran her finger underneath the text and read, "The hand is coming out." When asked to point to a particular word on the page, she was unable to do so. Fortunately, her teacher could see that Maria needed to acquire specific concepts about phoneme–grapheme relationships before she would develop a sight vocabulary.

Ehri's Phase Theory for Decoding and Encoding

Ehri (2005) preferred the term *phase theory* to stage theory, suggesting that phase theory provides a more accurate description of the course of development because the stages of reading and spelling are not qualitatively distinct. Essentially, the qualities of the connections that children make develop from visual nonalphabetic, to partial alphabetic, to full grapho-phonemic, to consolidated grapho-syllabic and grapho-morphemic (Ehri, 2014). Ehri (1998, 2000, 2005, 2014) described four

Instruction for the Processing Blocks

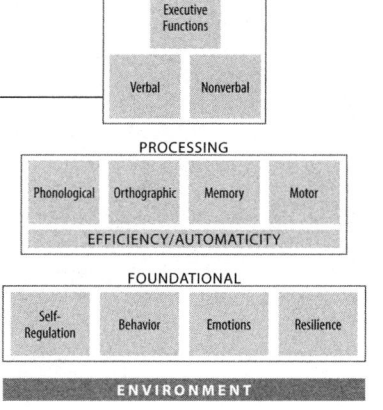

phases that underlie the development of both a sight vocabulary and spelling: prealphabetic, partial alphabetic, full alphabetic, and consolidated alphabetic. During the prealphabetic phase or visual nonalphabetic phase (Ehri, 2014), readers recognize words by selected visual attributes that are not connected to phoneme–grapheme relationships. They remember words by configuration or general visual appearance, and their spellings are often a string of letters in random order (Moats, 2010). In kindergarten, Maria knew the word *look* because her teacher had drawn eyes into the two *O*s. Once students begin to use alphabetic processes, the subsequent phases emerge successively (Ehri, 2005). In the partial alphabetic phase, readers discover the alphabetic principle and make connections between some of the letters and sounds in written words. In the full alphabetic phase, students make complete connections between letters and sounds, and they are able to pronounce phonically regular words. In the consolidated alphabetic phase, letter patterns that occur across many words are retained. These larger units consist of morphemes, syllables, or onsets and rimes.

Stage Theories and the Strategy Approach for Spelling

As with reading, students progress through developmental phases in learning to spell. Two theoretical approaches have been proposed to explain spelling development: stage theories and the strategy approach. Some theorists propose that children appear to progress through several developmental stages or phases when learning to spell (Ehri, 1986, 1989; Gentry, 1982, 1984, 1987; Henderson, 1990; Reid, 1988; Weiner, 1994). For example, Henderson (1990) outlined five development stages: 1) scribbles and pictures (i.e., the preliterate stage), 2) letter–name representation (i.e., letters are used to represent sounds), 3) recognition of within-word patterns (i.e., orthographic and morphological patterns are observed), 4) syllable juncture (i.e., consonants are doubled and patterns present in syllables are observed), and 5) derivational constancy (i.e., roots and derivations are used).

The strategy approach depicts spelling development as being more continuous, suggesting that children incorporate a variety of spelling strategies from the very beginning of their acquisition of writing skills (Treiman, 1998). Although they help depict spelling development, stage theories, unlike the strategy approach, do not capture fully the complexities of the phonological, orthographic, and morphological representations that are related to spelling (Treiman & Bourassa, 2000). However, even though many children do incorporate varied aspects of linguistic knowledge in their initial spellings and reveal sensitivity to orthographic and morphological influences, the proposed stages of development help explain how reading and spelling abilities evolve.

Similar Theories of Spelling Development

Other researchers in addition to Ehri (1998) have developed similar theories that focus primarily on spelling development (Gentry, 1984; Henderson, 1990). Although the stages or phases described vary somewhat in enumeration and description from Ehri's, they typically include five stages: 1) prephonetic, 2) semiphonetic, 3) phonetic, 4) transitional, and 5) conventional. Students with spelling difficulties appear to progress through similar stages as their peers, but their development is slower. Often, their difficulties appear indicative of arrest in one of the following stages in spelling development (Moats, 1991).

Prephonetic or Prephonemic In the initial and earliest phases of learning to spell, a child combines a string of unrelated letters to communicate a message. When first writing, many children are not aware of the alphabetic principle and simply write known letters. Figure 9.2 presents a story written by Maria in kindergarten. The first line contains both letters and numbers. At the bottom of the page, she wrote wavy lines as she made the comment, "I think I'll just write the rest in cursive." At this phase, the child knows little about the alphabetic system and recognizes words through memory of selected visual features (Ehri, 2005).

Semiphonetic or Partial Alphabetic In the semiphonetic phase, letters are used to represent sounds, but only a few sounds in words are represented. Children recognize some of the letters and sounds in words, such as the first and last letter sounds in the word. In some instances, students may use the names of letters rather than the letter sounds (Adams, 1990). For example, the word *while* may be written as *yl*. They may spell by writing a few consonants that are the most salient in speech, such as spelling the word *happy* as *hp* (Moats, 2010). During this phase, although spellings may follow logical linguistic patterns, children know very few correct spellings. A student may know consonant sounds, long vowel sounds, and an occasional sight word. Figure 9.3 illustrates Ryan's writing when he was in third grade. He is giving advice to Winnie the Pooh about when he should climb trees to avoid the bees. As can be seen, some of his attempted spellings are semiphonetic (e.g., *wn*), whereas others are phonetic (e.g., *clim*).

Many older children with reading disabilities would be identified as partial alphabetic phase readers (Ehri, 2005). Ehri suggested that partial alphabetic phase readers do not store sight words in memory in sufficient letter detail to recognize how they are similar yet different from other words.

Figure 9.2. Maria's kindergarten story.

Instruction for the Processing Blocks

Figure 9.3. Ryan's story about Winnie the Pooh: "He should climb when the bees are gone."

Phonetic or Full Alphabetic In the phonetic phase, students produce spellings that demonstrate grapheme–phoneme correspondence. When writing, they attempt to record all the sounds within a word and present them in the correct sound sequence. Students with weaknesses in the Orthographic block often overrely on sounds as a strategy for spelling (see Chapter 8). Even in eighth grade, Ben's attempted spellings revealed too much reliance on sounds. Individuals like Ben who have weaknesses in orthographic processing continue to produce phonetic spellings into adulthood.

Transitional or Consolidated Alphabetic In the transitional phase, the writer demonstrates awareness of many of the conventions of English orthography. For example, the student spells the ending of the past tense of a verb as *-ed* even when the ending sounds like a /t/, such as in the word *trapped*. Operating with chunks of words makes it easier for the student to decode and encode multisyllabic words (Ehri, 2000, 2005).

Conventional In this phase, the writer possesses multiple strategies for determining standard spelling. Although not all words are spelled correctly, the writer regularly employs information from all sources, sounds, sight, and meaning as an aid to English spelling.

Spelling Assessment and Instruction

As a general rule, teachers should not give students lists of words to memorize for a spelling test until students understand how the spelling system works (Ehri, 1998). Ehri indicated that children should be able to generate spellings that are phonetically complete and possible English spellings before they should be expected to memorize a list of words for a spelling test. She stated,

> Learning the spellings of specific words by memorizing word lists should not begin until students understand how the conventional system works graphophonically. Once this point is reached, remembering the spellings of specific words will be much easier, so spelling instruction can shift to this learning activity. (1998, p. 34)

Otaiba and Hosp (2010) summarized why assessment and instruction need to be linked for the area of spelling. Even though a variety of spelling assessments focus on different aspects of spelling at different grade levels, they present three main conclusions about spelling assessment and instruction:

1. Spelling assessment should not be restricted to certain grades or ability levels.
2. Detailed error analysis, when done systematically and in a standardized fashion, yields much richer data than simply examining correct–incorrect responses.
3. Different approaches to error analysis based on different theories have validity and utility, possibly for different purposes or at different levels of development. (2010, p. 5)

Spelling Flow List

An alternative to a traditional spelling test in which the teacher picks the words without any consideration to whether the child knows the word or not is a spelling flow list (Mather & Jaffe, in press; adapted from McCoy and Prehm, 1987). The main purpose of a spelling flow list is to give students considerable practice and review so that they can master the words. With a spelling flow list, students are tested daily on a few words. A word is kept on the list until it is spelled correctly 3 days in a row. Unlike a weekly spelling test in which the words are fixed, the words in a spelling flow list change as the student learns each word. Words are reviewed each week. When a word that was spelled correctly 3 days in a row is missed during review, the word is then added back to the spelling flow list.

A spelling flow list was used to help Ben improve his spelling skills when he was in fifth grade. He was still misspelling basic common words such as *they*. His teacher used the following steps:

1. Ben would identify six words that he uses in his writing but spells incorrectly. He could select the words either from his writing or from a high-frequency word list, such as the list presented in Appendix 9A.
2. The selected words were placed on the spelling flow list form.
3. Ben would study the words and then his teacher would test him daily on the words.
4. Ben's teacher marked each correctly spelled word with a *C* and each incorrect word with a check.
5. When a word was spelled correctly 3 days in a row, it would be crossed off the list, and a new word would be added. Ben would file all correct words alphabetically into a word bank.
6. One week later, Ben's teacher would check to make sure that he still knew how to spell words added to the bank. If a word were incorrect, Ben would add the word back on his list. A sample form is presented in Figure 9.4.

Struthers, Bartlamay, Dell, and McLaughlin (1994) investigated the use of an add-a-word spelling program for students with spelling difficulties. In this program,

Instruction for the Processing Blocks

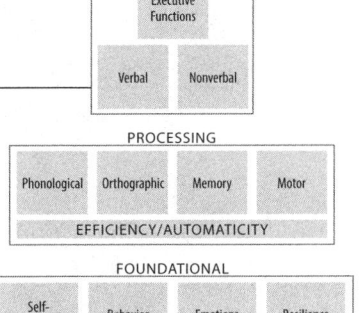

Spelling Flow List

Name: BenStarting Date: 11/12

Study word	M	T	W	TH	F	M	T	W	TH	F	M	T	W	TH	F
they	C	C	C			C									
said	C	✓	✓	C	C	C					✓				
people	✓	C	C	C			✓								
would	✓	C	✓	C	C	C					✓				
could	✓	C	C	C				C						C	
should	✓	C	C	C				C						C	
were			✓	C	C	C						C			✓
any				C	✓	✓	C	C	C						C
people										✓	C	C	✓	✓	C
said											C	✓	C	C	
would											C	C	C		
every											C	C	C		
busy														✓	✓
because															✓
any															C
friend															C

C = Correct
✓ = Incorrect

Figure 9.4. Sample spelling flow list.

students had individualized words presented on a flow list instead of a fixed spelling list. When the spelling of a word was correct on three consecutive daily tests, the word was replaced by another. The dropped words were retested at a later date. When mastery was demonstrated, they were removed from the list. The results of the study indicated that this type of procedure was more effective for struggling students than having traditional weekly spelling tests.

This procedure could also be adapted to assessing and learning sight words. Write or have the students write high-frequency words on cards. Have the students practice these words and then test the students on them daily. When a student identifies a word 3 days in a row correctly, file the word or have the student file the word in the student's word bank. A week later, review the word and replace it on the list for additional review, if needed.

Spelling Rubric

Another alternative to traditional spelling tests is a spelling rubric (Loeffler, 2005). Unlike traditional spelling tests that "do not provide insight into the spelling cues that students are using," a spelling rubric provides students opportunities to correct their own writing and use context clues (Loeffler, 2005, p. 24). As students with learning disabilities have been known to do well on traditional spelling tests by rote memorization, this strategy helps these students learn to internalize the strategies for spelling (Loeffler, 2005). Students work on their spelling by circling and correcting misspelled words in their own writing, which is then graded by a spelling rubric. Students are also praised for sounding out words, using the dictionary or spell checker to correct the word, or finding familiar words with similar patterns to help them spell unfamiliar words (Loeffler, 2005).

Curriculum-Based Measurement for Spelling

Curriculum-based measurement (CBM) was first developed more than 20 years ago by Stanley Deno and colleagues through a federal contract to develop a measurement system to evaluate students' basic growth skills (Deno, Mirkin, & Marston, 1982). CBM is used to monitor individual student short- and long-term progress in the areas of written expression, math, reading, and spelling (Riley-Heller, Kelly-Vance, & Shriver, 2005). CBM is simple, accurate, and an efficient indicator of student progress and achievement used to guide instruction. CBMs can be collected on an ongoing basis including weekly, biweekly, or even once a month. The following steps can be used to prepare probes:

1. Prepare a list of 12 (Grades 1–3) to 17 (Grades 4–8) spelling words from the end of the year curriculum.
2. Prepare a sheet with numbered lines to write words.
3. Announce a new spelling word each 10 seconds (Grades 1–3) and every 7 seconds (Grades 4–8).
4. Continue the administration for 2 minutes.

Although CBM spelling probes can be individually administered, they are typically given to a group of students. The teacher or examiner reads the first word and starts a stopwatch. Each word is only repeated twice, and homonyms (words that sound alike but have different meaning—e.g., *weak* and *week*) are used in a sentence to clarify their meaning (e.g., "Week. This is the last week of July.").

Scoring of CBM spelling probes provides students with partial credit for correct letter sequences (CLS) in contrast to traditional spelling tests that only give credit when all letters are in the correct order. Correct letter sequences are pairs of letters in a word that are right next to each other. A student receives a point for each CLS in the word. There is always an assumption that there is a phantom letter at the beginning of the word (_apple) and end of the word (apple_). The total possible correct letter sequences are obtained by adding the numbers of letters in a word plus one. Correct letter sequences are represented by carats (^). For instance, the word *apple* (^a^p^p^l^e^) has six CLS. If a student spells the word apple as *aple,* the student would receive five CLS (^a^p^l^e^) as opposed to being marked wrong for only forgetting one letter in the word. In eighth grade, Ben wrote *koma* instead of *coma.* The word *coma* has five CLS (^c^o^m^a^). If graded with traditional scoring, Ben would have gotten this word wrong, but with CBM scoring, Ben receives three CLS (k^o^m^a^). Using CBM spelling scoring could help Ben to see his progress in spelling instead of being discouraged by having words marked as incorrect by his teacher.

Instruction for the Processing Blocks

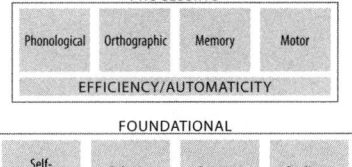

Metrics for Scoring Spelling

The Spelling Sensitivity Score (SSS) is a metric assessment created to be more sensitive to specific changes in a student's development of spelling throughout the year (Masterson & Apel, 2010, p. 37). In the SSS, each word is divided into specific elements (e.g., phonemes, juncture changes, affixes; Masterson & Apel, 2010). "When analyzing words with one morpheme, *butter* would be divided into B-U-TT-ER, *dog* into D-O-G, and *rain* into R-AI-N" (Masterson & Apel, 2010, p. 37). When analyzing words with more than one morpheme, the separation is between the base word and the affixes (prefixes or suffixes). For example, the word *dogs* has two morphemes: *dog* and *s*. In this case, *dog* is the base morpheme and *s* is the suffix.

After words are divided into specific elements, each element of a spelling word is scored on a scale of 0 to 3 points based on the following specific criteria (Masterson & Apel, 2010, p. 37):

3 points: All specific elements are spelled correctly.

2 points: The element is spelled incorrectly yet with a plausible or legal spelling (e.g., as in *bote* for *boat*).

1 point: The element is spelled incorrectly without a plausible or legal spelling (e.g., as in *ceke* for *cake*).

0 points: The element is omitted (as in in *sop* for *stop*).

Once all of the elements within each word have been scored 0 to 3 points within a student's writing sample, two scores are acquired. This includes the *SSS–Elements* (SSS-E) and the *SSS–Words* (SSS-W). SSS-E and SSS-W provide the kind of information that helps teachers monitor increases in word knowledge and spelling development (Masterson & Apel, 2010).

Ritchey, Coker, and McCraw compared four scoring metrics for two distinct data sets and found that using metrics can provide an "equivalent index" for spelling skills with just one assessment point (2009, pp. 78, 87). The four scoring metrics were total words correct, correct sounds, correct letter sequences, and phonological coding. For total words correct, the student receives one point for spelling the entire word correct (*dog* = 1) or no points for spelling the word incorrect (*dat* = 0). For correct sounds, the student is given points for each correct sound (phoneme) in the word even if the target letter is not used by the student. For the word *cat*, the following points would be given: *cat* = 3, *kat* = 3, *catc* = 3, *kaf* = 2, *ct* = 2, *k* = 1 (Ritchey et al., 2009, p. 81). Correct letter sequences are scored the same as CBMs for spelling, as one point is earned for the correct first letter, a point for the last letter, and an additional point is awarded for each correct letter sequence in the word. For example, the word *frog* has four letters and would therefore have five correct letter sequences (4 + 1 = 5): (^f^r^o^g^).

Spelling Rating Scales

When evaluating a student's spelling development, a spelling rating scale is more sensitive to measuring growth than the use of dichotomous scoring (i.e., correct or incorrect). Tangel and Blachman (1992) developed a scale based on phonological coding where spellings earn a score between 0 and 6:

0 = Random string of letters

1 = An initial sound represented by a phonologically related letter (e.g., *k, c*) or another sound in the word must be represented

2 = Initial sound represented by the correct letter

3 = Initial sound spelled correctly and has at least one additional sound spelled correctly, even if it is out of sequence

4 = All sounds represented, but one of them may be phonetically related

5 = All sounds represented with conventional letters and long vowel sounds must be attempted

6 = Correct spelling

As another example, the following scale, adapted from Tangel and Blachman (1992) and Kroese, Hynd, Knight, Hiemenz, and Hall (2000), can be used to evaluate spelling on tests:

0 points = Random letters

1 point = One phonetically related letter

2 points = Correct initial phoneme

3 points = Two correct phonemes (does not have to be correct grapheme)

4 points = Correct number of syllables represented (only used for multisyllabic words)

5 points = All phonemes in the word are represented

6 points = All phonemes in the word are represented with possible English spellings (e.g., *rane* for *rain*)

7 points = Correct spelling

Simpler scales could be used for younger students:

0 points = No correct phonemes

1 point = One correct phoneme

2 points = Two or more correct phonemes

3 points = All sounds represented

4 points = Correct spelling

This type of scoring system can help a teacher monitor a student's progress in sequencing sounds correctly.

Selecting Spelling Words

A serious mismatch is often found between a child's level of spelling development and the words that the student is assigned to memorize for a Friday spelling test. When Ryan was in third grade, he did not know how to spell many simple words, such as *they* and *was*. Despite this, his Friday spelling test contained the words *Chinese* and *chopsticks*. Ben was given lists of words to memorize that he could not even read in sixth grade. His spelling score almost every Friday was 0%. When selecting

Instruction for the Processing Blocks

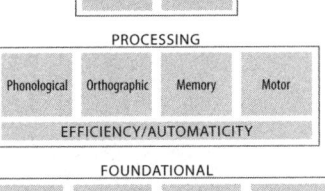
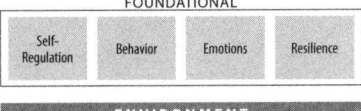

words for spelling practice, make sure that the child knows how to read each word, understands the meaning of the word, and uses the word in speaking and writing.

Scott (2000) suggested several ideas for selecting and using word lists for students having difficulty with spelling:

- Use high-frequency words.
- Use self-selected words.
- Use some irregular words.
- Use multisensory study techniques.
- Practice fewer words, more often, over longer time periods.
- Use computers to practice words.
- Use computer programs that allow teacher input of word lists.

Several instructional activities are described in the next section that can help students increase their knowledge of word spellings.

Phonological Awareness to Print

For students with weaknesses in phonology, explicit instruction in phonemic awareness should be coupled with instruction in phoneme–grapheme relationships (Calfee, 1998). By the end of kindergarten, children should be able to blend and segment sounds and use sounds to spell simple words (Chard & Dickson, 1999). As a first step, students must grasp the alphabetic principle. This principle has been defined simply as the understanding that the discrete letters of the alphabet represent the discrete sounds of speech (Liberman, Shankweiler, & Liberman, 1989). In other words, the beginning reader must discover that words have an internal phonemic structure that is represented by letters, and then they must be able to use and apply this knowledge.

When Maria was in fifth grade, she wrote the word *dentist* as *detestd*. Based on her spelling of the word *dentist*, it is apparent Maria has trouble with phonology or primarily phonological awareness, as she is leaving out sounds and confusing the sounds /d/ and /t/. Maria needs a teacher who can provide her with explicit instruction in phonological awareness, which contains direct teachings of letter–sound relationships. Several training programs are available that are designed to help teachers increase their abilities to teach and understand language structure, including the *Language Essentials for Teachers of Reading and Spelling* (LETRS) and *Mindplay Teacher's Companion, Companion Plus, and Understanding Dyslexia Courses.* (See Additional Resources.)

Invented or Temporary Spelling

One way to help students increase phonological awareness is to encourage the use of invented spelling. Invented spelling has been found to lead to a greater awareness of orthography and phonology (Ouellette & Sénéchal, 2008). Invented spelling does not mean that the word bears no resemblance to the correct spelling or that students simply make up the spellings of a word. Instead, invented spelling means that students listen carefully to the sounds in a word and then write the sounds in the correct order. Encouraging children to produce their own spellings requires them to think about the ways that words are written. Many teachers now refer to invented spelling as temporary spelling. The concept of temporary spelling communicates to parents that this type of spelling is only a stage in the developmental process and that it is important to teach correct spelling once students understand how to sequence the sounds in a word.

Ouellette and Sénéchal (2008) conducted a study in which students were split into three groups: One group received an invented-spelling training, one control group was asked to draw pictures for words, and one control group received an alternative phonological awareness training. Students in the invented-spelling training made the most gains in both reading and spelling. The use of "temporary" spelling helps students increase phonological awareness as well as skill in pairing sounds with letters.

When children are first learning to spell, they often pronounce the word and then attempt to write the sequence of sounds in order (phoneme to grapheme conversion). As skill progresses in spelling, children begin to incorporate orthographic and morphological strategies. They record memorized combinations of letter sequences, such as the *-ight* pattern in the word *night*. After writing a word, they may analyze the word to see if the sequence of letters looks right. They may also think that even though a word sounds like it ends in a /t/ (e.g., *jumped*), the spelling is likely to be *-ed* because *-ed* signifies past tense.

Because invented spelling reduces reliance on memory of how words appear, children who have difficulty picturing the visual appearance of words can increase their knowledge of sounds by writing words according to the way that they sound. When students are attempting to spell an unknown word, encourage them to pronounce the word slowly aloud while they attempt to sequence the sounds in the correct order.

For students who enter school with poor phonological awareness, more than just writing with invented spelling is needed to help them grasp phoneme–grapheme associations (Treiman, 1998). These students require instruction that is more explicit and intense. Liberman and colleagues (1989) noted that approximately 75% of students gain an understanding of the connection between spoken and written words without much explicit instruction but that the other 25% of children require explicit instruction or they remain locked into a sight word stage of reading. These children require direct, intensive, and systematic training in how phonological structure relates to reading and spelling. The earlier in a child's school career these difficulties are addressed, the better.

Many of the activities designed to build this knowledge involve moving around letters to form words by using letter cards, alphabet blocks, Scrabble tiles, or magnetic letters. In addition, words can be constructed by using a small pocket chart. Specific examples of activities used to help students increase their knowledge of phoneme–grapheme relationships are described in the following sections.

Teaching students about the regularities that exist in the language is more important than asking them to memorize phonic or spelling rules (Ehri, 2000). Teachers can foster linguistic awareness by engaging children in activities that involve active word study. Once students can sequence sounds, in-depth instruction in word structure is appropriate. The goal of this instruction is to help children understand (as much as possible) why English words are spelled the way that they are spelled.

Talk-to-Yourself Chart

Gaskins (1998) described a procedure called a talk-to-yourself chart that is used at the Benchmark School to help students learn common English spelling patterns. The purpose is to teach students to fully analyze keywords, or words that contain

Instruction for the Processing Blocks

high-frequency spelling patterns. This procedure is based on the premise that it is easier for students to segment a word into sounds if they do not already have a visual image.

The teacher introduces a keyword such as the word *right* and then asks students to stretch out the sounds and raise a finger for each sound that they hear. After the students respond by raising three fingers, the teacher places the word card up on the board and asks the students to count the number of letters that they see. Next, the students are asked to attempt to match the letters they hear with the letters that they see: The letters *r* and *t* each represent one sound and the three letters *igh* represent the vowel sound. The talk-to-yourself chart, adapted from this program (Gaskins, 1998), is placed on the board to remind the students of the steps involved:

1. The word is _____.
2. When I stretch the word, I hear _____ sounds.
3. There are _____ letters because _____.
4. The spelling pattern is _____.
5. This is what I know about the vowel: _____.
6. Another word I know with the same vowel sound is _____.
7. Other words that share this same spelling pattern are _____.

Using the example of the word *right*, students would say the following:

1. The word is *right*.
2. When I stretch the word, I hear three sounds.
3. There are five letters because it takes *igh* to represent the /i/ sound.
4. The spelling pattern is *ight*.
5. This is what I know about the vowel: The vowel is the only vowel in the word, and it says its own name.
6. Another word that I know with the same vowel sound is *ride*.
7. Other words that share this same spelling pattern are *night, might, fight, tight, sight, right, plight,* and *fright.*

This type of procedure can also help students such as Ryan, Maria, and Ben with spelling. The emphasis is not placed on teaching specific rules but rather on making explicit the connection between phonemes and graphemes. For instruction in both decoding and encoding, it is best to help children recognize and then internalize common English spelling patterns. Memorized rules do not improve spelling performance. A student must develop a working knowledge of the alphabetic system that he or she can apply to decoding or encoding (Ehri, 2000).

Adapted Elkonin Procedure

Elkonin (1973), a Russian psychologist, developed several simple procedures for explaining to students the relationship between speech sounds and printed letters. The following procedure, adapted from Elkonin, moves the student gradually from counting speech sounds to translating these sounds into letters.

1. Select a simple line drawing.
2. Place a rectangle for a word related to the drawing under the drawing. Divide the rectangle into squares equal to the number of phonemes. Begin with words

in which the number of phonemes matches the number of graphemes. In other words, the number of sounds should match the number of letters.

3. Ask the student to say the word slowly and push a marker forward for each sound, using poker chips or colored tiles. Once a student is able to perform Step 3 with confidence, progress to Step 4.

4. In Step 4, color-code markers for vowels and consonants, such as representing consonant sounds with blue poker chips and vowel sounds with red poker chips. Have the student push forward the blue chips for the consonant sounds and the red chips for the vowel sounds in the word. Once a student can identify and differentiate vowel and consonant sounds, proceed to Step 5.

5. In Step 5, use letter tiles, magnetic letters, or letter cards. At first, use words in which single phonemes are represented by single graphemes. Once a student is able to spell words with predictable spelling patterns, introduce additional graphemes. For example, demonstrate how the word *came* has three speech sounds but four letters. In these examples, the number of boxes does not match the number of speech sounds, so make larger squares for the speech sounds that can be heard and smaller boxes for the letters that are silent. The word *came* would have three large boxes (*c, a, m*) and one small box for the silent *e*. Write consonant and vowel digraphs (i.e., one speech sound spelled with two letters) in one box. For example, when writing the word *boat*, make three boxes, placing the *oa* into the middle box. Discuss with the student the difference between how a word is written and what is spoken. This type of instruction can improve both decoding and encoding ability because the emphasis is placed on segmenting and blending sounds. The Lanternfish web site allows teachers to create worksheets with pictures and Elkonin boxes with ease (http://www.bogglesworldesl.com).

Auditory Sequencing

Bannatyne (1971) discussed a similar procedure for helping students attend to the sequence of sounds when spelling.

1. Make small letter cards or use Scrabble tiles.
2. Sound out a word slowly and have the student attempt to place the letter tiles in correct sequence from left to right. When necessary, provide demonstrations on how to arrange the tiles before the child attempts to build the word.
3. After building the word, encourage the student to trace and then print the word.
4. As skill increases, use individual letter tiles to break words into syllables or to build several words around a root.

Teachers can also put dots under each letter or an arrow under the word to reinforce the concept of blending the sounds together. As skill develops, teachers can begin using an activity such as Making Words (Cunningham & Cunningham, 1992; Cunningham & Hall, 1994) to help students learn to sequence sounds in longer words.

Making Words

The purpose of Making Words, a guided invented spelling task, is to help students develop phonemic awareness and discover how the alphabetic system works by increasing their understanding of grapheme–phoneme relationships. This strategy

Instruction for the Processing Blocks

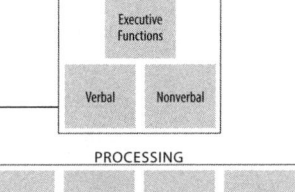
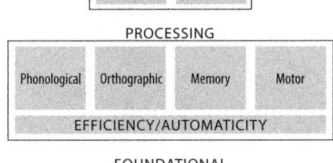
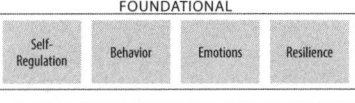

should be used along with typical writing activities. In this 15-minute activity, students are individually given letters that they will use to make 12–15 words. The activities begin with short easy words and end with a big word that uses all the letters. For the first lessons, students are given only one vowel letter, which is written in red, and several consonants. Later, students may be given two or more vowels. The patterns begin with two-letter words and increase in length. The final word, a six-, seven-, or eight-letter word, includes all the letters that the students have. In all activities, emphasis is placed on how the pronunciation of words changes when letters are moved and added.

Cunningham and Hall have presented lessons for this activity in several books (see Additional Resources). In addition, Lynch (1998) developed a book about Making Words–type activities targeted to the beginning reader from kindergarten to second grade. This program has also been included in a literacy model for classroom instruction called the Four-Blocks Way (Cunningham, Hall, & Cunningham, 2000). The four blocks include guided reading, self-selected reading, writing, and working with words.

Road to the Code

Blachman, Ball, Black, and Tangel (2000) prepared *Road to the Code: A Phonological Awareness Program for Young Children,* a research-based manual to help teachers incorporate phonological awareness and early literacy activities into the classroom (see Additional Resources). One activity, Say It and Move It, is used each day during this 11-week program. This activity is followed by instruction in letter names and sounds. The lessons are carefully sequenced and take 15–20 minutes a day. *Road to Reading: A Program for Preventing and Remediating Reading Difficulties* is a newer resource that includes multiple additional activities (Blachman & Tangel, 2008).

Phonics and Spelling Through Phoneme–Grapheme Mapping

Grace (2007) provided a sequential, systematic, explicit program for teaching students the relationships between letters and sounds. (See Additional Resources for more information.) This procedure is designed to be used three times a week for approximately 20 minutes. Six to ten colored tiles and phoneme–grapheme mapping paper (similar to graph paper) are used to teach students phonemes and graphemes. Lessons are organized around the six syllable types of English (i.e., closed syllables, syllables with vowels and the silent *e,* open syllables, syllables ending with *-le, r*-controlled syllables, and diphthong syllables). For the mapping procedure, students are instructed to do the following:

1. Say each phoneme and place one tile in each grid square for each sound.
2. Point to the first tile and say the sound and then move the tile up and write the grapheme in the square.
3. Continue with each tile until the exact spelling of the word is represented in the boxes based on phoneme–grapheme correspondences, not the number of letters in the word. For example, the digraph /sh/ would be written in one box because it only makes one sound.

Poor word recognition is a stumbling block for many young readers.

When Maria was in preschool, she had trouble pronouncing words. In second grade, she memorized many words. By the time Maria was in sixth grade, however, her word identification and spelling skills were several years below grade level. Her word reading was nonautomatic, and she did not understand how to pronounce common clusters in words. For example, when attempting to pronounce the word *wrestle,* Maria first made the /w/ sound and then the /r/ sound. When she came to the letters *le,* she attempted to pronounce the letters independently, producing two syllables. After repeated attempts, she commented, "Oh, the *e* doesn't make a sound." She still could not, however, produce the correct sound for this pattern. Maria knew individual letters and their corresponding sounds and could be described as fully alphabetic but had yet to master common syllable units and spelling patterns in the English language.

Reading Pen

One example of technology that may help a student such as Maria with word pronunciation is a talking or reading pen. The user scans the pen over a word, and it reads the word aloud. The reading pen (see Additional Resources) scans any word from printed text, displays a word in large characters, reads the word aloud through a built-in speaker or earphones, and defines the word. In addition, the pen can display syllable units and spell words out loud. Ben found that use of this pen enabled him to complete his assigned readings in a shorter amount of time because he no longer needed to rely on other people for help pronouncing certain words. John, a high school student, used the pen as an aid to better understand vocabulary.

Online Reading Programs

Within the last decade, an increasing number of online software programs have been developed to provide explicit reading instruction. Ideally, these web-based reading interventions have the potential to provide targeted instruction in the areas of phonemic awareness, letter–sound relationships, and oral reading fluency that are especially critical for students with reading disabilities. One example of a systematic, explicit program is *Mindplay Virtual Reading Coach* (http://www.mindplay.com). Consistent with the recommendations of the National Reading Panel, Mindplay Virtual Reading Coach (MVRC) is a recently released (March 2013) web-based reading intervention that provides direct instruction to students from kindergarten to Grade 12 in phonemic awareness, phonics, grammar, fluency, vocabulary, and comprehension. Ideally, a student would spend 30 minutes 5 days a week on the program. The design of the program balances technological resources and sound pedagogical principles, using a variety of approaches for each learning task; providing error correction and immediate, instructive feedback; and documenting each student's progress and mastery of content. MVRC has been under development for more than 30 years and is an online adaptation of the company's earlier computer-based reading program, *My Reading Coach.*

MVRC has two qualities that make it unique as a quality reading intervention that stands out from other web-based programs. First, explicit instruction is scaffolded, and lessons are presented in more than one way. For example, if a student struggles with a certain concept (e.g., the sound of letter *b*), MVRC presents a lesson on this sound in up to 20 different versions until the sound is mastered. Second, direct instruction is provided by "coaches" who are either speech-language therapists or experienced reading teachers. In brief video clips, these coaches explain and review concepts and lessons (and they pronounce speech sounds perfectly!). Students signing on to MVRC begin with a diagnostic assessment, RAPS 360, that identifies specific weaknesses in reading skills and then designs an individualized prescriptive intervention plan for each student.

Instruction for the Processing Blocks

PHONICS

Some children easily intuit phonics skills by being readers and writers and do not need to be taught the rules and principles of grapheme–phoneme relationships. For these children, a teacher may model and provide guided practice in word instruction within the context of connected text (Allen, 1998). Students with marked weaknesses in phonology or orthography, however, typically require more explicit instruction to learn to read and spell. These students can improve in reading performance when systematic phonics interventions are delivered. Results from a recent meta-analysis indicated that phonics instruction is the only treatment approach for students with severe reading disabilities where the effectiveness is statistically confirmed (Galuschka et al., 2014). Ryan, Ben, and Maria are all examples of students who need more intensive, systematic phonics instruction. Chard and Osborn (1999a, 1999b) provided a comprehensive set of guidelines to follow when providing word recognition instruction to children with reading disabilities, such as Maria. Essentially, two broad categories of phonics methods exist: synthetic and analytic.

Synthetic Phonics

With synthetic phonics instruction, a student is explicitly taught the relationships between letters and sounds using a part-to-whole approach. Sounds initially are taught in isolation, and then the student is taught how to blend the phonemes together to pronounce words (Ehri, 2006). Once the student can blend single phonemes, additional graphemes are introduced and emphasis is placed on learning to break words into their basic parts.

Two widely used synthetic phonics approaches are Orton-Gillingham (Gillingham & Stillman, 1973) and Slingerland (Slingerland, 1981). These methods provide instruction aimed at strengthening visual and auditory associations through tracing. Although both of these approaches are highly effective for students with reading disabilities, they require intensive teacher training. A typical Orton-Gillingham sequence would be to do the following:

1. Teach a letter and ask the student to repeat the letter name.
2. Form a letter and have the student trace over it, say the letter name, and write the letter from memory.
3. Present consonant letters on white cards and vowel letters on salmon-colored cards. Introduce letter sounds with a keyword (apple, /a/). Ask the student to repeat the keyword and provide the sound for the letter.
4. Start with these letter sounds: *a* (short sound as in cat), *b, f, h, j, k, m, p, t.*
5. Introduce blending with a consonant, vowel, and consonant. Ask the student to pronounce the whole word.
6. Pronounce a word slowly and separate the sounds. Ask the student to do the following:
   - Repeat the word.
   - Name the letters.
   - Write the word while naming each letter.
   - Read the word.
7. Introduce additional sounds: *g* (got), *o,* initial *r* and *l, n, th* (this), *u, ch, e, s, sh, d, w, wh, y, v, z, qu, x, ph.*

8. Introduce consonant blends.
9. Introduce long vowel sounds and the vowel consonant -*e* spelling pattern (e.g., *a-e, safe*).
10. Have the student practice reading decodable text.

This type of procedure forms the basis for most of the reading methods developed for students with dyslexia. In lieu of Orton-Gillingham, several other synthetic phonics programs are described in the following section. (See Additional Resources for information on ordering these programs.)

The Reading Lesson

The Reading Lesson (Levin & Langton, 1998) is a practical, structured approach designed for teaching children ages 3–7 years how to read. Although the program is designed for parents, the format is easy to use with a young child who is struggling with decoding. The program is divided into 20 easy-to-follow lessons. The method begins with the most common letters and sounds and teaches children how to put the sounds together to read simple words. There is also a Writing Lesson Companion course where the child can practice complementary writing skills that reinforce the connection between the sound and the letter. The program gradually progresses to longer words. After completing the last book in the series, a child can read with ease at the second-grade level.

The following supplementary materials provide additional support:

- *Giggle Bunny's StoryBook* is an animated, interactive CD with 40 stories that follow along with the *Reading Lesson* program. The stories are interactive as well as printable and start from a beginning reading level and progress as the child goes through them.
- *The Reading Lesson Animated Program* is a CD containing games and fun interactive content that also follows along with the book.
- *The Storymaker* e-book provides fun story writing for children who like to write. The stories come from the Storybook CD and follow the general structure of the *Reading Lesson* program.
- *The Reading Lesson Wordbook* is an e-book containing important sight words that are learned throughout the *Reading Lesson* book.

Reading Reflex

The *Reading Reflex* (McGuinness & McGuinness, 1998) program was designed for young children and elementary-age children who are struggling to learn to read. The program, which may be used by reading teachers or parents, provides a child with systematic instruction in the alphabetic code. The book includes simple diagnostic tests, lesson plans, word exercises, and games. Additional support materials are available that can be used in conjunction with the book.

Phonic Reading Lessons

The *Phonic Reading Lessons* (Kirk, Minskoff, Mather, & Roberts, 2007; Roberts & Mather, 2007) consist of two volumes: *Skills* and *Practice*. This systematic method is easy for teachers to learn to use and provides a step-by-step procedure for teaching phonics and reinforcing grapheme–phoneme relationships. No rules are taught. Instead, sounds are introduced one at a time in the *Skills* volume using a variety of

Instruction for the Processing Blocks

words so that the student develops an automatic response to each symbol. The *Practice* volume supports and reinforces the lessons from *Skills* through the use of story reading and spelling practice. As a supplement to the program, the child is asked to write words while carefully pronouncing each sound. In its third revision, this program has been used successfully with individuals of all ages.

Spalding Method

The Spalding Method, described in the book *The Writing Road to Reading* (Spalding & Spalding, 1990), is a language arts program that integrates handwriting, spelling, reading, speaking, and writing. Children are taught to recognize and write 70 common phonograms, which include single letters and sounds. The text includes a complete list of the rules to be taught and the individual phonograms. Phonogram cards are used to present the sounds. After the child has learned 54 phonograms, he or she receives instruction in spelling. To help with spelling, children learn to master the 70 phonograms and 29 spelling rules. The Spaldings claimed that, armed with sounds and rules, a child can spell about 80% of English words correctly. This method has been used successfully with students from first grade through college.

Other programs are designed to be more appealing to older students. Two examples of structured reading programs that are appropriate for upper elementary or secondary students are described briefly in the following sections.

LANGUAGE!

LANGUAGE! The Comprehensive Literacy Curriculum program, now in its fourth edition (Greene, 2008), is designed for students ranging from third grade through adulthood. The curriculum is designed for students who are not fluent readers, writers, and spellers and who are not making adequate gains with conventional methods. Effective use of the program requires background in structured language teaching. The program is based on building students' knowledge and mastery of phonological and linguistic awareness; decoding and encoding isolated words; and reading sentences, paragraphs, and passages for meaning. The curriculum contains instruction on reading, spelling, composition, comprehension, vocabulary, grammar, and usage, and it is designed to assist teachers in providing individualized instruction. The content is presented sequentially, and progress is based on each student's mastery of concepts. A supplementary reading series matches the language concepts that have been taught. Teachers may now present *LANGUAGE!* digitally from any device or with a blend of print and digital materials.

Specialized Program Individualizing Reading Excellence

Specialized Program Individualizing Reading Excellence (S.P.I.R.E.) is another example of a comprehensive multisensory program for struggling readers in kindergarten through eighth grade. (See Additional Resources.) Based on Orton-Gillingham methodologies, S.P.I.R.E. focuses on instruction in phonological awareness, phonics, fluency, comprehension, spelling, and handwriting. The integrated curriculum is designed to be used for 1 hour each day. Using magnetic boards, students engage in daily word-building activities. Decodable word cards are provided in the three colors of a stoplight: green (Go ahead, you know the sounds); yellow (Slow down because a part of the word has a less common pronunciation); and red (Stop, think, and remember because you cannot use the sounds to decode this word). Decodable texts and workbooks accompany the program to reinforce learning and provide additional practice in decoding, fluency, and comprehension.

Wilson Reading System

The *Wilson Reading System* (WRS) is based on Orton-Gillingham principles and is a multisensory, synthetic approach to teaching reading and writing (Wilson, 2004). The program was originally designed for older students in Grades 4–12, but adaptations have been made for younger students. *Fundations*® 2nd Edition (Wilson Language Training, 2012) is now available for K–3 students in general education classrooms. Teachers can incorporate a 30-minute daily *Fundations* lesson into their language arts classroom instruction with lessons that focus on carefully sequenced skills including print knowledge, alphabetic awareness, phonological awareness, phonemic awareness, and decoding.

The WRS is a research-based complete curriculum for teaching decoding and encoding beginning with phoneme segmentation. The program directly teaches the structure of English words so that students master the coding system for reading and spelling in a systematic and cumulative manner. This program uses multisensory structured language that is designed to teach step-by-step strategies for decoding and encoding. The English language is studied as a system with dependable rules. This program was designed with 10 underlying principles in mind:

1. Teach sounds to automaticity.
2. Teach total word structure—not just sounds.
3. Present concepts within context-controlled, written text.
4. Present the structure of language in a systematic, cumulative manner.
5. Teach all principles of English language structure directly.
6. Teach and reinforce concepts with visual-auditory-kinesthetic-tactile methods.
7. Teach phonemic and syllabic segmentation.
8. Include constant review and repetition.
9. Use questioning techniques for reinforcement and feedback.
10. Use diagnostic teaching to monitor progress.

In the beginning steps, phonological awareness, segmenting, and blending are stressed. Students use sound cards to learn and practice sounds and then to manipulate them to make words. Word cards are then used to present and practice words using the sounds on the sound cards. Students then read words from lists, and their progress is charted. Students read decodable text; practice spelling using sound, syllable, and suffix cards; and write dictated words and sentences in a dictation book.

The program is sequenced in 12 steps that are based on 6 syllable types (closed syllables, syllables with vowels and the silent *e,* open syllables, syllables ending with *-le, r*-controlled syllables, and diphthong syllables). Lessons are taught using the same basic structure. In Steps 1–6, the students learn to rely on the syllable rules; in Steps 7–12, students learn rules for adding suffixes to change base words. Examples of these six syllable types are provided:

Closed syllable: *cat*

Silent *e* syllable: *bike*

Instruction for the Processing Blocks

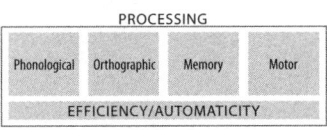

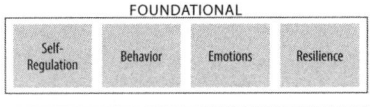

Open syllable: *motion*

Syllable ending with *-le*: *turtle*

R-controlled syllable: *car*

Diphthong syllable: *out*

A simple syllable marking is used to code for each of these syllable types. Using a left-to-right movement, a student draws a curved or straight line under each syllable. He or she then identifies the type of syllable, codes the vowels with a long or short marking, puts a slash through the *e* if it is a silent *e* or an *-le* syllable, and draws a circle around the vowels. Instruction in syllable types may also facilitate spelling, particularly mastery of words with a final silent *e*.

The WRS is one of the few structured reading methods that was originally designed for use with older students and adults, and the stories are written with the interests of older readers in mind. All the materials used in the program are carefully sequenced and color-coded for each step. In fifth grade, Ryan was taught using the WRS in the resource room. Instruction in the six syllable types helped Ryan to understand how to pronounce vowel sounds in unfamiliar words. The careful sequence of the program helped improve both his decoding and encoding skills.

If Maria had been provided with this type of program in sixth grade, her decoding and encoding skills would have improved. Unfortunately, this type of teaching was not available in her school. Students with severe weaknesses within the Processing blocks need to be provided with specifically designed and carefully sequenced reading programs. Although students with the most severe difficulties usually require a synthetic phonics approach, students with more moderate weaknesses can learn to read with an analytic phonics approach.

Analytic Phonics

Analytic phonics approaches use a whole-to-part approach that teaches children to analyze letter–sound patterns once the word has been identified as a whole (Ehri, 2006). Instruction begins with common words or word families. A student is shown the word *cat* and taught that *a* and *t* say /ăt/ and then is taught to read the many words in the /ăt/ family (e.g., *bat, cat, fat, hat, mat, pat, rat, sat, brat, chat, drat, flat, splat*). The student then practices reading these words in short, controlled stories.

Analogy Strategy

The basic idea of the analogy approach is that beginning readers can recognize unfamiliar words through knowledge of the letter patterns of similar, known words (Allen, 1998). This type of approach has also been referred to as a word family or linguistic approach. Teaching students to read and spell words by analogy includes instruction in the use of onsets (i.e., initial consonants and consonant clusters) and rimes (i.e., the ending portion of the syllable). As described in Chapter 8, in the word *hat,* the /h/ is the onset and the /ăt/ is the rime. Wylie and Durrell (1970) indicated that nearly 500 primary-grade words can be derived from a set of 37 rimes (see Figure 9.5).

To help children start to appreciate the relationship between spoken rhymes and written rimes, after reading a story, teachers or parents can discuss the rhyming words. Write the words on the board and show students how the spellings of the words are similar. For example, after reading a story that had the sentence,

-ack	-ain	-ake	-ale	-all	-ame	-an
-ank	-ap	-ash	-at	-ate	-aw	-ay
-eat	-ell	-est	-ice	-ick	-ide	-ight
-ill	-in	-ine	-ing	-ink	-ip	-ir
-ock	-oke	-op	-or	-ore	-uck	-ug
-ump	-unk					

Figure 9.5. Set of 37 rimes from which 500 primary words can be taught. (*Source:* Wylie & Durrell, 1970. As adapted in Wendling, B., & Mather, N. [2009]. *Essentials of evidence-based academic interventions.* New York, NY: John Wiley & Sons.)

"He turned off the light and said good night," Maria's first-grade teacher wrote the words *light* and *night* on the board and then discussed the shared spelling pattern.

Rhyming words that have the same rime can be placed on one side of a classroom word wall and words that rhyme but differ in spelling patterns can be placed on the other side for further study and review. Pinnell and Fountas (1998) presented a thorough reference for helping children learn about letters, sounds, and words, including a comprehensive list of phonograms.

Instruction with analogies focuses on both reading and spelling words. Englert, Hiebert, and Stewart (1985) presented an analogy strategy to help students notice orthographic similarities among words and then generalize this information to the spelling of new words. The following procedure is used:

1. Identify the words that a student misspelled on a pretest.
2. Develop a spelling bank of 15 words. Select words for the spelling bank by their similarity to the misspelled words. For example, the word *other* may be selected if the student misspelled the word *brother.*
3. Explain that the last parts of rhyming words are often spelled the same.
4. Present a list of words. Say one word and ask the student to identify the word in the spelling bank that rhymes with the stimulus word.
5. Using the rhyming rule, have the student identify which letters of the printed and orally presented words would be spelled the same.
6. Have the student practice the words by spelling them orally from memory.
7. Have the student write the words twice from memory.
8. Have the student write the words from memory in a test of delayed recall.

After developing the spelling bank, have students practice the transfer words in a cloze passage. Encourage students to fill in the missing words without looking at the analogous words. Ask students to think of the word from the spelling bank that rhymes with the transfer word.

The analogy strategy may also be used to teach words that have the same letter patterns but do not rhyme (e.g., *have, gave;* Gerber, 1993). Point out the similar spelling patterns and then discuss the exception to the spelling rules. Effective spelling instruction provides focus on three different language units: 1) phonemes to graphemes, 2) spoken words to whole written words, and 3) spoken and written onsets and rimes (Berninger et al., 2000). It is important to note that interventions for spelling and reading must address the morphophonemic principle in English. A constant trade-off exists in written English between representation of the sounds of the letters and preservation of the morphological roots of the words.

Instruction for the Processing Blocks

Glass Analysis Method for Decoding Only

Another easy-to-use method for helping students learn to recognize and pronounce common spelling units and pronounce words with more than one syllable is the Glass Analysis Method for Decoding Only (Glass, 1973). To begin, write several multisyllabic words on index cards. For practice, select words from the class reading material. Do not cover up parts of the word or present clusters separately from the word. Teach students only common letter clusters that can be generalized to new words. If possible, practice using this technique 10–15 minutes daily. Use these five general steps to present each word:

1. Identify the whole word. For example, present the word *carpenter* on an index card and say, "This word is *carpenter*."
2. Pronounce a sound in the word and ask students to name the letter or letters that make that sound. Say, "In the word *carpenter*, what letters make the /ar/ sound? What letters make the /pĕn/ sound?" and so forth. (For this step, say the letter sounds, not the letter names.)
3. Ask for the sound that certain letters or letter combinations make. Say, "What sound do the letters *er* make? What sound do the letters *ter* make?" and so forth. (For this step, say the letter names, not the letter sounds.)
4. Take away letters (auditorily, not visually) and ask for the remaining sound. Say, "In the word *carpenter*, if I took off /car/, how would you pronounce the word? If I took off /ter/, how would you pronounce the word? If I took off /pĕnter/, how would you say the word?" Think of as many combinations as you can.
5. Ask students to say the whole word.

Although the Glass Analysis Method was developed primarily for teaching decoding skills, it can be modified easily to work on encoding skills (Mather, 1991). For example, if students were learning to spell the word *consideration*, the following steps could be used:

1. Identify and discuss the visual and auditory clusters in the word.
2. Ask students to write the letters that make the /cŭn/ sound, then the /sid/ sound, then the /er/ sound, then the /ā/ sound, and finally the /shŭn/ or *-tion* sound.
3. Have students write the word *consideration* while pronouncing each part slowly: con•sid•er•a•tion.
4. Have students turn their papers over and write the word *consideration* from memory while saying the word as it is written.
5. Have students write the word from memory two more times.

When using this adapted method for spelling, emphasize ordering the sounds of a word in the correct sequence. This can be accomplished by presenting and practicing the visual and auditory clusters of a word in the order in which they appear. Other remedial spelling techniques encourage students to listen carefully to the sequence of sounds.

Although she had full alphabetic knowledge, Maria did not know how to break words into parts to aid in pronunciation. In light of Ehri's (1998) framework, Maria needed to move from the full alphabetic to the consolidated alphabetic phase. To do this, she required reading and spelling methods that would help her learn to group or chunk common word parts as an aid to pronunciation.

Spelling Grid

Just as chunking strategies are needed for reading, as skill progresses, the focus of spelling instruction should be directed to the correct spelling of word parts and syllable units. Some students can improve their spellings of multisyllabic words through the use of a spelling grid (Wong, 1986; see Figure 9.6 for an example). The purpose of a spelling grid is to promote structural analysis of words. Wong recommended the following steps:

1. Write the spelling word in column 1, and then pronounce the word and discuss its meanings.
2. Have the student say the word and put a checkmark in column 2.
3. In column 3, have the student write the number of syllables in the word.
4. In column 4, have the student divide the word into syllables and then write each syllable.
5. In column 5, have the student write and say the word.
6. As a final step, have the student turn over the paper and write the word from memory.

Reading Excellence: Word Attack and Rate Development Strategies

Reading Excellence: Word Attack and Rate Development Strategies (REWARDS; Archer, Gleason, & Vachon, 2000, 2014) is a program designed to teach upper elementary and secondary school students the pronunciation of multisyllabic words. The intermediate version is in the second edition and the secondary version is in the third edition. This specialized reading program teaches students the use of a flexible strategy for decoding multisyllabic words. The aim is to increase comprehension by increasing oral and silent reading fluency. Using REWARDS, readers are taught an overt and a covert strategy. The overt strategy involves circling the prefixes, circling the suffixes, and underlining the vowel sound in the root word. The

Write the word	Say the word	Write the # of syllables	Write each syllable				Write and say the word
			1	2	3	4	

Figure 9.6. Sample spelling grid. (*Source:* Wong, 1986.)

Instruction for the Processing Blocks

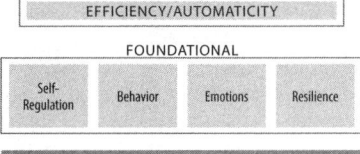

teacher then says, "What part? What part? What part?" while drawing scoops under the segments or decodable "chunks." Students are then instructed to say the words quickly. Eventually, the steps of underlining the vowel and circling the word parts are eliminated, leaving the student with the covert strategy of looking for the word parts and vowel sounds and saying the parts quickly to form a real word.

In addition to REWARDS, there is also REWARDS Plus (Archer, Gleason, & Vachon, 2006) for science or social studies targeted for students in Grades 6–12. REWARDS Plus should be used after a student has already been introduced to the REWARDS strategies. The main goal of REWARDS Plus is to develop the student's ability to successfully read science and social studies material.

Retrieval, Automaticity, Vocabulary, Engagement with Language, Orthography

Retrieval, Automaticity, Vocabulary, Engagement with Language, Orthography (RAVE-O; Wolf, 2012) is a small group reading intervention designated for Grades 2–5. RAVE-O is a multisensory program that allows students to play with language. Through hands-on activities, students learn core words and how they are related to other words. When working with a core word, students review the sound–symbol correspondences, the spelling of each word, what the meanings of a word are (if the word has multiple meanings), the part of speech, and how affixes change the meaning of the original core word. Then students read minute stories and practice and apply skills they have gained while also working on reading comprehension strategies such as "think thrice," in which the student is instructed to think ahead, think back, and think to him- or herself. RAVE-O also incorporates a variety of assessments for placement and progress monitoring. There are also additional online resources available for teachers at http://www.soprislearning.com/raveoresources. RAVE-O is a flexible program that can be used in a variety of settings such as general or special education classrooms, intensive summer school programs, individual tutoring, and before- or after-school tutoring.

TYPE OF TEXT

A critical factor for improving reading performance is the amount of time a student spends reading. Students are unlikely to spend time reading if they cannot read the books.

> Ryan would often sit in his fourth-grade class with a book placed in front of him, but it was too difficult for him to read. On occasion, he would turn a page, look at the pictures on the new page, and then glance around the room. The books used in the classroom were too difficult for Ryan to read independently. Although he sat quietly during reading time, the books he was given to read were inhibiting his reading development.

Instructional Level

An element of effective instruction in both decoding and encoding is to provide students with books that they are able to read independently and words that they are able to learn for spelling. Betts (1946) described three levels of reading material: 1) the independent level (99% accuracy), 2) the instructional level (95% accuracy), and 3) the frustration level (below 90% accuracy). In other words, out of 100 words, a student should mispronounce only 1 to be at the independent level and no more than 5 to be at the instructional level. This procedure has sometimes been referred to as the "rule of thumb" for choosing student texts. The teacher counts out a 100-word passage. As the child reads, the teacher presses down a finger each time that an error is made, starting with the little finger and moving toward the thumb. If the thumb is reached before the passage has been completed, the material is too difficult for the student. Although motivation and interest also play a major role in a student's willingness to read, these high values indicate that readers must be familiar with the majority of words for a text to be at an appropriate level.

Many students with reading disabilities spend the entire school day facing text at their frustration level. If teachers give all children in the classroom the same textbook, it is invariably too easy for some and too difficult for others. Betts provided the following description of rigid and prescriptive instruction:

> Once upon a time there was a third-grade teacher who was proud of the fact that she knew third-grade work and little about the nature of the experiences which came before or after. Now this teacher was immensely proud to be a specialist—she also might have been elated to be one of the three blind men who so surely described the elephant. Having some doubt in her mind regarding certain children in the room, she called in the researchers. By using a graded series of readers, these scientists found some children who could read with understanding nothing above a preprimer, the other pupils ranging from first- to average sixth-grade ability.
>
> When the evidence was placed before this teacher, she irately exclaimed to the principal, "See I knew that Miss So-and-So, the second-grade teacher, was sending me some children who were not ready for my third-grade work." During the ensuing conversation, it was explained that she had a somewhat typical third grade, composed of children who varied above as well as below the ability of the average third-grade child.
>
> But the conversation did not end here. After some explanation, she understood that because she only knew how to teach one third of the pupils, perhaps she should return $800 of her $1,200 salary to the school and that she should pay also an additional $800 for confusing the lower third of the class with third-grade materials and for failing to challenge the upper third with materials at their level. It took no specialist in mathematics to prove to this able teacher that she really owed the community $400 per year for the privilege of teaching in the school. (1946, pp. 542–543)

For home and school reading, both teachers and parents must consider each student's reading level when attempting to match books to his or her present skill level. Fountas and Pinnell (1999) provided a list of books for use in kindergarten through third grade organized by level of difficulty. Word counts are presented for most books. Although students with severe reading disabilities need to engage in authentic reading activities as part of their reading program, they also need to practice their developing skills using decodable text.

Decodable Text

Students with reading disabilities need extensive practice in applying their knowledge of phoneme–grapheme relationships to the task of reading (Grossen, 1997). The examples of programs described previously all include what is referred to as decodable text. When students are learning to read using a synthetic or analytic phonics approach, they need to practice the skills being taught in short passages that are controlled or easily decodable. Decodable text consists primarily of words with regular grapheme–phoneme relationships and a few sight words that have been taught systematically. This type of text allows beginning readers to integrate their knowledge in the context of connected reading and to practice and apply their developing knowledge of grapheme–phoneme correspondences to text. These materials are not to be viewed as a replacement for authentic, high-interest text but rather as a component of decoding instruction for reinforcing instruction in grapheme–phoneme

Instruction for the Processing Blocks

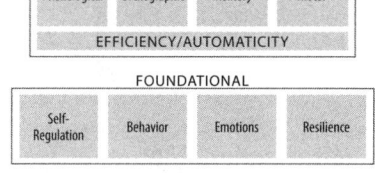

relationships. One example of a set of decodable texts that teachers can copy and that students can color is EZ2 Read Decodable Books. (See Additional Resources.)

Read Well

One example of a research-based primary reading program that uses decodable text is *Read Well* (Sprick, Howard, & Fidanque, 1998). This program provides systematic phonics instruction and fully decodable text and integrates reading and writing, including oral and written comprehension activities. The program provides expanded units for students who perform at a lower level and procedures for ongoing assessment for guiding instructional decisions. One of the nice features of this program is that decodable words are presented in large print, whereas words that are more difficult to pronounce are written in small print to be read by the teacher.

High-Frequency Words

One way to help students with reading and spelling is to focus on high-frequency words, the words that are most commonly used in writing. Some people refer to these words as "sight" words because they are supposed to be recognized instantly and easily without an analysis of sounds. As noted by Ehri (1998), with sufficient practice, all words acquire the status of sight words.

Instant Words

The most systematic way to work on high-frequency words is to provide practice with a carefully developed list of words, such as Fry's list of 600 instant words (Fry, 1977). The first 300 words make up about 60% of the words used in written material (see Appendix 9A). This list may be used to teach students high-frequency words for both reading and spelling.

As an informal assessment, a teacher may ask a student to read the words starting at the beginning of the list and to continue reading until an error is made. Instruction then begins at the point where the student does not immediately recognize or does not know how to spell a word. Next, the teacher can establish a program to help the student master the unknown words. This type of program does not need to be time consuming. An effective program can be conducted using only 10 minutes daily. The student starts at the beginning of the list and reads as many words as he or she can within 1 minute. After the minute, the teacher records the number of words read and then reviews any words that were not recognized instantly. A graph may be used to monitor progress. For the next few minutes, the student can practice spelling several of the unknown words and then review these words the following day. The teacher or student then checks off each word after the student has learned to read and spell it.

Flashcards

Students who have difficulty with memorizing benefit from rehearsal, review, and repetition, as well as from immediate feedback. Some students benefit from creating flashcards, particularly when extensive memorization is required. These cards should be viewed frequently for short periods of time. Several types of memorization software programs that may be used to create either virtual or printed flashcards with questions and answers are reviewed at the Quingle web site (http://www.xmarks.com/s/site/www.quingle.com/softarea/flash.htm). The features vary. For example, the Anki flashcard program provides a format so that users can embed audio clips, images, and videos on their cards (http://ankisrs.net).

Personalized Dictionary

Some students with spelling difficulties can benefit from keeping an individualized spelling dictionary that contains their own frequently misspelled words. Each letter of the alphabet is written in order on a separate page. In their dictionary, students then write words that they use in their writing but have difficulty spelling. They may then consult their dictionaries when writing or when editing.

Scheuermann, Jacobs, McCall, and Knies (1994) described the following process for making and using a personal spelling dictionary: 1) obtain a pocket-size notebook, 2) tab the pages in alphabetical order, and 3) if desired, laminate each page. Students may then write words on file folder labels to allow for easy removal once the words have been learned. As an alternative, students can use *A Spelling Dictionary for Beginning Writers* (Hurray, 1993). This dictionary contains the words most commonly used by novice writers. Another example is *Quick Word* (Sitton & Forest, 1994). This dictionary includes preprinted high-frequency words and provides blank spaces so that students can add words. Ben found that the easiest and quickest way to locate and correct misspelled words was to use his personalized dictionary.

Backward Spelling

Another activity that may help students such as Ben learn to form more complete orthographic images is backward spelling (Glenn & Hurley, 1993). For this procedure, a word is presented on a card and the student is asked to look at the word, look away from the card and attempt to visualize the word, and then check back and forth to confirm that the visualization is correct. Next, the card is turned over, and the student is asked to visualize the word and then spell the word forward and then backward. Backward spelling involves working memory and is only possible if the student forms a complete image of all the graphemes in the word (Apel & Swank, 1999). In turn, the ability to form a complete mental image of a word promotes the development of a sight vocabulary and reading fluency.

Self-Monitoring

Students should also be encouraged to monitor their own spelling development. If spelling tests are used, students can examine any missed words to determine what part of the word is incorrect. For example, were letters omitted or extra letters added? Misspelled words may also be taken from writing assignments and analyzed. Figure 9.7 depicts a sample self-monitoring form. By analyzing the parts of the words they are misspelling, students can focus on the specific orthographic patterns that occur within high-frequency words, such as the *-dge* or *-tch* spelling pattern.

Multisensory Procedures for Reading and Writing

Many of the programs designed for helping students with reading and writing problems are multisensory in nature. This means that the type of instruction incorporates abilities from four of the symbolic blocks: Phonological, Orthographic, Memory, and Motor. The student is encouraged to look at the word, say the word, and trace

Spelling Self-Monitoring Form

Name_____ Spelling self-analysis score_____ Pretest score_____ Posttest score_____

List word	Attempted spelling	Missing letters	Extra letters	Letters in wrong order	Cover list word and rewrite correct spelling

Figure 9.7. Sample spelling self-monitoring form.

the word. This type of procedure helps students with weaknesses in one or more of these blocks. Naming letters and words while tracing binds the orthographic, motor, and phonological images of the letter together at once (Adams, 1990). When Ryan traced each spelling word several times and then practiced writing the word from memory, he was able to recall the words on his spelling flow list more easily. The majority of these techniques involve three components: 1) multisensory word study, 2) emphasis on visual imagery, and 3) writing the word from memory.

Fernald Method

One example of a multisensory technique is called the Fernald Method (Fernald, 1943). Fernald stressed the importance of providing children with meaningful reading and writing activities. As she so aptly observed, "The child is much more interested in writing and reading fairly difficult material that is on the level of his understanding than simpler material which is below his mental age level" (p. 44). The method she created has been used effectively to teach struggling readers of all ages. The Fernald Method provides instruction aimed simultaneously at the Phonological, Orthographic, and Motor blocks. Because the method involves tracing, it can actually help children increase their abilities to picture words using the skills of the Orthographic block. The technique ensures that the student pays attention to the details of the word.

The Fernald Method is appropriate for students who have failed to learn to read with other instructional methods. This method consists of four stages through which students progress as their skill increases. Before starting, explain to the student that he or she will be shown a new way to learn words that has been successful with other learners.

In the first stage, the student selects a word that he or she cannot read but would like to learn. Discuss the meaning of the word with the student and then use the following steps to teach the word:

1. Write the word. Sit beside the student and ask the student to watch and listen while you 1) say the word, 2) use a crayon to write the word in large print in manuscript or cursive (depending on which writing style the child uses) on an index card, and 3) say the word again while running a finger underneath the word.

2. Model word tracing. Say, "Watch what I do and listen to what I say." Use the following steps: 1) Say the word; 2) trace the word using one or two fingers, saying each part of the word while tracing it; and 3) say the word again while running a finger underneath the word. Have the student practice tracing the word using these steps.

3. Have the student continue tracing the word until he or she can write the word from memory. Remind the student to say each part of the word while tracing it.

4. Have the student attempt to write the word from memory. When the student feels ready, remove the model and ask the student to write the word from memory. Make sure the student says the word while writing. If at any point the student makes an error, stop him or her immediately, cover the error, and model the tracing procedure again before proceeding.

5. File the word. After the student writes the word correctly three times without the model, have the student file the word in a word bank alphabetically to practice on a later date.

Instruction for the Processing Blocks

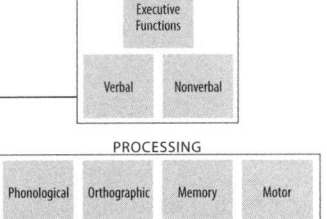

Although a few students continue to need tracing for word learning, most individuals progress through three more stages when using this method. By the second stage, the student no longer needs to trace words and can learn a word by looking at the word after it is written, saying the word, and then writing it. By the third stage, the student is able to learn new words directly from printed words without having them written. When reading with the student, help him or her with any words that are difficult for the student to pronounce. After reading, have the student review and write the unknown words. By the fourth stage, most students begin to notice similarities between unknown and known words and can recognize many new words without being told what they are.

A helpful technique is to ask the student to glance over a paragraph and underline any unknown words before reading. Tell the student how to pronounce the words and then ask the student to trace the words and then write the words from memory. This type of tracing technique is particularly useful for students such as Ryan and Ben, who have weaknesses in orthography and difficulty remembering how to spell commonly used words. Words may be selected from a high-frequency list or an assigned spelling list. Use the following procedures, adapted from Fernald (1943), for spelling:

1. Have the student select the word to learn.
2. Write the word on a card.
3. Pronounce the word clearly and distinctly. Ask the student to repeat the pronunciation while looking at the word.
4. Provide the student with time to develop a visual image of the word. A student who learns visually is encouraged to form a mental picture of the word; a student who learns auditorily is encouraged to say the word slowly; and a student with motor strengths is encouraged to trace the word with his or her finger.
5. When the student says that the word is known, erase or cover the word and have the student attempt to write the word from memory. If the word is incorrect, return to Step 3. If the word is correct, cover it and have the student write the word another time from memory.

Cover–Write Methods

Other remedial spelling methods use similar multisensory techniques to help students with word learning. As noted previously, these cover–write methods are most useful for students such as Ryan and Ben who have difficulty with forming and retrieving word images. Most of these methods include some variation of the following steps:

1. Select a word for the student to learn. Write the word on a card and pronounce it.
2. Have the student look at the word and then pronounce it.
3. Have the student say the letter sounds while tracing each letter.
4. Have the student continue to pronounce the word while tracing it several times.
5. Have the student turn over the word and then pronounce the word while writing it on paper. If the word is spelled incorrectly, repeat Step 4.

Continue the process until the student can write the word correctly three times.

305

READING FLUENCY

Reading fluency encompasses the speed or rate of reading as well as the ability to read materials with expression. Meyer and Felton defined fluency as "the ability to read connected text rapidly, smoothly, effortlessly, and automatically with little conscious attention to the mechanics of reading, such as decoding" (1999, p. 284). The core cognitive correlates of reading fluency involve rapid automatized naming, orthographic processing, attention, and lexical retrieval (Fletcher et al., 2007). Children are successful with decoding when the process used to identify words is fast and nearly effortless or automatic. As noted, the concept of automaticity refers to a student's ability to recognize words rapidly with little attention required to the word's appearance. The ability to read words by sight automatically is the key to skilled reading (Ehri, 1998).

Some children have developed accurate word pronunciation skills but read slowly. For these children, decoding is not automatic or fluent, and their limited fluency may affect performance in the following ways: they read less text than peers and have less time to remember, review, or comprehend the text; they expend more cognitive energy than peers trying to identify individual words; and they may be less able to retain text in their memories and less likely to integrate those segments with other parts of the text (Mastropieri, Leinart, & Scruggs, 1999).

The correlation between reading fluency and reading comprehension has been the most compelling reason to focus on reading fluency interventions (Allington, 1983; Johns, 1993; Samuels, 1988). Reading fluency has been described as the bridge between decoding and reading comprehension (Rasinski, 2004). Without accurate word reading, the reader will have no access to the author's intended meaning and will misinterpret the text (Hudson, Lane, & Pullen, 2005).

When Maria was in sixth grade, she still read very slowly. Although she pronounced most words correctly, she read with little expression. She complained that because she read so slowly, she could not understand what she was reading. She usually had to read materials several times in order to comprehend them. Students such as Maria, Ryan, and Ben require more exposures and more practice to recognize individual words easily and automatically. Even into middle school, these students often devote an inordinate amount of energy to word identification.

Determining a Student's Reading Rate

A student's reading rate may be calculated by dividing the number of words read correctly by the total amount of reading time. Count out 100 words in a passage and then time the student as he or she reads the passage. In the fall of sixth grade, Maria was given a passage to read with 100 words. She read 92 words correctly in 1.5 minutes, or 61 words per minute (wpm). Hasbrouck and Tindal (2005) completed an extensive study of oral reading fluency. The results of their study were published in a technical report titled *Oral Reading Fluency: 90 Years of Measurement.*

Table 9.1 shows the oral reading fluency rates for students in the fall, winter, and spring of Grades 1–8 as determined by Hasbrouck and Tindal (2005). The information in this table can be used to draw conclusions and make decisions about the oral reading fluency of students. Students scoring below the 50th percentile using the average score of two unpracticed readings from grade-level materials need a fluency-building program. In addition, teachers can use the table to set the long-term fluency goals for their students who are struggling with reading.

Instruction for the Processing Blocks

Table 9.1. Oral reading fluency data

Grade	Percentile	Percentile Fall WCPM*	Winter WCPM*	Spring WCPM*	Average weekly improvement**
1	90	–	81	111	1.9
	75	–	47	82	2.2
	50	–	23	53	1.9
	25	–	12	28	1.0
	10	–	6	15	0.6
2	90	106	125	142	1.1
	75	79	100	117	1.2
	50	51	72	89	1.2
	25	25	42	61	1.1
	10	11	18	31	0.6
3	90	128	146	162	1.1
	75	99	120	137	1.2
	50	71	92	107	1.1
	25	44	62	78	1.1
	10	21	36	48	0.8
4	90	145	166	180	1.1
	75	119	139	152	1.0
	50	94	112	123	0.9
	25	68	87	98	0.9
	10	45	61	72	0.8
5	90	166	182	194	0.9
	75	139	156	168	0.9
	50	110	127	139	0.9
	25	85	99	109	0.8
	10	61	74	83	0.7
6	90	177	195	204	0.8
	75	153	167	177	0.8
	50	127	140	150	0.7

From Hasbrouck, J., & Tindal, G. (2005). *Oral reading fluency: 90 years of measurement* (Tech. Rep. No. 33). Eugene: University of Oregon Press, College of Education, Behavioral Research and Teaching; reprinted with permission.

*WCPM = Words correct per minute.
**Average words per week improvement. Average weekly improvement is the average words per week growth you can expect from a student. It was calculated by subtracting the fall score from the spring score and dividing the difference by 32, the typical number of weeks between the fall and spring assessments. For Grade 1, because there is no fall assessment, the average weekly improvement was calculated by subtracting the winter score from the spring score and dividing the difference by 16, the typical number of weeks between the winter and spring assessments.

(continued)

Table 9.1. (continued)

Grade	Percentile	Percentile Fall WCPM*	Winter WCPM*	Spring WCPM*	Average weekly improvement**
	25	98	111	122	0.8
	10	68	82	93	0.8
7	90	180	192	202	0.7
	75	56	165	177	0.7
	50	128	136	150	0.7
	25	102	109	123	0.7
	10	79	88	98	0.6
8	90	185	199	199	0.4
	75	161	173	177	0.5
	50	133	146	151	0.6
	25	106	115	124	0.6
	10	77	84	97	0.6

In Table 9.1, average weekly improvement is shown by the average growth per week in words that can be expected from a student. It was calculated by subtracting the fall score from the spring score and dividing the difference by 32, the typical number of weeks between the fall and spring assessments. For Grade 1, because there is no fall assessment, the average weekly improvement was calculated by subtracting the winter score from the spring score and dividing the difference by 16, the typical number of weeks between the winter and spring assessments. Analysis of the Hasbrouck and Tindal table reveals that Maria is reading at a much slower rate than many of her peers.

Curriculum-Based Measurement for Reading

Curriculum-based measurement (CBM) can be used to monitor a student's reading progress throughout the year. CBM can be given as often as daily or as frequently as desired by the teacher in order to evaluate the progress or performance of the student. For CBM reading, a student reads aloud from a passage for 1 minute, and the errors are recorded. Errors in CBM reading include mispronunciations, substitutions, omissions, transpositions of word-pairs, and words read to the student by the examiner or teacher (words are read to the student if they are not produced within 3 seconds). Then the total number of words read correctly (WRC) is calculated by taking the total number of words attempted by the student in the timed reading subtracted by the total number of words read incorrectly. For example, Maria read 145 words with 5 errors. The steps would be the following:

Record total number of words read (145).

Record the number of errors (5).

Subtract the number of errors for the WRC (5).

Report in standard format of WRC/errors (140/5).

Instruction for the Processing Blocks

A few other general instructions are provided for CBM reading. During the timing, the teacher assesses and does not teach or correct errors. The student does not practice reading the passage, as this will influence the results of the timing. The student is told to do his or her best reading, not the fastest. The teacher sits across from the student, not beside the student.

Many web sites are available with supplementary CBM materials. The University of Oregon provides a free site focused solely on CBM reading for educators at http://www.cbmreading.com. The easy CBM lite edition provides free progress monitoring for students in Grades K–8 (http://www.easycbm.com). Intervention Central has numerous RTI checklists and probe generators (http://www.interventioncentral.org). In addition, an excellent CBM manual by Jim Wright, *Curriculum-Based Measurement: A Manual for Teachers,* can be downloaded at no cost from his web site (http://www.jimwrightonline.com/pdfdocs/cbaManual.pdf).

One important fact to remember is that before asking students to read quickly, they have to be able to read accurately. Hasbrouck and Glaser (2011) explained, "To be considered a fluent reader, reading must be accurate *first, foremost,* and *forever!*" (p. 11). In some situations, children are assessed before they have had sufficient instruction and have developed accuracy with the skills. Not long ago, one of our colleagues, Annmarie Urso, shared this story:

> Day 5 of kindergarten, and after testing her students, the classroom teacher is told that a full one third of her class is performing below expectations. As she struggled to explain to a young mother how her child needed extra help on Day 5, I witnessed the most insightful response from the mother. She asked, "How, with only 5 days of formal schooling and his first time not home, not taking a nap, and not playing during the day, can you tell he is behind? He's still adjusting to a new routine! How can this be a good thing to put children through their first week of school?" The teacher replied, "No one said it was a good thing." (Annmarie Urso, personal communication, September 4, 2013)

Adjusting Reading Rate

With CBM, students are reminded to do their best reading, not their fastest reading. For casual reading, most people have a constant rate. This rate is the fastest pace at which a person can understand complete thoughts in successive sentences of relatively easy material. As long as the material is relatively easy to read, a person's rate stays constant. For more complex reading materials, however, readers often alter their rate. Students with slow reading rates are often not aware that good readers adjust their rate depending on the purpose of reading. Learning how to make these types of adjustments is particularly important for a student with poor reading skills so that he or she will know to read more slowly when attempting to learn material or understand difficult concepts.

Carver (1990) used the analogy of adjusting reading speed to the shifting of gears in a car. First and second gears are the slowest, most powerful gears. First gear is used to memorize material. Second gear is used to learn material. Third gear is the typical reading rate. The fourth gear, skimming, and the fifth gear, scanning, are the fastest but least powerful gears. These gears are useful for locating a specific piece of information or trying to get the general sense of a passage without reading every word.

Adult readers monitor their reading pace and shift gears depending on the goals. If one is trying to memorize material for a test, the reading pace is slow and reflective, characterized by stopping and reviewing the material. If one is reading a novel for pleasure, the pace is steady and fluent. If one is searching for information in a catalog, the pace is rapid. Skilled readers know how to adjust the gears of their reading rate based on the purpose for reading.

Some children have not learned how to adjust their reading rates; they attempt to read information in an encyclopedia at the same pace that they read a novel. To help develop increased reading speed, encourage students to adjust their rate depending on the purpose of reading. Students can practice skimming through a chapter to get a sense of the information and then moving through the chapter more slowly to study for the weekly test. Model for the students how to change one's rate of reading for different types of materials.

Instructional Activities for Increasing Reading Rate

Teachers often describe students who would benefit from methods to increase reading speed as slow, laborious readers who read word by word with limited expression. Instructional activities for increasing reading rate are most useful with students who have acquired some proficiency in decoding skill but whose level of decoding skill is lower than their oral language abilities. Methods for increasing reading rate have several common features: 1) students listen to text as they follow along with the book, 2) students follow the print using their fingers as guides, and 3) reading materials are used that students would be unable to read independently. In addition, most of the fluency procedures involve repeated exposures to words with material at the student's instructional reading level (Fletcher et al., 2007). Chard and Osborn (1999a) suggested that a beginning reading program should provide opportunities for partner reading, practice reading difficult words prior to reading the text, timings for accuracy and rate, opportunities to hear books read, and opportunities to read to others. The following methods for increasing fluency are easy to use.

Speed Drills

For reading lists of words with a speed drill and a 1-minute timing, Fischer (1999) suggested using the following general guidelines: 30 correct wpm for first- and second-grade children, 40 correct wpm for beginning third-grade children, 60 correct wpm for mid–third grade, and 80 wpm for students in fourth grade and higher. To conduct a speed drill, the student reads a list of words for 1 minute as the number of errors is recorded. The list may be a high-frequency word list or the sample speed drills provided in Fischer's program, *Concept Phonics* (see Additional Resources). These drills are designed to develop automatic sight recognition of words.

Rapid Word Recognition Chart

An easy way to improve speed of recognition for words with an irregular element is the use of a rapid word recognition chart (Carreker, 2005). The chart is similar to a RAN task. It is a matrix that contains five rows of six exception words (e.g., *who, said*), with each row containing the same six words in a different order. After a brief review of the words and a warm-up during which the teacher points randomly to 8 to 10 words on the chart, students are timed for 1 minute as they read the words in the squares aloud. Students can then count and record the number of words they have read correctly. This type of procedure can help students such as Ben recognize words with irregular orthographic patterns more quickly.

Instruction for the Processing Blocks

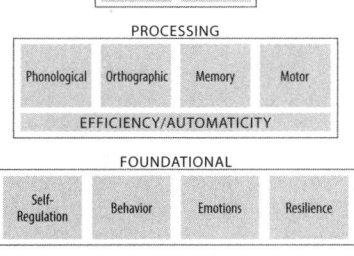

Great Leaps Reading Program

Great Leaps Reading (Campbell, 1998, 2005) was designed to help students build reading fluency and accuracy. One-minute timings employ three stimuli: phonics, sight phrases, and reading short stories, followed with a conversation intended to build expressive language. Each section is designed with a drill to be completed in 1 minute with 2 or less errors. When students master a page, they advance to the next page, which is slightly more difficult. The two main teaching interventions involved are immediate correction and modeling. The program is very adaptable to different educational settings, from the traditional to after-school programs, detention facilities, and home use.

Before beginning this program, teachers assess the student's present reading level either online or in person. Instruction begins at the level within the program at which reading rate first shows a slowdown or where the student makes several errors. In this way, students begin their remedial work obtaining a series of immediate successes.

After recording and discussing the data with the student, the teacher reviews the error or error patterns with the student and discusses strategies that he or she can use to improve performance. Instruction is then provided to develop expressive language with the goal of improving reading comprehension scores.

Performance is charted daily on graphs so that both students and teachers can keep track of progress and make data-based decisions. The program takes approximately 10 minutes per day. A K–2 version of this program also provides a phonological awareness instruction component (Mercer & Campbell, 1998). The activities in the book *Language Growth* (Campbell, 2013) completely cover the areas of phonological awareness for the emergent reader in a small group setting as well as through individual work.

Daily application of *Great Leaps* with middle school students with learning disabilities contributed to growth in reading and improvement in reading rate (Mercer, Campbell, Miller, Mercer, & Lane, 2000). The Mercer and colleagues study was replicated in Southern California 10 years later with the same results (Spencer & Manis, 2010). The average growth rates with these students from very disparate situations were remarkably similar: approximately two years of growth in a one year period. The author of the program is often available via telephone or e-mail to help parents and tutors with particular difficulties. *Great Leaps* strives to affordably bring all students to their reading potential in the shortest time possible.

Wilson Fluency/Basic

Wilson Fluency/Basic (Wilson Language Training, 2006) is a supplemental fluency program for students in early grades who are learning to read as well as older students who are struggling to learn to read. *Wilson Fluency/Basic* provides students with practice reading connected text so that they can develop rate-appropriate independent reading with ease and expression. The program includes four readers that focus on short vowel words with several 200–250 word passages composed of 90% decodable text.

Choral Reading or Neurological Impress Method

The neurological impress method (Heckelman, 1969, 1986) is a method for choral or concert reading. In this method, a teacher and student read aloud together for 10–15 minutes daily. To begin, select a high-interest book or a content-area textbook from the classroom. Sit next to the student and read aloud, pointing to each word. Read at a slightly faster pace than the student and encourage him or her to try to keep up with the person reading. When necessary, remind the student to keep his or her eyes on the words. Successful decoding requires the reader to connect the flow of spoken language with the flow of text (Carreker, 2005). Reading aloud with students can help them to practice phrasing and intonation.

Repeated Reading

The repeated reading technique is designed for children who read slowly despite adequate word recognition (Samuels, 1979). For this procedure, a child reads the same passage over again until a desired level of fluency is attained. To begin, the teacher may select an interesting passage that is 50–100 words long from a book that is slightly above the student's independent reading level. The teacher has the student read the selection orally and times the reading while counting the number of words that are pronounced incorrectly. The teacher then records the reading time and the number of words pronounced incorrectly. If desired, the teacher and student can set a realistic goal for speed and number of errors.

Figure 9.8 presents a sample recording form to use for repeated reading. The teacher may use two different color pencils for recording time and errors or a circle to indicate points on the line for time and an X or a square to indicate points on the line for errors. Between timings, the teacher may ask the student to look over the selection, reread it, and practice words that caused difficulty in the initial reading. When the student is ready, he or she rereads the same passage. Once again, the teacher times the reading and records the time and number of errors. The student repeatedly practices reading the selection as the teacher charts progress after each trial until a predetermined goal is reached or until the student is able to read the

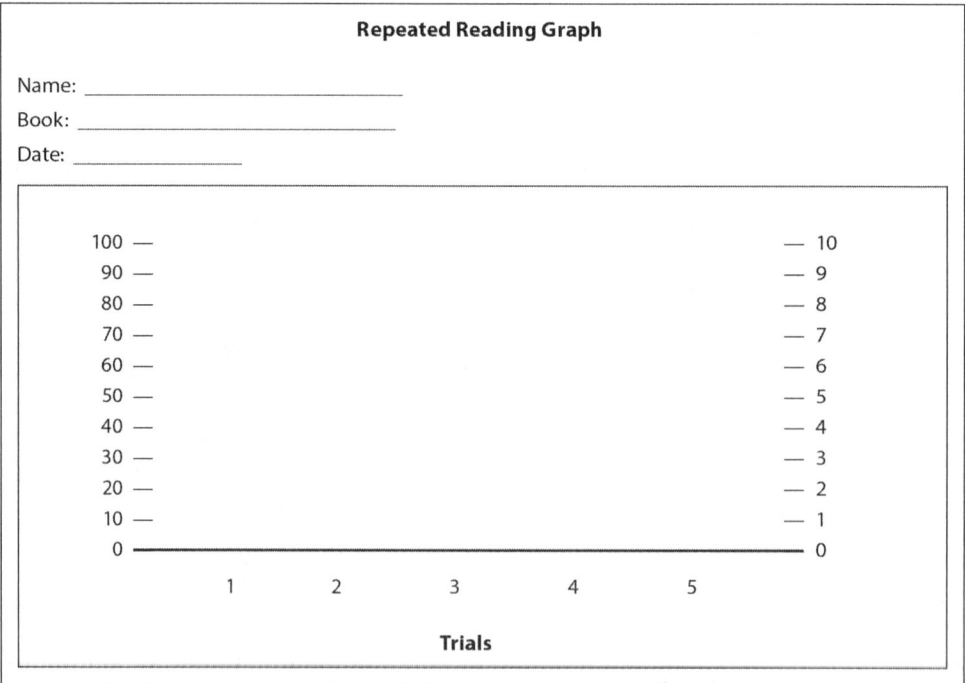

Figure 9.8. Sample repeated reading graph.

Instruction for the Processing Blocks

passage fluently with few mistakes. Research on repeated reading suggests that fluency can be improved as long as students are provided with specific instructions and procedures are used to monitor their progress (Mastropieri et al., 1999). An easy way to monitor student performance using this chart is for the teacher to keep a log of the dated charts. To control for a similar readability level, the teacher may select the passages to read from the same book. As performance improves, the time to perform the initial reading should decrease.

Repeated reading has also been used as a component of classwide peer tutoring (Mathes & Fuchs, 1993). In a study of this intervention, pairs of students in one group read continuously over a 10-minute period, whereas pairs of students in the other group read a passage together three times before going on to the next passage. Although both experimental conditions produced higher results than the typical reading instruction, no difference existed between the procedures, suggesting that the main benefit of the intervention is the student reading involvement and the increased time spent in reading (Mastropieri et al., 1999).

In a review of the effectiveness of repeated reading, Meyer and Felton (1999) concluded that the method of repeated reading improves reading speed for a wide variety of readers. They made the following recommendations for helping students to improve fluency: 1) have students engage in multiple readings (three to four times); 2) use instructional level text; 3) use decodable text with struggling readers; 4) provide short, frequent periods of fluency practice; and 5) provide concrete measures of progress. Base the amount of teacher guidance on each individual's characteristics. For students with poor reading skills, modeling and practicing of words between readings improve student performance and reduce frustration.

Previewing

Previewing is a technique similar to repeated reading, involving preexposure to materials before they are formally read (Rose, 1984). For this type of procedure, a student can preview the material silently, you may read the passage aloud as the student follows along, or the student may first listen to the recorded passage on tape. Rose and Sherry (1984) found that both silent previewing and teacher-directed previewing were more effective than no previewing. Maria found that, by hearing the passage before she was asked to read it, she made fewer errors and was more successful reading the text.

Recorded Books

Another way to help students practice reading is to use audiobooks. Have the student listen to the reading while he or she follows along with an unabridged copy of the book. Most public libraries provide a wide selection of recorded books for loan.

When Maria was in fifth grade, she was interested in horses. Her mother would take her to the library, and they would check out books and the corresponding CDs. Each evening, she would listen to classic stories about horses as she followed along with the text.

If a student has been identified as having SLD or dyslexia, recorded books are available from Learning Ally. Founded in 1948, Learning Ally is a national nonprofit that makes reading accessible for all. Learning Ally has a collection of more than 75,000 digitally recorded textbooks and literature. A paid membership is required to use Learning Ally. Learning Ally offers affordable and customizable packages for schools and schools districts. Information for contacting Learning Ally is provided in the Additional Resources.

Some commercial recordings, such as those obtained at the public library, go too fast for individuals with reading disabilities. In addition, because younger and struggling readers lose their place frequently, it is important to have a procedure for relocating the place at the top of each page. Many teachers prefer to make their own recordings of books so that they can select materials that are of high interest to students and control the rate of delivery.

Carbo Method

Carbo (1989) developed procedures for recording books to achieve maximum gains in fluency. The following is a brief description of how to record books using this method:

1. Decide which pages will be recorded on each cassette side.
2. Because every tape cassette has about 5–8 seconds of lead time, let the tape run for that amount of time before starting to record.
3. Speak into the microphone from a distance of approximately 6–8 inches.
4. Convey interest in the book through expression when reading.
5. Begin by reading the story title, providing a brief introduction, pausing, and then telling the student which page to turn to. Pause long enough so that the reader has enough time to turn pages and look at pictures.
6. Tell the student when to turn the page. In order not to distract from the content, soften your voice slightly when stating a page number.
7. Read the story in logical phrases, slowly enough so that most students can follow along but not so slowly that they become bored.
8. End each tape with, "Please rewind the tape for the next listener. This ends this recording."

As general guidelines, record 5–15 minutes at a typical pace for instructional level material and have the student listen to the tape once. For difficult material, record no more than 2 minutes at a slow pace with good expression and have the student listen to the passage two or three times. After listening, have the student read the passage aloud.

Read Naturally

Another program designed to build fluency in students from mid–first grade through sixth grade is called *Read Naturally* (see Additional Resources). Instruction is individualized and involves three main steps: 1) reading along with an audio recording of a story that provides a model of fluent reading; 2) intensive, repeated practice to build speed and accuracy; and 3) monitoring and evaluating performance through graphing. To use the program, students are placed into an appropriate level on the basis of their oral reading fluency. The sequenced reading levels range from beginning reading to sixth-grade level with 24 stories available for each level. In addition, the lower level materials have been translated into Spanish.

Fluency methods are designed to increase rate and automaticity. They should be taught as a part of an effective reading program along with instruction in phonological awareness and decoding in the younger grades and vocabulary and

Instruction for the Processing Blocks

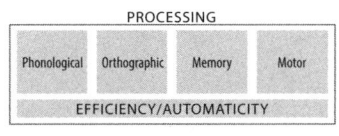

comprehension in all grades (Stahl & Stahl, 2004). Methods to increase rate are particularly beneficial for students such as Maria and Ben who have strong conceptual abilities but poor automaticity because of weaknesses within their phonological or orthographic abilities. These repeated readings of words and text provide repeated exposures that facilitate word mastery and automaticity. They can help a student move from Ehri's (1998) full alphabetic stage to the consolidated alphabetic stage, in which word learning is accomplished more easily.

CALCULATING

Parallels can be drawn among the development of decoding, encoding, and calculating skills. Acquisition of basic math skills may be affected by problems similar to those that affect decoding and encoding. A student who has trouble with memorizing basic math facts and developing numerical facility often has trouble solving mathematical problems. Students with math disabilities tend to have trouble retrieving basic math facts from memory, use procedures that are more commonly used by younger children, and tend to make more procedural errors (Geary, 2003, 2004, 2013a, 2013b). Just as with decoding and encoding, the lower-level skills of calculating must become increasingly automatized so that one may devote attention to problem solving.

More advanced levels of mathematics require rapid and accurate handling of numerical quantities (Carroll, 1993). Carroll defined numerical facility, which he identifies as Factor N, and explained the importance of this ability to mathematical thinking:

> Factor N refers simply to the degree to which the individual has developed skills in dealing with numbers, from the most elementary skills of counting objects and recognizing written numbers and their order, to the more advanced skills of correctly adding, subtracting, multiplying, and dividing numbers with an increasing number of digits, or with fractions and decimals. These are skills that are learned through experiences in the home, school, or even in the workplace. (1993, p. 469)

Carroll also explained the importance of this facility:

> In the early years, skills deal with simple numbers and operations, and the important object is to be able to deal with number problems correctly, at whatever speed. In later years, practice is aimed at handling computations with greater speed as well as accuracy. More complex problems can be dealt with effectively and efficiently only if skills with simple problems are increasingly automatized. (1993, p. 469)

Ryan's confusion with symbols extended into mathematics. He often reversed or transposed numbers (e.g., writing 12 for 21). He had trouble memorizing multiplication facts. He confused the directionality of symbols (e.g., the symbol for less than [<] and the symbol for greater than [>]), and he had trouble recalling the procedures for multiple steps, such as the steps required for long division. As with instruction in decoding and encoding, Ryan needed math instruction that was sequential, systematic, and multisensory in nature.

Failure in computation first occurs when the instruction is inappropriate or too limited to develop the skill being taught. Even though Ryan had only scored 30% correct on the chapter review, he was assigned problems from the next chapter along with his classmates. Unfortunately, Ryan was not experiencing immediate and continual success in his math program. With every chapter, he fell further behind. Ideally, a student should master concepts and skills before moving on to new information or the next chapter. This is not, however, always the case. When a teacher tries to keep all children in a classroom on the same page of a textbook, the pace becomes too fast for some and too slow for others. This type of instruction is ineffective.

In contrast, effective math instruction is based on the following seven principles (Fuchs et al., 2008, p. 85):

1. Instructional explicitness
2. Instructional design to minimize the learning challenge
3. Strong conceptual basis
4. Drill and practice
5. Cumulative review
6. Motivators to help students regulate their attention and behavior to work hard
7. Ongoing progress monitoring

Early Concepts

Just as the beginning reader/writer needs to acquire alphabetic knowledge, the beginning math student needs to acquire basic concepts for numeracy development. Some children acquire fundamental math skills in the preschool years. Maria always excelled in math, and by the time she entered kindergarten, she could count from 1 to 100 and add and subtract using objects. Learning number concepts was easy for Maria.

Children enter school with varying degrees of mathematical experiences so that some 6-year-olds have not acquired the math knowledge that other children acquire by the age of 3 (Clements & Sarama, 2011). Children's math competency at a young age has continuing significance for their achievement not only in school but also in life, as preschool children's math knowledge predicts their later school success into elementary and even high school (Clements & Sarama, 2011). Children need to have well-developed number sense that includes fluidity and flexibility with numbers, an understanding of what numbers mean, an ability to perform mental mathematics, and skill in making comparisons (Gersten & Chard, 1999, pp. 19–20). In kindergarten, a child's number sense was found to predict second-grade calculation fluency (Locuniak & Jordan, 2008). Number sense also supports more complex mathematics if developed before first grade (Jordan, Kaplan, Locuniak, & Rameneni, 2007). For children who lack the same mathematical knowledge as their peers, evidence-based mathematics interventions are necessary (Clements & Sarama, 2011). Without the proper intervention, students with less mathematical knowledge will continue to lag behind.

One-to-One Correspondence

One of the basic elements of number sense is accurate counting based on the concept of one-to-one correspondence. This means that one object in a group is represented by one number and that two sets of objects with the same number can be matched. In other words, two cookies can be matched to two glasses of milk. Children soon begin to realize that as each object is added to a set, the number increases by one. Most children master this concept between the ages of 4 and 5.

When Stephanie was in first grade, she was still having trouble with accurate counting. When given 10 objects to count, she would go around in a circle and count each object several times. She had trouble with remembering which ones she had already counted. Her teacher decided to line up the objects horizontally and have her count slowly as she pointed to each object in the line. Gradually,

Instruction for the Processing Blocks

she moved objects more and more away from a straight line. She encouraged Stephanie to touch each object as she counted it and to push it slightly away from the group.

An abacus can also be used for additional practice. Touching and moving the beads reinforce the concept of one-to-one correspondence and help a student develop an initial understanding of place value.

Drill

For cases in which a student has trouble with memory, daily trials may increase the speed and accuracy of recall. One way to help the student become more automatic with math facts is to practice with flashcards. First, identify the facts that the student does not know. Then practice three unknown facts at a time. Present the card and ask the student to respond. If the response takes longer than 2 seconds, tell the student the answer and move on to the next card. Once the student has mastered these three facts, place them in a pile for review on the following day. As an alternative to requiring an oral response, place three answers on the table and have the student point to the correct response. Once he or she can do this successfully, present the cards one at a time. When working with a student with weaknesses in memory, you may need to reduce the number of facts the student is expected to learn at any one time and repeat and practice the facts more often. Make a math flow list, similar to the spelling flow list, and do daily testing of a few facts. When the student remembers the fact correctly 3 days in a row, the fact can be removed from the list and then reviewed 1 week later. Research results support the importance of ongoing monitoring of performance coupled with student goal setting and feedback on fact retrieval (Fletcher et al., 2007).

The use of 1-minute timings is another evidence-based practice for increasing fluency with math computations (Miller & Hudson, 2007). Miller and Hudson describe the following procedure:

1. Provide students with a worksheet of problems that cannot typically be completed within 1 minute.
2. Tell students to begin and complete as many problems as they can within the minute.
3. Tell students to stop after 1 minute.
4. Score the sheet by counting the number of correct and incorrect digits written.
5. Plot the total number of correct digits on a graph.

Students may then review errors with the teacher or a peer or correct errors with a calculator.

Peer tutoring has also been used to help students improve math computation skill. In a meta-analysis of peer-mediated interventions, Kunsch, Jitendra, and Sood (2007) found that peer-mediated interventions were most effective for helping elementary-age students at risk for math failure improve computation skill in general education classrooms. Interventions were not as effective for addressing higher order mathematical skills.

Fact Charts

A pocket-size fact chart can also help students overcome computational weaknesses. Unlike a calculator, in which only one fact is viewed at a time, the chart allows students to view a full set of facts. Finding the same fact in the same location reinforces learning of the math fact. When facts have been mastered, they may be blackened over or removed from the pocket chart. Remember that the difference between students with weaknesses in memory and other learners is not the process by which they learn but rather the number of trials necessary for mastery. Patience, persistence, and frequent praise are essential in helping to motivate students to stick with it even though mastery may seem to be a slow, laborious process.

Software

Many software programs are available to help students practice and master basic math facts. A lot of these programs provide an engaging game format. Some students are more willing to practice with computers than with teachers. One nice thing about the computer is that it has unlimited patience.

One example is *Math Flash* (Fuchs, Hamlett, & Powell, 2003). In this program, the computer briefly displays a math fact, such as $8 \times 7 = 56$; then, after the prompt disappears, the student types the fact into the computer. If the fact is correct, it remains on the screen, the computer says the fact aloud, and the student receives points and prizes. If the response is incorrect, the student's response disappears and the computer says and shows the correct fact for the student to attempt again. The duration of the flash is increased or decreased depending on a student's performance during the session.

Calculation Assessment

Monitoring a student's progress is important in any subject; assessment is important, as it helps guide instruction. Math progress monitoring tools include daily or weekly assessments, such as curriculum-based measurement (CBM) in math. Without these data, teachers are unable to see what concepts students have grasped or in what areas they need additional support. Assessment is important not only during teaching but also to help plan for future instruction and remediation. Ultimately, assessment shows policy makers, teachers, administrators, and parents what students can do and are capable of doing. Other examples of ongoing or continuing assessment may include having each student make a portfolio of his or her work and having math assessments that include real-world problems embedded in them. Quick assessment for math can also be incorporated informally by having students respond with response cards or by taking a student poll.

Curriculum-Based Measurement for Math

CBM is a way to monitor student progress and also provide feedback regarding the effectiveness of instruction because it is sensitive to short-term gains. CBM math probes can be administered individually or in small groups. CBM math probes include either single-skill or multiskill worksheets. Single-skill worksheets include problems that are similar and focus on one skill, such as adding three to five 2-digit numbers with regrouping. Multi-skill worksheets contain a variety of problems with different math operations—for example, adding two 1-digit numbers in which the sum is 10 and adding two 2-digit numbers with regrouping. Students are given 2 minutes to work on the math probe.

CBM for math is scored by adding the total number of correct digits in a problem as opposed to tradition scoring of correct or incorrect. Specifically, the student is given one point for each correct digit in the problems on the worksheet. Separately

Instruction for the Processing Blocks

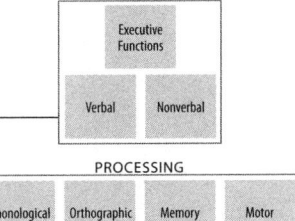
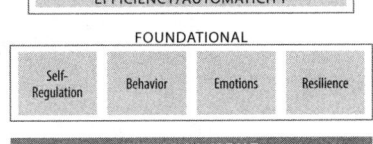

scoring digits allows a teacher to see where a student has a partial math competency as well as areas in which a student may need additional help. For example, 14 + 9 has a two-digit answer. If the student wrote the correct answer of 23, the student would earn two correct digits, one point for the 2 being in the correct place and one point for the 3 being in the correct place. Reversed digits are not counted as errors unless they become a new digit. Credit is also given for placeholders, such as in multidigit multiplication. Finally, credit is not given for regrouping, carries, and borrows from other numbers. The following is an example of an advanced multiplication problem and how it is scored using CBM math scoring. This problem has 11 total correct digits because there are 11 digits in 11 different place values. The zero counts as a placeholder; the student would also have been given credit if the space were left blank.

$$\begin{array}{r} 113 \\ \times\, 12 \\ \hline 226 \\ 1{,}130 \\ \hline 1{,}356 \end{array}$$

Dyscalculia

As with dyslexia in reading, dyscalculia refers to a learning disorder in mathematics. Students with dyscalculia may exhibit a variety of difficulties, including difficulty recognizing numbers and symbols (e.g., not knowing that an × indicates multiplication), poor number sense, difficulty counting, and problems with estimation and performing mental math. They may also struggle to recognize number patterns (1, 3, 5, 7. . . .) or understand the number line and place value. The most universal behavior characteristics of dyscalculia are 1) poor learning and retrieval of arithmetic facts from memory, 2) immature counting and problem-solving strategies, 3) slow number naming and calculation fluency, and 3) difficulty comparing the magnitudes of numbers (Price & Ansari, 2013). Thus, in the Building Blocks model, students with dyscalculia may have difficulty in memory as well as becoming efficient and automatic with memory and retrieval of number facts. Just as with dyslexia, from an instructional point of view, it is not enough to label someone as having "dyscalculia"; instead, one must describe the specific areas of math that are problematic for that student and then design a specific intervention plan.

Two other areas that can contribute to math learning disabilities are visual-spatial difficulties, represented by the Nonverbal block, and weaknesses in oral language, represented by the Verbal block. Students who have visual-spatial difficulties often have trouble with lining up numbers and seeing patterns. Verbal abilities come into play with learning math vocabulary and understanding story problems. Chapters 10 and 11 discuss these types of problems, as well as effective interventions.

Multisensory Procedures for Calculation

As with decoding and encoding, children with weaknesses in the Processing blocks often benefit from a multisensory approach to learning math facts. Similar to teaching reading and spelling, the abilities of the symbolic blocks are used to aid memorization. Students may need different approaches depending on their learning styles. Maria found it easiest to learn math facts if she would say the fact aloud while looking at it; Ben needed to look at the fact, say it, trace it, and then write it.

For many children, the act of saying the facts and then trying to write them from memory enhances learning. As with teaching spelling, encourage students to write answers from memory rather than simply copying. Use this simple procedure:

1. Have the student look at a fact with the answer.
2. Have the student say the fact. (Have the student say and trace the fact, if needed.)
3. Remove the fact.
4. Ask the student to say and write the fact and the answer.
5. Hold up the fact, and have the student check it.

Touch Points

For students who make frequent errors in computation but understand the basic operations, the teacher may place dot patterns on numbers (e.g., place four dots on the number 4) to help improve accuracy in addition and subtraction. As proficiency increases, students may just tap their pencils on each number as they count and perform simple addition and subtraction facts.

TouchMath

A multisensory approach for teaching four basic computational skills that uses touch points is called TouchMath (Bullock, 1991; see Additional Resources). For this approach, students are taught to touch the dots on each of the numbers when counting. Several steps are included in the process. To add a series of numbers, students touch the dots on the numbers and count forward. To subtract, students say the name of the larger number and then touch the dots while counting backward. Many first- and second-grade teachers use this type of method in conjunction with existing math programs to help children improve their accuracy in addition and subtraction and to aid with memorization of basic facts. Children are encouraged to eliminate touching the points as they become more proficient. Specific classroom sets are available for first and second grade. Figure 9.9 illustrates the touch points for the numbers.

Structural Arithmetic

Structural arithmetic is another multisensory teaching approach that helps children learn number concepts (Stern & Stern, 1971). This program encourages the use of manipulatives and exploration so that children can discover the basic principles underlying the arithmetic processes. Many sequenced activities and games are available. Stern (2005) provided a comprehensive overview of the basic features of this program.

For students whose problems are caused or compounded by poor handwriting, difficulty aligning figures, errors in transposing figures, or crowding figures on the page, the use of paper with boxes or columns marked on it may reduce problems. When Andy used graph paper with large boxes, he was able to align his numbers more accurately.

Mnemonics

Students who have difficulty with memorizing math facts may memorize facts more easily if instruction is linked with other stronger abilities. Greene (1999) found that

Instruction for the Processing Blocks

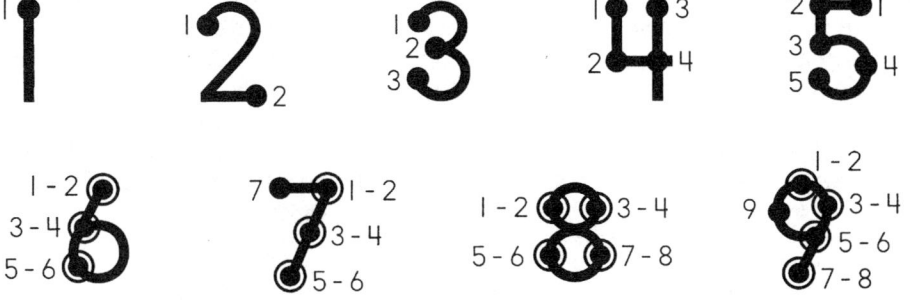
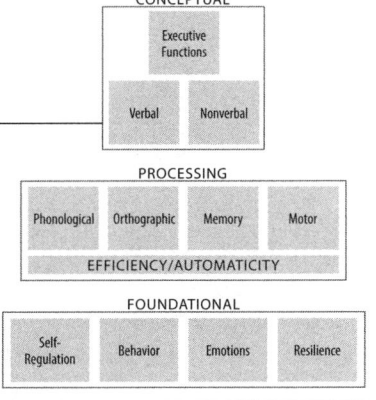

Figure 9.9. TouchMath touch points. (Source: From *Touch Math: The Touchpoint Approach for Teaching Basic Math Computation* [4th ed.], revised and enlarged. By permission of J. Bullock and Innovative Learning Concepts, Inc. Copyright 1984, 1986, 1992, by Innovative Learning Concepts, Inc., Colorado Springs. All rights reserved.)

students with LD learned multiplication facts more easily with mnemonic instruction. Students were taught facts associated with a pegword phrase for each number (e.g., 6 = sticks, 7 = heaven, 42 = warty shoe) and an associated picture (e.g., 6 × 7 = 42; sticks in heaven with a warty shoe).

If a student has strengths in the Verbal Conceptual block, facts may be learned most easily with the use of music or rhyme. Rap tapes are available that review multiplication facts. Inexpensive commercial rhyme cards, such as *Times Tables the Fun Way* and *Addition the Fun Way,* are also available; these rhymes for facts with associated picture cards are available from City Creek Press (http://www.citycreek.com; see Additional Resources). An example from these cards is "6 × 6 are very thirsty sixes" with a picture to reinforce the fact.

Calculators

In some math classes, a student's ability to remember formulas is critical; at other times, the student needs to demonstrate an ability to use formulas in order to perform a calculation. Students who are poor at calculating may have good problem-solving abilities. If the goal of a test or problem set is to demonstrate problem-solving skills rather than the ability to do calculations, use of a calculator is appropriate. Although tools such as a calculator or a software program can be helpful, students need to understand how to use the tools to solve problems.

A few teachers may feel that use of a calculator should be prohibited because it may inhibit learning of math facts.

Stephanie's individualized education program (IEP) stated that she should be encouraged to use a calculator for all math activities so that she could focus her attention on problem solving. She asked Ms. Taylor, her fourth-grade teacher, if she could use her calculator on her homework that evening. Ms. Taylor replied, "Yes, if you show your work." Stephanie said that she would, and the next day, she turned in the drawing shown in Figure 9.10.

Error Analysis

One of the most effective ways to help resolve a student's errors is to analyze any mistakes he or she makes on school papers or homework assignments. Attempt to determine exactly why the student has missed certain problems. The important point to realize is that students will continue to make the same type of errors unless intervention occurs. When you cannot determine why a student has missed a problem, ask the student to say aloud step by step what he or she was doing when attempting to solve the problem. Listen carefully to the student's explanation and ask questions as needed to discover why the student is making errors.

When Stephanie would add or subtract problems with a zero, she would always obtain a wrong answer. She would answer $7 + 0 = 0$. When asked to explain what she was doing, Stephanie reported, "Zero means that there is nothing there so you can't have anything when there is a zero." Using manipulatives, her teacher then showed her that when zero is added or subtracted, the number of objects in the set remains the same.

Modeling

When introducing new concepts and skills, use modeling and demonstrations. Have students watch how you perform a task as you talk yourself through it. Then students can perform the task as you talk the students through it. Finally, students can perform the tasks as they talk themselves through it. This procedure focuses on the Conceptual block of Executive Functions and helps students understand the basic process involved in computations.

Figure 9.10. Stephanie's calculator drawing.

Instruction for the Processing Blocks

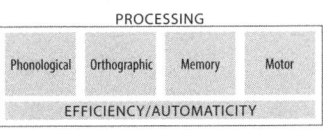
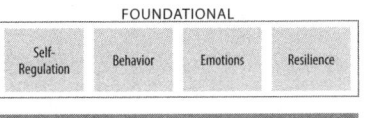

In fourth grade, Stephanie was having trouble understanding how to do division problems. Ms. Taylor, her teacher, showed her step by step how to solve 25 divided by 3:

1. Ask yourself, "Does 3 go into 25?" Because the answer is yes, count how many times.
2. Record 8 on the top of the line.
3. Multiply 8 × 3 and record 24 below 25.
4. Subtract.
5. Check to make sure all the 3s are out.
6. Record the remainder.

After they had talked through several different examples, Ms. Taylor summarized the steps of division on an index card.

1. Ask.
2. Write the number.
3. Multiply and write.
4. Subtract.
5. Check.
6. Bring down.

Stephanie then used this card to talk herself through the steps of the division problems that she was attempting to solve.

As described in Chapters 10 and 11, to increase understanding, students need to see, hear, perform, and talk about what they are learning. One fact is clear: A student's later mathematics achievement is compromised if he or she fails to acquire sufficient skill in performing basic operations with or without a calculator. In other words, limited fluency with the recall of basic facts hinders the development of higher level math skills. Although increasing a student's problem-solving skills is of the utmost importance, the student must also master basic math skills. When facts are mastered, the student is able to direct attention to the skills of the Conceptual blocks required for effective math problem solving.

HANDWRITING

Although some have called handwriting a lost art, ease with handwriting facilitates written expression, and the development of fine motor skills may affect other academic areas. For example, fine motor skills in preschool were found to be important predictors of later reading and math performance in second grade (Dinehart & Mandra, 2013). In a longitudinal study by Berninger et al. (2006), transcription skills in Grade 4 were strongly related to the quality of student compositions in Grade 8. Therefore, it is important for educators to spend time helping students develop fine motor skills such as handwriting even before kindergarten. Even though much research has focused on handwriting particularly in older grades, the development of handwriting skills are built on foundational skills acquired well before a student begins school. Extra support early on can help students who have difficulties in handwriting (Cahill, 2009).

All students should have specific instruction in handwriting, but students with weaknesses in the Motor block require even more time devoted to specific instruction. For children who struggle, handwriting can be a significant hindrance to written expression. They may even succumb to a self-filling proficiency where they avoid writing altogether (Graham, 2010). Thus, explicit instruction in handwriting in the early grades is important.

The basic goals of this instruction are to help students develop legible writing styles and be able to write quickly and easily without devoting conscious attention to letter formation (Graham, 1999). In addition to motor skills, handwriting involves knowledge of orthography and planning ability (Fletcher et al., 2007). Early intervention with students with handwriting difficulties should focus on forming letters automatically and retrieving them quickly from memory; this type of intervention can help prevent more serious writing problems later in school (e.g., Berninger & Amtmann, 2003).

Readiness

Some children begin attempting to write letters as young as age 2. They enjoy activities that involve small muscle control.

When Stephanie was 2 years old, she announced that she was writing a story. She had watched her older sister, Haley, who was in kindergarten, and wanted to engage in similar tasks. She informed her mother that she was going to sign her name. Stephanie's story is shown in Figure 9.11. Notice her attempt to write a small *HA* at the bottom of the page. Stephanie had watched her sister write her name enough times that she was trying to produce the first two letters.

Vast differences exist in the development of children's motor skills. By the time Stephanie entered kindergarten, her motor skills were well developed because she had already been drawing and attempting to write at the age of 2. Other children pick up a pencil for the first time when they enter a kindergarten classroom. Figure 9.12 shows a class of kindergarten children writing or attempting to write their names. Notice the difference in motor control among Kenneth, Dominic, Tony, and Sarah. Kenneth and Dominic already write stories. Clearly, Tony and Sarah are not ready to start writing letters.

Prior to handwriting instruction, children such as Tony and Sarah need to increase their fine motor coordination because forming letters requires controlled motor skill. Activities such as digging in the sand and playing with clay increase muscle tone. Encourage children to color and draw because these activities also help them strengthen their hands. As children begin using crayons, encourage scribbling. Scribbling builds strength and helps prepare children for the more precise motor movements that are needed for handwriting.

As a child's skill increases, you may provide him or her with more specific readiness activities, such as tracing and copying shapes and lines, completing dot-to-dot activity books, and drawing lines and circles. Unfortunately, children such as Tony and Sarah often do not like to color or draw, so extra time must be provided to develop readiness skills.

Letter formation requires the use of circles, lines, and curves. Sample prewriting activities include the following:

1. Producing scribbles
2. Drawing a horizontal line
3. Drawing a circle
4. Drawing a cross, square, and rectangle
5. Drawing lines that slant to the left and lines that slant to the right

Instruction for the Processing Blocks

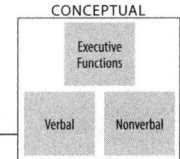

Figure 9.11. Stephanie's writing.

Teachers can encourage students to use these lines and shapes when drawing. For example, ask a child to draw a windy road, a long fence, a group of balls, some valleys and mountains, and a curvy snake. These forms can be drawn or painted on sheets of old newspaper.

Fundamentals

Prior to formal handwriting instruction, a few children need assistance with establishing hand preference. If a child has not developed a preferred hand by kindergarten, attempt to determine which hand is used more often and appears more coordinated. Although a child may switch back and forth, in most cases, he or she uses one hand more than the other. Through careful observation, a child's natural hand preference is likely to become apparent.

Andy tended to perform most activities with his right hand, although when he was using a pencil, he would sometimes pass the pencil from one hand to the other, depending on which side of the paper he was drawing on. Andy found it uncomfortable to cross the midline of his body, so his simple solution was to switch hands instead. Once his first-grade teacher decided that Andy should use his right hand for writing, Andy was not sure which hand was the right one. For a few weeks, he wore a ring on his hand as a reminder.

Some children have ineffective pencil grips. Most people hold the pencil between the thumb and index finger with the pencil resting on the middle finger, but Andy seemed to squeeze the pencil with an uncomfortable grip. After writing for a few

Figure 9.12. Kindergarten students' written names.

minutes, he always complained that his hand was tired. Several options are available for students such as Andy. Some students benefit from triangular pencil grips, available at most teaching supply stores. This type of rubber grip helps position the fingers around the pencil. As an alternative, rubber bands can also be wrapped around the pencil at the place where the middle finger rests. In addition, Pencil Grip manufactures special grips that position the hand so that the pencil rests on the first joint of the middle finger and the thumb and index fingers hold the pencil in place (see Additional Resources).

When a child is writing, he or she should be able to move his or her writing arm smoothly and easily across the paper. If the student is printing, the writing paper is usually positioned straight up and down in front of the body. When writing in

Instruction for the Processing Blocks

Figure 9.12. *(continued)*

manucursive or cursive style, right-handed students typically slant the paper to the left, whereas left-handed students slant the paper to the right. Some students have difficulty with keeping the writing paper positioned correctly on the table and find it easier to write if papers are attached to a clipboard.

Even though many children have trouble developing legible handwriting, some children receive very little instruction on how to form letters. The sample in Figure 9.13 demonstrates that the size and shape of Andy's letters are inconsistent and many of the words are hard to discern. He tried to form letters, but he had trouble controlling the pencil. He was trying to write a note to his friend, Dan, that said, "I'm sorry that I made you mad." Ms. Abram, his second-grade teacher, understands his difficulties and provides a supportive classroom for writing development; however, as Andy gets older, his teachers are likely to become less tolerant and more critical of his poor writing.

Handwriting that appears sloppy affects how people react to a paper. Picture yourself grading a large stack of papers. Think about how you feel when you look at a neatly written paper. It seems to invite you to read it. Think about how you feel when you come to a paper that is filled with smudge marks or seems only partially legible. Your eyes become tired, and you may even put the paper at the bottom of the stack and delay the grading. A neatly written paper implies effort, whereas a sloppy paper seems to reflect a lack of effort. Unfortunately, Andy is more likely to receive lower grades on writing assignments if his handwriting does not improve or if he does not develop keyboarding skill.

Developmental Stages

Like the development of decoding and encoding, the development of handwriting proficiency can be described by stages. Levine (1987) described several stages:

1. *Imitation:* From preschool to first grade, children pretend to write by copying others (e.g., by imitating her older sister, Stephanie was developing skill in letter formation).
2. *Graphic presentation:* During first and second grade, children learn how to form letters and to write on a line with proper spacing. Fine motor skills become better developed.
3. *Progressive incorporation:* From late second grade to fourth grade, letters are produced with less effort.
4. *Automatization:* In fourth through seventh grade, children write rapidly and efficiently.

In the final stages, children develop personalized styles and increase proficiency in writing. As with other instruction in basic skills, the goal is to establish automaticity, or rapid and easy production of letterforms. Writing should become both efficient and automatic.

General Principles

Graham and Madan (1981) noted that an effective program for teaching letter formation is based on the following four principles: 1) overlearning letters in isolation and then applying them in a written context; 2) forming letters with external cues, such as verbalizing and tracing until they become automatic; 3) encouraging students to evaluate their own handwriting; and 4) providing students with assistance in maintaining a consistent and legible writing style.

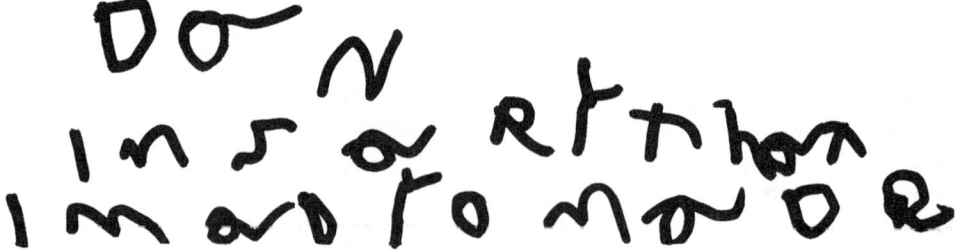

Figure 9.13. Andy's writing: "Dan. I'm sorry that I made you mad."

Instruction for the Processing Blocks

Important elements of handwriting instruction, therefore, include modeling and describing letter formation; discussing critical attributes; giving feedback and reinforcement; and having students practice tracing, self-verbalizing, and writing from memory (Graham & Madan, 1981; Graham & Miller, 1980). Many students require explicit and direct help to establish the patterns needed for legible, fluent writing (Graham, 1983). Skills are overlearned in isolation and then applied in meaningful assignments (Graham & Madan, 1981; Graham & Miller, 1980). In general, students benefit from supervised practice with immediate reinforcement and correction (Meese, 1994). As skill progresses, students can improve their handwriting as they write meaningful text, such as copying the final drafts of their own compositions. McCarney and Cummins (1988) summarized several general principles teachers should follow when helping students develop their handwriting skills:

1. Provide the student with ample opportunities to practice handwriting skill.
2. Model neat and correct handwriting at all times.
3. Have the student trace over model handwriting. As skill develops, slowly fade the model to promote independence.
4. Initially, provide the student with primary paper with a middle line in order to foster the correct size of letters. As skill develops, have the student use standard paper.
5. Provide the student with wide-ruled paper. As skill improves, gradually reduce the width of the lines.
6. If the student is having difficulty with spacing, provide him or her with paper that has both horizontal and vertical lines. Teach the student to write one symbol in each box and to leave one box empty after a comma and two empty boxes after a period.
7. If the student's handwriting is affected by poor positioning of the pencil, provide him or her with a triangular pencil grip.
8. When teaching handwriting to older students, provide them with functional opportunities to practice handwriting (e.g., filling out a job application or bank forms).
9. Recognize and reinforce improvement.

Choosing a Writing Style

Students may be taught several styles of script. The three most widely used writing styles are manuscript, manucursive, and cursive writing. Although most school districts adopt a certain approach to teaching handwriting, research has not demonstrated a clear advantage of one style over another (Graham, 1999; Graham & Miller, 1980). Traditionally, instruction in manuscript is provided in first and second grade, and then cursive instruction begins in second or third grade. Increasingly, schools are turning more to a manucursive method because it avoids devoting instructional time to a new writing style and eliminates the later transition from manuscript to cursive. In addition, improved technology has resulted in alternatives to handwriting: keyboarding and voice-activated word processing.

In a traditional manuscript instructional program, children are taught that letterforms are composed of simple sticks and circles. They are then taught how to make various combinations of circles and sticks to form the letters of the alphabet. This style is sometimes referred to as the ball-and-stick method.

Manucursive is a writing style that combines manuscript and cursive letter formation. The most widely used manucursive writing style is D'Nealian (Thurber, 1983). In this method, the majority of letters are formed using a continuous stroke motion. This provides a natural progression from manuscript to cursive letter formation because the letters are connected by adding joining strokes. In addition, D'Nealian offers visual, auditory, and tactile-kinesthetic clues to help children remember how the numbers and letters are formed. Figures 9.14a and 9.14b present D'Nealian number descriptions and lowercase manuscript letters with the suggested oral directions to use when teaching the letters. For cursive writing, all letters are formed with a continuous motion, and words are written as units.

Some individuals believe that manuscript is an easier style and the preferred method for young children to learn. Manuscript letters may be easier to form than cursive letters and are similar to the print that children see in books. In addition, cursive writing can pose problems for some children with motor weaknesses because they lack the fine motor coordination needed to sustain a rhythmic motion and make the required continuous strokes. Even after students have been taught cursive writing, they should not be discouraged from continuing to write in manuscript (Graham, 1999).

Other individuals believe that children should begin with manucursive or cursive writing styles. Manucursive and cursive approaches appear to be effective for some children with fine motor weaknesses for several reasons. First, in using these writing styles, children make fewer reversals because the letters are formed differently and are easier to discriminate. Second, they do not need to learn two different patterns of letter formation. Third, the continuous motion and rhythm can help a child with spacing and speed. Fourth, cursive writing can help reduce inconsistencies in the size and shape of letters.

Although Andy had problems with fine motor coordination, the occupational therapist recommended that he be taught cursive writing. She felt that cursive writing would help Andy keep the words together as a unit, so that the individual letters did not land above or below the writing line. In other words, cursive writing would eliminate having to pick up the pencil and replace it somewhere on the page. This method would reduce the frequency of letter reversals as well as the requirements for motor planning. Because cursive words are written as a unit, Andy would not have to relocate the line with formation of each letter. After 2 months of instruction, the legibility of Andy's writing improved. Figure 9.15 provides an illustration of his cursive writing: "I had camp today."

In general, as indicated by these various theories, there is a lack of evidence and consensus regarding what type of script to teach (Graham, 1999). Depending on a child's characteristics, one writing style may be easier than another. Some children learn to print easily but struggle to learn cursive. Others have tremendous difficulty learning to print and then experience similar difficulties in learning to write in cursive. In these cases, too much time can be wasted on developing an alternative writing style. The major goal of handwriting instruction is legibility, not proficiency or mastery of a certain style. For a child with weaknesses in motor skill, it is better to teach one system well than to insist on mastery of both manuscript and cursive writing.

Ultimately, handwriting is idiosyncratic: Each writer develops his or her own personal style that may sometimes involve a blending of different scripts. In fact, Graham, Weintraub, and Berninger (1998) found that students who used a mixed

Instruction for the Processing Blocks

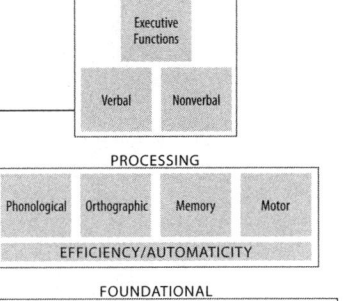

NUMBER DESCRIPTIONS

1 Start at the top, slant down to the bottom.
[Top start; slant down.]

2 Start a little below the top; curve up right to the top; curve down right to the middle; slant down left to the bottom; make a bar to the right.
[Start below the top; curve up, around; slant down left; and over right.]

3 Start a little below the top; curve up right to the top; curve down right to the middle; curve down right again to the bottom; curve up left, and stop.
[Start below the top; curve up, around halfway; around again, up, and stop.]

4 Start at the top; slant down to the middle; make a bar to the right. Start again at the top, to the right of the first start; slant down through the bar to the bottom.
[Top start; down halfway; over right. Another top start, to the right; slant down, and through.]

5 Start at the top; make a bar to the left; slant down to the middle; curve down right to the bottom; curve up left, and stop.
[Top start; over left; slant down halfway; curve around, down, up, and stop.]

6 Start at the top; slant down left to the middle; curve down left to the bottom; curve up right to the middle; curve left, and close.
[Top start; slant down and curve around; up, and close.]

7 Start at the top; make a bar to the right; slant down left to the bottom.
[Top start; over right; slant down left.]

8 Start a little below the top; curve up left to the top and down left to the middle; curve down right to the bottom; curve up left; slant up right, through the middle, to the beginning, and touch.
[Start below the top; curve up, around, down; a snake tail; slant up right; through, and touch.]

9 Start at the top; curve down left to the middle; curve up right to the beginning, and close; slant down to the bottom.
[Top start; curve down, around, close; slant down.]

10 Start at the top; slant down to the bottom. Start again at the top, to the right of the first start; curve down left to the bottom; curve up right to the top, and close.
[Top start; slant down. Another top start, to the right; curve down, around, and close.]

Figure 9.14a. D'Nealian script: Number descriptions. (From Thurber, D.N. [1993]. *D'Nealian Handwriting Book 4* [3rd ed.]. Glenview, IL: Scott Foresman & Co.; reprinted by permission. *D'Nealian Handwriting* is copyrighted by Pearson Education, Inc. or its affiliates. Used by permission. All Rights Reserved. D'Nealian is a registered trademark of Donald Neal Thurber.)

style received higher ratings for legibility than students who used either manuscript or cursive exclusively.

Letter Formation

Most children require some guidance as they are beginning to learn how to form letters. In these initial stages of learning, a child's hand may need to be physically guided as an adult reads aloud each letter name. This type of demonstration and practice can be provided easily on a chalkboard. As a general rule, teach the child how to form letters beginning at the top of the stroke. Although their first independent attempts at letter formation appear awkward, most children soon learn to form letters easily from memory.

When practicing letter formation with a student, begin with having him or her write letters in isolation. After the student has mastered the basic forms of the letters, progress to practicing letters within words and then within sentences. The following activities can be used to help students acquire legible, fluent writing.

LOWERCASE MANUSCRIPT LETTER DESCRIPTIONS

 Start at the middle line; curve down left to the bottom line; curve up right to the beginning, and close; retrace down, and swing up. [Middle start; around down, close up, down, and a monkey tail.]

 Start at the top line; slant down to the bottom line; curve up right to the middle line; curve left, and close. [Top start; slant down, around, up, and a tummy.]

 Start a little below the middle line; curve up left to the middle line; curve down left to the bottom line; curve up right, and stop. [Start below the middle; curve up, around, down, up, and stop.]

 Start at the middle line; curve down left to the bottom line; curve up right to the beginning; touch, and keep going up to the top line; retrace down and swing up. [Middle start; around down, touch up high, down, and a monkey tail.]

 Start between the middle line and the bottom line; curve up right to the middle line; curve down left; touch, and keep going down to the bottom line; curve up right, and stop. [Start between the middle and bottom; curve up, around, touch, down, up, and stop.]

 Start a little below the top line; curve up left to the top line; slant down to the bottom line. Make a crossbar on the middle line. [Start below the top; curve up, around, and slant down. Cross.]

 Start at the middle line; curve down left to the bottom line; curve up right to the beginning, and close; retrace down to halfway below the bottom line, and hook left. [Middle start; around down, close up, down under water, and a fishhook.]

 Start at the top line; slant down to the bottom line; retrace up halfway; make a hill to the right, and swing up. [Top start; slant down, up over the hill, and a monkey tail.]

 Start at the middle line; slant down to the bottom line, and swing up. Make a dot above the letter. [Middle start; slant down, and a monkey tail. Add a dot.]

 Start at the middle line; slant down to halfway below the bottom line, and hook left. Make a dot above the letter. [Middle start; slant down under water, and a fishhook. Add a dot.]

 Start at the top line; slant down to the bottom line; retrace up halfway; curve right; make a small loop left, and close; slant down right to the bottom line, and swing up. [Top start; slant down, up into a little tummy, and a monkey tail.]

Start at the top line; slant down to the bottom line, and swing up. [Top start; slant down, and a monkey tail.]

Start at the middle line; slant down to the bottom line; retrace up, and make a hill to the right; retrace up; make another hill to the right; and swing up. [Middle start; slant down, up over the hill, up over the hill again, and a monkey tail.]

 Start at the middle line; slant down to the bottom line; retrace up; make a hill to the right, and swing up. [Middle start; slant down, up over he hill, and a monkey tail.]

 Start at the middle line; curve down left to the bottom line; curve up right to the beginning, and close. [Middle start; around down, and close up.]

Figure 9.14b. D'Nealian script: Lowercase manuscript letter descriptions. (From Thurber, D.N. [1993]. *D'Nealian Handwriting Book 4* [3rd ed.]. Glenview, IL: Scott Foresman & Co.; reprinted by permission. *D'Nealian Handwriting* is copyrighted by Pearson Education, Inc. or its affiliates. Used by permission. All Rights Reserved. D'Nealian is a registered trademark of Donald Neal Thurber.)

Instruction for the Processing Blocks

Figure 9.14b.

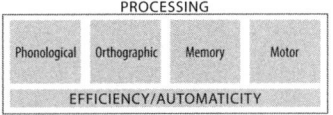
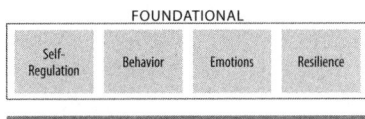

LOWERCASE MANUSCRIPT LETTER DESCRIPTIONS

 Start at the middle line; slant down to halfway below the bottom line; retrace up; curve down right to the bottom line; curve left, and close. [Middle start; slant down under water, up, around, and a tummy.]

 Start at the middle line; curve down left to the bottom line; curve up right to the beginning, and close; retrace down to halfway below the bottom line, and hook right. [Middle start; around down, close up, down under water, and a backwards fishhook.]

 Start at the middle line; slant down to the bottom line; retrace up; curve right, and stop. [Middle start; slant down, up, and a roof.]

 Start a little below the middle line; curve up left to the middle line and down left halfway; curve down right to the bottom line; curve up left, and stop. [Start below the middle; curve up, around, down, and a snake tail.]

 Start at the top line; slant down to the bottom line, and swing up. Make a crossbar on the middle line. [Top start; slant down, and a monkey tail. Cross.]

 Start at the middle line; slant down to the bottom line, and curve right; slant up to the middle line; retrace down, and swing up. [Middle start; down, around, up, down, and a monkey tail.]

 Start at the middle line; slant down right to the bottom line; slant up right to the middle line. [Middle start; slant down right, and slant up right.]

 Start at the middle line; slant down to the bottom line, and curve right; slant up to the middle line; retrace down, and curve right; slant up to the middle line. [Middle start; down, around, up, and down, around, up again.]

 Start at the middle line; slant down right to the bottom line, and swing up. Cross through the letter with a slant down left. [Middle start; down, around, up, and down, around, up again.]

 Start at the middle line; slant down to the bottom line, and curve right; slant up to the middle line; retrace down to halfway below the bottom line, and hook left. [Middle start; down, around, up, down under water, and a fishhook.]

Start at the middle line; make a bar to the right; slant down left to the bottom line; make a bar to the right. [Middle start; over right, slant down left, and over right.]

Multisensory Instruction for Writing

As with instruction in spelling, teaching handwriting for students with weaknesses in Orthographic and Motor blocks should be multisensory. Tracing exercises are critical for children who have severe weaknesses in fine motor skills. One of the most important ways to help a child who struggles with letter formation is to have him or her practice tracing letters until the motor movement becomes easy and automatic. Encourage younger children to trace letters made from sandpaper or felt.

Processing Blocks

Figure 9.15. Andy's cursive writing.

One easy multisensory way to make letters or numbers with a raised surface is to write letters on index cards in different colors. Draw the outline on top of the letter with Elmer's glue. Let the letters dry, and then have the child use the raised surface for tracing. At first, a teacher may need to guide the child's index finger over the letter. When the child is able to trace the letter easily, he or she can then trace the letter with a marking pen. Once the child is able to trace the letter successfully on paper, he or she can try to reproduce the letter on paper. Older children may use tracing paper or go over letters with a crayon or marking pen.

Many multisensory teaching techniques provide children with extensive practice in letter and number formation through repetitive tracings. This muscle movement and the development of motor memory help the child remember the specific patterns for letter formation.

The following simple procedure may be used for helping students learn how to form specific letters (Graham & Miller, 1980):

1. Write the letter with a crayon while the student observes.
2. Say the name of the letter with the student.
3. Have the student say the name of the letter while tracing it with his or her index finger.
4. Repeat Step 3 until the student is successful on five consecutive trials.
5. Have the student write the letter while looking at the model.
6. Repeat Step 5 until the student copies the letter successfully three times.
7. Have the student say the name of the letter while writing it from memory.
8. Repeat Step 7 until the student has written the letter successfully three times.

As another example of a multisensory procedure, Thurber (1983) described a six-step process for teaching letter formation that incorporates visual, auditory, and motor abilities using D'Nealian print.

Step 1: Tell the student which letter will be formed (e.g., "Now we will make the letter *a*").

Step 2: First, make eye contact with the student. Second, orally state the directions (e.g., up, around, down) for writing the letter while simultaneously writing the

Instruction for the Processing Blocks

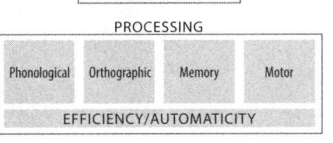
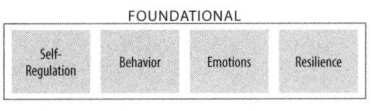

letter in the air. If facing the student, write the letter backward so that the child can see the correct formation.

Step 3: Have the student repeat the directions with you as you trace the letter in the air.

Step 4: When the student has mastered the letter formation, have him or her practice writing the letter on paper with a marker or pencil. Next, have the student write the letter with a few other letters in groups of three; two or three different groups may be needed for learning the correct formation. Then have the student repeat the directions for the letter when writing. At this point, do not allow the student to erase; have him or her simply cross out errors and practice again so that he or she may gauge his or her progress.

Step 5: Trace the letter on the student's arm, hand, or back with a finger while saying the directions. Repeat this step if necessary.

Step 6: Have the student trace the letter on your hand and say the directions. When the student succeeds, check to see if he or she has memorized the letter's formation. Do this by saying the directions and tracing the letter inaccurately on the child's hand. Encourage the student to indicate the error.

Directional Arrows

Placing numbered arrow cues on letters can increase automaticity of production (Brooks, Vaughan, & Berninger, 1999). Brooks and colleagues employed a procedure in which students were asked to look closely at the numbered arrow cues, cover the letter, and write the letter from memory. The interval of time for covering the letter before writing was increased systematically from 1 second (for the first four lessons) to 3 seconds (for the next four lessons) to 6 seconds (for the third set of four lessons), and so forth. This type of procedure is similar to the cover–write techniques discussed in the spelling section but includes the addition of numbered arrow cues to remind the student of how to form the letter. Berninger and colleagues (2006) found that direct instruction in letter writing that included following numbered arrow cues and writing letters from memory improved automaticity of legible letter writing.

Oral Descriptions

Another effective way to help a child with poor handwriting is to use the Verbal and Nonverbal skills of the Conceptual blocks to reinforce weaknesses in the Motor and Orthographic Processing blocks. Some children experiencing problems with letter formation have trouble getting a mental picture of a letter. As a child is tracing a letter or number, describe aloud the movement needed to form the symbol correctly. For example, when teaching a child to form the printed letter *a,* say, "Start up at the top and then swing around to the left in a circle and then come down." This verbal description helps the student remember the sequence of movements. Gradually encourage the child to say the verbal prompts.

In the Spalding method (Spalding & Spalding, 1990), children are prompted to visualize a clock face with all the numbers. Using a clock as a guide to teach formation of the letter *c,* say, "Start at 2:00 and drive back all the way around to 4:00." Or to teach the letter *a* with a clock, say, "Start at 2:00 and swing all the way back around to 2:00 and then draw a straight line down."

If the student is learning a manucursive writing style, the teacher may use the oral descriptions provided with the D'Nealian letters (Thurber, 1983). Gradually, students can describe the movements themselves as they write letters. For example, when printing the letter *n,* the student may say, "Down and then up. Make one hump."

Self-Guided Symbol Formation Strategy

Graham and colleagues (1998) examined the handwriting of 300 children in Grades 1–3. They found that the following six lowercase letters accounted for 48% of the omissions, miscues, and illegibilities: *q, j, z, u, n, k.* When only illegibilities were considered, five letters accounted for 54% of the errors. Thus, handwriting instruction may focus on mastery of specific letters.

Graham and Madan (1981) described an intensive remedial method for helping a student master the formation of a particular letter. The procedure is practiced on lined paper and can be used with either cursive or manuscript writing. The strategy consists of the following five steps:

1. Identify the letter that the student typically forms incorrectly. Ask the student to write a sample sentence that contains all the letters, such as "The quick brown fox jumps over the lazy dog."

2. Select one letter that the student has trouble forming. Model the correct letter formation with a crayon, marker, or chalk. Write the letter again while verbally describing the process. Continue until the student can repeat the verbal description with the teacher.

3. Have the student trace the letter until he or she can verbalize the steps alone. If needed, guide the student's tracing through the use of arrows or colored dots. Encourage the student to act as his or her own instructor by defining the task, correcting errors, and praising accurate letter formation. Continue with Step 3 until the student can copy the letter correctly five times.

4. Describe the formation of the target letter while the student attempts to visualize and write the letter. Provide corrective feedback. Continue until the student can write the letter five times from memory.

5. Have the student practice the target letter in meaningful contexts. Begin with practice of single words, phrases, and then sentences.

Persistent Reversals

A few students continue to reverse or invert letters and numbers past the age of 7. Even in eighth grade, Ben sometimes confused the letters *b* and *d.* Students who continue to reverse and invert letters often have weaknesses in the Orthographic block, the Phonological block, or both. They may have trouble recalling a mental image of a letter, forming letter images, or hearing subtle differences in sounds. Some types of errors (e.g., *b* and *d*) are more indicative of a weakness with orthographic images; other types (e.g., *b* and *p*) are more related to sound confusions (e.g., voiced and unvoiced consonant pairs).

The following simple suggestions can help a student reduce the frequency of reversed letters or numbers:

1. Have a student describe the movements for forming the letter. For example, if using the image of a clock face, the student can say for the letter *d,* "I begin at 2:00, swing back around, go up, and then go down."

Instruction for the Processing Blocks

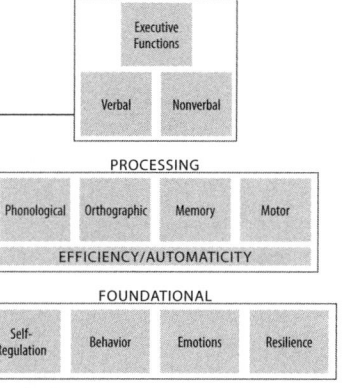

2. Have the student associate a problematic letter with another letter that does not cause confusion. The lowercase *b* can be related to the uppercase *B,* or a lowercase *a* can be associated as the beginning movement for making a lowercase *d.* The student may say, "I start the letter *d* just like the letter *a.*"
3. Use tracing to teach a simple, common word beginning with one of the problematic letters. For example, if the student reverses the letters *b* and *d,* teach the word *dad* and point out that all three letters are formed in the same way. Encourage the student to think of the word *dad* when uncertain of orientation.
4. Use a cue word, such as the word *bed,* which contains the two problematic letters. Draw a line across the word to show how the word looks like a bed. Encourage the student to think of the word *bed* when checking whether the letter is *b* or *d.*
5. Encourage the student to use cursive writing rather than manuscript because reversals appear less frequently in cursive writing.

Strategies to Build Writing Speed

As increased writing demands are placed on students, handwriting fluency increases in importance (Larsen, 1987). One instructional goal, therefore, is to help students develop a fluid, rapid style. Just as with decoding, encoding, and calculating, practice contributes to automaticity as the motor patterns needed for legible writing become more firmly established.

Timed Writing

One technique that may be used to improve writing rate and fluency and to encourage reluctant writers to increase their productivity is daily timed writings. Several variations are described briefly. The first variation, adapted from Houten, Morrison, Jarvis, and MacDonald (1974), uses the following steps:

1. Write a topic on the board.
2. Have students write about the topic for 10 minutes, trying to write more words than they did on the previous day.
3. At the end of the time period, have students count the number of words and record the word count on the top of the paper. Do not count words from repetitious or incomplete sentences.
4. Verify the scores and record the word count on a chart.

In a second variation, adapted from Alvarez (1983), students select their own topics. Sufficient knowledge of the topic helps students feel more comfortable in writing. For this procedure, use the following steps:

1. Have students select their own topics (although the teacher may choose to select the topic occasionally as a variation).
2. Have students write about their topics for 6 minutes, during which time the teacher spells words as requested.
3. At the end of the time period, have the student count the number of words.
4. Have the student record the number of words on the top of the paper and on individual graphs.

In another variation, suggested by Douglass (1984), the teacher writes along with the students. Teacher participation may increase the motivation of some individuals. Use the following procedure:

1. Have students select their own topics.
2. Spend 5 minutes writing about a topic of your choice while the students do the same.
3. Encourage the students to share their writing.

The fourth variation, adapted from several sources (Brigham, Graubard, & Stans, 1972; Rumsey & Ballard, 1985; Seabaugh & Schumaker, 1981), incorporates some reinforcement. For this procedure, use the following steps:

1. Have students write daily for an assigned time.
2. Have them count and record the number of letters, words, or sentences.
3. Provide individual reinforcements contingent on performance, such as points for an assigned number of letters, words, or sentences.
4. Provide students with opportunities to trade the reinforcements for various predetermined privileges.

By the time Ryan was in sixth grade, his cursive writing was neat and legible. Two years of instruction with a multisensory approach had helped him master the movements needed for writing. Although his difficulties with spelling were still apparent, he was clearly working carefully and taking pride in his writing. In his paragraph presented in Figure 9.16, he recounted one of his favorite jokes about a man going to visit a psychiatrist because his wife thinks that she is a chicken.

One of the best ways to work on handwriting is to have students practice their handwriting skills in interesting writing tasks. For example, a teacher could ask students to write wish lists, cards, jokes, or even stories. Students are more likely to write for a longer amount of time if they are interested in the topic (Cahill, 2009).

Computers

Computers can also be used to generate practice worksheets for handwriting or as an accommodation for poor handwriting. Many students complete the majority of their writing assignments on a computer. Students can also learn to use voice-activated software as an aid to writing.

Software

Two examples of flexible software programs for working on legibility and production speed are *Start Write* and *Fonts4Teachers* (see Additional Resources). These programs allow teachers to develop their own worksheets for handwriting practice. The teacher may select the style of writing—manuscript, modern manuscript (manucursive), or cursive—and can specify the font size, add directional arrows, and have letters presented with faded dots or light lines. In this way, students can practice handwriting on meaningful, individualized materials.

Andy's second-grade teacher, Ms. Abram, prepared daily, individualized worksheets for him to provide supplemental handwriting practice. On occasion, she had him write his spelling words. At

Instruction for the Processing Blocks

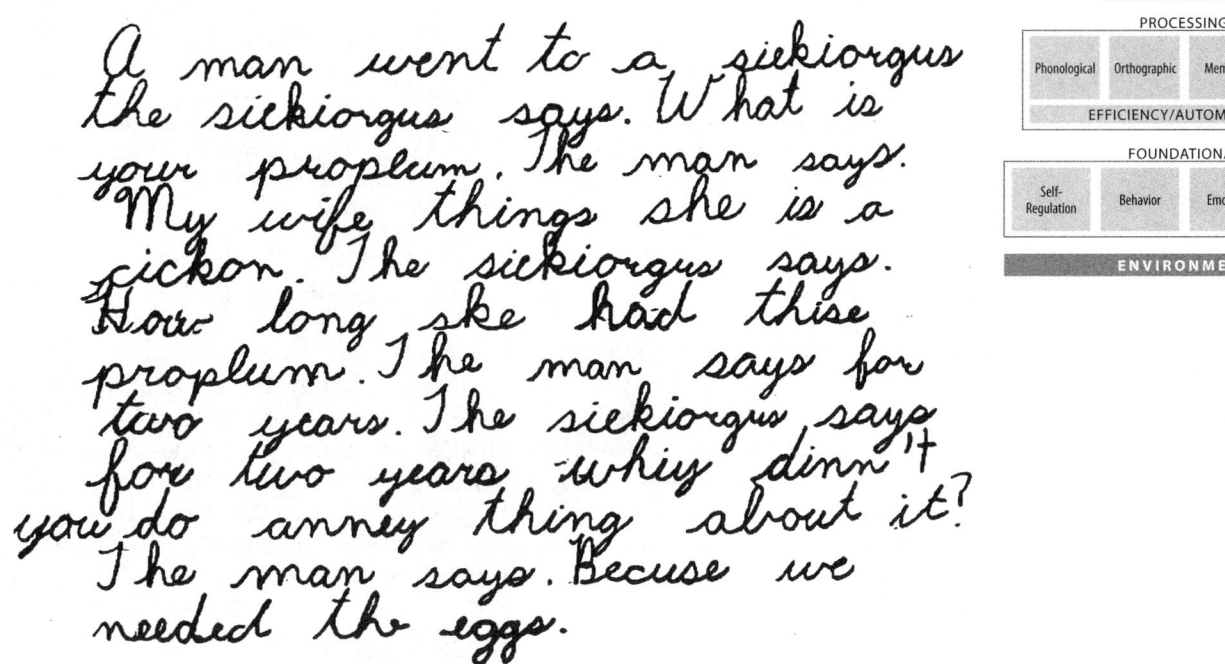

Figure 9.16. Ryan's cursive writing. (Provided by Wendy Wall.)

other times, she had him dictate a story that she typed and then he traced. The addition of the directional arrows reminded Andy of how to form letters properly.

Keyboarding

To compensate for severe fine motor difficulties, students such as Andy need to begin keyboarding instruction as early as possible. Several software programs are available that are designed to teach young children how to type. One interactive, carefully developed program called *Read, Write, and Type* is designed to increase beginning reading, writing, and keyboarding skills (see Additional Resources).

Voice-Activated Software

Older students with poor handwriting or spelling difficulties can be taught to use voice-activated word-processing programs or voice recognition software (VRS). The student speaks into a microphone, and the text is then translated into a word-processing format on the computer. Although this procedure is not error free, it can significantly reduce the demands on a student's secretarial skills, allowing a student to concentrate more fully on expressing and organizing ideas. These types of systems may allow students with LD to transcribe at rates closer to the speed of speech (de la Paz, 1999).

Sanderson (1999), however, described the frustration experienced by older students with reading impairments in training VRS systems. Common difficulties these students experience center on reading difficulties (the student must read phrases on the screen correctly on the first attempt), mispronunciations of known and unknown words, and lack of confidence while completing the training task.

339

Using a VRS system, Ben was able to complete the training session (independent reading of text for 30 minutes) with the assistance of a tutor over four short sessions. Prior to reading the paragraph, Ben would turn off the microphone and practice reading the passage with the tutor's assistance several times. The program would save the portion of the training that had been completed, and Ben could resume the training a few days later. Unfortunately for Ben, the program worked well for several months, but then his voice changed and he had to complete the training sessions all over again.

Fortunately, several of the newer programs do not require training. Examples include *Dragon Naturally Speaking* and *SpeakQ*, both designed specifically for students who cannot dictate at a fast rate, get through the training, or remember verbal commands with ease. (See Additional Resources.)

Even when individuals have been trained on the system, individuals with reading and spelling difficulties are likely to have difficulties correcting material that has not been transcribed accurately. Despite the limitations, VRS is likely to benefit many individuals with dyslexia or dysgraphia. As noted by de la Paz over 15 years ago, "In an age where electronic products rapidly become smaller and more sophisticated, we may all soon prefer to talk to our computers instead of struggling with keyboards or handwritten forms of composing" (1999, p. 181).

Dysgraphia

Dyslexia and dysgraphia are not the same but are both types of specific learning disabilities. Dysgraphia is a learning disability that directly affects writing production and makes the motor aspects of writing very difficult. The major difficulty is automatic legible letter writing, which then affects compositional fluency (Berninger & May, 2011). Students who have dysgraphia, such as Andy, have severe weaknesses in the fine motor skills needed for handwriting. They may have difficulty writing down thoughts, have trouble with spelling, have slow and labored writing, and confuse uppercase and lowercase letters. It is important that students with dysgraphia are identified early in their schooling and provided with appropriate handwriting instruction (Treiman & Kessler, 2014).

Teachers can assist students with dysgraphia by providing ongoing encouragement, helping students write an outline first, allowing students to write one draft without focusing on spelling and grammar, breaking large writing tasks into smaller tasks, and creating fun activities for writing. For example, a teacher may assist a student in writing an outline and then tell the student that only certain parts of the outline are due at certain times. This helps the student break apart a task to make it more manageable.

CONCLUSION

The basic skill areas of reading, writing, and math are linked to the acquisition and mastery of symbols. Students with weaknesses in processing struggle with the acquisition and mastery of basic reading, writing, and numeracy skills. As noted in Chapter 8, students with weaknesses in basic skills often require more time, shortened assignments, and specialized instruction. A teacher may need to manipulate other variables, such as the size of print, the color of the materials, or the kind of type or writing used. Ryan could not read the worksheets distributed in class; Ben complained that he had trouble reading cursive writing from the board; Maria rarely completed in-class reading assignments; Andy rarely finished writing assignments. For students with weaknesses in basic skills, selecting and implementing

Instruction for the Processing Blocks

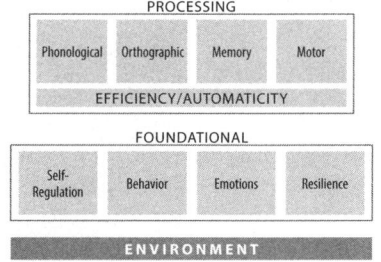

accommodations and instructional strategies require flexibility, adaptability, and patience. Some students with weaknesses in basic skills have strengths in conceptual abilities, and intervention plans should also include activities that focus on strong areas of performance in addition to weak areas of performance.

With all the skill areas, however, the most effective programs are explicit and directed to academic content, teach to mastery, provide scaffolding and emotional support, and monitor student progress (Fletcher et al., 2007). Students with LD require intensive, structured teaching that includes multisensory instruction, review, practice, and feedback, as well as opportunities to apply these skills in meaningful contexts. In addition, these students often require specific classroom accommodations and adjustments to promote classroom success. Several advances in technology can also be used to benefit students with weaknesses in the Processing blocks.

APPENDIX **9A**

Fry's 600 Instant Words

INSTANT WORDS: FIRST HUNDRED

___ 1. the	___ 26. he	___ 51. go	___ 76. who
___ 2. a	___ 27. I	___ 52. see	___ 77. an
___ 3. is	___ 28. they	___ 53. then	___ 78. their
___ 4. you	___ 29. one	___ 54. us	___ 79. she
___ 5. to	___ 30. good	___ 55. no	___ 80. new
___ 6. and	___ 31. me	___ 56. him	___ 81. said
___ 7. we	___ 32. about	___ 57. by	___ 82. did
___ 8. that	___ 33. had	___ 58. was	___ 83. boy
___ 9. in	___ 34. if	___ 59. come	___ 84. three
___ 10. not	___ 35. some	___ 60. get	___ 85. down
___ 11. for	___ 36. up	___ 61. or	___ 86. work
___ 12. at	___ 37. her	___ 62. two	___ 87. put
___ 13. with	___ 38. do	___ 63. man	___ 88. were
___ 14. it	___ 39. when	___ 64. little	___ 89. before
___ 15. on	___ 40. so	___ 65. has	___ 90. just
___ 16. can	___ 41. my	___ 66. them	___ 91. long
___ 17. will	___ 42. very	___ 67. how	___ 92. here
___ 18. are	___ 43. all	___ 68. like	___ 93. other
___ 19. of	___ 44. would	___ 69. our	___ 94. old
___ 20. this	___ 45. any	___ 70. what	___ 95. take
___ 21. your	___ 46. been	___ 71. know	___ 96. cat
___ 22. as	___ 47. out	___ 72. make	___ 97. again
___ 23. but	___ 48. there	___ 73. which	___ 98. give
___ 24. be	___ 49. from	___ 74. much	___ 99. after
___ 25. have	___ 50. day	___ 75. his	___ 100. many

(From Fry, E.B. [1977]. *Elementary reading instruction* [p. 73]. New York, NY: McGraw-Hill; reprinted by permission.)

Instruction for the Processing Blocks

INSTANT WORDS: SECOND HUNDRED

___ 1. saw	___ 26. big	___ 51. may	___ 76. ran
___ 2. home	___ 27. where	___ 52. let	___ 77. five
___ 3. soon	___ 28. am	___ 53. use	___ 78. read
___ 4. stand	___ 29. ball	___ 54. these	___ 79. over
___ 5. box	___ 30. morning	___ 55. right	___ 80. such
___ 6. upon	___ 31. live	___ 56. present	___ 81. way
___ 7. first	___ 32. four	___ 57. tell	___ 82. too
___ 8. came	___ 33. last	___ 58. next	___ 83. shall
___ 9. girl	___ 34. color	___ 59. please	___ 84. own
___ 10. house	___ 35. away	___ 60. leave	___ 85. most
___ 11. find	___ 36. red	___ 61. hand	___ 86. sure
___ 12. because	___ 37. friend	___ 62. more	___ 87. thing
___ 13. made	___ 38. pretty	___ 63. why	___ 88. only
___ 14. could	___ 39. eat	___ 64. better	___ 89. near
___ 15. book	___ 40. want	___ 65. under	___ 90. than
___ 16. look	___ 41. year	___ 66. while	___ 91. open
___ 17. mother	___ 42. white	___ 67. should	___ 92. kind
___ 18. run	___ 43. got	___ 68. never	___ 93. mist
___ 19. school	___ 44. play	___ 69. each	___ 94. high
___ 20. people	___ 45. found	___ 70. best	___ 95. far
___ 21. night	___ 46. left	___ 71. another	___ 96. both
___ 22. into	___ 47. men	___ 72. seem	___ 97. end
___ 23. say	___ 48. bring	___ 73. tree	___ 98. also
___ 24. think	___ 49. wish	___ 74. name	___ 99. until
___ 25. back	___ 50. black	___ 75. dear	___100. call

(continued)

INSTANT WORDS: THIRD HUNDRED

___ 1. ask	___ 26. hat	___ 51. off	___ 76. fire
___ 2. small	___ 27. car	___ 52. sister	___ 77. ten
___ 3. yellow	___ 28. write	___ 53. happy	___ 78. order
___ 4. show	___ 29. try	___ 54. once	___ 79. part
___ 5. goes	___ 30. myself	___ 55. didn't	___ 80. early
___ 6. clean	___ 31. longer	___ 56. set	___ 81. fat
___ 7. buy	___ 32. those	___ 57. round	___ 82. third
___ 8. thank	___ 33. hold	___ 58. dress	___ 83. same
___ 9. sleep	___ 34. full	___ 59. fell	___ 84. love
___ 10. letter	___ 35. carry	___ 60. wash	___ 85. hear
___ 11. jump	___ 36. eight	___ 61. start	___ 86. yesterday
___ 12. help	___ 37. sing	___ 62. always	___ 87. eyes
___ 13. fly	___ 38. warm	___ 63. anything	___ 88. door
___ 14. don't	___ 39. sit	___ 64. around	___ 89. clothes
___ 15. fast	___ 40. dog	___ 65. close	___ 90. through
___ 16. cold	___ 41. ride	___ 66. walk	___ 91. o'clock
___ 17. today	___ 42. hot	___ 67. money	___ 92. second
___ 18. does	___ 43. grow	___ 68. turn	___ 93. water
___ 19. face	___ 44. cut	___ 69. might	___ 94. town
___ 20. green	___ 45. seven	___ 70. hard	___ 95. took
___ 21. every	___ 46. woman	___ 71. along	___ 96. pair
___ 22. brown	___ 47. funny	___ 72. bed	___ 97. now
___ 23. coat	___ 48. yes	___ 73. fine	___ 98. keep
___ 24. six	___ 49. ate	___ 74. sat	___ 99. head
___ 25. gave	___ 50. stop	___ 75. hope	___ 100. food

Instruction for the Processing Blocks

INSTANT WORDS: FOURTH HUNDRED

___ 1. told	___ 26. time	___ 51. word	___ 76. wear
___ 2. miss	___ 27. yet	___ 52. almost	___ 77. Mr.
___ 3. father	___ 28. true	___ 53. thought	___ 78. slide
___ 4. children	___ 29. above	___ 54. send	___ 79. poor
___ 5. land	___ 30. still	___ 55. receive	___ 80. lost
___ 6. interest	___ 31. meet	___ 56. pay	___ 81. outside
___ 7. government	___ 32. since	___ 57. nothing	___ 82. wind
___ 8. feet	___ 33. number	___ 58. need	___ 83. Mrs.
___ 9. garden	___ 34. state	___ 59. mean	___ 84. learn
___ 10. done	___ 35. matter	___ 60. late	___ 85. held
___ 11. country	___ 36. line	___ 61. half	___ 86. front
___ 12. different	___ 37. remember	___ 62. fight	___ 87. built
___ 13. bad	___ 38. large	___ 63. enough	___ 88. family
___ 14. across	___ 39. few	___ 64. feel	___ 89. began
___ 15. yard	___ 40. hit	___ 65. during	___ 90. air
___ 16. winter	___ 41. cover	___ 66. gone	___ 91. young
___ 17. table	___ 42. window	___ 67. hundred	___ 92. ago
___ 18. story	___ 43. even	___ 68. week	___ 93. world
___ 19. sometimes	___ 44. city	___ 69. between	___ 94. airplane
___ 20. I'm	___ 45. together	___ 70. change	___ 95. without
___ 21. tried	___ 46. sun	___ 71. being	___ 96. kill
___ 22. horse	___ 47. life	___ 72. care	___ 97. ready
___ 23. something	___ 48. street	___ 73. answer	___ 98. stay
___ 24. brought	___ 49. party	___ 74. course	___ 99. won't
___ 25. shoe	___ 50. suit	___ 75. against	___100. paper

(continued)

INSTANT WORDS: FIFTH HUNDRED

___ 1. hour	___ 26. grade	___ 51. egg	___ 76. spell
___ 2. glad	___ 27. brother	___ 52. ground	___ 77. beautiful
___ 3. follow	___ 28. remain	___ 53. afternoon	___ 78. sick
___ 4. company	___ 29. milk	___ 54. feed	___ 79. became
___ 5. believe	___ 30. several	___ 55. boat	___ 80. cry
___ 6. begin	___ 31. war	___ 56. plan	___ 81. finish
___ 7. mind	___ 32. able	___ 57. question	___ 82. catch
___ 8. pass	___ 33. charge	___ 58. fish	___ 83. floor
___ 9. reach	___ 34. either	___ 59. return	___ 84. stick
___ 10. month	___ 35. less	___ 60. sir	___ 85. great
___ 11. point	___ 36. train	___ 61. fell	___ 86. guess
___ 12. rest	___ 37. cost	___ 62. hill	___ 87. bridge
___ 13. sent	___ 38. evening	___ 63. wood	___ 88. church
___ 14. talk	___ 39. note	___ 64. add	___ 89. lady
___ 15. went	___ 40. past	___ 65. ice	___ 90. tomorrow
___ 16. bank	___ 41. room	___ 66. chair	___ 91. snow
___ 17. ship	___ 42. flew	___ 67. watch	___ 92. whom
___ 18. business	___ 43. office	___ 68. alone	___ 93. women
___ 19. whole	___ 44. cow	___ 69. low	___ 94. among
___ 20. short	___ 45. visit	___ 70. arm	___ 95. road
___ 21. certain	___ 46. wait	___ 71. dinner	___ 96. farm
___ 22. fair	___ 47. teacher	___ 72. hair	___ 97. cousin
___ 23. reason	___ 48. spring	___ 73. service	___ 98. bread
___ 24. summer	___ 49. picture	___ 74. class	___ 99. wrong
___ 25. fill	___ 50. bird	___ 75. quite	___ 100. age

Instruction for the Processing Blocks

INSTANT WORDS: SIXTH HUNDRED

___ 1. become	___ 26. herself	___ 51. demand	___ 76. aunt
___ 2. body	___ 27. idea	___ 52. however	___ 77. system
___ 3. chance	___ 28. drop	___ 53. figure	___ 78. lie
___ 4. act	___ 29. river	___ 54. case	___ 79. cause
___ 5. die	___ 30. smile	___ 55. increase	___ 80. marry
___ 6. real	___ 31. son	___ 56. enjoy	___ 81. possible
___ 7. speak	___ 32. bat	___ 57. rather	___ 82. supply
___ 8. already	___ 33. fact	___ 58. sound	___ 83. thousand
___ 9. doctor	___ 34. sort	___ 59. eleven	___ 84. pen
___ 10. step	___ 35. king	___ 60. music	___ 85. condition
___ 11. itself	___ 36. dark	___ 61. human	___ 86. perhaps
___ 12. nine	___ 37. themselves	___ 62. court	___ 87. produce
___ 13. baby	___ 38. whose	___ 63. force	___ 88. twelve
___ 14. minute	___ 39. study	___ 64. plant	___ 89. rode
___ 15. ring	___ 40. fear	___ 65. suppose	___ 90. uncle
___ 16. wrote	___ 41. move	___ 66. law	___ 91. labor
___ 17. happen	___ 42. stood	___ 67. husband	___ 92. public
___ 18. appear	___ 43. himself	___ 68. moment	___ 93. consider
___ 19. heart	___ 44. strong	___ 69. person	___ 94. thus
___ 20. swim	___ 45. knew	___ 70. result	___ 95. least
___ 21. felt	___ 46. often	___ 71. continue	___ 96. power
___ 22. fourth	___ 47. toward	___ 72. price	___ 97. mark
___ 23. I'll	___ 48. wonder	___ 73. serve	___ 98. president
___ 24. kept	___ 49. twenty	___ 74. national	___ 99. voice
___ 25. well	___ 50. important	___ 75. wife	___ 100. whether

SECTION IV
Conceptual Blocks

CHAPTER 10 OUTLINE

VERBAL ABILITIES

- Components of Oral Language
- Receptive and Expressive Language
- Literacy Instruction for English Language Learners
- Instruction for Language Development

NONVERBAL ABILITIES

- Characteristics
- Interventions
- Instruction Using Visual Imagery

EXECUTIVE FUNCTIONS

- General Principles of Strategy Instruction
- Instruction in Strategies
- Notetaking Techniques
- Time Management and Organizational Strategies
- Test-Taking Strategies

CLASSROOM ADJUSTMENTS

- Alter the Difficulty Level
- Provide a Classroom Coach
- Allow More Time and Practice
- Consider Physical Classroom Arrangements
- Provide More than One Grade
- Base Grades on Individualized Education Program Goals
- Provide Opportunities for Improvement

CONCLUSION

APPENDIX 10A: ADDITIONAL STRATEGIES FOR TEST TAKING

APPENDIX 10B: INSTRUCTIONAL ACCOMMODATIONS SURVEY

APPENDIX 10C: APPS FOR VISUAL IMAGERY, NOTETAKING, TIME MANAGEMENT, AND TEST-TAKING INSTRUCTION

CHAPTER **10**

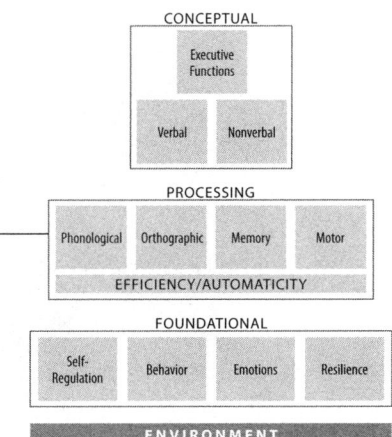

The Conceptual Blocks

Verbal, Nonverbal, and Executive Functions

with Ann M. Richards

With the passage of the No Child Left Behind Act of 2001 (PL 107-110) and its emphasis on academic content as well as the alignment of the school curriculum with the Common Core State Standards, many teachers have shifted the focus of their teaching from a developmental model to a primary focus on academic skill development. For the many students who struggle in school, this shift in instructional goals can leave them even further behind. Because of the diverse characteristics of students who struggle with aspects of learning, the range of instructional interventions that are needed can be vast. Some of these students are good at decoding but have difficulty understanding the overall meaning of what they read. Some have typical oral language abilities but struggle with tasks involving nonverbal abilities and spatial organization. Others seem attentive and motivated but are unable to develop or revise their plans for completing homework and tests. These types of difficulties often signify that the student has a weakness in the Conceptual blocks. This chapter reviews the abilities related to the Verbal, Nonverbal, and Executive Functions blocks.

VERBAL ABILITIES

Like the sea, talk is the environment that first incubates and then nurtures our development.

—Rubin, 1990, p. 3

The sea is a complex system of different ecological microcosms that come together to form one vast body of water. Oral language in this metaphor can then be considered one of the essential microcosms or building blocks for literacy-based academics. Considerable research has documented that students with limited verbal abilities often struggle to master the skills associated with reading (e.g., Bianco et al., 2012; Dickinson, Anastasopoulos, McCabe, Peisner-Feinberg, & Poe, 2003; Dickinson & McCabe, 2001; Fuchs et al., 2012; McArthur, Hogben, Edwards, Heath, & Mengler, 2000; Mengler, Hogben, Michie, & Bishop, 2005; Ricketts, Jones, Happe, & Charman, 2013). Students with weaknesses in verbal abilities can exhibit difficulties in understanding what they read or what is said to them and in formulating oral and written responses (Puranik & Lonigan, 2011). Essentially, a student's reading comprehension will be no stronger than his or her comprehension of oral language (Clarke, Snowling, Truelove, & Hulme, 2010; Fletcher, Lyon, Fuchs, & Barnes, 2007; Skebo et al., 2013). In fact, problems in reading comprehension and written expression typically stem from weaknesses in verbal abilities. Spencer, Quinn, and Wagner explained, "Individuals with problems in reading comprehension that are not attributable to poor word recognition have comprehension problems that are general to language comprehension rather than specific to reading" (2014, p. 3).

In addition to problems with reading comprehension, within the school environment, students with weaknesses in language may fail to understand the information that teachers are conveying. They may miss important points when the teacher is lecturing, or when they are asked to comprehend assignments and test questions, they may misinterpret the meaning. These difficulties can inhibit students' abilities to comprehend what is read, solve mathematical problems, and monitor their social and academic environments.

When John was in eighth grade, he was given a homework assignment to write an essay about a short story that was read in class. John had difficulty with understanding the story, so the special education teacher paraphrased and summarized the main events. She then attempted to explain the essay questions so that John could select the one he would attempt. After 40 minutes, John asked, "By the way, what is an essay?" His special education teacher then reviewed a standard process and structure for an essay: Begin with an introductory paragraph, add several supporting paragraphs to develop the topic introduced in the first paragraph, and summarize or draw conclusions in an ending paragraph. John then replied, "Oh, I thought she meant the letters *SA*." No wonder John had not been concerned that the assignment was due the following day!

Components of Oral Language

The following abilities are components of oral language: phonology, morphology, syntax, semantics, and pragmatics. Phonology refers to the sound system of a language. From birth to 4 years of age, children master sounds that are relevant to their native language (Ingram, 1986). Difficulties with the development of phonological awareness affect later success in reading. Chapter 8 provides a more comprehensive discussion of the difficulties associated with phonology.

Morphology refers to the meaning units of language. Just as a phoneme refers to the smallest unit of sound, a morpheme refers to the smallest unit of meaning. For example, the word *boys* is composed of two morphemes, the meaning unit *boy* and the plural marker *s*. An individual's understanding of the individual units of meaning can also influence his or her vocabulary, reading, and spelling development (Apel, Wilson-Fowler, Brimo, & Perrin, 2011). For example, understanding that past tense is typically spelled with the letters *-ed* can guide the student to spell the word *jumped* correctly, even though the word sounds like it ends with a /t/ sound.

Syntax refers to the underlying structure of language and the rules that guide word order. Students who have difficulties in the area of syntax often struggle to produce complex sentences in both oral and written exchanges. They may have difficulty formulating questions and using the correct verb tense when speaking.

Semantics refers to knowledge of word meanings. Difficulties in this area often affect a student's ability to comprehend information. John did not understand the meaning of the word *essay*, and, consequently, he constructed his own interpretation of the task based on the phonological features of the letters *SA*.

Verbal, Nonverbal, and Executive Functions

Pragmatics refers to the social aspects of language and the varied use of language in different social contexts. Students with pragmatic language disorders may fail to alter their language use on the basis of the situation and the listener. As a result, they may speak to the school principal in the same tone and manner as they would to a peer on the playground (e.g., "Hey, man, what's happening?"). Young children may also have difficulty adjusting to the more formal pragmatic language used in classrooms.

When Katy was in kindergarten, her teacher asked her, "Katy, can you pass the glue to Pablo?" Katy responded by stating, "No, I don't have time." Although the teacher made her request in a question format, Katy did not comprehend that the request actually was a statement of an action that an authority figure was asking her to complete. The learning behaviors of Katy suggest that she has difficulty with verbal processing, so her teacher filled out the 10 questions for the Verbal section in the Building Blocks Questionnaire. When doing so, she checked *Frequently* to indicate that Katy had limited speaking vocabulary and trouble retrieving specific words, answering questions, expressing ideas, and having meaningful conversations, resulting in her having trouble expressing ideas when writing as well as solving math story problems. Figure 10.1 illustrates the Verbal portion of the Building Blocks Questionnaire for Katy.

The first components of oral language are acquired in infancy. By the time many children are 9 months old, they understand that certain sounds represent words and that words represent objects, experiences, and feelings (Myklebust, 1965). Gradually, oral language develops as children learn to apply words to describe objects, experiences, and feelings. Children also begin to learn the rules of syntax by conversing with others. For example, a child might say to his mother, "Give blocks," to which his mother might respond, "Would you like me to give you the blocks?" Through an expansion of the original request, the mother has modeled to the child how language is used. In order to develop their abilities, children need to have practice using language for various tasks. Oral language provides the structure through which children interpret, organize, and store information about the world. Children with weaknesses in verbal abilities tend to struggle with language-based, higher

CONCEPTUAL

Verbal	Rarely	Sometimes	Frequently
Was slow to develop and use oral language	☐	✓	☐
Has limited speaking vocabulary	☐	☐	✓
Has problems retrieving specific words	☐	☐	✓
Has trouble answering questions	☐	☐	✓
Has difficulty organizing and expressing ideas when speaking	☐	☐	✓
Has difficulty sustaining meaningful conversations	☐	☐	✓
Makes grammatical errors when speaking or writing	☐	✓	☐
Has trouble understanding what is read	☐	✓	☐
Has trouble expressing ideas when writing	☐	☐	✓
Has trouble solving math story problems	☐	☐	✓

Figure 10.1. Building Blocks Questionnaire for Katy: Verbal Conceptual block.

level academic tasks, such as reading comprehension, written expression, and math problem solving.

Receptive and Expressive Language

Verbal abilities provide the foundation for success in tasks involving comprehension, problem solving, and self-monitoring. For each of these tasks, students must have strong receptive and expressive oral language abilities. Receptive oral language refers to an individual's ability to understand what is being said. The major skill needed for success in this area is listening. Listening requires that students receive and interpret correctly the message that is being conveyed. Many researchers have found that oral language abilities are a consistent predictor of comprehension skills as students progress throughout their elementary and middle school years (Cabell, Justice, Konold, & McGinty, 2011; Dickinson & McCabe, 2001; Kendeou, van den Brock, White, & Lynch, 2009; Nation, Cocksey, Taylor, & Bishop, 2010). Because language tasks increase in complexity, it is necessary to start building these skills at an early age.

Expressive oral language relates to an individual's ability to retrieve ideas and vocabulary and express these thoughts in an appropriate manner. The major ability needed for success in the area of expressive oral language is speaking. Speaking requires students to develop intent to speak, formulate what they are going to say, and finally produce the appropriate words and sentences. Deficiencies in the use of expressive language in preschool children have been found to predict subsequent academic difficulties (e.g., Berninger & Abbott, 2010; Cabell et al., 2011; Dickinson et al., 2003; Dickinson & McCabe, 2001; Justice, Turnbull, Bowles, & Skibbe, 2009; NICHD Early Child Care Research Network, 2005; Share & Leikin, 2004; Storch & Whitehurst, 2002). Some students have adequate receptive language but poor expressive language. They understand what is said to them but have trouble responding orally. Other students, such as Katy, have poor receptive and expressive language.

When children are in school, teachers expect them to be able to follow verbal instructions, lectures, and guidelines. Teachers also expect students to respond to academic exchanges using a certain vocabulary and structure. For students with difficulties in listening and limited experience in formal oral exchanges, the ability to follow through on a given verbal direction can be a challenge. Poor receptive language can result in lower grades, gaps in a knowledge base, and the inability to work effectively with others. Social interactions can also be affected by difficulties with listening to and understanding language. As children grow older and become employed, poor receptive oral language abilities can hinder vocational success and lower job performance.

John has a part-time job after school at Burger King. One afternoon, his supervisor stated, "Pull out the French fries after the timer goes off." Not understanding when he was supposed to remove the fries, he began wrapping hamburgers. When the timer went off, he did not remove the French fries. Smoke started to flow from the deep fryer. John's supervisor quickly pulled the French fries out of the oil and promptly informed John, "You've got to follow directions if you want to keep your job here."

Expressive language skills are needed consistently throughout school and in the work environment. Students are expected to give oral reports, engage in oral reading, and interact with their classmates daily. If a child's ability to tell stories or describe events is limited, performance in the areas of reading comprehension and written expression is affected (Catts, 1993; Roth & Speckman, 1994). When children have difficulties with acquiring and using language, academic performance is hindered (Bishop & Adams, 1990; Catts, 1993; Dickinson et al., 2003; Dickinson & McCabe, 2001; McArthur et al., 2000; Mengler et al., 2005; NICHD Early Child Care Research Network, 2005; Rissman, Curtiss, & Tallal, 1990; Roth & Speckman, 1994; Share & Leikin, 2004; Storch & Whitehurst, 2002).

Literacy Instruction for English Language Learners*

The importance of oral language proficiency is clearly demonstrated in the academic trajectory of students who are English language learners (ELLs); achievement of these learners lags behind that of English monolingual children (Lee, 2002; Lonigan, Farver, Nakamoto, & Eppe, 2013). The U.S. Department of Education reports a 36-point gap in reading scores between ELL and non-ELL students at the fourth-grade level on the National Assessment of Educational Progress (NAEP) and a 44-point gap at the eighth-grade level (National Center for Education Statistics [NCES], 2013). With these numbers in mind, it should not be surprising that ELLs drop out of high school at greater numbers than non-ELLs (Short & Fitzsimmons, 2007). Nor is this a small percentage of students: ELLs make up 10% of all public school children (Bunch, Kibler, & Pimentel, 2013). The percentage of students served within the ELL category within public schools has averaged 9.5% from 2002 to 2013 (NCES, 2013). This percentage is often thought to be an underestimate, as students who are reclassified as fluent English proficient (EP) are not being included in counts of ELLs consistently across school districts (Turkan & Scramm-Possinger, 2014). The five native languages most commonly spoken by ELLs in schools are Spanish, Vietnamese, Chinese, Arabic, and Hmong (U.S. Department of Education, 2013). ELLs face a unique set of challenges, from navigating everyday conversations to understanding course content in an unfamiliar language.

Academic language proficiency plays a critical role in the acquisition and assessment of content-area knowledge. Although ELLs vary in their academic outcomes and many thrive in schools, a significant proportion—some of whom have been designated as ELLs and are receiving support services for language development and some of whom have not—struggle considerably in developing English proficiency and meeting grade-level standards. For teachers, two major concerns exist regarding students who are ELLs: first, identifying what effective evidence-based interventions are for teaching academic skills and, second, determining a reasonable rate of growth in English competency.

Remember Beto, the fun-loving 8-year-old in third grade who was introduced in the first chapter? Although born in the United States, he spoke only Spanish until he began kindergarten. His parents immigrated to New Mexico just before his birth and speak very little English. Beto received English as a second language (ESL) support services from kindergarten to third grade. Throughout this time, many teachers were concerned with his limited progress in reading and writing in English. His third-grade teacher assumed it was due to his incomplete acquisition of English. This changed, however, once she completed the Building Blocks Questionnaire. After completing the questionnaire, she realized that the areas with *Frequently* marked most often were all in the Processing blocks. Although she did note occasional struggles with the Self-Regulation, Resilience, and Executive Functions blocks, she thought these were secondary to the struggles Beto was facing with reading and writing. In other

---

*Gratitude is expressed to Deborah Rhein, Ph.D., for her assistance on this section for this edition and to Annmarie Urso, Ph.D., for her assistance on this section in the second edition.

words, when Beto was inattentive, it was only when the task was too difficult for him. When he was slow on tasks, the material was above his ability to complete. Within the Processing blocks, she noted that Phonology appeared to be the area that was most problematic for Beto, with Orthography the next most problematic, and then Memory. She realized to make adequate progress that Beto would need more intensive instruction in both reading and writing.

Researchers studying ELLs and academic achievement have begun to identify evidence-based strategies and interventions that are effective in increasing literacy for this population. Crucial components of instruction include decoding, comprehension, and oral language skills (August & Shanahan, 2006, 2010; Gentile, 2004; Graves, Gersten, & Haager, 2004; Solari et al., 2014; Vadasy & Sanders, 2012). The need to focus on oral language skills when providing literacy instruction to ELLs cannot be overlooked. Gentile (2004) observed that instruction in literacy skills for ELLs without a corresponding emphasis on oral language development failed to yield positive results. Given that caveat, ELLs can meet with success when provided with effective intervention programs that address all areas of oral language development.

As with their native English-speaking peers, ELLs can learn to decode words when provided with skilled, explicit instruction (Graves et al., 2004). This instruction often focuses on ELLs learning phonemes within the English language that do not exist in their native language or are an allophonic variation of another phoneme. Allophonic variation means that in many languages, the phonemes have slight variations in the way they are produced. These variations are rule-governed within languages and are part of what infants learn as they attend to and develop an awareness of the phonemes of their native language. Some phonemes in a language have many allophones; some have just a few.

An example of an allophonic variation of the phoneme /p/ is the extra burst of air that is produced when saying the word *pit*. Say *pit* with your hand in front of your mouth, and you will notice a strong burst of air. Now say *splat* with your hand in front of your mouth and you will notice a very little air. The /p/ in *pit* is an aspirated /p/, which means it is a speech sound made with an audible puff of breath. Why does this matter? It relates to the idea that when infants develop this discriminatory ability for the sounds in their language, they are actually developing a representative schema for all the sounds, including when and where the allophonic variations occur.

This is especially important for second language learners. Not only do they have to learn the phonemes in a new language that may not exist in their native language, but they also have to learn the allophonic variations. In other words, the child may have learned to discriminate this sound and produce this sound but has it organized into the schema for another phoneme. Probably the most common example of this confusion for native Spanish speakers learning English is over the voiced /th/. In English, the voiced /th/ is a unique phoneme, as there are many high-frequency words such as "they, then, there, their, the" where the phoneme occurs. In most dialects of Spanish, however, the voiced /th/ exists, but it is actually an allophonic variation of the phoneme /d/. Thus, in English, it makes a big difference if we say "then we went into the den" versus saying "den we went into the then," but in most dialects of Spanish, it makes no difference.

Considering this, it makes sense that when Beto hears the voiced /th/ in English, he perceives this sound as part of the class of sounds related to the phoneme /d/. Of course, he could not explicitly state the rule as he knows it, but his implicit knowledge has an impact on how he perceives and spells English sounds. Another

Verbal, Nonverbal, and Executive Functions

area of confusion for native Spanish speakers learning English is the /ch/ and /sh/ in English. The speech sound /sh/ does not exist in Spanish, In Spanish, the /ch/ exists, but in most dialects, it is pronounced much softer than in English, resulting in a sound that is halfway between the English /ch/ and /sh/. In spite of the difficulties, studies have shown that when ELLs in kindergarten receive systematic instruction in phonological awareness, explicit instruction in phonics, opportunities for multiple reading experiences, and continual progress monitoring, their performance after 2 years is comparable to their English-speaking peers (Lesaux & Siegel, 2003; Stuart, 1999).

Although learning to decode comes rather quickly to ELLs who receive skilled, systematic, and explicit instruction, comprehending text is much more difficult. Several factors contribute to the complexity of comprehension instruction for ELLs, including native language literacy level, oral language skills using academic language in English, and oral language skills using conversational English. Many teachers are surprised to learn that good conversational English skills do not equate to the comprehension skills necessary for understanding academic language. Academic language, often referred to as academic English, includes a student's capacity to read, write, and engage in extensive conversations about content-area subjects. Most ELLs lag well behind their peers in the oral language skills and content knowledge needed for proficiency in academic English. For ELLs, the development of academic English to the competency level of their English-speaking peers can take between 4 and 12 years, depending on whether the nonnative speaker of English had any schooling in their native language (Collier, 1995; Collier & Thomas, 1989; Cummins, 1989).

Thirty years ago, Cummins, a Canadian psychologist who worked with many French-Canadian students, noticed that many of the children appeared to have good skills in English when interacting informally but tested poorly on more challenging tasks in English. Yet he did not think most of the children had any sort of disability. He posited there were two levels of second language acquisition. The first, called BICS, is an acronym for Basic Interpersonal Communication Skills. According to Cummins in his 1984 introduction, BICS is the kind of language used for social, informal purposes and can be acquired within 1–2 years. The other level of language described by Cummins is CALP, or Cognitive Academic Language Proficiency. Cummins indicated CALP is the language necessary to master academic concepts and takes between 5 to 7 years to develop.

These two major distinctions can be broken down further. For example, Krashen and Terrell (1983) described five stages of second language acquisition: 1) preproduction (also called the silent period), when students are absorbing the new language; 2) early production, when students have a vocabulary of approximately 1,000 words and can answer yes/no questions; 3) speech emergence, when students have a vocabulary of about 3,000 words and can usually sound out words phonetically and compose brief stories; 4) intermediate fluency, when students have a vocabulary of approximately 6,000 words and can use more complex language but still demonstrate many errors; and 5) advanced fluency, which can take between 4 and 10 years to develop.

Cummins (1989) also challenged the popular belief that successful learning of a second language had to occur at the expense of the first language. Instead, he posited, if the first language is stronger and more developed, then the acquisition of subsequent languages will be easier and more fluid. Cummins's theory is that as a person learns the first language, he or she learns a great deal about language in general that can be applied to learning a second language. This is the theory of common underlying proficiency (CUP).

For example, one of the earliest rules learned in English is that we mark plurals with an /s/ or /z/ sound—that is, the surface rule. The underlying knowledge that will apply to most languages is that plurals are marked in a special way. According to CUP, most if not all of the deep structure knowledge acquired for the first language will assist in learning the second language. Based on Cummins's theory of CUP, continued learning in the first language not only is not in competition with the second language but also directly enhances the learning of the second language.

Thus, one of the most important things educators can do is to encourage continued development of the first language. When talking to the parents, if they are literate in Spanish, encourage them to read to their child in Spanish, and have leveled books in Spanish available for home checkout (Kohnert, 2007). In addition, ensure that classroom materials include books relevant to the child's culture and country, even in English. Encourage the children to write about experiences related to their culture: For Beto, this may include writing about his summertime visits to Mexico with his cousins; for Marta, it could include journaling about differences in her educational experience in Honduras and the United States. Always praise the fact that they are bilingual and point out there will be more job opportunities for them if they remain proficient in Spanish. Remind them that they will become proficient in English in time, but they do not have to do it at the expense of their first language (Kohnert, 2007). When children already know words in their first language, they can often take everything they know about that word (the meaning, the part of speech) and only learn the new pronunciation. For example, a Spanish speaker who already knows the word *gato* in Spanish can take everything he or she knows about that word and only has to learn how to pronounce it in English: *cat.*

Vocabulary development is fundamental to the development of academic English (August, Carlo, Dressler, & Snow, 2005; Kelley, Lesaux, Kieffer, & Faller, 2010). Native English speakers enter kindergarten with a vocabulary of 5,000–7,000 words; they also have better access to verbal academic interactions as well as good role models. These factors place ELLs at a huge disadvantage compared with their native English-speaking peers (Hart & Risley, 1995; Kim & Linan-Thompson, 2013). If ELLs have developed literacy in their own language, developing vocabulary in English involves learning the English vocabulary equivalent for a known concept. However, if ELLs have not developed literacy in their native language, they must learn both the concept and the vocabulary for each new word. The latter is a much more complex and time-consuming task for both ELLs and their teachers.

Marta had already become literate in Spanish when she entered school in the United States in the sixth grade. Currently in the eighth grade, she continues to receive pull-out ESL services. She is now speaking in English but still has limited reading and writing skills. Marta told her teachers she felt inadequate because she didn't always understand what they were saying. For example, Marta called a plateau a *table* in her geology class. This is understandable, as the Spanish word *mesa* means a geologic plateau in Spanish and translates to *table* in English. Although *table* was not the correct term, Marta was demonstrating that she considered the meanings of *mesa* in Spanish and then applied them to English. In time, with more exposure, she will learn that the geologic structure of a high plateau is actually called a *mesa* in English. In the meantime, Marta is frustrated because she finds it hard to read and write in English, although she is an excellent reader in Spanish.

Mr. Kelly, Marta's language arts teacher, wanted to conduct an interview with Marta's mother to learn more about her developmental history. Mr. Kelly had read information about the process of collaborating with interpreters (Langdon & Cheng, 2002). Because Mr. Kelly did not speak Spanish,

Verbal, Nonverbal, and Executive Functions

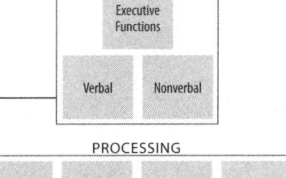

he enlisted the help of his neighbor, Ms. Gomez. Drawing from the rich body of work on professional interpreting used by the interpreters for American Sign Language, they discussed the three basic steps for working with interpreters: briefing, interaction, and debriefing (BID; Langdon & Cheng, 2002). In the briefing phase, educators are advised to meet with the interpreter before the actual interaction with the client. In this phase, the educator explains to the interpreter the purpose of the meeting, discusses questions that will be asked, addresses issues of dialect, and, if the interpreter is not a professional interpreter, lays the ground rules. Because Ms. Gomez was not a trained interpreter, Mr. Kelly discussed how he wanted her to translate everything that was said and to avoid adding anything. The interaction phase is the actual meeting. The debriefing phase is best accomplished as soon as possible after the meeting with the parent. In this phase, the goal is to review the interaction, clarify any areas that were unclear, and discuss any culturally relevant information that may have arisen during the meeting that needs explanation. During the meeting with Marta's mother, Mr. Kelly learned that Marta did very well in school in Mexico but was becoming increasingly anxious about her performance in her middle school. (Educators who need to learn about collaborating with an interpreter can also access a free tutorial at http://www.cehd.umn.edu/ssw/ContinuingEd/module5/default.html.)

Through explicit, meaningful, and structured conversations and listening opportunities, ELLs learn the words needed to engage in class discussions and the concepts needed to comprehend what they read in various content-area subjects. As with native English learners, memorizing word lists is inefficient and ineffective for learning vocabulary (Kauffman, 2007). The key to developing vocabulary concepts for ELLs is to provide meaningful, structured, and supported experiences adapted to the student's level of English development. Cooperative groupings, the use of selected videos and media, and the provision of enriching activities to support expository texts have all been found to increase vocabulary development and comprehension (Carlo et al., 2004; Lesaux, 2006). When teaching reading comprehension skills, evidence-based strategies have been identified for struggling readers that can be especially helpful for ELLs. One of the most relevant and effective strategies is to teach the skills and strategies necessary for comprehension of text explicitly (Aghaie & Zhang, 2012; Graves et al., 2004). For ELLs, explicitly teaching the syntax of language and the text structure of narrative, expository, and hypertext (i.e., text that is read on a computer that has links and connections to other related information), with special attention paid to vocabulary development, has been shown to increase comprehension skills (August & Shanahan, 2006; Kieffer & Lesaux, 2010; Minskoff, 2005; National Reading Panel, 2000). In addition to language development, educators must consider the impact of a student's environment as well.

Both Beto and Marta are children of immigrants and come from homes where no English is spoken. Although oral proficiency in English is clearly the most significant challenge facing ELLs, their families often face additional, less obvious challenges, which can include social isolation, culture shock, and poverty. Because proficiency in English and parental educational level is so closely tied to financial opportunities in the United States, children who come from homes where English is not spoken have a greater probability of living in poverty, putting them at greater risk for academic failure (Pagani, Boulerice, Vitaro, & Tremblay, 2003). Language development is greatly affected by factors related to poverty, including nutrition and parental modeling and interactions. Over time, some children from non–English-speaking homes may even feel shame or embarrassment regarding their parents' lack of English proficiency. An educator can help reduce this frustration in the following ways: 1) Provide the student with oral and written instructions, 2) use materials that the student can relate to, 3) refrain from correcting a student's oral errors but model correct grammar, and 4) remind students that learning a language takes time (Krough, 2014).

As discussed, one predictive factor is when ELLs have developed literacy skills in their first language in an academic setting for several years prior to entering English-speaking schools; this results in distinct advantages. First, word reading, reading comprehension, and the use of reading strategies in English are strongly related to these skills in an ELL's first language (August & Shanahan, 2006). In addition, the early stages of English spelling show the influence of the first language on the ELL's orthographic knowledge, as do aspects of their written expression (August & Shanahan, 2006).

The critical components of reading instruction for ELLs include 1) high-quality, explicit instruction in phonemic awareness, decoding, and vocabulary; 2) comprehension instruction using explicit and interactive teaching during all phases of reading; and 3) structured opportunities for oral language development, with a strong emphasis on daily oral language activities (Gentile, 2004; Graves et al., 2004; Kauffman, 2007; Lesaux, Kieffer, Faller, & Kelley, 2010). Short and Fitzsimmons indicate that educators and policy makers can improve literacy instruction for ELLs by

> integrating listening, speaking, reading, and writing skills into instruction from the start; teaching the components and processes of reading and writing; teaching reading comprehension strategies; focusing on vocabulary development; building and activating background knowledge; teaching language through content and themes; using native language strategically; pairing technology with existing interventions; and motivating adolescent ELLs through choice. (2007, p. 38)

As with Beto, extra time and instruction in literacy may also be necessary to ensure an appropriate rate of academic English achievement. Literacy instruction delivered by experienced, highly trained teachers must include several years of intensive, high-quality instruction with lots of practice and frequent assessment to identify students' strengths and weaknesses. In addition, awareness and development of the students' literacy skills in their native languages will enhance their English development (August & Shanahan, 2006; Lesaux, Crosson, Kieffer, & Pierce, 2010). In summary, ELLs need skilled teachers who can deliver intensive and explicit reading instruction using evidence-based reading strategies and interventions in a supportive environment. This type of instruction will assist ELLs in becoming fluent in speaking, reading, and writing academic English. This instruction should be accompanied by systematic progress monitoring to ensure appropriate skill development. Parents can also assist in this process. Cunningham and Zibulsky (2014) provide numerous activities that parents can implement to support their children as they are learning two languages.

If teachers have a basic understanding of the way a student's self-esteem can be affected by coming from a home and culture that is different from the majority, they can work to make the classroom a place that supports a student's first language and culture. If teachers understand the stages of second language development, it can help them monitor whether their ELL students are making progress toward English proficiency. When teachers learn about the differences between casual language and academic language, they will be better prepared to address the vocabulary learning of their ELL students. If classroom teachers learn about the phonemic differences between the first and second languages, it will help them interpret whether the errors students make are the result of those differences instead of evidence of a disability. It makes a big difference if Beto's teacher understands why he wrote "Den day go" instead of thinking he isn't paying attention or isn't listening. If teachers understand how well-developed literacy in the first language can be helpful in

Verbal, Nonverbal, and Executive Functions

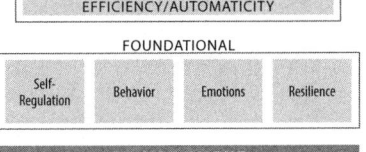

developing skills in English, then they can provide explicit instruction in the less regular aspects of English orthography. It matters if Marta's teachers see how hard she is trying and how capable she is in so many ways as she navigates the demands of a new language, a new school, and a new culture. Marta and Beto's teachers didn't have all the answers, but they were smart and caring, and they used resources to learn what they needed to do for these students. They understood that there needed to be some modifications to business as usual, and they wish to ensure their students will be successful.

Instruction for Language Development

The acquisition of language occurs by both implicit and explicit instruction (Brabham & Villaume, 2002). Vygotsky (1978) explained that one important way in which language develops is through social interactions with more knowledgeable language users. Hall (1987) supported Vygotsky's theory but added that children developing language need to 1) be the major constructors of language, 2) construct language in conjunction with placing meaning to their world and print, and 3) use language as a function to clarify information about themselves and others. As teachers and students work together to attain educational goals, they must model the process of learning by talking about these processes as they perform tasks. Englert (1992) provided an analogy to explain the mutual and reciprocal contributions of the teacher and students. Think of a team practicing volleyball. The team works together to keep the ball in play. As they practice, the teacher, like any good volleyball coach, stands by, ready to assist and provide instruction when needed.

Modeling

Verbal abilities form the basis for understanding what is read, expressing ideas in writing, and solving mathematical story problems. Through discussions with students, teachers can model the kind of thinking that people do while reading and problem solving, thus building the Conceptual block of Verbal abilities. What this means, quite simply, is that the teacher describes actions orally or the steps of a procedure while performing the activity. Teachers can use visual cues and talk aloud while students watch and listen. Through modeling, students become more strategic in their approaches and assume increasing responsibility for task completion.

Expansion and Elaboration

Another way to help students increase their understanding is to describe the actions that the student is performing. Two simple techniques are expansion and elaboration. For expansion, extend the student's remark to a more complete and correct form. So if the child said, "I keeped the book," you may remark, "Oh, you *kept* the book?" For elaboration, take the student's response, expand it to a correct form, and then add some additional information. You may say, "I am glad you kept that book. I knew you would think it was an interesting story." These types of simple activities help students increase language abilities as well as word knowledge.

Paraphrasing

When students have trouble remembering what they hear, make sure that the students understand oral directions. Ask students to paraphrase, repeat, or explain instructions, or ask students to repeat the questions they are being asked and rephrase the questions in their own words before answering. Students may also ask questions and respond in different ways (e.g., read the information aloud, say it aloud, describe a visual image). Several techniques, outlined in the "Instruction Using Visual Imagery" section, can help students learn how to form mental pictures.

Background Knowledge

One critical factor that influences oral expression, reading comprehension, and written expression is background knowledge, or what one already knows about a topic. When students do not understand what they hear or read or do not have much to write or say, it is usually because they have limited background knowledge about the topic. In other words, people understand most easily and write most fluently when the topics relate to or build on background and experiences. Cromley and Azevedo (2007) found that background knowledge and vocabulary made the strongest contributions to reading comprehension for students in ninth grade. They suggested that the most effective interventions for older students should focus on increasing academic vocabulary and background knowledge.

Both Katy and John have trouble understanding classroom instruction because many of the concepts are new and the vocabulary that is used is unfamiliar and difficult. The main reasons that they have trouble understanding are that they have limited vocabularies and lack the necessary background information to grasp the concepts presented.

John's high school biology teacher noted that John was highly motivated but did not retain the concepts that were presented in class and in the textbook. John had consequently failed the first three weekly biology examinations. John was also failing examinations in history. His history teacher, Dr. Mantell, commented that although John was attentive and participated actively in class, his oral answers to questions were often incorrect and, at times, not even related to the topic. Due to these learning behaviors, he decided to fill out the Executive Functions section of the Building Blocks Questionnaire. In doing so, he checked that John frequently had trouble developing a plan in order to complete a task, identifying and prioritizing relevant aspects of a task, developing an alternative strategy, and using techniques to study, all resulting in an inability to generalize and evaluate his performance. Figure 10.2 illustrates the Executive Functions section of the questionnaire for John.

In addition, when asked to define words as part of a reading evaluation, John appeared to have tangential knowledge of some of the words, but he seemed confused about the exact meanings. For example, John said that *equator* was an antonym

CONCEPTUAL

Executive Functions	Rarely	Sometimes	Frequently
Has trouble monitoring performance	☐	✓	☐
Has problems initiating activities or tasks	☐	✓	☐
Has trouble developing a plan to complete a task	☐	☐	✓
Has difficulty sustaining effort when problem solving	☐	✓	☐
Has trouble identifying and prioritizing the most relevant aspects of a task	☐	☐	✓
Has difficulty revising or generating an alternative plan or strategy	☐	☐	✓
Has trouble evaluating the quality of performance	☐	☐	✓
Has difficulty selecting and using techniques to memorize	☐	☐	✓

Figure 10.2. Building Blocks Questionnaire for John: Executive Functions Conceptual block.

Verbal, Nonverbal, and Executive Functions

for *latitude*. When asked for a synonym for *zero*, he responded, "One million because it has lots of zeros." For students such as John and Katy, the teacher should begin instruction by finding out what they already know about a topic and then relate the new information to the established concepts.

K-W-L Strategy

A simple strategy for helping students increase their knowledge is called the K-W-L strategy (Ogle, 1986). To begin, a teacher writes three columns across the top of a piece of paper, as illustrated in Figure 10.3, and then helps students complete the worksheet. In the first column, students brainstorm what they already know about the topic (What I Know [K]). In the second column, after group discussions, students list questions about what they want to learn about the topic (What I Want to Learn [W]). Students can then work in small groups to answer questions and record results in the third column (What I Learned [L]). For students with more limited abilities, a peer may help with notetaking.

After completing the worksheet, students may write a paragraph that summarizes what they have learned about the topic. K-W-L also provides the opportunity for the student to review and rehearse what has been learned. Katy completed a K-W-L sheet, presented in Figure 10.4, with a cooperative learning group in her fifth-grade classroom. The students were studying spiders.

Sampson (2002) suggested an adaptation to the K-W-L strategy that teaches students to support the statements they make with confirmed sources. She changed the first statement of the activity to read "What We Think We Know," followed by a column to confirm the idea in which students write down the correct information and another column to list the reference source. She then used the traditional "What I Want to Learn" and "What I Learned" columns but followed them with another column in which students would have to support what they learned with a source. Teachers reported that students benefited from this extension because it forced them to gather data from sources to support statements they had made. K-W-L can be used as part of the reading comprehension continuum integrating teacher-led instruction with independent practice (Hilden & Jones, 2011).

Vocabulary

The breadth and depth of an individual's vocabulary can affect school success. Because vocabulary knowledge is needed for most academic tasks, teachers must remember that "vocabulary is acquired both incidentally through indirect exposure and intentionally through explicit instruction in specific words and word-learning strategies" (Diamond & Gutlohn, 2006, p. 1). Students with well-established vocabularies tend to speak, read, and write more effectively.

K	W	L
What I Know	What I Want to Learn	What I Learned
Have students brainstorm and list any information that they already know about the topic.	Have students develop questions about what they want to learn about the topic.	Have students record what they have learned from reading and library research.

Figure 10.3. K-W-L sheet. (*Source:* Ogle, 1986.)

K What we know	W What we want to find out	L What we learned
- Spiders have 8 legs - Spider have sharp teeth - They climb in webs - Some spider bite people - Some can live under water - Some male spiders get killed	- Why do spider bite people? - Do all spider bite? - Why do spider have 8 eyes? - How many eggs do spiders lay? - Are spiders helpful to people? How? - Why do female spiders kill the male spiders?	- To protect themselves - No - Not all have 8 eyes. - More then 100 eggs in a sack for serten spicies) - They eat insects the plant we grow. - When there hungrey.

Figure 10.4. K-W-L on spiders. (*Source:* Ogle, 1986.)

Results from studies investigating the effects of vocabulary instruction with students with learning disabilities indicate that methods employing the direct teaching of vocabulary are effective and that systematic practice of word meanings is critical to vocabulary acquisition and maintenance (Burns, Dean, & Foley, 2004; Jitendra, Edwards, Sacks, & Jacobsen, 2004; Seifert & Espin, 2012). In addition, explicit teaching of word meanings within the context of shared storybook reading is effective for young children with reading difficulties (Coyne, Simmons, & Kame'enui, 2004) and is the most powerful way to help children develop new vocabulary (Stahl & Stahl, 2004). The teacher reads a book aloud several times with an explanation of 8–10 new vocabulary words (Biemiller, 2004). The use of e-books with dictionary support as an alternative to repeated readings has also been found to increase vocabulary development (Korat & Shamir, 2012; Shamir, Korat, & Fellah, 2012). Coyne, McCoach, and Kapp (2007) found that extended instruction that provided review of the target words in varied and meaningful contexts resulted in more complete knowledge of word meanings for students in kindergarten than simply providing definitions during story reading. They concluded that extended, direct vocabulary instruction could increase vocabulary knowledge. In contrast, for older students with learning challenges, methods such as looking up words in a dictionary and writing definitions or using context clues to determine a word's meaning are ineffective (Bryant, Goodwin, Bryant, & Higgins, 2003; Palmer, Boon, & Spencer, 2014).

Students with SLD as well as ELLs require multiple exposures to words to master word meaning. In addition to the need for more practice, a growing consensus exists regarding other elements of effective vocabulary instruction. In a review of four effective vocabulary programs, Foorman, Seals, Anthony, and Pollard-Durodola (2003) found that the programs were consistent on the following instructional

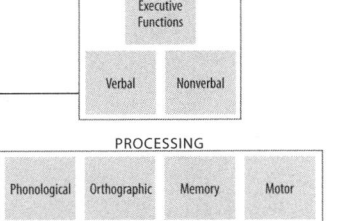

principles: 1) introduction of approximately 3 words per day, or no more than 12 to 15 words per week; 2) selection of words that could be extended derivationally and conceptually through discussion; 3) location and discussion of words in engaging text; and 4) provision of contextualized definitions with practice opportunities in new and multiple contexts. In addition, words are taught in a sequence with an attempt to determine which words should be learned next. The words to target for struggling readers are usually the ones that some children of that grade level know but others do not (Biemiller, 2005). Vocabulary instruction should focus on words that students will see or read often and will be useful (McKeown & Beck, 2011). Thus, the vocabulary words being taught need to be of appropriate complexity (Stahl & Stahl, 2004).

Based on their earlier work, Beck, McKeown, and Kucan (2013) described a three-tier framework for choosing words for vocabulary instruction. Tier 1 words are the basic and most familiar words that children encounter from an early age. Tier 1 words require little or no instruction (e.g., *apple, look*). Tier 2 words are of high utility for mature language users. They are found in various domains and are more common in written than spoken language (e.g., *perceive, contradict*). The most productive instruction is directed to these words. Tier 3 words are specialized words that are typically found in content areas (e.g., *mitosis, photosynthesis*). They are taught when needed to understand specific passages. Beck and colleagues encourage teachers to provide engaging instruction of about 400 Tier 2 words per year.

Beck and colleagues also explained how knowledge of a word's meaning is not simply known or not known. Often, students have some knowledge of a word's meaning but not complete knowledge. To explore word knowledge, teachers can make a chart that includes four categories: 1) know it well and can explain it, 2) know something about it, 3) have seen or heard the word before, and 4) do not know the word.

John had heard the word *sinister* before and knew it had something to do with "bad" but could explain it no further. His definitions presented in Figure 10.5 illustrate that he has some knowledge of what the words mean, but his definitions are not very precise. His teacher writes, "Where did you get these definitions?" It seems that John just wrote down what he thought the words meant.

John would benefit from explicit vocabulary instruction. Graves (2000) outlined four components of an effective vocabulary program with accompanying procedures that can help students increase vocabulary.

1. Encourage students to engage in wide or expanded independent reading to expand word knowledge.
   - Check first to see if students can define the new word by reading it in context (i.e., by reading the rest of the sentence or paragraph). This strategy can reduce the amount of time they spend looking up words. If they cannot define the word, looking it up in the dictionary and asking someone else are better strategies than skipping the word.

2. Provide instruction in specific words to enhance comprehension of texts containing those words.
   - Ask the students to select a word, relate it to other information, check the definition, write the definition, and use the word in a written sentence. Grouping words by similar meaning for practice can enhance recall.

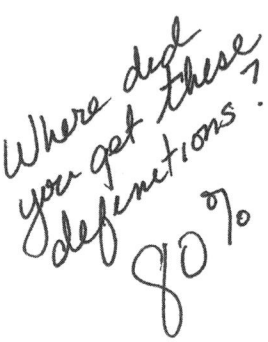

Figure 10.5. John's definitions.

3. Provide instruction in independent word-learning strategies.
   - Encourage students to write down and define unfamiliar words in a small notebook, inside the covers of their notebooks, or on the reverse side of the page when they first encounter them.
4. Encourage the development of word consciousness and word-play activities to motivate and enhance learning.
   - Encourage students to practice using new words in conversations and assignments, to listen for new words when watching television, and to play with words by doing crosswords and other word puzzles. Practice with using words increases the likelihood that students will retain word meanings.

Katy's fifth-grade teacher, Ms. McGrew, would log onto Puzzlemaker (http://www.puzzlemaker.com). This web site enables teachers to create word puzzles for students using any words they select.

As students progress through school, the vocabulary in classes becomes increasingly specialized. Many students benefit from direct instruction on the use of common prefixes and suffixes and the study of word origins (Anglo-Saxon, Latin, and Greek). For example, the Latin root *spect* means "to look." Knowledge of this root then helps students understand words such as *specimen, specific, spectator, spectacle,* and *aspect.* Students can also practice adding various prefixes and suffixes to alter the meaning of words, such as in *respect, disrespected, respectful,* and *inspector.* Greek roots are often called combining forms, as they combine together like Anglo-Saxon compound words, such as *bookend* and *sunset.* Students enjoy learning forms such as *auto,* meaning "self," combined with *graph,* meaning "written," to form *autograph* or *bio,* meaning "life," and *-ology,* meaning "the study of," to

Verbal, Nonverbal, and Executive Functions

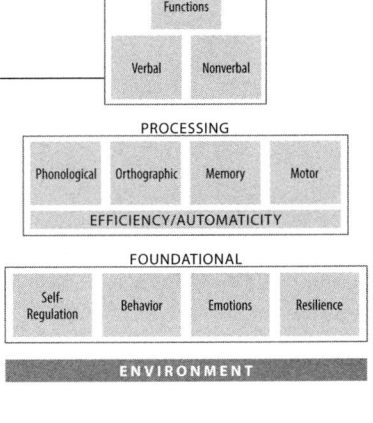

form *biology*. The Internet contains numerous lists of both Latin and Greek roots that teachers can use to enhance vocabulary instruction.

Students can also study the various derivations of words to increase their understanding of how common morphemes, prefixes, and suffixes alter word meaning. This type of instruction can be enhanced with a graphic organizer. Ms. McGrew, Katy's teacher, would place a word in the center of the map, such as the word *friend*, and then have students brainstorm all the words that are formed using this root. Figure 10.6 illustrates the completed class graphic.

Many texts have glossaries; when they do not, students can make a list of words with easy-to-understand definitions. John found that dictionaries sometimes offered definitions that were more confusing than helpful. He found that a glossary in an ability-appropriate text with a good index was far more useful. Many teachers

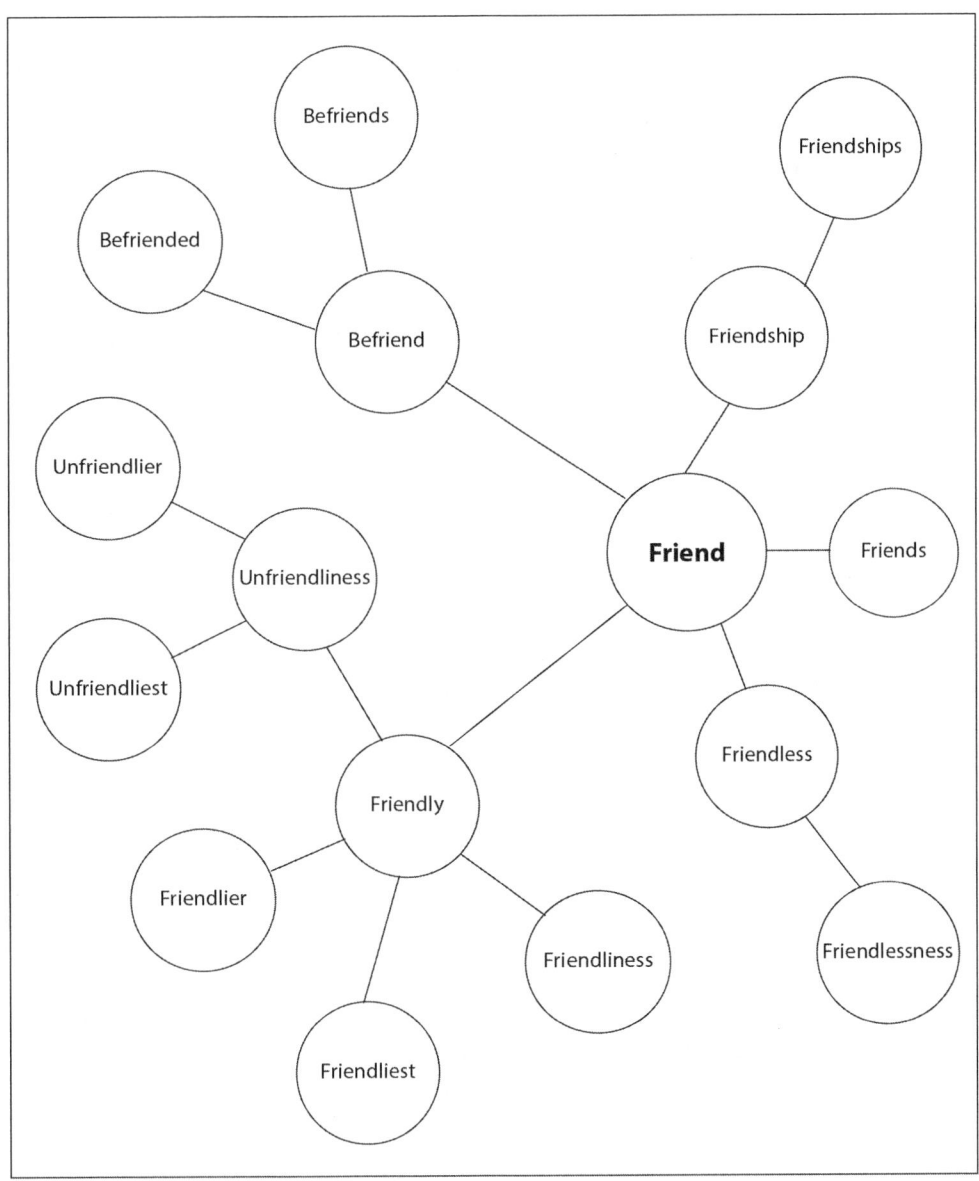

Figure 10.6. Map for derivations of the word *friend*.

367

post words on signs in their rooms to help reinforce new or important vocabulary words or phrases. Building a word wall around a specific content area is also useful for helping students increase their vocabulary. Modeling the use of different strategies in the classroom regularly helps students learn to apply them.

Students can also use technology to expand vocabulary. Students can use the Franklin Speaking Language Master or a software program that provides pronunciations and definitions orally. A reading pen such as the Quicktionary Reading Pen and other reading pens provide definitions of scanned words. There are also many apps that can be used with personal electronic devices such as smart phones and tablets for this purpose. See Appendix 11B and Additional Resources for numerous examples.

Adequate time and attention must be devoted to helping students such as Katy and John increase their word knowledge through multiple exposures to words and systematic and intensive instruction. Without this type of instruction, gaps in vocabulary knowledge will continue throughout elementary school, leaving students at greater risk for continued problems with reading comprehension and written expression as they progress through school.

Higher Level Questioning Skills

Some students need help developing the use of higher level questioning skills. As students progress in school, a greater emphasis is placed on assignments that require analytical and critical thinking. Asking questions presents an opportunity for active engagement with the material. Teachers often model how to ask questions during class discussions, encouraging students to formulate and discuss their own questions. As a result, more effective learning occurs. John found that it helped him to ask and try to answer questions in a variety of situations, such as taking notes from a text, writing a research paper, or studying a chapter in his math textbook.

Dr. Mantell, John's history teacher, encouraged students to recall related facts from several sources, express an opinion and give reasons, summarize what they had learned so far, predict the consequences of certain actions, and organize information in new ways. During class discussions, she asked the following types of questions:

- How are the ideas related to one another?
- How do they relate to what you already know?
- What is the main idea of _____?
- What if _____?
- How does it affect _____?
- What is the meaning of _____?
- Why is _____ important?
- Explain why _____.
- Explain how _____.
- How does this relate to what you've learned before?
- What conclusions can you draw?
- What is the difference between _____ and _____?
- How are _____ and _____ similar?
- How would you use _____?
- What are the strengths and weaknesses of _____?
- What is the best choice and why?

Verbal, Nonverbal, and Executive Functions

By using these types of questions, Dr. Mantell created an interactive classroom in which students are encouraged to discuss, clarify, compare, expand on, and review ideas.

NONVERBAL ABILITIES

Although much of the emphasis in the field of SLD has been placed on students who struggle with the acquisition and use of spoken and written language, a smaller subset of students show symptoms that are characteristic of what have been referred to as nonverbal learning disabilities (NVLDs). Although the characteristics of students with NVLD do not fit neatly into any one block of the Building Blocks model, two major characteristics are poor spatial organization and inattention to visual details, or abilities related to generating and using visual images.

Characteristics

Many students with NVLD are poorly organized and appear unfocused. Although they may be described as inattentive and distractible, these observed behaviors result from a reduced capacity for self-directed behavior rather than from attention-deficit/hyperactivity disorder (ADHD; Fletcher, Taylor, Levin, & Satz, 1995). A student with NVLD has strengths in word decoding, spelling, and rote memory but encounters difficulty with math computation and problem solving, visual-spatial tasks and motor coordination, and reading body language and social cues (Cortiella & Horowitz, 2014; Fletcher, 1985; Gathercole & Pickering, 2000; Miller, 2004; Rourke, 1995). Students often exhibit social difficulties, become overwhelmed by interacting with people, and have extreme difficulties in dealing with novel and complex materials. In addition, these students have difficulty acquiring new skills, particularly motor skills.

Because a student with NVLD presents early strengths in the development of general declarative knowledge and vocabulary, identification of these problems tends to occur in later grades. As the student moves through school, tasks that require higher level spatial-analytic abilities, such as those involved in mathematical problem solving, present increasing difficulty. Because a large proportion of the communication in an average conversation is nonverbal in nature, a student with NVLD may miss important information about what is being communicated and may be unsure of how to respond (Rothenberg, 1998). Students with Asperger syndrome often struggle with the same issues, and research suggests that NVLD may fall within the spectrum of autism disorders (Miller, 2004; National Research Council, 2001; Rourke et al., 2002).

Stephanie, a fourth-grade student, was often alone at lunchtime and recess. When she tried to engage her peers, she stood too close to them and asked in too loud of a voice if they would play with her. In the classroom, she often blurted out inappropriate answers. When she attempted to use a compass to draw a circle for her math assignment, she could not coordinate the series of movements. When she read aloud in class, she decoded words with ease but then had trouble responding to questions. Her responses often revealed lack of attention to critical details. For example, when asked, "Why did the children go into the cave?" she responded, "What cave?" Stephanie's teacher, Ms. Taylor, noticed that she was much more successful when ideas and concepts were presented to her sequentially within small groups of information and when she was provided with opportunities for repeated practice. Due to these concerns, Ms. Taylor filled out the 10 questions associated with nonverbal reasoning on the Building Blocks Questionnaire. She checked that Stephanie frequently had trouble with tasks involving spatial reasoning, developing mental images while reading, and the visual and spatial aspects of mathematics, as well as understanding maps, diagrams, and graphs. Figure 10.7 illustrates this part of the questionnaire for Stephanie.

Interventions

In general, students with NVLD benefit when interventions are highly concrete and as verbal as possible. Teachers can help a student with NVLD feel in control of the present academic environment before introducing new information or skills. Use methods that are highly structured and systematic and provide external guidance. Simplify, break down, or modify expectations. Establishing consistent expectations between home and school or from class to class is often beneficial and involves collaboration with family members and colleagues.

Stephanie had difficulties with generalization, and she had trouble recognizing which skills she should apply in new situations. Her performance improved when her teacher reviewed previous steps before introducing new information or processes.

Students with NVLD benefit from consistency and predictability, which helps them avoid becoming overwhelmed or confused. Thus, relatively static learning environments can be helpful. These students often require more time when processing information that requires visual imagery (Cornoldi, Rigoni, Tressoldi, & Vio, 1999). Verbal clarifications can also help students make meaningful connections among ideas (Foss, 1991; Vacca, 2001).

Ms. Taylor found that Stephanie was confused by the time line about ancient Egypt. Once she had explained why the period of time indicated by BCE (before the Common Era) decreased in years as time had passed, Stephanie was able to understand and interpret the timeline successfully.

Students with NVLD have difficulty with reading social cues, so they may misinterpret the actions of classmates and teachers. Direct teaching of cause-and-effect

CONCEPTUAL

Nonverbal	Rarely	Sometimes	Frequently
Has trouble putting puzzles together	☐	✓	☐
Has difficulty distinguishing left from right	☐	✓	☐
Has trouble judging distances	☐	✓	☐
Has trouble with tasks involving spatial reasoning	☐	☐	✓
Has difficulty creating mental images when reading	☐	☐	✓
Has difficulty with the visual and spatial aspects of mathematics	☐	☐	✓
Has trouble understanding maps, diagrams, or graphs	☐	☐	✓
Has difficulty interpreting body language or social cues	☐	✓	☐
Has poor social skills	☐	✓	☐
Has difficulty understanding humor	☐	✓	☐

Figure 10.7. Building Blocks Questionnaire for Stephanie: Nonverbal Conceptual block.

Verbal, Nonverbal, and Executive Functions

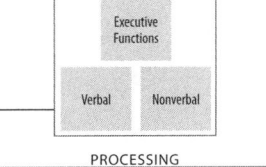
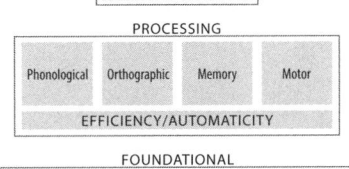

relationships for specific circumstances is helpful. Because verbal expression is typically considered a strength, teaching students how to use self-talk to reinforce routines or procedures can help them complete simple and complex tasks. Rourke (1995) recommended using a "part-to-whole" verbal teaching approach in which information is presented in a logical sequence. In this approach, the teacher helps students complete difficult tasks by encouraging them to proceed one step at a time, paying attention to details.

Ms. Taylor taught Stephanie the following strategy to employ when she was approaching novel tasks: When Stephanie started to work, she first asked herself, "What does the teacher want me to do?" If she could not come up with this answer, she asked other students who were seated nearby. Stephanie then found a partner and worked out the steps to take to complete the task. Stephanie organized the steps by placing picture cards that had been supplied to her on an outline. After she gained understanding of what was being asked and the steps to take, Stephanie asked herself the question "What do I need to accomplish this task?" She gathered the materials that she needed to complete the task and brought them into the working area. When Stephanie was unsure about a step, she first attempted to obtain clarification from a peer. If that failed, she would ask the teacher for clarification.

Instruction Using Visual Imagery

Both students with oral language impairments and students with NVLD can benefit from using techniques designed to structure information visually. When providing instruction in tasks that require visual imagery, create drawings, webs, or maps. Encourage students to try to create mental images of the information presented. Translating information into visual formats can help students such as John, Katy, and Stephanie store and retrieve important information. Appendix 10C provides examples of apps that are useful for instruction in visual imagery, notetaking, time management, and test-taking instruction.

Visualization

An easy way to encourage students to think with images is to help them learn to visualize words, settings, or scenes. Consider the expression "A picture is worth a thousand words." When students are shown pictures, it helps them expand their understanding. When students learn to form mental scenes, it enhances their expression.

When students in Stephanie's class were asked to write a story about traveling to the moon, Ms. Taylor asked Stephanie to close her eyes and imagine she was in a spaceship on her way to the moon. She then asked Stephanie to tell her everything that she could see. Ms. Taylor then wrote down Stephanie's observations so that Stephanie would be able to integrate the ideas into her writing assignment. She also asked Stephanie questions to help her expand information about the pictured scene.

Specialized vocabularies are part of most domains of study. These types of content-area words can be particularly difficult for students with weaknesses in language.

For biology class, John was attempting to learn the terms *mitosis* and *meiosis*. He was having difficulty with grasping that in mitosis, when a cell reproduces, it creates two genetically identical daughter cells. In meiosis, the cell divides into four gametes, each of which possesses half the number of chromosomes in the original cell. John's teacher provided two diagrams in which the stages were laid out in a circle in order to emphasize that the processes occur in a cycle. John's task was to fill in the names of the stages. Once John accomplished this, his teacher had John put this information into a hierarchy format so that he could see how his text described the process. To reinforce the information, the teacher then had John use materials—a sheet of paper as the cell; rubber bands for membranes; string for spindle fibers; and pennies, dimes, and quarters for chromosomes—so that he could create a visual display of the processes. John increased his understanding of the concepts by using materials that he could manipulate and by seeing the stages laid out in a visual sequence. He was able to pass the quiz and move on to the next biology lesson.

Often students do not view the diagrams, charts, graphs, and illustrations included in their texts as important pieces of information or they do not know how to use them. Helping students understand how to interpret these illustrations can also improve comprehension.

Ms. McGrew asked her students to develop posters for a section of her science class in which they were studying nutrition. Because Katy avoided the graphs and diagrams in her book (they look too much like math to her), she lacked important information, and, consequently, she failed to understand the assignment. Ms. McGrew asked Katy what aspect of nutrition interested her the most. Katy said that she often saw her mother making decisions about what to buy at the grocery store by reading information on labels, but she didn't know what it meant. Ms. McGrew used this example to develop Katy's understanding. She had her bring in labels from three brands of cereal and then helped her make a bar graph that compared the differences in amounts of vitamins, sugar, calories, fiber, and grams of fat visually through the use of color and proportion. Katy learned that a bar graph is a way to make comparisons, and she found out that her favorite cereal contained the most sugar and was the least nutritious. A few days later, she used her new knowledge to ask a question about a bar graph in her text.

Keyword Method

Some methods that are designed to help students recall vocabulary focus on the creation of visual images. These methods can help students recall more difficult terminology, such as new words to be learned for a math, science, or history class. Mastropieri (1988) described the keyword method, which involves tying new words to visual images to help students recall word meanings and learn new vocabulary. Three steps are used in the keyword method: recoding, relating, and retrieving. For recoding, students change the new vocabulary word into a known word that has a similar sound and is easily pictured, which is then used as the keyword. For relating, students associate the keyword with the definition of the new vocabulary word through a mental image or a sentence. For retrieving, students think of the keyword, remember the association, and then retrieve the definition. Research findings indicate that the keyword mnemonic strategy can both increase vocabulary knowledge and facilitate recall of words over time (Jitendra et al., 2004). This type of method can be beneficial for students with SLD because it emphasizes meaningfulness and concreteness in learning through memory of pictures and de-emphasizes memory for abstract or unfamiliar vocabulary (Scruggs & Mastropieri, 2013).

To use the keyword method, begin by defining and discussing the meaning of the new word with students. Next, discuss with the students various options for a keyword and then make a picture of the definition doing something with the keyword. The keyword may be a rhyming word or a word that evokes specific visual

Verbal, Nonverbal, and Executive Functions

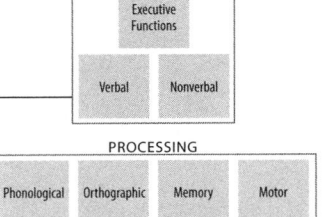

imagery. Students then study what they have imagined until they can recall the definition. For example, the special education teacher was trying to help Katy learn the meaning of the word *apex*. Katy created an image of a gorilla standing on a spot marked with the letter *X* on top of a mountain. When she was asked to produce the definition, this image came easily to mind. This strategy can also be used to develop mnemonic devices to assist students in remembering specific information.

Graphic Organizers

Graphic organizers provide a visual representation of main ideas or concepts. Together with the student, develop an idea framework in which information is organized to depict important relationships. Graphic organizers may take the form of maps, time lines, diagrams, pictures, flowcharts, pyramids, or webs.

Graphic organizers can be used for several different purposes. When teachers use graphic organizers as instructional tools in presenting new information to their classes, they often find that the graphic organizer helps them to formulate, clarify, and evaluate instructional objectives. When used in small-group discussions in class, students can be asked to analyze and visualize the relationships of key concepts. Students can generate their own graphic organizers after they read a selection. Because they are more actively engaged with the material, students who use postreading organizers grasp additional information. Graphic organizers can also be helpful when students write papers, serving as a method for organizing information that is then developed into text. Both students with oral language impairments and students with NVLD can benefit from using visually based techniques to support learning.

Mapping

One simple procedure for organizing information in a visual display is called mapping or webbing. This procedure focuses on using the images block to enhance memory and understanding. Maps or webs are graphic organizers that help children develop and organize their thoughts. Picture a spider web. Think of how all the threads connect and seem intertwined. Similar to a web, graphic organizers show connections. The visual display depicts the important ideas and the relationships among ideas. The illustrations of these relationships help students link together the information. Consequently, their understanding and ability to recall information improve.

To assist students in recalling specific vocabulary words using mapping, teachers and students can now use an online graphical dictionary called Visuwords (http://www.visuwords.com). When a student looks up a word using this web site, a map that represents the meaning of the chosen vocabulary word as well as the association to other words is displayed. This assists students in understanding the relationship between various vocabulary words as well as synonyms they can use to expand their writing. The visual representation provided also assists students in learning this information.

Mapping techniques work well for visual learners because visual memory reinforces the learning of information. Mapping requires the use of both hemispheres of the brain. Information is linked together or chunked. Relationships among pieces of information, particularly between facts and ideas, are developed. Mapping strategies do not require neat handwriting or presentation to be effective and can be used in conjunction with other notetaking techniques.

Adaptation of the K-W-L Strategy

An adaptation of the K-W-L strategy, described earlier in the chapter, adds mapping and summarization (Carr & Ogle, 1987). To add the mapping component, children categorize the information listed under L. The topic forms the center of the map. For example, because Katy was learning about spiders, she wrote *spiders* in the center of the map. Lines are then added to show the relationships between the main topic and the facts that are gathered.

Students then use the map to create a summary. The center of the map becomes the title of the essay, and each category is used as the topic for a new paragraph. Supporting details are then added to expand or explain the topic further. After practice with this procedure, some students are able to omit the mapping step and write their summaries directly from the K-W-L worksheet. The adapted K-W-L strategy using mapping helps students acquire, relate, and learn concepts; increase vocabulary; and discuss important points and keywords.

Brainstorming

Another use of mapping is as a brainstorming strategy that lets students rapidly produce and order a large number of ideas. Each idea is organized by placing it next to related ones. This creative visual process begins with a central word or concept that is placed at the center of the page or screen; then, approximately 5–10 main ideas that relate to that concept are added. As materials become more detailed and supporting ideas are articulated, several more words that relate to any of the first words are added. The use of shapes, such as circles, squares, and rectangles, along with symbols, such as arrows and equal signs, becomes the visual means to designate relationships among concepts. In this way, an exponential number of related ideas can be produced quickly. Students may place a page horizontally or use large sheets of paper for this process. Some students learn to use index cards for each subset of information. Students can follow these steps to create a map:

1. Write the topic in the middle of the page, and draw a circle around it.
2. Draw a line outward from the circle, and write a related main idea or word on it.
3. Place a border or shape around the new information.
4. Add branches, each with an idea or fact, generally becoming more specific in detail.
5. Draw branching lines out from these facts, and keep adding relevant information.
6. Personalize the map by adding pictures and symbols and by creating acronyms. (Illogical and humorous associations are sometimes effective ways to remember information.)
7. Use keywords when possible. Keywords, usually nouns or verbs, can represent summarized ideas, resulting in fewer words to write and remember.
8. Look for repetitions and for more accurate linking words. Add numbers if there is a sequence or hierarchy to the information.
9. Use colored pencils or pens, using one color for main ideas, another color for supporting ideas, and another color for details.

Verbal, Nonverbal, and Executive Functions

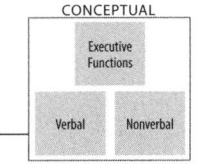
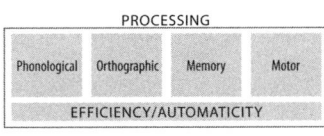
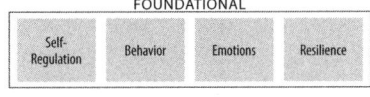

Maps can also be linked. One map can identify the five main ideas in a chapter, and the student can then create five individual maps, one for each idea. As a study strategy, students can try to reproduce the map from memory or arrange the same information in a different format. Students can post maps on the wall and embellish them with illustrations (in addition to using color).

Mapping can also facilitate active listening. During class discussions or lectures, help students identify a key idea or concept, which is then recorded in the center of the page. Ask the students to attempt to include each related idea. When discussions or presentations are not sequential, students may use mapping to isolate the key points that each speaker is adding to the discussions. Students can add the connections that were made among the points later. Taking the time to rearrange and review the map is a process that helps reinforce the important points of the discussion and helps clarify thinking and reduce the time needed to study. Some students prefer to make their maps after hearing the entire lecture or discussion in order to synthesize and review the information. Another effective strategy is to pair students together to create a map.

To create maps when reading text, ask a student to read the passage to be mapped, select the most important idea, and write it in the center of the page. As the student rereads the passage, he or she can identify key concepts and rank them in order of importance. The student can then arrange the concepts on the page, link the concepts by drawing circles and lines among them, and review the maps to determine if additional information needs to be added. By placing concepts on 3" × 5" cards or sticky notes, concepts can be rearranged easily. Students can also use the mapping technique for writing a paper. Students can take the notes that they have made (on either 3" × 5" index cards or on sticky notes) and place them in an order that structures the paper. Each card can then be expanded into a sentence or paragraph.

Figure 10.8 is an example of a mind map that John developed in his class on free enterprise. John's teacher assigned a chapter to be read and indicated that students should be prepared to join in a discussion about the reading the next day. The chapter was about marketing strategies and looked specifically at the advantages of selling to individuals versus selling to the mass market. John read the chapter and began to sort out the information. He decided that although the author seemed to him to be talking about marketing, the content was more about how one decides to sell something. As John identified this as the main focus of the chapter, he placed it in the middle of his map. When he thought about what he had just read, it occurred to him that the author was talking about selling to a mass market, which seemed large, and about selling to people more directly, which is interpersonal. He added two nodes, or branches, one on each side of the first, to indicate this distinction. He also knew he needed a bit more information in order to keep this in focus, so he added the cue that mass marketing means that a large audience gets the same message or sales pitch. The author emphasized several points about mass marketing, so John wrote down short phrases he felt he could remember in order to summarize each of them. He then found that the author had used the same approach when writing about interpersonal marketing, so he added brief summaries to his map about those as well.

John thought about what his teacher would ask them to discuss and decided that the topic would most likely be the advantages and disadvantages of each form of marketing. He noted that there were three advantages to selling to the mass market. He also recognized that there were three disadvantages. Because John was doing his map on the software program Inspiration (see Additional Resources), he was able to rearrange the placement of these points easily so that the advantages were above his main concept and the negatives were below the main concept. (Placing concepts on index cards would provide the student with an alternate way to accomplish the same goal.) As John was thinking about where the connections should be placed, he also added arrows to show the connections he thought he saw; he then began to realize that what was an advantage of one type of marketing strategy was not an advantage in the other marketing strategy (e.g., quick feedback is an advantage when using an interpersonal marketing strategy but is not possible when using a

Conceptual Blocks

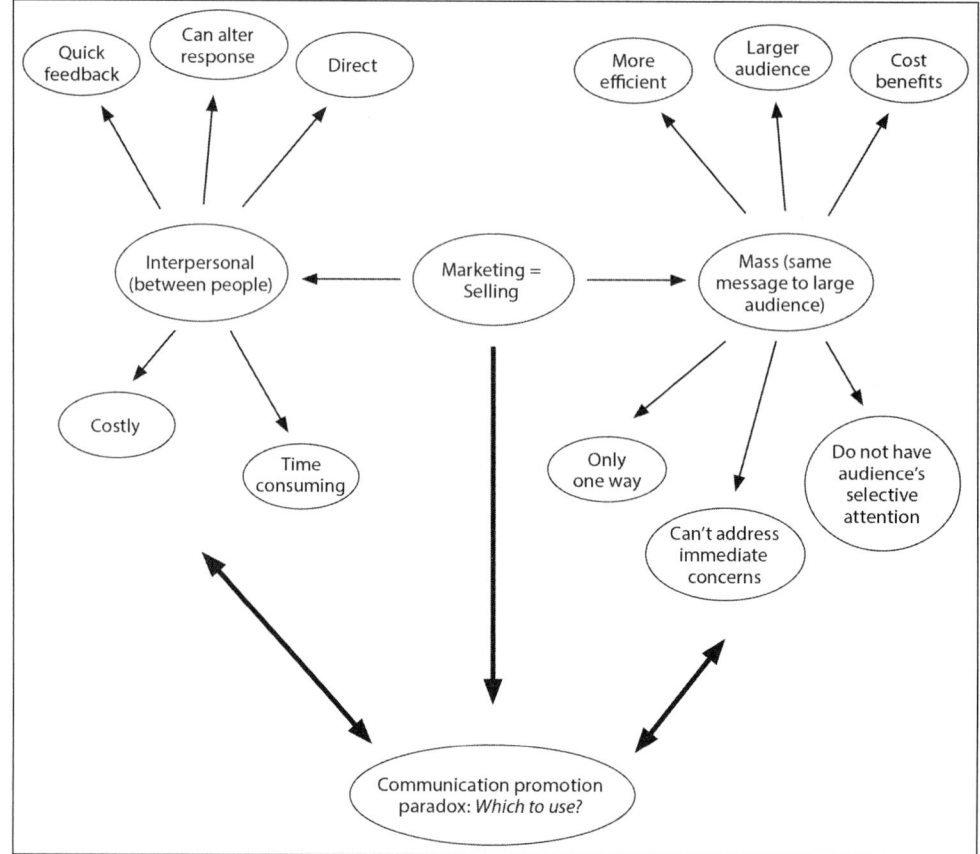

Figure 10.8. John's mind map.

mass-market strategy). John figured out that the really important point he was supposed to learn is that it is hard to decide which marketing strategy to use because there is no clear choice.

Creating the map helped John take charge of his learning. He had to focus on key concepts, select supporting details, compare and contrast information, and make decisions about what was and was not important. The week before, after reading a chapter, he had forgotten what he had read and was uncomfortable going into class. This week, he felt he had a much better grasp of the reading assignment because the information was now easier to recall. The map represented a summary of his reading, and he knew that if he forgot a point, he could review the map and refresh his memory quickly.

Spatial Outlining

Spatial outlining or three-column notetaking is another type of graphic organizer that can help a student learn how to take notes when a teacher talks quickly or when the class discussion or lecture seems to jump around. This procedure helps the learner determine how ideas and concepts are related. John's special education teacher taught him to use spatial outlining by following these steps:

1. Turn standard notebook paper sideways (11" × 8.5") to allow a wider space for recording ideas and separating concepts from details and examples.
2. Divide each page into three columns: a very narrow one on the left for very general topic words; a medium column in the middle for more specific sub-points; and the widest column on the right for facts, details, and examples.

Verbal, Nonverbal, and Executive Functions

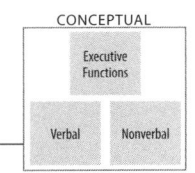
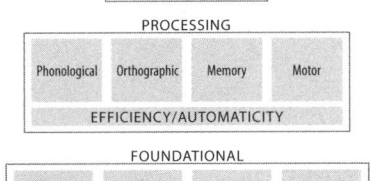

3. Decide which of the three columns each piece of information fits into and record it there. Leave plenty of white space for connecting ideas later. Use pauses in the discussion or presentation to draw arrows and other signals in order to remember which pieces go together.

4. Review the outline, connecting the general topics with the subpoints and details in order to identify any missing information and to determine ideas that need clarification.

Tables 10.1 and 10.2 illustrate two examples of three-column notetaking.

EXECUTIVE FUNCTIONS

The Building Block of Executive Functions is at the top of the Building Blocks model. This block is the most important because the abilities involved integrate language, reasoning, planning, self-monitoring, and self-evaluation. Evidence-based processing interventions tend to focus on higher level cognitive processes, such as working memory and executive functioning (Dehn, 2006). Most students can be successful in school if they learn how to be organized, reflective, and strategic. Unfortunately, many students with SLD have a limited repertoire of strategies and fail to monitor their academic performance (Montague, 2007).

Metacognition is the ability to think about one's own thinking. It is a capacity to adjust how one learns and what skills and strategies are needed to complete changing academic demands (Krawec, Huang, Montague, Kressler, & de Alba, 2012; Zimmerman, 1986). Weaknesses in metacognition appear to affect the development and use of strategies adversely and to impede progress in academic tasks (Cutting, Materek, Cole, Levine, & Mahone, 2009; Montague, 1997). Students who struggle in school often do not employ useful learning strategies. When students do not learn to use metacognitive strategies, their ability to complete tasks decreases. Students who are unable to choose the appropriate strategy to complete a task may be described as having deficient executive processing skills. Competency in metacognitive strategies has been found to be a strong predictor of academic success for students with SLD at the college level, further validating the need for such skills (Ruban, 2000; Smitely, 2001).

Executive functions are a portion of metacognition that relate to a student's ability to choose a strategy that will assist in problem-solving activities. Estimating memory capacity for specific tasks, predicting accuracy on a memory task, allotting appropriate time to study, and deciding when one has studied enough are all parts of executive functioning (Deshler, Ellis, & Lenz, 1996; Keeler & Swanson, 2001; Swanson & Siegel, 2001). Students must be able to recognize when the strategy they have chosen to solve a problem is ineffective so that they may alter their approach.

Students who lack problem-solving strategies generally need explicit instruction in specific cognitive strategies (e.g., visualization, verbal rehearsal,

Table 10.1. First example of three-column notetaking

Column 1	Column 2	Column 3
Old information	New information	Questions
Should be 2" wide	Should be 5" wide	Should be 1" wide
	Basic notetaking column	Questions or comments about notes that should be elaborated on or that are important for future assignments

Table 10.2. Second example of three-column notetaking

Column 1	Column 2	Column 3
Basic ideas	Background information	Questions
Basic notetaking column, stress on information for tests, reports, and so on	Related or interesting information	Questions or comments about notes that should be elaborated on or that are important for future assignments

paraphrasing, summarizing, estimating). Meaningful strategy instruction can occur only when the learner is developmentally ready. Students need to have the prerequisite skills necessary to employ a strategy. Students must also be reminded that strategies are flexible and can be adapted to fit different learning environments. Strategy instruction is a long-term process and not a quick fix to cure significant learning problems.

General Principles of Strategy Instruction

Regardless of whether a strategy is designed primarily to enhance reading comprehension, written expression, or math problem-solving ability, several general principles apply (Meltzer, Roditi, & Stein, 1998):

- Teach strategies in the context of the curriculum.
- Teach different strategies so students can choose among strategies.
- Provide a balance between instruction in strategies and skills.
- Encourage students to understand their own learning styles.
- Show children how to adapt strategies as needed.

Kaufman summarized seven core foundational teaching strategies, presented in Table 10.3, that are essential for students with weaknesses in executive functions (2010, pp. 81–94).

Instruction in Strategies

Students who struggle with aspects of executive functioning need to be taught how to use efficient strategies for problem solving. Although some students with SLD use a range of study strategies successfully, many students who struggle do not employ functional learning strategies (Lerner & Johns, 2014). Too often they have not learned to use strategies flexibly or do not know how to choose strategies that are appropriate to the demands of the task. These students tend to have difficulty with many of the tasks that are essential for successful participation in most classes, such as taking effective notes or preparing for and taking tests. As students such as Katy, Stephanie, and John learn strategies, they should be encouraged to submit the first drafts of their outlines, notes, or graphic organizers for review and feedback.

Many of the strategies described in the next section have several common elements:

- Teaching students to become active learners
- Helping students evaluate the effectiveness of a strategy
- Determining ways to modify the strategy for use in different settings

Verbal, Nonverbal, and Executive Functions

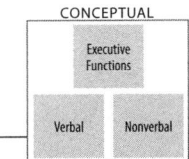
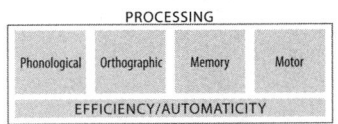
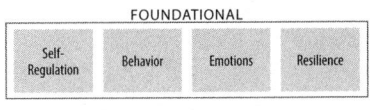

Table 10.3. Core strategies for teaching students with weaknesses in executive functions

Realize that these students will require greater levels of adult supervision. Take care to ensure that students are not asked to perform tasks that are beyond their current skill level.

Present new skills and content systematically and explicitly. Use highly explicit step-by-step instructions that link the unfamiliar to the familiar. Provide clear and repeated modeling of new skills.

Show how to apply new strategies in real-life contexts. Provide concrete methods for teaching students how to take notes, study for tests, and organize learning materials.

Minimize demands on working memory. Deliver instruction in a way that minimizes the amount of information presented at one time. Use a step-by-step design that requires only focusing on one element at a time.

Provide opportunities for guided and extended practice. Provide plenty of time for students to practice new skills and integrate new material into what they already know.

Keep schedules and routines as predictable and consistent as possible. Develop clear classroom routines and stick to them for the entire school year.

Anticipate the aspects of tasks and situations that students may find challenging or frustrating. Model how students should manage these challenges when they arise.

Source: Kaufman (2010).

Think-Alouds

Similar to the modeling techniques described earlier in this chapter, think-alouds can be used to explain to students which metacognitive and executive processes are effective when performing a skill, completing a task, or solving a problem (Davey, 1983). Think-alouds are a way for teachers to model how they think and learn. Davey (1983) listed the five major uses of think-alouds:

1. Making predictions or showing students how to develop a hypothesis
2. Describing visual images
3. Sharing an analogy or showing how prior knowledge applies
4. Verbalizing confusing points or demonstrating how to monitor understanding
5. Demonstrating repair strategies

When using think-alouds, develop guidelines for students' participation within the activity. The instruction should focus on the purpose, the relevant vocabulary, the organization, and the key points to observe (Good & Brophy, 1994). Guided instruction allows students to begin to think about what they are doing and what they can learn from it. After a presentation is done, a teacher may ask students to discuss what they learned and to summarize the key points. Teachers may also want to ask certain students to restate parts of the presentation for further rehearsal and review of concepts. Adults can also teach students how to ask questions such as the following (Gordon-Pershey, 2014):

- How did I find my answer?
- What is the reason for my answer?
- What was I thinking that helped me find the answer?
- When have I thought about this before and why is it important now?

Chapter 11 provides additional examples of the application of think-alouds for writing instruction.

Self-Regulated Strategy Development

Another procedure for promoting self-monitoring and regulation is self-regulated strategy development (SRSD; Graham & Harris, 1999; Graham & Harris, 2005; Graham, Harris, & McKeown, 2013). Using SRSD, students learn a task-specific strategy along with self-regulating strategies, such as goal setting, self-monitoring, and self-instruction (Mason, Harris, & Graham, 2013).

The following six instructional stages help students master task-specific strategies:

1. Develop and activate background knowledge. The teacher helps the students develop the background knowledge they need to use the strategy and teaches any preskills needed to learn the strategy.
2. Discuss it. The teacher and the students discuss the goals and benefits of the strategy.
3. Model it. The teacher demonstrates how to use the strategy.
4. Memorize it. The students memorize the steps of the strategy.
5. Support it. The students practice the strategy with teacher support.
6. Independent performance. The students apply the strategy independently.

The teacher should also explain how to use the strategy in different situations, how the procedures may be modified, and how to evaluate the success of the strategy, as well as provide reminders to use the strategy (Graham et al., 2013). Chapter 11 includes an application of this strategy to writing.

Mnemonics

The word *mnemonic* means "memory aid." One example was the keyword method described earlier in this chapter. By using mnemonics, many students can improve their recall of related facts and knowledge. Many learning strategies use first-letter mnemonics. With these strategies, each letter reminds the student of the next step. One example is "Kids prefer cheese over fried green spinach," which stands for the order of taxonomy in biology: kingdom, phylum, class, order, family, genus, and species. Mnemonics aid students in forming associations that do not exist naturally in the content (Eggen & Kauchak, 1992). By forming these associations, students are able to store information in their long-term memory and retrieve it later in an efficient manner. When teaching students to use mnemonics, include the following steps (Alsopp, 1999):

1. Model when to use the mnemonic (i.e., its purpose).
2. Model what each part of the mnemonic stands for.
3. Model how to attach the information that the mnemonic represents to previously learned knowledge.
4. Provide students with cue cards associated with the mnemonic to place at their desks.
5. Put up posters of mnemonics on classroom walls.
6. Use rapid-fire verbal rehearsal to help students remember mnemonics.

For rapid-fire verbal rehearsal, the teacher moves quickly from student to student, asking which steps are represented by the varying letters.

Verbal, Nonverbal, and Executive Functions

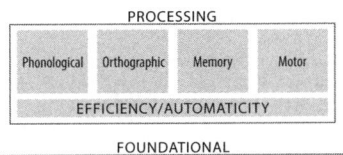
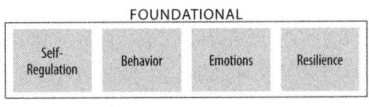

Cognitive Behavior Modification

Cognitive behavior modification is based on the belief that perceptions influence behaviors; therefore, by changing a student's perceptions, his or her behavior can be altered (Meichenbaum, 1977, 1983). Cognitive behavior modification combines aspects of behavior modification with monitoring instruction, evaluation, and verbalization. Change in behavior results from a change in thought processes. Common characteristics of these types of interventions include strategy steps, modeling, self-regulation, verbalization, and reflective thinking. The following general guidelines (Meichenbaum, 1977, 1983) help students be active participants in learning:

1. Analyze the target behavior.
2. Determine the strategies the student already uses (if any).
3. Select strategy steps that are as similar as possible to the strategy steps used by good problem solvers.
4. Work with the student in developing the strategy steps.
5. Teach the prerequisite skills.
6. Teach the strategy steps using modeling, self-instruction, and self-regulation.
7. Provide explicit feedback.
8. Teach strategy generalization.
9. Help the student maintain the strategy.

Many students with SLD require more repetition, more practice, and more reminders than their peers to learn a strategy.

Notetaking Techniques

As students progress through school, they need to develop an efficient method for notetaking. When reviewing pages of John's class notes, Dr. Mantell noted that John did not have a strategy for writing down important information presented during class lectures. He had trouble trying to decide what was important and what was unimportant, so he wrote down anything he could remember. As he tried to write everything down in class, he would often find that he did not understand what the teacher was saying.

As a first step for notetaking, check the student's understanding and use of notetaking systems. Notetaking involves listening, memory, writing, and reviewing information. Different notetaking abilities are needed before, during, and after information is presented. Before a lecture begins, students need to be ready to listen both physically (e.g., sitting up straight) and mentally, and they need to be familiar with the subject matter and vocabulary. During the lecture, students need to be able to pay attention, distinguish important and unimportant information, paraphrase the information given, and highlight keywords and concepts within their notes. Some students need direct instruction in order to develop notetaking strategies to use in different situations. For instance, a student may need to learn how to identify keywords and use abbreviations when taking notes. The use of an inexpensive laptop computer can make the process of taking notes more efficient. After the notes are taken, students must also be able to review, edit, and study the content of the notes. Several specific techniques for notetaking are described in the next sections.

AWARE Method

The AWARE method of notetaking was developed to help students remember all the skills associated with notetaking (Suritsky & Hughes, 1993). This strategy teaches students to identify important information presented in a lecture. Table 10.4 presents the steps involved in the AWARE method.

> Dr. Mantell, John's history teacher, modeled the use of this strategy for her students. John could immediately see how this method would help him improve his notetaking skills. He also realized the importance of allotting a brief period of time each day for reviewing his notes.

Students who have difficulty with organization are also likely to have difficulty locating their notes later. John uses a separate notebook or folder for each subject; Stephanie likes having one notebook with sections for each subject.

When Ms. McGrew introduced notetaking skills to students, she modeled proper techniques by showing students a PowerPoint presentation with a handout. She demonstrated to students what they should be writing in their notes and what speakers may do to stress important information. For example, she explained that when teachers move closer to the class, the information is usually important. When teachers move away and lower their voices, the information is often less important. Other ways that teachers can assist students in notetaking include the following (Deshler et al., 1996):

1. Alter the rate at which material is presented during a lecture.
2. Provide visual aids.
3. Provide verbal and nonverbal lecture cues.
4. Use advance and post organizers.
5. Insert questions into the lecture.

When teachers incorporate each of these ideas, students can become more effective in their notetaking skills.

Table 10.4. Steps for the AWARE method of notetaking

Step 1	**A**rrange to take notes	Arrive early
		Take a seat near the front or center
		Obtain a pen and notebook
		Make note of the date
Step 2	**W**rite quickly	Indent minor points
		Record some words without vowels
Step 3	**A**pply cues	Attend to accent and organizational verbal cues
		Record cued lecture ideas
		Make a checkmark before cued ideas
Step 4	**R**eview notes as soon as possible	
Step 5	**E**dit notes	Add information you forgot to record
		Add personal details
		Supplement notes with details from readings

Source: Suritsky and Hughes (1993).

Verbal, Nonverbal, and Executive Functions

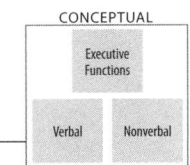
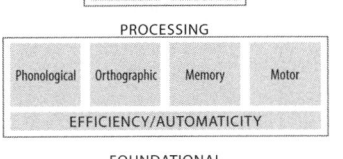
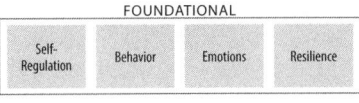

Time Management and Organizational Strategies

Time management can be a problem for any student, but effective time management skills are especially critical for secondary students with SLD or ADHD. These students may need extra time for completing reading and writing assignments, learning material from class notes, preparing for examinations, arranging for support services, scheduling appointments with instructors or tutors, and taking breaks to maintain focus during study sessions. Some students have problems with concepts of time (e.g., difficulty with being able to tell whether an impromptu conversation lasts 10 minutes or an hour, trouble estimating how long it will take to complete an activity). Setting priorities requires an additional set of skills. In addition, elementary school programs typically provide much more structure than is found in the high school environment, so secondary students have to take more responsibility for making decisions about how to manage their time themselves. The following strategies are recommended for students who need help learning to manage their time efficiently. Students should try a technique that appeals to them and then adopt it or modify it as needed. If the strategy seems ineffective, students can then discard it in favor of an alternative approach. The first step is determining an approach that works for the individual student.

How Hours Are Spent

Everyone has the same amount of time available—168 hours per week. Although much of that time is spent sleeping, an analysis of how the waking hours are spent may help students use their time more efficiently. Keeping a log of their activities for a week can help students develop an overview of how their time is spent.

　John complained that he was spending all his time at school or working on homework. His special education teacher encouraged him to keep a log of his activities. After completing his record, John and his teacher looked at it for patterns: how much time was spent in class; on entertainment and recreation; and on studying, sleeping, waiting, running errands, meeting family responsibilities, sending text messages, or engaging in extracurricular activities. His teacher asked John to identify which areas require more time and which areas consume more time than necessary. The teacher then asked John to make a plan for the next week in which he would indicate when he intended to do certain things: attend class, study, meet with tutors, meet with study groups and instructors, do chores, see friends, send text messages, watch television, play video games, and so forth. Throughout the next week, John recorded what he actually did.

At the end of that week, the log was compared with the plan. John discovered that he had spent more time playing video games and sending text messages to his friends than he thought that he would. He decided that the following week, he would spend less time on the computer and more time studying. Students need to learn to use time management tools, including daily planners, weekly schedules (a master list with recurring events recorded on it can be copied to save time), a monthly schedule, and a summary of major assignments. They need to be taught how to record information for each class systematically. John also found that he accomplished more when he developed a daily to-do list in the front of his daily planner. He also put the list on a dry-erase board in his bedroom.

Making Lists

Adults learn to write daily lists of what they hope to accomplish during a day or a week. Students can also make daily to-do lists that they carry with them. Younger students or students with writing difficulties can be asked to compose their lists aloud while someone else records what they describe or to dictate their list into a cell phone. The list can be created the night before in the daily planner, on a piece of notebook paper, on an index card, or on a cell phone. Once the list has been made, the student can number the tasks in order of priority. Students can add to the list as they realize that other tasks need to be done. Students also need to step back and look at the items on their lists that they do not accomplish. If the tasks are important, the student may need to work on strategies to accomplish more; if items aren't important, they should be removed from the list. Both Stephanie and Katy got more done in the classroom when tasks were explained and then written down in a series of steps. When they checked off completed items, they felt a sense of accomplishment.

Using Time Efficiently

As students progress through school, they need to take increased responsibility for using their time efficiently. A good study environment and a routine to make the most efficient use of study time become increasingly important; students, and sometimes their parents, can often use assistance in figuring out ways to minimize problems. At home, distractions can be avoided by hanging a "Do not disturb" sign on the door; turning off the television, computer, or stereo; and limiting telephone calls, text messaging, and video games to certain times. Teachers can encourage students to do the following:

- Develop specific agreements with their families about study time.
- Study the hardest or least interesting subject during their prime time. Prime time varies from student to student; more often than not, daylight hours are best.
- Include time for exercise, study breaks, and rewards. As students become older and homework assignments increase, they need to plan frequent breaks.
- Break term projects and big assignments into manageable, logical subgoals, and plot target completion dates on a time line and in a daily planner. Some students need assistance in determining the steps they need to take; others may have difficulty estimating the time they should allot. Assist the student in a review of how the project developed, identifying those steps they did well and those that need further attention.
- Take advantage of brief periods of time by having index cards with vocabulary words or key concepts that will be covered on a quiz.

Some students need a greater amount of time to complete their homework assignments. In the lower grades, a teacher often has a good sense of the effort that a project or assignment requires and how the child copes. Once students reach the point at which they have classes with several instructors, it can be hard to know the effect of multiple assignments. Asking students at the beginning of the school year about how they approach their assignments and what kind of time is required can help reduce the possibility of future homework problems.

Managing Procrastination

If students find themselves continually procrastinating, the following suggestions may help. Encourage students to do the following:

- Write down what is important about the task.
- Make large tasks manageable by breaking them into subgoals. Model this behavior routinely in the classroom.

Verbal, Nonverbal, and Executive Functions

- Tell others what they will do by a certain date and then have others check to see if they have met their goals.
- Earn a reward only when goals (or subgoals) are accomplished.
- Reschedule tasks that get postponed.
- Resist postponing important tasks. Identify one specific subgoal that can be accomplished; completing small steps can create the motivation to move forward with the larger task.

Getting Organized

Students can work on setting goals or establishing priorities by doing the following:

- Identify specific and realistic long-term and short-term goals. These should be used to provide structure for each class.
- Determine a plan to help attain goals by looking at the specific actions that need to be taken for each class, looking at what has worked in the past, and setting aside time each week to monitor progress.

Teach students to develop systems for organization that will help them retrieve information when they need it. Helpful strategies include the use of index cards or colored sticky notes, taking all notes in one notebook or on a computer, or placing all materials in labeled envelopes or file folders.

Organizing Materials

Students with SLD and ADHD often have difficulty with organizing materials for class. Although the selection of notebooks and folders is usually a matter of personal preference, a single-subject spiral notebook for each class that is color-coordinated with folders is an efficient way to organize. For classes in which many handouts are distributed, students may prefer a loose-leaf notebook. They may divide notebooks into sections chronologically, by topic, or by component (e.g., class notes, notes on readings, handouts, maps). Notes may be taken in a spiral notebook with perforations for neat removal after class to be filed in the loose-leaf notebook. A plastic zipper pencil case can be used for items such as pencils, disks, concept cards, or highlighters; inside pockets of loose-leaf notebooks are handy for storing frequently used items such as the syllabus. When using a loose-leaf notebook, all papers should be three-hole punched and put into the notebook in a logical place, and index dividers should be used and labeled appropriately. Teachers can help students learn to keep their backpacks, book bags, and so forth neat and organized and encourage students to get into the habit of keeping certain items, such as their daily planner, calculator, and pens and pencils, in certain pockets of the backpack. Another good habit for students to learn is to check their backpacks or desks at the end of every day for items that need to be filed or thrown out. John found that if he cleaned out the papers, organized his homework, and packed his backpack the night before, it saved time and reduced stress in the morning.

Most students benefit from the use of a clutter-free study area. Everyday materials, such as a hole punch, dictionary, index cards, highlighters, and an assignment calendar, can be arranged in a convenient place. Students can organize materials by class. For example, John found that by using and labeling folders and then keeping them in a plastic box, he could locate the materials for each class more easily. In addition, an area that is regularly identified for study often prompts or encourages the student to adopt behaviors that facilitate his or her studying.

Test-Taking Strategies

Students such as Katy and John find test taking frustrating. Their problems with language, in addition to problems with providing correct responses, often prevent them from understanding the tasks that they are expected to perform. They are also less likely to employ appropriate strategies in preparing for tests and are therefore more likely to develop test anxiety as a result of previous negative experiences.

Test-taking strategies can be grouped into two categories: 1) strategies for preparing for the examination and 2) strategies for taking the examination. Test taking is a way for teachers to evaluate knowledge, but students' performances depend not only on how hard they study and what they know but on how strategic they are in their approaches to tests. Davis, Sirotowitz, and Parker (1996) provided an extensive set of test-taking strategies. Appendix 10A contains a list of additional test-taking strategies.

Preparing for Tests

Attending class regularly, keeping current with assignments, using appropriate support (e.g., peer tutors, study groups, study guides), meeting with teachers, and making arrangements for appropriate accommodations (e.g., recorded textbooks, in-class notetakers, extended time for tests, alternative testing sites, alternative formats) set the stage for successful test taking. When a student is able to anticipate what the test will be like (i.e., what the format of the test will be, how much time will be allotted for the test, what material will be covered, and what types of answers the teacher expects), these skills become the basis for an effective study plan.

Dr. Mantell helped John plan backward from the date of the test for his history class. They talked about how much time would be needed to prepare for the test and how important the test was. They then used this information to formulate a study plan and timetable. John used his calendar and daily planner to record the steps of test preparation. Dr. Mantell shared a practice examination with the students in the class that was written in the same format. This helped John anticipate what types of questions would be on the test.

Two weeks before the test, John worked on bringing his assignments up to date. He then reviewed readings (e.g., annotations, notes, highlighted passages) and class notes and began to practice with study aids. Dr. Mantell encouraged him to ask questions and request clarification of information he found difficult. John made a point of identifying what had been emphasized in class and in his notes and identified key concepts and important details.

One week before the test, John wrote practice questions in the format of the test (i.e., multiple choice, matching, short answer, essay) and answered the practice test items. He outlined responses to essay questions, used flashcards for material that needed to be memorized, and made condensed study notes based on study materials. He also checked the end of his chapter units for sample questions. During the week of the test, John reviewed annotated and highlighted readings, notes, and handouts and made several critical concept cards (i.e., he reduced study notes to index cards). The day before the test, John reviewed his notes, reading material, and concept cards. Dr. Mantell also recognized that John sometimes had problems with understanding how to frame his responses. By helping him understand keywords often used in questions (e.g., *describe, discuss, analyze, outline, explain, illustrate, contrast*), John was able to improve the quality of his written responses.

When it was time to take his history test, John made sure that he had the materials he needed. He looked over the entire test and determined how much time he needed for each part before starting. For this test, John jotted down several dates he thought he might be asked about and quickly sketched out a mind map to help him remember. He also made sure to underline important

Verbal, Nonverbal, and Executive Functions

words in each of the questions. Then he did the shortest, easiest part of the test first. He saved the essay question for last because the objective questions would serve as warm-up exercises. He tried looking for information in subsequent test questions that he could use to answer other test items. He put a mark in the margin of the test page by questions that he wanted to come back to if he had enough time.

When John got his test results back, he had a B, two letter grades higher than on his last examination. Dr. Mantell asked him to look at which part of the test had the best score, and they talked about the strategies he had used and how they had helped. They also discussed what John had found difficult and looked carefully at his mistakes. Although John had responded to two questions quite well, he had misread instructions on one question. It was apparent that he had not yet grasped an important concept. They then discussed ways to use this information when it was time for John to prepare for his next test. Fortunately, John is highly motivated and wants to do well in his history class. He also has an extremely supportive teacher who understands John's difficulties with learning and is willing to take time to help John improve his study and test-taking skills.

Reducing Test Anxiety

Most people experience some level of anxiety when taking tests. Given the nature of SLD, students with a history of learning difficulties may be more vulnerable to test anxiety because of past failures. In addition, external distractors (e.g., noise, lighting, movement) and internal distractors (e.g., negative thoughts; bodily sensations such as tense muscles, increased heart rate, shallow breathing) can contribute to an already elevated level of anxiety.

In general, anxiety results from a sense of loss of control. Students need to understand that what is being tested is their knowledge, not their self-worth. John noted that sometimes, even when he felt well prepared, his mind would go totally blank when the test was placed in front of him. Several strategies, in addition to adequate preparation, can help students such as John reduce their anxiety.

Simple breathing and relaxation exercises (e.g., taking several deep breaths) can help students regain focus. Sitting up straight gives the body the message that it is time to be in a state of readiness; slouching tends to confirm that one should feel bad. Using a pen or pencil to underline or circle keywords in directions or in a question begins to shift the focus away from how the body is reacting. Covering questions with a blank piece of paper or with an arm can help keep the focus on the question at hand. Students can also practice positive self-talk. Johnson (1997) described several positive statements that a student might practice, such as the following:

- I can feel anxious and think at the same time.
- This is only anxiety. I've been through this before, and I can wait it out.
- Everything is going to be okay.
- I can do well on this test even though I feel afraid. (Or I think I can try this one question.)
- Take it slowly, one step at a time.
- Lots of people feel this way when they take tests; I'm not the only one.
- All I can do is my best.

CLASSROOM ADJUSTMENTS

Students with difficulties in language and reasoning often require specific adjustments in the curriculum to succeed. They may need a different set of instructional materials, simplified assignments, or shortened assignments. When selecting accommodations, teachers should check with the students to see whether or not they think that the accommodation would be beneficial. Students of any age do not like to feel that they differ significantly from peers, so sometimes it is necessary to make an accommodation available to all students. Appendix 10B (also available as a download) is a survey to use with students to help determine and discuss appropriate accommodations. If a student can read the survey, he or she may complete it independently. If not, the teacher can conduct the survey as an oral interview.

Alter the Difficulty Level

Students with difficulties in language and reasoning often need the difficulty level of assignments to be adjusted so that reading, writing, and problem-solving activities are geared to match their verbal ability. Again, this does not mean that the assignments are not challenging but rather that they are at an appropriate instructional level. Vygotsky (1978) described a concept that he referred to as the "zone of proximal development." This zone represents the gap between present performance levels and the level of learning that may be obtained when the student is paired with more knowledgeable others, such as a teacher or more knowledgeable peer. Good instruction, therefore, is provided at the upper bounds of an individual's knowledge when teachers and students work together to construct new knowledge (Englert, 1992).

Provide a Classroom Coach

Vygotsky (1978) also stressed the importance of social interaction as a means for expanding understanding. A student with weaknesses in verbal abilities may not understand classroom instructions or may need more guidance to interpret assignments. A simple way to resolve this difficulty is to find a peer who is willing and able to clarify class instructions as needed.

Katy knew that she could ask Stacy for clarification of instructions. Stacy was able to paraphrase the information and help Katy understand what she was supposed to do. Katy also knew that she could call Stacy at night when she needed clarifications about homework assignments.

Allow More Time and Practice

As a general rule, students with weaknesses in language often need more time than other students to process responses to questions. Attempt to break down and simplify information and tasks and encourage students to begin their response to oral questions by restating the question in their own words. Students such as Katy and John need many opportunities for repetition, rehearsal, practice, and feedback. They need to practice specific strategies and use the strategies in various settings. Whenever possible, demonstrate and discuss connections among concepts and do not let the textbook control the content delivered to the student. In other words, students must master concepts before moving on to new sets of information. It is far better for the students to complete several chapters successfully than to flounder through an entire book without ever grasping any of the ideas and concepts presented.

Verbal, Nonverbal, and Executive Functions

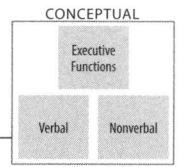
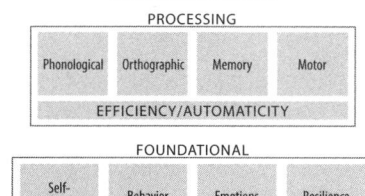

Consider Physical Classroom Arrangements

Some students benefit from sitting near the instructor or away from distracting noises such as air conditioners, heating systems, or doors that open and close frequently. The most effective seats for listening are often described as being in the "T" of the classroom. The front row forms the top of the T and the center row forms the line. John found it was easier for him to pay attention when sitting closer to where the teacher lectured.

Provide More than One Grade

Students with learning difficulties often feel discouraged when a paper is returned with a low grade and lots of corrections or comments. Provide feedback in ways that allow students to see the progress they have made as well as what they need to continue to work on. Positive feedback can help keep students motivated. Separate grades for content and presentation help students see the progress they are making while they struggle with difficulties such as poor spelling and punctuation. A grade can also be based on the amount of improvement from pretest to posttest. A student who went from 70% to 90% would receive the same grade as the student who went from 10% to 30%.

Base Grades on Individualized Education Program Goals

Some students need to have their grades based on accomplishment of their individualized education program (IEP) goals. Because of weaknesses in language and reasoning, they cannot be expected to accomplish the same tasks at the same rate as other students. The IEP is written to formulate appropriate goals and objectives on the basis of the learner's needs and characteristics. This does not mean that the curriculum is compromised but rather that the goals set for each student are realistic, challenging, and yet possible to achieve.

Provide Opportunities for Improvement

Students can quickly become overwhelmed by classes in which they perceive they only have one chance to "get it right." Motivation to improve can quickly be undermined. Devise assignments that can be developed in stages or that students can resubmit, in whole or part, to gain additional feedback, credit, or points.

CONCLUSION

To succeed in school, students need to possess a range of strategies that they can apply in varied settings. Instruction in strategies is an ongoing endeavor that varies according to the tasks students are asked to perform and the goals they are expected to meet. Modeling, demonstrations, and explanations are valuable approaches that help students increase verbal abilities and acquire an understanding of strategic approaches to learning. Active engagement in applying strategies such as those described in this chapter enables students to take control of their education, resulting in increased motivation and learning. Incorporating a variety of graphic organizers and visual supports can help students envision relationships among concepts and improve recall of information. Students also benefit from time spent teaching them how to study, take lecture notes, and prepare for examinations.

One fact is clear: Students with weaknesses in verbal abilities, nonverbal abilities, and executive functions need to have teachers who establish realistic expectations and set clear educational goals and objectives. Teachers must attempt to adjust explanations to the level of the student's understanding. This does not mean lowered expectations; it means formulating a program that is challenging but possible for the student to learn and succeed. As Vygotsky (1978) noted, good instruction is one step above a student's present performance level. With carefully designed instruction, students such as Katy, Stephanie, and John can become more strategic and successful in their learning.

APPENDIX 10A

Additional Strategies for Test Taking

This appendix outlines some ways in which students can improve their test-taking skills. Students can often improve their grades and test performance simply by paying attention to accuracy in recording answers and developing explicit strategies for answering different kinds of test questions.

RECORDING ANSWERS

Tests that require the use of a bubble sheet to record answers can be particularly problematic for some students. Students who have difficulty with lining up numbers to solve math problems or copying information from a chalkboard are also likely to have difficulty with transferring the response from the test to the sheet. Recording the answers directly in the text booklet allows a student to demonstrate command of the subject without being penalized for copying errors. If this is not possible, a teacher may remind the student to do the following:

- Check to be sure that the number on the answer sheet coincides with the number of the test item in the test booklet. Recheck when turning a page and when moving to a new row or column on the answer sheet.
- Consider completing the test by recording answers on the test pages and then transposing answers to the answer sheet.

PIRATES TEST-TAKING STRATEGY

The PIRATES test-taking strategy (Hughes, Schumaker, Deshler, & Mercer, 1988) was developed to help students in middle and high school improve performance on objective tests. Table 10A.1 outlines the steps included in the PIRATES strategy.

TEST FORMATS

Although some students seem to understand how to address test questions, other students need to develop overt strategies and practice step-by-step approaches that they can apply when trying to respond to test questions.

Multiple-Choice Questions

The following suggestions can be helpful for students to keep in mind while answering multiple-choice questions:

- Cover the answers, read the stem of the question, and predict what answer should follow before looking at the choices.

Table 10A.1. The steps for the PIRATES test-taking strategy

Step 1	**P**repare to succeed	Put your name and PIRATES on the test
		Allot time and order to sections
		Say affirmations
		Start within 2 minutes
Step 2	**I**nspect the instructions	Read instructions carefully
		Underline what to do and where to respond
		Notice special requirements
Step 3	**R**ead, remember, reduce	
Step 4	**A**nswer or abandon	
Step 5	**T**urn back	
Step 6	**E**stimate	Avoid absolutes
		Choose the longest or most detailed choice
		Eliminate similar choices
Step 7	**S**urvey	Review the answers before handing it in

Source: Hughes, Schumaker, Deshler, and Mercer (1988).

- Read the stem with each choice.
- Read each answer choice and try to eliminate obviously incorrect or impossible options. If writing on the test is permitted, cross out incorrect options to help focus on the right response. Eliminating obviously incorrect options can help significantly if you are unsure about the answer. For a question that has four options, if you eliminate two options, the possibility of guessing the right answer is 50%.
- Code the question to make it easier to go back to later if you are uncertain of the correct response and watch for information in subsequent test items that may help answer the question.
- Reread the test question with the option that has been chosen. Subvocalizing the answer can help you make sure that it sounds correct and can help you read exactly what is there.
- Be sure that the answer sounds right grammatically.
- Watch out for phrases such as "All the following except...."
- When answering a question stated in the negative, try stating it in the positive first and consider the answers. Then select the best answer after rereading the question in the negative.
- Ask for clarification if a question seems ambiguous. If clarification is not an option, select the best answer and briefly indicate why that answer seems best, perhaps adding a note that indicates that the question was difficult to understand.

If the student has no idea of the correct answer, teach him or her the ACE strategy, which is part of the PIRATES strategy (Hughes et al., 1988):

A: Avoid absolutes (*always, never*).

C: Choose the longest and most detailed answer.

E: Eliminate similar answers.

Verbal, Nonverbal, and Executive Functions

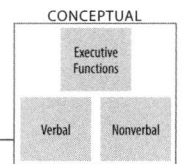
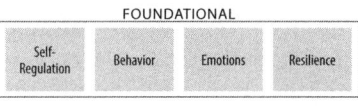

Fill-in-the-Blank Questions

The following suggestions are helpful to keep in mind while answering fill-in-the-blank questions:

- Try to predict what is being asked and how the question should be answered while reading it.
- Write enough to let the instructor know that you understand the concept even if you cannot provide the specific response.
- Search for information in other test items that may help with fill-in-the-blank questions.

Matching Questions

The following suggestions are helpful to keep in mind while answering matching questions:

- Check directions to determine if answers may be used more than once.
- Try to determine what would be an appropriate answer before looking at the options.

True/False Questions

The following suggestions are helpful to keep in mind while answering true/false questions:

- Read each statement carefully.
- Beware of words such as *always, never, all,* and *none*; these words frequently are used in statements that are false.

Short-Answer Questions

The following suggestions are helpful to keep in mind while answering short-answer questions:

- Read each question carefully.
- Be brief but complete.
- Make sure the response answers the question asked.
- If you are unsure, use information from the rest of the test to help jog your memory or confirm your answers.

Essay Questions

The following suggestions can be helpful to keep in mind while answering essay questions:

- Read directions carefully. Do all questions require an answer? If not, how many need to be answered?
- Read each question carefully.
- Develop a topic sentence that paraphrases the main question (e.g., The major reasons that the . . .).

- Outline a response. If time runs out, partial credit might be given for the information in the outline.
- Be sure to respond to all parts of the question.
- Start with the strongest point. Be clear and concise.
- Get to the point relatively quickly and avoid adding irrelevant information.
- Be familiar with key essay words (for specific suggestions, see Ellis, 1994).

APPENDIX **10B**

Instructional Accommodations Survey

Instructional Accommodations Survey

Student Name: _____   Teacher: _____

Directions: Indicate whether you think you would benefit from the following instructional accommodations if your teachers provided them for you.

If you think the accommodation would be helpful for you, mark *Yes*. If you think it would not be helpful, mark *No*. If you are unsure if it would be helpful, mark *Unsure*.

Yes	Unsure	No	**INSTRUCTION**
☐	☐	☐	1. For topics the class is studying, have the teacher suggest videos to help you learn the material.
☐	☐	☐	2. Have more time to think about the teacher's question before answering.
☐	☐	☐	3. Have a secret way for the teacher to remind you to go back to work when you are distracted.
☐	☐	☐	4. For social studies or science, have the teacher show an outline of the lesson before it starts.

CLASSWORK AND HOMEWORK

Yes	Unsure	No	**Reading**
☐	☐	☐	1. Have shorter reading assignments.
☐	☐	☐	2. Have larger print on reading materials.
☐	☐	☐	3. Have more space between lines of print on reading materials.
☐	☐	☐	4. Have reading assignments available on a computer or audio recording so you can listen and follow the text at the same time.
☐	☐	☐	5. Be given easier reading but on the same topics that the class is studying.
☐	☐	☐	6. Use an electronic dictionary.

Instructional Accommodations Survey *(continued)*

Yes	Unsure	No	**Writing**
☐	☐	☐	1. Have shorter writing assignments.
☐	☐	☐	2. Dictate papers rather than write them.
☐	☐	☐	3. Have a proofreader check your written work.
☐	☐	☐	4. Substitute oral presentations for written projects.
☐	☐	☐	5. Have class notes given to you, rather than take notes yourself.
☐	☐	☐	6. Use an electronic spell checker.
☐	☐	☐	7. Have fewer spelling words to study on spelling tests.

Yes	Unsure	No	**Math**
☐	☐	☐	1. On math assignments, have fewer problems to complete.
☐	☐	☐	2. On math worksheets, have more space between the problems.
☐	☐	☐	3. Have math problems on a worksheet rather than copying them from the book.
☐	☐	☐	4. Use a calculator or table of math facts.

Yes	Unsure	No	**General**
☐	☐	☐	1. Have extra time to complete class assignments.
☐	☐	☐	2. Use a timer to help keep track of how much time is left to finish an assignment.
☐	☐	☐	3. Have a check-off list for tasks that have a lot of parts or steps.

Yes	Unsure	No	**HOMEWORK**
☐	☐	☐	1. Do extra credit projects.
☐	☐	☐	2. Have an extra set of books to keep at home.
☐	☐	☐	3. Have help or reminders to write assignments in assignment book.
☐	☐	☐	4. Have a reminder to hand in homework.

Instructional Accommodations Survey (continued)

Yes	Unsure	No	**TESTS**
☐	☐	☐	1. Have extra time to complete tests.
☐	☐	☐	2. Take tests in a quiet place.
☐	☐	☐	3. Answer test questions orally rather than in writing.
☐	☐	☐	4. Take multiple-choice tests instead of essay tests.
☐	☐	☐	5. Take essay tests instead of multiple-choice tests.
☐	☐	☐	6. Take tests on a computer so you can type your answers.
☐	☐	☐	7. Use a calculator on math tests.
☐	☐	☐	8. Mark answers on the question sheet rather than on a bubble sheet.
☐	☐	☐	9. Have short quizzes on smaller portions of a unit.

Yes	Unsure	No	**SEATING**
☐	☐	☐	1. Sit in or near the front of the room.
☐	☐	☐	2. Sit near the board.
☐	☐	☐	3. Sit close to the teacher.
☐	☐	☐	4. Sit near students who won't distract you.

APPENDIX **10C**

Apps for Visual Imagery, Notetaking, Time Management, and Test-Taking Instruction

Visual imagery apps	
Popplet by Notion Students can capture facts, thoughts, and images and learn to create relationships among them.	$4.99
MindMeister by MeisterLabs Students can create mind maps that allow them to see relationships within and between topics. Maps created can be worked on at home and school as well as on the go.	Free
MindMash by Numlock Business Solutions Co. Students can create ideas and mash them up by combining and manipulating text, images, and drawings in a visual and free-form manner.	Free
iBrainstorm by Universal Mind Students are able to share thoughts and ideas on a variety of topics with others.	Free
Inspiration Maps VVP by Inspiration Software, Inc. Students can use diagrams and plots to display, integrate, and critically analyze large amounts of information in ways that are easy to understand and help reveal relationships and patterns.	$9.99
Kidspiration Maps Lite by Inspiration Software, Inc. Students combine pictures, text, numbers, and spoken words to develop vocabulary, word recognition, reading for comprehension, writing, and critical thinking skills.	Free
Notetaking apps	
Notability by Ginger Labs Students are able to import the teachers' materials onto their devices so that they have the ability to add their own thoughts during class.	$4.99
EverClip 2 by Ignition Soft Ltd. Students can copy any class handout or document; automatically import it to EverClip; edit, annotate, and organize it; and then send it to Evernote.	$5.99
iNotes for iPad by Anson Li This app allows students to type text, draw lines to annotate the text, draw charts by hand, or take pictures to enhance their notetaking abilities.	Free
N+OTES by REIU Ltd. Students can take notes and then create folders based on subject, date, or time for easy organization. Students can e-mail, tweet, and set simple reminders with this app.	Free
Write 2 Lite by Daniel V.W. Students can take notes, write, and edit on documents. Once all edits are complete, students can synch notes to Dropbox.	Free
Penultimate by Evernote This app allows students to utilize digital handwriting on all class handouts and documents as well as take notes during class. Once done, these notes can be organized within Evernote.	Free

(continued)

Conceptual Blocks

Time-management apps

MyLifeOrganized 2 by Andriy Tkachuk — Free
Tasks and subtasks can be created to assist students in keeping track of their commitments.

Toggl Time by Toggl — Free
Students are able to type in the task they are working on, turn the timer on while working on the task, and then turn it off when the task is complete. Students can then develop spreadsheets and graphs that give the insight into how they are using their time.

Tooledo by Toodledo — $2.99
Students can use this productivity tool to organize to-do lists and notes.

To-Do Lists Mobile by Antlogic — $1.99
This app allows students to manage all tasks.

Focus Time by Peer Assembly — $4.99
This app assists students in focusing on task at hand by breaking up tasks into 25-minute intervals with 5-minute breaks. It can also track how long students are taking on different tasks to assist students in better utilizing their time.

Test-taking apps

Prepzilla by gWhiz, LLC — Free
Students can browse test preparation titles from various sources and choose to prepare on their own or challenge friends on the chosen topic.

Flashcards+ by Connor Zwick — Free
Students can create and study flashcards without the hassle of writing them out by hand. They also can choose from decks made by others. The audio feature allows flashcards to be read to students if needed.

gFlash+ Flashcards & Tests by gWhiz, LLC — Free
Students can create, download, and manipulate flashcards and tests in all subject areas. Students can also develop a matching game study mode.

Flash cards by Anki — Free
Students and teachers can create flashcards and decks for studying any type of material.
  http://ankisrs.net/
This web site links to Windows, MacOS, Linux/BSD, IOS, and Android clients.
  https://ankiweb.net/
This is the web version and the place to get shared decks. Most shared decks are for foreign language study or test preparation.

Algebra Touch by Regular Berry Software, LLC — $2.99
This app allows students to brush up on their overall algebra skills.

Khan Academy by Khan Academy — Free
This application offers students a video education system covering subjects such as biology, chemistry, physics, math, civics, finance, art history, and much more.

Exam Support with Andrew Johnson by Michael Schnieder — $2.99
This app helps students deal with the nerves they encounter before an exam. It offers guided meditation sessions to help students improve focus or concentration and overcome anxiety.

CHAPTER 11 OUTLINE

READING COMPREHENSION AND WRITTEN EXPRESSION

TEXT STRUCTURE

- Narrative Text Structure: Story Grammar
- Expository Text Structure

READING COMPREHENSION STRATEGIES

- RAP
- Reciprocal Teaching
- Collaborative Strategic Reading
- SQ3R
- ReQuest Procedure
- Multipass
- PORPE

WRITTEN LANGUAGE STRATEGIES

- The Process of Writing
- Self-Regulated Strategy Development
- Cognitive Strategy in Writing Program
- Cohesion
- Paragraphs
- Essays
- Research

MATH PROBLEM SOLVING

- Mathematical Knowledge
- Instructional Concerns
- Instructional Format
- Instructional Sequence
- Language and Mathematics
- Story or Word Problem Strategies
- Cue Cards
- Effective Strategy Instruction
- Effective Teaching Strategies for Advanced Math Courses
- Software Selection and Math Instruction

CONCLUSION

APPENDIX 11A: SYNONYMS FOR WORDS THAT CHILDREN COMMONLY USE IN WRITING

APPENDIX 11B: APPS TO SUPPORT LITERACY INSTRUCTION

CHAPTER **11**

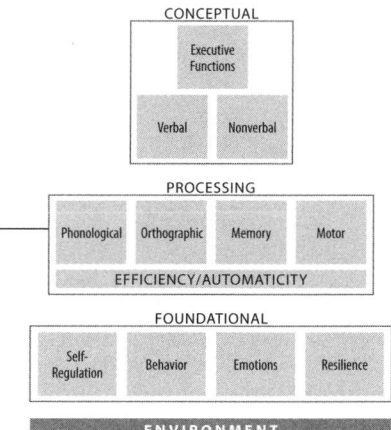

Instruction in Reading Comprehension, Written Expression, and Math Problem Solving

with Ann M. Richards

Our abilities to understand what we read, express our ideas in writing, and solve math story problems are based on several factors: fluent reading and writing, background and conceptual knowledge, vocabulary, and interest. These abilities are supported by the three higher level abilities in the Conceptual blocks: Verbal, Nonverbal, and Executive Functions. This chapter addresses instruction in reading comprehension, written expression, and math problem solving.

READING COMPREHENSION AND WRITTEN EXPRESSION

To date, most states have adopted the Common Core State Standards (CCSS). Regardless of whether or not a state follows the standards, they do outline many of the critical skills that students need to acquire in school. The CCSS (2014) delineate skills in reading, writing, speaking, listening, and language under the category of English Language Arts Standards. This supports the research that contends that teaching students strategy instruction in one of these domains affects the others (e.g., Ahmed, Wagner, & Lopez, 2014; Herbert, Gillespie, & Graham, 2013; Senokossoff & Fine, 2013). The CCSS state that students who achieve these standards are able to demonstrate independence; build strong content knowledge; respond to the varying demands of audience, task, purpose, and discipline; comprehend as well as critique; value evidence; use technology and digital media strategically and capably; and demonstrate the understanding of other perspectives and cultures. To accomplish these standards, teachers must instruct students in how to elicit key ideas and details, integrate knowledge and ideas, and understand how the craft and structure of different texts affect content and style.

These types of skills are difficult for students with weaknesses in the Conceptual blocks.

John, a high school student, struggled with the concepts presented in his content-area textbooks because of limited knowledge. He had trouble answering test questions based on the information presented. For John, summarizing what he had read seemed impossible because he had trouble distinguishing important from unimportant information, which then made it difficult to organize his thoughts for writing.

Fortunately, strategies exist that can help students such as John understand and recall information from text and express their ideas in writing.

TEXT STRUCTURE

One important aspect of instruction is to teach students about how different texts are structured. Comprehension of text often improves if students understand how texts are structured and then write about the topics that they have read. This increased level of comprehension occurs because, to write, students must remember, analyze, connect, and manipulate information to justify their point of view (Graham & Hebert, 2011). Explicit instruction in text structure strategies helps students increase their knowledge and use of text structure and improves the cohesion and organization of their writing (Lienemann, Graham, Leader-Janssen, & Reid, 2006; Williams, 2005; Williams, Hall, & Lauer, 2004). Two basic types of text structure exist: narrative and expository. Narrative text typically refers to fictional stories, whereas expository text refers to nonfictional passages.

Narrative Text Structure: Story Grammar

An effective way to help students increase understanding of narrative text and improve narrative writing is to teach them how to use story grammar. Story grammar simply refers to the underlying structure of a story. Story grammar instruction can be used as a prereading or prewriting strategy or as a postreading activity. Koutsoftas and Gray (2012) suggested that the oral storytelling aspect of story grammar also be included when teaching writing so skills from each task can support the other.

As noted previously, many children do not realize that comprehension requires attention, effort, and monitoring.

Shannon, one of Katy's classmates in fifth grade, wrote the story, presented in Figure 11.1, about a "qwen." After she had written her first draft, Katy was assigned as a peer editor to read her story and make suggestions for revision. Katy told Shannon that she thought her story was just fine but reminded her that she was supposed to write along the line at the left side of the paper. Shannon then added in the arrows. Shannon did not describe the character of Tammy in much detail, other than that she was "pretty" and had "pretty shoes." Direct instruction in story grammar can help students such as Katy and Shannon improve their narrative writing skills.

Simple Story Grammars

Students may be introduced to the concept of story grammar as early as kindergarten or first grade. When first discussing story grammar, a teacher may tell students that every story has three parts—a beginning, a middle, and an end—and then draw three circles and connect them with arrows to illustrate this sequence. To practice this concept, a teacher may review a common fairy tale or fable, such as *The Tortoise and the Hare,* and ask the students, "What happened at the beginning? The middle? The end?" The students can then retell the main events of the fable in their own words.

Instruction in Reading Comprehension, Written Expression, and Math Problem Solving

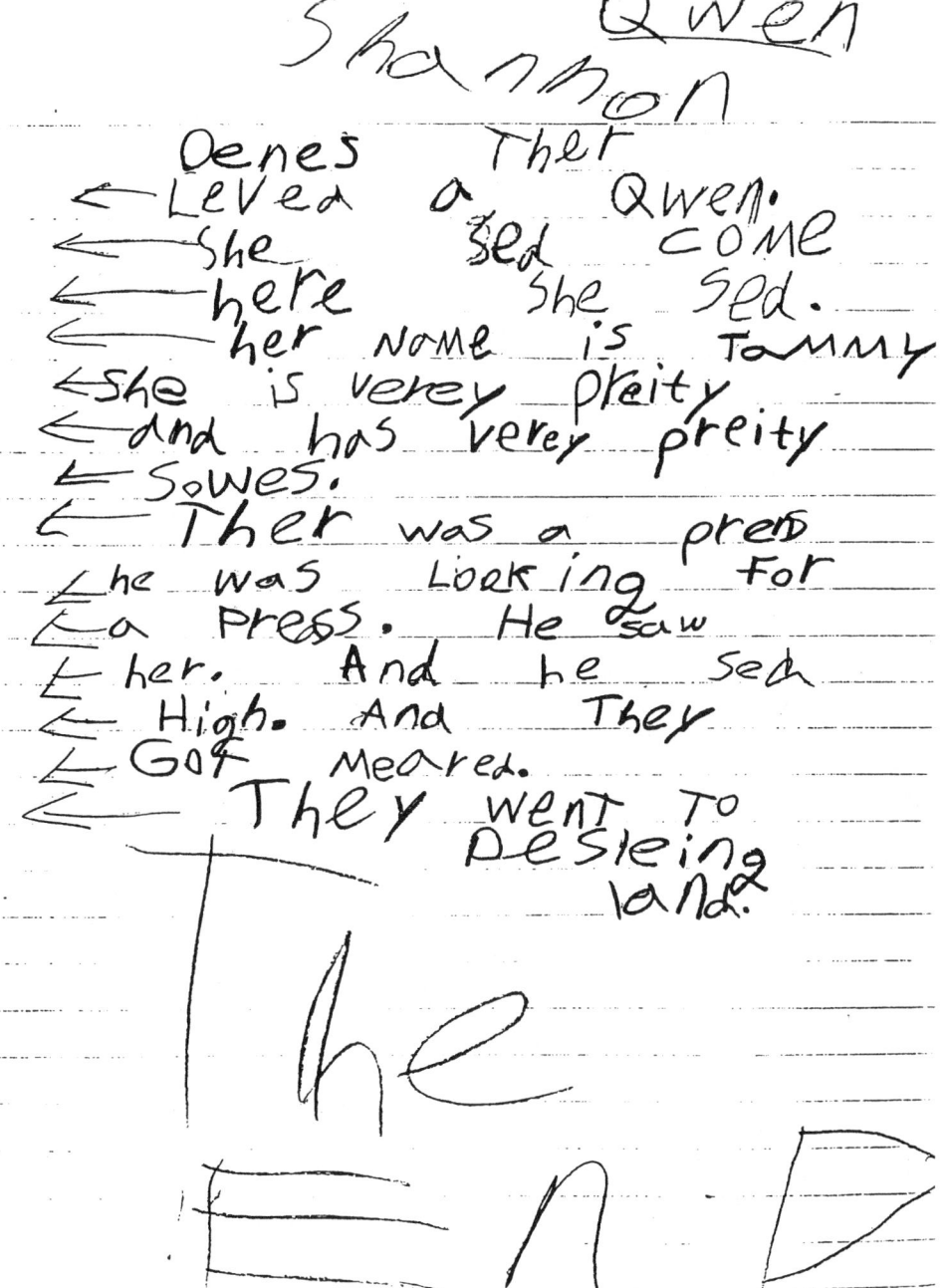

Figure 11.1. Shannon's story.

Story Grammar Components

By second or third grade, teachers can introduce more detailed story grammars, including the following general elements:

405

1. *The setting:* Where and when does the story take place?
2. *The main characters:* Who is the story about?
3. *The problem:* What happens to the main character?
4. *The solution:* What does the main character do to solve the problem?
5. *The ending:* How is the story resolved?

As students increase their knowledge about story grammar, more complex elements can be introduced. Ms. Moore, John's English teacher, used the following seven categories of story elements (Montague & Graves, 1993; Stein & Glenn, 1979):

1. *Major setting:* The main character is introduced.
2. *Minor setting:* The time and place of the story are described.
3. *Initiating event:* The atmosphere is changed and the main character responds.
4. *Internal response:* The characters' thoughts, ideas, emotions, and intentions are noted.
5. *Attempt:* The main character's goal-related actions are represented.
6. *Direct consequence:* The attainment of the goal is noted; if the goal is not attained, the changes resulting from the attempt are noted.
7. *Reaction:* The main character's thoughts and feelings in regard to the outcome are specified, along with the effect of the outcome on the character.

Thinking about these categories improved John's comprehension of short stories.

When asking students to recall a story that they have read or when helping them prepare to write a story, use story grammar to guide points for the discussion. Provide students with a list of elements to include in their story. When students with learning disabilities are given cue cards, check-off systems, mnemonics to implement, and self-regulation techniques for story parts, the quality of their story writing improves (Graves & Montague, 1991; Lane et al., 2010; Watanabe & Hall-Kenyon, 2011). Figure 11.2 presents a sample cue card.

Character Development

In addition to strategies to assist with organization, some students benefit from instruction in character development. The following questions help students expand their descriptions of the physical appearance, the speech and actions, and the thoughts and emotions of the main characters (Leavell & Ioannides, 1993):

1. *Physical appearance:* What does the person look like?
2. *Speech and actions:* What does the person say? What does the person do?
3. *Thoughts and emotions:* What does the character think about? What emotions does the person display? How does the character feel about the outcome?

☐ Describe the main characters.
☐ Describe the setting.
☐ Explain how a problem develops.
☐ Explain how the characters attempt to solve the problem.
☐ Describe how the characters feel.
☐ Create an ending.

Figure 11.2. Sample cue card.

Instruction in Reading Comprehension, Written Expression, and Math Problem Solving

Before using this strategy, read two paragraphs to students: one paragraph in which the main character has been fully developed and another in which only minimal information is given. Encourage students to discuss the differences between the two paragraphs and note how detailed descriptions can help readers increase their understanding of the appearance and feelings of characters.

Story Maps

Graphic organizers can also help students pay attention to relevant information and to understand story elements. The ability to understand these details can help students plan a story prior to writing. Story maps provide a structure in which to record and organize elements of a story. These simple steps can be used to create a map:

1. Have students brainstorm ideas.
2. Help them organize the ideas on the map and then subcategorize these ideas under characters, setting, problem, and ending.
3. Help students incorporate the information on the map into a story.
4. As skill increases, encourage students to take more responsibility for developing and organizing their own maps.

Story maps can also help students with a particular aspect of story grammar. By using story mapping to teach story grammar, teachers assist students in identifying story grammar elements when reading narrative texts (Boulineau, Fore, Hagan-Burke, & Burke, 2004).

John was reading a novel for his English class that involved many characters. He was having trouble remembering the relationships among the characters. To help organize and remember the characters, John constructed a character map. He wrote each character's name in a circle, drew lines between characters with a relationship, and then wrote the relationship on the line, such as "sisters." Whenever he needed clarification regarding the characters, he consulted the map.

Questioning

Initially, some students will require increased structure to incorporate elements of story grammar into their writing. Prior to writing, ask students to answer specific questions pertaining to the setting, problem, and ending.

Setting

Characters

Who is the main character?

Who are the other characters?

What do you know about these characters?

What do they look like?

What do they act like?

What do they do?

How do they feel about what is happening?

What emotions do they display?

How are the characters alike? How do they differ?

Time

When does the story occur?

What is the time of year?

Place

Where does the story occur?

What is the place like?

The Problem

What is the main problem?

Are there other, minor problems?

How does the main character plan to solve the problem?

How do other characters respond to the problem?

The Solution

How is the problem resolved?

How does the story end?

How do the characters feel at the end?

STATE the Story

Some students benefit from having a mnemonic to help them remember the steps of strategies more easily. One example is STATE the story (Goldstein & Mather, 1998):

Setting (Who? What? Where? When?)

Trouble (What is the trouble or problem?)

Action (What happens?)

Turning point (What is done to resolve the problem?)

End (How does the story end?)

As students are reviewing a story or planning to write a story, encourage them to answer each of these elements. These steps can be written on the board or students can keep cue cards on their desks.

STORE the Story

Another example of a first-letter mnemonic strategy is STORE the story (Schlegel & Bos, 1986):

Setting (Who? What? Where? When?)

Trouble (What is the trouble or problem?)

Order of action (What happens?)

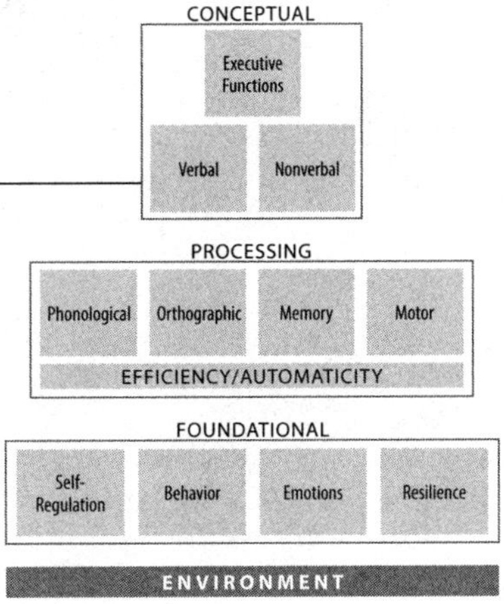

Instruction in Reading Comprehension, Written Expression, and Math Problem Solving

Resolution (What is done to solve the problem?)

End (How does the story end?)

To introduce the strategy, discuss the meaning of the verb *to store* (e.g., save, hold, keep for a while, put away) and explain to the students that the purpose of the strategy is to help them understand and remember (i.e., store) any story that they read by recognizing and recalling each part or to help them organize the components of a story prior to writing.

Using the STORE format, guide the students to create a group story. Then brainstorm ideas for the story and fill in the STORE cue sheet, crossing out ideas and adding others until satisfied. Students next read over the cue sheet to make sure that all parts make sense and fit in relation to other parts. When students need additional support, provide them with certain elements of the story or have them work with peers to complete the cue sheet. Figure 11.3 provides a sample cue sheet for using the STORE strategy.

C-SPACE

The mnemonic C-SPACE (MacArthur, Schwartz, & Graham, 1991) may be used as a prewriting strategy. Prior to writing, ask the students to think about 1) who will read the story and 2) what kind of story he or she wants to write. Next, the student takes notes on the story, using the following mnemonic:

C Who is the *character*?

S What is the *setting*?

P What is the *problem* or *purpose*?

STORE the Story

Name _____ Date _____

Title _____

SETTING
  Who _____
  Where _____
  When _____

TROUBLE _____
_____
_____

ORDER
  OF ACTION 1. _____
                2. _____
                3. _____
                4. _____

RESOLUTION _____
_____
_____

ENDING _____
_____

Figure 11.3. Sample cue sheet for the STORE strategy.

A What *action* occurs?

C What is the *conclusion?*

E What is the *emotion* of the character?

As the final step, have students write stories by expanding on their notes.

W-W-W, What = 2, How = 2 Strategy

A similar mnemonic strategy, W-W-W, What = 2, How = 2 (Graham & Harris, 1989), may be used as a prewriting strategy. Prior to writing, students answer the following questions:

1. *Who* is the main character? *Who* else is in the story?
2. *When* does the story take place?
3. *Where* does the story take place?
4. *What* does the main character do?
5. *What* happens when he or she tries to do it?
6. *How* does the story end?
7. *How* does the main character feel?

This strategy may be used with a picture stimulus as a basis for writing. Before a student attempts to use the self-instructional strategy, model and demonstrate it while thinking out loud using these steps:

1. Instruct students to look at the picture.
2. Tell students to use their imaginations.
3. Have students write down the story-part reminder (W-W-W, What = 2, How = 2).
4. Have students write down ideas for each part.
5. Have students write their stories.
6. Have students read their stories as a group activity.
7. Have the group discuss which elements of the stories are missing and how and where they can be added.
8. Have students add the missing elements.

Provide guidance until students can compose stories independently using the strategy.

Expository Text Structure

Although instruction in story narratives is often an appropriate place to begin with young readers and writers, specific instruction in expository structures is needed at all levels (Englert & Mariage, 1991; Jitendra, Burgess, & Gajria, 2011). Expository text differs from narrative text in that it is written to represent the relationship between ideas; it is not simply a telling of a sequence of events. Students must learn the underlying concepts in several different types of expository structures to succeed in higher grades (Watson, Gable, Gear, & Hughes, 2012; Westby, 1994). Examples of expository text structures are sequential, description, compare and contrast, and cause and effect. A writer can also combine two or more different structures. Beginning in first grade, students can be taught to write simple expository paragraphs about interesting topics, such as dinosaurs, insects, and animals.

A three-phase study by Williams (2005) explored the effects of explicitly teaching a text structure program to second-grade at-risk readers. The following components and key elements of a successful text structure program were identified: 1) instruction in clue words; 2) trade book reading and discussion to supplement expository sources (i.e., encyclopedias, text books); 3) vocabulary development; 4) reading and analysis of target paragraphs focusing on compare–contrast structure; 5) graphic organizers; 6) compare–contrast strategy questions; 7) written summaries with a paragraph frame as support; and 8) review of vocabulary and the strategies at the end of each lesson. The results suggested that when provided with highly structured and explicit instruction that focuses on text structure, children at risk for reading failure show gains in comprehension, including the ability to transfer what they have learned to novel texts.

In later grades, different text structures can form the basis for instruction in paragraph and essay writing. Using a student's writing, model the process and provide positive and corrective feedback (Moran, 1988). Whichever strategies are employed, the structures and processes of writing need to be made apparent to students (Englert & Mariage, 1991). Stewart (1992) provided the following general guidelines for teaching specific writing skills, including text structure organization:

1. Provide direct instruction in writing by modeling and teaching writing strategies.
2. Emphasize high-level skills that focus on content and organization.
3. Control the task difficulty by isolating target objectives.
4. Teach students to use text structure to plan, generate, and monitor their writing.
5. Teach students to plan, implement, and monitor their use of strategies.
6. Integrate writing instruction with the curriculum.

Summarization

Findings from a literature review conducted by Kim, Linan-Thompson, and Misquitta (2012) indicated that summarization was one of the leading strategies that affected reading outcomes. One easy method for helping students learn to summarize that integrates a reading comprehension and writing strategy is to have students ask two questions after reading a paragraph: 1) Who or what was the paragraph about? 2) What was happening in the paragraph? (Malone & Mastropieri, 1992). Place a blank line or sticky note after each paragraph and have students write a summary sentence for each. Many e-books now come with the ability to write a "sticky" note and attach them to the text while reading.

When Katy was reading a chapter in her content-area textbooks, her teacher had her place a sticky note by the side of each paragraph. After reading each paragraph, Katy would then write a summary sentence on the note. She then moved all her sentences in order onto a page in her notebook and used them to guide her writing. Using this technique, she was able to write a complete and accurate summary of the chapter events. This summary then served as a study guide for quizzes.

READING COMPREHENSION STRATEGIES

The National Reading Panel (2000) found that students' text comprehension improved when teachers demonstrated and then had students apply various strategies, such as answering and generating questions and summarizing what was read. This section describes several easy-to-use examples of research-based strategies. The purpose of these strategies is to help students recognize important information, formulate and answer questions, and increase their ability to explain and discuss what they have read. Instruction in these strategies can help students improve their understanding and increase their retention of information. Several of these strategies use a first-letter mnemonic. These types of strategies can help students remember the various steps of a task.

RAP

As an upper-elementary school student, Katy benefited from a simple paraphrasing strategy developed by Schumaker, Denton, and Deshler (1984). The acronym RAP represents three steps:

Read the paragraph.

Ask what the main ideas and details in this paragraph were.

Put the main ideas into your own words.

By using this strategy for each paragraph, Katy became actively involved and increased her understanding of the material. By attempting to transform the text into her own words, she was able to monitor her level of understanding.

Reciprocal Teaching

The reciprocal teaching procedure (Palinscar & Brown, 1986) can be used with small groups in general education classrooms. This procedure includes the following four skills: questioning, summarizing, clarifying, and predicting. The first two skills, questioning and summarizing, help students learn to identify and paraphrase the most important information in the text. To begin, students may read a paragraph or passage together. After the passage is completed, they generate questions together about what has been read and then summarize the content in a sentence or two. For clarifying, students discuss any difficult or hard-to-understand sections and review the meaning of any new vocabulary. For the final skill, students predict what will happen in the next passage. The process of making predictions helps students link background knowledge with the new information. As students practice these procedures, they can take more responsibility for developing questions, summarizing the content, and making predictions about the next section. Activities involving self-questioning and comprehension monitoring promote active involvement with the reading process.

Collaborative Strategic Reading

Collaborative strategic reading (CSR) is an intensive classroom or group-based reading comprehension strategy similar to reciprocal teaching that is designed to be used with expository text (Vaughn & Klingner, 1999). The focus of the strategy is to assist readers in gaining skills on how to think and interact with the text (Vaughn et al., 2011). CSR works best when implemented within an elementary or high school class structure so that students use it over time and with a series of instructors. Vaughn and colleagues found that CSR was easily included into English language arts classrooms and resulted in increased reading comprehension scores.

Instruction in Reading Comprehension, Written Expression, and Math Problem Solving

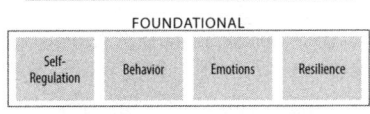

Successful implementation requires that teachers model the strategies, provide ongoing examples and opportunities, and guide and provide feedback over an extended period of time. CSR integrates four specific reading comprehension strategies to teach students how to become active, effective readers.

Step 1: Preview

The first step develops students' interest in what they are reading, activates background knowledge, and encourages students to make predictions about what they will read. To illustrate the concept of previewing, discuss how movie previews make viewers begin to develop expectations and interest in upcoming movies. Once students understand the concept, model the tasks of previewing: Read the title; look at any pictures, graphs, or diagrams; read the headings and try to anticipate what they mean; look for keywords (e.g., words that are underlined, italicized, in bold, or set off); and read the first and last paragraphs. As a final task, have students predict what they think will be learned from the reading. After this procedure has been demonstrated, the class practices the preview step several times over the next few days, and the teacher provides feedback and support.

Step 2: Click and Clunk

In the second step, students learn to monitor their reading, determining what they already know and what causes difficulty. A click occurs when the reader identifies something he or she knows (it clicks because it makes sense). A clunk is a word or point that the student does not understand. For this step, the teacher can model clicks and clunks and then ask students to write down their own clunks after reading a short assignment. Once students learn to recognize clunks, demonstrate strategies to address them. Strategies might include use of a glossary or a dictionary, rereading, discussion with a peer, and so forth. The teacher asks the students to identify the strategy they would choose to address each clunk so that they learn which strategies work best in which situations.

Step 3: Get the Gist

For the third step, each student summarizes the main idea of a paragraph in 10–12 words and then discusses and offers different versions. Students provide evidence to support their summary and exclude unnecessary details. The students then vote on which summary is best. After making their choices, they must also explain why.

Step 4: Wrap-Up

During wrap-up, the students review the reading and what has been learned by asking and responding to questions. Depending on the age group, the teacher may provide question stems, such as the following:

How would you compare and contrast ____?

How were they the same or different?

How would you interpret ____?

Eventually, students are encouraged to write their own questions. To improve students' abilities to ask higher level questions, the teacher may assign values to questions. A $10 question is one in which the answer is located in the text and requires a short response; a $20 question is located in the text but requires more than two or three words to answer; a $30 question is found in the text but, in order to respond, students need to reread the text and compose an answer based on the reading; and a $40 question requires inference and generalization. Students have to integrate responses with previous knowledge and experience. Each group can generate questions and place them on one side of color-coded index cards with the answers on the reverse side. These cards can be used for review, as the basis for questions on future tests, and as a resource for students to learn to ask good questions. The cards can also be used in a game in which members of one group quiz members of other groups.

To make the collaborative groups successful, students from a variety of reading levels (including both an advanced and a struggling reader) need to be present in each group, and at least one student member should have leadership skills. The following roles may be assigned:

- The leader, who focuses the group on using the four strategies
- The clunk expert, who reminds the group of strategies for figuring out a clunk
- The gist expert, who reminds the group about steps to use to figure out the main idea
- The announcer, who calls on students to read or share an idea and who reports back to the entire class

The group of individuals may write or submit the reports. As a final recommendation, students can keep a CSR learning log, modeled after the K-W-L strategy described in Chapter 10.

SQ3R

The **S**urvey, **Q**uestion, **R**ead, **R**ecite, and **R**eview (SQ3R; Robinson, 1970) strategy is best used when reading textbooks and articles. The steps help a student learn how to study the material and increase concentration. SQ3R is most useful for secondary students such as John who have trouble learning the information presented in textbook chapters. For students who also have decoding issues, teaching students to use text-to-speech software in conjunction with this strategy can further assist students in gaining access to grade-level materials (Roberts, Takahashi, Park, & Stodden, 2012). For increased structure and active involvement with the reading material, a student may both recite and write responses to questions. A modified SQ3R procedure is presented in the following sections.

Step 1: Have a Purpose for Reading

When a student does not understand why a reading has been assigned or why a text is important, problems often arise. Some classes are based on a developmental model that requires students to learn the previous material thoroughly before proceeding with the subsequent reading. In other subjects, the goal may be to introduce students to the breadth and scope of materials that are used rather than to expect students to master all the details. Students who perceive reading requirements as something they have been told to do are likely to have difficulty motivating themselves to read. In contrast, students who understand the purpose of the reading assignment within the context of the class are more likely to complete the assignment. Initially, you can assist by making explicit the purpose behind the reading.

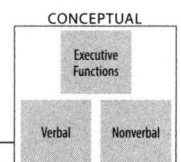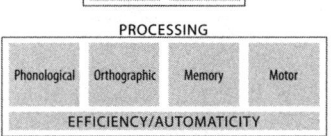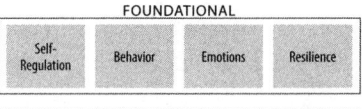

Step 2: Survey the Text

In this step, the reader becomes familiar with the organization and general content of the material to be read. As John uses this strategy, he follows these steps:

- Note the author, title, and publication date.
- Read the preface or foreword (the preface often contains the author's explanation of his or her purpose in writing the text).
- Preview the table of contents.
- Scan the book and read any chapter summaries.
- Take note of the kinds of illustrative materials included, such as maps, charts, graphs, diagrams, and pictures.
- Look to see if the text contains an index (i.e., topics and page locations), an appendix (i.e., supplementary material such as tables or maps), a glossary (i.e., definitions of specific terms), or references and a bibliography (i.e., credits for other authors and their works and suggested additional readings).
- Read headings if the material contains them (a list of headings in sequence almost always forms an outline of the main ideas; the text gives the supporting details).
- Read the first and the last sentence of each paragraph in order to grasp the general idea of the chapter or article.

Although a thorough survey of a textbook may take as much as a half-hour, the survey reduces time spent reading later because students can identify sections that are more important to read than others.

Step 3: Ask Questions

As John surveys his text, he asks questions about what he is reading so that he stays actively engaged in the reading process. He is able to follow these steps:

- Turn each heading into a question by using words such as *who, what, when,* and *where.* Higher level questions (i.e., questions using words such as *how, why, explain, discuss, criticize, compare,* and *contrast*) foster more abstract thinking.
- Use the questions asked to set a purpose for reading, which, in turn, increases motivation and understanding. Asking questions can take up to 15 minutes per chapter; trying to answer the questions should be delayed until later. Some readers benefit from listing their questions in order to refer to them as they read.

Step 4: Read the Selection and Recite Important Information

Good readers spend more time on important sections. As an example, good readers may spend 80% of the time allotted for reading on the 20% of the text that they find important or difficult to understand (Robinson, 1993). During this step, students should keep in mind the questions that they formulated earlier. If the assignment is long, students can divide it into segments and respond to their questions as they finish each segment. If the reading is particularly difficult or the content is unfamiliar, students may need to proceed on a paragraph-by-paragraph basis. Short breaks with preplanned limits may allow students to continue with renewed concentration. After finishing reading, students may ask the questions orally and respond in complete sentences. As noted previously, some students may want to write down their answers in order to maximize recall.

Step 5: Review the Selection

Because most forgetting occurs within the first 24 hours, setting aside time for review daily can save a lot of study time later on. John found that if he attempted to explain the reading to a friend or classmate, his understanding and retention of the material improved. Older students can be encouraged to form study groups so that this type of review and rehearsal can occur regularly.

ReQuest Procedure

The **re**ciprocal **quest**ioning procedure (ReQuest) is designed for older students who have more advanced reading skills (Manzo, 1969, 1985). The purposes of this simple but effective procedure are to help students 1) set their own goals for reading and 2) learn how to ask and answer questions while they read. Before beginning, discuss with the student the purpose for reading the selection and then model how to ask questions. These questions may require factual recall, recognition, evaluation, or critical thinking.

Read the first sentence of a passage silently with the student. Close your book, and then have the student ask as many questions as he or she can. Have the student close his or her book, and then ask as many questions as you can. Continue this process sentence by sentence until the student can provide a reasonable prediction of what is going to happen next in the rest of the selection. At this point, tell the student to finish the passage to see whether the prediction is correct.

When Katy was first introduced to this strategy, she had trouble formulating questions. She would just say that she could not think of anything to ask. Her teacher then adjusted the level of the instructional material. She taught Katy how to paraphrase what she was reading and then how to use that content to formulate simple questions.

Multipass

Another example of a textbook study strategy designed for secondary students is Multipass, an adaptation of SQ3R. This strategy improves comprehension of content-area textbooks (Schumaker, Deshler, Alley, Warner, & Denton, 1982). By using the three steps, the student never reads the passage in its entirety. The teacher explains the three steps and the rationale for the strategy and then demonstrates the use of the strategy in a chapter by thinking aloud. Students verbally rehearse the three steps.

Step 1: Survey

The student surveys the textbook by reading the chapter title, introductory paragraph, table of contents (in order to understand the relationship of the chapter to others in the text), subtitles, illustrations, diagrams, and summary paragraphs. The student then paraphrases all the information gained from the first pass through the reading.

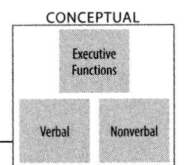
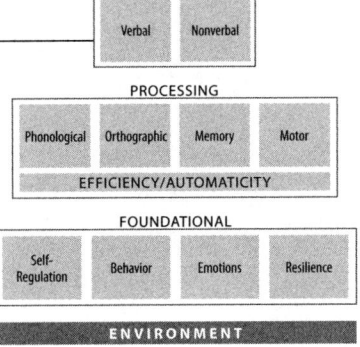

Step 2: Size Up

In the second step, the student sizes up by reading the questions at the end of the chapter and checking off those already known. The student then looks through the text for headings and parts of the text that are in italics, bold, or colored print to identify cues. The student turns each of these cues into a question and skims the text for an answer. At the end of the chapter, the student paraphrases all remembered facts and ideas.

Step 3: Sort Out

The student sorts out by reading the questions at the end of the chapter again and marking those questions that can be answered immediately. If a question cannot be answered, the student attempts to locate the answer by skimming the text.

PORPE

PORPE (Simpson & Stahl, 1987) is an approach for studying textbook materials in which the reader creates and answers essay questions. John found that this strategy was particularly useful for preparing to take an in-class essay test on the assigned reading. Although time consuming, PORPE is an excellent strategy to use when a student needs to develop mastery of the content. The five steps include the following:

Step 1: Predict

After reading a chapter or section, John predicts possible essay questions from the information contained in the text by constructing questions using keywords such as *explain, discuss, criticize, compare,* and *contrast.*

Step 2: Organize

John organizes, summarizes, and synthesizes the key points in each chapter in his own words. Then he outlines answers to the questions.

Step 3: Rehearse

As he reads, John rehearses by reciting aloud the information and asking himself questions to check for retention. This stage helps the reader place the key ideas, examples, and overall organization in long-term memory. This step is repeated over the next couple of days.

Step 4: Practice

John practices by attempting to answer the questions from memory. Students can sketch an outline or talk through an answer but need to make sure to include enough information.

Step 5: Evaluate

John evaluates his work by asking if there are enough concrete examples and if his answers are complete, accurate, and appropriate.

To check a student's knowledge of strategies, ask a student questions (Reid, 1988), such as the following:

- What is the most important reason for reading this material? Why does your teacher want you to read this material?
- What makes a person a good reader?
- How good are you at reading this material? How do you know?
- What would be the best way to remember information from this text?
- What would be the best way to find answers in this book?
- What is the hardest part about answering questions like the ones in this book?

WRITTEN LANGUAGE STRATEGIES

The next sections review several easy-to-use examples of strategies for writing. The purpose of these strategies is to help students formulate and write different types of texts. Instruction in these strategies can help students improve their understanding and increase their retention of important information. As with other strategies, several of these techniques use a first-letter mnemonic. These types of strategies can help students remember the various steps involved in a task.

The CCSS (2014) has divided written expression into four skill areas: text types and purposes, production and distribution of writing, research to build and present knowledge, and range of writing. Graham and Harris operationalize these four areas as

> learning to write for multiple purposes; producing and publishing well-organized text appropriate to task and purpose by planning, revising, editing, and collaborating with others; using writing to recall, organize, analyze, interpret, and build knowledge about a topic, or materials read; and applying both extended and shorter writing tasks to facilitate learning in a range of discipline-specific subjects and across purposes and audiences. (2013, p. 28)

Students need to be taught how to increase their understanding, organize their thoughts, and structure their writing to achieve these skills.

The Process of Writing

Although the actual process of writing does not follow discrete steps, the activities involved include brainstorming or getting ideas, outlining and planning, writing a draft, revising the ideas, and editing or proofreading. Often, after writing a first draft, the student has to go back to brainstorming to come up with additional ideas. A student may also return to outlining or rethinking the organizational format of a paper during revision. Some students like to write down the main thesis and list the subjects for each paragraph or section prior to writing.

Many students are writing on computers using word-processing programs. Using computers, the process of writing becomes even more recursive as one easily moves back and forth among drafting, revising, brainstorming, and editing. John found that he could start on a paper by entering in all his ideas. By cutting and pasting, he could then easily rearrange his thoughts into a more organized sequence.

Brainstorming

Encourage students to talk with people who can help clarify their assignments. Classmates, teaching assistants, teachers, and librarians can offer useful information and help identify sources. Procedures such as the K-W-L strategy described in Chapter 10 are also useful at this stage. Some students find it helpful to record their ideas and then play them back to assess how good the ideas sound. Students can also play the recording to ensure that everything they want to include in the paper is there. John found that it was helpful to go on walking brainstorms during which he would take his smart phone and record his ideas about one section of the paper while walking in one direction and then plan the second section on his return.

Outlining

Prior to writing, students need to have a sense of how their paper will be organized. Some students benefit from looking at a model paper to see how it is structured. Practice with highlighting or outlining a model can help students identify the component parts as well as the organization. Software programs such as Inspiration and Kidspiration for younger children assist students in using techniques such as semantic webbing and mind maps and then change these graphic organizers into outlines. With one push of a key, the student can move between maps and traditional linear outlines. It can also be helpful to talk about the paper's organization with someone else. Paying close attention to questions the listener asks can help the student identify revisions that would improve the paper.

Some writing assignments require the use of specialized vocabulary. Prior to writing, a student can make a vocabulary list of keywords. The student might type keywords in a large font so that they will be easier to check for spelling or usage.

Composing

When writing the first draft, encourage the student to focus on one section at a time because the sections can be easily reordered. The student may leave white space to separate parts of the paper and to make it easier to review. When reviewing the organization, the student may highlight the topic sentence (by using italics, underlining, bold print, or large font) in each paragraph. This helps emphasize the topic focus of each paragraph and is helpful if the sequence of thoughts needs to be rearranged.

Another option is to give each section or paragraph a title; repeating the titles may help the writer to stay focused. At the end of the writing process, the student eliminates the highlighting. If the student is having particular difficulty with one section, it often helps to talk aloud. Many times people are able to say something more simply and directly than when they attempt to write it. Students can record their thoughts to remind them of what they have said.

Ryan was writing his first draft of a commercial. He decided he would try to sell someone a car. Before writing, he jotted down a few ideas and the names of his favorite cars: Mazda, Baboa (?), and Ferrari. He thought about the way people pay for cars and wrote, "check, credit cards, or cash." Figure 11.4 depicts his first draft.

Revising

When revising a paper, encourage the student to read topic sentences aloud. This provides a summary of the paper. The student should also check the transitions between paragraphs. If the sentences do not fit together, either the organization or the content needs more work. The student may also have someone else read the paper. If both the reader and the writer have a copy, the writer can make notes while the reader is reading. If the reader has trouble or hesitates, the student should make

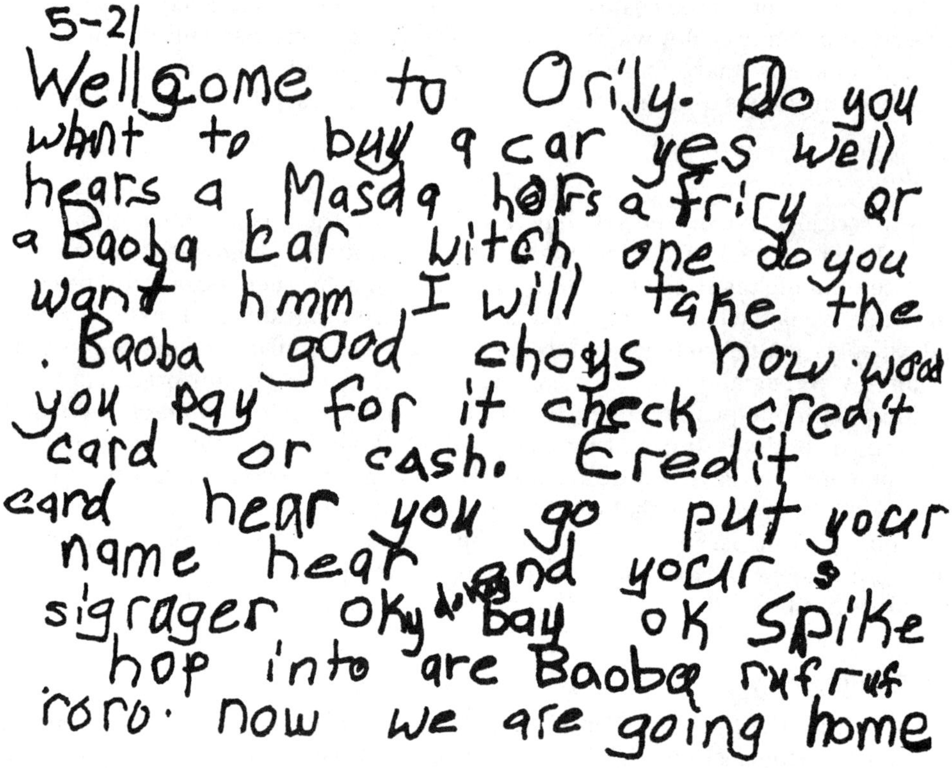

> 5-21
> Wellcome to Orily. Do you whnt to buy a car yes well hears a Masda hors a friry or a Baoba car witch one do you want hmm I will take the Baoba. good choys how wod you pay for it check credit card or cash. Credit card hear you go put your name hear and your sigrager oky day ok Spike hop into are Baoba ruf ruf roro. now we are going home

Figure 11.4. Ryan's commercial.

a note to check for coherence or usage errors. (Spelling and punctuation can also make a reader hesitate.) These errors can be corrected during the editing stage.

Students who have a limited vocabulary can be encouraged to take the time to vary their word usage by using a strategy in which they receive additional points when they use "$5 words."

> When Katy would write first drafts of papers, she would repeat the same words and same ideas over and over again. In her journal, she wrote, "Today, when I got up, I was happy. I was happy today because we were going to have a party, and I will be happy. I was happy. I looked at the board. It said 'journal.' I was happy." Katy needs to have someone help her develop her ideas prior to writing and to help her select and use more varied vocabulary.

Appendix 11A presents a list of words that children commonly use in their writing with some possible synonyms. A peer could help Katy consider alternative words to use when revising drafts.

Another strategy that is successful in encouraging students to make revisions that are more substantial and meaningful is based on peer response. Once in partners of two, one student is assigned to read the paper (the writer) to another student (the editor), who also reads along. The editor responds by telling the writer two or three positive things about the writing. The editor then looks at the paper and indicates if certain places are not clear or if there are places where more information should be added. The writer then revises the paper. The process is then reversed, with the

Instruction in Reading Comprehension, Written Expression, and Math Problem Solving

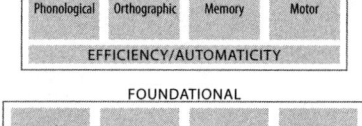

other student reading his or her paper. Initially, monitor the exchange between the students until they have learned how to give both positive and constructive feedback.

Editing and Proofreading

For editing, students can create a checklist of editing tasks (e.g., using a spell checker, checking for proper annotation of quotes, adding page numbers, eliminating highlighting). Students can check off each task as it is completed. John learned to keep a manual nearby that reminded him of specific rules that he found problematic, such as using quotation marks or citing quotations. He also made a list of words he had trouble spelling in the back of his notebook.

Revision and editing should be separated, not combined in one step. Students should review for content first; then for organization; then for transitions; and, finally, when it is time to create the final draft, for spelling, capitalization, and punctuation. Teachers who separate their comments on content from their comments about written presentation help students develop a clearer sense of the content problems they need to address. Chapter 9 provides specific suggestions for helping students with basic writing skills.

Some students benefit from a process approach to both narrative and expository structures that emphasizes writing and revising. Try using the following procedure, adapted from Wong, Wong, Darlington, and Jones (1991):

1. Teach students that writing is a process involving planning, generating sentences, and revising.
2. Discuss with students the relevance of planning in real-life situations.
3. Elicit from students why planning is useful in writing (i.e., to direct them toward a topic and to clarify their writing goals).
4. Select a strategy for the specific essay type: narrative or expository (e.g., compare and contrast).
5. Model the planning strategy.
6. Have students take turns thinking aloud their essay plans.
7. Have students write a first draft.
8. Read the draft and ask for clarification of unclear sentences using an interactive teaching style, ensuring that the student understands why a sentence is unclear.
9. Have each student clarify and expand on sentences deemed unclear.
10. Work with the student to improve the clarity of the essay.
11. Explain how the revised sentences are better.
12. Repeat Steps 8–11 as often as necessary.
13. Have the student rewrite the essay.
14. When message clarity has been attained, work with the student at correcting spelling and grammatical errors.
15. Have the student write the final draft.

Students who struggle with basic writing skills need feedback prior to making edits. A child who spells the word *any* as *eney* cannot find the word in a dictionary and cannot use a spell checker. When Ryan was in third grade, he wrote a first draft of an expository paragraph about the importance of being healthy, presented in

Figure 11.5. His only feedback was a failing grade and a comment that he must edit. Clearly, this type of limited feedback is not helpful.

POWER

Some students need assistance in understanding the phases of the writing process, often requiring guidance throughout the process. In her classroom, Katy would often start writing before she had spent time developing and organizing ideas. To help students such as Katy remember that writing is a process that requires planning, Englert, Raphael, Anderson, Anthony, and Stevens (1991) developed the acronym POWER to represent the following steps:

Plan

Organize

Write

Edit

Revise

Self-Regulated Strategy Development

Self-regulated strategy development (Graham & Harris, 1999; Graham, Harris, & McKeown, 2013; Harris, Graham, Mason, & Friedlander, 2008) can be employed to help a student to plan and organize writing. Harris and colleagues (2008) provided an in-depth description of this strategy. Use of this approach can improve writing quality and a student's ability to plan and revise writing. To begin, the teacher schedules a conference with the student to discuss his or her approach to writing. The student then learns three steps:

1. Think about who will read this (the audience) and why you are writing it.
2. Plan what to say (i.e., generate ideas and plan organization).
3. Write and say more (i.e., continue to improve the piece).

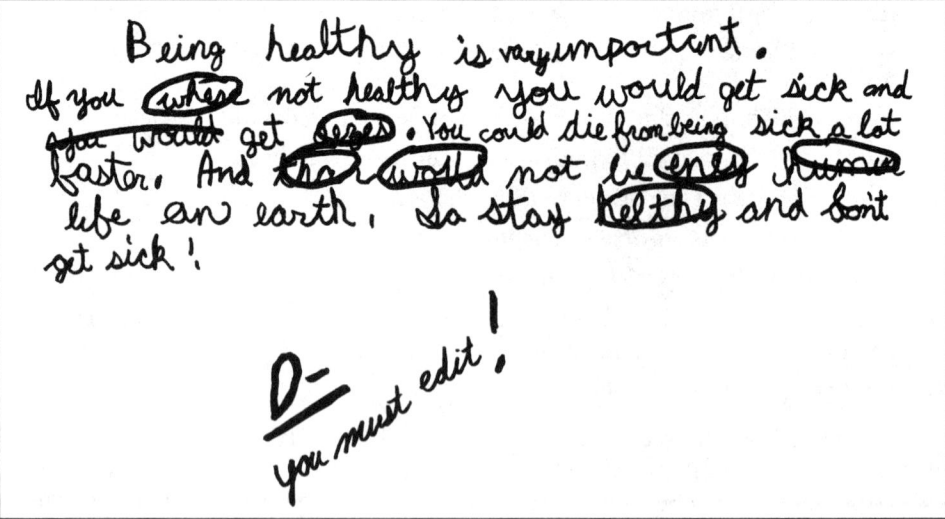

Figure 11.5. Ryan's first draft.

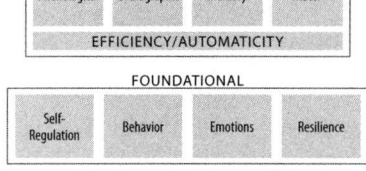

The teacher follows up by describing the planning and writing strategy appropriate to the type of writing assignment (e.g., opinion piece, compare and contrast) and discusses the concept of progress monitoring (i.e., the steps to use to complete work). The student may count and graph elements that should be addressed in the assignment as one way to monitor progress.

With this approach, the teacher also discusses with the student or the class the importance of what people say to themselves while working. Students may have two positive statements to use while they are working. As needed, the teacher continues to model the use of appropriate strategies, such as planning, reviewing, and self-evaluation.

Cognitive Strategy in Writing Program

To become members of the literacy community, students need to learn to talk about literacy (Englert, 1992). The Cognitive Strategy in Writing (CSIW) program (Englert, 1990; Englert & Raphael, 1989) emphasizes the dialogic and social nature of writing (Englert, 1992). Students must be able to convey ideas in a conventional format to a distant audience (Kozulin, 2003). This approach has been particularly successful for upper-elementary and middle school students with writing difficulties. When used with adolescents with LD, having students focus on the purpose of writing, as well as the brainstorming and expansion of ideas, improved students' abilities to generate and organize ideas (Hallenbeck, 1996, 2002). As Hallenbeck so aptly observed about students with writing difficulties, "Writing a paper is like building a house without a blueprint; they don't know where they are going or how to begin" (1996, p. 107).

Englert (1992) described three principles for teaching students how to write expository text: 1) writers should engage in strategies related to planning, organizing, revising, and editing text; 2) writers benefit from teachers modeling the inner talk and thinking involved in effective writing; and 3) writers need to learn about the social nature of writing by collaborating with each other and writing for authentic purposes. The program emphasizes teacher modeling through think-alouds and student rehearsal of modeled strategies through the use of think sheets.

For the CSIW think-alouds, describe aloud your inner thinking by verbalizing the steps of a strategy, asking questions, and providing answers. Use various think sheets that contain a set of self-questions intended to guide the writing process until the strategies and questions are internalized. The purpose of these think sheets is to make strategies visible to students and to provide them with a vocabulary for talking about writing (Englert, 1992). The sheets guide students in strategy use as they engage in text construction and monitoring activities and can be adapted to meet particular writing assignments.

Englert and Raphael (1989) described several types of think sheets. The plan think sheet includes a series of prompts that help the writer focus on the audience. Questions may include the following:

Who am I writing for?

Why am I writing this?

What do I already know about the topic?

How can I organize my ideas?

The organize think sheet presents a series of text structure questions, such as the following:

What is being explained?

What materials are needed?

What are the steps?

What do you do first, second, third, fourth?

The self-edit think sheet has the writer rate performance on the questions included in the plan think sheet. The writer places a star by his or her favorite parts of the paper and question marks by parts that seem unclear. A peer editor then completes an editor think sheet. The author and editor then talk about ways to make the paper better.

Katy's compositions improved dramatically when she was given a series of think sheets to guide her writing. The provision of a series of questions helped her learn how to self-monitor and self-regulate. Prior to writing, Katy learned how to select a topic, identify her audience, brainstorm ideas, and then organize her ideas. In addition, the use of two software programs, *Co:WriterSolo* and *Write:Outloud*, provided additional support and helped her concentrate more fully on expressing her ideas.

In high school, John found that using the software program *Draft Builder* provided him with a strategic approach to planning, organizing, and drafting essays and research projects.

Appendix 11B provides a list of various apps that can be useful for helping students with reading and writing challenges.

Cohesion

Cohesion refers to the organization and unity of the text. Writers use various strategies and techniques to help readers understand their messages. Cohesive ties are words that signal the organization of text and provide transitions that show how a previous clause or statement is related to another. Explicit instruction in the use of cohesive ties helps students learn to organize and integrate concepts in writing. This instruction is aimed at helping students connect the sentences and paragraphs within their compositions by using words that signify a variety of types of relationships. Wallach and Miller (1988) described several types of cohesive ties:

1. Additive (*and, also, in addition*)
2. Amplification (*furthermore, moreover*)
3. Adversative (*but, however, in contrast, nevertheless*)
4. Causal (*if/then, because, due to, as a result*)
5. Conclusion (*therefore, accordingly, consequently*)
6. Temporal (*after, meanwhile, whenever, previously*)
7. Spatial (*next to, between, in front of, adjacent to*)
8. Continuative (*after all, again, finally, another*)
9. Likeness (*likewise, similarly*)
10. Example (*for example, as an illustration*)
11. Restatement (*in other words, that is, in summary*)
12. Exception (*except, barring, beside, excluding*)

Instruction in Reading Comprehension, Written Expression, and Math Problem Solving

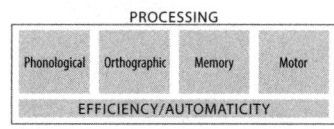

Katy was able to organize a sequential paragraph about the steps involved in brushing her teeth by introducing the four sentences with the words *first, next, then,* and *finally.* At first, her teacher had her fold her paper into four squares and then write a linking word in the upper left corner of each square. Katy drew a picture of four steps and then wrote a sentence to describe each step.

Paragraphs

Many strategies can help students improve their skills in collecting and organizing the factual information that they wish to include in paragraphs, essays, or reports. In general, students benefit from formal instruction that presents organizational models and includes practice writing in a variety of modes (Vogel & Moran, 1982). As with other areas of achievement related to the Conceptual blocks, students benefit from strategies that provide direct instruction in strategies paired with teacher modeling. For example, Wallace and Bott (1989) found that use of a metacognitive text structure strategy that involved completing a paragraph planning guide improved student skill in paragraph writing.

A key to teaching paragraph writing is to help students learn how to subordinate.

John had trouble distinguishing main ideas from details. His English teacher demonstrated how to write a topic sentence for a paragraph and then how to support this sentence with details. She then showed John how to link paragraphs together to form an essay. She also spent time teaching the class how to turn essay questions on examinations into topic sentences.

Statement Pie

Statement pie is an easy-to-use strategy for helping students develop expository paragraphs (Englert & Lichter, 1982; Hanau, 1974). In this strategy, *statement* refers to a topic statement and *pie* refers to the details, which may be categorized as follows:

Proofs

Information

Examples

Wallace and Bott (1989) described the following adaptation:

1. Give students a completed paragraph guide as a model of the strategy.
2. Explain the meaning of *statement* and *pie.*
3. Model the detection and generation of pies.
4. Give students a statement.
5. Have students verbally generate appropriate pies using the following guide:

   Statement: topic statement

   Pie: a detail related to the topic statement

   Pie: another detail related to the topic statement

   Pie: another detail related to the topic statement
6. Give immediate feedback in regard to the appropriateness of each pie.
7. Give students another topic sentence in an area that is age appropriate and in which students have background knowledge.

8. Have students generate and write appropriate pies to be used as paragraph planning guides on the given topic.
9. Give immediate feedback in regard to the appropriateness of each pie.

Use the following steps for outlining statements and pies in expository paragraphs:

1. Model the outlining of statements and pies in chosen expository paragraphs.
2. Give students paragraphs for guided practice.
3. Circle the statements, and underline the pies.
4. Write the statements and pies in a planning guide.

Use the following steps for writing paragraphs:

1. Model paragraph writing by doing the following:
   - Selecting a topic
   - Writing a paragraph planning guide
   - Using the guide to construct sentences
   - Forming the sentences into a paragraph
   - Emphasizing keywords and cohesive ties (e.g., *first, next, afterward, finally*)
2. Have students choose a topic from a list you have generated.
3. Have students generate statement-pie paragraph planning guides.
4. Have students write a paragraph.
5. Provide immediate feedback with regard to the appropriateness of the pies.

When he was in seventh grade, Samuel's English teacher was attempting to teach the class how to write descriptive paragraphs. She first had the class read sample paragraphs and then asked them to write a paragraph that was similar to the model. Figure 11.6 presents Samuel's first draft. He selected the topic "Monday has been very boring." Notice the teacher's feedback and grade. Experienced teachers know not to grade the first drafts of assignments but rather to give feedback about ways to improve the writing. What Samuel needed as a writer was increased modeling and support, not a failing grade and a recommendation for a more interesting topic.

Essays

As students are learning to write paragraphs, they can be taught how to link the paragraphs together to form an essay. Several simple approaches exist for teaching students how to construct essays.

Kerrigan's Method

Kerrigan (1979) described a comprehensive procedure for teaching students how to write essays with the following six steps for theme organization and composition writing.

1. Have the student write a sentence in which a person or an object is/was something or does/did something. The sentence must adhere to the following rules:
   - Create a sentence about which you can say something more.
   - Concentrate on what the person or object does.
   - Be specific—what exactly did the person or object do?

Instruction in Reading Comprehension, Written Expression, and Math Problem Solving

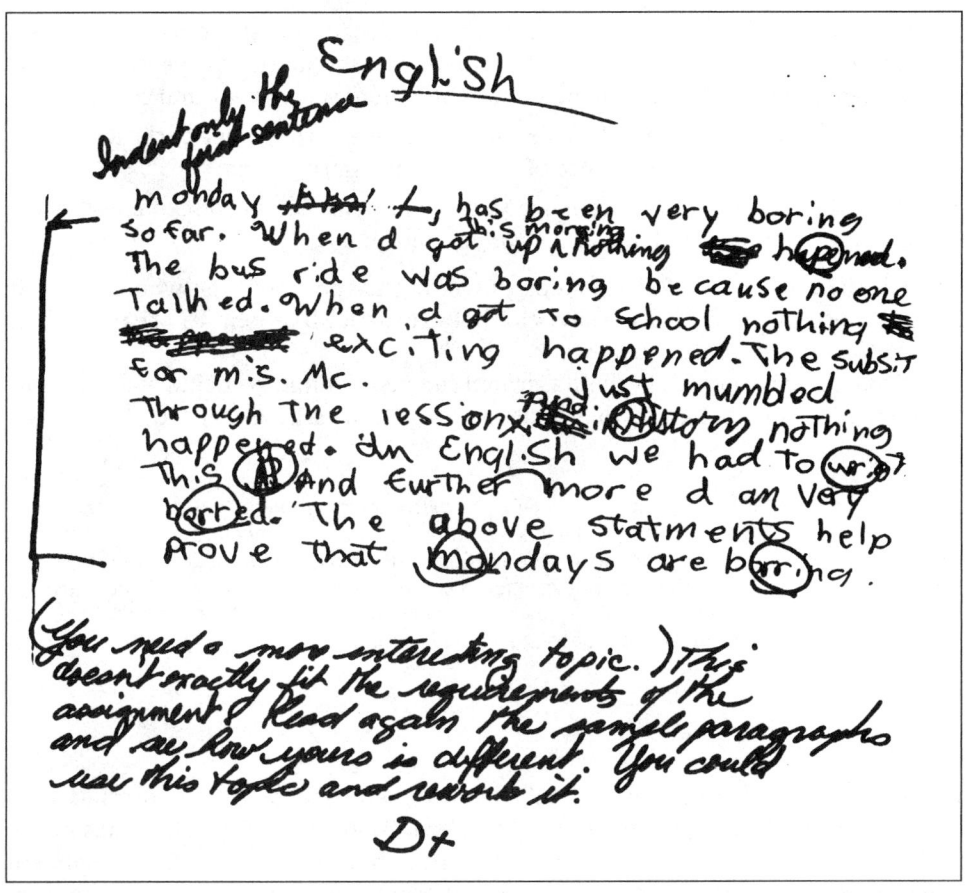

Figure 11.6. Samuel's first draft.

- Keep the sentence short until you become proficient.
- Keep the sentence as a statement, not a question or command.
- Ensure you have only one statement.
- Do not use a descriptive or narrative sentence.

2. Have the student write three sentences about the original sentence. Encourage the student to use simple, declarative sentences that give information clearly and directly about the original sentence. The information given must pertain to the whole of the original sentence and not to only a piece of it. Help the student provide more specific information rather than repeating the same idea in different words.

3. Ask the student to write four or five sentences about each of the three sentences in Step 2.

4. The sentences in Step 3 must be specific and concrete. Encourage the student to go into detail and use examples. Specify that the goal is to give more information about what has already been introduced, thus there must be no new ideas. Sharing short anecdotal stories with the student can be effective during the fourth stage.

   At this point, help the student review the content to ensure that the subject has not changed and that the central idea or theme is obvious from the first paragraph. Have the student focus on being understood by the prospective audience. Encourage the student to use vocabulary that is pertinent to the audience and to concentrate on making the theme clear, real, and convincing.

5. Have the student insert a clear, explicit reference to the theme of the preceding paragraph in the first sentence of the following paragraphs.
6. Have the student work to ensure that every sentence is connected with the previous sentence and makes a clear reference to it.

Use of Kerrigan's (1979) six steps to writing ensures that the whole theme is thoroughly connected. This method can help students like John to organize their ideas within a meaningful framework.

Visual displays posted in the classroom can also remind students of what information they should include as they write a paragraph, essay, or report.

Ryan's teacher, Mr. Steen, created a poster in his room using the image of a dinosaur to remind the students of the elements of essays. He explained that the head represented the introduction; the body was supported by the facts and details, represented by the legs; and the tail served as a reminder that every good essay has a clear-cut ending. Figure 11.7 shows the visual mnemonic that he used.

Ms. McGrew used a similar visual display, Ms. Edith Essay. Her head represented the introduction and her body was the main part of the text. The legs and arms were topic sentences for the paragraphs.

Research

As students progress through school, they are required to work more independently and are asked to present work with a greater scope or depth than has previously been required. To begin, assess a student's abilities to engage in independent research. Students with learning difficulties may need to practice the steps required for effective research before being able to work independently, or they may need to have the steps simplified or repeated over a period of time.

Some students find that conducting research on the computer is exciting; others find it frustrating and difficult. Poor spelling skills can prevent entering a correctly spelled item in a keyword search. Trouble identifying specific words to narrow a search can frustrate those with poor word retrieval skills. When a topic is too broad or general, students may find that their search results in hundreds of sites or articles and quit working in frustration. As with other areas of academic performance, students need explicit instruction and practice in using the Internet to retrieve information for a report.

MATH PROBLEM SOLVING

As with reading comprehension and written expression, multiple factors can affect a student's ability to solve math problems effectively. Many students with math difficulties also struggle with reading and writing. In fact, Koepke and Miller reported that "in the United States, roughly 7% of all children suffer from a math disability, and of these, an estimated 17% to 66% also has a comorbid reading disability" (2013, p. 483). The Building Block of Verbal abilities plays a key role in math problem solving, as does the ability to move between verbal and spatial (nonverbal) representations.

In recent literature, the focus on working memory—for example, the ability to store numbers while calculating problems—has also been noted as both a predictor

Instruction in Reading Comprehension, Written Expression, and Math Problem Solving

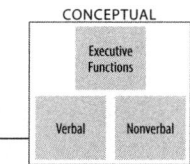

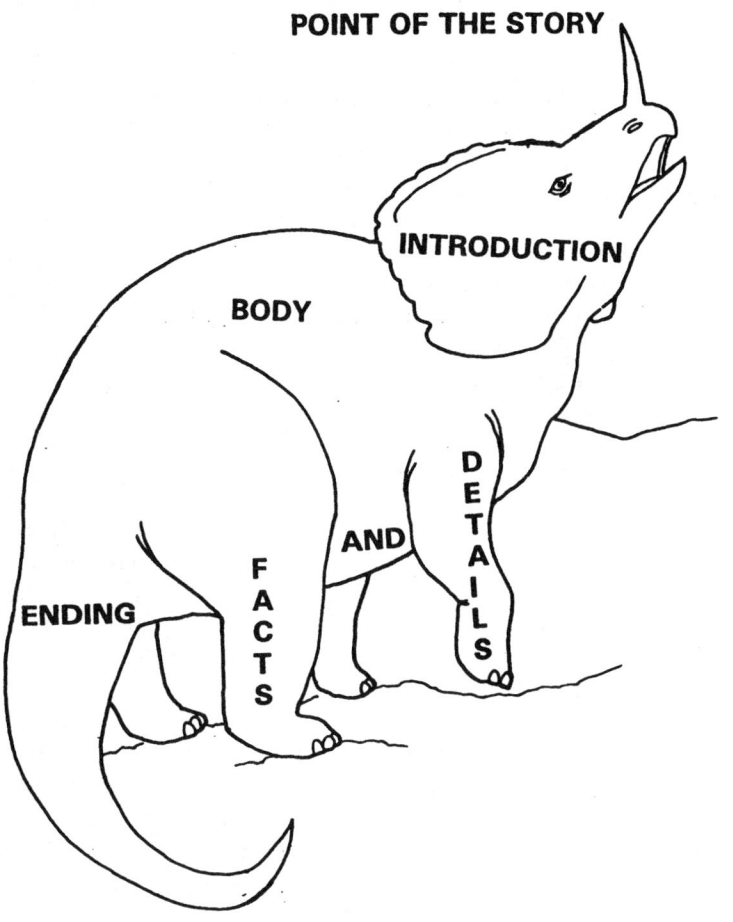

Figure 11.7. Dinosaur for essay structure.

and assessment area in relation to computational and problem-solving abilities (e.g., Alloway & Passolunghi, 2011; Raghubar, Barnes, & Hecht, 2010; Toll, Van der Ven, Kroesbergen, & Van Luit, 2011; Watson & Gable, 2012).

Poor planning processes, slow execution rates, and deficient reading skills are also common problems for students with math difficulties (Ashkenazi, Black, Abrams, Hoeft, & Menon, 2013). Students who lack awareness of the skills, strategies, and resources that are needed to perform a task and who fail to use self-regulatory mechanisms to perform a task will undoubtedly have difficulty with mathematics (Montague & van Garderen, 2008; Swanson & Jerman, 2006; Swanson & Saez, 2003; Vukovic & Siegel, 2010; Wong, Harris, Graham, & Butler, 2003). Similar to reading comprehension and written language, success in mathematics is dependent largely on background knowledge, symbolic facility, and the use of strategies.

   John's limited acquired knowledge also affected his ability to solve mathematical problems. When John was asked the question, "If a foot-long ruler were divided into six equal parts, how long would each part be?" he responded, "One tenth." He did not know that a foot was composed of 12 inches. When he was asked the question, "If three people each have $4, how much money do they have all together?" he responded, "Between $13 and $14." John did not understand that this type of question has one correct response and does not require estimation.

Because of the complexity of mathematics, different students demonstrate problems with different applications. To explore the areas in which a student has particular difficulty, a teacher could conduct an individualized oral math interview. The teacher would consider the full range of mathematical abilities, such as the student's ability to make predictions on the basis of patterns, to sort, to measure, to organize space, and to follow steps in completing problems. Students need to know multiple concepts and show competence in a variety of skills to be successful across different mathematical domains (e.g., algebra, geometry) (Andersson, 2008; Montague, 2007). Also the teacher would check to see what strategies the student employs (e.g., does the student talk to him- or herself, draw pictures to help understand problems, ask for clarifications, check his or her answers, or estimate an answer before solving a problem?). The teacher would attempt to discover the student's problem-solving strengths as well as weaknesses.

Mathematical Knowledge

While conducting these assessments, teachers should consider the three types of knowledge students need to be successful in mathematics: declarative, procedural, and conceptual (Hasselbring, Lott, & Zydney, 2006; Mancl et al., 2012). Declarative knowledge refers to a student's abilities in the area of factual knowledge, or the information that students retrieve from memory without hesitation (Miller & Hudson, 2007). Examples of this knowledge are the facts that 6 + 4 = 10 and that a square is a four-sided polygon with equal-length sides that meet at right angles. Procedural knowledge is the understanding of rules, algorithms, and procedures used to solve various mathematical tasks. Examples of this knowledge are the order of operations and the sequential steps used to solve long division or algebraic expressions. Conceptual knowledge is an overarching piece that represents a student's knowledge and understanding of the meaning of how declarative and procedural knowledge work together to solve mathematical equations.

As with reading, students need to be provided with enough instructional examples and opportunities for practice. Several examples can be provided to define a given concept in order to help students develop accurate conceptualizations. For example, both Katy and John struggled with the concept of estimation. To help them improve this ability, their teachers provided examples from real-life situations (e.g., show how long it will take, what is the actual approximate temperature) and varied the language that was used (e.g., *between, approximately, about, close to*) in each example. Teachers can continue to model each step of the problem-solving sequence until students acquire the skill and then provide adequate practice so that they retain the skill.

Katy didn't look for patterns or meaning when she completed math problems, and she was often puzzled when other students seemed to solve problems easily. Her teacher noted that Katy tried to memorize everything, as if remembering the response was the only way she could get the right answer. Many times the answers that she wrote were not even close to the correct solution. Katy's teacher was trying to find ways to ensure that Katy understood the procedures and was not just trying to imitate them.

Instructional Concerns

The CCSS in relation to mathematics have been developed due to the belief that mathematics education in the United States needs to become more focused and coherent

Instruction in Reading Comprehension, Written Expression, and Math Problem Solving

in order for students to achieve. The standards call for shifts in mathematics education that include "(1) greater focus on fewer topics, (2) linking of topics and thinking across grades, and (3) perusal of conceptual understanding, procedural skills and fluency, as well as application with equal intensity" (CCSS, 2014). The National Council of Teachers of Mathematics (NCTM, 2014) have come out in support of CCSS for mathematics and look to support this effort by using research on learning as well as practitioner experience to modify and develop standards that emphasize conceptual understanding, mathematical reasoning, and real-world applications for problem-solving skills. Because of the self-regulated nature of the activities that adhere to these standards, students with LD have struggled to succeed with these curricular changes (Woodward, 2006).

Another concern is that both the CCSS and the NCTM do not explicitly outline research-based strategies for teaching mathematics to students who have disabilities (Mancl, Miller, & Kennedy, 2012). The National Assessment of Educational Progress (NAEP, 2013) reported that 65% of students with disabilities compared with 21% of students without disabilities score below the basic level on mathematics performance assessments at the eighth-grade level, supporting the idea that systematic research-based instruction is needed to assist students with disabilities in mathematics.

According to Jones, Wilson, and Bhojwani (1997), teachers tend to direct their instruction, in terms of the difficulty of the material, to students of higher achievement. Many students, particularly at the secondary level, do not have the skills needed to meet the demands of a traditional curriculum (Miller, 1996). To involve students with lower achievement, teachers should strive to do the following:

- Maintain a lively pace of instruction.
- Obtain frequent active responses from all students.
- Monitor individual students' attention and accuracy.
- Provide feedback and positive reinforcement for correct responses.
- Offer corrective feedback for errors.

Achievement will be highest when all five of these principles are part of the instruction.

Instructional Format

An effective format for a session in math instruction is to 1) begin with a short period of review of previously covered materials, 2) follow with teacher-directed instruction of the concept of the day including guided practice, and 3) conclude with independent practice with corrective feedback. Students need enough time for instruction as well as for practice. In many classrooms, students' difficulties are compounded by long stretches of independent practice in which they receive little feedback prior to completion of the assignment. In addition to providing ongoing feedback, one successful variation is to engage students in small-group practice in which students can ask questions and check answers. Thus, essential teaching practices include advance organizers, communication of lesson objectives, teacher demonstration, guided practice, independent practice, and maintenance checks (Doabler et al., 2012; Miller & Hudson, 2007).

Another example of a problem-solving format a teacher can use is to provide a 10-minute working period in which students work on solving problems, a 5-minute period of teacher-guided self-reflection, and finally another 10-minute working period (Naglieri & Gottling, 1995). During the self-reflection period, students can think about how they tried to solve the problems and then comment on what they did well and what they could do to improve their performance. Students can answer questions such as the following:

- What did you notice about the strategies you used to solve the problem?
- How did you solve this problem?
- I noticed you had some trouble with _____. What did you do?
- What could you do to get more problems right?

The task of the instructor is to encourage students to verbalize the strategies they could use and explain why they might use those strategies. When using this exercise, place the emphasis on the strategies students are using rather than the number of correct answers they have (Naglieri & Gottling, 1995).

Students become discouraged when they receive problem sets or tests back with marks indicating they have answered questions incorrectly but with no other feedback. In a short period of time, they may come to feel that they have no control over doing math problems and lose the incentive to try. Rather than viewing problems as correct or incorrect, reinforce students by providing positive feedback on the steps of the problem that have been done correctly. Varied reinforcement strategies can also reduce the need for constant help (Miller & Mercer, 1997).

Within class sessions, teachers may present problems in four modes: 1) active construction or manipulation of objects, 2) fixed visual displays, 3) oral statements, and 4) written or symbolic presentations. The student's response may also be presented using one of these four options. In some instances, a teacher may present the problem in one mode and ask the student to respond in the same mode. In other instances, a teacher may ask the student to respond in an alternate mode from the one used to present the problem. Students who have the opportunity to work with varied response presentations and options are more likely to generalize skills than students who spend the greatest proportion of their time writing responses to problems in workbooks (Jones et al., 1997).

Just as with reading and writing, explicit instruction for students with math disabilities results in more predictable and functional achievement (Gersten, Chard, Jayanthi, Baker, Morphy, & Flojo, 2009; Kroesbergen & Van Luit, 2003; Swanson & Hosykn, 2001; Zheng, Flynn, & Swanson, 2012). Teachers need to plan and structure the learning experience, emphasizing mastery of concepts and skills and providing students with time to master those skills. In their book, *Guiding Children's Learning of Mathematics,* Tipps, Johnson, and Kennedy (2011) describe many mathematical techniques and experiences that emphasize the teacher's role as a guide to children's learning. The book includes many practical resources and interesting activities to use with children in preschool through sixth grade. The text focuses on both the conceptual and procedural aspects of teaching and learning mathematics with specific information about what teachers need to know, as well as specific learning objectives for students.

Although the use of basal materials for classroom instruction in the area of mathematics is a successful strategy for some students, it is problematic for students with LD. Most textbooks rely on a spiraling approach to teaching math skills in which numerous skills are introduced rapidly and reintroduced at different levels. Opportunities for mastery of individual concepts or for adequate practice and review are limited. Other concerns include inadequately sequenced problems and a

Instruction in Reading Comprehension, Written Expression, and Math Problem Solving

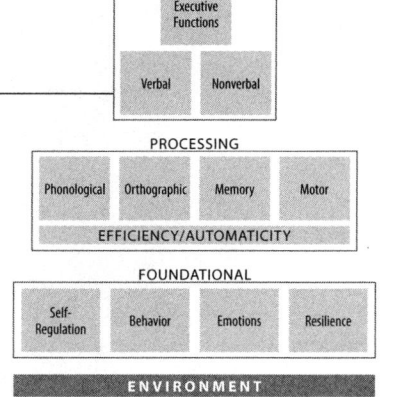

lack of strategy instruction. Students who move through a math textbook without understanding concepts continue to experience failure. For students who struggle with mathematical concepts, prerequisite skills need to be introduced and practiced for several days (or even weeks). Review needs to be distributed over time so that students do not forget the concepts they are learning. For example, when Katy was asked to point to the shape that was a triangle, she responded that the class was not doing that kind of problem anymore.

When only those problems presented in texts or workbooks are used, difficulty with generalization of processes can occur. The worksheets provided by publishers often fail to provide opportunities for enough practice to achieve mastery. Adequate sampling of a range of real-life examples needs to be given for students to avoid limited or erroneous understanding of the concept (Jones et al., 1997). As an example, Jones and colleagues described the way in which students are often taught to understand fractions as lesser parts of one whole (e.g., ¼, ⅓). Because some fractions are greater than the whole (e.g., 9/8), the original presentation limits students' understanding of computation with fractions and, as a result, can affect their problem-solving skills.

Instructional Sequence

When he was in fifth grade, John had memorized many multiplication facts but did not understand the basic process of multiplication. If he forgot the solution, he could not come up with the answer in another way. He also could not check to see if his answers were reasonable.

As a general rule for teaching mathematical concepts to a student, follow a sequence that goes from concrete (objects) to semiconcrete (drawings or representations) to abstract (numbers), which is commonly referred to as a concrete-representation-abstract (CRA) or concrete-semiconcrete-abstract (CSA) teaching sequence (Maccini, Mulcahy, & Wilson, 2007; Mercer, 1992; Miller, 1996; Miller & Hudson, 2007). This sequence is important because if a student has problems with concepts and skills in the lower elementary years, these difficulties will continue to compound without targeted intervention (Mancl et al., 2012). With this progression, students such as Katy and John develop mental representations of the meaning of numbers.

Concrete

In this beginning stage of understanding, children see and manipulate objects to solve problems. To count from 1 to 10, for example, students would move and count 10 objects. To add, students would put together two or more groups and then count the total number. To subtract, students would remove a specified number of objects from the group. The basic purpose of working with manipulatives is to help students form mental images of the processes and an understanding of what numbers represent. In other words, by learning to perform problems with concrete objects, students understand how numbers (abstractions) relate to the objects. Sometimes, however, children do not fully grasp the connection between the use of manipulatives and math facts.

Students can also use an act-it-out strategy to simulate a story or word problem (Tipps et al., 2011). Provide simple story problems and have children act out the problems using real props as other students observe the acting out. Tipps and colleagues suggested that younger students act out experiences such as "buying" items at a classroom store in order to solve math problems. Older students can simulate a microeconomics society by buying and selling products. Some problems may require several steps. Tipps and colleagues described the use of the classic handshake problem: A basketball team has a meeting with five players attending. If each player shakes hands with each of the other players, how many handshakes occur among players at the meeting? As they act out the handshakes, students must determine a way to systematically record the number of handshakes.

Manipulatives can be used in many different ways when providing math instruction at all levels. The National Library of Virtual Manipulatives (http://nlvm.usu.edu/en/nav/vlibrary.html) provides a library of web-based and interactive manipulatives and concept tutorials at all levels for teachers' use. An extension and enhancement of this resource, including interactive online tutorials, can be found at its web site (http://enlvm.usu.edu/ma/nav/doc/intro.jsp).

Even secondary-level students can benefit from the use of manipulatives (Allsopp, 1999; Allsopp, Kyger, & Lovin, 2007; Cass, Cates, Smith, & Jackson, 2003). Allsopp suggested a variety of manipulatives to use when teaching concepts at the concrete level:

- *Angles:* protractors, compasses, geoboards, rulers, tangrams, pattern blocks
- *Area:* geoboards, color tiles, base-10 blocks, decimal squares, cubes, tangrams, pattern blocks, rulers, fraction models
- *Volume:* capacity containers, cubes, geometric solids
- *Probability:* spinners, number cubes, fraction models, color tiles, cubes
- *Ratio/proportion:* color tile cubes, Cuisenaire rods, tangrams, pattern blocks
- *Polynomials:* algebra tiles, base-10 materials
- *Symmetry:* geoboards, pattern blocks, tangrams, cubes, attribute blocks

John's geometry teacher incorporated manipulatives into his daily schedule. Before working with geometric shapes on paper, the teacher made sure that students understood concepts such as points, corners, edges, sides, roundness, flatness, solids, stacks, and rolls. When these terms were understood, more difficult terms such as *faces* and *vertices* were easier to understand. He also used tangrams, a puzzle game with seven pieces, and geoboards, pegboards that come in various shapes and sizes, to improve spatial pattern recognition and spatial coordination. By using string or rubber bands or by drawing lines around the pegs or pins on the grid of a geoboard, students invent shapes. For one assignment, the teacher asked students to make as many quadrilateral shapes as they could using the geoboard and then to count the number of parallel lines in each shape. Students recorded their answers on paper that had dots to represent the pegs in order to have a permanent record of what they had done.

A geoboard also works well as a manipulative for teaching the Pythagorean theorem. This type of instruction helps students learn to think with images and to relate concepts to visual representations, critical skills for increasing conceptual understanding.

Allsopp and colleagues (2007) cautioned, however, that teachers should not assume that students understand the same underlying mathematical ideas as teachers do when using manipulatives. Just because students have a visual representation of something does not mean that they are grasping the principle behind it. Be careful to continue to teach the ideas as they are using the manipulatives. Once

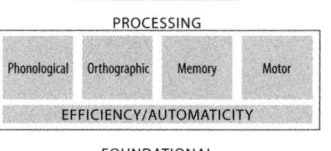
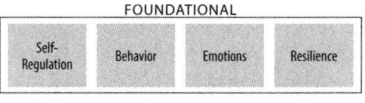

students have demonstrated mastery of concepts with manipulatives, instruction can move to activities at the semiconcrete stage.

Semiconcrete or Representational

In this stage, a student is shown that tallies or pictures can be drawn to represent objects. You may help students develop understanding at the semiconcrete level by representing physical objects with dots, lines, sticks, or pictures. Students may be shown how to use popsicle sticks to represent each member of a set with a tally. This type of procedure encourages students to focus on the number properties of sets rather than other characteristics of the objects, such as color or size. The basic purpose of this level is to help students make associations between visual pictures and symbolic processes. Using manipulatives and pictorial representations is particularly beneficial for helping students with LD develop conceptual knowledge (Miller & Hudson, 2007).

Children with difficulties in either the Processing or Conceptual blocks need a lot of experience at the concrete and semiconcrete levels before they can use numbers meaningfully. When John was in third grade, he still counted on his fingers when solving simple addition and subtraction problems. His teacher showed him how to draw lines to add or subtract so that he did not have to rely on his fingers. For students with memory problems, working with manipulatives and pictorial representations improves their ability to retain what they are learning. When memory fails, recall of pictorial information may help them rediscover needed information.

Abstract

At the abstract level, students learn to solve problems by using numbers. Some students memorize formulas or steps in a sequence without understanding the concepts behind them; when this is the case, they are unable to apply the information to different problems. Other children are asked to use numbers to solve problems when they really do not understand the meaning of numbers. Their first experience with numbers is at the abstract level rather than at the concrete level. Use of the CRA or CSA sequence ensures that concepts are taught to students with both three-dimensional (manipulatives) and two-dimensional representations (pictures) (Miller & Hudson, 2007)).

In first grade, Katy's teacher showed the class the number four and said, "This is the number four." Although she had learned to count by rote from 1 to 20, Katy did not understand that the number 4 represented 4 objects. To her, numbers were no different from letters of the alphabet. In fact, sometimes when she was writing, she would create a word that was composed of letters and numbers. Before engaging in problems with numbers at the abstract level, Katy needed to go back to the concrete and then semiconcrete stages to learn that numbers represent a set of objects. Once she mastered this concept, she was ready to solve problems using numbers.

Language and Mathematics

Students who struggle to develop mathematical concepts require careful instruction. In thinking about the various strategies and methods used to teach mathematics, consider the ways in which comprehension of language may affect the learning process. Students who experience problems with language are likely to have difficulty with mathematics. Like Katy, they may be more likely to rely on memorization of facts and procedures rather than to develop a solid understanding of mathematical concepts and applications.

As with strategies for improving reading comprehension, students need opportunities to discuss, clarify, and state what is being learned. In addition, students need explicit instruction in the language of mathematics, which includes signs, symbols, and terms, as well as the vocabulary used to express mathematical ideas. A teacher has two main roles: interpreting the language of mathematics and clarifying a student's attempts to use the language of mathematics.

Students who have difficulty using language need to try out possible answers to word problems (Tobias, 1993). All word problems contain assumptions. Asking students to talk through their approach helps them to identify incorrect assumptions. In a situation described previously, Katy was asked how many half of four trees would be. Katy envisioned that the trees would be cut in half horizontally, not separated into two groups. Her misunderstanding is based on an incorrect assumption. To correct this assumption, a teacher could have Katy practice this same type of problem using manipulatives.

When students do not have a strong language base, explanations need to be simple, accurate, and concise. Give the explanation just once, provide the student with the opportunity to think about the explanation, and encourage the student to ask meaningful questions.

Students also need language skills to recall and use the many steps and rules involved in math. Some students, although they may have memorized terms and signs, fail to understand how meanings change in different contexts. For instance, a student who associates the word *multiply* with the idea of becoming larger may not grasp the concept that numbers become smaller when multiplying fractions. Tobias (1993) described the confusion of the student who understands the minus sign in subtraction and then tries to apply the same meaning to the interpretation of negative numbers.

Although so-called keywords often appear in problems and may be relevant to the solution, they may not be relevant to the process of solving the problem. For example, a student may believe that the phrase "How many in all" means that the problem is asking them to add. Clearly, problems can be written so that the phrase signifies another process. Unfortunately, many students with poor math concepts may rely more on keywords instead of attempting to understand the more critical information presented in the problem. They then have difficulty with solving problems that do not use keywords or that use keywords in ways that are irrelevant to the solution (Cawley, Miller, & School, 1987; Jones et al., 1997).

Story or Word Problem Strategies

When students work on story or word problems, they draw on two critical skills: comprehension and translation. Students need to understand what is being asked (to interpret the goal of the problem), and they need to be able to represent that information by planning and executing a solution. Polloway and Patton (1993) noted that students with math disabilities improve their problem-solving abilities through teacher-directed activities that include several key stages: 1) having students read the problem carefully, 2) helping students focus on significant information, 3) involving students in stating a solution, 4) developing strategies for solving the problem, and 5) performing the necessary calculations.

Instruction in Reading Comprehension, Written Expression, and Math Problem Solving

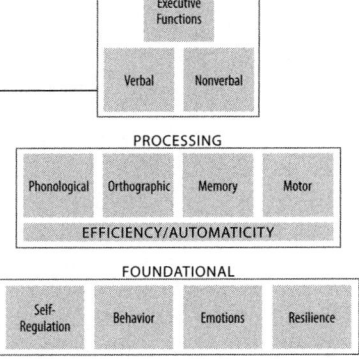

To assist students who experience difficulty and require explicit instruction in both representing and solving the problem, Maccini (1998) developed the acronym STAR:

Search the word problem.

Translate the words into an equation in picture form.

Answer the problem.

Review the solution.

This strategy can be helpful for students such as John who recognize the value of strategies when attempting to solve word problems.

John began by employing the first step (**S**earch the word problem). While searching the problem, he asked himself, "What facts do I know?" and "What do I need to find?" Once these questions were answered, John then wrote down the facts. In the second step (**T**ranslate the words into an equation in picture form), John attempted to do the following:

- *Choose the variable and identify the operations.* Translate the English terms into mathematical or algebraic terms, being careful to check the sequence in which the information needs to be conveyed. John used a chart of terms and their symbols that he had developed from his notes in order to double-check his translation.
- *Represent the equation using a drawing and concrete manipulatives.* Make a simple drawing of the problem in order to make it more meaningful or create a table of information, leaving blank spaces for any unknown information. Teach students to use as few unknowns as possible because a separate equation has to be developed to solve each unknown.

In the third step (**A**nswer the problem), John answered the problem using cues and a work mat. He then performed the fourth step (**R**eview the solution) and reread the problem while asking, "Does the answer make sense?" and "Why?" to make a final check of his answer.

When John's algebra teacher talked to John's history teacher, he learned that John understood the value of using preorganizers and postorganizers when studying for tests and when writing papers. Because the first two steps in the STAR procedure represent preorganizers and the last two steps represent postorganizers, the algebra teacher could help John see the value of working problems through on a step-by-step basis rather than guessing at the answer.

Through modeling and guided practice, students can learn how to plan what they need to do to solve problems. Students can be asked to solve different types of problems and obtain solutions depending on the type of question asked. Examples of different math problems include the following (Mather & Jaffe, in press):

- Decide which operations to use. (For example, Harry weighed 250 pounds. He weighed 72 more pounds than James. How much did James weigh?)
- Make a table, graph, or chart of the information provided. (For example, Hansel and Gretel went to the witch's house every day except Sunday. On Mondays and Thursdays, Hansel went twice. On Wednesday, Gretel went in the morning, at noon, and once after Hansel was in bed. Who traveled to the witch's house more times in a month?)
- Make a drawing of the information provided. (For example, Mehitabel planted a square garden with 12 garlic plants on each side to keep the snails away. How many garlic plants did she plant?)
- Make inferences and logical deductions. (For example, the Carsons went to Jack in the Box and spent $20.75 for lunch. An adult meal costs $4.95 and lunch for

a child costs $2.95. How many people are in the family? How many of them are children?)

Cue Cards

As students are learning a new algorithm (i.e., a set of rules for solving a kind of problem in a finite number of steps), they are likely to benefit from having an index card that lists several sequenced steps to follow when solving story problems. A sample card could list for students to 1) read and reread the problem, 2) draw or mentally picture what is happening, 3) restate what is being asked, 4) choose the operation or operations, and 5) compute and check the answer. Another example of steps to write on an index card would be 1) read the problem, 2) reread the problem to determine what is known, 3) identify the question that is being asked, 4) identify the operation or operations to use, 5) use objects or drawings to solve the problem, 6) write the problem, and 7) write the solution.

As a final step in problem solving, encourage students to check that their answer makes sense. Training students to estimate and evaluate their answers allows them to gain experience in testing their assumptions and in understanding when various processes are appropriate and when they are not. Another way to help students internalize important concepts is to ask them to explain the problem in their own words, try to explain it by putting it into a teacher's words, and, as a final step, translate the problem into mathematical language. Because students do not often get to see that even accomplished mathematicians often try several solutions, they need active modeling of the process.

John was having trouble understanding the meaning of place value when numbers included decimals. He thought that longer numbers would always be the bigger numbers. Therefore, he stated that 12.008 was larger than 12.8. John needed to review the concept of place value and the meaning of numbers containing fractions.

As discussed in Chapter 10, teachers need to help students resolve conceptual difficulties by using manipulatives, drawings, and think-alouds.

Effective Strategy Instruction

As with reading and writing, students who have difficulties with mathematics may require additional time for processing and learning skills and can benefit from self-questioning strategies, guided practice, and modeling. These strategies often focus on assisting students in developing and using systematic procedures to solve problems, finding the key that is appropriate for the kind of problem that is being solved, and helping students identify the necessary and unnecessary details within problems. Students who learn to be active and successful participants in their learning perceive themselves as competent problem solvers (Jones et al., 1997). Teachers can aid students by writing out basic processes and the necessary steps to procedures, drawing diagrams, and rewording problems in language closer to the students' own. Teachers can also create a variety of instructional techniques as they sequence tasks carefully. Miller (1996, p. 357) presented the following sequence for mastery of word problems:

Word problems with single words or phrases

Word problems with sentences; numbers still aligned vertically

Instruction in Reading Comprehension, Written Expression, and Math Problem Solving

Word problems in a traditional paragraph format

Word problems without extraneous information

Word problems with extraneous information

Word problems students create

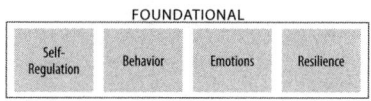

For students such as Ben, difficulties with reading and spelling can also affect math performance. Figure 11.8 presents several story problems Ben wrote when he was in third grade. Students were asked to write problems for peers to solve. After writing the problems, Ben drew illustrations. When he passed his problems to Marcos, Marcos replied, "I can't read these." Ben understands how to create and solve story problems, but other students cannot read his writing because of his misspelled words.

In addition, Ben has trouble reading the chapters presented in the math textbook. Cawley and Miller advised the following:

> If problem solving is truly the goal, obstacles to problem solving must be removed. A child who cannot solve problems because he or she cannot read the problems is not involved in problem solving but is involved in reading. (1986, p. 47)

As with instruction in reading comprehension and written expression, effective mathematics instruction involves teacher modeling, demonstrations, and student rehearsal. When introducing new concepts and skills, perform the task while talking and then ask the student to perform the task while talking it through. Describe and model how to solve the math problem several times using both visual and auditory cues (Allsopp, 1999). Then move from a teacher think-aloud (i.e., the teacher asks and then answers a question) to a teacher–student think-aloud (i.e., the teacher asks a question and then students help provide the answer). Students can then begin to help frame questions.

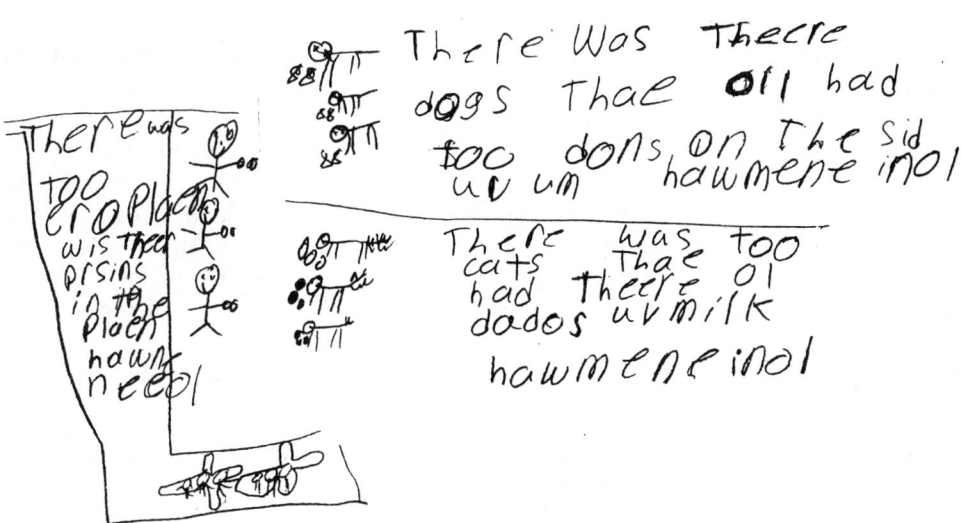

Figure 11.8. Ben's story problems.

John's algebra teacher used this procedure, adapted from Allsopp (1999), to demonstrate how to solve two-variable math equations. He wrote the following equation on the board: $2a + 3b = 20$. He then stated,

> I see that I have the letter a in this problem. What does the letter a stand for? I know that a letter stands for an unknown variable. I also know that when a letter is next to a number that it means multiplication. Now I also see that I have the letter b. Who can tell me what the b stands for in this problem?

A student answered, "Another unknown variable." The teacher said, "That's right, and who can tell me what it means when a letter is next to a number?" Another student answered, "It means to multiply." These types of think-alouds make the steps involved in problem solving apparent.

Sometimes students fail to understand that math is unlike other subjects. In most subjects, students learn content by starting with general concepts and then learning more specific information. In math, they need to start with very specific information that they then need to generalize. In teaching math problem solving, students need to learn information and then how to apply the information.

Some students have trouble understanding story problems. These students tend to make judgments about how to solve the problem on the basis of surface structure (i.e., the words or situation in the problem) rather than on an understanding of the mathematical structure of the problem (Hutchinson, 1993). Instruction is most effective when it focuses on mathematical structure.

In class, present clear, straightforward examples and have students take notes. Students can then explain the steps in their own words. Then present problems to be solved in which the rules or principles that the students need to remember are clearly illustrated. Students can state the rule, principle, or formula that will be used to solve the problem. Once students know how to solve the problem, present problems that differ or vary by one step. As time goes on, the sequence or types of problems assigned can be varied, but students should continue to state the rule or principle they must follow prior to attempting to solve it. Fuchs, Fuchs, and Hollenbeck (2007) suggested that teachers can change problems in the following four ways—referred to as transfer features—without altering their structure and the solution: a different look, different vocabulary or use of an unfamiliar keyword, a different or additional question, or an irrelevant number or information. Students can work with problems classifying how a feature has changed. Table 11.1 provides examples of these ways to change problems.

Hutchinson (1993) described ways to present problems at three levels of difficulty. Introduce a problem (e.g., relational, proportional, a two-equation problem) and practice it in its simplest form. Once the student has demonstrated mastery, alter the problem by maintaining the mathematical structure of the problem and changing its surface structure or storyline (i.e., a near-transfer problem). Once mastery is achieved, present students with problems in which the storyline of the problem is maintained but an additional step is added (i.e., a far-transfer problem). Hutchinson (1993, p. 38) provided the following example of a proportional problem at each of the three levels.

Problem: On a map, a distance of 2 centimeters (cm) represents 120 kilometers (km). What distance is represented on this map by 4 cm?

Near-transfer problem: The ratio of the mass of the big box to the mass of the little box is 3:2. If the mass of the big box is 42 pounds, find the mass of the small box.

Instruction in Reading Comprehension, Written Expression, and Math Problem Solving

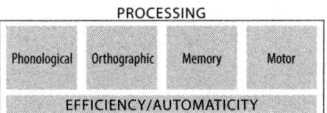
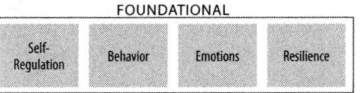

Table 11.1. Five ways to change math problems

Original problem
Ann wants to buy her dog Maggie some pork pizzle dog treats. Pork pizzle dog treats come in packages that contain 12 in each package. How many packages should she buy to get 36 pork pizzle dog treats?
Different look

• Ann wants to buy some pork pizzle dog treats for Maggie.
• The sign she sees at the store says,
 	
    On Sale Here Pork Pizzle Dog Treats!!!
    12 in Each Package!!
 	
• How many packages should you buy to get 36 pork pizzle dog treats?
  a. 2
  b. 3
  c. 4
  d. 5

Different vocabulary
Ann wants to buy her dog Maggie some pork pizzle dog treats. Pork Pizzle dog treats come in bags that contain 12 in each bag. How many bags should she buy to get 36 pork pizzle dog treats?
Different question
Ann wants to buy her dog Maggie some pork pizzle dog treats. Pork pizzle dog treats come in packages that contain 12 in each package and cost $5.00 per package. How many packages can she buy with $15.00?
Irrelevant number
Ann wants to buy her dog Maggie some pork pizzle dog treats. Pork pizzle dog treats come in bags that contain 12 in each bags. Maggie eats 4 pork pizzle dog treats a day. How many bags should she buy to get 36 pork pizzle dog treats?
Combined problems
Ann wants to buy her dog Maggie some pork pizzle dog treats. Pork pizzle dog treats come in packages that contain 12 in each package and cost $5.00 per package. How many packages does she need to buy and how much will she spend?

Far-transfer problem: Emma's family is walking to raise money. For every 14 km that Emma walks, her brother walks 10 km, and her father walks 2 km. Emma's father walks 18 km. Find the distance walked by Emma and her brother. (p. 38)

Because of his past difficulties with acquiring mathematical concepts, John frequently felt like giving up before he even attempted to solve a problem. Fortunately, his teacher took an active role and employed multisensory approaches. In class, he used colored highlighters to emphasize key terms, operations, symbols, and numbers, and he drew visual breaks between each step. He had his students talk about the problem by having them say the numbers aloud as they wrote them, recite formulas, and put problems into their own words. He encouraged students to do the following:

- Read a problem twice before attempting to solve it.
- Look for key terminology or essential features.
- Eliminate unnecessary details and ask how the problem can be rephrased.
- Consider what this problem reminds them of (do they see similar patterns in other problems they have done?).
- Use a variation of the K-W-L (Know-Want-Learned) strategy described in Chapter 10. Have students ask themselves, "What do I already know? What do I want to find out? What relates the two?"
- Determine principles and relationships involved, and determine the strategy to use to arrive at a solution.
- Make a guess about what the result or answer would be.

- Do each step on paper, not mentally.
- Use summary sheets.
- Check results.
- Pay attention to special cases.
- Explore alternative solutions.

This step-by-step approach allowed both John and his teacher to determine where he encountered difficulty. Although John initially needed to have his teacher model the steps a number of times, he knew that he was making progress in solving math problems.

A think-aloud strategy that encourages a student to describe how he or she approaches a set of problems in a homework assignment or on a quiz or test can help the student see the value inherent in using a strategic approach. Naglieri and Gottling (1995) found that some students start with random strategies, setting themselves up to encounter frustration.

John initially failed to understand when he was taking an algebra test that it was to his advantage to go through and solve the easier problems first rather than spending too much time on just one problem. In addition, John would not check his answers before handing in his test. The teacher asked him to use a think-aloud approach in describing how he solved the assigned problems. At that point, John came to understand that his low grade was as much a result of carelessness as it was a lack of knowledge. On his next test, he made the effort to solve the easiest problems first and then check his responses. His score improved several points.

For other students, a think-aloud strategy helps them to recognize that they have a number of strategies or techniques already available to them. Montague (2003) and Montague, Enders, and Dietz (2011) recommended that teachers assist students in learning to do the following:

- Read the problem aloud for understanding.
- Paraphrase the problem.
- Visualize or draw a picture of the problem.
- Hypothesize and plan a way to solve the problem.
- Estimate the answer.
- Compute the answer.
- Check the answer.

Effective Teaching Strategies for Advanced Math Courses

As special educators work with students with LD, it is important to provide balanced instruction across mathematics standards (i.e., numbers and operations, algebra, geometry, measurement, data analysis, probability) (Miller & Hudson, 2007). Adolescents with SLD can be taught to solve more complex problems than their teachers generally expect as long as they are provided with guided instruction and sufficient opportunity to solve problems (Jones et al., 1997). Despite significant problems with computation, some students understand mathematical concepts quite well and succeed in math courses at the secondary level. Students need to make a persistent effort at strengthening their computational weaknesses and developing their

Instruction in Reading Comprehension, Written Expression, and Math Problem Solving

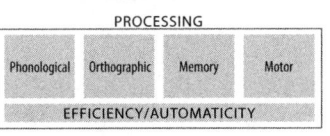
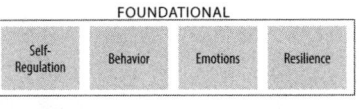

self-monitoring skills. Teach students the full range of upper-level math concepts, including more complex equations and applications.

For algebra instruction, the most effective teachers engage in modeling, provide guided practice activities, and check students' responses (Maccini, McNaughton, & Ruhl, 1999). Maccini and colleagues recommended that instructors employ the following principles to help students with SLD succeed in higher level mathematics courses:

Before beginning instruction, do the following:

- Administer a daily quiz of previously learned skills.
- Give a general orientation to introduce the strategy; explain the rationale for self-questioning strategies.

During instruction, do the following:

- Provide a clear and precise presentation of the skill or concept with a range of examples and nonexamples.
- Make use of manipulatives and computer-assisted instruction when possible.
- Teach students self-questioning strategies.
- Provide guided practice, reinforcing instruction with structured worksheets.
- Provide feedback and reinforcement by offering opportunities for monitoring students' level of understanding and providing corrective and positive reinforcement.

Maccini and colleagues (1999) also recommended requiring a level of mastery, using set criteria, providing independent practice, and assessing students frequently using a variety of measures, such as oral and written responses. Use the following types of self-questioning strategies to help students learn how to represent algebra word problems (Hutchinson, 1993):

- Have I read and understood each sentence? Are there any words whose meaning I need to ask?
- Have I understood the whole picture of the problem?
- Have I written down my representation of the problem on my worksheet (e.g., goals, unknowns, knowns, type of problem, equation)?
- What should I look for in a new problem to see if it is the same kind of problem?

For solving algebra word problems, use the following types of self-questioning strategies:

- Have I written an equation?
- Have I expanded the terms?
- Have I written out the steps of my solution on the worksheet (e.g., collected like terms, isolated unknowns, solved for unknowns, checked my answer with the goal, highlighted my answer)?
- What should I look for in a new problem to see if it is the same kind of problem?

In a review of effective math interventions for secondary students, Maccini and colleagues (2007) concluded that student performance can be improved through the use of 1) effective teaching principles, 2) a CRA sequence in teaching,

3) methods to teach the structure of word problems, 4) peer-mediated instruction for basic skills, and 5) videos that provide contextualized instruction in problem solving.

Software Selection and Math Instruction

Students who use appropriate technology persist longer, enjoy learning more, and make gains in math performance (Babbitt & Miller, 1997). Babbitt (2000) recommended the following principles for using mathematical software:

- Choose programs that minimize the clutter on the screen; too much stimuli is a problem and often distracts from the math concept being presented.
- Match the procedures used in the software with those being taught in class. If there are differences, take the time to point them out to students.
- Choose software that can be modified to meet students' needs. Some students thrive on timed responses; others find the time limits frustrating. Students also vary with regard to their need for feedback or breaks. Also check to see if the software provides helpful feedback or if it limits the number of wrong answers for a single problem.
- Watch for increments between levels. Software programs often have jumps that are too large for struggling students. Choose software that has built-in instructional aids or that simulates real-life solutions and has good record-keeping capabilities. A variety of software programs, ranging in content from basic math skills to advanced algebra, are available from Riverdeep (http://www.riverdeep.com). The Destination Math series, which focuses on real-word mathematics, provides instruction in basic skills, math reasoning, conceptual understanding, and problem solving. Software programs such as Access to Math, MathPad, Arithmefonts, and Math Type allow teachers to create calculations or word problems while controlling the number of problems on the page, the type size, the graphics, and many other features.

Numerous online programs are now also available such as WebMath (http://www.webmath.com/wsheet.html), Math Composer (http://www.mathcomposer.com), and the Math Worksheet Site (http://themathworksheetsite.com), as well as many other web sites described in Table 11.2.

One particularly comprehensive program is ALEKS (http://www.aleks.com). Through adaptive questioning, ALEKS accurately assesses a student's knowledge and then provides specific instruction targeted to each student's needs. ALEKS has been in thousands of K–12 schools, colleges, and universities throughout the world. Numerous free mathematical tutorials are also provided through the Khan Academy (http://www.khanacademy.org).

CONCLUSION

Students with weaknesses in reading comprehension, written expression, and math problem solving benefit from specific explicit instruction to develop conceptual, procedural, and declarative knowledge as well as the use of strategies. These strategies are taught most effectively when coupled with discussion, modeling, practice, rehearsal, and application of the strategies in differing contexts. When students such as John and Katy are actively involved in their learning and practice using strategies in the context of academic subjects, their understanding of concepts and

Instruction in Reading Comprehension, Written Expression, and Math Problem Solving

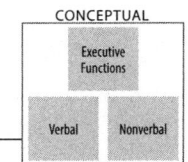

Table 11.2. Web sites and software for mathematics

Name / web site	Application
Motion Math Zoom (http://motionmathgames.com/motion-math-zoom)	Allows kids to navigate among concrete objects (animals) that represent abstract numbers, from *dinosaurs in the thousands* to *amoebas in the thousandths,* assisting them in learning the concept of place value.
Quick Graph (http://downloads.zdnet.com/product/20415-10946482)	This application allows students to have a graphing calculator. With this application it is easy to enter and/or edit equations and visualize them in mathematical notation. It is capable of displaying explicit and implicit (opt) equations as well as inequalities (opt) in both 2D and 3D, in all standard coordinate systems—Cartesian, polar, spherical, and cylindrical—all with amazing speed and beautiful results, which can be copied, e-mailed, or saved to the photograph library.
Questimate (http://www.graphite.org/app/questimate)	Students are exposed to estimating real-world items in unique ways that focus on how math—not just guessing—can be used to estimate. From how many bread loaves equal the length of the average couch to how far a hippo can run in a minute, kids get to choose from various topics with types of estimation (length, speed, height, and more) via a fill-in-the-blank template with real-world options.
Algebra Touch (http://www.graphite.org/app/algebra-touch)	Students learn the basics of algebra step by step. They will learn addition, variables, basic equations, negatives, and more, with a total of 20 topics.
Dragon Box Algebra 5+ (http://www.graphite.org/app/dragonbox-algebra-5)	Algebra is taught to students in a refreshing and unique way. Ten increasingly complex chapters teach students to solve, balance, and reduce multivariable equations.
Einstein Math Academy (https://play.google.com/store/apps/details?id=com.eddiehsu.mathgame)	K–5 students practice and strengthen their arithmetic skills using basic operations. Students move through problem sets and receive gold or silver pieces to boost their scores as they complete problem sets correctly.
Mathmateer (https://itunes.apple.com/us/app/mathmateer/id393989284?mt=8)	Students use this math app to build a rocket ship and launch it into space but must complete basic math challenges in order to earn money. Challenges include patterns and shapes, telling time, and fractions.
Counting Money Bingo (https://itunes.apple.com/us/app/counting-money-by-abcya!/id571405765?mt=8)	Students learn about U.S. currency and how to count, add, and subtract with it.

relationships improves. Although they are still likely to need adaptations within classroom settings and adjustments in the difficulty level of assignments, repeated opportunities to engage in the problem-solving activities of understanding and producing text, as well as solving mathematical problems, can increase their knowledge and academic success.

APPENDIX 11A

Synonyms for Words that Children Commonly Use in Writing

amazing   astonishing, astounding, dazzling, extraordinary, fabulous, fantastic, impressive, superb, unbelievable, wonderful

anger   aggravate, agitate, annoy, arouse, displease, enrage, exasperate, incense, inflame, infuriate, irritate, madden

angry   annoyed, exasperated, furious, indignant, inflamed, infuriated, irritated, mad, peeved, raging, vexed, wrathful

answer   acknowledge, reply, respond, retort

ask   beckon, demand, inquire, interrogate, invite, query, question, quiz, request, solicit, summon

awful   base, contemptible, direful, distasteful, dreadful, grotesque, nasty, repulsive, terrible, unpleasant

bad   contemptible, corrupt, criminal, dangerous, dark, deplorable, depraved, despicable, disgusting, dismal, evil, execrable, foul, ghastly, grisly, gruesome, heinous, horrid, immoral, insidious, malevolent, malicious, nasty, nefarious, noxious, putrid, rank, reprehensible, rotten, sinful, sinister, villainous, wicked

beautiful   alluring, attractive, captivating, charming, comely, dazzling, delicate, engaging, enthralling, enticing, fascinating, glamorous, glowing, gorgeous, handsome, heavenly, lovely, pretty, radiant, ravishing, resplendent, sparkling, splendid, stunning

begin   actuate, commence, embark, initiate, instigate, introduce, launch, open, originate, start

big   capacious, colossal, elephantine, enormous, expansive, extensive, gargantuan, gigantic, huge, immense, large, mammoth, massive, robust, titanic, vast

brave   audacious, bold, chivalric, courageous, daring, dashing, dauntless, fearless, gallant, heroic, plucky, valiant, valorous

break   atomize, crack, demolish, destroy, fracture, pulverize, rupture, shatter, smash, splinter, wreck

bright   colorful, gleaming, incandescent, intellectual, luminous, radiant, shimmering, shining, smart, sparkling, vivid

calm   aloof, collected, composed, detached, level-headed, mild, peaceful, quiet, serene, smooth, still, tranquil, unexcited, unruffled

come   advance, approach, arrive, near, reach

cool   chilly, cold, frigid, frosty, icy, wintry

crooked   bent, curved, hooked, twisted, zigzag

cry   bawl, bellow, roar, scream, shout, sob, wail, weep, yell, yowl

cut   carve, chop, cleave, crop, gash, lop, nick, prick, reduce, sever, slash, slice, slit

dangerous   hazardous, perilous, risky, uncertain, unsafe

dark   black, dim, dismal, dusky, gloomy, murky, sad, shaded, shadowy, sunless, unlit

decide   choose, determine, resolve, settle

definite   certain, clear, determined, distinct, obvious, positive, sure

Instruction in Reading Comprehension, Written Expression, and Math Problem Solving

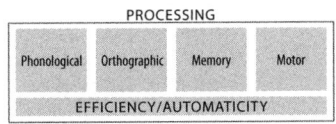
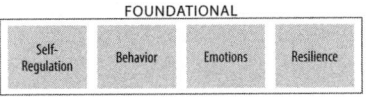

delicious appetizing, delectable, delightful, enjoyable, exquisite, luscious, palatable, savory, scrumptious

describe characterize, narrate, picture, portray, record, recount, relate, report, represent

destroy demolish, end, extinguish, kill, raze, ruin, slay, waste

difference contrast, disagreement, dissimilarity, incompatibility, inequality

do accomplish, achieve, attain, carry out, conclude, effect, enact, execute, finish

dull boring, dead, dreary, dumb, expressionless, humdrum, insensible, lifeless, listless, monotonous, plain, slow, stupid, tedious, tiresome, tiring, unimaginative, uninteresting, wearisome

eager enthusiastic, fervent, interested, involved, keen

end cease, close, conclude, discontinue, finish, halt, stop, terminate

enjoy appreciate, bask in, be pleased, delight in, devour, indulge in, like, luxuriate in, relish, savor

explain account for, clarify, define, elaborate, interpret, justify

fair honest, impartial, just, objective, unbiased, unprejudiced

fall descend, drop, plunge, topple, tumble

false counterfeit, deceptive, erroneous, fake, fallacious, fraudulent, groundless, spurious, unfounded, untrue

famous celebrated, distinguished, eminent, famed, illustrious, noted, notorious, renowned, well-known

fast expeditiously, fleet, hastily, hasty, lickety-split, like a flash, mercurial, posthaste, quick, quickly, rapid, rapidly, snappily, snappy, speedily, speedy, swift, swiftly

fat bulky, burly, chubby, corpulent, obese, overweight, paunchy, portly, pudgy, rotund, stout, tubby

fear alarm, anxiety, apprehension, awe, dismay, dread, fright, horror, panic, scare, terror

fly coast, cruise, flee, flit, glide, hover, sail, skim, soar, waft, wing

funny amusing, comic, comical, droll, humorous, laughable, silly

get accept, accumulate, acquire, bag, catch, collect, come by, derive, earn, fetch, find, gain, gather, glean, net, obtain, pick up, procure, reap, regain, salvage, score, secure, win

go depart, disappear, fade, move, proceed, recede, travel

good agreeable, apt, capable, edifying, excellent, fine, first-rate, friendly, generous, gracious, grand, honorable, kindly, marvelous, obedient, obliging, pleasant, pleasurable, proper, qualified, reliable, respectable, satisfactory, sterling, suitable, suited, superb, superior, top-notch, trustworthy, well-behaved, wonderful

great considerable, distinguished, grand, mighty, much, noteworthy, powerful, remarkable, worthy

gross coarse, crude, extreme, grievous, improper, indecent, low, obscene, outrageous, rude, shameful, uncouth, vulgar

happy blissful, cheerful, contented, delighted, ecstatic, elated, gay, glad, gratified, joyful, jubilant, overjoyed, pleased, satisfied, tickled

hate abhor, abominate, despise, detest, disapprove, disfavor, dislike, loathe

have absorb, acquire, bear, beget, believe, contain, enjoy, fill, gain, hold, maintain, occupy, own, possess

help abet, aid, assist, attend, back, befriend, benefit, encourage, relieve, serve, succor, support, wait on

hide camouflage, cloak, conceal, cover, mask, screen, shroud, veil

hurry accelerate, bustle, hasten, race, run, rush, speed, urge

hurt afflict, damage, distress, harm, injure, pain, wound

idea belief, concept, conception, notion, opinion, plan, thought, understanding, view

important considerable, critical, distinguished, essential, famous, indispensable, necessary, notable, primary, principal, significant, valuable, vital, well-known

interesting absorbing, animated, appealing, arresting, attractive, bewitching, bright, captivating, challenging, consuming, curious, enchanting, engaging, engrossing, entertaining, enthralling, exciting, fascinating, gripping, inspiring, intelligent, intriguing, inviting, involving, keen, lively, moving, piquant, provocative, racy, sharp, spellbinding, spicy, spirited, tantalizing, thought-provoking, titillating

keep hold, maintain, preserve, retain, support, sustain, withhold

kill abolish, assassinate, cancel, destroy, execute, murder, slay

lazy idle, inactive, indolent, slothful, sluggish

little cramped, diminutive, dinky, exiguous, itsy-bitsy, limited, microscopic, miniature, minute, petite, puny, runty, shrimpy, slight, small, tiny

look behold, contemplate, discover, examine, explore, eye, gape, gawk, gaze, glance, glimpse, inspect, leer, notice, observe, ogle, peek, peep, peer, perceive, peruse, recognize, scrutinize, search for, see, seek, sight, spy, stare, study, survey, view, watch, witness

love admire, adore, appreciate, care for, cherish, esteem, fancy, like, savor, treasure, worship

make accomplish, acquire, beget, build, compose, construct, create, design, develop, do, earn, effect, execute, fabricate, form, gain, get, invent, manufacture, obtain, originate, perform, produce

mark brand, designate, effect, heed, impress, imprint, label, note, notice, price, sign, stamp, tag, ticket, trace

mischievous impish, naughty, playful, prankish, roguish, sportive, waggish

move accelerate, amble, bolt, bound, breeze, budge, chase, coast, crawl, creep, dart, dash, dawdle, drag, fling, flow, gallop, glide, go, hasten, high-tail, hobble, hotfoot, hump, hurry, inch, jog, journey, lag, lope, lumber, lunge, meander, mosey, pace, paddle, perambulate, plod, plug, poke, prance, promenade, race, ride, roam, run, rush, sail, saunter, scamper, scoot, scramble, scurry, scuttle, shuffle, skedaddle, slide, slip, slither, slouch, spin, sprint, stagger, stir, straggle, streak, stride, stump, swagger, tear, toddle, trail, traipse, travel, trek, trip, trot, trudge, waddle, walk, wander, whisk, wobble

moody changeable, fretful, glum, irritable, mopish, morose, peevish, short-tempered, spiteful, sulky, sullen, temperamental, testy, touchy

neat clean, dapper, desirable, elegant, orderly, shapely, shipshape, smart, spruce, super, tidy, trim, well-kept, well-organized

new current, fresh, modern, novel, original, recent, unusual

old aged, ancient, archaic, broken-down, conventional, customary,

Instruction in Reading Comprehension, Written Expression, and Math Problem Solving

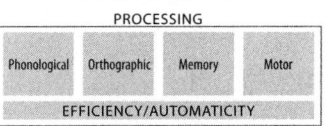
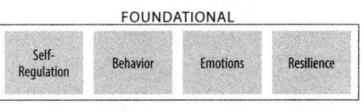

dilapidated, extinct, faded, feeble, former, frail, mature, musty, obsolete, old-fashioned, outmoded, passé, primitive, ragged, stale, traditional, used, venerable, veteran, weak, worn

part allotment, fraction, fragment, piece, portion, section, share

place area, dwelling, location, plot, position, region, residence, set, site, situation, space, spot, state, station, status

plan arrangement, blueprint, contrivance, design, device, diagram, draw, intention, map, method, plot, procedure, scheme, way

popular accepted, approved, celebrated, common, current, favorite, well-liked

predicament dilemma, jam, pickle, plight, problem, quandary, scrape, spot

put achieve, assign, attach, build, do, effect, establish, keep, place, save, set, set aside

quiet calm, mute, peaceful, restful, silent, soundless, still, tranquil

right accurate, apt, correct, factual, fair, good, honest, just, lawful, legal, moral, proper, suitable, true, upright

run dash, elope, escape, flee, hasten, hurry, race, rush, speed, sprint

say/tell advise, affirm, allege, announce, articulate, assert, assure, bellow, bid, boom, command, contend, converse, convey, declare, deliver, deny, dispute, direct, disclose, divulge, drawl, enlighten, exclaim, explain, express, grunt, hiss, impart, inform, insist, instruct, issue, jabber, lisp, mumble, mutter, narrate, negate, notify, order, philosophize, pronounce, protest, recount, relate, remark, reveal, roar, scream, screech, shriek, sigh, sing, snarl, snort, speak, squawk, stammer, state, stutter, suppose, swear, teach, thunder, train, utter, verbalize, voice, vow, whine, whisper, yell, yelp

scared afraid, alarmed, apprehensive, disquieted, disturbed, fearful, frightened, haunted, horrified, insecure, jumpy, panicked, paralyzed, petrified, shocked, shrinking, shy, skittish, stunned, stupefied, terrified, terrorized, timid, timorous, tremulous, troubled, unnerved, vexed, worried

show demonstrate, display, exhibit, explain, expose, indicate, note, point to, present, prove, reveal

slow behind, gradual, late, leisurely, slack, tedious, unhurried

stop cease, conclude, discontinue, end, finish, halt, pause, quit

story account, anecdote, chronicle, epic, fable, legend, memoir, myth, narrative, record, sage, tale, yarn

strange curious, exclusive, irregular, odd, outlandish, peculiar, queer, uncommon, unfamiliar, unique, unusual, weird

take acquire, assume, bewitch, buy, capture, catch, choose, consume, engage, grasp, hold, lift, occupy, pick, prefer, purchase, recall, remove, retract, rob, seize, select, steal, win

tell advise, bid, command, declare, disclose, divulge, explain, expose, inform, narrate, order, recount, relate, repeat, reveal, show, uncover

think assume, believe, consider, contemplate, deem, judge, meditate, reflect

trouble anguish, anxiety, concern, danger, difficulty, disaster, distress, effort, exertion, grief, inconvenience, misfortune, pain, peril, worry, wretchedness

true accurate, actual, dependable, exact, genuine, loyal, precise, proper, real, right, sincere, staunch, steady, trusty, valid

ugly evil, frightening, frightful, ghastly, grisly, gross, gruesome, hideous, homely, horrible, horrid, monstrous, plain, repugnant, repulsive, shocking, terrifying, unpleasant, unsightly

unhappy dejected, depressed, discouraged, dismal, downhearted, gloomy, glum, heartbroken, melancholy, miserable, poor, sad, sorrowful, uncomfortable, unfortunate, wretched

use consume, employ, exercise, exhaust, expend, spend

wrong erroneous, improper, inaccurate, inappropriate, incorrect, mistaken, unsuitable

APPENDIX 11B

Apps to Support Literacy Instruction

Purposeful, effective literacy instruction explicitly and systematically links instruction with essential content that is appropriate for the learner's needs. This list of apps is organized by their intended use: utility/presentation, dictionaries, word recognition skills, and language comprehension strategies.

UTILITY/PRESENTATION

SoundLiteracy by 3D Literacy

SoundLiteracy features electronic "tiles" with blanks, letters, graphemes, prefixes, suffixes, Latin roots, and Greek combining forms. The tiles are arranged by category. Instructional videos guide the user.

Dropbox by Dropbox

Dropbox lets you access any file saved to your Dropbox account from any computer, smartphone, or tablet. You can share a link to one file or set up shared files with other Dropbox account holders. Users get 2 GB of free data storage.

Doodle Buddy for iPad by Pinger, Inc.

Users can paint with their fingers or drawing tools and add sounds and stamps. You can import documents and photos from your Dropbox account.

Flashcards [+] by NKO Ventures, LLC

This versatile and powerful app allows the user to create custom flashcards with pictures or download sets made by "experts and novices" on Quizlet or Flashcards Exchange. The user can organize flashcards into categories. Text-to-speech in different languages is available for a fee.

Explain Everything by MorrisCooke

Explain Everything has an easy-to-use design, screencasting, and an interactive whiteboard tool that allows the teacher to annotate, animate, narrate, import, and export almost anything to and from almost anywhere. Export MP4 movies, PDF documents, PNG images, or XPL project files directly from your iPad.

VisTimer by Mindfultools

VisTimer utilizes an animated shrinking pie chart to depict elapsed time. It provides a visual reminder of time remaining and has an optional early warning setting. The user can select the sounds and colors.

The authors thank Elaine Cheesman, Ph.D., for contributing this resource material to the third edition.

Socrative Teacher Clicker and Student Clicker by Socrative

This is an iPad/iPhone version of an audience response technology (clickers). It provides clear definitions using only 2,000 common words and has special features for education (e.g., flashcards, teacher resources, printable worksheets, idiomatic phrases, synonyms, and word histories).

DICTIONARIES

Dictionary.com Dictionary and Thesaurus for iPad by Dictionary.com

This app version of the popular online dictionary provides standard and International Phonetic Alphabet (IPA) pronunciations, orally pronounces words, and identifies the origin and history of words. Several upgrades provide additional information (e.g., rhyming words, grammar tips, slang dictionary). It also works offline.

Longman Dictionary of Contemporary English—5th Edition by Pearson Education

The digital version of the latest print edition features a spelling suggestion dictionary, custom flashcards, a word of the day, and much more.

WORD RECOGNITION SKILLS

Phonological and Phonemic Awareness

Partners in Rhyme by Preschool University

This app helps the user to recognize rhyme using four games.

Blending SE by 95 Percent Group Inc.

Blending SE teaches students to recognize spoken words that are pronounced blended and sound-by-sound. It is an excellent and effective app for students who have difficulty blending sounds.

SmallTalk Phonemes by Lingraphica

Interactive "flashcards" show the phoneme written on one side. Touch it, and a video of a real person's mouth demonstrates how to pronounce the phoneme. This uses symbols of speech and language therapists (e.g., /ch/ is shown as /tsh/), so classroom teachers may need to modify some "cards." Disappointingly, /ng/ is pronounced /ing/.

Beginning Sounds Interactive Game by Lakeshore Learning Materials

Match words that share the same beginning sound using a drag-and-drop format. The user selects three sounds to play.

ABC MAGIC 3 by Preschool University

Draw lines to match initial sounds and letters. There are two formats: pictures to pictures or letters to pictures.

Sound Beginnings by Preschool University

Spelling starts with phonemic awareness (sequencing speech sounds in oral words). This app matches pictures at the beginning, middle, and ends of

Instruction in Reading Comprehension, Written Expression, and Math Problem Solving

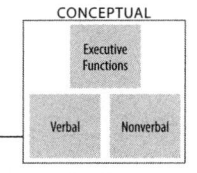
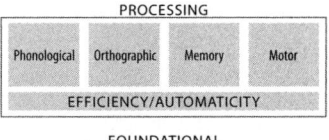
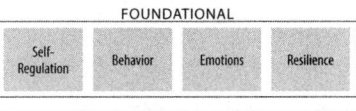

consonant-vowel-consonant (CVC) words and by matching letters to sounds. By touching the letter, the user can hear the associated sound (spoken by a child's voice); touching pictures allows the player to hear the name of the picture.

ABC Reading Magic Series by Preschool University

This series of apps blends and segments oral words presented as photographs.
- Reading Magic 1: three-phoneme, closed-syllable words
- Reading Magic 2: four- and five-phoneme, closed-syllable words with initial and final consonant blends
- Reading Magic 3: six-phoneme words with two syllables; contains a few vowel pronunciation errors
- Reading Magic 4: three-phoneme words with vowel-consonant-silent *e* and closed-syllable words

Letter Identification, Handwriting, and Spelling-Sound Correspondences

Handwriting Without Tears: Wet Dry Try by No Tears Learning

The app allows each student in a classroom to sign in and practice his or her letters while the app records their progress and errors. Via the Live Insights web site, the instructor can access reports, view graphs, and analyze the data for each student individually or collectively as a class.

StarDot Handwriting by TrishCO

This handwriting app has "kinesthetic" and alphabetic sequence, supports unlimited users, and provides reports. The web site (http://www.stardothandwriting.com) also has printable worksheets.

iTrace (Handwriting for Kids) by iTrace

This app teaches manuscript letters, words, and numbers. It provides three repetitions, supports multiple users, and monitors progress. The user can add his or her own words. Options include left-handed functionality and different instructional styles.

Letter Quiz by Tantrum

Letter Quiz features four learning modes to identify and write the letters of the alphabet, match upper- and lowercase letters, and learn the associated sound (not all are the most common sound, though).

Writing Wizard and Cursive Writing Wizard by L'Escapadou

This app uses both upper- and lowercase letters. The user can add words with audio.

LetterSchool by Boreaal

LetterSchool provides three modes of progressively difficult letter-forming practice (with mostly correct associated sounds and key words). The scaffolding and instant feedback are brilliant! Note: The *x* keyword and sound is "xylophone," /z/, rather than "box," /k-s/.

Letter Find by Matthew Thomas

This app is a letter-matching activity. The "negative" feedback buzzer sound proved to be too tempting for children over age 8.

Intro to Cursive by Montessorium, LLC

This app helps the user associate a letter shape with the most common sound by providing a model with a sound or name of the letter in upper- and lowercase cursive. Touch the eye to reveal the user's writing without the model. Note: *x* is pronounced /ks/.

Cursive Writing HD by Jiwoo Studio

This app lets the user practice writing single letters with stroke guidelines and pronunciation of each letter name. The user can input words or original sentences.

Conquering Cursive by Write-On Handwriting LLC

This app uses simple cursive letter formations and easy-to-understand terminology to explain the letter patterns.

Alphabetic Principle and Reading (Decoding)

Sound Beginnings by Preschool University

Sound Beginnings matches sounds with letters at the beginning, middle, and ends of pictures representing consonant-vowel-consonant (CVC) words.

Alphabetics by For Dyslexia S.L.

Using a multisensory approach, Alphabetics connects the names, shapes, and most common sounds via hearing, tracing, and pronouncing (with recording of user's voice!). The letter *q* is for /k/ in "quetzal" rather than the grapheme "qu" for /kw/.

Talking Shapes by Talking Fingers

Talking Shapes introduces the alphabetic principle via a fictitious story. Letters are introduced as "talking shapes."

ABC Reading Magic Series by Preschool University

This series of apps helps the user to read words using photographs for support to confirm reading accuracy.
- Reading Magic 1: three-phoneme, closed-syllable words
- Reading Magic 2: four- and five-phoneme, closed-syllable words with initial and final consonant blends
- Reading Magic 3: six-phoneme words with two syllables; contains a few vowel pronunciation errors
- Reading Magic 4: three-phoneme words with vowel-consonant-silent *e* and closed-syllable words

Sentence Reading Magic by Preschool University

This app bridges the gap between reading CVC words and reading decodable text in either print or cursive! This app has three modes. The first mode is sentence building, where children can move the words into their correct sentence position.

Instruction in Reading Comprehension, Written Expression, and Math Problem Solving

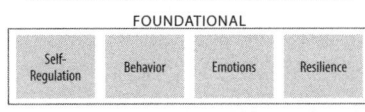

The second mode is the reading mode, where children can read the words of the phrase or sentence and then check their work by touching the hidden picture. The third mode challenges the user to match spoken and written high-frequency words. The picture is hidden so that the child will read the words first and then only look at the picture to check his or her work.

Bob Books—Reading Magic by Learning Touch

This decodable app is identical to the popular beginning reading book series. These interactive books put decodable words into a story to read. The user also spells target words by dragging and dropping letters to form a spoken word from the story. There are four levels of difficulty.

Starfall Learn to Read by Starfall Education

This app is identical to the popular beginning reader web site.

High-Frequency (Sight) Words

Fry Words by Innovative Mobile Apps

This "flashcard" app has two modes: learn and practice. In the "learn" mode, the user can choose to have the words pronounced or not. In the practice mode, the user has the option of selecting the pronounced word from a presented list of two to five words, and the user can set the display time as low as 0.7 seconds per word, spoken or not.

English Words 1–300: Everyone Learns by Teacher Created Materials

This app offers seven interactive games and four learning activities designed to read and spell 300 of the most common high-frequency words. One can also purchase sets of 100 words for half the price.

Sentence Reading Magic by Preschool University

One option in this app challenges the user to match spoken and written high-frequency words in either cursive or manuscript.

Spelling

ABC SPELLING MAGIC by Preschool University

The Word Building game includes only the three letters needed; the Movable Alphabet includes all letters. Touch the letters and pictures for audio. The app also uses an easy drag-and-drop format. Positive feedback is a short snippet of classical music!

- Spelling Magic 1: CVC words
- Spelling Magic 2: CCVC and CVCC words with beginning and ending consonant blends and double-letter spellings (e.g., *ff, ll, ss*)
- Spelling Magic 3: two-syllable words with closed and open syllables
- Spelling Magic 4: vowel-consonant-silent-*e* syllables

abc PocketPhonics by Apps in My Pocket Ltd

This app combines handwriting practice and spelling individual letters as well as letter combinations, or digraphs (e.g., *th, ea*). This app reinforces spellings by using the target spelling-sound correspondence to spell spoken words. This app could be improved with more inspiring feedback and rewards, but educationally, it is very sound.

Spel It Rite Pro by Todor Dimitrov

Note: This is listed under iPhone apps but can be played on an iPad.

This is for mature spellers. The objective is to select the correctly spelled word from two choices (e.g., epicurean/eppicurian). The word is presented orally (requires an Internet connection). Instant feedback quickly corrects errors. The user can review the spelling, pronunciation, definition, and synonyms.

A+ Spelling Test by Innovative Mobile Apps

The parent, teacher, or older student must type and record spelling lists, which takes just a minute from prepared lists. Several activities and a test track progress; reports can be e-mailed. The teacher or student can turn the instant feedback on or off during the spelling test. The user can also clear the test scores for another student to complete the test on the same device.

SpellingCity by SpellingCity

Although the provided word lists are not particularly useful for increasing spelling achievement, the user can easily create customized lists to suit any purpose. This is particularly useful for students learning to spell advanced words. The adult creates an account at the web site (http://www.vocabularyspellingcity.com). The user can then easily create a new list with a specific focus. After the words are entered, the user selects definitions and sentences or creates original text. Once done, users can play a game on the iPad or computer. Appealing bonuses are the alphabetized lists and handwriting features! The user can create a PDF of the word list in manuscript, D'Nealian, cursive, or American Sign Language, with a choice of sizes.

Spelling and Word Games

Spellvetica by Chudchud Industries

Like Letris, letter tiles fall down, and the user must use adjacent tiles to spell a word before all the tiles reach to the top. Tap the screen to move or flip the tiles to a strategic order. Longer words generate more points. You can play against friends on the same network.

Letris 2: Word Puzzle Game by Ivanovich Games

Play alone or split the screen and play with a friend or connect online. It includes seven languages! Like Tetris, the tiles drop from the top of the screen. Spelling words keeps the board clean, which encourages spelling longer words. When the board fills, the game is over. As the player improves, the game gives you the choice to say on the current level or progress to a more difficult level. There are several game modes, from calm to frenetic!

Letris and Friends: Word Puzzle Game by Ivanovich Games

This features the same game as Letris 2, only the Game Center automatically seeks opponents depending on your rank.

Instruction in Reading Comprehension, Written Expression, and Math Problem Solving

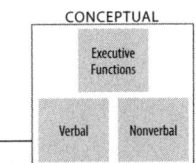
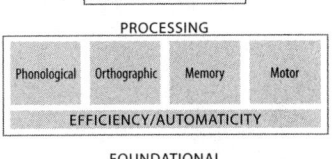

UPWORDS Free by Lonely Star Software, Inc.

This app is just like the traditional board game. You play against an opponent, which can be your alter ego!

SpellTower by Zach Gage

As you tap out adjacent letters to form words, more letter tiles rise from the bottom of the screen. When the columns reach the top of the screen, the game is over. There are five levels.

LANGUAGE COMPREHENSION

Vocabulary

Kids iHelp—Word Analogy by John Talavera

Kids iHelp is an intuitive analogies game that requires reading skills.

Categories Learning Center by Smarty Ears

Categories Learning Center can be used to help individuals sort items that belong to a certain category. There are several levels of play: Level 1 sorts dissimilar objects, and Level 2 sorts similar objects. Activities include "where does it go?" (placing an object in the correct category of three), category naming (providing the correct category name for a group of objects without prompts), and category selection (identifying which of four category names a group of objects belongs to). A progress monitoring feature showing treatment effectiveness with a report is presented at the end of each session, which may be e-mailed, printed, or stored.

The Right Word by Dactyl Applications

This app features a comprehensive list of frequently misused words within the context of a sentence. It is very challenging, even at the "easy" level.

Word Wit by Ballpoint Inc.

For both iPhone and iPad, this app presents a word and its "evil twin" (e.g., averse and adverse), the definitions, a quote, a "Master It" game for the user to select the correct word for the presented sentence, and a quiz. It is excellent for advanced word-learning skills.

Quizzative by Merriam-Webster

The goal of this app is to master "1000 words worth knowing."

Vocab Rootology HD—Greek and Latin Roots and Etymology by PrepInteractive

This app has a flashcard format for instruction plus interactive games. It offers letter "grades" for work done. It contains more than 5,000 combined flashcards and multiple-choice questions designed by Harvard, INSEAD, and University of Chicago graduates.

Find the Synonym by FreshLogo

The user's goal is to combine the provided letters to find the synonym/antonym before time runs out.

Language and Text Structure

Rainbow Sentences by Mobile Education Store

Rainbow Sentences is designed to help students improve their ability to construct grammatically correct sentences by using color-coded visual cues. The parts of sentences can be color-coded to help students recognize and understand how combinations of these parts create basic sentence structure.

Syntax City by Smarty Ears

This app features different locations with practice on usage. Categories include the gym (do/does), the beach (third-person singular agreement), the bakery (was/were), a ski resort (he/she), a farm (past tense verb agreement), the grocery store (has/have), the park (is/are), and the zoo (regular and irregular plurals).

Felt Board by Software Smoothie

With this app, the user is provided with a wide variety of backgrounds and figures for storytelling or summarizing text. It includes shapes, numbers, and letters, plus animals and settings for popular nursery and preschool songs like "Itsy Bitsy Spider," "Old MacDonald," and more.

SpellingCity by SpellingCity

SpellingCity is a sentence unscrambling game. It must be connected to the Internet to use the custom lists feature.

Inspiration Maps/Kidspiration by Inspiration Software

Students build their knowledge by creating diagrams, maps, and organizers that help them brainstorm, plan, organize, and build thinking skills. Tap to transform visual work into outlines that export for writing. Kidspiration includes math concepts.

Phrase Wit by Ballpoint Inc.

This app challenges the user to select the correct form of common figurative phrases (e.g., bated/baited breath). By providing explanations of the origins, the user discovers how they are spelled and why. Included are descriptions, origins, and quotes from literature with the phrase used in the correct sense. It also provides repetition through games.

Poems By Heart from Penguin Classics by Penguin Group USA

This app provides a structured, drag-and-drop format to memorize classic poems from master wordsmiths including Shakespeare, Edgar Allan Poe, Emily Dickinson, and more. The free trial version comes with two poems.

Interactive Books (Children)

The Monster at the End of This Book and **Another Monster at the End of This Book!** by Sesame Street

Beginning readers can follow along with an interactive version of the classic book narrated by Grover. The sequel also includes Elmo. Words are highlighted to help early readers follow along.

Instruction in Reading Comprehension, Written Expression, and Math Problem Solving

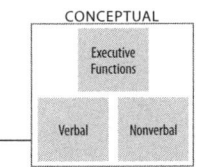
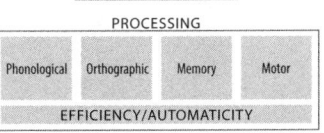
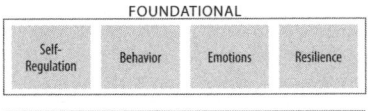

Dr. Seuss Series Interactive Books by Oceanhouse Media

These digital versions of the Dr. Seuss classics feature narrated text with simultaneous highlighting. When pictures are touched, the written word appears, accompanied by spoken text.

Interactive Books by Loud Crow Interactive Inc.

Loud Crow Interactive offers a large selection of interactive books for young children. The growing collection includes classic literature (e.g., Peter Rabbit), Sandra Boynton titles (e.g., *Blue Hat, Green Hat*), and *Peanuts* (e.g., *A Charlie Brown Christmas*). Each title has two options: "Read to Me," with professional narration accompanied by word highlighting, or "Read it Myself." In both formats, words are pronounced with the tap of a finger.

Nursery Rhymes with StoryTime by ustwo

This app lets the user play with Humpty Dumpty, Jack and Jill, Three Blind Mice, and other classic nursery rhyme characters.

Interactive Books (Teens and Adults)

Shakespeare in Bits by Mindconnex Learning Ltd.

Available in a free trial version, this is a multimedia approach to learning Shakespeare through reenactments with professional audio and unabridged text. Each title includes professional animation and soundtrack. The text, presented side by side with animated action, has portions highlighted as they are spoken. It also includes study notes and integrated analyses. A single purchase can be used on multiple iOS devices. The following titles are available for in-app purchase: *Romeo and Juliet, Macbeth, A Midsummer Night's Dream, Hamlet,* and *Julius Caesar.*

Poems by Heart from Penguin Classics by Penguin Group USA

This app provides a structured, drag-and-drop format to memorize classic poems from master wordsmiths including Shakespeare, Edgar Allan Poe, Emily Dickinson, and more. The free trial version comes with two poems.

WEB SITES WITH TABLET APP REVIEWS

http://www.interdys.org (Publication: IDA *Examiner*)

http://appsplayground.com

http://dyslexiahelp.umich.edu

http://www.teachthought.com

http://a4cwsn.com (apps for children with special needs)

http://pinterest.com (search for "educational iPad apps")

http://www.kirkusreviews.com (search for "top book app")

http://www.parents-choice.org/allawards.cfm (mobile app category)

http://www.apphalloffame.com (unfiltered content)

http://www.smartappsforkids.com

http://www.teachthought.com (iPad link)

http://www.ipadineducation.co.uk/iPad_in_Education/Literacy.html (British list)

http://teacherswithapps.com

http://appsforclass.com

https://www.appolearning.com

http://www.commonsensemedia.org

http://www.flashcardapps.info (reviews and filters for hundreds of flashcards)

SECTION V
Conclusion

CHAPTER 12 OUTLINE

HARPER UNIFIED SCHOOL DISTRICT REVISITED

THE CHANGING ROLE OF EDUCATION

WHAT TEACHERS WANT FROM STUDENTS

WHAT STUDENTS NEED FROM TEACHERS

   Essential Guidelines

CONCLUSION

CHAPTER **12**

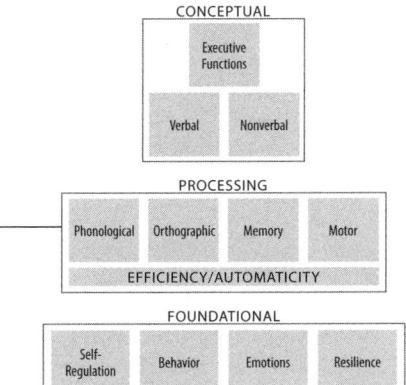

The Classroom Environment as a Microcosm of the World

The secret of education lies in respecting the pupil.

—Ralph Waldo Emerson

HARPER UNIFIED SCHOOL DISTRICT REVISITED

It has been 10 years since the school day described in Chapter 1. As time passes, students and teachers change, but the educational process of preparing children for their future continues. Teachers continue to be concerned about their students who have learning disabilities and behavior problems. What effect do those teachers have on their students? What strategies truly make a difference? Are educational plans, additional time engaged in one-to-one instruction, specialized tutoring, or counseling effective?

For the children described 10 years ago, life has changed. As a second grader, Andy struggled with fine and gross motor skills. Similar to the children in educator Rick Lavoie's (1994) description, Andy was the last one picked on the playground and often the first one his peers picked on. Now 10 years later, as a graduating senior, Andy has been accepted to a 4-year college. His handwriting is still hard to read. In fact, he describes it as "chicken scratchings," but he has become proficient on the keyboard and still loves to draw. He has also learned to play the piano and spends much of his free time practicing with a local band. Andy still experiences problems with coordination, but years of karate have helped him with balance and muscle tone. As he leaves high school, Andy is happy and on the road to a successful academic career.

Beto was a fun-loving 8-year-old boy born and raised in New Mexico. He arrived in the United States with his parents just before his birth. Beto spoke only Spanish at home until he attended kindergarten. Beto continued to struggle in elementary school but was subsequently identified as a child with a specific learning disability. It was eventually determined that his learning disability was not a consequence of English as a second language. Although academics were difficult for Beto, he continued to attend school and participated in a number of high school sports. He also completed vocational training and earned a certificate as a certified nurse assistant.

Ryan was the fourth grader with limited reading skills. He felt dumb because of his difficulty with reading and the need to receive support services in the resource room. As school progressed, Ryan's reading skills and self-confidence improved, but he continued to struggle with reading and writing even as he graduated. He required accommodations in complex academic subjects. Ryan is now completing a community college program in computer science. He has good friends and has not experienced any significant behavioral or emotional concerns. Now in his second year, he has been nominated for an award in mathematics. When he completes his 2-year college degree, he plans to enter the work force as a computer programmer.

During high school, Stephanie, the fourth-grade girl with nonverbal learning disabilities (NVLDs), continued to have few friends and had a hard time working in groups. In spite of these difficulties, Stephanie graduated a year ago and has taken a job as a semiconductor assembler. Stephanie enjoys the job because of its repetitive nature. Since she has started working at the company, she has made a few friends and has joined a bowling league. Her manager at the plant states,

> Stephanie is a hard worker, but I have come to realize that I need to show her how to do things step by step. She needs to repeat things several times before she catches on. Once Stephanie can perform the task, she works diligently to do what is asked of her.

Also, because of the patience of her manager, Stephanie can now complete three different jobs on the assembly line.

In fifth grade, Katy possessed good rote skills but struggled when attempting to learn new concepts and vocabulary. This continued throughout school. In high school, she received resource services to provide support for complex classes, such as history and science. During her senior year in high school, Katy decided to become a beautician. After graduating high school, she attended beauty school for 6 months and earned her license. Katy now works for a local hairdresser and has developed a good clientele.

As a fifth grader, Anthony was depressed and increasingly isolated from family and friends. That year Anthony was referred to the school psychologist for an evaluation. During a visit with Anthony's mother, the school psychologist learned that Anthony's father and many of his relatives were diagnosed with depression. Anthony was placed in therapy with a community-based psychologist and soon after began taking an antidepressant medication. Anthony still takes a medication for depression and periodically visits his psychologist. Though still prone to bouts of unhappiness, Anthony is finishing his third year of college and planning to become an accountant.

Mark was the fifth-grade student whom Ms. Perry wished she could adopt. He had good abilities, but his home life was chaotic and inconsistent. Mark's mother eventually moved out of state, taking all her children. Despite Mark's chaotic life, he continued to do well in school, and his school success provided an island of competence. He joined the track team in high school and was one of the school's top two runners. The combination of his good grades, achievement in track, and financial need enabled Mark to obtain a full scholarship to a 4-year college. Presently, Mark rarely visits his family. He

The Classroom Environment as a Microcosm of the World

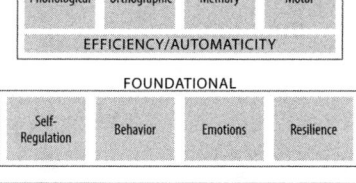

has pledged a fraternity and, through his friendships, developed an extended family. He is now successfully completing his junior year of college and would like to be a teacher.

Jeremy was the boy who was diagnosed with attention-deficit/hyperactivity disorder (ADHD). His grades were marked by inconsistencies in middle school. Within the same class, he had As, Cs, and Fs, depending on the type of task. In high school, he attended an alternative school that provided students with more structure and support. During these years, Jeremy became an avid skier and spent weekends working for the ski patrol. Although Jeremy plans to go to college someday, as of 2014, he is working on the ski patrol in the winter and doing construction work in the summer.

Mr. Arnold was concerned about Maria as she finished sixth grade. Despite extended instruction, Maria continued to demonstrate problems with aspects of reading and spelling. Maria had an accommodation plan in high school that allowed her to have extended time on all tasks and tests requiring reading and writing. With these accommodations, she was able to stay on the honor role. After graduating from high school, she applied to a 4-year college with outstanding support services for students with LD. She was accepted, received tutorial support, and is now completing her junior year. On her application to the LD program, she was asked to write a personal statement describing how her LD has affected her school career (see Figure 12.1). Maria will succeed. She understands her learning problems, can explain how these problems affected her school performance, and recognizes how these experiences have shaped her personality.

Samuel was the sixth-grade student who appeared to be in trouble for something every day. Despite support at school and through community resources, Samuel continued to struggle. He began experimenting with drugs and alcohol and eventually dropped out of school during his junior year. As a teenager, he ended up repeatedly in the juvenile court for status offenses and received several felony charges for drug possession. Though he works doing manual labor, he rarely keeps a job longer than a month. Samuel is constantly in financial trouble and continues to abuse both alcohol and drugs.

Marta was shy and pleasant but spoke very little English in eighth grade. Her family had emigrated from Honduras 2 years earlier. Despite support, Marta struggled in school, eventually dropping out. Today she works in the food service industry, is married, and has two children.

Remember Ben, the eighth grader who would rather walk over hot coals than write? Well, he still dislikes writing. Ben received resource support throughout high school and improved his writing immensely. After leaving high school, he spent 2 years in the Air Force. He is now a tennis professional at a local country club and has developed a well-known tennis academy for children. Although he e-mails friends regularly, he spends little time reading or writing.

John, a junior 10 years ago, was an enthusiastic student who had poor study skills and difficulty with grasping concepts. John attempted several courses at the local community college but struggled with the content. He decided to forego college for now and take a job working with a friend who owned a furniture store. He has now worked successfully at the store for 5 years. John is presently in his mid-20s. He and his wife have two children and have just bought their first home.

Personal Statement –

I think my learning disability has impacted my education in many ways, both good and bad. My learning disability caused me to have a hard time with reading and writing, which seemed to cause me to learn slower then others when it came to reading. This kind of upset me because, for example, I never got to read the same kind of books my friends were reading when I was younger, like the Baby Sitters Club. My disability also caused a problem when I tryed to read outloud because I wasn't at the same level as everyone else. So sometimes people would make fun of me which caused me to be hesitant to read to people, which I still have today. But on the other hand, I think that having this disability caused me to work harder because I knew that I could never slack off or do anything to, half of my obility, otherwise I wouldn't be able to pass my classes. Also when it came to reading I always had to put in double the time that was expected, which caused me to learn how to mannage my time.

Figure 12.1. Maria's personal statement for her application to her college's specific learning disabilities program.

The Classroom Environment as a Microcosm of the World

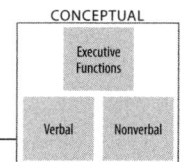

Figure 12.1.

> too. I also think that having this disability made me more assertive and confident in myself. Because I always had to standup for myself to other kids, when they made fun of me, and to my instructors by asking them for more time or more help with something. This made me realize that if I needed something I had to be the one to say it, and that you aren't going to lose anything by asking, you just gain. I find that even today some of my friend will need something or will have a problem and they are to afraid to talk to their teachers about it. But with myself, I have always had really great relationships with my teachers and always keep in comunication with them at all times, telling them how I am doing and how I think everything is going, good or bad. I think my disability played a big part in this. So as you can see my disability has effected my education and life, but I feel like I have learned from it and that it make me a better person.

Are these the typical outcomes for students with histories of emotional, behavior, and academic problems at school? As a microcosm of the world, do school problems predict future lives? For some students, it would appear to be so. Yet for others, struggling in school does not appear to be a life sentence or a particularly negative predictor that one's adult life will be unfulfilled or disrupted. If success is defined as personal and vocational satisfaction, all but one of these students successfully made the transition into adult life. It is unknown whether this group represents a better outcome than most because few large-scale studies explore the outcomes of the 15%–20% of students struggling at school. The available data, however, suggest that these students do not succeed at anywhere near the rate of the general population (Goldstein, 1995; Goldstein & Brooks, 2007; Sprague & Walker, 2000).

Most educational personnel understand that certain characteristics place children at risk in school, and these characteristics decrease their chances for future success. Although the majority of school problems cannot be resolved quickly or cured easily, the first step in helping is to possess a working model to understand these problems. By focusing on strengths first and foremost and recognizing weaknesses in learning abilities, appropriate expectations and interventions can be developed. Understanding a student's unique disposition, support system, characteristics, and abilities empowers adults to create positive change and make a difference in an individual's life.

THE CHANGING ROLE OF EDUCATION

By the very nature of their work, teachers are futurists. They are entrusted with the important though at times underappreciated job of preparing children for a successful adulthood. Growth of formal education in the United States came about as a means of socializing a diverse group of immigrants. Teachers were entrusted with instilling not only academic information but also a set of values and ideals consistent with the culture. During the past fifteen years, however, the teaching of social and cultural values is no longer of paramount importance for teachers. Instead, parents look to teachers primarily to convey academic information to their children. In the early grades, parents expect teachers to teach basic skills and, in the later grades, to help children acquire complex information about the world around them. But is this all society demands of teachers and the educational system at this time? What has replaced teachers' primary charge of socializing culturally diverse immigrants? What is it that society and culture require from the educational system beyond imparting academic knowledge to students?

Certainly, at the very least, society expects the educational system, including the postsecondary school system, to prepare students to enter a work force that has become technologically and intellectually more demanding and complex. It is no longer enough for a student to be the holder of many facts. One has to learn to think, reason, judge, and cope with complex information.

The secondary role that the schools and teachers have been given is to prepare children who are at risk. Students such as Andy, Beto, Ryan, Stephanie, Katy, Mark, Jeremy, Maria, Anthony, Ben, Marta, Samuel, and John can no longer afford to simply leave school because they are academically unsuccessful and expect success in adult life. Teachers are increasingly required to help prepare those at greatest risk for making a successful transition into adult life. This is what society wants from schools and teachers. Society expects educators to be futurists: to gaze into the proverbial crystal ball; identify those students at risk; and, through their expertise, help students develop skills to overcome adversities.

WHAT TEACHERS WANT FROM STUDENTS

Teachers want students to be successful. In the classroom, students who are at risk may demonstrate inappropriate behavior, participate in less academically engaged

The Classroom Environment as a Microcosm of the World

time, struggle with academic success, and often develop very different relationships with their teachers (Skiba, McLeskey, Waldron, & Grizzle, 1993; Sprague & Walker, 2000; Walker, Cheney, Stage, & Blum, 2005). In response, teachers engage in an increased variety and frequency of behavior and educational management strategies. Walker and Rankin (1983) suggested eight student qualities that predict classroom success. These qualities are still relevant today:

1. The ability to follow teacher directions consistently
2. The ability to follow classroom rules without the need for extensive teacher supervision
3. The ability to complete all or the majority of schoolwork without extensive teacher support
4. The ability to follow group rules and norms in all school situations
5. The ability to follow social rules while interacting with classmates without extensive teacher support
6. The ability and willingness to follow teacher instructions and assignment directions without significant assistance
7. Flexibility, or the ability to adjust to changes during the educational day
8. The capacity to respond to conventional classroom management techniques and to not stand apart from others behaviorally, academically, or socially

In one aspect or another, the students described in this text struggled to develop most of the attributes for becoming and being a successful student. Often, in a frustrating cycle, students' inabilities to be successful shape the nature and quality of the interactions they have with their teachers, which further shapes students' mind-sets about school and their capabilities. A successful student then appears to be one who does not experience a learning or developmental problem; is not depressed, anxious, or experiencing significant life adjustment problems; resides in a stable family; does not experience problems with temperament resulting in an excessive activity level, inattention, or impulsivity; and does not exhibit disruptive behavior problems.

Unfortunately, successful students are viewed as those who do not possess liabilities that interfere with school performance. Of paramount importance for helping children who struggle in school is adoption of a new vision of what it means to be a successful student. Despite his struggles with motor development, Andy found success in music and other academic areas. If success is defined as entering adult life and finding a comfortable niche, Ryan and Katy too were successful, although they continued to struggle with reading. Even Mark, the boy who struggled because of problems in the home environment, managed to find an island of competence in his life. Thus, school success comes in many shapes and forms. The definition of a successful student must begin with an understanding of what students need from teachers. This definition must begin with the belief that all children can be successful at school.

WHAT STUDENTS NEED FROM TEACHERS

First and foremost, students need empathetic teachers who possess a reasoned and reasonable understanding of how children learn, think, feel, and behave. Teachers must be charismatic adults in the lives of children for whom school is unrewarding. Students need effective teachers capable of exuding an aura of authority and affection. Effective teachers 1) focus on academic goals, 2) carefully set instructional goals and materials, 3) structure and plan learning activities, 4) involve students in the learning process, 5) closely monitor students' progress, and 6) provide frequent feedback on progress and accomplishments (Goldstein & Brooks, 2007). They are capable of organizing and maintaining the classroom learning environment by maximizing time spent engaged in productive activity and minimizing time lost during transitions or disruptions. Effective teachers are proactive and work to avoid problems rather than respond to them. They can develop a workable set of student expectations; respond consistently and quickly to inappropriate behavior; do not take students' misbehaviors personally; and have at their disposal a repertoire of behavioral and educational strategies to help every student succeed. Most importantly, they know how to help every child feel competent, accepted, respected, and valued in the process.

Students need teachers who are helpers and ready to assist when needed. Cunningham and Zibulsky provide the following explanation of how parents can assist their children as they develop reading skills:

> Remember that reading really is like helping your child learn to ride a bicycle. You'll adjust the level of support you provide over time, as your child begins to become more independent and wobble less as he makes his way down the street, but you will always keep your eyes on him and be ready to help if he hits a bump in the road. (2014, p. 400)

So it is with effective teachers: they watch and support their students as they grow and are ready to come to assistance when they see that a student is struggling.

Students also require teachers who are capable of developing clear student expectations for behavior, learning, and consequences; who are prepared for class lessons; and who understand the learning characteristics of their students and provide appropriate instructions. They also need teachers who emphasize success rather than failure; who model appropriate behavior; and who communicate with students in positive, sensitive, and constructive ways. Students with learning and behavior difficulties benefit from teachers who communicate high expectations for student efforts and accomplishments while providing a supportive classroom environment. These teachers foster student success and use the power of success as effective motivators. They incorporate different types of approaches in teaching and allow adequate time for learning to take place through practice and application of skills. In discussing the experiences of adults with histories of LD, Reiff, Gerber, and Ginsberg (1993) stated that in many cases, adults found innovative ways to teach themselves. In other words, the student's ability to learn was always present, but the teacher's knowledge of how to teach was lacking.

Walker and Shea (1991) described effective teachers as "authentic teachers." This description focused on the personal traits that teachers as human beings bring with them into the classroom that foster successful students. These traits are perhaps most needed by students who are at risk. Authentic teachers choose their vocation and know why they make this choice. They accept children for the individuals they are rather than trying to make them someone they are not. They possess a workable model about how children learn, think, and feel. They are willing to examine their own behavior critically, learn new strategies for reaching at-risk students, and make changes as needed. They are patient, flexible, consistent, and supportive. The ideal teacher sounds very much like the ideal spouse, friend, or boss. Effective teachers can honestly respond that they would enjoy being a student in their own class. Perhaps the golden rule for being an effective teacher and meeting students' needs is striving to be a good human being.

The Classroom Environment as a Microcosm of the World

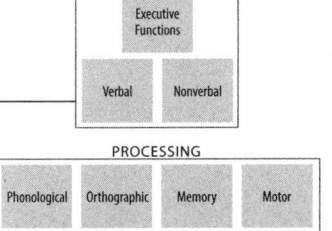

The message in this text is that when a child struggles in school, teachers must first understand and determine the underlying factors contributing to learning, behavior, or emotional problems. When children misbehave, their reasons may not be readily apparent. When a child fails or refuses to complete work, it is rarely due to poor motivation. As discussed within the text, the classroom behavior, emotional, and learning problems of children can be placed within a triangular framework reflecting foundational abilities, processing abilities, and conceptual abilities. This model offers a bridge between scientific research and educational practice. The model is designed to increase understanding of the reasons students struggle and, more important, the ways educators can help them, not just today, but throughout their entire lives.

Essential Guidelines

Effective teachers follow these essential guidelines:

- *Want to teach.* If teachers do not enjoy being in classrooms, they should seek other professions. Models, guidelines, knowledge, or management strategies will not fill the void of an unfulfilling vocation.

- *Respect all students.* This chapter began with a quote by Emerson suggesting that the secret of education lies not in strategy or technique but in respecting the student. If teachers set out to fix students; to shape, chip, or otherwise force them into their own preconceived notions of success; and to convey to students that who they are is not good enough, these students will most likely not be successful in the classroom.

- *Work from a model.* One of every five children in the classroom experiences some type of foundational, processing, or thinking problem. Many experience multiple problems that impair their abilities to be successful in the traditional way at school. Teachers should begin with a model or framework for seeing the world through the eyes of these students and work to understand how to help them.

- *Understand the forces that shape student outcomes.* Effective teachers recognize that student, setting, teacher, and strategy are all variables that affect classroom behavior and student functioning. Modifying any one of these can successfully change outcomes.

- *Accept the fact that children think.* There is no doubt that behavior is shaped, developed, maintained, and modified on the basis of consequences. It is also equally important, however, to recognize that the methods and means by which children interpret, process, think, and talk to themselves about their experiences affect their self-esteem, their relationships with adults and other students, and their behavior. Effective teachers take the time to understand how students think and feel about their lives.

- *Focus on the work.* E.B. White (1999), the author of the fabled children's classic *Stuart Little,* once wrote, "I'll make the work interesting, and the discipline will take care of itself." When classroom work and activities are interesting, engaging, and enjoyable, children become active participants in the educational process. Such participation is incompatible with classroom misbehavior and a lack of motivation.

- *Remember that schools cannot resolve family problems.* Families may be coping with increased stress, transitions, or other impediments to successful family functioning. Effective teachers understand and accept that children come to the classroom with an outside history that can significantly affect their functioning. By understanding and accepting individual differences in family background and functioning, teachers can make school a safe haven and an important place for many children.

- *Recognize the importance of friends.* Socialization is a powerful force, not only for shaping children's happiness, but also as a predictive influence in shaping a positive future. All students need to have opportunities to socialize with peers.
- *Keep learning and growing.* As with any other skill, teaching is learned by trial and error, success and failure. Teachers must be honest and avoid being defensive when more experienced teachers provide guidance or advice. Take advantage of the knowledge of others. The advances in knowledge about the brain's role in learning, emotions, and behavior continue to grow at an exponential pace. The more teachers learn, the more effective they become in developing strategies to help students experience success. The commitment to teach is also a commitment to a lifelong process of continued learning to maintain excellence in education.

Effective teachers help students develop the capacity to confront and overcome the various challenges that they will encounter in academic environments. To confront these challenges, a student must 1) understand his or her strengths and weaknesses, 2) acknowledge and confront his or her academic challenges, 3) want to succeed, and 4) set achievable goals (Gerber & Ginsberg, 1990). In other words, success depends on the individual's resilience, persistence, and motivation to accomplish goals. Successful students have a solid understanding and acceptance of their strengths and weaknesses and are persistent, motivated, hardworking, and goal oriented. Perhaps most importantly, students who succeed develop a supportive environment that includes friends and family as well as their teachers. They find people who believe in their learning abilities.

CONCLUSION

What will be the future of education in America? How will classrooms appear 20, 30, or 50 years from today? Some have suggested that in the future, classrooms will be eliminated because the "world will be a child's classroom." Perhaps the days of classrooms in which the teacher sits at his or her desk in the front of the room, students' desks are neatly aligned in rows, and teaching takes place on a chalkboard are over. A diverse set of technologies is changing how we teach and how children learn. Children are now exposed to technology at a very young age and enter school extremely sophisticated in the use of computers, tablets, and cell phones. To keep pace, education and educators must be prepared to embrace and employ this technology, changing how children are taught as well as the physical environments in which they are taught. A study completed by the Herman Miller Company in 2011 titled "Our Journey to a Better World" reported, "Emerging discoveries about how people learn, rapid advancements in technology and heightened awareness of student expectations drive pedagogical changes. In order for teachers to take advantage of these changes, teaching space and theory must be modified" (p. 2). Classrooms must be sufficiently flexible to accommodate different teaching styles, technologies, and needs. They must be designed to encourage students to feel comfortable in asking questions, work effectively in groups, and feel valued and connected. These are not necessarily new goals, but the means and manner by which they will be conducted and carried out in classrooms are new. Teachers must be trained to collaborate

The Classroom Environment as a Microcosm of the World

with students and administrators. Classrooms of the future must facilitate learning by using technology, supporting students in virtual and physical learning spaces. Classrooms of the future may be paper free. They may be more focused on project-based curricula and test scores based on problem solving rather than rote recitation of knowledge. Classrooms of the future must be sustainable and capable of meeting children's social, emotional, and academic needs while simultaneously setting goals for academic, citizenship, and life skills. As Siegal (2012) has pointed out, caregivers and educators are architects of the way in which experience influences genetically preprogrammed but experience-dependent brain development. Caregivers and teachers create an environment in which instinctual optimism, resilience, and self-discipline flourish. While children acquire knowledge and learn to apply that knowledge effectively, teachers must provide opportunities for students to assimilate and accommodate information, foster executive functioning, and, most importantly, begin to view teachers as engagement coaches. Such coaches are prepared, strategic, and efficient in designing classrooms in which children of all abilities are able to succeed, acquire knowledge, and problem-solve.

Education is the legacy teachers provide to our children and the gateway to their successful future. The future lies in their hands. Unlike snakes and salmon that never need to meet their mothers or bear cubs and primates that require only a few years with adults before they can survive alone, children need to be nurtured throughout their school years. Students who struggle with school can succeed when they have support from teachers or possess the persistence and resilience of Maria. As she described in her personal statement, one major factor contributing to her success was that she always knew she could count on her teachers. As a result of their support, she believed her struggles helped her to become a better, more understanding person. Ginott (1972, p. 13) wrote the following poem as a young teacher; teachers are the decisive element.

> I have come to a frightening conclusion.
> I am the decisive element in the classroom.
> It is my personal approach that creates the climate.
> It is my daily mood that makes the weather.
> As a teacher, I possess tremendous power to make a child's life miserable or joyous.
> I can be a tool of torture or an instrument of inspiration.
> I can humiliate or humor, hurt or heal.
> In all situations, it is my response that decides whether a crisis will be escalated or de-escalated, and a child humanized or dehumanized.

References

Aaron, P.G., & Simurdak, J. (1991). Reading disorders: Their nature and diagnosis. In J.E. Obrzut & G.W. Hynd (Eds.), *Neuropsychological foundations of learning disabilities: A handbook of issues, methods, and practice* (pp. 549–571). San Diego, CA: Academic Press.

Aase, H., Meyer, A., & Sagvolden, T. (2006). Moment-to-moment dynamics of ADHD behaviour in South African children. *Behavioral and Brain Functions, 2*(11), 1–13.

Abramowitz, A.J., & O'Leary, S.G. (1991). Behavior interventions for the classroom: Implications for students with ADHD. *School Psychology Review, 20,* 220–234.

Achenbach, T., & Rescorla, L. (2000). *Achenbach Child Behavior Checklist (CBCL).* Burlington, VT: ASEBA.

Adams, M.J. (1990). *Beginning to read: Thinking and learning about print.* Cambridge, MA: MIT Press.

Adams, M.J., Foorman, B.R., Lundberg, I., & Beeler, T. (1998). *Phonemic awareness in young children: A classroom curriculum.* Baltimore, MD: Paul H. Brookes Publishing Co.

Aghaie, R., & Zhang, L.J. (2012). Effects of explicit instruction in cognitive and metacognitive reading strategies on Iranian EFL students' reading performance and strategy transfer. *Instructional Science, 40,* 1063–1081. doi:10.1007/s11251-011-9202-5

Ahmed, Y., Wagner, R.K., & Lopez, D. (2014). Developmental relations between reading and writing at the word, sentence, and texts levels: A latent range score analysis. *Journal of Educational Psychology, 106,* 416–434. doi:10.1037/a0035692

Ahrentzen, S., & Evans, G.W. (1984). Distraction, privacy, and classroom design. *Environment and Behavior, 16,* 437–454.

Alberto, P.A., & Troutman, A.C. (2013). *Applied behavior analysis for teachers* (9th ed.). Upper Saddle River, NJ: Pearson.

Alcott, L.M. (1868). *Little women.* Boston, MA: Roberts Brothers.

Allen, L. (1998). An integrated strategies approach: Making word identification instruction work for beginning readers. *Reading Teacher, 52,* 254–268.

Allington, R.L. (1983). Fluency: The neglected reading goal. *Reading Teacher, 36,* 556–561.

Alloway, T.P., & Passolunghi, M.C. (2011). The relationship between working memory IQ, and mathematical skill in children. *Learning and Individual Differences, 21,* 133–137. doi:10.1016/j.lindif.2010.09.013

Allsopp, D.H. (1999). Using modeling, manipulatives, and mnemonics with eighth-grade math students. *Teaching Exceptional Children, 32*(2), 74–81.

Allsopp, D.H., Kyger, M.M., & Lovin, L.H. (2007). *Teaching mathematics meaningfully: Solutions for reaching struggling learners.* Baltimore, MD: Paul H. Brookes Publishing Co.

Alvarez, M.C. (1983). Sustained timed writing as an aid to fluency and creativity. *Teaching Exceptional Children, 15,* 160–162.

American Psychiatric Association (APA). (1980). *Diagnostic and statistical manual of mental disorders* (3th ed.). Washington, DC: Author.

American Psychiatric Association (APA). (1994). *Diagnostic and statistical manual of mental disorders* (4th ed.). Washington, DC: Author.

American Psychiatric Association (APA). (2000). *Diagnostic and statistical manual of mental disorders* (4th ed., text rev.). Washington, DC: Author.

American Psychiatric Association (APA). (2013). *Diagnostic and statistical manual of mental disorders* (5th ed.). Washington, DC: Author.

Anastopoulos, A.D., Barkley, R.A., & Shelton, T. (1994). The history and diagnosis of attention-deficit/hyperactivity disorder. *Therapeutic Care and Education, 3,* 96–110.

Anderson, H.H., & Brewer, J.E. (1946). Studies of teachers' classroom personalities: II. Effects of teachers' dominative and integrative contacts on children's classroom behavior. *Applied Psychological Monographs,* no. 8.

Andersson, U. (2008). Mathematical competencies in children with different types of learning difficulties. *Journal of Educational Psychology, 100,* 48–66. doi:10.1037/0022-0663.100.1.48

Andrade, B.F., Waschbusche, D.A., Doucet, A., King, S., MacKinnon, M., McGraath, P.J., . . . Corkum, P. (2012). Social information processing of positive and negative hypothetical events in children with ADHD and conduct problems and controls. *Journal of Attention Disorders, 16,* 491–504. doi:10.1177/1087054711401346

Anthony, J.L., & Francis, D.J. (2005). Development of phonological awareness. *Current Directions in Psychological Science, 14,* 255–259.

References

Apel, K., & Swank, L.K. (1999). Second chances: Improving decoding skills in the older student. *Language, Speech, and Hearing Services in Schools, 30,* 231–242.

Apel, K., Wilson-Fowler, E.R., Brimo, D., & Perrin, N. (2011). Metalinguistic contributions to reading and spelling in second and third grade students. *Reading and Writing: An Interdisciplinary Journal, 25,* 1283–1305. doi:10.1007/s11145-011-9317-8

Archer, A.L., Gleason, M.M., & Vachon, V. (2000). *Reading excellence: Word attack and rate development strategies.* Longmont, CO: Sopris West.

Archer, A.L., Gleason, M.M., & Vachon, V. (2006). *Reading excellence: Word attack and rate development strategies plus.* Longmont, CO: Sopris West.

Archer, A.L., Gleason, M.M., & Vachon, V. (2014). *Reading excellence: Word attack and rate development strategies.* Longmont, CO: Sopris West.

Artiles, A.J., Rueda, R., Salazar, J.J., & Higareda, I. (2005). Within-group diversity in minority disproportionate representation: English language learners in urban school districts. *Exceptional Children, 71,* 283–300.

Ashkenazi, S., Black, J.M., Abrams, D.A., Hoeft, F., & Menon, V. (2013). Neurobiological underpinnings of math and reading learning disabilities. *Journal of Learning Disabilities, 46,* 549–569. doi:10.1177/0022219413483174

Ashman, A.F., & Conway, R.N.F. (1997). *An introduction to cognitive education: Theory and application.* London, England: Routledge.

Athanasiou, M.S., Geil, M., Hazel, C.E., & Copeland, E.P. (2002). A look inside school-based consultation: A qualitative study of the beliefs and practices of school psychologists and teachers. *School Psychology Quarterly, 17,* 258–298.

August, D., Carlo, M., Dressler, C., & Snow, C. (2005). The critical role of vocabulary development for English language learners. *Learning Disabilities Research & Practice, 20,* 50–57.

August, D., & Shanahan, T. (Eds.). (2006). *Developing literacy in second-language learners: Report of the National Literacy Panel on language-minority children and youth.* London, England: Routledge.

August, D., & Shanahan, T. (2010). Response to a review and update on developing literacy in second-language learners: Report of the National Literacy Panel on language minority children and youth. *Journal of Literacy Research, 42,* 341–348. doi:10.1080/1086296X.2010.503745

Babbitt, B.C. (2000). 10 tips for software selection for math instruction (LD Online Reprint). *The CDA Gram, 34*(2), 11–12.

Babbitt, B.C., & Miller, S.P. (1997). Using hypermedia to improve the mathematics problem solving skills of students with learning disabilities. In K. Higgins & R. Boone (Eds.), *Technology for students with learning disabilities* (pp. 91–108). Austin, TX: PRO-ED.

Baddeley, A.D. (1986). *Working memory.* New York, NY: Oxford University Press.

Baddeley, A.D. (2000). The episodic buffer: A new component of working memory? *Trends in Cognitive Sciences, 4,* 417–423.

Baddeley, A.D. (2003). Working memory: Looking back and looking forward. *Nature Reviews Neuroscience, 4,* 829–839.

Baddeley, A.D., & Hitch, G. (1974). Working memory. *Psychology of Learning and Motivation, 8,* 47–89.

Badian, N.A. (1997). Dyslexia and the double deficit hypothesis. *Annals of Dyslexia, 47,* 69–87.

Badian, N.A. (1998). A validation of the role of preschool phonological and orthographic skills in the prediction of reading. *Journal of Learning Disabilities, 31,* 472–481.

Badian, N.A. (2005). Does a visual-orthographic deficit contribute to reading disability? *Annals of Dyslexia, 55*(1), 28–52.

Bagwell, C.L., Molina, D.S., Pelham, W.E., & Hoza, B. (2001). ADHD and problems in peer relations: Predictions from childhood to adolescence. *Journal of the American Academy of Child and Adolescent Psychiatry, 40,* 1285–1299.

Bailet, L.L. (1991). Beginning spelling. In A.M. Bain, L.L. Bailet, & L.C. Moats (Eds.), *Written language disorders: Theory into practice* (pp. 1–21). Austin, TX: PRO-ED.

Baker, J.A. (2008). Assessing school risk and protective factors. In B. Doll & J.A. Cummings (Eds.), *Transforming school mental health services* (pp. 43–65). Thousand Oaks, CA: Corwin Press.

Baker, L., & Brown, A. (1980). *Metacognitive skills and reading* (Tech. Rep. No. 188). Urbana: University of Illinois, Center for the Study of Reading.

Baker, L., & Cantwell, D.P. (1992). Attention deficit disorder and speech/language disorders. *Comprehensive Mental Health Care, 2,* 3–16.

Bakker, D.J. (1972). *Temporal order in disturbed reading: Developmental and neuropsychological aspects in normal and reading-retarded children.* Rotterdam, Netherlands: Rotterdam University Press.

Bakker, D.J. (1979). Hemisphere differences and reading strategies: Two dyslexias? *Bulletin of the Orton Society, 29,* 84–100.

Bakker, D.J. (1980). Hemisphere-specific dyslexia models. In R.N. Malatesha & L.C. Hastlage (Eds.), *Lateralization of language in the child* (pp. 310–351). Amsterdam, Netherlands: Swets & Zeitlinger.

Bakker, D.J. (1992). Neuropsychological classification and treatment of dyslexia. *Journal of Learning Disabilities, 25,* 102–109.

Balthazor, M.J., Wagner, R.K., & Pelham, W.E. (1991). The specificity of the effects of stimulant medication on classroom learning related measures of cognitive processing for attention deficit disorder children. *Journal of Abnormal Child Psychology, 19,* 35–52.

Bandura, A. (1969). *Principles of behavior modification.* New York, NY: Holt, Rinehart & Winston.

Bannatyne, A. (1971). *Language, reading and learning disabilities.* Springfield, IL: Charles C. Thomas.

References

Barbe, W.B., Lucas, V.H., Wasylyk, T.M., Hackney, C.S., & Braun, L.A. (1987). *Zaner-Bloser handwriting: Book 1. Basic skills and application.* Columbus, OH: Zaner-Bloser.

Barkley, R.A. (1981). *Hyperactive children: A handbook for diagnosis and treatment.* New York, NY: Guilford Press.

Barkley, R.A. (1990). *Attention deficit hyperactivity disorder: A handbook for diagnosis and treatment.* New York, NY: Guilford Press.

Barkley, R.A. (1994). What to look for in a school for a child with ADHD. *The ADHD Report, 2*(3), 1–3.

Barkley, R.A. (1995). ADHD and IQ. *The ADHD Report, 3*(2), 1–3.

Barkley, R.A. (1997). *The nature of self-control.* New York, NY: Guilford Press.

Barkley, R.A. (2000). *Taking charge of ADHD: The complete, authoritative guide for parents.* New York, NY: Guilford Press.

Barkley, R.A. (2002). Psychosocial treatments for attention-deficit/hyperactivity disorder in children. *Journal of Clinical Psychiatry, 63*(Suppl. 12), 36–43.

Barkley, R.A. (2005). *Attention deficit hyperactivity disorder* (3rd ed.). New York, NY: Guilford Press.

Barkley, R.A., Fischer, M., Edelbrock, C.S., & Smallish, L. (1990). The adolescent outcome of hyperactive children diagnosed by research criteria: I. An eight-year prospective follow-up study. *Journal of the American Academy of Child and Adolescent Psychiatry, 29,* 546–557.

Barkley, R.A., & Gordon, M. (2002). Research on comorbidity, adaptive functioning and cognitive impairments in adults with ADHD: Implications for a clinical practice. In S. Goldstein & A. Teeter Ellison (Eds.), *Clinician's guide to adult ADHD: Assessment and intervention* (pp. 46–73). New York, NY: Academic Press.

Barkley, R.A., McMurray, M.B., Edelbrock, C.S., & Robbins, K. (1990). Side effects of methylphenidate in children with attention deficit hyperactivity disorder: A systemic placebo-controlled evaluation. *Pediatrics, 86,* 184–192.

Barkley, R.A., & Murphy, K.R. (2006). Identifying new symptoms for diagnosing ADHD in adulthood. *The ADHD Report, 14*(4), 7–11.

Barkley, R.A., Murphy, K.R., & Fischer, M. (2010). *ADHD in adults: What the science says.* New York, NY: Guilford Press.

Barrett, P.M. (2004). *FRIENDS for Life group leaders' manual for youth.* Bowen Hills, Queensland: Australian Academic Press.

Barrett, P.M., & Turner, C. (2001). Prevention of anxiety symptoms in primary school children: Preliminary results from a universal school-based trial. *British Journal of Clinical Psychology, 40,* 399–410.

Barrett, S., Eber, L., & Weist, M. (2012). *Advancing education effectiveness: Interconnecting school mental health and school-wide positive behavior support.* OSEP Technical Assistance Center on Positive Behavioral Interventions & Support. Retrieved from http://www.pbis.org/school/school-mental-health/interconnected-systems

Bateman, B. (1992). Learning disabilities: The changing landscape. *Journal of Learning Disabilities, 25,* 29–36.

Bauermeister, J.J., Barkley, R.A., Bauermeister, J.A., Martinez, J.V., & McBurnett, K. (2012). Validity of the sluggish cognitive tempo, inattention, and hyperactivity symptom dimensions: Neuropsychological and psychosocial correlates. *Journal of Abnormal Child Psychology, 40,* 683–697.

Baydala, L., Sherman, J., Rasmussen, C., Wikman, E., & Janzen, H. (2006). ADHD characteristics in Canadian Aboriginal children. *Journal of Attention Disorders, 9,* 642–647.

Bear, D.R., Invernizzi, M., Templeton, S., & Johnston, F. (2011). *Words their way: Word study for phonics, vocabulary, and spelling instruction* (5th ed.). Upper Saddle River, NJ: Merrill Prentice Hall.

Bear, G.G. (2005). *Developing self-discipline and preventing conduct misbehavior.* Boston, MA: Allyn & Bacon.

Beck, J.S., Beck, A.T., & Jolly, J.B. (2005). *Beck Youth Inventories (2nd ed.) (BYI–II).* Upper Saddle River, NJ: Pearson.

Beck, I.L., McKeown, M.G., & Kucan, L. (2013). *Bringing words to life: Robust vocabulary instruction* (2nd ed.). New York, NY: Guilford Press.

Beesdo, K., Knappe, S., & Pine, D.S. (2009). Anxiety and anxiety disorders in children and adolescents: Developmental issues and implications for *DSM-V. Psychiatric Clinics of North America, 32,* 483–524.

Beidel, D.C., & Turner, S.M. (2005). *Childhood anxiety disorders: A guide to research and treatment.* New York, NY: Routledge/Taylor & Francis.

Belfiore, P.J., Grskovic, J.A., Murphy, A., & Zentall, S.S. (1996). The effects of antecedent color on reading for students with learning disabilities and co-occurring attention deficit/hyperactivity disorder. *Journal of Learning Disabilities, 29,* 432–438.

Belsky, J. (2005). Differential susceptibility to rearing influence: An evolutionary hypothesis and some evidence. In B.J. Ellis & D.F. Bjorklund (Eds.), *Origins of the social mind: Evolutionary psychology and child development* (pp. 139–163). New York, NY: Guilford Press.

Belzer, K., & Schneier, F.R. (2004). Comorbidity of anxiety and depressive disorders: Issues in conceptualization, assessment, and treatment. *Journal of Psychiatric Practice, 10,* 296–306. doi:10.1097/00131746-200409000-00003

Bender, W.N. (1997). *Understanding ADHD: A practical guide for teachers and parents.* Englewood Cliffs, NJ: Prentice Hall.

Bener, A., Al Qahtani, R., & Abdelaal, I. (2006). The prevalence of ADHD among primary school children in an Arabian society. *Journal of Attention Disorders, 10*(1), 77–82.

Bergman, R.L., Piacentini, J., & McCracken, J.T. (2002). Prevalence and description of selective mutism in a school-based sample. *Journal of the American Academy of Child and Adolescent Psychiatry, 41,* 938–946.

Berk, L.E., & Landau, S. (1993). Private speech of learning disabled and normally achieving children in classroom academic and laboratory contexts. *Child Development, 64,* 556–571.

Berlin, R. (1884). Uber Dyslexie [About dyslexia]. *Archiv fur Psychiatrie, 15,* 276–278.

Berninger, V.W. (1996). *Reading and writing acquisition: A developmental neuropsychological perspective.* Boulder, CO: Westview.

Berninger, V.W., & Abbott, R.D. (1994). Redefining learning disabilities: Moving beyond aptitude–achievement discrepancies to failure to respond to validated treatment protocols. In G.R. Lyon (Ed.), *Frames of reference for the assessment of learning disabilities: New views on measurement issues* (pp. 163–183). Baltimore, MD: Paul H. Brookes Publishing Co.

Berninger, V., & Abbott, R. (2010). Listening comprehension, oral expression, reading comprehension, and written expression: Related yet unique language systems in Grades 1, 3, 5, and 7. *Journal of Educational Psychology, 10,* 635–651. doi:10.1037/a0019319

Berninger, V.W., Abbott, R.D., Jones, J., Wolf, B.J., Gould, L., Anderson-Youngstrom, M., . . . Apel, K. (2006). Early development of language by hand: Composing, reading, listening, and speaking connections; three letter-writing modes; and fast mapping in spelling. *Developmental Neuropsychology, 29,* 61–92.

Berninger, V., & Amtmann, D. (2003). Preventing written expression disabilities through early and continuing assessment and intervention for handwriting and/or spelling problems: Research into practice. In H.L. Swanson, K. Harris, & S. Graham (Eds.), *Handbook of research on learning disabilities* (pp. 345–363). New York, NY: Guilford Press.

Berninger, V.W., Mizokawa, D., & Bragg, R. (1991). Theory-based diagnosis and remediation of writing disabilities. *Journal of School Psychology, 29,* 57–97.

Berninger, V., & May, M. (2011). Evidence-based diagnosis and treatment for specific learning disabilities involving impairments in written and/or oral language. *Journal of Learning Disabilities, 44,* 167–183. doi:10.1177/0022219410391189

Berninger, V., Rutberg, J., Abbott, R., Garcia, N., Anderson-Youngstrom, M., Brooks, A., & Fulton, C. (2006). Tier 1 and tier 2 early intervention for handwriting and composing. *Journal of School Psychology, 44,* 3–30.

Berninger, V.W., Vaughan, K., Abbott, R.D., Brooks, A., Begay, K., Curtin, G., . . . Graham, S. (2000). Language-based spelling instruction: Teaching children to make multiple connections between spoken and written words. *Learning Disability Quarterly, 23,* 117–135.

Betts, E.A. (1946). *Foundations of reading instruction.* New York, NY: American Book.

Bianco, M., Pellenq, P., Lambert, E., Bressoux, P., Lima, L., & Doyen, A. (2012). Impact of early code-skill and oral-comprehension training on reading achievement in first grade. *Journal of Research in Reading, 35,* 427–455. doi:10.1111/j.1467-9817.2010.01479.x 427

Biederman, J., Faraone, S.V., Mick, E., & Lelon, E. (1995). Psychiatric comorbidity among referred juveniles with major depression: Fact or artifact? *Journal of the American Academy of Child and Adolescent Psychiatry, 34,* 579–590.

Biederman, J., Faraone, S.V., Mick, E., Williamson, B.A., Wilens, T.E., Spencer, T.J., . . . Zallen, B. (1999). Clinical correlates of ADHD in females. *Journal of the American Academy of Child and Adolescent Psychiatry, 38,* 966–975.

Biederman, J., Faraone, S.V., Milberger, S., Curtiss, S., Chen, L., Marrs, A., . . . Spencer, T. (1996a). Predictors of persistence and remissions of ADHD in adolescence: Results from a 4-year prospective follow-up study. *American Journal of Child and Adolescent Psychiatry, 35,* 343–351.

Biederman, J., Faraone, S.V., Milberger, S., Jetton, J.G., Chen, L., Mick, E., . . . Russell, R.L. (1996b). Is childhood oppositional defiant disorder a precursor to adolescent conduct disorder? Findings from a 4-year follow-up study of children with ADHD. *Journal of the American Academy of Child and Adolescent Psychiatry, 35,* 1193–1204.

Biederman, J., Monuteaux, M., Mick, E., Spencer, T., Wilens, T., Silva, J., . . . Faraone, S.V. (2006). Young adult outcome of attention deficit hyperactivity disorder: A controlled 10-year follow-up study. *Psychological Medicine, 36,* 167–179.

Biederman, J., Munir, K., Knee, D., Amermentano, M., Waternaux, C., & Tsuang, M. (1987). High rate of affective disorder in probands with attention deficit disorder in their relatives: A controlled family study. *American Journal of Psychiatry, 144,* 330–333.

Biemiller, A. (2004). Teaching vocabulary in the primary grades. In J.F. Baumann & E.J. Kame'enui (Eds.), *Vocabulary instruction: Research to practice* (pp. 28–40). New York, NY: Guilford Press.

Biemiller, A. (2005, July). *Teaching vocabulary in the primary and upper elementary grades.* Paper presented at the meeting of the International Dyslexia Association's Special Conference, Research to Practice, Advances in Reading and Literacy, Washington, DC.

Birsh, J.R. (Ed.). (2005). *Multisensory teaching of basic language skills* (2nd ed.). Baltimore, MD: Paul H. Brookes Publishing Co.

Bishop, D.V.M., & Adams, C. (1990). A prospective study of the relationship between specific language impairment, phonological disorders and reading retardation. *Journal of Child Psychology and Psychiatry, 31,* 1027–1050.

Blachman, B.A. (1994). Early literacy acquisition: The role of phonological awareness. In G.P. Wallach & K.G. Butler (Eds.), *Language learning disabilities in school-age children and adolescents* (pp. 253–274). New York, NY: Merrill.

References

Blachman, B.A., Ball, E.W., Black, R., & Tangel, D.M. (2000). *Road to the code: A phonological awareness program for young children.* Baltimore, MD: Paul H. Brookes Publishing Co.

Blachman, B.A., & Tangel, D.M. (2008). *Road to reading: A program for preventing & remediating reading difficulties.* Baltimore, MD: Paul H. Brookes Publishing Co.

Blick, D.W., & Test, D.W. (1987). Effects of self recording on high-school students' on-task behavior. *Learning Disability Quarterly, 10,* 203–213.

Block, J.H. (1977). Hyperactivity: A cultural perspective. *Journal of Learning Disabilities, 10,* 236–240.

Boder, E. (1973). Developmental dyslexia: A diagnostic approach based on three atypical reading patterns. *Developmental Medicine and Child Neurology, 15,* 663–687.

Boets, B., Smedt, B., Cleuren, L., Vandewalle, E., Wouters, J., & Ghesquiere, P. (2010). Towards a further characterization of phonological and literacy problems in Dutch-speaking children with dyslexia. *British Journal of Developmental Psychology, 28*(1), 5–31.

Boulineau, T., Fore, C., III, Hagan-Burke, S., & Burke, M.D. (2004). Use of story-mapping to increase the story-grammar text comprehension of elementary students with learning disabilities. *Learning Disabilities Quarterly, 27,* 105–121.

Bowers, P.G., Sunseth, K., & Golden, J. (1999). The route between rapid naming and reading progress. *Scientific Studies of Reading, 3,* 31–53.

Bowers, P.G., & Wolf, M. (1993). Theoretical links between naming speed, precise timing mechanisms, and orthographic skill in dyslexia. *Reading and Writing: An Interdisciplinary Journal, 5,* 69–85.

Bowley, B., & Walther, E. (1992). Attention deficit disorders and the role of the elementary school counselor. *Elementary School Guidance and Counseling, 27,* 39–46.

Brabham, E., & Villaume, S. (2002). Vocabulary instruction: Concerns and visions. *Reading Teacher, 55,* 264–267.

Bradley, R., Doolittle, J., & Bartolotta, R. (2008). Building on the data and adding to the discussion: The experiences and outcomes of students with emotional disturbance. *Journal of Behavioral Education, 17*(1), 4–23.

Braswell, L., & Bloomquist, M.L. (1991). School consultation and school based intervention. In L. Braswell & M.L. Bloomquist (Eds.), *Cognitive-behavioral therapy with ADHD children: Child, family and school interventions* (pp. 201–212). New York, NY: Guilford Press.

Breen, M.J., & Barkley, R.A. (1988). Child psychopathology and parenting stress in girls and boys having attention deficit hyperactivity disorder with hyperactivity. *Journal of Pediatric Psychology, 13,* 265–280.

Brendtro, L.K., Brokenleg, M., & Van Bockern, S. (1990). *Reclaiming youth at risk: Our hope for the future.* Bloomington, IN: National Educational Service.

Brewer, D.M., Fowler, C.H., Test, D.W., & Wood, W.M. (2005). A content and methodological review of self-advocacy intervention studies. *Exceptional Children, 72,* 101–139.

Briere, J. (1996). *Trauma Symptom Checklist for Children (TSCC).* Lutz, FL: Psychological Assessment Resources, Inc.

Brigham, T.A., Graubard, P.S., & Stans, A. (1972). Analysis of the effects of sequential reinforcement contingencies on aspects of composition. *Journal of Applied Behavior Analysis, 5,* 421–429.

Brinckerhoff, L.C. (1993). Self-advocacy: A critical skill for college students with learning disabilities. *Family Community Health, 16*(3), 23–33.

Brizzolara, D., Chilosi, A., Cipriani, P., Di Filippo, G., Gasperini, F., Mazzotti, S., . . . & Zoccolotti, P. (2006). Do phonologic and rapid automatized naming deficits differentially affect dyslexic children with and without a history of language delay? A study of Italian dyslexic children. *Cognitive and Behavioral Neurology, 19,* 141–149.

Broca, P. (1861). Nouvelle observation d'aphemia produite par une lésion de la moitié posterieure des deuxième et troisième circonvolutions frontales [The novel observation of aphasia produced by a lesion in the second and third posterior frontal convolution]. *Bulletin de la Société Anatomie, 6,* 398–407.

Brooks, A., Vaughan, K., & Berninger, V. (1999). Tutorial interventions for writing difficulties: Comparison of transcription and text generation processes. *Learning Disability Quarterly, 23,* 183–190.

Brooks, R.B. (1991). *The self-esteem teacher.* Circle Pines, MN: American Guidance Service.

Brooks, R.B. (1999a). Creating a positive school climate: Strategies for fostering self-esteem, motivation, and resilience. In J. Cohen (Ed.), *Educating hearts and minds: Social emotional learning and the passage into adolescence* (pp. 61–73). New York, NY: Teachers College Press.

Brooks, R.B. (1999b). Fostering resilience in exceptional children: The search for islands of competence. In V. Schwean & D. Saklofske (Eds.), *Handbook of psychosocial characteristics of exceptional children* (pp. 563–586). New York, NY: Kluwer Academic/Plenum.

Brooks, R.B. (2002). Creating nurturing classroom environments: Fostering hope and resilience as an antidote to violence. In S. Brock, P. Lazarus, & S. Jimerson (Eds.), *Best practices in school crisis prevention and intervention* (pp. 67–93). Bethesda, MD: NASP Publications.

Brooks, R.B. (2004). To touch the hearts and minds of students with learning disabilities: The power of mindsets and expectations. *Learning Disabilities: A Contemporary Journal, 2,* 9–18.

Brooks, R., Brooks, S., & Goldstein, S. (2012). The power of mindsets: Nurturing engagement, motivation, and resilience in students. In S.L. Christenson, A.L. Reschly, & K. Wylie (Eds.), *Handbook of research on student engagement* (pp. 541–562). New York, NY: Springer.

Brooks, R., & Goldstein, S. (2001). *Raising resilient children: Fostering strength, hope, and optimism in your child.* New York, NY: Contemporary Books.

Brooks, R., & Goldstein, S. (2007). *Raising a self-disciplined child.* New York, NY: McGraw-Hill.

Brooks, R., & Goldstein, S. (2013). *Handbook of resilience in children* (2nd ed.). New York, NY: Springer.

Brown, A.L., & Palinscar, A.S. (1982). Inducing strategic learning from texts by means of informed self-control training. *Topics in Learning and Learning Disabilities, 2,* 1–18.

Bruck, M. (1993). Component spelling skills of college students with childhood diagnoses of dyslexia. *Learning Disability Quarterly, 16,* 171–184.

Brunsdon, R., Coltheart, M., & Nickels, L. (2005). Treatment of irregular word spelling in developmental surface dysgraphia. *Cognitive Neuropsychology, 22,* 213–251.

Bryan, T., & Nelson, C. (1994). Doing homework: Perspectives of elementary and junior high school students. *Journal of Learning Disabilities, 27,* 488–499.

Bryant, D.P., Goodwin, M., Bryant, B.R., & Higgins, K. (2003). Vocabulary instruction for students with learning disabilities. *Learning Disability Quarterly, 26,* 117–128.

Buchoff, R. (1990). Attention deficit disorder: Help for the classroom teacher. *Childhood Education, 67,* 86–90.

Bugental, D.B., Lyon, J.E., Lin, E.K., McGrath, E.P., & Binbela, A. (1999). Children tune out in response to the ambiguous communication style of powerless adults. *Child Development, 70,* 214–230.

Bullock, J. (1991). *TouchMath: The touchpoint approach for teaching basic math computation* (4th ed.). Colorado Springs, CO: Innovative Learning Concepts.

Bunch, G.C., Kibler, A., & Pimentel, S. (2013). *Realizing opportunities for English learners in the Common Core English language arts and disciplinary literacy standards.* Retrieved from http://ell.stanford.edu/sites/default/files/pdf/academic-papers/01_Bunch_Kibler_Pimentel_RealizingOpp%20in%20ELA_FINAL_0.pdf

Burcham, B., Carlson, L., & Milich, R. (1993). Promising school-based practices for students with attention deficit disorder: Issues in the education of children with attentional deficit disorder [Special issue]. *Exceptional Children, 60,* 174–180.

Burke, J.D., Loeber, R., & Birmaher, B. (2002). Oppositional defiant disorder and conduct disorder: A review of the past 10 years, part II. *Journal of the American Academy of Child and Adolescent Psychiatry, 41*(11), 1275–1293. doi:10.1097/00004583-200211000-00009

Burns, M.K., Dean, V.J., & Foley, S. (2004). Preteaching unknown key words with incremental rehearsal to improve reading fluency and comprehension with children identified as reading disabled. *Journal of School Psychology, 42,* 303–314.

Busch, B. (1993). Attention deficits: Current concepts, controversies, management and approaches to classroom instruction. *Annals of Dyslexia, 43,* 5–26.

Bushell, D. (1973). *Classroom behavior.* Englewood Cliffs, NJ: Prentice Hall.

Cabell, S.Q., Justice, L.M., Konold, T.R., & McGinty, A.S. (2011). Profiles of emergent literacy skills among preschool children who are at risk for academic difficulties. *Early Childhood Research Quarterly, 26,* 1–14. doi:10.1016/j.ecresq.2010.05.003

Cahill, S.M. (2009). Where does handwriting fit in? Strategies to support academic achievement. *Intervention in School and Clinic, 44,* 223–228. doi:10.1177/1053451208328826

Calfee, R.C. (1998). Phonics and phonemes: Learning to decode and spell in a literature based program. In J.L. Metsala & L.C. Ehri (Eds.), *Word recognition in beginning literacy* (pp. 315–340). Mahwah, NJ: Erlbaum.

Calfee, R.C., Lindamood, P., & Lindamood, C. (1973). Acoustic–phonic skills in reading: Kindergarten through twelfth grade. *Journal of Educational Psychology, 64,* 293–298.

Callinan, S., Cunningham, E., & Theiler, S. (2013). Revisiting discrepancy theory in learning disabilities: What went wrong and why we should go back. *Australian Journal of Guidance and Counselling, 23*(1), 1–17.

Campbell, K.U. (1998). *Great leaps reading program* (4th ed.). Gainesville, FL: Diarmuid.

Campbell, K.U. (2005). *Great leaps reading program: Grades 3–5.* Gainesville, FL: Diarmuid.

Campbell, K.U. (2013). *Language growth: Phonological awareness and language activities for the emergent reader.* Gainesville, FL: Diarmuid.

Campbell, S.B., Endman, M.W., & Bernfeld, G. (1977). A 3-year follow-up of hyperactive preschoolers into elementary school. *Journal of Child Psychology and Psychiatry, 18,* 239–249.

Cantwell, D.P., & Baker, L. (1985). Psychiatric and learning disorders in children with speech and language disorders: A descriptive analysis. *Advances in Learning and Behavioral Disabilities, 4,* 29–47.

Cantwell, D.P., & Baker, L. (1991). Association between attention-deficit/hyperactivity disorder and learning disorders. *Journal of Learning Disabilities, 24,* 88–95.

Caravolas, M., Snowling, M., & Hulme, C. (1999, April). *Emergent spelling: Initial skills and concurrent predictors.* Paper presented at the annual meeting of the Society for the Scientific Study of Reading, Montreal, Quebec, Canada.

Caravolas, M., Volín, J., & Hulme, C. (2005). Phoneme awareness is a key component of alphabetic literacy skills in consistent and inconsistent orthographies: Evidence from Czech and English children. *Journal of Experimental Child Psychology, 92,* 107–139.

Carbo, M. (1989). *How to record books for maximum reading gains.* New York, NY: National Reading Styles Institute.

References

Carlisle, J.F. (1993). Selecting approaches to vocabulary instruction for the reading disabled. *Learning Disabilities Research & Practice, 8,* 97–105.

Carlisle, J.F., & Rice, M.S. (2002). *Improving reading comprehension: Research-based principles and practices.* Timonium, MD: York Press.

Carlo, M.S., August, D., McLaughlin, B., Snow, C., Dressler, C., Lippman, D.N., . . . White, C.E. (2004). Closing the gap: Addressing the vocabulary needs of English-language learners in bilingual and mainstream classrooms. *Reading Research Quarterly, 39,* 118–215.

Carnine, D.W., Silbert, J., Kame'enui, E.J., & Tarver, S.G. (2010). *Direct instruction reading* (5th ed.). Upper Saddle River, NJ: Pearson.

Carr, E., & Ogle, D. (1987). K-W-L Plus: A strategy for comprehension and summarization. *Journal of Reading, 30,* 626–631.

Carreker, S. (2005). Teaching reading: Accurate decoding and fluency. In J.R. Birsh (Ed.), *Multisensory teaching of basic language skills* (2nd ed., pp. 141–182). Baltimore, MD: Paul H. Brookes Publishing Co.

Carroll, J.B. (1993). *Human cognitive abilities: A survey of factor-analytic studies.* New York, NY: Cambridge University Press.

Carter, E.W., Lane, K.L., Pierson, M.R., & Glaeser, G. (2006). Self-determination skills and opportunities for transition-age youth with emotional disturbances and learning disabilities. *Exceptional Children, 72,* 333–346.

Carver, R.P. (1990). *Reading rate: A review of research and theory.* San Diego, CA: Academic Press.

Cash, S., & Bridge, J. (2009). Epidemiology of youth suicide and suicidal behavior. *Current Opinion in Pediatrics, 21,* 613–619.

Cass, M., Cates, D., Smith, M., & Jackson, C. (2003). Effects of manipulative instruction on solving area and perimeter problems by students with learning disabilities. *Learning Disabilities Research & Practice, 18,* 112–120.

Castellanos, F.X., Giedd, J.N., Marsh, W.L., Hamburger, S.D., Vaituzis, A.C., Dickstein, D.P., . . . Rapport, J.L. (1996). Quantitative brain magnetic resonance imaging in attention-deficit hyperactivity disorder. *Archives of General Psychiatry, 53,* 607–616.

Castles, A., & Coltheart, M. (1993). Varieties of developmental dyslexia. *Cognition, 47,* 149–180.

Catts, H.W. (1993). The relationship between speech-language impairments and reading disabilities. *Journal of Speech and Hearing Research, 36,* 948–958.

Cawley, J.F., & Miller, J.H. (1986). Selected views on metacognition, arithmetic problem solving, and learning disabilities. *Learning Disabilities Focus, 2*(1), 36–48.

Cawley, J.F., Miller, J.H., & School, B.A. (1987). A brief inquiry of arithmetic word-problem solving among learning disabled secondary students. *Learning Disabilities Focus, 2*(2), 87–93.

Centers for Disease Control and Prevention. (2010, November 12). Increasing prevalence of parent-reported attention-deficit/hyperactivity disorder among children—United States, 2003 and 2007. *Morbidity and Mortality Weekly, 59*(44), 1439–1443. Retrieved from http://www.cdc.gov/mmwr/preview/mmwrhtml/mm5944a3.htm?s_cid=mm5944a3_w

Chafouleas, S.M., Riley-Tillman, T.C., & Christ, T.J. (2010). *Direct Behavior Ratings Smiley Face Form.* Retrieved from http://www.directbehaviorratings.org/cms/files/pdf/V%201.0%20DBR%20Smiley%20Face%20Form%20with%20Fill-In%20Behaviors.pdf

Chafouleas, S., Riley-Tillman, T.C., & Sugai, G. (2007). *School-based behavioral assessment: Informing intervention and instruction.* New York, NY: Guilford Press.

Chard, D.J., & Dickson, S.V. (1999). Phonological awareness: Instructional and assessment guidelines. *Intervention in School and Clinic, 34,* 261–270.

Chard, D.J., & Osborn, J. (1999a). Phonics and word recognition instruction in early reading programs: Guidelines for accessibility. *Learning Disabilities Research & Practice, 14,* 107–117.

Chard, D.J., & Osborn, J. (1999b). Word recognition instruction: Paving the road to successful reading. *Intervention, 34,* 271–277.

Chess, S., & Thomas, A. (1986). *Temperament in clinical practice.* New York, NY: Guilford Press.

Christensen, C.A. (2005). The role of orthographic-motor integration in the production of creative and well-structured written text for students in secondary school. *Educational Psychology: An International Journal of Experimental Educational Psychology, 25,* 441–453.

Clark, D.B., & Uhry, J.K. (1995). *Dyslexia: Theory and practice of remedial instruction* (2nd ed.). Timonium, MD: York Press.

Clarke, P.J., Snowling, M.J., Truelove, E., & Hulme, C. (2010). Ameliorating children's reading-comprehension difficulties: A randomized controlled trial. *Psychological Science, 21,* 1106–1116. doi:10.1177/0956797610375449

Clements, D.H., & Sarama, J. (2011). Early childhood mathematics intervention. *Science, 333,* 968–970. doi:10.1126/science.1204537

Clements, S.D., & Peters, J.E. (1962). Minimal brain dysfunctions in the school-age child: Diagnosis and treatment. *Archives of General Psychiatry, 6*(3), 185–197.

Cohen, J. (2006). Social, emotional, ethical, and academic education: Creating a climate for learning, participation in democracy, and well-being. *Harvard Educational Review, 76,* 201–237.

Cohen, J.A., Mannarino, A.P., & Deblinger, E. (2006). *Treating trauma and traumatic grief in children and adolescents.* New York, NY: Guilford Press.

Cohen, J., McCabe, L., Michelli, N.M., & Pickeral, T. (2009). School climate: Research, policy, teacher education, and practice. *Teachers' College Record, 111,* 180–213.

Cohen, M.J., Sullivan, S., Minde, K.K., Novak, C., & Helwig, C. (1981). Evaluation of the relative effectiveness of methylphenidate and cognitive behavior modification in the treatment of kindergarten-aged hyperactive children. *Journal of Abnormal Child Psychology, 9,* 43–54.

Collier, V.P. (1995). Acquiring a second language for school. *Directions in Language & Education National Clearinghouse for Bilingual Education, 1*(4). Retrieved May 1, 2007, from http://www.usc.edu/dept/education/CMMR/CollierThomas_Acquiring_L2_for_School

Collier, V.P., & Thomas, W.P. (1989). How quickly can immigrants become proficient in school English? *Journal of Educational Issues of Language Minority Students, 5,* 26–38.

Coltheart, M. (1978). Lexical access in simple reading tasks. In G. Underwood (Ed.), *Strategies of information processing* (pp. 151–216). San Diego, CA: Academic Press.

Common Core State Standards Initiative. (2014a). *English language arts standards, writing, Grade 4.* Retrieved from http://www.corestandards.org/ELA-Literacy/W/4

Common Core State Standards Initiative. (2014b). *Key shifts in mathematics.* Retrieved from http://www.corestandards.org/other-resources/key-shifts-in-mathematics

Common Core State Standards Initiative. (2014c). *Mathematics standards.* Retrieved from http://www.corestandards.org/Math

Conners, C.K. (2008). *Conners 3rd edition: Manual.* Toronto, Canada: Multi-Health Systems.

Connor, D.F., & Doerfler, L.A. (2008). ADHD with comorbid oppositional defiant disorder or conduct disorder: Discrete or nondistinct disruptive behavior disorders? *Journal of Attention Disorders, 12*(2), 126–134. doi:10.1177/1087054707308486

Conyers, C., Miltenberger, R., Maki, A., Barenz, R., Jurgens, M., Sailer, A., . . . & Kopp, B. (2004). A comparison of response cost and differential reinforcement of other behavior to reduce disruptive behavior in a preschool classroom. *Journal of Applied Behavior Analysis, 37,* 411–415.

Cooper, H., & Nye, B. (1994). Homework for students with learning disabilities: The implications of research for policy and practice. *Journal of Learning Disabilities, 27,* 470–479.

Copeland, W.E., Angold, A., Shanahan, L., & Costello, E.J. (2014). Longitudinal patterns of anxiety from childhood to adulthood: The Great Smoky Mountains study. *Journal of the American Academy of Child and Adolescent Psychiatry, 53*(1), 21–33. Retrieved from http://download.journals.elsevierhealth.com/pdfs/journals/0890-8567/PIIS0890856713006989.pdf

Corcos, E., & Willows, D.M. (1993). The processing of orthographic information. In D.M. Willows, R.S. Kruk, & E. Corcos (Eds.), *Visual processes in reading and reading disabilities* (pp. 163–190). Mahwah, NJ: Erlbaum.

Corkin, S. (1974). Serial-ordering deficits in inferior readers. *Neuropsychologia, 12,* 347–354.

Cornoldi, C., Rigoni, F., Tressoldi, P.E., & Vio, C. (1999). Imagery deficits in nonverbal learning disabilities. *Journal of Learning Disabilities, 32,* 48–58.

Cortiella, C., & Horowitz, S.H. (2014). *The state of learning disabilities: Facts, trends and emerging issues.* New York, NY: National Center for Learning Disabilities.

Costello, E.J., Erklani, A., & Angold, A. (2006). Is there an epidemic of child or adolescent depression? *Journal of Child Psychology and Psychiatry, 47,* 1263–1271.

Costello, E.J., Mustillo, S., Erkanli, A., Keeler, G., & Angold, A. (2003). Prevalence and development of psychiatric disorders in childhood and adolescence. *Archives of General Psychiatry, 60,* 837–844. doi:10.1001/archpsyc.60.8.837

Cowan, N. (2014). Working memory underpins cognitive development, learning, and education. *Educational Psychology Review, 26,* 197–223.

Coyne, M.D., McCoach, B.D., & Kapp, S. (2007). Vocabulary intervention for kindergarten students: Comparing extended instruction to embedded instruction and incidental exposure. *Learning Disability Quarterly, 30,* 74–88.

Coyne, M.D., Simmons, D.C., & Kame'enui, E.J. (2004). Vocabulary instruction for young children at risk of experiencing reading difficulties: Teaching word meanings during shared storybook readings. In J.F. Baumann & E.J. Kame'enui (Eds.), *Vocabulary instruction: Research to practice* (pp. 41–58). New York, NY: Guilford Press.

Crepeau-Hobson, F., & Bianco, M. (2011). Identification of gifted students with learning disabilities in a response-to-intervention era. *Psychology in the Schools, 48,* 102–109. doi:10.1002/pits.20528

Critchley, M. (1964). *Developmental dyslexia.* Westport, CT: Heinemann.

Cromley, J.G., & Azevedo, R. (2007). Testing and refining the direct and inferential mediation model of reading comprehension. *Journal of Educational Psychology, 99,* 311–325.

Cruickshank, W.M. (1977). Least-restrictive placement: Administrative wishful thinking. *Journal of Learning Disabilities, 10,* 193–194.

Cummings, C.M., Caporino, N.E., & Kendall, P.C. (2013). Comorbidity of anxiety and depression in children and adolescents: 20 years after. *Psychological Bulletin, 140,* 816–845. doi:10.1037/a0034733

Cummins, J. (1989). *Empowering minority students.* Sacramento, CA: California Association for Bilingual Education.

Cunningham, A.E., & Stanovich, K.E. (1998). The impact of print exposure on word recognition. In J.L. Metsala & L.C. Ehri (Eds.), *Word recognition in beginning literacy* (pp. 235–262). Mahwah, NJ: Erlbaum.

Cunningham, A.E., Stanovich, K.E., & Wilson, M.R. (1990). Cognitive variation in adult college students

References

differing in reading ability. In T.H. Carr & B.A. Levy (Eds.), *Reading and its development: Component skills approaches* (pp. 129–159). San Diego, CA: Academic Press.

Cunningham, A.E., & Zibulsky, J. (2014). *Book smart: How to develop and support successful, motivated readers.* New York, NY: Oxford University Press.

Cunningham, P.M., & Cunningham, J.W. (1992). Making words: Enhancing the invented spelling–decoding connection. *Reading Teacher, 46,* 106–115.

Cunningham, P.M., & Hall, D.P. (1994). *Making words: Multilevel, hands-on, developmentally appropriate spelling and phonics activities.* Torrance, CA: Frank Schaffer.

Cunningham, P.M., Hall, D.P., & Cunningham, J.W. (2000). *Guided reading: The Four-Blocks way.* Greensboro, NC: Carson-Dellosa.

Curby, T.W., Rudasill, K.M., Edwards, T., & Perez-Edgar, K. (2011). The role of classroom quality in ameliorating the academic and social risks associated with difficult temperament. *School Psychology Quarterly, 26,* 175–188.

Cutting, L.E., & Denckla, M.B. (2003). Attention: Relationships between attention-deficit hyperactivity disorder and learning disabilities. In H.L. Swanson, K.R. Harris, & S. Graham (Eds.), *Handbook of learning disabilities* (pp. 125–139). New York, NY: Guilford Press.

Cutting, L.E., Materek, A., Cole, C.A.S., Levine, T.M., & Mahone, E.M. (2009). Effects of fluency, oral language, and executive function on reading comprehension performance. *Annals of Dyslexia, 59,* 34–54. doi:10.1007/s11881-009-0022-0

Daigneault, S., Braun, C.M.J., & Whitaker, H.A. (1992). An empirical test of two opposing theoretical models of prefrontal function. *Brain and Cognition, 19,* 48–71.

Das, J.P. (1980). Planning: Theoretical considerations and empirical evidence. *Psychological Research* (W. Germany), *41,* 141–151.

Das, J.P., Kar, B.C., & Parrila, R.K. (1996). *Cognitive planning: The psychological basis of intelligent behavior.* Thousand Oaks, CA: Sage.

Das, J.P., Naglieri, J.A., & Kirby, J.R. (1994). *Assessment of cognitive processes.* Needham Heights, MA: Allyn & Bacon.

Davey, B. (1983). Think-aloud: Modeling the cognitive processes for reading comprehension. *Journal of Reading, 27,* 44–47.

Davis, L., Sirotowitz, S., & Parker, H.D. (1996). *Study strategies made easy: A practical plan for school success.* Plantation, FL: Specialty Press.

de la Paz, S. (1999). Composing via dictation and speech recognition systems: Compensatory technology for students with learning disabilities. *Learning Disability Quarterly, 22,* 173–182.

De Pry, R.L., & Sugai, G. (2002). The effect of active supervision and pre-correction on minor behavioral incidents in a sixth grade general education classroom. *Journal of Behavioral Education, 11,* 255–264.

de Zwaan, M., Gruß, B., Müller, A., Graap, H., Martin, A., Glaesmer, H., . . . & Philipsen, A. (2012). The estimated prevalence and correlates of adult ADHD in a German community sample. *European Archives of Psychiatry and Clinical Neuroscience, 262*(1), 79–86. doi:10.007/s00406-011-0211-9.

Deblinger, E., Cohen, J., & Mannarino, A. (2003). *Child and parent trauma-focused cognitive behavioral therapy treatment manual.* Pittsburgh, PA: Allegheny General Hospital Center for Traumatic Stress in Children and Adolescents.

Deci, E.L., & Flaste, R. (1995). *Why we do what we do: Understanding self-motivation.* New York, NY: Penguin Books.

Decker, S. (2012). Dimensional integration of assessment outcomes with intervention services for children with specific learning disabilities. *Journal of Applied School Psychology, 28,* 175–199. doi:10.1080/15377903.2012.669745

Decker, S.L., Roberts, A.M., & Englund, J.A. (2013). Cognitive predictors of rapid picture naming. *Learning and Individual Differences, 25,* 141–149.

DeFries, J.C., Olson, R.K., Pennington, B.F., & Smith, S.D. (1991). The Colorado Reading Project: An update. In D.D. Duane & D.B. Gray (Eds.), *The reading brain: The biological basis of dyslexia* (pp. 53–87). Timonium, MD: York Press.

Dehn, M.J. (2006). *Essentials of processing assessment.* New York, NY: Wiley.

Denckla, M.B. (1972a). Clinical syndromes in learning disabilities: The case for splitting versus lumping. *Journal of Learning Disabilities, 5,* 401–406.

Denckla, M.B. (1972b). Color-naming defects in dyslexic boys. *Cortex, 8,* 164–176.

Denckla, M.B. (1979). Childhood learning disabilities. In K.M. Heilman & E. Valenstein (Eds.), *Clinical neuropsychology* (pp. 535–573). New York, NY: Oxford University Press.

Denckla, M.B., & Cutting, L.E. (1999). History and significance of rapid automatized naming. *Annals of Dyslexia, 49,* 29–42.

Denckla, M.B., & Rudel, R.G. (1974). Rapid automatized naming of pictured objects, colors, letters and numbers by normal children. *Cortex, 10,* 186–202.

Denckla, M.B., & Rudel, R.G. (1976). Rapid "automatized" naming (RAN): Dyslexia differentiated from other learning disabilities. *Neuropsychologia, 14*(4), 471–479.

Deno, S.L., Mirkin, P., & Marston, D. (1982). Valid measurement procedures for continuous evaluation of written expression. *Exceptional Children, 48,* 368–371.

Deshler, D.D., Ellis, E.S., & Lenz, B.K. (1996). *Teaching adolescents with learning disabilities: Strategies and methods* (2nd ed.). Denver, CO: Love.

Diamond, L., & Gutlohn, L. (2006). *Teaching vocabulary.* Retrieved from http://www.ldonline.org/article/9943

Dickinson, D.K., Anastasopoulos, L., McCabe, A., Peisner-Feinberg, E.S., & Poe, M.D. (2003). The comprehensive language approach to early literacy:

The interrelationships among, vocabulary, phonological sensitivity, and print knowledge among preschool-aged children. *Journal of Educational Psychology, 95,* 465–481.

Dickinson, D.K., & McCabe, A. (2001). Bringing it all together: The multiple origins, skills and environmental supports of early literacy. *Learning Disabilities Research & Practice, 16,* 186–202.

Dickstein, D.P., Garvey, M., Pradella, A.G., Greenstein, D.K., Sharp, W.S., Castellanos, F.X., . . . Leibenluft, E. (2005). Neurologic examination of abnormalities in children with bipolar disorder or ADHD. *Biological Psychiatry, 58,* 517–524.

Diller, L. (1998). *Running on Ritalin.* New York, NY: Bantam.

Diller, L.N. (2006a). *Last normal child.* Westport, CT: Greenwood.

Diller, L.N. (2006b). Science, ethics and the psychosocial treatment of ADHD: Editorial. *Journal of Attention Disorders, 9,* 571–574.

Dinehart, L., & Manfra, L. (2013). Association between early fine motor development and later math and reading achievement in early elementary school. *Early Education and Development, 24,* 138–161. doi:10.1080/10409289.2011.636729

Ding, C., & Hall, A. (2007). Gender, ethnicity, and grade differences in perceptions of school experiences among adolescents. *Studies in Educational Evaluation, 33,* 159–174.

Doabler, C.T., Cary, M.S., Jungjohann, K., Clarke, B., Fien, H., Baker, S., . . . Chard, D. (2012). Enhancing core mathematics instruction for students at risk for mathematics disabilities. *Teaching Exceptional Children, 44*(4), 48–57.

Dolch, E.W. (1939). *A manual for remedial reading.* Champaign, IL: Garrard Press.

Doll, B., & Brehm, K. (2010). *Resilient playgrounds.* New York, NY: Routledge.

Doll, B., Brehm, K., & Zucker, S. (2014). *Resilient classrooms: Creating healthy environments for learning.* New York, NY: Guilford Press.

Doll, B., Kurien, S., LeClair, C., Spies, R., Champion, A., & Osborn, A. (2009). The ClassMaps Survey: A framework for promoting positive classroom environments. In R. Gilman & E.S. Huebner (Eds.), *Handbook of positive psychology schools* (pp. 213–227). New York, NY: Routledge/Taylor & Francis.

Douglas, V.I. (1983). Attentional and cognitive problems. In M. Rutter (Ed.), *Developmental neuropsychiatry* (pp. 280–329). New York, NY: Guilford Press.

Douglas, V.I. (1985). The response of ADD children to reinforcement: Theoretical and clinical implications. In L.N. Bloomingdale (Ed.), *Attention deficit disorder: Identification, course and rationale* (pp. 87–99). Jamaica, NY: Spectrum.

Douglas, V.I., Barr, R.G., O'Neil, M.E., & Britton, B.G. (1986). Short-term effects of methylphenidate on the cognitive, learning, and academic performance of children with attention deficit disorder in the laboratory and classroom. *Journal of Child Psychology and Psychiatry, 27,* 191–211.

Douglas, V.I., & Peters, K.G. (1979). Toward a clear definition of the attentional deficit of hyperactive children. In G.A. Hale & M. Lewis (Eds.), *Attention and the development of cognitive skills* (pp. 41–62). New York, NY: Kluwer Academic/Plenum.

Douglass, B. (1984). Variation on a theme: Writing with the LD adolescent. *Academic Therapy, 19,* 361–363.

Downing, J. (1973). *Comparative reading: Cross national studies of behavior and processes in reading and writing.* New York, NY: Macmillan.

Dunlap, G., & Kern, L. (1996). Modifying instructional activities to promote desirable behavior: A conceptual and practical framework. *School Psychology Quarterly, 11,* 297–312.

DuPaul, G.J. (1991). Attention-deficit hyperactivity disorder: Classroom intervention strategies. *School Psychology International, 12,* 85–94.

DuPaul, G.J., Guevremont, D.C., & Barkley, R.A. (1992). Behavioral treatment of attention-deficit hyperactivity disorder in the classroom: The use of the attention training system. *Behavior Modification, 16,* 204–225. doi:10.1177/01454455920162004

DuPaul, G.J., McGoey, K.E., Eckert, T.L., & VanBrakle, J. (2001). Preschool children with attention-deficit/hyperactivity disorder: Impairments in behavioral, social, and school functioning. *Journal of the American Academy of Child and Adolescent Psychiatry, 40,* 508–515.

DuPaul, G.J., & Rapport, M.D. (1993). Does methylphenidate normalize the classroom performance of children with attention deficit disorder? *Journal of the American Academy of Child and Adolescent Psychiatry, 32,* 190–198.

DuPaul, G.J., & Stoner, G.D. (2003). *ADHD in the schools: Assessment and intervention strategies* (2nd ed.). New York, NY: Guilford Press.

DuPaul, G.J., & Weyandt, L.L. (2006). School-based intervention for children with attention deficit hyperactivity disorder: Effects on academic, social, and behavioral functioning. *International Journal of Disability, Development, and Education, 53,* 161–176.

Dweck, C. (2006). *Mindset: The new psychology of success.* New York, NY: Ballantine Books.

Eaves, L., Rutter, M., Silberg, J.L., Shillady, L., Maes, H., & Pickles, A. (2000). Genetic and environmental causes of covariation in interview assessments of disruptive behavior in child and adolescent twins. *Behavior Genetics, 30*(4), 321–334. doi:10.1023/A:1026553518272

Eccles, J.S., & Wigfield, A. (2002). Motivational beliefs, values, and goals. *Annual Review of Psychology, 53,* 109–132.

Edelbrock, C., Rende, R., Plomin, R., & Thompson, L.A. (1995). A twin study of competence and problem behavior in childhood and early adolescence. *Journal of Child Psychology and Psychiatry, 36,* 775–785.

Edelen-Smith, P.J. (1997). How now brown cow: Phoneme awareness activities for collaborative classrooms. *Intervention in School and Clinic, 33,* 103–111.

Eden, G.F., & Vaidya, C.J. (2008). ADHD and developmental dyslexia: Two pathways leading to impaired

References

learning. *Annals of the New York Academy of Sciences, 1145,* 316–327.

Education for All Handicapped Children Act of 1975, PL 94-142, 20 U.S.C. §§ 1400 *et seq.*

Education of the Handicapped Act of 1970, PL 91-230, 84 Stat. 121-154, 20 U.S.C. §§ 1400 *et seq.*

Edwards, D., Hunt, D., Meyers, M.H., Grogg, K.R., & Jarrett, O. (2005). Acceptability and student outcomes of a violence prevention curriculum. *Journal of Primary Prevention, 26,* 401–418.

Eggen, P.D., & Kauchak, D. (1992). *Educational psychology: Classroom connections.* New York, NY: Macmillan.

Ehri, L.C. (1986). Sources of difficulty in learning to read and spell. In M.L. Wolraich & D. Routh (Eds.), *Advances in developmental and behavioral pediatrics* (pp. 121–195). Greenwich, CT: JAI Press.

Ehri, L.C. (1989). The development of spelling knowledge and its role in reading acquisition and reading disability. *Journal of Learning Disabilities, 22,* 356–365.

Ehri, L.C. (1994). Development of the ability to read words: Update. In R. Ruddell, M. Ruddell, & H. Singer (Eds.), *Theoretical models and processes of reading* (4th ed., pp. 323–358). Newark, DE: International Reading Association.

Ehri, L.C. (1997). Learning to read and learning to spell are one and the same, almost. In C.A. Perfetti, L. Rieben, & M. Fayol (Eds.), *Learning to spell: Research, theory, and practice across languages* (pp. 237–270). Mahwah, NJ: Erlbaum.

Ehri, L.C. (1998). Grapheme–phoneme knowledge is essential for learning to read words in English. In J.L. Metsala & L.C. Ehri (Eds.), *Word recognition in beginning literacy* (pp. 3–40). Mahwah, NJ: Erlbaum.

Ehri, L.C. (2000). Learning to read and learning to spell: Two sides of a coin. *Topics in Language Disorders, 20*(3), 19–36.

Ehri, L.C. (2005). Learning to read words: Theory, findings, and issues. *Scientific Studies of Reading, 9,* 167–188.

Ehri, L.C. (2006). Alphabetics instruction helps students learn to read. In R.M. Joshi & P.G. Aaron (Eds.), *Handbook of orthography and literacy* (pp. 649–677). Mahwah, NJ: Erlbaum.

Ehri, L.C. (2014). Orthographic mapping in the acquisition of sight word reading, spelling memory, and vocabulary learning. *Scientific Studies of Reading, 18,* 5–21.

Ehri, L.C., & Roberts, T. (2006). The roots of learning to read and write: Acquisition of letters and phonemic awareness. *Handbook of Early Literacy Research, 2,* 113–131.

Eisenman, L., Chamberlin, M., & McGahee-Kovac, M. (2005). A teacher inquiry group on student-led IEPs: Starting small to make a difference. *Teacher Education and Special Education, 28,* 195–206.

Eisenman, L., & Tascione, L. (2002). "How come nobody told me?" Fostering self-realization through a high school English curriculum. *Learning Disabilities Research & Practice, 17,* 35–46.

Elementary and Secondary Education Act Amendments of 1969: Title VI, Education of the Handicapped Act of 1970, PL 91-230, 84 Stat. 121-154, 20 U.S.C. §§1400 *et seq.*

Elia, J., Borcherding, B.G., Rapoport, J.L., & Keysor, C.S. (1991). Methylphenidate and dextroamphetamine treatments of hyperactivity: Are there true nonresponders? *Psychiatry Research, 36*(2), 141–155.

Elias, M.J., Zins, J.E., Graczyk, P.A., & Weissberg, R.B. (2003). Implementation, sustainability and scaling up of social, emotional and academic innovations in public schools. *School Psychology Review, 32,* 303–319.

Elkonin, D.B. (1973). U.S.S.R. In J. Downing (Ed.), *Comparative reading: Cross national studies of behavior and processes in reading and writing* (pp. 551–579). New York, NY: Macmillan.

Ellis, A.W. (1985). The cognitive neuropsychology of developmental (and acquired) dyslexia: A critical survey. *Cognitive Neuropsychology, 2,* 169–205.

Ellis, E.S. (1994). An instructional model for integrating content-area instruction with cognitive strategy instruction. *Reading and Writing Quarterly: Overcoming Learning Difficulties, 1,* 63–90.

Englert, C.S. (1990). Unraveling the mysteries of writing through strategy instruction. In T.E. Scruggs & B.Y.L. Wong (Eds.), *Intervention research in learning disabilities* (pp. 186–223). New York, NY: Springer-Verlag.

Englert, C.S. (1992). Writing instruction from a sociocultural perspective: The holistic, dialogic, and social enterprise of writing. *Journal of Learning Disabilities, 25,* 153–172.

Englert, C.S., Hiebert, E.H., & Stewart, S.R. (1985). Spelling unfamiliar words by an analogy strategy. *Journal of Special Education, 19,* 291–306.

Englert, C.S., & Lichter, A. (1982). Using statement-pie to teach reading and writing skills. *Teaching Exceptional Children, 14*(5), 164–170.

Englert, C.S., & Mariage, T.V. (1991). Shared understandings: Structuring the writing experience through dialogue. *Journal of Learning Disabilities, 24,* 330–342.

Englert, C.S., & Raphael, T.E. (1989). Developing successful writers through cognitive strategy instruction. In J. Brophy (Ed.), *Advances in research on teaching* (Vol. 1, pp. 105–151). Greenwich, CT: JAI Press.

Englert, C.S., Raphael, T.E., Anderson, L.M., Anthony, H.M., & Stevens, D.D. (1991). Making strategies and self-talk visible: Writing instruction in regular and special education classrooms. *American Educational Research Journal, 23,* 337–372.

Ericsson, K.A., & Kintsch, W. (1995). Long-term working memory. *Psychological Review, 102,* 211–245.

Ernst, M., Cohen, R.M., Liebenauer, L.L., Jons, P.H., & Zametkin, A.J. (1997). Cerebral glucose metabolism in adolescent girls with attention-deficit/hyperactivity disorder. *Journal of the American Academy of Child and Adolescent Psychiatry, 36,* 1399–1406.

Evans, J.J., Floyd, R.G., McGrew, K.S., & Leforgee, M.H. (2002). The relations between measures of

Cattell-Horn-Carroll (CHC) cognitive abilities and reading achievement during childhood and adolescence. *School Psychology Review, 31,* 246–262.

Express Scripts Report. (2014, March). *Turning attention to ADHD: U.S. medication trends for attention deficit hyperactivity disorder.* Retrieved from http://lab.express-scripts.com/publications/turning-attention-to-adhd-report

Faraone, S.V., & Biederman, J. (2005). What is the prevalence of adult ADHD? *Journal of Attention Disorders, 9,* 384–391.

Faraone, S.V., Biederman, J., & Mick, E. (2006). The age dependent decline of ADHD: A meta-analysis of follow-up studies. *Psychological Medicine, 36,* 159–165.

Faraone, S.V., Perlis, R.H., Doyle, A.E., Smoller, J.W., Goralnick, J.J., Holmgren, M.A., & Sklar, P. (2005). Advancing the neuroscience of ADHD: Molecular genetics of attention-deficit/hyperactivity disorder. *Biological Psychiatry, 57,* 1313–1323.

Fay, J., Cline, F.W., & Sornson, B. (2005). *Meeting the challenge.* Golden, CO: Love and Logic Institute.

Felton, R.H. (1993). Effects of instruction on the decoding skills of children with phonological-processing problems. *Journal of Learning Disabilities, 26,* 583–589.

Felton, R.H., & Wood, F.B. (1989). Cognitive deficits in reading disability and attention deficit disorder. *Journal of Learning Disabilities, 22,* 3–13.

Fernald, G.M. (1943). *Remedial techniques in basic school subjects.* New York, NY: McGraw-Hill.

Ferrer, E., Shaywitz, B.A., Holahan, J.M., Marchione, K., & Shaywitz, S.E. (2010). Uncoupling of reading and IQ over time: Empirical evidence for a definition of dyslexia. *Psychological Science, 21*(1), 93–101. doi:10.1177/0956797609354084

Fiedler, C.R., & Danneker, J.E. (2007). Self-advocacy instruction: Bridging the research-to-practice gap. *Focus on Exceptional Children, 39*(8), 1–20.

Fiorello, C.A., Flanagan, D.P., & Hale, J.B. (2014). The utility of the pattern of strengths and weaknesses approach. *Learning Disabilities: A Multidisciplinary Journal, 20,* 55–59.

Fischer, P. (1999). Getting up to speed. *Perspectives (The International Dyslexia Foundation), 25*(2), 12–13.

Fisher, S.E., Francks, C., McCracken, J.T., McGough, J.J., Marlow, A.J., MacPhie, L., . . . Smalley, S.L. (2002). A genomewide scan for loci involved in ADHD. *American Journal of Human Genetics, 70,* 1183–1196.

Fletcher, J.M. (1985). Memory for verbal and nonverbal stimuli in learning disability subgroups: Analysis by selective reminding. *Journal of Experimental Child Psychology, 40,* 244–259.

Fletcher, J.M., Francis, D.J., Shaywitz, S.E., Lyon, G.R., Foorman, B.R., Stuebing, K.K., & Shaywitz, B.A. (1998). Intelligence testing and the discrepancy model for children with learning disabilities. *Learning Disabilities Research & Practice, 13,* 186–203.

Fletcher, J.M., Lyon, G.R., Fuchs, L.S., & Barnes, M.A. (2007). *Learning disabilities: From identification to intervention.* New York, NY: Guilford Press.

Fletcher, J.M., Taylor, H.G., Levin, H.S., & Satz, P. (1995). Neuropsychological and intellectual assessment of children. In H. Kaplan & B. Sadock (Eds.), *Comprehensive textbook of psychiatry* (pp. 581–601). Baltimore, MD: Williams & Wilkins.

Floyd, R.G., Evans, J.J., & McGrew, K.S. (2003). Relations between measures of Cattell-Horn-Carroll (CHC) cognitive abilities and mathematics achievement across the school-age years. *Psychology in the Schools, 60,* 155–171.

Foa, E.B., Johnson, K.M., Feeny, N.C., & Treadwell, K.R.H. (2001). *Child PTSD Symptom Scale (CPSS).* Deerfield, IL: International Society for Traumatic Stress Studies. Retrieved from http://www.istss.org/AM/Template.cfm?Section=ResourcesforClinicians&Template=/CM/ContentDisplay.cfm&ContentID=1579

Foorman, B.R. (2007). Primary prevention in classroom reading instruction. *Teaching Exceptional Children, 39*(5), 24–30.

Foorman, B.R., Seals, L.M., Anthony, J., & Pollard-Durodola, S. (2003). A vocabulary enrichment program for third and fourth grade African-American students: Description, implementation, and impact. In B.R. Foorman (Ed.), *Preventing and remediating reading difficulties: Bringing science to scale* (pp. 419–441). Timonium, MD: York Press.

Forehand, R., & McMahon, R. (1981). *Helping the noncompliant child.* New York, NY: Guilford Press.

Foss, J.M. (1991). Nonverbal learning disabilities and remedial interventions. *Annals of Dyslexia, 41,* 128–140.

Fountas, I.C., & Pinnell, G.S. (1999). *Matching books to readers: Using leveled books in guided reading, K–3.* Westport, CT: William Heinemann.

Frankenberger, W., & Fronzaglio, K. (1991). A review of states' criteria and procedures for identifying children with learning disabilities. *Journal of Learning Disabilities, 24,* 495–500.

Freda, L. (2010). Suicide risk assessment and prevention in children and adolescents. *The Brown University Child and Adolescent Behavior Letter, 26,* 1–7. doi:10.1002/cbl.2012

Freebody, P., & Byrne, B. (1988). Word-reading strategies in elementary school children: Relations to comprehension, reading time, and phonemic awareness. *Reading Research Quarterly, 23,* 441–453.

Frisby, B.N., & Martin, M.M. (2010). Instructor-student and student-student rapport in the classroom. *Communication Education, 59*(2), 146–164.

Fry, E.B. (1977). *Elementary reading instruction.* New York, NY: McGraw-Hill.

Fuchs, D., Compton, D., Fuchs, L., Bryant, V.J., Hamlett, C., & Lambert, W. (2012). First-grade cognitive abilities as long-term predictors of reading comprehension and disability status. *Journal of Learning Disabilities, 45,* 217–231. doi:10.1177/0022219412442154

Fuchs, D., & Deshler, D.D. (2007). What we need to know about responsiveness to intervention (and shouldn't be afraid to ask). *Learning Disabilities Research & Practice, 22,* 129–136.

Fuchs, D., Fuchs, L.S., & Compton, D. (2012). Smart RTI: A next-generation approach to multilevel

References

prevention. *Exceptional Children, 78,* 263–279. doi:10.1177/0022219412442167

Fuchs, D., Fuchs, L.S., & Fernstrom, P. (1993). A conservative approach to special education reform: Mainstreaming through transenvironmental programming and curriculum-based measurement. *American Educational Research Journal, 30,* 149–177.

Fuchs, D., Mock, D., Morgan, P.L., & Young, C.L. (2003). Responsiveness-to-intervention: Definitions, evidence, and implications for the learning disabilities construct. *Learning Disabilities Research & Practice, 18,* 157–171.

Fuchs, L.S., Fuchs, D., & Hollenbeck, K.N. (2007). Extending responsiveness to intervention to mathematics at first and third grades. *Learning Disabilities Research & Practice, 22,* 13–24.

Fuchs, L.S., Fuchs, D., Powell, S.R., Seethaler, P.M., Cirino, P.T., & Fletcher, J.M. (2008). Intensive intervention for students with mathematics disabilities: Seven principles of effective practice. *Learning Disability Quarterly, 31,* 79–92. doi:10.2307/20528819

Fuchs, L.S., Fuchs, D., Steubing, K., Fletcher, J.M., Hamlett, C.L., & Lambert, W.E. (2008). Problem solving and calculation skill: Are they shared or distinct aspects of mathematical cognition? *Journal of Educational Psychology, 100*(1), 30–47. doi:10.1037/0022-0663.100.1.30

Fuchs, L.S., Hamlett, C.L., & Powell, S.R. (2003). *Math Flash* [Computer software]. (Available from L.S. Fuchs, 328 Peabody, Vanderbilt University, Nashville, TN 37203).

Fuchs, L.S., & Vaughn, S.R. (2005). Response-to-intervention as a framework for the identification of learning disabilities. *Trainer's Forum: Periodical of the Trainers of School Psychologists, 25*(1), 12–19.

Fuhs, M.W., Farran, D.C., & Nesbitt, K.T. (2013). Preschool classroom processes are predictors of children's cognitive self-regulation skills development. *School Psychology Quarterly, 28,* 347–359.

Furnes, B., & Samuelsson, S. (2011). Phonological awareness and rapid automatized naming predicting early development in reading and spelling: Results from a cross-linguistic longitudinal study. *Learning and Individual Differences, 21*(1), 85–95.

Fuster, J.M. (1989). A theory of prefrontal functions: The prefrontal cortex and the temporal organization of behavior. In J.M. Fuster (Ed.), *The prefrontal cortex: Anatomy, physiology, and neuropsychology of the frontal lobe* (pp. 1–32). New York, NY: Raven Press.

Gallagher, K.C. (2002). Does child temperament moderate the influence of parenting on adjustment? *Developmental Review, 22,* 623–643.

Galuschka, K., Ise, E., Krick, K., & Schulte-Köme, G. (2014). Effectiveness of treatment approaches for children and adolescents with reading disabilities: A meta-analysis of randomized controlled trials. *PLoS ONE, 9*(2), e89900. doi:10.1371/journal.pone.0089900

Garber, J., & Weersing, V.R. (2010). Comorbidity of anxiety and depression in youth: Implications for treatment and prevention. *Clinical Psychology: Science and Practice, 17,* 293–306. doi:10.1111/j.1468-2850.2010.01221.x

Gaskins, I.W. (1998). A beginning literacy program for at-risk and delayed readers. In J.L. Metsala & L.C. Ehri (Eds.), *Word recognition in beginning literacy* (pp. 209–232). Mahwah, NJ: Erlbaum.

Gathercole, S.E., & Holmes, J. (2014). Developmental impairments of working memory: Profiles and interventions. *Perspectives on Language and Literacy, 40*(2), 36–39.

Gathercole, S.E., & Pickering, S.J. (2000). Working memory deficits in children with low achievements in the national curriculum at 7 years of age. *British Journal of Educational Psychology, 70,* 177–194.

Geary, D.C. (2003). Learning disabilities in arithmetic: Problem-solving differences and cognitive deficits. In H.L. Swanson, K.R. Harris, & S. Graham (Eds.), *Handbook of learning disabilities* (pp. 199–212). New York, NY: Guilford Press.

Geary, D.C. (2004). Mathematics and learning disabilities. *Journal of Learning Disabilities, 37,* 4–15.

Geary, D.C. (2013a). Early foundations for mathematics learning and their relations to learning disabilities. *Current Directions in Psychological Science, 22,* 23–27.

Geary, D.C. (2013b). Learning disabilities in mathematics: Recent advances. In H.L. Swanson, K.R. Harris, & S. Graham (Eds.), *Handbook of learning disabilities* (2nd ed., pp. 239–255). New York, NY: Guilford Press.

Geary, D.C., Hoard, M.K., Nugent, L., & Bailey, D.H. (2012). Mathematical cognition deficits in children with learning disabilities and persistent low achievement: A five-year prospective study. *Journal of Educational Psychology, 104,* 206–223.

Gentile, L. (2004). *The oracy instructional guide.* Carlsbad, CA: Dominie Press.

Gentry, J.R. (1982). An analysis of developmental spelling in GYNS AT WRK. *Reading Teacher, 36,* 192–200.

Gentry, J.R. (1984). Developmental aspects of learning to spell. *Academic Therapy, 20,* 11–19.

Gentry, J.R. (1987). *Spel... is a four-letter word.* Westport, CT: Heinemann.

Georgiou, G.K., & Parrila, R. (2013). Rapid automatized naming and reading. In H.L. Swanson, L.R. Harris, & S. Graham (Eds.), *Handbook of Learning Disabilities* (2nd ed., pp. 169–185). New York, NY: Guilford Press.

Georgiou, G.K., Parrila, R., & Kirby, J. (2006). Rapid naming speed components and early reading acquisition. *Scientific Studies of Reading, 10*(2), 199–220.

Gerber, A. (1993). *Language-related learning disabilities: Their nature and treatment.* Baltimore, MD: Paul H. Brookes Publishing Co.

Gerber, P.J., & Ginsberg, R.J. (1990). *Identifying alterable patterns of success in highly successful adults with learning disabilities.* Washington, DC: Office of Special Education and Rehabilitation Services.

Gersten, R., & Chard, D. (1999). Number sense: Rethinking arithmetic instruction for students with mathematical disabilities. *Journal of Special Education, 33,* 18–28.

Gersten, R., Chard, D.J., Jayanthi, M., Baker, S.K., Morphy, P., & Flojo, J. (2009). Mathematics instruction for students with learning disabilities: A meta-analysis of instructional components. *Review of Educational Research, 79,* 1202–1242. doi:10.3102/0034654309334431

Geschwind, N. (1982). Why Orton was right. *Annals of Dyslexia, 32,* 13–30.

Geschwind, N., & Fusillo, M. (1966). Color-naming defects in association with alexia. *Archives of Neurology, 15*(2), 137.

Gillberg, C., Gillberg, I.C., Rasmussen, P., Kadesjo, B., Soderstrom, H., Rastam M., . . . Niklasson, L. (2004). Co-existing disorders in ADHD—implications for diagnosis and intervention. *European Child Adolescent Psychiatry, 13*(Suppl.1), 80–92.

Gillingham, A., & Stillman, B.W. (1973). *Remedial training for children with specific disability in reading, spelling, and penmanship.* Cambridge, MA: Educators Publishing Service.

Ginott, H. (1972). *Teacher and child.* New York, NY: Avon Books.

Ginsburg, K.R. (2011). *Building resilience in children and teens* (2nd ed.). Elk Grove Village, IL: American Academy of Pediatrics.

Glasgow, K.L., Dornbusch, S.M., Troyer, L., Steinberg, L., & Ritter, P.L. (1997). Parenting styles, adolescents' attributions, and educational outcomes in nine heterogeneous high schools. *Child Development, 68,* 507–529.

Glass, G.G. (1973). *Teaching decoding as separate from reading.* New York, NY: Adelphi University Press.

Glasser, W. (1997). A new look at school failure and school success. *Phi Delta Kappan, 78,* 596–602.

Glenn, P., & Hurley, S. (1993). Preventing spelling disabilities. *Child Language, Teaching, and Therapy, 9,* 1–12.

Goldberg, E. (2001). *The executive brain: Frontal lobes in the civilized mind.* New York, NY: Oxford University Press.

Goldman, E. (1910). *Anarchism and other essays.* New York, NY: Mother Earth Publishing Association.

Goldstein, S. (1995). *Understanding and managing children's classroom behavior.* New York, NY: Wiley.

Goldstein, S. (1997). *Managing attention deficit disorder and learning disabilities in late adolescence and adulthood: A guide for practitioners.* New York, NY: Guilford Press.

Goldstein, S. (1999). Attention-deficit/hyperactivity disorder. In C.R. Reynolds & S. Goldstein (Eds.), *Handbook of neurodevelopmental and genetic disorders* (pp. 154–184). New York, NY: Guilford Press.

Goldstein, S. (2006). Is ADHD a growth industry? *Journal of Attention Disorders, 9,* 461–464.

Goldstein, S., & Brooks, R. (2007). *Understanding and managing children's classroom behavior: Creating sustainable, resilient schools* (2nd ed.). New York, NY: Wiley.

Goldstein, S., & Brooks, R. (2013). *Handbook of resilience in children* (2nd ed.). New York, NY: Springer.

Goldstein, S., & Goldstein, M. (1990). *Managing attention deficit disorder in children: A guide for practitioners.* New York, NY: Wiley.

Goldstein, S., & Goldstein, M. (1992). *Hyperactivity: Why won't my child pay attention?* New York, NY: Wiley.

Goldstein, S., & Goldstein, M. (1998). *Understanding and managing attention-deficit/hyperactivity disorder in children: A guide for practitioners* (2nd ed.). New York, NY: Wiley.

Goldstein, S., & Gordon, M. (2003). Gender issues and ADHD: Sorting fact from fiction. *The ADHD Report, 11*(4), 7–16.

Goldstein, S., & Jones, C.B. (1998). Managing and educating children with ADHD. In S. Goldstein & M. Goldstein (Eds.), *Understanding and managing attention-deficit/hyperactivity disorder in children: A guide for practitioners* (2nd ed., pp. 545–591). New York, NY: Wiley.

Goldstein, S., & Mather, N. (1998). *Overcoming underachieving: An action guide for helping your child succeed in school.* New York, NY: Wiley.

Goldstein, S., & Naglieri, J.A. (2006). The role of intellectual processes in the *DSM-V* diagnosis of ADHD: Editorial. *Journal of Attention Disorders, 10*(1), 3–8.

Goldstein, S., & Naglieri, J.A. (2014). *Handbook of executive functioning.* New York, NY: Springer.

Goldstein, S., & Rider, R. (2013). Resilience and the disruptive disorders of childhood. In S. Goldstein, & R.B. Brooks (Eds.), *Handbook of resilience in children* (pp. 183–200). New York, NY: Springer Science and Business Media. doi:10.1007/978-1-4614-3661-4_11

Goldstein, S., & Teeter-Ellison, A. (2002). *Clinician's guide to adult ADHD: Assessment and intervention.* New York, NY: Academic Press.

Good, T.L., & Brophy, J.E. (1994). *Looking in classrooms* (6th ed.). New York, NY: HarperCollins.

Good, T.L., & Grouws, D. (1977). Teaching effects: A process-product study in fourth grade mathematics classrooms. *Journal of Teacher Education, 28,* 49–54.

Goodman, G., & Poillion, M.J. (1992). ADD: Acronym for any dysfunction or difficulty. *Journal of Special Education, 26,* 37–56.

Gordon, M., Thomason, D., Cooper, S., & Ivers, C.L. (1991). Nonmedical treatment of ADHD/hyperactivity: The attention training system. *Journal of School Psychology, 29,* 151–159.

Gordon, S.D., & Davidson, N. (1981). Behavioral parent training. In N. German & L. Kriskern (Eds.), *Handbook of family therapy* (pp. 236–251). New York, NY: Brunner/Mazel.

Gordon-Pershey, M. (2014). Executive functioning and language: A complementary relationship that supports learning. *Perspectives on Language and Literacy, 40*(2), 23–26.

Goswami, U. (2006). Orthography, phonology, and reading development: A cross-linguistic perspective. In R.M. Joshi & P.G. Aaron (Eds.), *Handbook of*

References

orthography and literacy (pp. 463–480). Mahwah, NJ: Erlbaum.

Goulandris, N.K., & Snowling, M. (1991). Visual memory deficits: A plausible cause of developmental dyslexia? Evidence from a single case study. *Cognitive Neuropsychology, 8,* 127–154.

Gould, M., King, R., Greenwald, S., Fisher, P., Schwab-Stone, M., Kramer, R., . . . Shaffer, D. (1998). Psychopathology associated with suicidal ideation and attempts among children and adolescents. *Journal of the American Academy of Child and Adolescent Psychiatry, 37,* 915–923.

Grace, K.E.S. (2007). *Phonics and spelling through phoneme-grapheme mapping.* Longmont, CO: Sopris West.

Graham, S. (1983). The effect of self-instructional procedures on LD students' handwriting performance. *Learning Disability Quarterly, 6,* 231–234.

Graham, S. (1999). Handwriting and spelling instruction for students with learning disabilities: A review. *Learning Disability Quarterly, 22,* 78–98.

Graham, S. (2010). Want to improve children's writing? Don't neglect their handwriting. *American Educator, 33*(4), 20–27, 40.

Graham, S., Berninger, V., Weintraub, N., & Schafer, W. (1999). The development of handwriting speed and legibility in grades 1 through 9. *Journal of Educational Research 92*(1), 42–52.

Graham, S., & Harris, K.R. (1989). Components analysis of cognitive strategy instruction: Effects on learning disabled students' compositions and self-efficacy. *Journal of Educational Psychology, 81,* 353–361.

Graham, S., & Harris, K.R. (1999). Assessment and intervention in overcoming writing difficulties: An illustration from the Self-Regulated Strategy Development model. *Learning, Speech, and Hearing Services in Schools, 30,* 255–264.

Graham, S., & Harris, K. (2005). *Writing better: Effective strategies for teaching students with learning difficulties.* Baltimore, MD: Paul H. Brookes Publishing Co.

Graham, S., & Harris, K.R. (2013). Common core state standards, writing, and students with LD: Recommendations. *Learning Disabilities Research & Practice, 28,* 28–37.

Graham, S., Harris, K.R., & McKeown, D. (2013). Students with learning disabilities and the process of writing: A meta-analysis of SRSD studies. In H.L. Swanson, K.R. Harris, & S. Graham (Eds.), *Handbook of learning disabilities: Second edition* (pp. 405–438). New York, NY: Guilford Press.

Graham, S., & Hebert, M.A. (2010). *Writing to read: Evidence for how writing can improve reading. A Carnegie Corporation Time to Act Report.* Washington, DC: Alliance for Excellent Education.

Graham, S., & Hebert, M. (2011). Writing to read: A meta-analysis of the impact of writing and writing instruction on reading. *Harvard Educational Review, 81,* 710–745.

Graham, S., & Madan, A.J. (1981). Teaching letter formation. *Academic Therapy, 16,* 389–396.

Graham, S., & Miller, L. (1980). Handwriting research and practice: A unified approach. *Focus on Exceptional Children, 13*(2), 1–16.

Graham, S., Weintraub, N., & Berninger, V. (1998). The relationship between handwriting style and speed and legibility. *Journal of Educational Research, 91,* 290–296.

Graves, A.W., Gersten, R., & Haager, D. (2004). Literacy instruction in multiple-language first-grade classrooms: Linking student outcomes to observed instructional practice. *Learning Disabilities Research & Practice, 19,* 262–272.

Graves, A.W., & Montague, M. (1991). Using story grammar cueing to improve the writing of students with learning disabilities. *Learning Disabilities Research & Practice, 6,* 246–250.

Graves, F. (2000). A vocabulary program to complement and bolster a middle-grade comprehension program. In B.M. Taylor, M.F. Graves, & P. Van Den Broek (Eds.), *Reading for meaning: Fostering comprehension in the middle grades* (pp. 116–135). New York, NY: Teachers College Press.

Greene, G. (1999). Mnemonic multiplication fact instruction for students with learning disabilities. *Learning Disabilities Research & Practice, 14,* 141–148.

Greene, J.F. (2008). *LANGUAGE! The comprehensive literacy curriculum* (4th ed.). Longmont, CO: Sopris West.

Greene, R. (1993). Hidden factors affecting the education success of ADHD students. *The ADHD Report, 2,* 8–9.

Greenhill, L.L., & Osman, B.B. (1991). *Ritalin: Theory and patient management.* Larchmont, NY: Mary Ann Liebert.

Greenwood, C., Hops, H., Walker, H.M., Guild, J.J., Young, K.R., Keleman, K., & Willardson, M. (1979). Standardized classroom management programs: Social validation replication studies in Utah and Oregon. *Journal of Applied Behavioral Analysis, 12,* 235–253.

Griggs, M.S., Rimm-Kaufman, S.E., Merritt, E.G., & Patton, C.L. (2013). The responsive classroom approach and fifth grade students' math and science anxiety and self-efficacy. *School Psychology Quarterly, 28,* 360–373.

Grossen, B. (1997). *Thirty years of research: What we now know about how children learn to read.* Santa Cruz, CA: Center for the Future of Teaching & Learning.

Guardino, C.A., & Fullerton, E. (2010). Changing behaviors by changing the classroom environment. *Teaching Exceptional Children, 42*(6), 8–13.

Haenlein, M., & Caul, W.F. (1987). Attention deficit disorder with hyperactivity: A specific hypothesis of reward dysfunction. *Journal of the American Academy of Child and Adolescent Psychiatry, 26,* 356–362.

Hagerman, R. (1991). Organic causes of ADHD. *ADDVANCE, 3,* 4–6.

Hale, J.B., & Fiorello, C.A. (2004). *School neuropsychology: A practitioner's handbook.* New York, NY: Guilford Press.

Hall, N. (1987). *The emergence of literacy.* Portsmouth, NH: Heinemann.

Hallahan, D. (2007). Learning disabilities: Whatever happened to intensive instruction? *LDA Newsbriefs, 42*(1), 1, 3–5, 24.

Hallahan, D.P., & Sapona, R. (1983). Self-monitoring of attention with learning disabled children: Past research and current issues. *Journal of Learning Disabilities, 16,* 616–620.

Hallenbeck, M.J. (1996). The cognitive strategy in writing: Welcome relief for adolescents with learning disabilities. *Learning Disabilities Research & Practice, 11,* 107–119.

Hallenbeck, M.J. (2002). Taking charge: Adolescents with learning disabilities assume responsibility for their own writing. *Learning Disability Quarterly, 25,* 227–246.

Hamlet, C.C., Axelrod, S., & Kuerschner, S. (1984). Eye contact as an antecedent to compliant behavior. *Journal of Applied Behavior Analysis, 17,* 553–557.

Hammill, D.D., Leigh, E., McNutt, G., & Larsen, S. (1981). A new definition of learning disabilities. *Learning Disability Quarterly, 4,* 336–342.

Hamre, B.K., & Pianta, R.C. (2005). Can instructional and emotional support in the first-grade classroom make a difference for children at risk of school failure? *Child Development, 76,* 949–967.

Hamstra-Bletz, L., & Blote, A.W. (1993). A longitudinal study on dysgraphic handwriting in primary school. *Journal of Learning Disabilities, 26,* 689–699.

Hanau, L. (1974). *The study game: How to play and win with statement-pie.* New York, NY: Barnes & Noble.

Harnadek, M.C.S., & Rourke, B.P. (1994). Principal identifying features of the syndrome of nonverbal learning disabilities in children. *Journal of Learning Disabilities, 23,* 108–113.

Harrier, L.K., & DeOrnellas, K. (2005). Performance of children diagnosed with ADHD on selected planning and reconstitution tests. *Applied Neuropsychology, 12,* 106–119.

Harris, K.R., Graham, S., Mason, L.H., & Friedlander, B. (2008). *Powerful writing strategies for all students.* Baltimore, MD: Paul H. Brookes Publishing Co.

Hart, B., & Risley, T.R. (1995). *Meaningful differences in the everyday experience of young American children.* Baltimore, MD: Paul H. Brookes Publishing Co.

Hart, E.L., Lahey, B.B., Loeber, R., Applegate, B., & Frick, P. (1995). Developmental change in attention deficit hyperactivity disorder in boys: A four-year longitudinal study. *Journal of Abnormal Child Psychology, 23,* 729–749.

Hart, J. (2008). *Understanding today's learner.* Retrieved from http://www.learningsolutionsmag.com/articles/80/understanding-todays-learner

Harvey, E.A., Lugo-Candelas, C.I., & Breaux, R.P. (in press). Longitudinal changes in individual symptoms across the preschool years in children with ADHD. *Journal of Clinical Child and Adolescent Psychology.* doi:10.1080/15374416.2014.886253.

Hasbrouck, J., & Glaser, D. (2011). *Fluency: Understanding and teaching this complex skill: Training manual.* Wellesley Hills, MA: Gibson Hasbrouck & Associates.

Hasbrouck, J., & Tindal, G. (2005). *Oral reading fluency: 90 years of measurement* (Tech. Rep. No. 33). Eugene: University of Oregon Press.

Hasbrouck, J., & Tindal, G.A. (2006). Oral reading fluency norms: A valuable assessment tool for reading teachers. *Reading Teacher, 59,* 636–644.

Hasselbring, T.S., Lott, A.C., & Zydney, J.M. (2006). *Technology-supported instruction for students with disabilities: Two decades of research and development.* Washington, DC: American Institutes for Research. Retrieved from http://www.ntuaft.com/Departments/Research___Communication/SpecialEd/Training%20Modules/Training%20Modules/Access%20Folder/Computer%20Assisted%20Instruction/Tech-SupportedMathInstruction-FinalPaper_early.pdf

Hayes, S.C., & Nelson, R.O. (1983). Similar reactivity produced by external cues and self-monitoring. *Behavior Modification, 7,* 193–196.

Hecht, S.A., Torgesen, J.K., Wagner, R.K., & Rashotte, C.A. (2001). The relations between phonological processing abilities and emerging individual differences in mathematical computational skills: A longitudinal study from second to fifth grades. *Journal of Experimental Child Psychology, 79,* 192–227.

Heckelman, R.G. (1969). A neurological impress method of remedial-reading instruction. *Academic Therapy, 4,* 277–282.

Heckelman, R.G. (1986). N.I.M. revisited. *Academic Therapy, 21,* 411–420.

Heim, S., Tschierse, J., Amunts, K., Wilms, M., Vossel, S., Willmes, K., . . . & Huber, W. (2008). Cognitive subtypes of dyslexia. *Acta neurobiologiae experimentalis, 68*(1), 73–82.

Hektner, J.M., August, G.J., Bloomquist, M.L., Lee, S., & Klimes-Dougan, B. (2014). A 10-year randomized controlled trial of the early risers conduct problems preventive intervention: Effects on externalizing and internalizing in late high school. *Journal of Consulting and Clinical Psychology, 82,* 355–360. doi:10.1037/a0035678

Henderson, E.H. (1990). *Teaching spelling* (2nd ed.). Boston, MA: Houghton Mifflin.

Herbert, M., Gillespie, A., & Graham, S. (2013). Comparing effects of different writing analysis on reading comprehension: A meta-analysis. *Reading and Writing, 26,* 111–138. doi:10.1007/s11145-012-9386-3

Herman Miller Company. (2011). *Adaptable spaces and their impact on learning.* Retrieved from http://www.hermanmiller.com/researc/research-summaries/adaptablespacesandtheirimpactonlearning.html

Herr, C.M., & Bateman, B.D. (2013). Learning disabilities and the law. In H.L. Swanson, K.R. Harris, & S. Graham (Eds.), *Handbook of learning disabilities* (2nd ed., pp. 51–68). New York, NY: Guilford Press.

Herrenkohl, T.L., Maguin, E., Hill, K.G., Hawkins, J.D., Abbott, R.D., & Catalano, R.F. (2000). Developmental

References

risk factors for youth violence. *Journal of Adolescent Health, 26,* 76–186.

Hilden, K., & Jones, J. (2011). Comprehension and authentic reading: Putting the power back into K-W-L. *Reading Today, 29*(3), 15–16.

Hinshaw, S. (1992). Academic underachievement, attention deficits, and aggression: Comorbidity and implications for intervention. *Journal of Consulting and Clinical Psychology, 60,* 893–903.

Hinshelwood, J. (1895). Word-blindness and visual memory. *Lancet, 2,* 1564–1570.

Hinshelwood, J. (1902). *Congenital wordblindness with reports of two cases.* London, England: John Bale, Sons & Danielsson Ltd.

Hinshelwood, J. (1917). *Congenital wordblindness.* London, England: Lewis.

Hobbs, N. (1966). Helping the disturbing child: Psychological and ecological strategies. *American Psychologist, 21,* 1105–1115.

Hogan, T.P., Catts, H.W., & Little, T.D. (2005). The relationship between phonological awareness and reading: Implications for the assessment of phonological awareness. *Language, Speech, and Hearing Services in Schools, 36,* 285–293.

Hohman, L.B. (1922). Post-encephalitic behavior disorders in children. *Johns Hopkins Hospital Bulletin, 33,* 372–375.

Hooper, S.R. (1996). Subtyping specific reading disabilities: Classification approaches, recent advances, and current status. *Mental Retardation and Developmental Disabilities, 2,* 14–20. doi:10.1002/(SICI)1098-2779(1996)2:1<14::AID-MRDD4>3.0.CO;2-X

Horn, J.L., & Cattell, R.B. (1966). Refinement and test of the theory of fluid and crystallized intelligence. *Journal of Educational Psychology, 57,* 253–270.

Houten, R.V., Morrison, E., Jarvis, R., & McDonald, M. (1974). The effects of explicit timing and feedback on compositional response rate in elementary school children. *Journal of Applied Behavior Analysis, 7,* 547–555.

Hudson, R.F., Lane, H.B., & Pullen, P.C. (2005). Reading fluency assessment and instruction: What, why, and how? *International Reading Association, 58,* 702–714. doi:10.1598/RT.58.81

Hughes, C.A., Schumaker, J., Deshler, D., & Mercer, C. (1988). *The test-taking strategy.* Lawrence, KS: Edge Enterprises.

Hughes, J., & Kwok, O. (2007). Influence of student–teacher and parent–teacher relationships on lower achieving readers' engagement and achievement in the primary grades. *Journal of Educational Psychology, 99,* 39–51.

Hulme, C. (1981). *Reading retardation and multisensory teaching.* London, England: Routledge & Kegan Paul.

Hurray, G. (1993). *A spelling dictionary for beginning writers.* Cambridge, MA: Educators Publishing Service.

Hutchinson, N.L. (1993). Effects of cognitive strategy instruction on algebra problem solving of adolescents with learning disabilities. *Learning Disability Quarterly, 16,* 34–50.

Hynd, G.W., Hern, K.L., Novey, E.S., & Eliopulos, D. (1993). Attention-deficit/hyperactivity disorder and asymmetry of the caudate nucleus. *Journal of Child Neurology, 8,* 339–347.

Individuals with Disabilities Education Act (IDEA) Amendments of 1997, PL 105-17, 20 U.S.C. §§ 1400 et seq.

Individuals with Disabilities Education Improvement Act (IDEA) of 2004, PL 1U08-446, 20 U.S.C. §§ 1400 et seq.

Ingalls, S.I. (1991). *Levels of processing related to learning disability and disability characteristics.* Unpublished manuscript, Department of Special Education, University of Utah.

Ingersoll, B., & Goldstein, S. (1993). *Attention deficit disorder and learning disabilities: Myths, realities and controversial treatments.* New York, NY: Doubleday.

Ingersoll, B.D., & Goldstein, S. (1995). *Attention deficit disorder and learning disabilities: Realities, myths and controversial treatments.* New York, NY: Doubleday.

Ingram, D. (1986). Phonological development: Production. In P. Fletcher & M. Garman (Eds.), *Language and acquisition* (pp. 223–239). Cambridge, England: Cambridge University Press.

Interagency Committee on Learning Disabilities. (1987). *Learning disabilities: A report to Congress.* Bethesda, MD: National Institutes of Health.

Isaacson, S.L. (1989). Role of secretary vs. author in resolving the conflict in writing instruction. *Learning Disability Quarterly, 12,* 200–217.

Iseman, J.S. (2005). *A cognitive instructional approach to improving math calculation of children with ADHD: Application of the PASS theory.* (Unpublished doctoral dissertation). George Mason University, Fairfax County, VA.

Izzo, M., & Lamb, P. (2002). *Self-determination and career development: Skills for successful transition to postsecondary education and employment.* Retrieved from http://www.ncset.hawaii.edu/publications/pdf/self_determination.pdf

Jacobson, L.A., Ryan, M., Martin, R.B., Ewen, J., Mostofsky, S.H., Denckla, M.B., & Mahone, E.M. (2011). Working memory influences processing speed and reading fluency in ADHD. *Child Neuropsychology, 17,* 209–224.

Jensen, P.S. (2000). Pediatric psychopharmacology in the United States: Issues and challenges in the diagnosis and treatment of attention-deficit/hyperactivity disorder. In L.L. Greenhill & B.B. Osman (Eds.), *Ritalin: Theory and practice* (2nd ed., pp. 1–3). Larchmont, NY: Mary Ann Liebert.

Jensen, P.S., & Cooper, J.R. (2004). *Attention deficit hyperactivity disorder: State of the science.* Kingston, NJ: Civic Research Institute.

Jensen, P.S., Kettle, L., Roper, M.T., Sloan, M.T., Dulcan, M.K., Hoven, C., . . . Payne, J.D. (1999). Are stimulants overprescribed? Treatment of ADHD in four U.S. communities. *Journal of the American Academy of Child and Adolescent Psychiatry, 38,* 797–804.

Jiron, C., Sherrill, R., & Chiodo, A. (1995, November). Is ADHD being overdiagnosed? Paper presented at the National Academy of Neuropsychology, San Francisco.

Jitendra, A.K., Burgess, C., & Gajria, M. (2011). Cognitive strategy instruction for improving expository text comprehension of students with learning disabilities: The quality of evidence. *Exceptional Children, 77,* 135–159.

Jitendra, A.K., Edwards, L.L., Sacks, G., & Jacobsen, L.A. (2004). What research says about vocabulary instruction for students with learning disabilities. *Exceptional Children, 70,* 299–322.

Johns, J.L. (1993). *Informal reading inventories.* DeKalb, IL: Communitech.

Johnson, D.J. (1995). An overview of learning disabilities: Psychoeducational perspectives. *Journal of Child Neurology, 10*(1), 2–5.

Johnson, D.J., & Myklebust, H.R. (1971). *Learning disabilities: Educational principles and practices* (2nd ed.). New York, NY: Grune & Stratton.

Johnson, S. (1997). *Taking the anxiety out of taking tests: A step-by-step guide.* Oakland, CA: New Harbinger.

Jones, C.B. (1989, November/December). Managing the difficult child. *Family Day Caring,* 6–7.

Jones, C.B. (1991). *Sourcebook on attention disorders: A management guide for early childhood professionals and parents.* Tucson, AZ: Communication Skill Builders.

Jones, C.B. (1994). *Attention deficit disorder: Strategies for school-age children.* Tucson, AZ: Communication Skill Builders.

Jones, E.D., Wilson, R., & Bhojwani, S. (1997). Mathematics instruction for secondary students with learning disabilities. *Journal of Learning Disabilities, 30,* 151–163.

Jordan, N.C., Kaplan, D., Locuniak, M.N., & Ramineni, C. (2007). Predicting first-grade math achievement from developmental number sense trajectories. *Learning Disabilities Research & Practice, 22*(1), 36–46. doi:10.1111/j.1540-5826.2007.00229.x

Joshi, R.M., Hoien, T., Feng, X., Chengappa, R., & Boulware-Gooden, R. (2006). Learning to spell by ear and by eye: A cross-linguistic comparison. In R.M. Joshi & P.G. Aaron (Eds.), *Handbook of orthography and literacy* (pp. 569–577). Mahwah, NJ: Erlbaum.

Jurbergs, N., Palcic, J., & Kelley, M. (2007). School-home notes with and without response cost: Increasing attention and academic performance in low-income children with attention-deficit/hyperactivity disorder. *School Psychology Quarterly, 22,* 358–379. doi:10.1037/1045-3830.22.3.358

Justice, L., Turnbull, K., Bowles, R., & Skibbe, L. (2009). School readiness among children with varying histories of language difficulties. *Developmental Psychology, 45*(2), 460–476. doi:10.1037/a0014324

Kail, R. (1991). Developmental change in speed of processing during childhood and adolescence. *Psychological Bulletin, 109,* 490–501.

Kail, R., & Hall, L.K. (1994). Processing speed, naming speed, and reading. *Developmental Psychology, 30,* 949–954.

Kail, R., Hall, L.K., & Caskey, B.J. (1999). Processing speed, exposure to print, and naming speed. *Applied Psycholinguistics, 20,* 303–314.

Kame'enui, E.J. (1993). Diverse learners and the tyranny of time: Don't fix blame; fix the leaky roof. *Reading Teacher, 46,* 376–383.

Kaplan, L. (1970). *Mental health and education.* New York, NY: Harper & Row.

Kataoka, S., Stein, B.D., Jaycox, L.H., Wong, M., Escudero, P., Tu, W., . . . Fink, A. (2003). Effectiveness of a school-based mental health program for traumatized Latino immigrant children. *Journal of the American Academy of Child and Adolescent Psychiatry, 42,* 311–318.

Katz, M. (1994, May). From challenged childhood to achieving adulthood: Studies in resilience. *CH.A.D.D.E.R.,* 8–11.

Katz, M. (1997). *Playing a poor hand well.* New York, NY: W.W. Norton.

Katzir, T., Kim, Y., Wolf, M., O'Brien, B., Kennedy, B., Lovett, M., & Morris, R. (2006). Reading fluency: The whole is more than the parts. *Annals of Dyslexia, 56*(1), 51–82.

Kauffman, D. (2007). *What's different about teaching reading to students learning English?* Washington, DC: Center for Applied Linguistics.

Kauffman, J.M. (2005). *Characteristics of emotional and behavioral disorders of children and youth* (8th ed.). Upper Saddle River, NJ: Pearson.

Kauffman, J.M., & Landrum, T.J. (2012). *Characteristics of emotional and behavioral disorders of children and youth* (10th ed.). Upper Saddle River, NJ: Merrill Prentice Hall.

Kaufman, A.S., & Kaufman, N.L. (2004). *Kaufman Assessment Battery for Children—Second Edition.* Circle Pines, MN: American Guidance Service.

Kaufman, C. (2010). *Executive function in the classroom.* Baltimore, MD: Paul H. Brookes Publishing Co.

Kavale, K.A. (2005). Identifying specific learning disability: Is responsiveness to intervention the answer? *Journal of Learning Disabilities, 38,* 553–562.

Kavale, K.A., Kauffman, J.M., Bachmeier, R.J., & LeFever, G.B. (2008). Response-to-intervention: Separating the rhetoric of self-congratulation from the reality of specific learning disability identification. *Learning Disability Quarterly, 31,* 135–150. doi:10.1111/j.1540-5826.2008.00274.x

Kavale, K.A., Kaufman, A.S., Naglieri, J.A., & Hale, J. (2005). Changing procedures for identifying learning disabilities: The danger of poorly supported ideas. *The School Psychologist, 59,* 16–25.

Kavanagh, J.F. (1988, October). *New federal biological definition of learning and attentional disorders.* Speech given at the 15th Annual Conference of the New York branch of the Orton Society.

Kazdin, A. (2012). *Behavior modification in applied settings* (7th ed.). Long Grove, IL: Waveland Press.

Keeler, C.E., & Swanson, H.L. (2001). Does strategy knowledge influence working memory in children with mathematical disabilities? *Journal of Learning Disabilities, 34,* 418–434.

References

Keller, C.E., & Sutton, J.P. (1991). Specific mathematics disorders. In J.E. Obrzut & G.W. Hynd (Eds.), *Neuropsychological foundations of learning disabilities: A handbook of issues, methods, and practice* (pp. 549–571). San Diego, CA: Academic Press.

Kelley, J.G., Lesaux, N.K., Kieffer, M.J., & Faller, S.E. (2010). Effective academic vocabulary instruction in the urban middle school. *Reading Teacher, 64,* 5–14. doi:10.1598/RT.64.1.1

Kendall, P.C., & Hedtke, K.A. (2006). *Cognitive-behavioral therapy for anxious children: Therapist manual.* Ardmore, PA: Workbook Publishing.

Kendeou, P., van den Brock, P., White, M.J., & Lynch, J. (2009). Predicting reading comprehension in early elementary school: The independent contributions of oral language and decoding skills. *Journal of Educational Psychology, 101,* 765–778. doi:10.1037/a0015956

Keogh, B. (2003). *Temperament in the classroom: Understanding individual differences.* Baltimore, MD: Paul H. Brookes Publishing Co.

Kerrigan, W.J. (1979). *Writing to the point: Six basic steps* (2nd ed.). New York, NY: Harcourt Brace Jovanovich.

Kessler, R.C., Berglund, P., Demler, O., Jin, R., & Walters, E.E. (2006). Lifetime prevalence and age-of-onset distributions of *DSM-IV* disorders in the national comorbidity survey replication. *Archives of General Psychiatry, 62,* 593–602.

Kessler, R.C., Birnbaum, H., Bromet, E., Hwang, I., Sampson, N., & Shahly, V. (2010). Age differences in major depression: Results from the National Comorbidity Survey Replication (NCS-R). *Psychological Medicine, 40,* 225–237.

Kieffer, M.J., & Lesaux, N.K. (2010). Morphing into adolescents: Active word learning for English-language learners and their classmates in middle school. *Journal of Adolescent & Adult Literacy,* 54(1), 47–56. doi:10.1598/JA AL.54.1.5

Kim, O.H., & Kaiser, A.P. (2000). Language characteristics of children with ADHD. *Communication Disorders Quarterly, 21,* 154–165.

Kim, W., & Linan-Thompson, S. (2013). The effects of self-regulation on science vocabulary acquisition of English language learners with learning difficulties. *Remedial and Special Education, 34,* 225–236. doi:10.1177/0741932513476956

Kim, W., Linan-Thompson, S., & Misquitta, R. (2012). Critical factors in reading comprehension instruction for students with learning disabilities: A research synthesis. *Learning Disabilities Research & Practice,* 27(2), 66–78. doi:10.1111/j.1540-5826.2012.00352.x

Kirk, S.A., & Bateman, B. (1962/1963). Diagnosis and remediation of learning disabilities. *Exceptional Children, 29,* 73–78.

Kirk, S.A., & Kirk, W.D. (1971). *Psycholinguistic learning disabilities: Diagnosis and remediation.* Urbana, IL: University of Illinois Press.

Kirk, S.A., Kirk, W.D., Minskoff, E.H., Mather, N., & Roberts, R. (2007). *Phonic reading lessons: Skills.* Novato, CA: Academic Therapy.

Kirk, S.A., McCarthy, J.J., & Kirk, W. (1968). *Examiner's manual: Illinois Test of Psycholinguistic Abilities* (Rev. ed.). Urbana: University of Illinois Press.

Klein, D.N., & Riso, L.P. (1993). Psychiatric disorders: Problems of boundaries and comorbidity. In C.G. Costello (Ed.), *Basic issues in psychopathology* (pp. 19–66). New York, NY: Guilford Press.

Klingner, J., Sorrells, A.M., & Barrera, M.T. (2007). Considerations when implementing response to intervention with culturally and linguistically diverse students. In D. Haager, J. Klingner, & S. Vaughn (Eds.), *Evidence-based reading practices for response to intervention* (pp. 223–244). Baltimore, MD: Paul H. Brookes Publishing Co.

Klingner, J.K., Vaughn, S., Hughes, M.T., Schumm, J.S., & Elbaum, B. (1998). Outcomes for students with and without learning disabilities in inclusive classrooms. *Learning Disabilities Research & Practice, 13,* 153–161.

Koenen, K.C., Moffitt, T.E., Caspi, A., Gregory, A., Harrington, H., & Poulton, R. (2008). The developmental mental-disorder histories of adults with posttraumatic stress disorder: A prospective longitudinal birth cohort study. *Journal of Abnormal Psychology, 117,* 460–466. doi:10.1037/0021-843X.117.2.460

Koepke, K.M., & Miller, B. (2013). At the intersection of math and reading disabilities: Introduction to the special issue. *Journal of Learning Disabilities, 46,* 483–489. doi:10.1177/0022219413498200

Koeppen, A.S. (1974). Relaxation training for children. *Elementary School Guidance and Counseling, 9,* 14–21.

Kohnert, K. (2007). *Language disorders in bilingual children and adults.* San Diego, CA: Plural.

Kollins, S.H., Lane, S.D., & Shapiro, S.K. (1997). Experimental analysis of childhood psychopathology: A laboratory analysis of the behavior of children diagnosed with ADHD. *Psychological Record, 47,* 25–44.

Koplow, L. (2002). *Creating schools that heal.* New York, NY: Teachers College Press.

Korat, O., & Shamir, A. (2012). Direct and indirect teaching: Using e-books for supporting vocabulary, word reading, and story comprehension for young children. *Journal of Educational Computing Research, 46,* 135–152.

Korhonen, T.T. (1991). Neuropsychological stability and prognosis of subgroups of children with learning disabilities. *Journal of Learning Disabilities, 24,* 48–57.

Kosc, L. (1974). Developmental dyscalculia. *Journal of Learning Disabilities, 7,* 164–167.

Koutsoftas, A.D., & Gray, S. (2012). Comparison of narrative and expository writing in students with and without language-learning disabilities. *Language, Speech, and Hearing Services in Schools, 43,* 395–409.

Kovacs, M. (2010). *Children's Depression Inventory 2 (CDI 2).* Upper Saddle River, NJ: Pearson.

Kozulin, A. (2003). Psychological tools and mediated learning. In A. Kozulin, B. Gindis, V.S. Ageyev, & S.M. Miller (Eds.), *Vygotsky's educational theory in cultural context* (pp. 15–38). New York, NY: Cambridge University Press.

Krashen, S.D., & Terrell, T. (1983). *The natural approach: Language acquisition in the classroom.* Hayward, CA: Alemany Press.

Krawec, J., Huang, J., Montague, M., Kressler, B., & de Alba, A. (2012). The effects of cognitive strategy instruction on knowledge of math problem-solving processes of middle school students with learning disabilities. *Learning Disability Quarterly, 36*(2), 80–92. doi:10.1177/0731948712463368

Kroesbergen, E.H., & Van Luit, J.E.H. (2003). Mathematics interventions for children with special educational needs. *Remedial and Special Education, 24,* 97–114.

Kroese, J.M., Hynd, G.W., Knight, D.F., Hiemenz, J.R., & Hall, J. (2000). Clinical appraisal of spelling ability and its relationship to phonemic awareness (blending, segmenting, elision, and reversal), phonological memory, and reading in reading disabled, ADHD, and normal children. *Reading and Writing: An Interdisciplinary Journal, 13,* 105–131.

Krogh, K. (2014). *Understanding Stephen Krashen's affective filter hypothesis.* Retrieved from http://suite.io/kristin-krog/5c27243

Kunsch, C.A., Jitendra, A.K., & Sood, S. (2007). The effects of peer-mediated instruction in mathematics for students with learning problems: A research synthesis. *Learning Disabilities Research & Practice, 22,* 1–12.

Kussmaul, A. (1877a). Die Storungen der Sprache. Ziemssen's Handbuch d. Speciellen. *Pathologie u. therapie, 12,* 1–300.

Kussmaul, A. (1877b). Disturbances of speech. In H. von Ziemssen (Ed.) & J.A. McCreery (Trans.), *Cyclopedia of the practice of medicine* (p. 595). New York, NY: William Wood.

La Greca, A.M., Boyd, B.A., Jaycox, L.H., Kassam-Adams, N., Mannarino, A.P., Silverman, W.K., . . . Wong, M. (2008). *Children and trauma: Update for mental health professionals.* American Psychological Association Presidential Task Force on Posttraumatic Stress Disorder in Children and Adolescents. Washington, DC: American Psychological Association.

Lahey, B.B., Applegate, B., McBurnett, K., Biederman, J., Greenhill, L., Hynd, G., . . . Shaffer, D. (1994). *DSM-IV* field trial for attention deficit/hyperactivity disorder in children and adolescents. *American Journal of Psychiatry, 151,* 1673–1685.

Lahey, B.B., Pelham, W.E., Loney, J., Lee, S., & Willcutt, E. (2005). Instability of the *DSM-IV* subtypes of ADHD from preschool through elementary school. *Archives of General Psychiatry, 62,* 896–902.

LaNae', T. (Interviewer) & Angelou, M. (Interviewee). (2012). *A conversation with Dr. Maya Angelou* [Interview transcript]. Retrieved from Beautifully Said Magazine Web site: http://beautifullysmagazine.com/201207feature-of-the-month-3/

Lane, K.L., Graham, S., Harris, K.R., Little, M.A., Sandmel, K., & Brindle, M. (2010). The effects of self-regulated strategy development for second-grade students with writing and behavioral difficulties. *Journal of Special Education, 44,* 107–128. doi:10.1177/0022466908331044

Lane, K.L., Menzies, H.M., Bruhn, A.L., & Crnobori, M. (2011). *Managing challenging behaviors in schools: Research-based strategies that work.* New York, NY: Guilford Press.

Lane, K.L., Wehby, J., Menzies, H.M., Doukas, G.L., Munton, S.M., & Gregg, R.M. (2003). Social skills instruction for students at risk for antisocial behavior: The effects of small-group instruction. *Behavior Disorders, 28,* 229–248.

Langdon, H., & Cheng, L. (2002). *Interpreting and translating in speech-language pathology and audiology.* Eau Claire, WI: Thinking Publications.

Larsen, S.C. (1987). *Assessing the writing abilities and instructional needs of students.* Austin, TX: PRO-ED.

Lavoie, R. (1994). *Last one picked, first one picked on* [Videotape]. (Available from PBS Video, P.O. Box 279, Melbourne, FL 32902 [800] 752-9727).

Leavell, A., & Ioannides, A. (1993, Summer). Using character development to improve story writing. *Teaching Exceptional Children (Special Edition),* 41–45.

Lee, J. (2002). Racial and ethnic achievement gap trends: Reversing the progress towards equity. *Educational Researcher, 32,* 3–12.

Leitchman, H.M. (1993). *Attention deficit disorder subgroups: ADD outcome matrix.* Boston, MA: Wediko Children's Services.

Lerner, B. (1996). Self-esteem and excellence: The choice and the paradox. *American Educator, 20,* 14–19.

Lerner, J.W., & Johns, B.H. (2011). *Learning disabilities and mild disabilities* (12th ed.). Belmont, CA: Wadsworth Cengage Learning.

Lerner, J.W., & Johns, B.H. (2014). *Learning disabilities and related disabilities: Strategies for success* (13th ed.). Belmont, CA: Wadsworth Cengage Learning.

Lerner, J.W., & Lowenthal, B. (1992). Attention deficit disorders: New responsibilities for the special educator. *Learning Disabilities, 4,* 1–8.

Lervåg, A., & Hulme, C. (2009). Rapid automatized naming (RAN) taps a mechanism that places constraints on the development of early reading fluency. *Psychological Science, 20,* 1040–1048.

Lesaux, N.K. (2006). Building a consensus: Future directions for research on English language learners at risk for learning difficulties. *Teachers' College Record, 108,* 2406–2438.

Lesaux, N.K., Crosson, A.C., Kieffer, M.J., & Pierce, M. (2010). Uneven profiles: Language minority learners' word reading, vocabulary, and reading comprehension skills. *Journal of Applied Developmental Psychology, 31,* 475–483. doi:10.1016/j.appdev.2010.09.004

Lesaux, N.K., Kieffer, M.J., Faller, S.E., & Kelley, J.G. (2010). The effectiveness and ease of implementation of an academic vocabulary intervention for linguistically diverse students in urban middle

References

schools. *Reading Research Quarterly, 45,* 196–228. doi:10.1598/RRQ.45.2.3

Lesaux, N.K., & Siegel, L.S. (2003). The development of reading in children who speak English as a second language. *Developmental Psychology, 39,* 1005–1019.

Levin, M., & Langton, C. (1998). *The reading lesson.* San Ramon, CA: Mountcastle.

Levine, M. (1987). *Developmental variations and learning disorders.* Cambridge, MA: Educators Publishing Service.

Levine, M. (1990). *Keeping a head in school.* Cambridge, MA: Educators Publishing Service.

Levine, M.D. (2002). *A mind at a time.* New York, NY: Simon & Schuster.

Lezak, M.D. (1995). *Neuropsychological assessment.* New York, NY: Oxford University Press.

Liaupsin, C., Umbreit, J., Ferro, J.B., Urso, A., & Upreti, G. (2006). Improving academic engagement through systematic, function-based intervention. *Education and Treatment of Children, 29,* 573–592.

Liberman, I.Y. (1973). Segmentation of the spoken word and reading acquisition. *Bulletin of the Orton Society, 23,* 65–77.

Liberman, I.Y., & Shankweiler, D. (1985). Phonology and the problems of learning to read and write. *Remedial and Special Education, 6,* 8–17.

Liberman, I.Y., Shankweiler, D., & Liberman, A.M. (1989). The alphabetic principle and learning to read. In D. Shankweiler & I.Y. Liberman (Eds.), *Phonology and reading disability: Solving the reading puzzle* (pp. 1–33). Ann Arbor: University of Michigan Press.

Lieberman, L.M. (1992). Preserving special education... for those who need it. In W. Stainback & S. Stainback (Eds.), *Controversial issues confronting special education* (pp. 29–43). Boston, MA: Allyn & Bacon.

Lienemann, T.O., Graham, S., Leader-Janssen, B., & Reid, R. (2006). Improving the writing performance of struggling writers in second grade. *Journal of Special Education, 40*(2), 66–78.

Lindamood, C.H., & Lindamood, P.C. (1998). *Lindamood phoneme sequencing program (LiPS) for reading, spelling, and speech.* Austin, TX: PRO-ED.

Lindstrom, J.H., & Sayeski, K. (2013). Identifying best practice in a shifting landscape: Making sense of RTI in the context of SLD identification. *Exceptionality, 21,* 5–18.

Lingo, A.S. (2014). Tutoring middle school students with disabilities by high school students: Effects on oral reading fluency. *Education and Treatment of Children, 37,* 53–76. doi:10.1353/etc.2014.0005

Lipka, O., Lesaux, N.K., & Siegel, L.S. (2006). Retrospective analyses of the reading development of Grade 4 students with reading disabilities: Risk status and profiles over 5 years. *Journal of Learning Disabilities, 39,* 364–378.

Lloyd, J.W., Landrum, T.J., & Hallahan, D.P. (1991). Self-monitoring applications for classroom intervention. In H.M. Walker, M.R. Shinn, & G. Stoner (Eds.), *Interventions for achievement and behavior problems* (pp. 310–311). Silver Spring, MD: National Association of School Psychologists.

Locuniak, M.N., & Jordan, N.C. (2008). Using kindergarten number sense to predict calculation fluency in second grade. *Journal of Learning Disabilities, 41,* 451–459. doi:10.1177/0022219408321126

Loe, I.M., & Feldman, H.M. (2007). Academic and educational outcomes of children with ADHD. *Journal of Pediatric Psychology, 32,* 643–654.

Loeber, R., Burke, J.D., Lahey, B.B., Winters, A., & Zera, M. (2000). Oppositional defiant and conduct disorder: A review of the past 10 years, part I. *Journal of the American Academy of Child and Adolescent Psychiatry, 39,* 1468–1484. doi:10.1097/00004583-200012000-00007

Loeber, R., Burke, J.D., & Pardini, D.A. (2009). Development and etiology of disruptive and delinquent behavior. *Annual Review of Clinical Psychology, 5,* 291–310. doi:10.1146/annurev.clinpsy.032408.153631

Loeffler, K.A. (2005). No more Friday spelling tests? *Teaching Exceptional Children, 37*(4), 24–27.

Lomas, B., & Gartside, P. (1999). ADHD in adult psychiatric outpatients. *Psychiatric Services, 5,* 705.

Loney, J., Kramer, J., & Milich, R. (1981). The hyperkinetic child grown up: Predictors of symptoms, delinquency and achievement at follow-up. In K.D. Gadow & J. Loney (Eds.), *Psychosocial aspects of drug treatment for hyperactivity* (pp. 181–211). Boulder, CO: Westview.

Lonigan, C.J., Farver, J.M., Nakamoto, J., & Eppe, S. (2013). Developmental trajectories of preschool early literacy skills: A comparison of language-minority and monolingual-English children. *Developmental Psychology, 49,* 1943–1957. doi:10.1037/a0031408

Lopez-Vergara, H.I., & Colder, C.R. (2013). An examination of the specificity of motivation and executive functioning in ADHD symptom-clusters in adolescence. *Journal of Pediatric Psychology, 38,* 1081–1090.

Lovett, M.W. (1987). A developmental approach to reading disability: Accuracy and speed criteria of normal and deficient reading skill. *Child Development, 58,* 234–260.

Luria, A.R. (1966). *Human brain and psychological processes.* New York, NY: Harper and Row.

Luria, A.R. (1973). The origin and cerebral organization of man's conscious action. In S.G. Sapir and A.C. Nitzburg (Eds.), *Children with learning problems* (pp. 109–130). New York, NY: Brunner/Mazel.

Luria, A.R. (1980). *Higher cortical functions in man* (2nd ed.). New York, NY: Basic Books.

Lynch, J. (1998). *Easy lessons for teaching word families.* New York, NY: Scholastic.

Lyon, G.R. (1995). Toward a definition of dyslexia. *Annals of Dyslexia, 45,* 3–27.

Lyon, G.R., Shaywitz, S.E., & Shaywitz, B.A. (2003). A definition of dyslexia. *Annals of Dyslexia, 53,* 1–14.

Lyon, G.R., & Watson, B. (1981). Empirically derived subgroups of learning disabled readers: Diagnostic characteristics. *Journal of Learning Disabilities, 14,* 256–261.

MacArthur, C.A., Schwartz, S.S., & Graham, S. (1991). A model for writing instruction: Integrating word processing and strategy instruction into a process approach to writing. *Learning Disabilities Practice, 6,* 230–236.

Maccini, P. (1998). *Effects of an instructional strategy incorporating concrete problem representation on the introductory algebra performance of secondary students with learning disabilities.* (Unpublished doctoral dissertation). Pennsylvania State University, University Park, PA.

Maccini, P., McNaughton, D., & Ruhl, K.L. (1999). Algebra instruction for students with learning disabilities: Implications from a research review. *Learning Disability Quarterly, 22,* 113–119.

Maccini, P., Mulcahy, C.A., & Wilson, M.G. (2007). A follow-up of mathematics interventions for secondary students with learning disabilities. *Learning Disabilities Research & Practice, 22,* 58–74.

Macklem, G.L. (2011). Evidence-based tier 1, tier 2, and tier 3 mental health interventions in schools. In G.L. Macklem (Ed.), *Evidence-based school mental health services affect education, emotion regulation training, and cognitive behavioral therapy* (pp. 19–37). New York, NY: Springer Science and Business Media.

Mahone, E. (2011). The effects of ADHD (beyond decoding accuracy) on reading fluency and comprehension. *New Horizons for Learning, 9*(1). Retrieved from http://education.jhu.edu/PD/newhorizons/Journals/Winter2011/Mahone

Mallett, C.A. (2014). Child and adolescent behaviorally based disorders: A critical review of reliability and validity. *Research on Social Work Practice, 24*(1), 96–113. doi:10.1177/1049731512464275

Malone, L.D., & Mastropieri, M.A. (1992). Reading comprehension instruction: Summarization and self-monitoring training for students with learning disabilities. *Teaching Exceptional Children, 58,* 270–279.

Mammarella, I.C., Ghisi, M., Bomba, M., Bottesi, G., Caviola, S., Broggi, F., & Nacinovich, R. (2014). Anxiety and depression in children with nonverbal learning disabilities, reading disabilities, or typical development. *Journal of Learning Disabilities.* Advance online publication, April 14, 2014. http://ldx.sagepub.com/content/early/2014/04/14/0022219414529336. doi:10.1177/0022219414529336

Mancl, D., Miller, S.P., & Kennedy, M. (2012). Using the concrete-representation-abstract sequence with integrated strategy instruction to teach subtraction with regrouping to students with learning disabilities. *Learning Disabilities Research & Practice, 27,* 152–166. doi:10.1111/j.1540-5826.2012.00363.x

Manis, F.R., Seidenberg, M.S., & Doi, L.M. (1999). See Dick RAN: Rapid naming and the longitudinal prediction of reading subskills in first and second graders. *Scientific Studies of Reading, 3,* 129–157.

Manis, F.R., Seidenberg, M.S., Doi, L.M., McBride-Chang, C., & Petersen, A. (1996). On the bases of two subtypes of development [sic] dyslexia. *Cognition, 58,* 157–195.

Mann, V.A. (2003). Language processes: Keys to reading disability. In H.L. Swanson, K.R. Harris, & S. Graham (Eds.), *Handbook of learning disabilities* (pp. 213–228). New York, NY: Guilford Press.

Mannuzza, S., Klein, R.G., Bonagura, N., Malloy, P., Giampino, T.L., & Addalli, K.A. (1991). Hyperactive boys almost grown up: V. Replication of psychiatric status. *Archives of General Psychiatry, 48,* 77–83.

Manzo, A.V. (1969). The ReQuest procedure. *Journal of Reading, 13,* 123–126.

Manzo, A.V. (1985). Expansion modules for the ReQuest, CAT, GRP, and REAP reading/study procedures. *Journal of Reading, 28,* 498–502.

Marshall, J.C., & Newcombe, F. (1978). Patterns of paralexia: A psycholinguistic approach. *Journal of Psycholinguistic Research, 2,* 178–199.

Martella, R.C., Nelson, J.R., & Marchand-Martella, N.E. (2003). *Managing disruptive behavior in the schools: A schoolwide, classroom, and individualized social learning approach.* Boston, MA: Allyn & Bacon.

Martin, R. (2005). The future of learning disabilities as federal laws change again. *Learning Disability Quarterly, 28,* 144–146.

Marx, I., Höpcke, C., Berger, C., Wandschneider, R., & Herpertz, S.C. (2013). The impact of financial reward contingencies on cognitive function profiles in adult ADHD. *PLOS Collections, 8*(6). doi:10.1371/journal.pone.0067002

Masi, G., Mucci, M., & Millepiedi, S. (2001). Separation anxiety disorder in children and adolescents: Epidemiology, diagnosis, and management. *CNS Drugs, 15,* 93–104.

Mason, L.H., Harris, K.R., & Graham, S. (2013). Strategies for improving student outcomes in written expression. In M. Tankersley & B. Cook (Eds.), *Effective practices in special education* (pp. 86–97). Upper Saddle River, NJ: Pearson.

Masten, A.S. (2001). Ordinary magic: Resilience processes in development. *American Psychologist, 56,* 227–238.

Masterson, J.J., & Apel, K. (2010). The spelling sensitivity score: Noting developmental changes in spelling knowledge. *Assessment for Effective Intervention, 36,* 35–45. doi:10.1177/1534508410380039

Mastropieri, M.A. (1988). Using the keyword method. *Teaching Exceptional Children, 20*(2), 4–8.

Mastropieri, M.A., Leinart, A., & Scruggs, T.E. (1999). Strategies to increase reading fluency. *Intervention in School and Clinic, 34,* 278–283.

Mather, N. (1991). *An instructional guide to the Woodcock-Johnson Psycho-Educational Battery—Revised.* New York, NY: Wiley.

Mather, N., Bos, C., Podhajski, B., Babur, N., & Rhein, D. (2000). *Screening of early reading processes.* Unpublished manuscript, Department of Disability and Psychoeducational Studies, University of Arizona–Tucson.

Mather, N., & Goldstein, S. (2001). *Learning disabilities and challenging behaviors: A guide to intervention*

References

and classroom management. Baltimore, MD: Paul H. Brookes Publishing Co.

Mather, N., & Gregg, N. (2006). Specific learning disabilities: Clarifying, not eliminating, a construct. *Professional Psychology, 37,* 99–106.

Mather, N., & Healey, W.C. (1990). Deposing aptitude–achievement discrepancy as the imperial criterion for learning disabilities. *Learning Disabilities: A Multidisciplinary Journal, 1,* 40–48.

Mather, N., & Jaffe, L. (in press). *Woodcock-Johnson IV: Reports, Recommendations, and Strategies*. New York, NY: John Wiley & Sons.

Mather, N., & Kaufman, N. (2006). It's about the *what,* the *how well,* and the *why*. *Psychology in the Schools, 43,* 747–752.

Mather, N., Sammons, J., Podhajski, B., Kroese, J., & Varricchio, M. (2000). *Phonological Awareness Skills Screener*. Unpublished manuscript, Department of Disability and Psychoeducational Studies, University of Arizona–Tucson.

Mather, N., Shaywitz, B.A., & Shaywitz, S. (2013). Toward a synthesis of cognitive-psychological, medical/neurobiological, and educational models for the diagnosis and management of dyslexia. In D. Saklofske, C.R. Reynolds, & V.L. Schwean (Eds.). *The Oxford handbook of child psychological assessment* (pp. 698–721). New York, NY: Oxford University Press.

Mather, N., Wendling, B.J., & Roberts, R. (2009). *Writing assessment and instruction for students with learning disabilities*. New York, NY: Jossey-Bass.

Mathers, M.E. (2006). Aspects of language in children with ADHD: Applying functional analyses to explore language use. *Journal of Attention Disorders, 9,* 523–533.

Mathes, P.G., & Fuchs, L.S. (1993). Peer mediated reading instruction in special education resource rooms. *Learning Disabilities Research & Practice, 8,* 233–243.

Mattis, S., French, J.H., & Rapin, I. (1975). Dyslexia in children and young adults: Three independent neuropsychological syndromes. *Developmental Medicine and Child Neurology, 17,* 150–163.

Maughan, B., Messer, J., Collishaw, S., Pickles, A., Snowling, M., Yule, W., & Rutter, M. (2009). Persistence of literacy problems: Spelling in adolescence and at mid-life. *Journal of Child Psychology and Psychiatry, 50,* 893–901.

McArthur, G.M., Hogben, J.H., Edwards, V.T., Heath, S.M., & Mengler, E.D. (2000). On the "specifics" of specific reading disability and specific language impairment. *Journal of Child Psychology and Psychiatry, 41,* 869–874.

McCardle, P., Scarborough, H.S., & Catts, H.W. (2001). Predicting, explaining, and preventing children's reading difficulties. *Learning Disabilities Research & Practice, 16,* 230–239.

McCarney, S.B., & Cummins, K.K. (1988). *The pre-referral intervention manual: The most common learning and behavior problems encountered in the educational environment*. Columbia, MO: Hawthorne Educational Services.

McConville, D.W., & Cornell, D.G. (2003). Aggressive attitudes predict aggressive behavior in middle school students. *Journal of Emotional and Behavioral Disorders, 11,* 179–187.

McCoy, K.M., & Prehm, H.J. (1987). *Teaching mainstreamed students: Methods and techniques*. Denver, CO: Love.

McDuffie, K.A., Mastropieri, M.A., & Scruggs, T.E. (2009). Differential effects of peer tutoring in co-taught and non-co-taught classes: Results for content learning and student-teacher interactions. *Exceptional Children, 75,* 493–510. doi:10.1177/001440290907500406

McGee, R., & Share, D.L. (1988). Attention deficit hyperactivity disorder and academic failure: Which comes first and what should be treated? *Journal of the American Academy of Child and Adolescent Psychiatry, 27,* 251–259.

McGrew, K.S. (2005). The Cattell-Horn-Carroll (CHC) theory of cognitive abilities: Past, present and future. In D. Flanagan & P. Harrison (Eds.), *Contemporary intellectual assessment: Theories, tests, and issues* (2nd ed., pp. 136–202). New York, NY: Guilford Press.

McGrew, K.S., & Knopik, S.N. (1993). The relationship between the WJ-R *Gf-Gc* cognitive clusters and writing achievement across the life span. *School Psychology Review, 22,* 687–695.

McGrew, K.S., LaForte, E.M., & Schrank, F.A. (2014). Technical Manual. *Woodcock-Johnson IV*. Rolling Meadows, IL: Riverside.

McGrew, K.S., & Wendling, B.J. (2010). Cattell-Horn-Carroll cognitive-achievement relations: What we have learned from the past 20 years of research. *Psychology in the Schools, 47,* 651–675. doi:10.1002/pits.20497

McGuinness, C., & McGuinness, G. (1998). *Reading reflex: The foolproof phono-graphix method for teaching your child to read*. New York, NY: The Free Press.

McKenzie, R.G. (2009). Obscuring vital distinctions: The oversimplification of learning disabilities within RTI. *Learning Disability Quarterly, 32,* 203–215.

McKeown, M.G., & Beck, I.L. (2011). Making vocabulary interventions engaging and effective. In R.E. O'Connor & P.F. Vadasy (Eds.), *Handbook of reading interventions* (pp. 138–168). New York, NY: Guilford Press.

McLoyd, V.C. (1998). Socioeconomic disadvantage and child development. *American Psychologist, 53*(2), 185–204.

McNamara, J.J. (1972). Hyperactivity in the apartment bound child. *Clinical Pediatrics, 11,* 371–372.

Meese, R.L. (1994). *Teaching learners with mild disabilities: Integrating research and practice*. Pacific Grove, CA: Brooks/Cole.

Mehrabian, A., & Ferris, S.R. (1967). Inference of attitudes from nonverbal communication in two channels. *Journal of Consulting Psychology, 31,* 248.

Mehta, P., Foorman, B.R., Branum-Martin, L., & Taylor, P.W. (2005). Literacy as a unidimensional construct: Validation, sources of influence, and implications in a longitudinal study in Grades 1 to 4. *Scientific Studies of Reading, 9,* 85–116. doi:10.1207/s1532799xssr0902_1

Meichenbaum, D. (1977). *Cognitive-behavior modification: An integrative approach.* New York, NY: Kluwer Academic/Plenum.

Meichenbaum, D. (1983). *Teaching thinking: A cognitive-behavioral approach.* Austin, TX: PRO-ED.

Meltzer, L.J. (1994). Assessment of learning disabilities: The challenge of evaluating the cognitive strategies and processes underlying learning. In G.R. Lyon (Ed.), *Frames of reference for the assessment of learning disabilities: New views on measurement issues* (pp. 571–606). Baltimore, MD: Paul H. Brookes Publishing Co.

Meltzer, L.J., Roditi, B., & Stein, J. (1998). Strategy instruction: The heartbeat of successful inclusion. *Perspectives (The International Dyslexia Foundation), 24*(3), 10–13.

Mengler, E.D., Hogben, J.H., Michie, P., & Bishop, D. (2005). Poor frequency discrimination is related to oral language disorder in children: A psychoacoustic study. *Dyslexia, 11,* 155–173.

Mercer, C.D. (1992). *Students with learning disabilities* (4th ed.). New York, NY: Macmillan.

Mercer, C.D. (1995, March). *Perspectives on the future of learning disabilities: The main thing is to keep the main thing the main thing.* Paper presented at the Learning Disabilities Association of America International Conference, Orlando, FL.

Mercer, C.D., & Campbell, K.U. (1998). *Great leaps reading program.* Gainesville, FL: Diarmuid.

Mercer, C.D., Campbell, K.U., Miller, M.D., Mercer, K.D., & Lane, H.B. (2000). Effects of a reading fluency intervention for middle schoolers with specific learning disabilities. *Learning Disabilities Research & Practice, 15,* 179–189.

Mercugliano, M., Power, T.J., & Blum, N.J. (1999). *The clinician's practical guide to attention-deficit/hyperactivity disorder.* Baltimore, MD: Paul H. Brookes Publishing Co.

Merikangas, K.R., He, J., Burstein, M., Swanson, S.A., Avenevoli, S., Cui, L., ... Swendsen, J. (2010). Lifetime prevalence of mental disorders in U.S. adolescents: Results from the national comorbidity survey replication-adolescent supplement (NCS-A). *Journal of the American Academy of Child and Adolescent Psychiatry, 49,* 980–989. doi:10.1016/j.jaac.2010.05.017

Merrell, K.W. (2002). Social-emotional intervention in schools: Current status, progress, and promise. *School Psychology Review, 31,* 143–147.

Mesmer, H.A.E., & Griffith, P.L. (2005). Everybody's selling it—but just what is explicit, systematic phonics instruction? *Reading Teacher, 59,* 366–376.

Meyer, M.S., & Felton, R.H. (1999). Repeated reading to enhance fluency: Old approaches and new directions. *Annals of Dyslexia, 49,* 283–306.

Meyer, M.S., Wood, F.B., Hart, L.A., & Felton, R.H. (1998). Selective predictive value of rapid automatized naming in poor readers. *Journal of Learning Disabilities, 31,* 106–117.

Miciak, J., Fletcher, J.M., Steubing, K.K., Vaughn, S., & Tolar, T.D. (2014). Patterns of cognitive strengths and weaknesses: Identification rates, agreement, and validity for learning disabilities identification. *School Psychology Quarterly, 29,* 21–37.

Milich, R., Ballentine, A.C., & Lynam, D.R. (2001). ADHD/combined type and ADHD predominantly inattentive type are distinct and unrelated disorders. *Clinical Psychology: Science and Practice, 8,* 463–488.

Miller, C.J., Miller, S.R., Bloom, J.S., Jones, J., Lindstrom, W., Craggs, J., ... Hynd, G.W. (2006). Testing the double-deficit hypothesis in an adult sample. *Annals of Dyslexia, 56,* 83–102.

Miller, D.J., & Daniel, B. (2007). Competent to cope, worthy of happiness? How the duality of self-esteem can inform a resilience-based classroom environment. *School Psychology International, 28,* 605–622.

Miller, K. (2004). When Asperger's syndrome and a nonverbal learning disability look alike. *Pediatrics, 114,* 1458–1463.

Miller, S.P. (1996). Perspectives on mathematics instruction. In D.D. Deshler, E.S. Ellis, & B.K. Lenz (Eds.), *Teaching adolescents with learning disabilities* (2nd ed., pp. 313–367). Denver, CO: Love.

Miller, S.P., & Hudson, P.J. (2007). Using evidence-based practices to build mathematics competence related to conceptual, procedural, and declarative knowledge. *Learning Disabilities Research & Practice, 22,* 47–57.

Miller, S.P., & Mercer, C.D. (1997). Educational aspects of mathematics disabilities. *Journal of Learning Disabilities, 30,* 47–56.

Miltenberger, R.G. (2012). *Behavior modification: Principles and procedures.* Belmont, CA: Wadsworth.

Minskoff, E. (2005). *Teaching reading to struggling learners.* Baltimore, MD: Paul H. Brookes Publishing Co.

Moats, L.C. (1991). Spelling disability in adolescents and adults. In A.M. Bain, L.L. Bailet, & L.C. Moats (Eds.), *Written language disorders: Theory into practice* (pp. 23–42). Austin, TX: PRO-ED.

Moats, L.C. (1995). *Spelling: Development, disability, and instruction.* Timonium, MD: York Press.

Moats, L.C. (2010). *Speech to print: Language essentials for teachers* (2nd ed.). Baltimore, MD: Paul H. Brookes Publishing Co.

Moats, L., & Tolman, C. (2009). The development of phonological skills. Excerpted from *Language Essentials for Teachers of Reading and Spelling (LETRS): The Speech Sounds of English: Phonetics, Phonology, and Phoneme Awareness (Module 2).* Boston, MA: Sopris West. Retrieved from http://www.readingrockets.org/article/28759

Monroe, M. (1932). *Children who cannot read.* Chicago, IL: University of Chicago Press.

Monroe, M., & Backus, B. (1937). *Remedial reading: A monograph in character education.* Boston, MA: Houghton Mifflin.

References

Montague, M. (1997). Cognitive strategy instruction in mathematics for students with learning disabilities. *Journal of Learning Disabilities, 30,* 164–177.

Montague, M. (2003). *Solve it! A mathematical problem solving instructional program.* Reston, VA: Exceptional Innovations.

Montague, M. (2007). Self-regulation and mathematics instruction. *Learning Disabilities Research & Practice, 22,* 75–83.

Montague, M., Enders, C., & Dietz, S. (2011). Effects of cognitive strategy instruction on math problem solving of middle school students with learning disabilities. *Learning Disability Quarterly, 34,* 262–272.

Montague, M., & Graves, A. (1993). Improving students' story writing. *Teaching Exceptional Children, 25*(4), 36–37.

Montague, M., & van Garderen, D. (2008). Effective mathematics instruction. In R. Morris & N. Mather (Eds.), *Evidence-based interventions for students with learning and behavioral challenges* (pp. 236–257). New York, NY: Routledge.

Moran, M.R. (1988). Reading and writing disorders in the learning disabled student. In N.J. Lass, L.V. McReynolds, J.L. Northern, & D.E. Yoder (Eds.), *Handbook of speech–language pathology and audiology* (pp. 835–857). Philadelphia, PA: Brian C. Decker.

Mordre, M., Groholt, B., Kjelsberg, E., Sandstad, B., & Myhre, A. (2011). The impact of ADHD and conduct disorder in childhood on adult delinquency: A 30 years follow-up study using official crime records. *Biomedcentral Psychiatry, 11,* 1–10. doi:10/1186/1471-24X-11-57.

Morgan, W.P. (1896, November 7). Word blindness. *British Medical Journal, 1378,* 98.

Morris, R., Blashfield, R.K., & Satz, P. (1986). Developmental classification of reading disabled children. *Journal of Clinical and Experimental Neuropsychology, 8,* 371–392.

Morris, R.D., Stuebing, K.K., Fletcher, J.M., Shaywitz, S., Lyon, G.R., Shankweiler, D.P., . . . Shaywitz, B.A. (1998). Subtypes of reading disability: Variability around a phonological core. *Journal of Educational Psychology, 90,* 347–373.

Morsette, A., Swaney, G., Stolle, D., Schuldberg, D., van den Pol, R., & Young, M. (2009). Cognitive behavioral intervention for trauma in schools (CBITS): School-based treatment on a rural American Indian reservation. *Journal of Behavioral Therapy & Experimental Psychiatry, 40*(1), 169–178. doi:10.1016/j.jbtep.2008.07.006

Mottram, L.M., Bray, M.A., Kehle, T.J., Broudy, M., & Jenson, W.R. (2002). A classroom-based intervention to reduce disruptive behaviors. *Journal of Applied School Psychology, 19*(1), 65–74.

Mouridsen, S.E., Rich, B., & Isager, T. (2014). The sex ratio of full and half siblings of people diagnosed with ADHD in childhood and adolescence: A Danish nationwide register-based cohort study. *Journal of Attention Disorders.* Advance online publication. PMID: 24752665

Muenke, M. (2006). *The genetics of ADHD.* Presentation at the 19th annual meeting of Children and Adults with Attention Deficit Hyperactivity Disorder (CHADD), Chicago, IL.

Myklebust, H.R. (1965). *Development and disorders of written language* (Vol. 1). New York, NY: Grune & Stratton.

Naglieri, J.A., & Das, J.P. (1997). Intelligence revised. In R. Dillon (Ed.), *Handbook on testing* (pp. 136–163). Westport, CT: Greenwood.

Naglieri, J.A., & Das, J.P. (2007). Planning, attention, simultaneous, successive (PASS) theory: A revision of the concept of intelligence. In D.P. Flanagan P.L. Harrison (Eds.), *Contemporary intelligence assessment* (2nd ed., pp. 136–182). New York, NY: Guilford Press.

Naglieri, J., Das, J.P., & Goldstein, S. (2014a). *Cognitive Assessment System 2.* Austin, TX: PRO-ED.

Naglieri, J.A., Das, J.P., & Goldstein, S. (2014b). *Cognitive Assessment System 2 Rating Scale.* Austin, TX: PRO-ED.

Naglieri, J., & Goldstein, S. (2012). *Comprehensive Executive Functioning Inventory Technical Manual.* Toronto, Canada: Multi-Health Systems.

Naglieri, J., Goldstein, S., Iseman, J.S., & Schwebach, A. (2003). Performance of children with attention deficit hyperactivity disorder and anxiety/depression on the WISC-III and Cognitive Assessment System (CAS). *Journal of Educational Assessment, 21,* 32–42.

Naglieri, J.A., & Gottling, S.H. (1995). Mathematics instruction and learning disabilities. *Psychological Reports, 76,* 1343–1354.

Naglieri, J.A., & Gottling, S.H. (1997). Mathematics instruction in PASS cognitive processes: An intervention study. *Journal of Learning Disabilities, 30,* 513–520.

Naglieri, J.A., & Pickering, E.B. (2010). *Helping children learn: Intervention handouts for use in school and at home* (2nd ed.). Baltimore, MD: Paul H. Brookes Publishing Co.

Naglieri, J.A., Salter, C.J., & Edwards, G.H. (2004). Assessment of ADHD and reading disabilities using the PASS Theory and Cognitive Assessment System. *Journal of Psychoeducational Assessment, 22,* 93–105.

Nation, K., Cocksey, J., Taylor, J.S.H., & Bishop, D.V.M. (2010). A longitudinal investigation of early reading and language skills in children with poor reading comprehension. *Journal of Child Psychology and Psychiatry, 51,* 1031–1039. doi:10.1111/j.1469-7610.2010.02254.x

National Advisory Committee on Handicapped Children. (1968, January 31). *Special education for handicapped children: First annual report.* Washington, DC: U.S. Department of Health, Education, and Welfare.

National Assessment of Educational Progress. (2013). *2013 mathematics and reading: Which student groups are making gains.* Retrieved from http://nationsreportcard.gov/reading_math_2013/#/gains-by-group

National Center for Education Statistics (NCES). (2010). Table 5. Percentage of public schools reporting that corporal punishment was allowed as a disciplinary action, and used during the school year: School year 2009–2010. *Crime and Safety Surveys.* Retrieved from http://nces.ed.gov/surveys/ssocs/tables/all_2010_tab_05.asp?referrer=css

National Center for Education Statistics (NCES). (2012). *Children living in poverty.* Retrieved from https://nces.ed.gov/programs/coe/pdf/coe_cce.pdf

National Center for Education Statistics (NCES). (2013). *English language learners.* Retrieved from http://nces.ed.gov/programs/coe/indicator_cgf.asp

National Council of Teachers of Mathematics (NCTM). (2014). *Supporting the common core state standards for mathematics.* Retrieved from http://www.nctm.org/uploadedFiles/About_NCTM/Position_Statements/Common%20Core%20State%20Standards.pdf

National Joint Committee on Learning Disabilities (NJCLD). (2005). Responsiveness to intervention and learning disabilities. *Learning Disability Quarterly, 28,* 249–260.

National Joint Committee on Learning Disabilities (NJCLD). (2010). *Comprehensive assessment and evaluation of students with learning disabilities* (pp. 1–15). Retrieved from http://www.ldonline.org/?module=uploads&func=download&fileId=802

National Joint Committee on Learning Disabilities (NJCLD). (2011). Learning disabilities: Implications for policy regarding research and practice: A report by the National Joint Committee on Learning Disabilities March 2011. *Learning Disability Quarterly, 34,* 237–241.

National Reading Panel. (2000). *Report of the National Reading Panel. Teaching children to read: An evidence-based assessment of the scientific research literature on reading and its implications for reading instructions* (NIH Publication No. 00-4769). Washington, DC: U.S. Government Printing Office.

National Research Council, Committee on Education Intervention for Children with Autism, Division of Behavioral and Social Sciences Education. (2001). *Educating children with autism.* Washington, DC: National Academies Press.

Nelson, J., Martella, R.M., & Marchand-Martella, N. (2002). Maximizing student learning: The effects of a comprehensive school-based program for preventing problem behaviors. *Journal of Emotional and Behavioral Disorders, 10,* 136–148. doi:10.1177/10634266020100030201

Nelson, N.W., & Van Meter, A.M. (2006). The writing lab approach for building language, literacy, and communication abilities. In R.J. McCauley & M.E. Fey (Eds.), *Treatment of language disorders in children* (pp. 383–422). Baltimore, MD: Paul H. Brookes Publishing Co.

Newby, R.F., Recht, D.R., & Caldwell, J.A. (1993). Validation of a clinical method for the diagnosis of two subtypes of dyslexia. *Journal of Psychoeducational Assessment, 11,* 72–83.

NICHD Early Child Care Research Network. (2005). Pathways to reading: The role of oral language in the transition to reading. *Developmental Psychology, 41,* 428–442.

Nicholls, J.G., McKenzie, M., & Shufro, J. (1994). Schoolwork, homework, life's work: The experience of students with and without learning disabilities. *Journal of Learning Disabilities, 27,* 562–569.

No Child Left Behind Act of 2001, PL 107-110, 115 Stat. 1425, 20 U.S.C. §§ 6301 *et seq.*

Noblit, G.W., Rogers, D.L., & McCadden, B.M. (1995). In the meantime: The possibilities of caring. *Phi Delta Kappan, 76,* 680–685.

Nock, M.K., & Kurtz, S.M.S. (2005). Direct behavioral observation in school settings: Bringing science to practice. *Cognitive and Behavioral Practice, 12,* 359–370. doi:10.1016/S1077-7229(05)80058-6.

Nolan, J.D., & Filter, K.J. (2012). A function-based classroom behavior intervention using non-contingent reinforcement plus response cost. *Education and Treatment of Children, 35,* 419–430. doi:10.1353/etc.2012.0017

Norton, E.S., & Wolf, M. (2012). Rapid automatized naming (RAN) and reading fluency: Implications for understanding and treatment of reading disabilities. *Annual Review of Psychology, 63,* 427–452. doi:10.1146/annurev-psych-120710-100431

Novick, B.Z., & Arnold, M.M. (1988). *Fundamentals of clinical child neuropsychology.* New York, NY: Grune & Stratton.

O'Connor, R.E., & Jenkins, J.R. (1999). Prediction of reading disabilities in kindergarten and first grade. *Scientific Studies of Reading, 3,* 159–197.

Ogle, D.M. (1986). K-W-L: A teaching model that develops active reading of expository text. *Reading Teacher, 39,* 564–570.

O'Leary, K.D., & O'Leary, S.G. (1977). *Classroom management: The successful use of behavior modification* (2nd ed.). Elmsford, NY: Pergamon Press.

O'Malley, M., & Eklund, K. (2012). Creating safe and supportive learning and working environments. In S.E. Brock & S.R. Jimerson (Eds.), *Best practices in school crisis prevention and intervention* (pp. 151–176). Bethesda, MD: National Association of School Psychologists.

O'Neil, K.A., Conner, B.T., & Kendall, P.C. (2011). Internalizing and substance use disorders in youth: Comorbidity, risk, temporal order, and implications for intervention. *Clinical Psychology Review, 31*(1), 104–112. doi:10.1016/j.cpr.2010.08.002

O'Neil, K.A., Podell, J.L., Benjamin, C.L., & Kendall, P.C. (2010). Comorbid depressive disorders in anxiety-disordered youth: Demographic, clinical, and family characteristics. *Child Psychiatry & Human Development, 41,* 330–341. doi:10.1007/s10578-009-0170-9

References

Orton, J. (1966). The Orton-Gillingham approach. In J. Money (Ed.), *The disabled reader: Education of the dyslexic child* (pp. 119–145). Baltimore, MD: Johns Hopkins University Press.

Orton, S.T. (1925). Word-blindness in school children. *Archives of Neurology and Psychiatry, 14,* 581–615.

Orton, S.T. (1937). *Reading, writing, and speech problems in children.* New York, NY: W.W. Norton.

Osgood, C.E. (1957). Motivational dynamics of language behavior. In M.R. Jones (Ed.), *Nebraska symposium on motivation* (pp. 348–424). Lincoln: University of Nebraska Press.

Otaiba, S.A., & Hosp, J.L. (2010). Spell it out: The need for detailed spelling assessment to inform instruction. *Assessment for Effective Intervention, 36,* 3–6. doi:10.1177/1534508410384478

Ouellette, G., & Sénéchal, M. (2008). Pathways to literacy: A study of invented spelling and its role in learning to read. *Child Development, 79,* 899–913. doi:10.1111/j.1467-8624.2008.01166.x

Owens, J.S., & Murphy, C.E. (2004). Effectiveness research in the context of school-based mental health. *Clinical Child and Family Psychology Review, 7,* 195–209.

Pagani, L., Boulerice, B., Vitaro, F., & Tremblay, R.E. (2003). Effects of poverty on academic failure and delinquency in boys: A change and process model approach. *Journal of Child Psychology and Psychiatry, 40,* 1209–1219.

Paine, S.C., Radicchi, J., Rosellini, L.C., Deutchman, L., & Darch, C.B. (1983). *Structuring your classroom for academic success.* Champaign, IL: Research Press.

Palinscar, A.S., & Brown, A.L. (1986). Interactive teaching to promote independent learning from text. *Reading Teacher, 39,* 771–777.

Palmer, J., Boon, R.T., & Spencer, V.G. (2014). Effects of concept mapping instruction on the vocabulary acquisition skills of seventh-graders with mild disabilities: A replication study. *Reading & Writing Quarterly: Overcoming Learning Difficulties, 30,* 165–182. doi:10.1080/10573569.2013.818890

Pancheri, C., & Prater, M.A. (1999, March/April). What teachers and parents should know about Ritalin. *Teaching Exceptional Children,* 20–26.

Paolito, A.W. (1999). Clinical validation of the Cognitive Assessment System for children with ADHD. *The ADHD Report, 1,* 1–5.

Patrick, H., Ryan, A.M., & Kaplan, A. (2007). Early adolescents' perceptions of the classroom social environment, motivational beliefs, and engagement. *Journal of Educational Psychology, 99,* 83–98.

Pelham, W.E. (1986). The effects of psychostimulant drugs on learning and academic achievement in children with attention deficit disorders and learning disabilities. In J.K. Torgesen & B.Y.L. Wong (Eds.), *Psychological and educational perspectives on learning disabilities* (pp. 333–364). San Diego, CA: Academic Press.

Pelham, W.E., & Bender, M.E. (1982). Peer relationships in hyperactive children. In K.D. Gadow & I. Bialer (Eds.), *Advances in learning and behavioral disabilities* (Vol. 1, pp. 365–436). Greenwich, CT: JAI Press.

Pelham, W.E., & Milich, R. (1984). Peer relations of children with hyperactivity/attention deficit disorder. *Journal of Learning Disabilities, 17,* 560–568.

Pennington, B.F. (1991). *Diagnosing learning disorders: A neuropsychological framework.* New York, NY: Guilford Press.

Pennington, B.F. (2009). *Diagnosing learning disorders: A neuropsychological framework* (2nd ed.). New York, NY: Guilford Press.

Pennington, B.F., Peterson, R.L., & McGrath, L.M. (2009). Dyslexia. In B.F. Pennington, *Diagnosing learning disorders* (2nd ed., pp. 45–82). New York, NY: Guilford Press.

Perfetti, C.A. (1992). The representation problem in reading acquisition. In P.B. Gough, L.C. Ehri, & R. Treiman (Eds.), *Reading acquisition* (pp. 145–174). Mahwah, NJ: Erlbaum.

Perfetti, C.A., Marron, M.A., & Foltz, P.W. (1996). Sources of comprehension failure: Theoretical perspectives and case studies. In C. Cornoldi & J. Oakhill (Eds.), *Reading comprehension difficulties: Processes and intervention* (pp. 137–165). Mahwah, NJ: Erlbaum.

Peterson, R.L., & Pennington, B.F. (2012). Developmental dyslexia. *The Lancet, 379*(9830), 1997–2007.

Pfiffner, L.J., & O'Leary, S.G. (1993). School based psychological treatments. In J.L. Matson (Ed.), *Handbook of hyperactivity in children* (pp. 234–255). Boston, MA: Allyn & Bacon.

Phillips, G.W. (1983). Learning the conservation concept: A meta-analysis. *Dissertation Abstracts International, 44,* 1990B. (University Microfilms No. 83-22983).

Phillips, P. (1990). A self-advocacy plan for high school students with learning disabilities: A comparative case analysis of students', teachers', and parents' perceptions of program effects. *Journal of Learning Disabilities, 28,* 466–471.

Pierrehumbert, B., Bader, M., Thévoz, S., Kinal, A., & Halfon, O. (2006). Hyperactivity and attention problems in a Swiss sample of school-aged children: Effects of school achievement. *Journal of Attention Disorders, 10*(1), 65–76.

Pinnell, G.S., & Fountas, I.C. (1998). *Word matters: Teaching phonics and spelling in the reading/writing classroom.* Westport, CT: William Heinemann.

Platzman, K.A., Stoy, M.R., Brown, R.T., Coles, C.D., Smith, I.E., & Falek, A. (1992). Review of observational methods in attention deficit hyperactivity disorder (ADHD): Implications for diagnosis. *School Psychology Quarterly, 7,* 155–177.

Pliszka, S.R. (1992). Comorbidity of attention deficit hyperactivity disorder and overanxious disorder. *Journal of the American Academy of Child and Adolescent Psychiatry, 31,* 197–203.

Pliszka, S.R. (2005). The neuropsychopharmacology of attention-deficit/hyperactivity disorder. *Biological Psychiatry, 57,* 1385–1390.

Polloway, E.A., Epstein, M.H., Bursuck, W.D., Madhavi, J., & Cumblad, C. (1994). Homework practices of general education teachers. *Journal of Learning Disabilities, 27,* 500–509.

Polloway, E.A., & Patton, J.R. (1993). *Strategies for teaching learners with special needs* (5th ed.). New York, NY: Merrill.

Posthuma, D., & Polderman, T.J. (2013). What have we learned from recent twin studies about the etiology of neurodevelopmental disorders? *Current Opinion in Neurology, 26,* 111–121.

Powell, D., Stainthorp, R., Stuart, M., Garwood, H., & Quinlan, P. (2007). An experimental comparison between rival theories of rapid automatized naming performance and its relationship to reading. *Journal of Experimental Child Psychology, 98*(1), 46–68.

Pribram, K., & Luria, A.R. (Eds.). (1973). *Psychophysiology of the frontal lobes.* New York, NY: Academic Press.

Price, G.R., & Ansari, D. (2013). Dyscalculia: Characteristics, causes and treatments. *Numeracy, 6*(1), Article 2. Retrieved from http://scholarcommons.usf.edu/numeracy/vol6/iss1/art2

Price, L.A., Wolensky, D., & Mulligan, R. (2002). Self-determination in action in the classroom. *Remedial and Special Education, 23*(2), 109–115.

Puranik, C., & Lonigan, C. (2011). Early writing deficits in preschoolers with oral language difficulties. *Journal of Learning Disabilities, 45,* 179–190. doi:10.1177/0022219411423423

Qiu, M., Ye, Z., Li, Q., Lieu, G., Xie, B., & Wang, J. (2011). Changes of brain structure and function in ADHD children. *Brain Topography, 24,* 243–252.

Rack, J.P., Snowling, M.J., & Olson, R.K. (1992). The nonword reading deficit in developmental dyslexia: A review. *Reading Research Quarterly, 27*(1), 28–53.

Raggi, V.L., & Chronis, A.M. (2006). Interventions to address the academic impairment of children and adolescents with ADHD. *Clinical Child and Family Psychology Review, 9*(2), 85–111.

Raghubar, K.P., Barnes, M.A., & Hecht, S.A. (2010). Working memory and mathematics: A review of the developmental, individual, and cognitive approaches. *Learning and Individual Differences, 20,* 110–122. doi:10.1016/j.lindif.2009.10.005

Ramirez de Arellano, M.A., Lyman, D.R., Jobe-Shields, L., George, P., Dougherty, R.H., Daniels, A.S., . . . & Delphin-Rittmon, M.E. (2014). Trauma-focused cognitive-behavioral therapy for children and adolescents: Assessing the evidence. *Psychiatric Services, 65,* 591–602. doi:10.1176/appi.ps.201300255

Rapport, M.D. (1987). *The attention training system.* DeWitt, NY: Gordon Systems.

Rapport, M.D. (1989). The classroom functioning and treatment of children with ADHD: Facts and fictions. *CH.A.D.D.E.R., 3,* 4–5.

Rapport, M.D., Murphy, H.A., & Bailey, J.S. (1982). Ritalin vs. response cost in the control of hyperactive children: A within-subject comparison. *Journal of Applied Behavior Analysis, 15,* 205–216.

Rasinski, T.V. (2004). *Assessing reading fluency.* Honolulu, HI: Pacific Resources for Education and Learning.

Raver, C.C., Jones, S.M., Li-Grining, C., Zahi, F., Bub, K., & Pressler, E. (2011). CSRP'S impact on low income preschoolers' pre-academic skills: Self-regulation as a mediating mechanism. *Child Development, 82,* 362–378.

Read, C. (1971). Pre-school children's knowledge of English phonology. *Harvard Educational Review, 41*(1), 1–34.

Redd, W.H., Morris, E.K., & Martin, J.A. (1975). Effects of positive and negative adult–child interactions on children's social preferences. *Journal of Experimental Child Psychology, 19,* 153–164.

Rehabilitation Act Amendments of 1992, PL 102–569, 29 U.S.C. §§ 701 *et seq.*

Reid, D.K. (1988). *Teaching the learning disabled: A cognitive developmental approach.* Boston, MA: Allyn & Bacon.

Reid, R., Maag, J.W., & Vasa, S.F. (1994). Attention deficit hyperactivity disorder as a disability category: A critique. *Exceptional Children, 60,* 198–214.

Reiff, H.B., Gerber, P.J., & Ginsberg, R. (1993). Definitions of learning disabilities from adults with learning disabilities: The insiders' perspectives. *Learning Disability Quarterly, 16,* 114–125.

Reinke, W.M., Herman, K.C., Petras, H., & Ialongo, N.S. (2008). Empirically derived subtypes of child academic and behavior problems: Co-occurrence and distal outcomes. *Journal of Abnormal Child Psychology, 36,* 759–770.

Reitsma, P. (1989). Orthographic memory and learning to read. In P.G. Aaron & R.M. Joshi (Eds.), *Reading and writing disorders in different orthographic systems* (pp. 51–73). New York, NY: Kluwer Academic/Plenum.

Reynolds, C.R., & Horton, M. (2008). Assessing executive functions: A life span perspective. *Psychology in the Schools, 45,* 875–892.

Reynolds, C.R., & Kamphaus, R.W. (2004). *Behavior Assessment System for Children* (2nd ed.). San Antonio, TX: Psychological Corporation.

Reynolds, C.R., & Richmond, B.O. (1985). *Revised Children's Manifest Anxiety Scales (RCMAS).* Los Angeles: Western Psychological Services.

Rhode, G., Jenson, W.R., & Reavis, H.K. (1992). *The tough kid book: Practical classroom management strategies.* Longmont, CO: Sopris West.

Richardson, E., & DiBenedetto, B. (1996). Identifying dyslexic students. In L.R. Putnam (Ed.), *How to become a better reading teacher: Strategies for assessment and intervention* (pp. 53–63). Englewood Cliffs, NJ: Prentice Hall.

Richardson, E., Kupietz, S., & Maitinsky, S. (1986). What is the role of academic intervention in the treatment of hyperactive children with reading disorders? *Journal of Children in Contemporary Society, 19,* 153–167.

References

Richardson, S.O. (1992). Historical perspectives on dyslexia. *Journal of Learning Disabilities, 25,* 40–47.

Ricketts, J., Jones, C.R.G., Happe, F., & Charman, T. (2013). Reading comprehension in autism spectrum disorders: The role of oral language and social functioning. *Journal of Autism and Developmental Disorders, 43,* 807–816. doi:10.1007/s11145-013-9434-7

Riley-Heller, N., Kelly-Vance, L., & Shriver, M. (2005). Curriculum-based measurement. *Journal of Applied School Psychology, 21,* 141–162. doi:10.1300/J370v21n01_07

Rissman, M., Curtiss, S., & Tallal, P. (1990). School placement outcomes of young language-impaired children. *Journal of Speech-Language Pathology & Audiology, 14*(2), 49–58.

Ritchey, K.D., Coker, D.L., Jr., & McCraw, S.B. (2009). A comparison of metrics for scoring beginning spelling. *Assessment for Effective Intervention, 35,* 78–88. doi:10.1177/1534508409336087

Roberts, K.D., Takahashi, K., Park, H.J., & Stodden, R.A. (2012). Supporting struggling readers in secondary school science classes. *Teaching Exceptional Children, 44*(6), 40–48.

Roberts, R., & Mather, N. (2007). *Phonic reading lessons: Practice.* Novato, CA: Academic Therapy.

Robin, A.L. (1998). *ADHD in adolescents: Diagnosis and treatment.* New York, NY: Guilford Press.

Robinson, A. (1993). *What smart students know.* New York, NY: Crown.

Robinson, F.P. (1970). *Effective study* (5th ed.). New York, NY: HarperCollins.

Roffman, A.J. (2000). *Meeting the challenge of learning disabilities in adulthood.* Baltimore, MD: Paul H. Brookes Publishing Co.

Rose, T.L. (1984). The effects of two prepractice procedures on oral reading. *Journal of Learning Disabilities, 17,* 544–548.

Rose, T.L., & Sherry, L. (1984). Relative effects of two previewing procedures on LD adolescents' oral reading performance. *Learning Disability Quarterly, 7,* 39–44.

Rosenfeld, S. (2008). Best practice in instructional consultation and instructional consultation teams. In A. Thomas & J. Grimes (Eds.) *Best practices in school psychology* (pp. 1645–1660). Bethesda, MD: National Association of School Psychologists.

Rosenshine, B. (2012, Spring). Principles of instruction: Research-based strategies that all teachers should know. *American Educator,* 12–39.

Roth, F.P., & Speckman, N.J. (1994). Oral story production in adults with learning disabilities. In R.L. Bloom, L.K. DeSanti, & J.S. Ehrlich (Eds.), *Discourse analysis and applications: Studies in adult clinical populations* (pp. 131–148). Mahwah, NJ: Erlbaum.

Roth, R.M., Erdodi, L.A., McCulloch, L.J., & Isquith, P.K. (in press). Much ado about norming: The behavior rating inventory of executive functioning. *Child Neurology.* doi:10.1080/09297049.2014.897312

Rothenberg, S. (1998). Nonverbal learning disabilities and social functioning: How can we help? *Journal of the Learning Disabilities Association of Massachusetts, 8*(4), 10.

Rourke, B.P. (1989). *Nonverbal learning disabilities: The syndrome and the model.* New York, NY: Guilford Press.

Rourke, B.P. (1995). *Syndrome of nonverbal learning disabilities: Neurodevelopmental manifestations.* New York, NY: Guilford Press.

Rourke, B., Ahmad, S., Collins, D., Hayman-Abello, B., Hayman-Abello, S., & Warriner, E. (2002). Child clinical/pediatric neuropsychology: Some recent advances. *Annual Review of Psychology, 53,* 309–339.

Routh, D.K. (1978). Hyperactivity. In P.R. Magrab (Ed.), *Psychological management of pediatric problems* (Vol. 2, pp. 71–98). Baltimore, MD: University Park Press.

Rowe, R., Costello, E.J., Angold, A., Copeland, W.E., & Maughan, B. (2010). Developmental pathways in oppositional defiant disorder and conduct disorder. *Journal of Abnormal Psychology, 119,* 726–738. doi:10.1037/a0020798

Ruban, L.M. (2000). Patterns of self-regulated learning and academic achievement among university students with and without learning disabilities. *Dissertation Abstracts International, 61,* 1296.

Rubin, D.L. (1990). *Perspectives on talking and learning.* Urbana, IL: National Council of Teachers of English.

Rueda, R., & Windmueller, M.P. (2006). English language learners, LD, and overrepresentation: A multiple-level analysis. *Journal of Learning Disabilities, 39,* 99–107.

Rumsey, I., & Ballard, K.D. (1985). Teaching self-management strategies for independent story writing to children with classroom behavior difficulties. *Educational Psychology, 5,* 147–157.

Rutter, M. (1978). Prevalence and types of dyslexia. In A.L. Benton & D. Pearl (Eds.), *Dyslexia: An appraisal of current knowledge* (pp. 3–28). New York, NY: Oxford University Press.

Rutter, M. (1985). Resilience in the face of adversity: Protective factors and resistance to psychiatric disorder. *British Journal of Psychiatry, 147,* 598–611.

Rutter, M. (1987). Psychosocial resilience and protective mechanisms. *American Journal of Orthopsychiatry, 57,* 316–331.

Rutter, M. (2006). Implications of resilience concepts for scientific understanding. *Annals of the New York Academy of Sciences, 1094,* 1–12.

Ryder, J.F., Tunmer, W.E., & Greaney, K.T. (2008). Explicit instruction in phonemic awareness and phonemically based decoding skills as an intervention strategy for struggling readers in whole language classrooms. *Reading and Writing, 21,* 349–369.

Sabol, T.J., Hong, S.L., Pianta, R.C., & Burchinal, M.R. (2013). Can rating pre-K programs predict children's learning? *Science, 341,* 845–846.

Safer, D.J., Zito, J.M., & Fine, E.M. (1996). Increased methylphenidate usage for attention deficit disorder in the 1990s. *Pediatrics, 98,* 1084–1088.

Saigh, P.A. (2003). *Children's PTSD Inventory (CPTSDI)*. Upper Saddle River, NJ: Pearson.

Salvia, J., & Ysseldyke, J.E. (2010). *Assessment in special and inclusive education* (11th ed.). Boston, MA: Wadsworth/Cengage.

Sampson, M.B. (2002). Confirming a K-W-L: Considering the source. *Reading Teacher, 55,* 528–532.

Samuels, S.J. (1979). The method of repeated readings. *Reading Teacher, 32,* 403–408.

Samuels, S.J. (1988). Decoding and automaticity: Helping poor readers become automatic at word recognition. *Reading Teacher, 41,* 756–760.

Sanderson, A. (1999). Voice recognition software: A panacea for dyslexic learners or a frustrating hindrance? *Dyslexia, 5,* 113–122.

Satterfield, J.H., Hoppe, C.M., & Schell, A.M. (1982). A perspective study of delinquency in 110 adolescent boys with attention deficit disorder and 88 normal adolescent boys. *American Journal of Psychiatry, 139,* 795–798.

Satz, P., & Morris, R. (1981). Learning disability subtypes: A review. In F.J. Pirozzolo & M.C. Wittrock (Eds.), *Neuropsychological and cognitive processes in reading* (pp. 109–141). New York, NY: Academic Press.

Savage, R., & Frederickson, N. (2005). Evidence of a highly specific relationship between rapid automatic naming of digits and text-reading speed. *Brain and Language, 93,* 152–159.

Sawyer, D.J. (1987). *Test of Awareness of Language Segments*. Austin, TX: PRO-ED.

Scarborough, H.S. (1991). Antecedents to reading disability: Preschool language development and literacy experiences of children from dyslexic families. In B.F. Pennington (Ed.), *Reading disabilities: Genetic and neurological influences* (pp. 31–45). New York, NY: Kluwer Academic/Plenum.

Scarborough, H.S. (2009). Connecting early language and literacy to later reading (dis)abilities: Evidence, theory, and practice. In F. Fletcher-Campbell, J. Soler, & G. Reid (Eds.), *Approaching difficulties in literacy development: Assessment, pedagogy, and programmes* (pp. 23–38). London, England: Sage.

Schatschneider, C., Carlson, C.D., Francis, D.J., Foorman, B.R., & Fletcher, J.M. (2002). Relationship of rapid automatized naming and phonological awareness in early reading development: Implications for the double-deficit hypothesis. *Journal of Learning Disabilities, 35,* 245–256.

Schatz, D.B. (2006). ADHD with comorbid anxiety. *Journal of Attention Disorders, 10,* 141–149. doi:10.1177/1087054706286698

Scheeringa, M., & Zeanah, C. (2008). Reconsideration of harm's way: Onsets and comorbidity patterns in preschool children and their caregivers following Hurricane Katrina. *Journal of Clinical Child and Adolescent Psychology, 37,* 508–518. doi:10.1080/15374410802148178

Scheuermann, B., Jacobs, W.R., McCall, C., & Knies, W.C. (1994). The personal spelling dictionary: An adaptive approach to reducing the spelling hurdle in written language. *Intervention in School and Clinic, 29,* 292–299.

Schlegel, M., & Bos, C.S. (1986). *STORE the story: Fiction/fantasy reading comprehension and writing strategy.* Unpublished manuscript, Department of Disabilities and Psychoeducational Studies, University of Arizona–Tucson.

Schleifer, M., Weiss, G., Cohen, N.J., Elman, M., Cvejic, H., & Kruger, E. (1975). Hyperactivity in preschoolers and the effect of methylphenidate. *American Journal of Orthopsychiatry, 45,* 35–50.

Schneider, W., & Shiffrin, R.M. (1977). Controlled and automatic human information processing: Detection, search, and attention. *Psychological Review, 84,* 1–66.

Scholnick, E.K. (1995, Fall). Knowing and constructing plans. *SRCD Newsletter,* 1–3.

Schrank, F.A., McGrew, K.S., & Mather, N. (2014). *Woodcock-Johnson IV Tests of Cognitive Abilities.* Rolling Meadows, IL: Riverside.

Schuldheisz, J.M., & van der Mars, H. (2001). Active supervision and students' physical activity in middle school physical education. *Journal of Teaching in Physical Education, 21,* 75–90.

Schultz, K.S., Simpson, C., & Lynch, S. (2012). Specific learning disability identification: What constitutes a pattern of strengths and weaknesses? *Learning Disabilities: A Multidisciplinary Journal, 18,* 87–97.

Schumaker, J.B., Denton, P.H., & Deshler, D.D. (1984). *The paraphrasing strategy.* Lawrence: University of Kansas Press.

Schumaker, J.B., Deshler, D.D., Alley, G.R., Warner, M.M., & Denton, P.H. (1982). MULTIPASS: A learning strategy for improving reading comprehension. *Learning Disability Quarterly, 5,* 295–304.

Schwean, V.L., Parkinson, M., Francis, G., & Lee, F. (1993). Educating the ADHD child: Debunking the myths [Special issue]. *Canadian Journal of School Psychology, 9,* 37–52.

Scott, C.M. (2000). Principles and methods of spelling instruction: Applications for poor spellers. *Topics in Language Disorders, 20*(3), 66–82.

Scruggs, T.E., & Mastropieri, M.A. (2013). Teaching students with high-incidence disabilities. In B.G. Cook & M. Tankersley (Eds.), *Research-based practices in special education* (pp. 342–352). Boston, MA: Pearson.

Seabaugh, G.O., & Schumaker, J.B. (1981). *The effects of self-regulation training on academic productivity of LD and NLD adolescents* (Research Report No. 37). Lawrence: University of Kansas Press.

Segal, J. (1988). Teachers have enormous power in affecting a child's self-esteem. *Brown University Child Behavior and Development Newsletter, 4,* 1–3.

Seifert, K., & Espin, C. (2012). Improving reading of science text for secondary students with learning disabilities: Effects of text reading, vocabulary learning, and combined approaches to instruction. *Learning Disabilities Quarterly, 35,* 236–247. doi:10.1177/0731948712444275

Semrud-Clikeman, M. (1996). Neuropsychological evidence for subtypes in developmental dyslexia. In

References

L.R. Putnam (Ed.), *How to become a better reading teacher: Strategies for assessment and intervention* (pp. 43–52). Englewood Cliffs, NJ: Prentice Hall.

Semrud-Clikeman, M. (2005). Neuropsychological aspects for evaluating learning disabilities. *Journal of Learning Disabilities, 38,* 563–568.

Semrud-Clikeman, M., & Hynd, G.W. (1991). Specific nonverbal and social-skills deficits in children with LD. In J.E. Obrzut & G.W. Hynd (Eds.), *Neuropsychological foundations of learning disabilities: A handbook of issues, methods, and practice* (pp. 603–629). San Diego, CA: Academic Press.

Senokossoff, G.W., & Fine, J.C. (2013). Supporting teachers of inclusive classrooms: Using visible thinking (VT) and writing with adolescents to develop reading comprehension. *Journal of Reading Education, 38,* 39–45.

Severson, H.H., Walker, H.M., Hope-Doolittle, J., Kratochwill, T.R., & Gresham, F.M. (2007). Proactive, early screening to detect behaviorally at-risk students: Issues, approaches, emerging innovations, and professional practices. *Journal of School Psychology, 45,* 193–223.

Seymour, P.H., & Evans, H.M. (1999). Foundation-level dyslexia: Assessment and treatment. *Journal of Learning Disabilities, 32,* 394–405.

Shamir, A., Korat, O., & Fellah, R. (2012). Promoting vocabulary awareness and concept print among children at risk for learning disability: Can e-books help? *Reading & Writing, 25*(1), 45–69. doi:10.1007/s11145-010-9247-x

Shanahan, M.A., Pennington, B.F., Yerys, B.E., Scott, A., Boada, R., Willcutt, E.G., ... DeFries, J.C. (2006). Processing speed deficits in attention deficit/hyperactivity disorder. *Journal of Abnormal Child Psychology, 34,* 585–602. doi:10.1007/s10802-006-9037-8

Share, D.L., & Leikin, M. (2004). Language impairment at school entry and later reading disability: Connections at lexical versus supralexical levels of reading. *Scientific Studies of Reading, 8*(1), 87–110.

Shaw, D.S., Owens, E.B., Giovannelli, J., & Winslow, E.B. (2001). Infant and toddler pathways leading to early externalizing disorders. *Journal of the American Academy of Child and Adolescent Psychiatry, 40*(1), 36–43. doi:10.1097/00004583-200101000-00014

Shaywitz, S. (2003). *Overcoming dyslexia: A new and complete science-based program for reading problems at any level.* New York, NY: Alfred A. Knopf.

Shaywitz, S.E., & Shaywitz, B.A. (2003). Neurobiological indices of dyslexia. In H.L. Swanson, K.R. Harris, & S. Graham (Eds.), *Handbook of learning disabilities* (pp. 514–531). New York, NY: Guilford Press.

Shea, T.M., & Bauer, A.M. (1987). *Teaching children and youth with behavior disorders* (2nd ed.). Englewood Cliffs, NJ: Prentice Hall.

Shea, T.M., & Bauer, A.M. (2012). *Behavior management: A practical approach for educators* (10th ed.). Upper Saddle River, NJ: Pearson.

Sherman, L.W. (1993). Defiance, deterrence, and irrelevance: A theory of the criminal sanction. *Journal of Research in Crime and Delinquency, 30,* 445–473.

Short, D., & Fitzsimmons, S. (2007). *Double the work: Challenges and solutions to acquiring language and academic literacy for adolescent English language learners—a report to the Carnegie Corporation of New York.* Washington, DC: Alliance for Excellent Education.

Shure, M., & Aberson, A. (2005). Enhancing the process of resilience through effective thinking. In S. Goldstein & R. Brooks (Eds.), *Handbook of resilience* (pp. 373–396). New York, NY: Academic Press.

Siegal, D.J. (2012). *The developing mind* (2nd ed.). New York, NY: Guilford Press.

Siegel, L.S. (2007). Perspectives on dyslexia. *Paediatrics & Child Health, 11,* 581–588.

Silver, A.A., & Hagin, R.A. (1990). *Disorders of learning in childhood.* New York, NY: John Wiley & Sons.

Simmons, D.C., Fuchs, L.S., & Fuchs, D. (1995). Effects of explicit teaching and peer tutoring on reading achievement of learning-disabled and low-performing students in regular classrooms. *Elementary School Journal, 95,* 387–408.

Simon, N.M. (2009). Generalized anxiety disorder and psychiatric comorbidities such as depression, bipolar disorder, and substance abuse. *Journal of Clinical Psychiatry, 70,* 10–14. doi:10.4088/JCP.s.7002.02

Simonsen, B., Fairbanks, S., Briesch, A., Myers, D., & Sugai, G. (2008). Evidence-based practices in classroom management: Considerations for research to practice. *Education and Treatment of Children, 31,* 351–380.

Simpson, M.L., & Stahl, N.A. (1987). PORPE: A comprehensive study strategy using self assigned writing. *Journal of College Reading and Learning, 20,* 51–57.

Simpson, R.G., & Buckhalt, J.A. (1990). A non-formula discrepancy model to identify learning disabilities. *School Psychology International, 11,* 273–279.

Sitton, R.A., & Forest, R.G. (1994). *QuickWord.* North Billerica, MA: Curriculum Associates.

Skebo, C., Lewis, B., Freebairn, L., Tag, J., Ciesta, A., & Stein, C. (2013). Reading skills of students with speech sound disorders at three stages of literacy development. *Language, Speech, and Hearing Services in Schools, 44,* 360–373.

Skiba, R.J., McLeskey, J., Waldron, N.L., & Grizzle, K. (1993). The context of failure in the primary grades: Risk factors in low and high referral rate classrooms. *School Psychology Quarterly, 8,* 81–98.

Slingerland, B.H. (1981). *A multisensory approach to language arts for specific language disability children: A guide for primary teachers* (Book 3). Cambridge, MA: Educators Publishing Service.

Smitely, B.L. (2001). *Factors predicting academic adjustment among college students with learning disabilities* (Unpublished doctoral dissertation). University of Miami, FL.

Solari, E., Aceves, T., Higareda, I., Richards-Tutor, C., Filippini, A., Gerber, M., & Leafstedt, J. (2014). Longitudinal prediction of 1st and 2nd grade English oral reading fluency in English language learners: Which early reading and language skills are better predictors? *Psychology in the Schools, 51,* 126–142. doi:10.1002/pits.21743

Somech, L.Y., & Elizur, Y. (2012). Promoting self-regulation and cooperation in pre-kindergarten children with conduct problems: A randomized controlled trial. *Journal of the American Academy of Child and Adolescent Psychiatry, 51,* 412–422. doi:10.1016/j.jaac.2012.01.019

Spalding, R.B., & Spalding, W.T. (1990). *The writing road to reading* (4th ed.). New York, NY: William Morrow.

Spear-Swerling, L., & Sternberg, R.J. (1996). *Off track: When poor readers become "learning disabled."* Boulder, CO: Westview.

Speece, D.I. (2005). Hitting the moving target known as reading development: Some thoughts on screening first-grade children for secondary interventions. *Journal of Learning Disabilities, 38,* 437–493.

Spielberger, C.D. (1973). *Manual for the State-Trait Anxiety Inventory for Children.* Palo Alto, CA: Consulting Psychologists Press.

Spencer, M., Quinn, J.M., & Wagner, R.K. (2014). Specific reading comprehension disability: Major problem, myth, or misnomer? *Learning Disabilities Research & Practice, 29,* 3–9.

Spencer, S.A., & Manis, F.R. (2010). The effects of a fluency intervention program on the fluency and comprehension outcomes of middle-school students with severe reading deficits. *Learning Disabilities Research & Practice, 25,* 76–86.

Spinelli, C.G. (1997). Accommodating the adolescent with attention deficit disorder: The role of the resource center teacher. *Journal of Attention Disorders, 1,* 209–216.

Sprague, J., & Horner, R. (2007). School-wide positive behavioral support. In S.R. Jimerson & M.J. Furlong (Eds.), *Handbook of school violence and school safety: From research to practice* (pp. 412–428). Mahwah, NJ: Erlbaum.

Sprague, J., & Walker, H. (2000). Early identification and intervention for youth with antisocial and violent behavior. *Exceptional Children, 66,* 367–379.

Spreen, O. (2011). Nonverbal learning disabilities: A critical review. *Child Neuropsychology, 17,* 418–443.

Sprick, M., Howard, L., & Fidanque, A. (1998). *Read well.* Longmont, CO: Sopris West.

Spring, C., Yellin, A.M., & Greenberg, L.M. (1976). Effects of imipramine and methylphenidate on perceptual-motor performance of hyperactive children. *Perceptual and Motor Skills, 43,* 459–470.

Srebnicki, T., Kolakowski, A., & Wolańczyk, T. (2013). Adolescent outcome of childhood ADHD in primary care setting: Stability of diagnosis. *Journal of Attention Disorders, 17,* 655–659.

Stahl, S.A., & Stahl, K.A.D. (2004). Word wizards all! Teaching word meanings in preschool and primary education. In J.F. Baumann & E.J. Kame'enui (Eds.), *Vocabulary instruction: Research to practice* (pp. 59–78). New York, NY: Guilford Press.

Stanovich, K.E. (1982a). Individual differences in the cognitive processes of reading: I. Word decoding. *Journal of Learning Disabilities, 15,* 485–493.

Stanovich, K.E. (1982b). Individual differences in the cognitive processes of reading: II. Textlevel processes. *Journal of Learning Disabilities, 15,* 549–554.

Stanovich, K.E. (1991). Conceptual and empirical problems with discrepancy definitions of reading disability. *Learning Disability Quarterly, 14,* 269–280.

Stanovich, K.E. (1994). Are discrepancy-based definitions of dyslexia empirically defensible? In K.P. van den Bos, L.S. Siegel, D.J. Bakker, & D.L. Share (Eds.), *Current directions in dyslexia research* (pp. 15–30). Lisse, Netherlands: Swets & Zeitlinger.

Stanovich, K.E. (1999). The sociopsychometrics of learning disabilities. *Journal of Learning Disabilities, 32,* 350–361.

Stanovich, K.E. (2005). The future of a mistake: Will discrepancy measurement continue to make learning disabilities a pseudoscience? *Learning Disability Quarterly, 28,* 103–106.

Stanovich, K.E., Siegel, L.S., & Gottardo, A. (1997). Converging evidence for phonological and surface subtypes of reading disability. *Journal of Educational Psychology, 89,* 114–127.

Stark, K., Krumholz, L., Ridley, K., & Hamilton, A. (2009). Cognitive behavioral therapy for youth depression: The ACTION treatment program. In S. Nolen-Hoeksema & L.M. Hilt (Ed.), *Handbook of depression in adolescents* (pp. 475–509). New York, NY: Routledge/Taylor & Francis.

Stecher, B.M., Hamilton, L.S., & Gonzlaez, G. (2003). *Working smarter to leave no child behind: Practical insights for school leaders.* White paper prepared for the William and Flora Hewlett Foundation. Santa Monica, CA: RAND.

Stein, B.D., Jaycox, L.H., Kataoka, S.H., Wong, M., Tu, W., Elliott, M.N., & Fink, A. (2003). A mental health intervention for schoolchildren exposed to violence: A randomized controlled trial. *Journal of the American Medical Association, 290,* 603–611.

Stein, M. (1997). We have tried everything and nothing works: Family-centered pediatrics and clinical problem solving. *Journal of Developmental and Behavioral Pediatrics, 18,* 114–119.

Stein, N., & Glenn, C.G. (1979). An analysis of story comprehension in elementary school children. In R.O. Freedle (Ed.), *New directions in discourse processes* (Vol. 2, pp. 53–120). Norwood, NJ: Ablex.

Stern, C., & Stern, M. (1971). *Children discover arithmetic: An introduction to structural arithmetic.* New York, NY: HarperCollins.

Stern, M.B. (2005). Multisensory mathematics instruction. In J.R. Birsh (Ed.), *Multisensory teaching of basic language skills* (2nd ed., pp. 457–479). Baltimore, MD: Paul H. Brookes Publishing Co.

Stewart, S.R. (1992). Development of written language proficiency: Methods for teaching text structure.

References

In C.S. Simon (Ed.), *Communication skills and classroom success* (pp. 419–432). Eau Claire, WI: Thinking Publications.

Stokes, T.R., & Baer, D.M. (1977). An implicit technology of generalization. *Journal of Applied Behavior Analysis, 10,* 349–367.

Stoner, G., & Carey, S.P. (1992). Serving students diagnosed with ADD: Avoiding deficits in professional attention. *School Psychology Quarterly, 7,* 302–307.

Storch, S.A., & Whitehurst, G.J. (2002). Oral language and code-related precursors to reading: Evidence from a longitudinal structural model. *Developmental Psychology, 38,* 934–937.

Strang, J.D., & Rourke, B.P. (1985). Arithmetic disability subtypes: The neuropsychological significance of specific arithmetical impairment in childhood. In B.P. Rourke (Ed.), *Neuropsychology of learning disabilities: Essentials of subtype analysis* (pp. 167–183). New York, NY: Guilford Press.

Strauss, A.A., & Lehtinen, L.E. (1947). *The psychopathology and education of the brain-injured child* (Vol. 1). New York, NY: Grune & Stratton.

Strickland, G. (1998). *Bad teachers.* New York, NY: Pocket Books.

Stringaris, A., & Goodman, R. (2009). Three dimensions of oppositionality in youth. *Journal of Child Psychology and Psychiatry, 50,* 216–223.

Strother, D.B. (1984). Another look at time on task. *Phi Delta Kappan, 66,* 714–717.

Struthers, J.P., Bartlamay, H., Dell, S., & McLaughlin, T.F. (1994). An analysis of the Add-a-Word spelling program and public posting across three categories of children with special needs. *Reading Improvement, 31,* 28–36.

Stuart, M. (1999). Getting ready for reading: Early phoneme awareness and phonics teaching improves reading and spelling in inner-city second language learners. *British Journal of Educational Psychology, 69,* 587–605.

Suhr, J.A. (2008). Assessment versus testing and its importance in learning disability diagnosis. In E. Fletcher-Janzen & C.R. Reynolds (Eds.), *Neuropsychological perspectives on learning disabilities in the era of RTI: Recommendations for diagnosis and intervention* (pp. 99–114). Hoboken, NJ: John Wiley & Sons.

Suritsky, S.K., & Hughes, C.A. (1993). *Note taking strategy training for college students with learning disabilities.* Unpublished manuscript, Pennsylvania State University, University Park, PA.

Sutherland, K.S., Alder, N., & Gunter, P.L. (2003). The effect of varying rates of opportunities to respond to academic requests on the classroom behavior of students with EBD. *Journal of Emotional and Behavioral Disorders, 11,* 239–248.

Swanson, H.L. (2013). Meta-analysis of research on children with learning disabilities. In H.L. Swanson, M.R. Harris, & S. Graham (Eds.), *Handbook of learning disabilities* (2nd ed., pp. 627–642). New York, NY: Guilford Press.

Swanson, H.L., & Hoskyn, M. (1998). Experimental intervention research on students with learning disabilities: A meta-analysis of treatment outcomes. *Review of Educational Research, 68,* 277–321.

Swanson, H.L., & Hoskyn, M. (2001). A meta-analysis of intervention research for adolescent students with learning disabilities. *Learning Disabilities Research & Practice, 16,* 109–119.

Swanson, H.L., & Jerman, O. (2006). Math disabilities: A selective meta-analysis of the literature. *Review of Educational Research, 76,* 249–274.

Swanson, H.L., & Saez, L. (2003). Memory difficulties in children and adults with learning disabilities. In H.L. Swanson, K.R. Harris, & S. Graham (Eds.), *Handbook of learning disabilities* (pp. 182–198). New York, NY: Guilford Press.

Swanson, H.L., & Siegel, L. (2001). Learning disabilities as a working memory deficit. *Issues in Education, 7,* 1–48.

Swanson, H.L., Trainin, G., Necoechea, D.M., & Hammill, D.D. (2003). Rapid naming, phonological awareness, and reading: A meta-analysis of the correlational evidence. *Review of Educational Research, 73,* 407–444. doi:10.3102/00346543073004407

Swanson, H.L., & Zheng, X. (2013). Memory difficulties in children and adults with learning disabilities. In H.L. Swanson, K. Harris, & S. Graham (Eds.), *Handbook of learning disabilities* (2nd ed., pp. 214–238). New York, NY: Guilford Press.

Swanson, H.L., Zheng, X., & Jerman, O. (2009). Working memory, short-term memory, and reading disabilities: A selective meta-analysis of the literature. *Journal of Learning Disabilities, 42,* 260–287.

Swanson, J.M., Cantwell, D., Lerner, M., McBurnett, K., & Hanna, G. (1991). Effects of stimulant medication on learning in children with ADHD. *Journal of Learning Disabilities, 24,* 219–230.

Takeda, T., Ambrosini, P.J., deBerardinis, R., & Elia, J. (2012). What can ADHD without comorbidity teach us about comorbidity? *Research in Developmental Disabilities, 33,* 419–425.

Tangel, D.M., & Blachman, B.A. (1992). Effect of phoneme awareness instruction on kindergarten children's invented spelling. *Journal of Literacy Research, 24,* 233–261. doi:10.1080/1086296920954777

Tanol, G., Johnson, L., McComas, J., & Cote, E. (2010). Responding to rule violations or rule following: A comparison of two versions of the good behavior game with kindergarten students. *Journal of School Psychology, 48,* 337–355. doi:10.1016/j.jsp.2010.06.001

Temple, E., Poldrack, R.A., Salidis, J., Deutsch, G.K., Tallal, P., Merzenich, M.M., . . . Gabrieli, J.D. (2001). Disrupted neural responses to phonological and orthographic processing in dyslexic children: An fMRI study. *NeuroReport, 12,* 299–307.

Templeton, S. (2004). The vocabulary–spelling connection: Orthographic development and morphological knowledge at the intermediate grades and beyond. In J.F. Baumann & E.J. Kame'enui

(Eds.), *Vocabulary instruction: Research to practice* (pp. 118–138). New York, NY: Guilford Press.

Tenenbaum, H.R., & Ruck, M.D. (2007). Are teachers' expectations different for racial minority than for European American students? A meta-analysis. *Journal of Educational Psychology, 99,* 253–273.

Terestman, N. (1980). Mood quality and intensity in nursery school children as predictors of behavior disorder. *American Journal of Orthopsychiatry, 50,* 125–138.

Thomas, A., & Chess, S. (1977). *Temperament and development.* Levittown, PA: Brunner/Mazel.

Thome, J., Ehlis, A.C., Fallgatter, A.J., Krauel, K., Lange, K.W., Riederer, P., . . . Gerlach, M. (2012). Biomarkers for attention-deficit/hyperactivity disorder (ADHD): A consensus report of the WFSBP task force on biological markers and the World Federation of ADHD. *World Journal of Biological Psychiatry, 13,* 379–400. doi:10.3109/15622975.2012.690535

Thomsen, K. (2002). *Building resilient students.* Thousand Oaks, CA: Corwin Press.

Thomson, J.M., Richardson, U., & Goswami, U. (2005). Phonological similarity neighborhoods and children's short-term memory: Typical development and dyslexia. *Memory & Cognition, 33,* 1210–1219.

Thurber, D.N. (1983). Write on! With continuous stroke point. *Academic Therapy, 18,* 389–395.

Thurber, D.N., & Scott, Foresman and Company. (1993). *Manuscript and cursive alphabets and number descriptions. D'Nealian handwriting: Book 4.* Glenview, IL: Addison-Wesley.

Tienken, C.H., & Orlich, D.C. (2013). Translating the common core state standards. *AASA Journal of Scholarship & Practice, 10*(1). Retrieved from https://aasa.org/uploadedFiles/Publications/Journals/AASA_Journal_of_Scholarship_and_Practice/Spring2013.FINAL_v3.pdf#page=3

Tipps, S., Johnson, A., & Kennedy, L.M. (2011). *Guiding children's learning of mathematics* (12th ed.). Independence, KY: Cengage Learning.

Tobias, S. (1993). *Overcoming math anxiety.* New York, NY: W.W. Norton.

Toll, S.W.M., Van der Ven, S.H.G., Kroesbergen, E.H., & Van Luit, J.E.H. (2011). Executive functions as predictors of math learning disabilities. *Journal of Learning Disabilities, 44,* 521–532. doi:10.1177/0022219410387302

Torgesen, J.K. (1992). Learning disabilities: Historical and conceptual issues. In B.Y.L. Wong (Ed.), *Learning about learning disabilities* (pp. 3–38). San Diego, CA: Academic Press.

Torgesen, J.K. (1993). Variations on theory in learning disabilities. In G.R. Lyon, D.B. Gray, J.F. Kavanagh, & N.A. Krasnegor (Eds.), *Better understanding learning disabilities: New views from research and their implications for education and public policies* (pp. 153–170). Baltimore, MD: Paul H. Brookes Publishing Co.

Torgesen, J.K. (1994). Issues in the assessment of executive function: An information processing perspective. In G.R. Lyon (Ed.), *Frames of reference for the assessment of learning disabilities: New views on measurement issues* (pp. 143–162). Baltimore, MD: Paul H. Brookes Publishing Co.

Torgesen, J.K. (2005). Recent discoveries from research on remedial interventions for children with dyslexia. In M. Snowling and C. Hulme (Eds.), *The science of reading* (pp. 521–537). Oxford: Blackwell.

Torgesen, J.K., Alexander, A.W., Wagner, R.K., Rashotte, C.A., Voeller, K., & Conway, T. (2001). Intensive remedial instruction for children with severe reading disabilities: Immediate and long-term outcomes from two instructional approaches. *Journal of Learning Disabilities, 34,* 33–58.

Torgesen, J.K., & Burgess, S.R. (1998). Consistency of reading-related phonological processes throughout early childhood: Evidence from longitudinal-correlational and instructional studies. In J.L. Metsala & L.C. Ehri (Eds.), *Word recognition in beginning literacy* (pp. 161–188). Mahwah, NJ: Erlbaum.

Treiman, R. (1998). Why spelling? The benefits of incorporating spelling into beginning reading instruction. In J.L. Metsala & L.C. Ehri (Eds.), *Word recognition in beginning literacy* (pp. 289–313). Mahwah, NJ: Erlbaum.

Treiman, R., & Bourassa, D.C. (2000). The development of spelling skill. *Topics in Language Disorders, 20*(3), 1–18.

Treiman, R., & Kessler, B. (2014). *How children learn to write words.* New York, NY: Oxford University Press.

Treuting, J.J., & Hinshaw, S.P. (2001). Depression and self-esteem in boys with attention-deficit/hyperactivity disorder: Associations with comorbid aggression and explanatory attributional mechanisms. *Journal of Abnormal Child Psychology, 29*(1), 23–39.

Tripp, G., & Alsop, B. (2001). Sensitivity to reward delay in children with attention deficit hyperactivity disorder (ADHD). *Journal of Child Psychology and Psychiatry, 42,* 691–698.

Troia, G.A., & Olinghouse, N.G. (2013). The common core state standards and evidence-based educational practices: The case of writing. *School Psychology Review, 42,* 343–357.

Turgay, A. (2005). Comorbidity of dysthymic disorders in children and adolescents. *Psychiatric Times, 22,* 34–36.

Turkan, S., & Schramm-Possinger, M. (2014). Teaching content to English learners in the era of the common core standards. *R & D Connections, 23,* 1–9. Retrieved from http://www.ets.org/Media/Research/pdf/RD_Connections_23.pdf

Umbreit, J., Ferro, J.B., Liaupsin, C.J., & Lane, K.L. (2007). *Functional behavioral assessment and function-based intervention: An effective, practical approach.* Upper Saddle River, NJ: Pearson Education.

Ungar, J. (2010). Cultural dimensions of resilience among adults. In J.W. Reich, A.J. Zautra, and S. Hall (Eds.), *Handbook of adult resilience* (pp. 404–426). New York, NY: Guilford Press.

U.S. Census Bureau. (2013). *Language use in the United States: 2011.* U.S. Department of Commerce.

References

Retrieved from http://www.census.gov/prod/2013pubs/acs-22.pdf

U.S. Department of Education, Office of English Language Acquisition, Language Enhancement, and Academic Achievement for Limited English Proficient Students. (2013). *The biennial report to Congress on the implementation of the Title III state formula grant program, school years 2008–10.* Retrieved from http://www.ncela.us/files/uploads/3/Biennial_Report_0810.pdf

Vacca, D.M. (2001). Confronting the puzzle of nonverbal learning disabilities. *Educational Leadership, 59*(3), 26–32.

Vadasy, P.F., & Sanders, E.A. (2012). Two-year follow-up of a kindergarten phonics intervention for English and native speakers: Contextualizing treatment impacts by classroom literacy instruction. *Journal of Educational Psychology, 104,* 987–1005. doi:10.1037/a0028163

Vaillancourt, K., Cowan, K.C., & Kalamaros Skalski, A. (n.d.). Providing mental health services within a multi-tiered system of supports. *Depression in children and adolescents: Guidelines for school practice,* Handout K. Bethesda, MD: National Association of School Psychologists. Retrieved from http://www.nasponline.org/resources/handouts/depression/handout_MTSS_key_points.pdf

Van Hoorn, J.F., Maathuis, C.G., & Hadders-Algra, M. (2013). Neural correlates of paediatric dysgraphia. *Developmental Medicine and Child Neurology, 55*(4), 65–68.

Vaughn, S., & Klingner, J.K. (1999). Teaching reading comprehension through collaborative strategic reading. *Intervention in School and Clinic, 34,* 284–292.

Vaughn, S., Klingner, J.K., Swanson, E.A., Boardman, A.G., Roberts, G., Mohammed, S.S., & Stillman-Spisak, S.J. (2011). Efficacy of collaborative strategic reading with middle school students. *American Educational Research Journal, 28,* 938–964. doi:10.3102/0002831211410305

Vaughn, S., & Wanzek, J. (2014). Intensive interventions in reading for students with reading disabilities: Meaningful impacts. *Learning Disabilities Research & Practice, 29,* 46–53.

Vellutino, F.R. (1979). *Dyslexia: Theory and research.* Cambridge, MA: MIT Press.

Vellutino, F.R., & Scanlon, D.M. (1987). Phonological coding, phonological awareness, and reading ability: Evidence from a longitudinal and experimental study. *Merrill Palmer Quarterly, 33,* 321–363.

Vellutino, F.R., Scanlon, D.M., & Tanzman, M.S. (1994). Components of reading ability: Issues and problems in operationalizing word identification, phonological coding, and orthographic coding. In G.R. Lyon (Ed.), *Frames of reference for the assessment of learning disabilities: New views on measurement issues* (pp. 279–332). Baltimore, MD: Paul H. Brookes Publishing Co.

Visser, J. (2001). Aspects of physical provision for pupils with emotional and behavioural difficulties. *Support for Learning, 16,* 64–66.

Visser, S.N., Danielson, M.L., Bitsko, R.H., Holbrook, J.R., Kogan, M.D., Ghandour, R.M., . . . Blumberg, S.J. (2014). Trends in the parent-report of health care provider-diagnosed and medicated attention-deficit / hyperactivity disorder: United States, 2003–2011. *Journal of the American Academy of Child & Adolescent Psychiatry, 53*(1), 34–46.

Voeller, K.S. (1991). Towards a neurobiologic nosology of attention deficit hyperactivity disorder. *Journal of Child Neurology, 6,* S2–S8.

Vogel, S., & Moran, M.R. (1982). Written language disorders in learning disabled college students: A preliminary report. In W. Cruickshank & J. Lerner (Eds.), *The Best of ACLD 1981: Vol 3. Coming of age* (pp. 211–225). Syracuse, NY: Syracuse University Press.

Vukovic, R.K., & Siegel, L.S. (2010). Academic and cognitive characteristics of persistent mathematics difficulty from first through fourth grade. *Learning Disabilities Research & Practice, 25*(1), 25–38. doi:10.1111/j.1540-5826.2009.00298.x

Vygotsky, L.S. (1978). *Mind in society.* Cambridge, MA: Harvard University Press.

Wadlington, E.M., & Wadlington, P.L. (2005). What educators really believe about dyslexia. *Reading Improvement, 42*(1), 16–33.

Wagner, R.K., & Torgesen, J.K. (1987). The nature of phonological processing and its causal role in the acquisition of reading skills. *Psychological Bulletin, 101,* 192–212.

Wagner, R.K., Torgesen, J.K., Laughon, P., Simmons, K., & Rashotte, C.A. (1993). The development of young readers' phonological processing abilities. *Journal of Educational Psychology, 85,* 1–20.

Walker, B., Cheney, D., Stage, S., & Blum, C. (2005). Schoolwide screening and positive behavior supports: Identifying and supporting students at risk for school failure. *Journal of Positive Behavior Interventions, 7,* 194–204.

Walker, H.M., Ramsey, E., & Gresham, F. (2004). *Antisocial behavior in school: Evidence-based practices.* Belmont, CA: Thomson/Wadsworth.

Walker, H.M., & Rankin, R. (1983). Assessing the behavioral expectations and demands of less restrictive settings. *School Psychology Review, 12,* 274–284.

Walker, J., & Shea, T.M. (1991). *Behavior management: A practical approach for educators.* New York, NY: Macmillan.

Wallace, G.W., & Bott, D.A. (1989). Statement pie: A strategy to improve the paragraph writing skills of adolescents with learning disabilities. *Journal of Learning Disabilities, 22,* 541–543, 553.

Wallach, G.P., & Miller, L. (1988). *Language intervention and academic success.* New York, NY: Little, Brown.

Warner, C.M., Fisher, P.H., Shrout, P.E., Rathor, S., & Klein, R.G. (2007). Treating adolescents with social anxiety disorder in school: An attention control trial. *Journal of Child Psychology and Psychiatry, 48,* 676–686.

Watanabe, L.M., & Hall-Kenyon, K.M. (2011). Improving young children's writing: The influence of story structure on kindergartners' writing complexity. *Literacy Research and Instruction, 50,* 272–293. doi:10.1080/19388071.2010.514035

Watson, S.M.R., & Gable, R.A. (2012). Unraveling the complex nature of mathematics learning disability: Implications for research and practice. *Learning Disability Quarterly, 36,* 178–187. doi:10.1177/0731948712461489

Watson, S.M.R., Gable, R.A., Gear, S.B., & Hughes, K.C. (2012). Evidence-based strategies for improving the reading comprehension of secondary students: Implications for students with learning disabilities. *Learning Disabilities Research & Practice, 27*(2), 79–89. doi:10.1111/j.1540-5826.2012.00353.x

Way, S.M. (2011). School discipline and disruptive classroom behavior: The moderating effects of student perceptions. *Sociological Quarterly, 52,* 346–375. doi:10.1111/j.1533-8525.2011.01210.x

Wechsler, D. (1991). *Wechsler Intelligence Scale for Children* (3rd ed.). San Antonio, TX: Psychological Corporation.

Weiner, B. (1974). *Achievement motivation and attribution theory.* Morristown, NJ: General Learning Press.

Weiner, S. (1994). Four first graders' descriptions of how they spell. *Elementary School Journal, 94,* 315–332.

Weintraub, N., & Graham, S. (1998). Writing legibly and quickly: A study of children's ability to adjust their handwriting to meet common classroom demands. *Learning Disabilities Research & Practice, 13,* 146–152.

Weintraub, S., & Mesulum, M.M. (1983). Developmental learning disabilities of the right hemisphere. *Archives of Neurology, 40,* 463–468.

Weiss, G., & Hechtman, L. (1993). *Hyperactive children grown up: ADHD in children, adolescents, and adults* (2nd ed.). New York, NY: Guilford Press.

Weist, M.D. (2003). Commentary: Promoting paradigmatic change in child and adolescent mental health and schools. *School Psychology Review, 32,* 336–341.

Wellington, T.M., Semrud-Clikeman, M., Gregory, A.L., Murphy, J.M., & Lancaster, J.L. (2006). Magnetic resonance imaging volumetric analysis of the putamen in children with ADHD: Combined type versus control. *Journal of Attention Disorders, 10,* 171–180.

Wender, P.H. (1979). The concept of adult minimal brain dysfunction. In L. Bellak (Ed.), *Psychiatric aspects of minimal brain dysfunction in adults* (pp. 97–115). New York, NY: Grune & Stratton.

Wentzel, K.R., & Watkins, D.E. (2002). Peer relationships and collaborative learning as contexts for academic enablers. *School Psychology Review, 31,* 366–377.

Werner, E.E. (1993). Risk, resilience, and recovery: Perspectives from the Kauai longitudinal study. *Development and Psychopathology, 5,* 503–515.

Werner, E.E. (2013). What can we learn about resilience from large-scale longitudinal studies? In S. Goldstein & R.B. Brooks (Eds.), *Handbook of resilience in children* (pp. 87–104). New York, NY: Springer.

Werner, E.E., & Smith, R.S. (1992). *Overcoming the odds: High risk children from birth to adulthood.* Ithaca, NY: Cornell University Press.

Westby, C.E. (1994). The effects of culture on genre, structure, and style of oral and written texts. In G.P. Wallach & K.G. Butler (Eds.), *Language learning disabilities in schoolage children and adolescents* (pp. 180–218). New York, NY: Merrill.

Westman, J.C. (1996). Concepts of dyslexia. In L.R. Putnam (Ed.), *How to become a better reading teacher: Strategies for assessment and intervention* (pp. 65–73). Upper Saddle River, NJ: Prentice Hall.

Whalen, C.K., & Henker, B. (1991). Therapies for hyperactive children: Comparisons, combinations, and compromises. *Journal of Consulting and Clinical Psychology, 59,* 126–137.

Wheldall, K., & Lam, Y.Y. (1987). Rows versus tables: The effects of two classroom seating arrangements on classroom disruption rate, on-task behavior and teacher behavior in three special school classes. *Educational Psychology: An International Journal of Experimental Educational Psychology, 7,* 303–312.

White, E.B. (1999). *Stuart Little.* New York, NY: HarperCollins. (Original work published 1945).

Wight, V.R., Chau, M., & Artaani, Y. (2010). *Who are America's poor children?* New York, NY: National Center for Children in Poverty, Columbia University.

Wilde, S. (1997). *What's a schwa sound anyway?* Westport, CT: William Heinemann.

Williams, J.P. (2005). Instruction in reading comprehension for primary-grade students: A focus on text structure. *Journal of Special Education, 39*(1), 6–18.

Williams, J.P., Hall, K.M., & Lauer, K.D. (2004). Teaching expository text structure to young at-risk learners: Building the basics of comprehension instruction. *Exceptionality, 12*(3), 129–144.

Willows, D.M., Kruk, R.S., & Corcos, E. (Eds.). (1993). *Visual processes in reading and reading disabilities.* Mahwah, NJ: Erlbaum.

Willows, D.M., & Terepocki, M. (1993). The relation of reversal errors to reading disabilities. In D.M. Willows, R.S. Kruk, & E. Corcos (Eds.), *Visual processes in reading and reading disabilities* (pp. 31–56). Mahwah, NJ: Erlbaum.

Wilson, B. (2004). *Wilson Reading/System®, instructor manual* (3rd ed.). Oxford, MA: Wilson Language Training.

Wilson Language Training. (2012). *Fundations®* (2nd ed.). Oxford, MA: Wilson Language Training.

Wilson Language Training. (2006). *Wilson Fluency/Basic.* Oxford, MA: Wilson Language Training.

Wolf, M. (1999). What time may tell: Towards a new conceptualization of developmental dyslexia. *Annals of Dyslexia, 49,* 3–28.

Wolf, M. (2012). *The RAVE-O Program* (2nd ed.). Longview, CO: Cambium/Sopris Learning.

Wolf, M., & Bowers, P.G. (1999). The double deficit hypothesis for the developmental dyslexias. *Journal of Educational Psychology, 91,* 415–438.

References

Wolf, M., Bowers, P.G., & Biddle, K. (2000). Naming-speed processes, timing, and reading: A conceptual review. *Journal of Learning Disabilities, 33,* 387–407.

Wolf, M., & Denckla, M.B. (2006). *Rapid Automatized Naming and Rapid Alternating Stimulus tests.* Austin, TX: PRO-ED.

Wolf, M., O'Rourke, A.G., Gidney, C., Lovett, M., Cirino, P., & Morris, R. (2002). The second deficit: An investigation of the independence of phonological and naming-speed deficits in developmental dyslexia. *Reading and Spelling, 15*(1–2), 43–72.

Wolraich, M.L., McKeown, R.E., Visser, S.N., Baird, D., Cuffe, S., Neas, B., . . . Danielson, M. (2012). The prevalence of ADHD: Its diagnosis and treatment in four school districts across two states. *Journal of Attention Disorders, 18,* 563–575. doi:10.1177/1087054712453/69

Wong, B.Y.L. (1986). A cognitive approach to spelling. *Exceptional Children, 53,* 169–173.

Wong, B.Y.L., Harris, K.R., Graham, S., & Butler, D. (2003). Cognitive strategies instruction research in learning disabilities. In H.L. Swanson, K.R. Harris, & S. Graham (Eds.), *Handbook of learning disabilities* (pp. 383–402). New York, NY: Guilford Press.

Wong, B.Y.L., Wong, R., Darlington, D., & Jones, W. (1991). Interactive teaching: An effective way to teach revision skills to adolescents with learning disabilities. *Learning Disabilities Research & Practice, 6,* 117–127.

Woodward, J. (2006). Making reform-based mathematics work for academically low-achieving middle school students. In M. Montague & A. Jitendra (Eds.), *Teaching mathematics to middle school students with learning difficulties* (pp. 29–50). New York, NY: Guilford Press.

Wylie, R., & Durrell, D. (1970). Teaching vowels through phonograms. *Elementary English, 47,* 787–791.

Wyman, P.A., Cowen, E.L., Work, W.C., Hoyt-Meyers, L.A., Magnus, K.B., & Fagen, D.B. (1999). Caregiving and developmental factors differentiating young at-risk urban children showing resilient versus stress-affected outcomes: A replication and extension. *Child Development, 709,* 645–659.

Zagar, R., & Bowers, N. (1983). The effect of time of day on problem solving and classroom behavior. *Psychology in the Schools, 20,* 337–345.

Zahn-Waxler, C., Schmitz, S., Fulker, D., Robinson, J., & Ende, R. (1996). Behavior problems in five-year-old monozygotic and dizygotic twins: Genetic and environmental influences, patterns of regulation and internationalization of control. *Developmental Psychopathology, 8,* 103–122.

Zametkin, A.J., & Rapoport, J.L. (1987). Neurobiology of attention-deficit disorder with hyperactivity: Where have we come in 50 years? *Journal of the American Academy of Child and Adolescent Psychiatry, 36,* 676–686.

Zentall, S.S. (1989). Attentional cuing and spelling tasks for hyperactive and comparison regular classroom children. *Journal of Special Education, 23,* 83–93.

Zentall, S.S. (1995). Modifying classroom tasks and environments. In S. Goldstein (Ed.), *Understanding and managing children's classroom behavior* (pp. 356–374). New York, NY: Wiley.

Zentall, S.S. (2006). *ADHD and education: Foundations, characteristics, methods, and collaborations.* New York, NY: Merrill.

Zentall, S.S., & Goldstein, S. (1999). *Seven steps to homework success.* Plantation, FL: Specialty Press.

Zentall, S.S., & Kruczek, T. (1988). The attraction of color for active attention-problem children. *Journal of Abnormal Child Psychology, 15,* 519–536.

Zheng, X., Flynn, L.J., & Swanson, H.L. (2012). Experimental intervention studies on word problem solving and math disabilities: A selective analysis of the literature. *Journal of Learning Disabilities, 36,* 97–111. doi:10.1177/0731948712444277

Zigmond, N. (2004). Searching for the most effective service delivery model for students with learning disabilities. In H.L. Swanson, K.R. Harris, & S. Graham (Eds.), *Handbook of learning disabilities* (pp. 110–122). New York, NY: Guilford Press.

Zigmond, N., Jenkins, J., Fuchs, L., Deno, S., Fuchs, D., Baker, J.N., . . . Couthino, M. (1995). Special education in restructured schools: Findings from three multi-year studies. *Phi Delta Kappan, 76,* 531–540.

Zimmerman, B.J. (1986). Becoming a self-regulated learner: Which are the key subprocesses? *Contemporary Educational Psychology, 11,* 307–313.

Zirkel, P.A. (1992). A checklist for determining legal eligibility of ADD/ADHD students. *Special Educator, 8,* 93–97.

Additional Resources

READING

Alphabetic Phonics

(A.R. Cox)
Educators Publishing Service
P.O. Box 9031
Cambridge, MA 02139-9031
800-435-7728
Fax: 888-440-2665
http://eps.schoolspecialty.com

Benchmark Phonetic Connections

BuildUp Phonics
BuildUp Phonics Readers
Benchmark Education Company
145 Huguenot Street
New Rochelle, NY 10801
877-236-2465
Fax: 877-732-8273
info@benchmarkeducation.com
http://www.benchmarkeducation.com

Concept Phonics

(P.E. Fischer)
Oxton House Publishers
P.O. Box 209
Farmington, ME 04938
800-539-7323
Fax: 207-779-0623
http://www.oxtonhouse.com

Corrective Reading

McGraw-Hill
McGraw-Hill School Education
P.O. Box 182605
Columbus, OH 43218
800-334-7344
Fax: 800-953-8691
http://www.mheonline.com

Doors to Discovery

McGraw-Hill
McGraw-Hill School Education
P.O. Box 182605
Columbus, OH 43218
800-334-7344
Fax: 800-953-8691
http://www.mheonline.com

Early Intervention in Reading (EIR)

McGraw-Hill
McGraw-Hill School Education
P.O. Box 182605
Columbus, OH 43218
800-334-7344
Fax: 800-953-8691
http://www.mheonline.com

Earobics Literacy Launch

Earobics / Houghton Mifflin Harcourt Learning Technology
222 Berkeley Street
Boston, MA
888-242-6747
Fax: 800-567-2714
http://www.earobics.com

Easy Lessons for Teaching Word Families

(J. Lynch)
Scholastic
800-724-6527
http://www.scholastic.com

Edmark Reading Program

PRO-ED
8700 Shoal Creek Boulevard
Austin, TX 78757-6897
800-897-3202

The authors thank Sarah Goldman, M.A., for updating this resource material for the third edition.

Fax: 800-397-7633
http://www.proedinc.com

EPS Phonics Plus

EPS Phonics Plus Readers

Educators Publishing Service
P.O. Box 9031
Cambridge, MA 02139-9031
800-435-7728
Fax: 888-440-2665
http://eps.schoolspecialty.com

Explode the Code

(N.M. Hall)
Educators Publishing Service
P.O. Box 9031
Cambridge, MA 02139-9031
800-435-7728
Fax: 888-440-2665
http://eps.schoolspecialty.com

EZ2 Read Barbara Nicholson Books and Material

EZ2 Read Decodable Set

(B. Nicholson)
916-933-4329
ez2read@ez2read.com
http://www.ez2read.com

Fast ForWord

Scientific Learning
300 Frank H. Ogawa Plaza
Suite 600
Oakland, CA 94612-2040
888-665-9707
Fax: 510-444-3580
support@scilearn.com
http://www.scilearn.com

Fluency First

(T. Rasinski & N. Padak)
McGraw-Hill
McGraw-Hill School Education
P.O. Box 182605
Columbus, OH 43218
800-334-7344
Fax: 800-953-8691
http://www.mheonline.com

Flyleaf Publishing (Decodable Books K–3)

400 Bedford Street
1st Floor SW03
Manchester, NH 03101
800-449-7006
info@flyleafpublishing.com
http://www.flyleafpublishing.com

Fundations® (2nd ed.)

(B. Wilson)
Wilson Language Training
47 Old Webster Rd.
Oxford, MA 01540-2705
800-899-8454
Fax: 508-368-2300
http://www.wilsonlanguage.com

Glass Analysis for Decoding Only

(G.G. Glass & E.W. Glass)
Easier to Learn, Inc.
P.O. Box 259
Blue Point, NY 11715
Phone and fax: 631-475-7693
info@glassanalysis.com
http://www.glassanalysis.com

Great Leaps Reading

(K.U. Campbell)
Diarmuid, Inc.
P.O. Box 357580
Gainesville, FL 32635
877-475-3277
Fax: 352-384-3883
http://www.greatleaps.com

Herman Method

(R. Herman)
Voyager Sopris Learning
Cambium Learning Group
17855 Dallas Parkway
Suite 400
Dallas, TX 75287
800-547-6747
Fax: 888-819-7767
http://www.voyagersopris.com

1000 Instant Words: The Most Common Words for Teaching Reading, Writing, and Spelling

(E. Fry)
Teacher Created Resources
6421 Industry Way
Westminster, CA 92683
888-343-4335
Fax: 800-525-1254
custserv@teachercreated.com
http://www.teachercreated.com

Additional Resources

Ladders to Literacy: A Kindergarten Activity Book (2nd ed.)

(R. O'Conner, A. Notari-Syverson, & P.F. Vadasy)
Paul H. Brookes Publishing Co.
P.O. Box 10624
Baltimore, MD 21285-0624
800-638-3775
Fax: 410-337-8539
http://www.brookespublishing.com

Language! The Comprehensive Literacy Curriculum
Language! (4th ed.)

(J.F. Greene)
Voyager Sopris Learning
Cambium Learning Group
17855 Dallas Parkway
Suite 400
Dallas, TX 75287
800-547-6747
Fax: 888-819-7767
http://www.voyagersopris.com

Let's Begin with the Letter People

Abrams Learning Trends
16310 Bratton Lane
Suite 250
Austin, TX 78728-2403
800-227-9120
Fax: 800-737-3322
http://www.abramslearningtrends.com

Let's Go Read! 1: An Island Adventure
Let's Go Read! 2: An Ocean Adventure

Riverdeep, Inc., LLC
100 Pine Street
Suite 1900
San Francisco, CA 94111
888-242-6747
Fax: 415-659-2020
info@riverdeep.net

LETRS (2nd ed.)

(S. Hall, D. Glaser, S. Baker, M. Davidson, C. Hancock, J.R. Nelson, A. Fierro, N. Hennessey, C. Tolman, M.E. Arguelles, L. Moats, & L.H. Paulson)
Voyager Sopris Learning
Cambium Learning Group
17855 Dallas Parkway
Suite 400
Dallas, TX 75287
800-547-6747
Fax: 888-819-7767
http://www.voyagersopris.com

Lexia Reading Core5

Lexia Learning Systems
200 Baker Ave Ext.
Concord, MA 01742
800-435-3942
Fax: 978-287-0062
info@lexialearning.com
http://www.lexialearning.com

Lindamood Phoneme Sequencing Program for Reading, Spelling, and Speech (LiPS)

(P.C. Lindamood & P.D. Lindamood)
PRO-ED
8700 Shoal Creek Boulevard
Austin, TX 78757-6897
800-897-3202
Fax: 800-397-7633
http://www.proedinc.com

Literacy Express

Lakeshore
2695 E. Dominguez Street
Carson, CA 90895
800-778-4456
Fax: 800-537-5403
lakeshore@lakeshorelearning.com
http://www.lakeshorelearning.com

Making Words, Making Big Words

(P.M. Cunningham & D.P. Hall)
School Specialty
P.O. Box 1579
Appleton, WI 54912-1579
888-388-3224
Fax: 888-388-6344
http://www.schoolspecialty.com

Megawords: Decoding, Spelling, and Understanding Multisyllabic Words (2nd ed.)

(K. Johnson & P. Bayrd)
Educators Publishing Service
P.O. Box 9031
Cambridge, MA 02139-9031
800-435-7728
Fax: 888-440-2665
http://eps.schoolspecialty.com

MindPlay

4400 E. Broadway
Suite 400
Tucson, AZ 85711

800-221-7911
http://www.mindplay.com
(RAPS 360, Virtual Reading Coach, Fluent Reading Trainer, Understanding Dyslexia, Teacher Companion Course, Teacher Companion Plus Course)

Neuhaus Education Center

Practices for Developing Accuracy and Fluency
Reading Readiness
Scientific Spelling Manual
4433 Bissonnet
Bellaire, TX 77401
713-664-7676
Fax: 713-664-4744
http://www.neuhaus.org

Onset Rime Cards

Teaching Resource Center
P.O. Box 443
West Linn, OR 97068
800-833-3389
Fax: 866-850-4456
http://www.trcabc.com

Open Court Phonemic Awareness and Phonics Kits
Open Court Reading Series

(A. Archer, J. Flood, D. Lapp, & L. Lungren)
McGraw-Hill
McGraw-Hill School Education
P.O. Box 182605
Columbus, OH 43218
800-334-7344
Fax: 800-953-8691
http://www.mheonline.com

Orton-Gillingham

Institute for Multi-Sensory Education
19720 Gerald Street
Northville, MI 48167
800-646-9788
Fax: 248-735-2927
imse@orton-gillingham.com
http://www.orton-gillingham.com

Patterns for Success in Reading and Spelling

(M.K. Henry & N.C. Redding)
PRO-ED
8700 Shoal Creek Boulevard
Austin, TX 78757-6897
800-897-3202
Fax: 800-397-7633
http://www.proedinc.com

Peer Assisted Learning Strategies (PALS) Reading

Vanderbilt University
PMB 228
110 Magnolia Circle
Suite 418
Nashville, TN 37203
Peabody Box 228
615-343-4782
PALS@vanderbilt.edu

Phonemic Awareness in Young Children

(M. Adams, B. Foorman, I. Lundberg, & T. Beeler)
Paul H. Brookes Publishing Co.
P.O. Box 10624
Baltimore, MD 21285-0624
800-638-3775
Fax: 410-337-8539
http://www.brookespublishing.com

Phonic Reading Lessons

(S.A. Kirk, W. Kirk, E. Minskoff, N. Mather, & R. Roberts)
Academic Therapy Publications/High Noon Books
20 Leveroni Court
Novato, CA 94949-5746
800-422-7249
Fax: 888-287-9975
customerservice@academictherapy.com
http://www.academictherapy.com

Phonics and Spelling Through Phoneme-Grapheme Mapping

(K.E.S. Grace)
Voyager Sopris Learning
Cambium Learning Group
17855 Dallas Parkway
Suite 400
Dallas, TX 75287
800-547-6747
Fax: 888-819-7767
http://www.voyagersopris.com

Phonics from A to Z: A Practical Guide (2nd ed.)

(W. Blevins)
Scholastic
800-724-6527
http://www.scholastic.com

Phonics Q: The Complete Cueing System

(P. Herzog)
P.O. Box 22825
Seattle, WA 98122-0825

206-325-7989
Fax: 206-325-5066
info@phonicsq.com
http://www.phonicsq.com

Phonological Awareness Kit

(C. Robertson & W. Salter)
Primary (Grades K–3)
Intermediate (Grades 3–8)
LinguiSystems
3100 4th Avenue
East Moline, IL 61244
800-776-4332
Fax: 800-577-4555
service@linguisystems.com
http://www.linguisystems.com

Project Read

(V.E. Greene & M.L. Enfield)
Language Circle Enterprises, Inc.
1620 West 98th Street
Suite 130
Bloomington, MN 55431
800-450-0343
Fax: 952-884-6787
languagecircle@projectread.com
http://www.projectread.com

Retrieval, Automaticity, Vocabulary, Elaboration, and Orthography (RAVE-O)

Center for Reading and Language Research
Tufts University
School of Arts and Sciences
Miller Hall, North Wing
Medford, MA 02155
617-627-3815
Fax: 617-627-3827
http://ase.tufts.edu/crlr/RAVE-O

Read 180

(T. Hasselbring)
Scholastic
800-724-6527
http://www.scholastic.com

Read Naturally

(C. Ihnot)
2945 Lone Oak Drive
Suite 190
Saint Paul, MN 55121
800-788-4085
651-452-4085
Fax: 651-452-9204
customerservice@readnaturally.com
http://www.readnaturally.com

Read Well

(M. Sprick)
Voyager Sopris Learning
Cambium Learning Group
17855 Dallas Parkway
Suite 400
Dallas, TX 75287
800-547-6747
Fax: 888-819-7767
http://www.voyagersopris.com

Read, Write, and Type Learning System Computer Software: Wordy Qwerty

Talking Fingers, Inc.
830 Rincon Way
San Rafael, CA 94903
800-674-9126
415-472-3103
contact@talkingfingers.com
http://www.talkingfingers.com

Reading A–Z

Learning A–Z
1840 East River Rd, #320
Tucson AZ 85718
866-889-3729
520-232-5000
Fax: 520-327-9934
support@learninga-z.com
http://www.readinga-z.com

Reading Horizons

800-333-0054
Fax: 801-295-7088
info@readinghorizons.com
http://www.readinghorizons.com

The Reading Lesson

(M. Levin & C. Langton)
Mountcastle Company
2305 Camino Ramon #217
San Ramon, CA 94583
925-548-5402
Fax: 925-476-1525
Nlevin@readinglesson.com
http://www.readinglesson.com

Reading Mastery Classic II 2008 Edition

McGraw-Hill
McGraw-Hill School Education
P.O. Box 182605

Columbus, OH 43218
800-334-7344
Fax: 800-953-8691
http://www.mheonline.com

Reading Milestones

PRO-ED
8700 Shoal Creek Boulevard
Austin, TX 78757-6897
800-897-3202
Fax: 800-397-7633
http://www.proedinc.com

Reading Reflex

(C. McGuinness & G. McGuinness)
Free Press
Trade Paperback
Simon & Schuster, Inc.
1230 Avenue of the Americas
New York, NY 10020
212-698-7000
http://www.simonandschuster.com
http://www.successforall.org

Recipe for Reading: New Century Edition

(N. Traub, & F. Bloom)
Educators Publishing Service
P.O. Box 9031
Cambridge, MA 02139-9031
800-435-7728
Fax: 888-440-2665
http://eps.schoolspecialty.com

REWARDS

(A.L. Archer, M.M. Gleason, & V. Vachon)
Voyager Sopris Learning
Cambium Learning Group
17855 Dallas Parkway
Suite 400
Dallas, TX 75287
800-547-6747
Fax: 888-819-7767
http://www.voyagersopris.com

Road to the Code: A Phonological Awareness Program for Young Children

(B. Blachman, E.W. Ball, R. Black, & D.M. Tangel)
Paul H. Brookes Publishing Co.
P.O. Box 10624
Baltimore, MD 21285-0624
800-638-3775
Fax: 410-337-8539
http://www.brookespublishing.com

Scott Foresman Early Reading Intervention

(D.C. Simmons & E.J. Kame'enui)
Pearson
K12 Customer Service
P.O. Box 2500
Lebanon, IN 46052
800-848-9500
Fax: 877-260-2530
http://www.pearsonschool.com

Simon S.I.O. (Sounds It Out)

Don Johnston, Inc.
26799 West Commerce Drive
Volo, IL 60073
800-999-4660
Fax: 847-740-7326
info@donjohnston.com
http://www.donjohnston.com

Six-Minute Solution: A Reading Fluency Program

(G. Adams & S. Brown)
Voyager Sopris Learning
Cambium Learning Group
17855 Dallas Parkway
Suite 400
Dallas, TX 75287
800-547-6747
Fax: 888-819-7767
http://www.voyagersopris.com

Slingerland

Slingerland Institute for Literacy
12729 Northup Way
Suite 1
Bellevue, WA 98005
425-453-1190
Fax: 425-635-7762
mail@slingerland.org
http://www.slingerland.org

Sonday System

Winsor Learning, Inc.
1620 West Seventh Street
St. Paul, MN 55102
800-321-7585
Fax: 651-222-3969
http://www.winsorlearning.com

Sounds Abound Listening, Rhyming, and Reading

PRO-ED
8700 Shoal Creek Boulevard

Austin, TX 78757-6897
800-897-3202
Fax: 800-397-7633
http://www.proedinc.com

Sounds Abound Interactive Software

(H. Catts & T. Williamson)
PRO-ED
8700 Shoal Creek Boulevard
Austin, TX 78757-6897
800-897-3202
Fax: 800-397-7633
http://www.proedinc.com

Sounds Abound Program Teaching Phonological Awareness in the Classroom

(O. Lenchner & B. Podhajski)
PRO-ED
8700 Shoal Creek Boulevard
Austin, TX 78757-6897
800-897-3202
Fax: 800-397-7633
http://www.proedinc.com

Sound Partners

(P. Vadasy, S. Wayne, R. O'Connor, J. Jenkins, K. Pool, M. Firebaugh, & J. Peyton)
Voyager Sopris Learning
Cambium Learning Group
17855 Dallas Parkway
Suite 400
Dallas, TX 75287
800-547-6747
Fax: 888-819-7767
http://www.voyagersopris.com

Sounds Great!

McGraw-Hill
McGraw-Hill School Education
P.O. Box 182605
Columbus, OH 43218
800-334-7344
Fax: 800-953-8691
http://www.mheonline.com

Spalding: The Writing Road to Reading

Spalding Education International
23335 N. 18th Drive
Suite 102
Phoenix, AZ 85027
623-434-1204
Fax: 623-434-1208
staff@spalding.org
http://www.spalding.org

Specialized Program Individualizing Reading Excellence (S.P.I.R.E.)

(S. Clark-Edmands)
Educators Publishing Service
P.O. Box 9031
Cambridge, MA 02139-9031
800-435-7728
Fax: 888-440-2665
http://eps.schoolspecialty.com

Story Grammar Marker

MindWing Concepts, Inc.
One Federal Street, #103-1
Springfield, MA 01105
413-734-7476
866-851-2415
Fax: 413-734-0075
info@mindwingconcepts.com
http://www.mindwingconcepts.com

Teacher-Directed PALS: Path to Achieving Literacy Success

(P. Mathes, J. Howard Allor, J.K. Torgesen, & S.H. Allen)
Voyager Sopris Learning
Cambium Learning Group
17855 Dallas Parkway
Suite 400
Dallas, TX 75287
800-547-6747
Fax: 888-819-7767
http://www.voyagersopris.com

WatchWord

(K. Lacey & W. Baird)
Voyager Sopris Learning
Cambium Learning Group
17855 Dallas Parkway
Suite 400
Dallas, TX 75287
800-547-6747
Fax: 888-819-7767
http://www.voyagersopris.com

Wilson Reading System

(B. Wilson)
Wilson Language Training
47 Old Webster Rd.
Oxford, MA 01540-2705
800-899-8454
Fax: 508-368-2300
http://www.WilsonLanguage.com

Word Journeys: Assessment-Guided Phonics, Spelling, and Vocabulary Instruction (2nd ed.)

(K. Ganske)
Guilford Press
72 Spring Street
New York, NY 10012
800-365-7006
Fax: 212-966-6708
info@guilford.com
http://www.guilford.com

WORDS: Integrated Decoding and Spelling Instruction Based on Word Origin and Word Structure (2nd ed.)

(M.K. Henry)
PRO-ED
8700 Shoal Creek Boulevard
Austin, TX 78757-6897
800-897-3202
Fax: 800-397-7633
http://www.proedinc.com

Wright Skills Decodable Books

McGraw-Hill
McGraw-Hill School Education
P.O. Box 182605
Columbus, OH 43218
800-334-7344
Fax: 800-953-8691
http://www.mheonline.com

Zoo-Phonics

20950 Ferretti Rd.
Groveland, CA 95321
800-622-8104
Fax: 209-962-4320
info@zoo-phonics.com
http://www.zoo-phonics.com

SPELLING AND VOCABULARY

Saxon Phonics and Spelling
Saxon Phonics Intervention

Houghton Mifflin Harcourt
Saxon Publishing
Specialized Curriculum Group
9205 Southpark Center Loop
Orlando, FL 32819
800-289-4490
Fax: 800-289-3994
http://www.hmhco.com

Scholastic Spelling

(L. Moats & B. Foorman)
Scholastic
800-724-6527
http://www.scholastic.com

Sitton Spelling Series

(R. Sitton)
Educators Publishing Service
P.O. Box 9031
Cambridge, MA 02139-9031
800-435-7728
Fax: 888-440-2665
http://www.eps.schoolspecialty.com
http://www.sittonspelling.com

Spellography

(B. Rosow & L.C. Moats)
Voyager Sopris Learning
Cambium Learning Group
17855 Dallas Parkway
Suite 400
Dallas, TX 75287
800-547-6747
Fax: 888-819-7767
http://www.voyagersopris.com

Words Their Way: Word Study for Phonics Vocabulary, and Spelling Instruction (5th ed.)

(D.R. Bear, M. Invernizzi, S. Templeton, & F. Johnston)
Pearson Higher Education
800-922-0579
http://www.pearsonhighered.com

WRITTEN LANGUAGE AND GRAPHIC ORGANIZERS

Co-Writer 7
Draft: Builder
Solo 6
Write: Outloud 6

Don Johnston, Inc.
26799 West Commerce Drive
Volo, IL 60073
800-999-4660
Fax: 847-740-7326
info@donjohnston.com
http://www.donjohnston.com

Additional Resources

Inspiration

Kidspiration

Inspiration Software, Inc.
6443 SW Beaverton-Hillsdale Hwy
Suite 370
Portland, OR 97221
503-297-3004
800-877-4292
Fax: 503-297-4676
customerservice@inspiration.com
http://www.inspiration.com

HANDWRITING RESOURCES

Fonts4Teachers

DownHill Publishing
80 8th Avenue
Suite 1107
New York, NY 10011-7166
800-203-0612
Fax: 212-661-5757
info@downhillpublishing.com
http://www.fonts4teachers.com

Pencil Grip

The Pencil Grip, Inc.
P.O. Box 67096
Los Angeles, CA 90067
888-736-4747 (PEN-GRIP)
info@thepencilgrip.com
http://www.thepencilgrip.com

Start Write 6

The Handwriting Worksheet Wizard

Startwrite, Inc.
P.O. Box 540531
North Salt Lake, UT 84054
801-359-2173
888-974-8322
Fax: 801-770-2009
http://www.startwrite.com

ASSISTIVE TECHNOLOGY

Books on Tape

Random House, LLC
Attn: Library and School Services
400 Hahn Road
Westminster, MD 21157
800-733-3000
Fax: 800-940-7046
http://www.booksontape.com

Dragon Naturally Speaking

Nuance Communications, Inc.
1 Wayside Road
Burlington, MA 01803
781-565-5000
Fax: 781-565-5001
http://www.nuance.com

Franklin Speaking Language Master

Franklin Electronic Publishers, Inc.
2 Manhattan Drive
Burlington, NJ 08016
800-266-5626
Fax: 609-239-5950
service@franklin.com
http://www.franklin.com

Learning Ally

National Headquarters
20 Roszel Road
Princeton, NJ 08540
800-221-4792
http://www.learningally.org

Quicktionary Reading Pens

WizCom Technologies Ltd.
support@wizcomtech.com
http://www.wizcomtech.com

Recorded Books, LLC

270 Skipjack Road
Prince Frederick, MD 20678
877-732-2898
Fax 410-535-5499
http://www.recordedbooks.com

SpeakQ

Quillsoft Ltd.
Go Q Software
75 Mary Street
Unit #1
Aurora, Ontario
Canada
L4G 1G3
877-674-7687
Fax: 888-908-4765
info@goQsoftware.com
http://www.goqsoftware.com

MATHEMATICS

Childrens' Mathematics/Cognitively Guided Instruction

Heinemann
P.O. Box 6926
Portsmouth, NH 03802-6926
800-225-5800
603-431-7894
Fax: 877-231.6980
custserv@heinemann.com
http://www.heinemann.com

Connecting Math Concepts

McGraw-Hill
McGraw-Hill School Education
P.O. Box 182605
Columbus, OH 43218
800-334-7344
Fax: 800-953-8691
http://www.mheonline.com

Great Leaps Math Package and Great Leaps Oral Calculation Program

Diarmuid, Inc.
P.O. Box 357580
Gainesville, FL 32635
877-475-3277
Fax: 352-384-3883
http://www.greatleaps.com

Hand-Made Math Manipulatives Instructions

http://mason.gmu.edu/~mmankus/Handson/manipulatives.htm

Math Their Way (K–2)

Baretta-Lorton, M.
Center for Innovation in Education, Inc.
P.O. Box 2070
Saratoga, CA 95070-0070
800-395-6088
Fax: 408-725-8146
http://www.center.edu
maththeirway.com

Mathematics . . . A Way of Thinking (3–6)

Baretta-Lorton, R.
Center for Innovation in Education, Inc.
P.O. Box 2070
Saratoga, CA 95070-0070
800-395-6088
Fax: 408-725-8146
http://www.center.edu
maththeirway.com

Multiplication Rap CD + Tape

Teacher's Paradise
Fax: 800-371-0579
http://www.teachersparadise.com

National Library of Virtual Manipulatives

http://nlvm.usu.edu/en/nav/vlibrary.html

Peer Assisted Learning Strategies (PALS) Math

Vanderbilt University
PMB 228
110 Magnolia Circle
Suite 418
Nashville, TN 37203
Peabody Box 228
615-343-4782
PALS@vanderbilt.edu

Times Tables and Addition the Fun Way

City Creek Press, Inc.
P.O. Box 8415
Minneapolis, MN 55408
800-585-6059
Fax: 877-286-1163
info@citycreek.com
http://www.CityCreek.com

TouchMath

(J. Bullock)
Innovative Learning Concepts, Inc.
5445 Mark Dabling Boulevard
Colorado Springs, CO 80918
800-888-9191
Fax: 719-593-2446
http://www.touchmath.com

Two Plus Two Is Not Five

(S. Greenwald)
Longevity Publishing
10179 E. Pinewood Avenue
Englewood, CO 80111
720-489-7243
info@longevitypublishing.com
http://www.longevitypublishing.com

Web Sites and Professional Organizations

WEB SITES

Center for Applied Technology (CAST)

CAST develops innovative, technology-based educational resources and strategies based on the principles of Universal Design for Learning (UDL). The products resource page contains interactive UDL tools for teachers, parents, and students. The Book Builder is an interactive online tool that enables educators to develop their own digital books to support reading instruction for children ages 3 and up. Teachers can create, edit, and save universally designed texts that support diverse learners.
http://www.cast.org

Center for Improving Learning of Fractions (CILF)

CILF is a project funded by the Institute of Education Sciences of the U.S. Department of Education in order to promote understanding of mathematics difficulties and appropriate interventions. The CILF web site lists publications and a description of current research goals. The resources page provides recommendations and strategies for implementation of an intervention to help students learn fractions.
http://www.udel.edu/soe/fractions

Center for Parent Information and Resources (CPIR)

CPIR is a national center that provides resources on disabilities and information about parent training centers across the country. The CPIR web site also includes resources from the former National Dissemination Center for Children with Disabilities (NICHCY). Information on disabilities, links to web sites and national organizations devoted to different disability topics, and research-based educational information are available on this site.
http://www.parentcenterhub.org

Center for Response to Intervention in Early Childhood (CRTIEC)

CRTIEC was developed in order to advance research on early childhood literacy assessment and intervention. The CRTIEC web site includes a resources page with links to various tools to aid in the implementation of response to intervention programs for young children. In addition, current CRTIEC publications and presentations are posted.
http://www.crtiec.org

The Center on Response to Intervention at the American Institutes of Research

The Center on Response to Intervention provides support in the implementation of response to intervention (RTI) programs as a follow-up to the National Center on Response to Intervention (NCRTI), which was funded by the Office of Special Education Programs. This web site describes the components of effective RTI programs, including multilevel prevention systems, universal screening, progress monitoring, and data-based decision making. In addition, webinars, publications, and family resources are available.
http://www.rti4success.org

Equity Alliance

Equity Alliance provides a variety of resources aimed at promoting educational equity for all students. It is focused on closing achievement gaps, inclusive education, and increasing family and community involvement. This web site also includes resources from the former National Center for Culturally Responsive Educational Systems (NCCRESt).
http://www.equityallianceatasu.org

The Florida Center for Reading Research (FCRR)

The FCRR contains a wealth of information on reading for both educators and researchers. Its web site includes resources to enhance instruction, an

---

The authors thank Annmarie Urso, Ph.D., for contributing this resource material to the third edition.

extensive collection of reading activities, and presentations hyperactivity made by FCRR faculty members.
http://www.fcrr.org

Intervention Central

Intervention Central provides a collection of free tools and resources for differentiating instruction, monitoring progress, academic assessment, and behavioral interventions.
http://www.interventioncentral.org

The IRIS Center

The IRIS Center offers a wide variety of instructional and intervention practices that are evidence based and designed specifically for use in college instruction, professional development activities, and independent learning opportunities for educators. Modules, case studies, activities, expert video and audio clips, as well as other web-based tools are offered.
http://iris.peabody.vanderbilt.edu

LD Online

LD Online is a service of the Washington Educational Television Association, a public broadcasting station in Washington, D.C. The site provides comprehensive information on special education services, learning disabilities, and attention-deficit/hyperactivity disorder (ADHD) for parents, teachers, and other professionals.
http://ldonline.org

The Learning Toolbox

This web site, developed by the James Madison University Special Education Program, contains tools and resources to assist secondary and postsecondary students who have learning disabilities and attention-deficit/hyperactivity disorder (ADHD). The web site provides strategies for test taking, studying, taking notes, solving problems, and remembering information. The toolbox has three access areas—one for parents, explaining the strategies children may be using and how to help support them at home; one for teachers, outlining the steps for selecting and teaching the strategies; and last, an area for students, helping them select and learn appropriate strategies.
http://coe.jmu.edu/Learningtoolbox

National Assistive Technology Research Institute (NATRI)

This web site provides a clearinghouse for the latest assistive technology information and resources.
http://natri.uky.edu

National Center for Learning Disabilities (NLCD)

This web site offers information about various types of learning disabilities and resources for both adults with learning disabilities and parents. The parent resources are devoted to such topics as warning signs and evaluation, post–high school transition, and understanding the Individuals with Disabilities Education Act. The school section includes information concerning accommodations, assistive technology, response to intervention, and study skills.
http://www.ncld.org

National Center on Assessment and Accountability for Special Education (NCAASE)

This project is funded by the Institute of Education Sciences of the U.S. Department of Education. The goal of NCAASE is to determine appropriate learning acquisition trajectories for students with disabilities in order to improve intervention, progress monitoring, and accountability. This site provides relevant references, a glossary of related terms, links to tools, technical reports, presentations, and manuscripts.
http://www.ncaase.com

National Center on Intensive Intervention

The National Center on Intensive Intervention is housed at the American Institutes for Research and works in conjunction with many of our nation's most distinguished data-based individualization experts. It is funded by the U.S. Department of Education's Office of Special Education Programs (OSEP) and is part of OSEP's Technical Assistance and Dissemination Network. Online modules, tool charts, implementation reports, and resources provide support to teachers implementing intensive interventions.
http://www.intensiveintervention.org

National Center on Student Progress Monitoring

The National Center on Student Progress Monitoring was funded by the Office of Special Education Programs (OSEP) in order to conduct research and disseminate findings in order to improve the implementation of progress-monitoring systems. The project has now concluded; however, its web site continues to provide access to tools for teachers, information for parents, and a library of resources on progress monitoring.
http://www.studentprogress.org

National Institute for Direct Instruction

The National Institute for Direct Instruction is a nonprofit organization; its web site provides access to research on direct instruction and tools to support its implementation.
http://www.nifdi.org

Office of Special Education Programs (OSEP) Ideas that Work

This web site is designed to provide easy access to information from research to practice initiatives funded by the Office of Special Education Programs (OSEP) that address the provisions of the Individuals with Disabilities Education Act 2004 (PL 108-446) and the No Child Left Behind Act of 2001 (PL 107-110). This web site includes resources, links, and other important information that supports OSEP's research to practice efforts.
https://www.osepideasthatwork.org

Public Broadcasting Service (PBS) LearningMedia

PBS LearningMedia is your destination for direct access to thousands of classroom-ready, curriculum-targeted digital resources. PBS LearningMedia provides free access to public media resources and is designed to improve teacher effectiveness and student achievement. Resources are aligned to the Common Core State Standards and national standards and include videos and interactives, as well as audio, documents, and in-depth lesson plans. You can browse by standards, grade level, subject area, and special collections. You can also identify and share resources with your class and colleagues through folders and social media. PBS LearningMedia's basic service is free for pre-K–12 educators and teaching faculty.
http://www.pbslearningmedia.org

Read, Write, Think

ReadWriteThink is a partnership between the International Reading Association (IRA), the National Council of Teachers of English (NCTE), and Verizon Thinkfinity. The web site provides access to materials that promote professional development as well as to instructional resources in reading and language. Lesson plans, standards, web resources, and supplemental student materials are available for download.
http://www.readwritethink.org

Special Education Resources on the Internet (SERI)

SERI is a library of resources related to special education. It includes links to resources on various disabilities, special education law, health, and transition.
http://seriweb.com

TeachingLD

This web site is provided by the Division for Learning Disabilities of the Council for Exceptional Children, which is the largest international professional organization focused on learning disabilities and giftedness. The site features current practice alerts and information about related organizations.
http://www.teachingld.org

The Technical Assistance Center on Positive Behavioral Interventions and Supports

The Technical Assistance Center on Positive Behavioral Interventions and Supports is established by the U.S. Department of Education's Office of Special Education Programs (OSEP) to define, develop, implement, and evaluate a multitiered approach to technical assistance that improves the capacity of states, districts, and schools to establish, scale up, and sustain the positive behavioral interventions and supports (PBIS) framework. Emphasis is given to the impact of implementing PBIS on the social, emotional, and academic outcomes for students with disabilities. The site contains training materials, modules, resources, and digital media supports. Many resources are available in French and Spanish.
http://www.pbis.org

The Technical Assistance Center on Social Emotional Intervention (TACSEI) for Young Children

TACSEI provides evidence-based tools, resources, interventions, and modules for training teachers and others on how to support and respond to the needs of young children with social and emotional behavior disorders.
http://challengingbehavior.fmhi.usf.edu/index.htm

Understood.org

This web site provides numerous resources and materials for parents who wish to gain a deeper understanding of their child's learning and behavioral challenges. Materials can be accessed in either English or Spanish. A parent toolkit provides practical ideas for students with social, emotional, and behavioral challenges.

Vaughn Gross Center for Reading and Language Arts, University of Texas at Austin

This web site has a materials download section with free booklets, videos, and professional development guides appropriate for pre-K–secondary schools as well as English language learner (ELL), English as a

second language (ESL), and special education. The web site also highlights research being conducted at the center.
http://www.meadowscenter.org/vgc

What Works Clearinghouse

What Works Clearinghouse was established in 2002 by the U.S. Department of Education's Institute of Education Sciences to provide educators, policy makers, researchers, and the public with a central source for evidence-based practices in education.
http://www.whatworks.ed.gov

PROFESSIONAL ASSOCIATIONS/ORGANIZATIONS

Council for Exceptional Children (CEC)

The CEC is a major international professional association focused on enhancing educational outcomes for students participating in special and/or gifted educational programs. The CEC aims to provide support to educators through its influence on government policy, professional guidelines, and opportunities for professional development. The CEC offers professional journals, online seminars, and networking groups.
http://www.cec.sped.org

International Dyslexia Association (IDA)

IDA supports achievement for students with reading disabilities through disseminating research, providing information on effective interventions, and offering access to a variety of resources and professional development opportunities.
http://www.interdys.org

Learning Disabilities Association of America (LDA)

LDA provides support to individuals with learning disabilities in order to promote success in both school and the community. This web site has information for adults, parents, teachers, and other professionals. LDA provides resources about educational law and advocacy as well as access to current research.
http://www.ldaamerica.org

Learning Disabilities Worldwide (LDW)

LDW is an organization that aims to support individuals with learning disabilities in achieving success both inside and outside of the classroom. This international web site contains separate pages of resources; tips for success; and support for children, adolescents, young adults, and adults with learning disabilities. It also includes resources for educators, researchers, clinicians, and parents.
http://www.ldworldwide.org

National Association of School Psychologists (NASP)

NASP is a professional organization for school psychologists and related professionals that aims to support actions and activities that seek to positively influence outcomes directly affecting the lives of the students, their families, and the schools the psychologists serve. The site provides a plethora of free resources, recommended practices, strategies for intervention, and support for a range of social, emotional, behavioral, and mental health issues.
http://www.nasponline.org

Index

Note: The letters *f* and *t* indicate that the entry refers to a page's figure or table, respectively.

ABC Reading Magic Series, 453, 454
Ability–achievement discrepancy model, 211–214, 216–217
   as a diagnostic tool, 214, 217
   problems with, 212
   response to intervention (RTI) versus, 216
   strengths of, 214
   over successive grade levels, 213–214
   validity of, 212–213
Academic performance
   academic language proficiency, 355, 357–358, 360
   Building Blocks of Learning model and, 49, 50*t*–51*t*, 52*f*
   effect of stimulants on, 103
   improving, 443–444
   linguistic and neuropsychological functions underlying, 215–216, 218
   math skills for, 49, 51*t*, 52*f*
   metacognition and, 377
   rapid automatized naming (RAN) as predictor of, 249–250
   reading fluency and, 49, 50*t*, 52*f*
   rote memorization and, 15, 35, 35*t*, 36*t*, 464, 473
   spelling development and, 49, 50*t*, 52*f*
   see also Background knowledge; Common Core State Standards (CCSS)
Access to Math, 444
Accommodations, 253–254, 387–389
   ability–achievement discrepancy in determining, 214
   assignments, 254
   classroom coaches, 388
   classwork adjustments, 396
   copying, 253
   difficulty level, 388
   fairness of, 191–193
   feedback and, 389
   homework adjustments, 396, 397
   individualized education program (IEP), 199, 321–322, 389
   Instructional Accommodations Survey, 396–399
   math instruction adjustments, 397
   opportunities for improvement, 388–389
   physical classroom arrangements, 65, 389
   seating adjustments, 398
   Section 504 of the Rehabilitation Act Amendments of 1992 (PL 102-569), 94, 95*f*–97*f*
   test-taking adjustments, 198
   time and practice, 388
   timed tests, 254–254
   transitions, 65
   visual-motor skill developmental disorders and, 247
   worksheets, 118–120, 397
   writing instruction adjustments, 397
   see also Instructional Accommodations Survey; Specific learning disabilities (SLD)
ACE strategy, 392
Achenbach Child Behavior Checklist (CBCL), 162*f*
ACTION program, 168
Act-it-out strategy, 433
Active learning, 378
Acute stress disorder, 158, 178
Adaptive functioning, 162*t*
Add-a-word spelling program, 280–281
Adderall (dextroamphetamine sulfate), 102–103
Addition the Fun Way cards, 321, 522
ADHD, *see* Attention-deficit/hyperactivity disorder
Adjustment disorders, 158, 178–179
Adolescence
   attention-deficit/hyperactivity disorder (ADHD) in, 100, 107
   cognitive behavior therapy (CBT) and, 167–169
   functional impairments among, 156
   internalizing disorders and, 156–157, 167–168, 171–175
   oppositional behaviors and, 125–127, 128*t*, 146
   resilience among, 189, 195, 198
   suicide risk and, 157
Adulthood
   attention-deficit/hyperactivity disorder (ADHD) in, 83, 100–101
   reading fluency difficulties into, 237
   spelling difficulties in, 235–236, 238*f*, 279
   transition to, 468
   unipolar depression in, 174
Affricates, 266, 267, 268*t*
Age, *see* Adolescence; Adulthood; Students
Aggressive behaviors, 33, 123–126, 185–186
   attention-deficit/hyperactivity disorder (ADHD), 84*t*, 98–99
   internalizing disorders and, 157–158, 174
   modeling behaviors and, 128*t*
   peers and, 123, 126, 132–133
   systematic direct observations (SDOs) and, 135*f*
   see also Behavior modification; Challenging behaviors
Agoraphobia, 173
Algebra, 430, 437
   apps for learning, 440, 445*t*
   effective instruction techniques in, 442–443
   see also Math instruction; Math knowledge
Alphabetic Phonics, 513
Alveolar sounds, 266, 266*t*, 267*t*
American Institutes of Research, 523, 524
Analogy strategy, 295–296, 296*f*
Analytic phonics, 295–299
Anki flashcard program, 301–302, 400
Antecedent manipulation, 69, 111
Anxiety disorders, 10, 156, 171–173
   agoraphobia, 173
   Diagnostic and Statistical Manual of Mental Disorders, Fifth Edition (DSM-5) diagnostic criteria for, 156
   due to medical condition, 173
   educator strategies for coping with student's, 163, 164*t*
   formal assessment of, 162*f*
   generalized anxiety disorder, 173
   normative fear versus, 156
   panic disorder, 172
   selective mutism, 171–172
   separation anxiety disorder, 171, 178
   social anxiety disorder, 167–168, 172
   specific phobias, 172, 173
   substance/medication-induced anxiety disorder, 173

Anxiety disorders—*continued*
see also Cognitive behavioral therapy (CBT); Emotions block; Internalizing disorders
Aphasia, 208, 232
Apps
dictionaries, 452
for executive functions (EFs), 399–400
handwriting, 453–455
high-frequency words, 455
interactive books, 458–459
language and text structure, 458
language comprehension, 457–459
letter identification, 453–455
for literacy instruction, 451–459
spelling, 455–457
spelling-sound correspondences, 453–455
utility/presentation, 451–452
vocabulary, 457
web sites with reviews of tablet, 460
word games, 456–457
word recognition skills, 452–453
see also Technology
Aptitude–achievement discrepancy model, see Ability–achievement discrepancy model
Asperger syndrome, 369
Assessments
anxiety disorders, 162*f*
attention-deficit/hyperactivity disorder (ADHD) with, 101, 102*f*
Building Blocks Questionnaire, 21–28
depressive disorders, 162*f*
Emotions block, 159–162, 162*f*
English language learners (ELLs) with, 355
formal, 61, 159–160, 162, 162*f*
informal, 160–162, 224–226, 228, 235–236, 236*t*
learning environments, 63, 126
math skills, 318–319
orthographic dyslexia, 235–236, 236*t*
phonological awareness, 224–226
Phonological block, 224–227, 224–227
reading fluency progress, 308
specific learning disabilities (SLD) with, 48–49
spelling development and, 228, 277–285
vocabulary knowledge, 365
see also Building Blocks Questionnaire; Classroom observations; Curriculum-based measures (CBM); Feedback; Instructional Accommodations Survey
Assistive technology, 218, 521, 524
Associative memory, see Rote memory
Atomoxetine (Strattera), 103
ATS, see Attention Training System
Attention Training System (ATS), 151
Attentional control, 8–9, 38, 40, 238
Attention–arousal system, 44–45
Attention-deficit/hyperactivity disorder (ADHD), 5, 33, 81–121
adapting the curriculum, 119–120
in adulthood, 83, 100–101
age of diagnosis for, 98
behavior management strategies, 111
behavior problems, 100–101
biology and environment, 86
building success, 116–117
causes of, 94–97
characteristics of, 82–94, 106*t*
classroom adjustments for, 94
classroom model for managing, 109, 109*f*, 104–112
as a cluster of symptomatic problems, 87–89
color coding, 120
cues, 113–114, 114*t*
definition of, 92
development course and comorbidity, 98–101
diagnostic criteria, 90–94
Building Blocks Questionnaire and, 101, 102*f*
Diagnostic and Statistical Manual of Mental Disorders, Fifth Edition (DSM-5) criteria for, 82, 88, 90–91
early symptoms of, 98
emotional regulation, 93–94
feedback, 92–94, 113, 116, 118
flagging attention, 107
gender and, 81–82, 87, 102
general guidelines when working with students with, 118
genetics and, 88, 94, 97
as a "hidden" disability, 192
hyperactivity, 93
impulsivity and planning, 92
inattention, 92–93
incidence of, 86–87
interactive issues, 118–120
interventions, 102, 109–110
keeping things changing, 116
key goals for children with, 107
language disorders, 98
learning disabilities, 98–99
legal protections, 94, 95*f*–97*f*
major misconceptions about, 91
medications, 102–104
dopamine and, 104
effects of, 103–104
neurotransmitters, 104
Ritalin, 83, 91, 102–104, 105*f*
stimulant use and, 102–104, 151
need for brevity, 107
nondisruptive movement, 116
other impairments
antisocial personality disorder and, 100
disorders that seem like, 87–88
language-based learning or reading disability, 98–99
nonverbal learning disability (NVLD) versus, 369
oppositional and conduct disorders and, 126
risk of developing internalizing disorders, 100
pairing undesirable tasks with desirable ones, 116
peer tutoring, 111
pervasive impairments and, 89
planning facilitation, 111–112, 112*f*
poor working memory and, 106*t*
preparing for changes, 117
preventive strategies, 117
as a problem of faulty performance, 89
problems modulating gratification, 93
processing speed and, 252–253
reasons for increased diagnoses of, 86
remedial strategies, 106*t*
routines, 115
school problems, 82–83
Section 504 of the Rehabilitation Act Amendments of 1992 (PL 102-569), 94, 95*f*–97*f*
self-monitoring program, 113, 114*t*, 115*f*
social difficulties, 99–100
structure and transitions, 114–115
student performance and, 83, 83*t*–84*t*
subtypes of, 90–91
teacher's role in evaluating, 83, 83*t*–84*t*, 101–102, 102*f*
teacher–student interactions, 108–109, 112–113, 108*f*
traditional disease model and, 89
using class time effectively, 117–118
variety and, 107
working memory problems in students with, 88, 92, 106*t*, 252
worksheet adjustments for students with, 118–120
see also Behavior modification; Challenging behaviors; Oppositional and conduct disorders; Specific learning disabilities (SLD)
Attribution theory, 187–189, 200–202
Auditory processing (Ga) ability, 36*t*, 47, 47*t*, 218, 249–250
Automatization, see Efficiency/automaticity block; Rapid automatized naming (RAN)
AWARE method, 382, 382*t*

Background knowledge, 41, 60
collaborative strategic reading (CSR) and, 413
language development and, 362
math knowledge and, 429
reciprocal teaching and, 412
self-regulated strategy development, 380
statement pie writing strategy and, 426
vocabulary knowledge and, 223, 360, 362
Basal ganglia, 97
BASC-2, see *Behavior Assessment System for Children, Second Edition*
Basic Interpersonal Communication Skills (BICS), 357
Beck Youth Inventories, 162*f*
Behavior Assessment System for Children, Second Edition (BASC-2), 101–102, 162*f*

Index

Behavior block, 9–10, 33–34
    Building Blocks Questionnaire and, 18*f*, 21, 23, 123, 124*f*
    see also Attention-deficit/hyperactivity disorder (ADHD); Behavior modification; Challenging behaviors; Foundational blocks; Oppositional and conduct disorders
Behavior logs, 159–161, 161*f*, 163, 383
Behavior modification, 134–153
    behavior management versus, 152
    behavior planning with parents, 133–134
    classroom observations, 134–137
    Direct Behavior Ratings (DBRs) form, 137, 138*f*
    effective preventive disciplinary approaches, 132
    examples of schedules, 137–139
    extinction, 139*t*
    on-task behaviors, 136
    Premack principle, 110
    punishment, 148–153, 139*t*
    reinforcement, 137–148
    see also Challenging behaviors; Classroom observations; Punishment; Reinforcement
Benchmark Phonetic Connections, 513
BICS, *see* Basic Interpersonal Communication Skills
BID, *see* Briefing, interaction, and debriefing
Bilabial sounds, 265, 266*t*, 267*t*
Brain anatomy
    attention–arousal system, 44–45
    basal ganglia, 97
    cerebellum, 97
    functional magnetic resonance imaging (fMRI), 37
    occipitoparietal regions, 37
    prefrontal cortex, 43, 45–46, 97
    "right-brained," 42
    temporoparietal cortex, 37
    see also Theories of intelligence
Brainstorming, 418–419, 374–376, 376*f*, 418–419
Briefing, interaction, and debriefing (BID), 359
Building Blocks of Learning, 7–9, 8*f*
    academic performance and, 49, 50*t*–51*t*, 52*f*
    Building Blocks Questionnaire, 16–17, 18*f*, 21–28, 102*f*
    Cattell-Horn-Carroll (CHC) theory, 46–49, 47*t*
    common children's profiles, 15–17
    Conceptual blocks, 13–14, 18*f*, 27–28
        Executive Functions (EF) block, 14, 18*f*, 21, 28, 362, 362*f*
        Nonverbal block, 13, 18*f*, 21, 27, 369–370
        Verbal block, 13, 18*f*, 21, 27, 253, 253*f*
    corresponding academic skills in, 52*f*
    Foundational blocks, 9–10, 18*f*, 21–24
        Behavior block, 9–10, 18*f*, 21, 23, 33–34, 123, 124*f*
        Emotions block, 10, 18*f*, 21, 23, 34, 159, 160*f*
        Resilience block, 10, 18*f*, 21, 24, 34, 185, 186*f*
        Self-Regulation block, 9, 18*f*, 21, 22, 33, 101, 102*f*
    how the blocks work together, 14
    intent of, 7
    learning environment, 9, 31–32
    overlap among, 8–9
    Planning, Attention, Simultaneous, Successive (PASS) theory, 44–46, 46*t*
    Processing blocks, 10–13, 18*f*, 24–26
        Memory block, 12, 18*f*, 21, 25, 38, 241, 242*f*
        Motor block, 12, 18*f*, 21, 26, 38, 243–244, 244*f*
        Orthographic block, 12, 18*f*, 21, 25, 37–38, 231, 232*f*
        Phonological block, 11–12, 18*f*, 21, 24, 37–38, 220, 220*f*
    theoretical foundations, 31–52
    theories of intelligence and, 44–49, 46*t*, 47*t*
    see also Building Blocks Questionnaire; Conceptual blocks; Foundational blocks; Learning environment; Processing blocks
Building Blocks Questionnaire, 21–28
    assessments
        attention-deficit/hyperactivity disorder (ADHD), 101, 102*f*
        English language learners (ELLs), 355
        specific learning disabilities (SLD), 48–49
    completing the, 16–17, 18*f*
    Conceptual blocks, 18*f*, 21, 26–28
        Executive Functions (EF) block, 18*f*, 21, 28, 362, 362*f*
        Nonverbal block, 18*f*, 21, 27, 369–370
        Verbal block, 18*f*, 21, 27, 253, 253*f*
    Foundational blocks on the, 18*f*, 21, 22–24
        Behavior block, 18*f*, 21, 23, 123, 124*f*
        Emotions block, 18*f*, 21, 23, 159, 160*f*
        Environment, 18*f*, 21, 22
        Resilience block, 18*f*, 21, 24, 185, 186*f*
        Self-Regulation block, 18*f*, 21, 22, 101, 102*f*
    Processing blocks on the, 18*f*, 21, 24–26
        Efficiency/Automaticity block, 18*f*, 21, 26, 248, 249*f*
        Memory block, 18*f*, 21, 25, 241, 242*f*
        Motor block, 18*f*, 21, 26, 243–244, 244*f*
        Orthographic block, 18*f*, 21, 25, 231, 232*f*
        Phonological block, 18*f*, 21, 24, 220, 220*f*
    see also Accommodations; Assessments; Building Blocks of Learning; Instructional Accommodations Survey
Bullying, 186, 189

Calculating, *see* Dyscalculia; Math instruction; Math knowledge; Math problem solving
CALP, *see* Cognitive Academic Language Proficiency
Carbo Method, 314
CAS-2, *see* Cognitive Assessment System 2
CASEL, *see* Collaborative for Academic, Social, and Emotional Learning
Catapres-TTS (clonidine), 103
Cattell-Horn-Carroll (CHC) theory of intelligence, 46–49, 47*t*
    auditory processing (Ga) ability, 36*t*, 47, 47*t*, 218, 249–250
    comprehension–knowledge (Gc) ability, 47, 47*t*
    fluid reasoning (Gf) ability, 47, 47*t*
    long-term retrieval (Glr) ability, 47, 47*t*
    processing speed (Gs), 47, 252
    visual-spatial thinking (Gv), 42, 47–48, 47*t*
CBCL, *see Achenbach Child Behavior Checklist*
CBITS, *see* Cognitive Behavioral Intervention for Trauma in Schools
CBT, *see* Cognitive-behavioral therapy
CCSS, *see* Common Core State Standards
CDC, *see* Centers for Disease Control and Prevention
CDI 2, *see Children's Depression Inventory 2*
CEC, *see* Council for Exceptional Children
Center for Applied Technology (CAST), 523
Center for Improving Learning of Fractions (CILF), 523
Center for Parent Information and Resources (CPIR), 523
Center for Response to Intervention in Early Childhood (CRTIEC), 523
Centers for Disease Control and Prevention (CDC), 86–87
Cerebellum, 97
Challenging behaviors, 123–153
    addressing classroom conflicts, 131–133
    behavior logs, 159–161, 161*f*, 163, 383
    Building Block Questionnaire, 123, 124*f*
    building parent partnerships, 133–134
    characteristics of, 155–159
    classroom expectations, 128–129, 129*f*
    common features of models and techniques to manage, 127
    cooling-off periods, 133
    cooperative time-outs, 133
    developing a hierarchy of the desirable behaviors, 142
    differential attention (ignoring), 145–146
    dimensions of, 123–124
    escalating pattern of noncompliance, 69
    externalizing disorders, 9, 162*t*

Challenging behaviors—*continued*
   factors shaping student response to modeling, 146–148
   impulsivity, 82
   mediation, 133
   nature versus nurture, 126
   oppositional and conduct disorders, 123–126
   passive-aggressive behavior, 186
   preventative approaches, 127*t*, 128–134
   proactive classroom management strategies, 130–131, 130*t*
   reflective listening, 133
   ripple effect in, 147
   role-playing or role reversal, 133
   sample behavior log
   self-defeating behaviors, 185–187
   self-regulation, 128*t*
   setting time-related goals, 139
   steps for effective shaping, 147–148
   student ownership of actions and sense of fairness, 196
   "think time," 149–150
   see also Attention-deficit/hyperactivity disorder (ADHD); Anxiety disorders; Behavior modification; Depressive disorders; Trauma and stress disorders
CHC, *see* Cattell-Horn-Carroll (CHC) theory
Cheating, 186
Child PTSD Symptom Scale (CPSS), 162*f*
Children's Depression Inventory 2 (CDI 2), 162*f*
Children's Mathematics/Cognitively Guided Instruction, 522
Choral or concert reading, 311–312
Choral responding, 65
Classroom activities
   choral responding, 65
   to improve grapheme–phoneme awareness, 288–289, 291–293, 300–301
   for increasing reading rate, 310–315
   promoting phonological awareness, 226
   see also Instructional strategies; Interventions; Mnemonics
Classroom adjustments and accommodations, *see* Accommodations
Classroom environments, 62–66
   addressing classroom conflicts, 131–133
   class meetings, 132–133
   classroom as central learning environment, 32
   classroom expectations, 128–129, 129*f*
   classrooms of the future, 473
   inclusive, 63–64, 184, 523
   key factors, 62
   as a microcosm of the world, 463–473
   most effective seats for listening, 389
   out-of-classroom services, 63–64
   physical arrangement of the classroom, 32, 62–63
   proactive strategies to manage challenging behaviors, 130–131, 130*t*
   process to assess, 63
   questions to consider about, 56*t*
   student and classroom variables, 62
   student engagement, 62–66, 140
   transitions, 64–65
   what students need from teachers, 469–471
   what teachers want from students, 468–469
   see also Learning environment; School environments
Classroom observations, 134–137
   behavior logs, 159–161, 161*f*, 163, 383
   peer comparison observation method, 136–137, 136*f*
   response discrepancy observation method, 136*f*
   systematic direct observations (SDOs), 134–136, 135*f*
   see also Behavior modification; Challenging behaviors
Clickers, 65, 452
Clonidine (Catapres-TTS), 103
Clowning and regressing, 186
CLS, *see* Correct letter sequences
Cognitive Academic Language Proficiency (CALP), 357
Cognitive Assessment System 2 (CAS-2), 43, 46
Cognitive Behavioral Intervention for Trauma in Schools (CBITS), 169–170
Cognitive Strategy in Writing (CSIW) program, 423–424
   evidence-based strategies in, 167
   FRIENDS program, 168
   trauma-focused cognitive-behavioral therapy (TF-CBT), 169–170
   see also Behavior modification; Challenging behaviors; Self-monitoring programs
Cognitive-behavioral therapy (CBT), 167–170
Collaborative strategic reading (CSR), 412–414
Collaborative for Academic, Social, and Emotional Learning (CASEL), 166
Color coding, 117, 120, 288, 295, 385, 414
Common Core State Standards (CCSS), 59–60, 182, 351, 403, 525
   English language arts/literacy (ELA) standards, 59, 403
   evidence-based strategies, 59–60
   mathematics standards, 59, 418–419, 430–431
   school environments and, 59–60
Common underlying proficiency (CUP), 357–358
Comorbidity, 98–101, 158–159, 174
   attention-deficit/hyperactivity disorder (ADHD), 98–101
   learning disabilities (LD) and, 126
   math and reading disabilities, 428
   oppositional and conduct disorders, 100–101, 125–126, 174
Compositional fluency, *see* Handwriting; Written expression, 340
Compound word deletion, 225
Comprehension–knowledge (Gc) ability, 47, 47*t*
Comprehensive Executive Functioning Inventory, 43
Concept Phonics program, 310, 513
Conceptual blocks, 13–14
   Building Blocks Questionnaire and, 18*f*, 21, 26–28
   Executive Functions (EF) block, 14, 18*f*, 21, 28, 362, 362*f*
   Nonverbal block, 13, 18*f*, 21, 27, 369–370
   rationale for, 34–35, 35*t*, 36*t*, 38–44
   Verbal block, 13, 18*f*, 21, 27, 253, 253*f*
   see also Executive Functions (EF) block; Nonverbal block; Verbal block
Concrete-representation-abstract (CRA) teaching sequence, 433, 435, 443–444
Concrete-semiconcrete-abstract (CSA) teaching sequence, 433, 435
Conduct disorder, 9, 33, 125–127
   comorbidity with attention-deficit/hyperactivity disorder (ADHD), 100–101, 174
   parenting behaviors and, 127
   prevalence of, 81–82, 125–126
   see also Attention-deficit/hyperactivity disorder (ADHD); Behavior modification; Challenging behaviors
Connecting Math Concepts, 522
Conners' Rating Scales, Third Edition, 101–102
Consonants, 264–268
   affricates, 266, 267, 268*t*
   classification of, 265
   fricatives, 266, 267, 267*t*
   glides, 266, 267, 268*t*
   liquids, 266, 268, 268*t*
   manner of articulation, 266
   nasals, 266, 267*t*
   place of articulation, 265–266
   sibilants, 267
   stops, 266, 266*t*, 267
   trigraphs. 265
   voicing, 265, 265*t*
Consonant-vowel-consonant (CVC) words, 452–453, 454
Continuous schedules of reinforcement (CRF), 138–139
Correct letter sequences (CLS), 282–283
Corrective Reading, 513
Coteaching, 275
Council for Exceptional Children (CEC), 525, 526
Cover–write methods, 305, 335
CPSS, *see* *Child PTSD Symptom Scale*
CRA, *see* Concrete-representation-abstract (CRA) teaching sequence

Index

CRF, *see* Continuous schedules of reinforcement
Critical thinking, 58*t*, 368, 416
CSA, *see* Concrete-semiconcrete-abstract (CSA) teaching sequence
CSIW, *see* Cognitive Strategy in Writing (CSIW) program
C-SPACE mnemonic, 409–410
CSR, *see* Collaborative strategic reading
Cue cards, 380, 406, 406*f*, 408, 438
Cultural and linguistic diversity, 57, 58*t*, 60, 66, 69–71, 468
  see also English language learners (ELLs)
CUP, *see* Common underlying proficiency
Curriculum-based measures (CBM)
  for math, 318–319
  for reading, 308–309
  response to intervention (RTI) and, 215
  for spelling, 282
  web sites with supplementary materials, 309
Cursive writing
  apps for, 453–456
  Building Blocks Questionnaire and, 26, 243–244, 244*f*
  choosing a writing style, 329–330, 331*f*, 332*f*, 334*f*
  Fernald Method and, 304–305
  levels of processing related to learning disabilities (LD), 36*t*
  preferred hand and, 326–327
  preventing letter reversals with, 330
  self-guided symbol formation strategy, 336–340, 338*f*
  see also Handwriting; Letter formation
CVS, *see* Consonant-vowel-consonant (CVC) words
Cylert (pemoline), 102–103

Daily planner schedules, 117, 383–386
DBRs, *see* Direct Behavior Ratings
Declarative knowledge, 369, 430, 444
Decoding, 222, 230, 273–279
  as an academic skill in relation to the Building Blocks model, 52*f*
  central goal of instruction, 276
  Ehri's phase theory for, 276–277
  encoding and, 275*f*
  language systems of phonology, orthography, and morphology in, 274
  skill development in, 275–276
  see also Encoding; Phonics; Phonological awareness to print; Reading comprehension; Speech sounds; Verbal block; Written expression
Dental sounds, 267*t*
Depressive disorders, 10, 156–157, 174–176
  Diagnostic and Statistical Manual of Mental Disorders, Fifth Edition (*DSM-5*) diagnostic criteria for, 156, 174–175

differences among specific, 156–157
disruptive mood dysregulation disorder, 174
educator strategies for coping with student's, 163, 164*t*
formal assessment of, 162*f*
major depressive disorder, 157, 174–175
due to medical condition, 157, 176
mood dysregulation disorder, 157
persistent depressive disorder (dysthymia), 157, 175
premenstrual dysphoric disorder, 157, 175
substance/medication-induced depressive disorder, 157, 176
unipolar depression in adolescence and adulthood, 174
  see also Cognitive behavioral therapy (CBT); Emotions block; Internalizing disorders
Desipramine hydrochloride (Norpramin), 102–103
Desoxyn (methamphetamine hydrochloride), 102–103
Destination Math series, 444
Developmental disorders, *see* Specific learning disabilities (SLD)
Developmental dyslexia, *see* Dyslexia; Specific learning disabilities (SLD)
Developmental motor coordination disorder, 242
Dextroamphetamine sulfate (Adderall), 102–103
Diagnostic and Statistical Manual of Mental Disorders, Fifth Edition (*DSM-5*)
  attention-deficit/hyperactivity disorder (ADHD) diagnostic criteria, 82, 88, 90–91
  anxiety-related disorders diagnostic criteria, 156
  depressive disorders diagnostic criteria, 156, 174–175
  trauma and stress-related disorders diagnostic criteria, 158, 177–179
Diagnostic and Statistical Manual of Mental Disorders, Fourth Edition, Text Revision (*DSM-IV-TR*), 91
Dictionaries, 302
  as an accommodation, 396
  apps, 452
  e-books with dictionary support, 364
  electronic, 396
  glossaries versus, 367
  limits of, 367, 421
  online graphical, 373
  personalized, 302
Differential attention (ignoring), 145–146
Digraphs, 269
Diphthongs, 267–267, 289, 294–295
Direct Behavior Ratings (DBRs), 137, 138*f*
Disinhibited social engagement disorder, 158, 179
Disruptive behaviors, *see* Challenging behaviors

Diversity, *see* Cultural and linguistic diversity
Division for Learning Disabilities of the Council for Exceptional Children, 525
D'Nealian script, 330–334, 331*f*, 332*f*, 336, 456
Doors to Discovery, 513
Double-deficit hypothesis, 39–40
Dr. Seuss Series Interactive Books, 459
Dragon Naturally Speaking, 340, 521
Drills, 310, 317
Dry-erase boards, 383
DSM-5, *see Diagnostic and Statistical Manual of Mental Disorders, Fifth Edition*
DSM-IV-TR, *see Diagnostic and Statistical Manual of Mental Disorders, Fourth Edition, Text Revision*
Dyscalculia, 15, 35
  Building Blocks of Learning model and, 319
  incidence of, 428
  individualized oral math interview, 430
  instructional strategies for, 431–433, 436
  subtypes of developmental, 40–41
  universal behavior characteristics of, 319
  working memory and, 35, 315, 428–429
Dyseidetic reading impairments, 39, 231–232
Dysgraphia, 340
  Building Blocks of Learning model and, 12, 15–16
  handwriting rate and, 245, 247*f*
  voice recognition software (VRS) and, 340
  see also Handwriting; Letter formation
Dyslexia, 11
  definitions and terminology, 222–223, 232
  International Dyslexia Association (IDA), 42, 222–223, 526
  logographic, 232
  L-type, 231–232
  orthographic, 228, 231–236
  other speed-related impairments, 252
  phonological, 221–223
  problems processing symbolic information in, 252
  processing speed and, 252–253
  P-type, 223
  rate-disabled, 232
  small-group instruction and, 274
  surface, 39, 232
  timed tests, 253–254
  visual, 231–232
  see also Orthographic dyslexia; Phonological dyslexia
Dysphonetic reading impairments, 39, 223
Dysthymia (persistent depressive disorder), 157, 175

531

Early intervention, *see* Response to intervention (RTI)
Early Intervention in Reading (EIR), 513
Earobics Literacy Launch, 513
Easy Lessons for Teaching Word Families, 513
E-books, 292, 364, 411
Edmark Reading Program, 513
Education for All Handicapped Children Act of 1975 (PL 94-142), 208, 209t, 212
Educators, *see* Effective educators
Effective educators
 activities of, 470
 attribution theory, 187–189, 200–202
 as "authentic teachers," 470
 changing role of education, 468
 core foundational teaching strategies, 378, 379t
 essential guidelines, 471–472
 fostering self-esteem, 190–202
 helping students overcome challenges, 472
 instructional principles for effective early instruction among diverse learners, 66
 instructional stages help students master task-specific strategies, 380
 internal attributional style of, 61
 islands of competence, 189–190
 mind-sets of, 182–190
 professional development, 55, 57–60, 58t, 62, 524–426
 resilience in students, 184, 190–202
 understanding students' basic needs, 188–189
 see also Learning environments; Teacher–student interactions
Efficiency/automaticity block, 13, 18f, 21, 26, 248–253
 Building Blocks Questionnaire and, 18f, 21, 26, 248, 249f
 Cattell-Horn Carroll (CHC) theory and, 47–48, 47t
 processing speed, 252–253
 rapid automatized naming (RAN), 13, 39–40, 248–252
 see also Processing blocks; Rapid automatized naming (RAN)
Ehri's phase theory for decoding, 276–277
EIR, *see* Early Intervention in Reading
ELA, *see* English language arts/literacy (ELA) standards
Elkonin procedure, 287–288
ELLs, *see* English language learners
Emotions block, 10, 34, 123–153
 assessment of, 159–162, 162f
 Building Blocks Questionnaire and, 18f, 21, 23, 159, 160f
 cognitive-behavioral therapy (CBT), 167–168
 management and intervention, 162–170, 165f–166f
 multi-tiered systems of support, 163–167

oppositional and conduct disorders and, 126
 progressive muscle relaxation (PMR), 163, 165f–166f
 referrals for care, 101
 reinforced practice and participant modeling, 168–169
 theory of observational learning, 168–169
 trauma-focused cognitive-behavioral therapy (TF-CBT), 169–170
 see also Anxiety disorders; Behavior modification; Challenging behaviors; Depressive disorders; Foundational blocks; Trauma and stress-related disorders
Encephalitis, 97, 208
Encoding, 41, 273–279, 311, 354–355
 as an academic skill in relation to the Building Blocks model, 52f
 central goal of instruction, 276
 decoding and, 275f
 Ehri's phase theory for, 276–277
 language systems of phonology, orthography, and morphology in, 274
 skill development in, 275–276
 spelling development and assessment, 277–285
 stage theories and the strategy approach for spelling, 277–279
 see also Decoding; Handwriting; Phonics; Phonological awareness to print; Speech sounds; Spelling development; Verbal block; Written expression
English as a second language (ESL), *see* English language learners (ELLs)
English language arts/literacy (ELA) standards, 59, 403
English language learners (ELLs)
 academic language proficiency and, 357
 allophonic variations of phonemes, 356–357
 Building Blocks Questionnaire and, 355
 embarrassment about parents, 359–360
 encouraging continued development of the first language, 358
 evidence-based strategies, 355–356, 359–360
 gap in reading scores, 355
 interpreters and, 359
 literacy instruction for, 355–361
 misconceptions about relationship between first and second languages among, 357–358
 native languages most commonly spoken by, 355
 native Spanish speakers, 356–357
 new phonemes for, 356–357
 poverty among, 359
 predicting school success for, 360
 pull-out services, 6
 reading comprehension among, 357

reclassified as fluent English proficient (FEP), 355
 stages of second language acquisition, 357
 unique challenges for families of, 359
 vocabulary instruction for, 364–365
Environment, *see* Learning environment
EPS Phonics Plus Readers, 514
Equity Alliance, 523
"Equivalent index," 283
ESL (English as a second language), *see* English language learners (ELLs)
Essay writing, 426–428
 Dinosaur for essay structure, 428, 429f
 Kerrigan's method for, 426–428
 paragraphs, 425–426
 research, 428
 statement pie writing strategy, 425–426
 steps for theme organization and composition writing, 426–428
 in tests, 352, 387, 393–394, 417, 425
 see also Written expression
EverClip 2, 399
Evidence-based strategies
 Common Core State Standards (CCSS), 59–60
 core components of, 66–68
 for English language learners (ELLs), 355–356, 360
 for math instruction, 316–317
 response to intervention (RTI), pattern of strength and weaknesses (PSW) approach, and, 218–219
 school environments, 56–57
 in tiered cognitive behavioral therapy (CBT), 167
 What Works Clearinghouse, 526
Executive Functions (EF) block, 14, 377–390
 apps for, 399–400
 Building Blocks Questionnaire and, 18f, 21, 28, 362, 362f
 Cattell-Horn Carroll (CHC) theory and, 47–48, 47t
 explicit instruction in specific cognitive strategies, 377–378
 measures of, 88
 Planning, Attention, Simultaneous, Successive (PASS) theory and, 44–46, 46t
 strategy instruction, 378–381
 test-taking strategies, 386–387
 time management and organizational strategies, 383–386
 verbal abilities and, 43
 see also Conceptual blocks; Notetaking techniques; Strategy instruction; Test-taking strategies; Time management and organizational strategies
Explode the Code, 514
Expressive language skills, *see* Encoding
Externalizing disorders, *see* Attention-deficit/hyperactivity disorder (ADHD); Behavior modification;

Index

Challenging behaviors; Oppositional and conduct disorders
EZ2 Read Barbara Nicholson Books and Material, 514

Fairness, 191–193, 196
Far-transfer problem, 440–441
Fast ForWord, 514
FBA, *see* Functional behavior assessment
FCRR, *see* The Florida Center for Reading Research
Feedback
    as a component of effective interventions, 66, 130*t*, 132
    Direct Behavior Ratings (DBRs) and, 137
    fairness and, 192
    on homework assignments, 72, 74, 201
    if-then rule, 67
    negative, 93–94, 108, 125
    nonverbal, 110
    parents and behavior planning with, 133–134
    prevention-oriented approaches to promote positive, 130, 130*t*
    self-regulation and, 104, 108
    specific learning disabilities (SLD) and, 110
    students with attention-deficit/hyperactivity disorder (ADHD) and, 92–94, 113, 116, 118
    teacher–student interactions and encouragement, 60, 62, 64, 108, 198–199
    see also Assessments; Teacher–student interactions
FEP, *see* Fluent English proficient
Fernald Method, 304–305
Fine motor skills, 244–248
    artistic expression, 12
    dysfunction as a sign of attention-deficit/hyperactivity disorder (ADHD), 106*t*
    handwriting rate, 245–248, 248*t*
    legibility, 245
    symbol production, 12
    see also Dysgraphia; Gross motor skills; Handwriting; Letter formation
Flashcards
    apps, 302, 400, 451, 452, 455, 460
    color coding and, 120
    high-frequency words, 301–301, 455
    irregular words, 237
    math drill, 317
    test preparation and, 386, 400
    word formation, 457
Florida Center for Reading Research, The (FCRR), 66, 228, 523–524
Fluency First, 514
Fluent English proficient (FEP), 355
Fluid reasoning (Gf) ability, 47, 47*t*
Fluoxetine hydrochloride (Prozac), 103
Flyleaf Publishing (Decodable Books K–3), 514

fMRI, *see* Functional magnetic resonance imaging
Focus Time, 400
Fonts4Teachers, 338, 521
Foundational blocks, 9–10, 18*f*, 21–24, 79–203
    Behavior block, 9–10, 18*f*, 21, 23, 33–34, 123, 124*f*
    Building Blocks Questionnaire and, 18*f*, 21, 22–24
    Emotions block, 10, 18*f*, 21, 23, 34, 159, 160*f*
    environment, 18*f*, 21, 22
    rationale for, 9–10, 32–34
    Resilience block, 10, 18*f*, 21, 24, 34, 185, 186*f*
    Self-Regulation block, 9, 18*f*, 21, 22, 33, 101, 102*f*
    see also Behavior block; Emotions block; Learning environments; Resilience block; Self-Regulation block
Fragile X syndrome, 97
Franklin Speaking Language Master, 368, 521
Fricatives, 266, 267, 267*t*
FRIENDS program, 168
Fry's 600 Instant Words, 301, 342–347, 455, 514
Functional behavior assessment (FBA), 134
Functional impairments, 156, 158
Functional magnetic resonance imaging (fMRI), 37
Fundations, 294, 514

Ga, *see* auditory processing (Ga) ability *under* Cattell-Horn-Carroll (CHC) theory of intelligence
Gc, *see* comprehension–knowledge (Gc) ability *under* Cattell-Horn-Carroll (CHC) theory of intelligence
Gender
    attention-deficit/hyperactivity disorder (ADHD) and, 81–82, 87, 102
    handwriting and, 246, 248*t*
    prevalence of disruptive problems across, 81–82
    suicide risk and, 157
Generalized anxiety disorder, 173
Genetics, 88, 94, 97, 124
Geoboards, 434
Geometry, 430, 434, 442
Gf, *see* fluid reasoning (Gf) ability *under* Cattell-Horn-Carroll (CHC) theory of intelligence
Gf-Gc theory, 46
Glass Analysis for Decoding Only, 297, 514
Glides, 266, 267, 268*t*
Glossaries, 367–368, 413, 415
Glr, *see* long-term retrieval (Glr) ability *under* Cattell-Horn-Carroll (CHC) theory of intelligence
Grammar, 38, 50*t*, 120, 290, 293, 340, 360–361

Graph paper, 119, 247, 320
Grapheme–phoneme awareness, 39, 224, 265
    activities to improve, 288–289, 291–293, 300–301
    apps for, 453–455
    charts and recording sheets, 261*f*, 262*f*–263*f*
    orthographic dyslexia and, 234–235
    phonics and spelling through mapping, 289–290, 516
    spelling development and, 279
    see also Orthographic blocks; Phonological awareness; Phonological awareness to print; Phonological Awareness Skills Screener (PASS); Phonological blocks; Reading fluency; Spelling development; Vocabulary instruction; Vocabulary knowledge
Graphic organizers, 367, 373, 376, 378, 389, 407, 411, 419, 520
Graphic presentation, 328
Great Leaps Math Package, 522
Great Leaps Oral Calculation Program, 522
Great Leaps Reading program, 514
Gross motor skills, 3, 12, 242–243, 463
Gs, *see* long-term retrieval (Gs) ability *under* Cattell-Horn-Carroll (CHC) theory of intelligence
Guanfacine hydrochloride (Tenex), 103
Gv, *see* visual-spatial thinking (Gv) ability *under* Cattell-Horn-Carroll (CHC) theory of intelligence

Hand-Made Math Manipulatives Instructions, 522
Handwriting, 323–341
    as an academic skill in relation to the Building Blocks model, 52*f*
    apps for, 453–455
    assessing, 245
    ball-and-stick method, 329
    computers, 338–340
    correlation between writing rate and preferred hand, 246
    developmental stages of, 328
    fundamentals, 325–328
    gender, 246, 248*t*
    general principles, 328–329
    helping students develop, 329
    as idiosyncratic, 330–331
    letter formation, 331–337
    most common letters in error, 336
    pencil grips, 253, 325–326, 329, 521
    preferred hand, 246, 325
    prewriting activities, 324
    readiness, 324–325
    resources for, 453–455, 521
    software to assist learning, 338
    stages of development, 247, 328
    strategies to build writing speed, 337–338
    styles of script, 329–337, 331*f*, 332*f*

Handwriting—*continued*
  timed writing, 337–338
  traditional instruction in, 329
  visual and motor skills for, 243*f*
  worksheets for, 338–339, 521
  writing styles
    choosing among, 329–330
    D'Nealian writing style, 330–334, 331*f*, 332*f*, 336, 456
    initial style for children, 330
    manucursive style, 326–327, 329–330, 336, 338
    manuscript writing, 329
    Zaner-Bloser proficiency scale, 245–246
  see also Cursive writing style; Dysgraphia; Letter formation
Herman Method, 514
"Hidden disabilities," *see* Attention-deficit/hyperactivity disorder (ADHD); Specific learning disabilities (SLD)
High-frequency words, 39, 230, 275, 280–281, 285
  apps for, 455
  backward spelling, 302
  flashcards, 301–302
  Fry's 600 Instant Words, 301, 342–347, 455, 514
  personalized dictionary, 302
  self-monitoring, 302
Home environments, 126–127, 385–386, 471–472
Homework assignments, 71–75, 76*f*
  accommodations for, 396, 397
  completing, 74–75, 74*f*, 76*f*
  creating, 73, 75*t*, 76*f*
  extra time for, 193
  feedback on, 72, 74, 201
  guidelines for teachers, 75, 76*f*
  Instructional Accommodations Survey and, 396, 397
  meaningfulness, difficulty, and length of, 73, 76*f*
  as punishment, 75
  purpose of, 72
  time limit for doing and measures of success, 192–193

IDA, *see* International Dyslexia Association
IDEA, *see* Individuals with Disabilities Education Improvement Act (IDEA) of 2004 (PL 108-446)
IEP, *see* Individualized education program
Illinois Test of Psycholinguistic Abilities (*ITPA*), 34–35
Imipramine (Tofranil), 102–103
Imitation, 146, 328
Impaired functioning, *see* Functional impairments
Inclusion, 63–64, 184, 523
Index cards
  for brainstorming, 374–375
  in collaborative strategic reading (CSR), 414
  color coding and, 334, 414
  Fernald Method for word study, 304
  Glass Analysis Method for Decoding Only, 297
  for letter formation, 334
  for math instruction, 323, 438
  for test preparation, 384, 414
  for time management and organization, 384–386
Individualized education program (IEP), 199, 321–322, 389
Individualized instruction, 4, 63, 66, 217, 293
Individuals with Disabilities Education Improvement Act (IDEA) of 2004 (PL 108-446), 94, 210–212, 525
  amendments of 1997 (PL 105-17), 94
  identification of specific learning disability (SLD), 210–211, 214–215, 217–219
  response to intervention (RTI) and, 210, 214–215
  resources for, 524, 525
  legal mandates of, 210–212, 217–219
  see also Accommodations; Dyscalculia; Dysgraphia; Dyslexia; Specific learning disabilities (SLD)
Instant words, 301, 342–347, 455, 514
Institute for Multi-Sensory Education, 516
Institute of Education Sciences, 523, 524
Instructional Accommodations Survey, 396–398
  classwork, 396
  homework, 396, 397
  instruction, 396
  math instruction, 397
  seating, 398
  test-taking, 198
  writing instruction, 397
  see also Accommodations
Instructional strategies
  for algebra, 442–443
  for dyscalculia, 431–433, 436
  effective early instruction among diverse learners, 66
  for English language learners (ELLs), 355–361
  explicit instruction, 377–378, 404
  individualized instruction, 4, 63, 66, 217, 293
  "instructional triangle" to evaluate student–task mismatch, 61
  for language development, 361–369
  in letter formation, 304, 328, 334–337
  math problem solving sequences, 433–435
  principles of instruction, 67–68
  reading comprehension, 404
  reading fluency, 310–315
  sequential mastery of topics, 66
  specific cognitive strategies, 377–378
  spelling development and, 277–285
  strategy instruction, 378–381
  whole-class instruction, 32, 62, 101, 130*t*, 136, 164–165
  see also Accommodations; Classroom activities; Effective teachers; Evidence-based strategies; Handwriting; Manipulatives; Math instruction; Multisensory techniques; Reading comprehension; Reading fluency; Response to intervention (RTI); Small-group instruction; Student engagement; Visual imagery; Vocabulary instruction
"Instructional triangle," 61
Interactions, *see* Classroom environments; Student–parent interactions; Student–student interactions; Teacher–parent interactions
Interactive books, 455, 458–459
Interagency Committee on Learning Disabilities, 209
Interdental sounds, 266
Internalizing disorders, *see* Anxiety disorders; Depressive disorders; Trauma and stress-related disorders
International Dyslexia Association (IDA), 42, 222–223, 526
International Reading Association (IRA), 525
Intervention Central, 309, 524
Interventions
  attention-deficit/hyperactivity disorder (ADHD), 102, 109–110
  in the Emotions block, 162–170
  how rigid discrepancy can prevent early, 213
  multimodal short-term, 102
  in the Nonverbal block, 370–371
  nonverbal learning disabilities (NVLDs) and, 370–371
  oppositional and conduct disorders, 127, 128*t*
  for the Orthographic block, 236–237, 238*f*
  positive behavioral interventions and supports (PBIS) framework, 59, 525
  prereferral, 216
  school based, 169–170
  tertiary system of, 164
  see also Behavior modification; Challenging behaviors; Classroom activities; Cognitive behavioral therapy (CBT); Instructional strategies; Learning environments; Response to intervention (RTI); *specific interventions and programs*
IRA, *see* International Reading Association
IRIS Center, The, 524
Irregular words, 25, 230, 234, 236–238, 276, 285
ITPA, *see Illinois Test of Psycholinguistic Abilities*

Index

James Madison University Special Education Program, 524

Kaufman Assessment Battery for Children–II (KABC–II), 48
K-W-L (Know-Want-Learned) strategy, 363, 363f, 364f, 374, 418–419, 441

Labiodental sounds, 265, 267t
Language development, 41
  background knowledge, 362
  components of oral, 352–353
  developmental stages of, 277
  English language learners (ELLs) and, 355–360
  first components of, 353
  instruction for, 361–369
  social interactions and, 361
  see also Orthographical block; Phonological block; Reading comprehension; Reading fluency; Verbal block; Written expression
Language Essentials for Teachers of Reading and Spelling (LETRS), 285, 515
Language! The Comprehensive Literacy Curriculum, 293, 515
LD Online, 210, 524
LDA, *see* Learning Disabilities Association of America
LDW, *see* Learning Disabilities Worldwide
Learning Ally, 313–314, 521
Learning disabilities (LD), 94
  consensus definition for, 208–209
  Interagency Committee on Learning Disabilities definition of, 209
  National Advisory Committee on Handicapped Children definition of, 208
  oppositional and conduct disorders comorbid with, 126
  see also Accommodations; Dyscalculia; Dysgraphia; Dyslexia; Interventions; Reading disabilities; Specific learning disabilities (SLD)
Learning Disabilities Association of America (LDA), 526
Learning Disabilities Worldwide (LDW), 526
Learning disorders, *see* Learning disabilities; Specific learning disabilities (SLD)
Learning environments, 55–77
  antecedent manipulation, 69, 111
  Building Blocks Questionnaire and, 18f, 21, 22
  classroom environment, 62–66
  communication with parents, 69, 70f
  communication with students, 68–69
  conditions and components of, 66–69
  diverse backgrounds, 69–71
  individualized and small-group instruction, 66–67
  "instructional triangle" to evaluate student–task mismatch, 61
  principles of instruction, 67–68
  relationships, 68
  school environments, 56–60, 58t
  see also Classroom environments; Homework assignments; School environment; Teacher–parent interactions; Teacher–student interactions
Learning Toolbox, The, 524
Least restrictive placement, 63–64
LETRS, *see* Language Essentials for Teachers of Reading and Spelling
Let's Begin with the Letter People, 515
Let's Go Read! series, 515
Letter formation, 26, 50t, 324–325
  directional arrows, 335
  fine motor skills and, 242, 244
  increasing automaticity of, 335
  instruction strategies in, 304, 328, 334–337
  letter reversals, 330, 336–337
  mirror writing, 236
  multisensory instruction for writing, 333–335
  oral descriptions, 335–336
  self-guided symbol formation strategy, 336
  see also Dysgraphia; Handwriting
letter identification, 453–455
Letter–sound identification, *see* Grapheme–phoneme awareness
Lexia Reading Core5, 515
Lindamood Phoneme Sequencing Program for Reading, Spelling, and Speech (LiPS) program, 265, 515
Liquids, 266, 268, 268t
Literacy Express, 515
Logographic dyslexia, 232
Long-term retrieval (Glr) ability, 47, 47t
L-type dyslexia, 231–232
Luria model, 48

Making Words task, 288–289, 515
Manipulatives
  for algebra instruction, 443
  for hand-made, 522
  limits of, 434–435
  for math instruction, 320, 322, 434–435, 522
  for math problem solving, 433–438
  National Library of Virtual Manipulatives, 434, 522
  for spelling development, 120, 227, 288
Manucursive writing style, 326–327, 329–330, 336, 338
Math disabilities, *see* Dyscalculia
Math Flash software program, 318
Math instruction
  acting out concrete experiences, 433–434
  additional resources, 522
  drills, 317
  effective format for, 431
  evidence-based strategies, 316–317
  examples from real-life situations, 430
  explicit, 432
  face charts, 317–318
  Instructional Accommodations Survey and, 397
  involving students with lower achievement, 431
  manipulatives in, 320, 322, 434–435, 522
  mnemonics, 320–321
  modeling, 322–323
  multisensory techniques for, 319–321
  one-to-one correspondence, 316–317
  online programs, 444
  pegword phrase mnemonic, 321
  planning facilitation for, 111–112, 112f
  principles of effective, 316
  real-life examples, 433
  rhyme cards for multiplication, 321
  software, 318, 444, 445t
  structural arithmetic, 320
  students with learning disabilities and, 432–433
  Touch Points, 320
  TouchMath, 320–321, 321f, 522
  worksheets and, 317–319, 397, 433, 443–444
  see also Dyscalculia; Math knowledge; Math problem solving
Math knowledge, 316, 397
  as an academic skill in relation to the Building Blocks model, 52f
  assessing, 318–319
  basic skills necessary for academic performance, 49, 51t, 52f
  Common Core State Standards (CCSS) on, 59, 418–419, 430–431
  curriculum-based measures (CBM), 318–319
  early concepts, 316–318
  error analysis, 321–322
  numerical facility (Factor N) and, 315
  procedural knowledge, 430
  role of memory in children with specific learning disabilities (SLD), 40
  rote memorization and, 435
  types of knowledge, 430
  understanding zero, 322
  uniqueness of, 440
  see also Dyscalculia; Math instruction; Math problem solving
Math problem solving, 428–445
  abstract instruction, 435
  as an academic skill in relation to the Building Blocks model, 51t, 52f
  act-it-out strategy, 433
  classic handshake problem, 434
  comorbid reading disability, 428
  conceptual knowledge, 430
  concrete instruction in, 433–435
  cue cards, 437

Math problem solving—*continued*
  declarative knowledge, 430
  example of a classroom activity format, 431–432
  identifying important keywords, 436
  instructional concerns, 430–431
  instructional format, 431–432
  instructional sequences, 433–435
  language and, 435–436
  manipulatives in, 433–438
  math disability as a cause of difficulty in, 428
  mathematical knowledge, 430
  modes of presenting problems in class, 432
  presenting problems at three levels of difficulty, 440–441
  procedural knowledge, 430
  role of semantic memory in, 40–41
  semiconcrete or representational instruction, 435
  sequence for mastery of word problems, 438–439
  software selection and math instruction, 318, 444, 445t
  STAR acronym, 437
  story or word problem strategies, 436–437
  strategies for advanced math courses, 442–444
  strategy instruction, 437–442
  ways to change problems to solve them, 440, 441t
  working memory and, 428–429
  see also Algebra; Dyscalculia; Math instruction; Math knowledge
Math Their Way (K–2), 522
Math Type software program, 444
Math Worksheet Site, 444
Mathematics . . . A Way of Thinking (3–6), 522
MathPad, 444
Memory aids, *see* Mnemonics
Memory block, 21, 25, 238–241
  Building Blocks Questionnaire and, 18f, 21, 25, 242f
  Cattell-Horn Carroll (CHC) theory and, 47–48, 47t
  memory span, 38
  Planning, Attention, Simultaneous, Successive (PASS) theory and, 44–46, 46t
  students with specific learning disabilities (SLD) and problems with, 38
  visual memory, 373
  working memory, 240–241, 428–429
  see also Processing blocks; Rote memory; Short-term memory; Working memory
Memory span, *see* Short-term memory
Metacognition, 14, 43–44, 377
Methamphetamine hydrochloride (Desoxyn), 102–103
Methylphenidate hydrochloride (Ritalin), 83, 91, 102–104, 105f
MindPlay, 515–516

Mindplay Teacher's Companion, Companion Plus, and Understanding Dyslexia Courses, 285
Mindplay Virtual Reading Coach (MVRC), 290
Minimal brain dysfunction, *see* Specific learning disabilities (SLD)
Mnemonics
  C-SPACE mnemonic, 409–410
  defined, 380
  keyword method for vocabulary, 372–373, 380
  math related, 119, 320–321
  modeling the use of, 380
  pegword phrase mnemonic, 321
  poor working memory and, 241
  STAR math problem-solving mnemonic, 437
  STATE the Story mnemonic, 408
  STORE the story mnemonic, 408–409, 409f
  story recall and, 406
  strategy instruction, 380
  students with attention-deficit/hyperactivity disorder (ADHD), 106t
  W-W-W, What = 2, How = 2 mnemonic, 410
Modeling behaviors
  aggression and, 128t
  challenging behaviors and, 146–148
  desired behaviors, 132
  factors shaping student response to modeling, 146–148
  handwriting, 329
  math calculation, 322–323
  mnemonics, 380
  notetaking techniques, 382
  peer, 147
  reinforced practice and participant modeling, 168–169
  reinforcement and, 146–147
  self-talk, 164t, 371, 387
  written expression and, 338
Morphology, 8, 49, 274, 352
Motor block, 21, 26, 241–248
  Building Blocks Questionnaire and, 18f, 21, 26, 243–244, 244f
  fine motor skills, 244–248
  gross motor skills, 3, 12, 242–243, 463
  handwriting rate, 245–248, 248t
  occupational therapy, 9, 242–244, 247, 330
  Planning, Attention, Simultaneous, Successive (PASS) theory and, 44–46, 46t
  questionnaire, 243–244
  see also Dysgraphia; Fine motor skills; Handwriting; Letter formation; Processing blocks
Multipass reading strategy, 416–417
Multiplication Rap CD + Tape, 522
Multisensory techniques, 441
  cover-write methods, 305, 335
  Fernald Method, 304–305
  for handwriting, 333–335
  for math instruction, 319–321

  mnemonics, 320–321
  pegword phrase mnemonic, 321
  for reading fluency, 302–305
  structural arithmetic, 320
  Touch Points, 320
  TouchMath, 320–321, 321f, 522
MVRC, *see* Mindplay Virtual Reading Coach

NAEP, *see* National Assessment of Educational Progress
Narrative text structure, *see* Story grammars
Nasals, 266, 267t
NASP, *see* National Association of School Psychologists
National Advisory Committee on Handicapped Children, 208, 209t
National Assessment of Educational Progress (NAEP), 355, 431
National Assistive Technology Research Institute (NATRI), 524
National Association of School Psychologists (NASP), 526
National Center for Culturally Responsive Educational Systems (NCCRESt), 523
National Center for Learning Disabilities (NLCD), 524
National Center on Assessment and Accountability for Special Education (NCAASE), 524
National Center on Intensive Intervention, 524
National Center on Response to Intervention (NCRTI), 523
National Center on Student Progress Monitoring, 524
National Council of Teachers of English (NCTE), 525
National Council of Teachers of Mathematics (NCTM), 431
National Dissemination Center for Children with Disabilities (NICHCY), 523
National Institute for Direct Instruction, 525
National Institute of Child Health and Human Development (NICHD), 222
National Joint Committee on Learning Disabilities (NJCLD), 66, 215, 217
National Library of Virtual Manipulatives, 434, 522
NATRI, *see* National Assistive Technology Research Institute
NATs, *see* Negative automatic thoughts
NCAASE, *see* National Center on Assessment and Accountability for Special Education
NCCRESt, *see* National Center for Culturally Responsive Educational Systems
NCTE, *see* National Council of Teachers of English
NCTM, *see* National Council of Teachers of Mathematics

Index

Near-transfer problem, 440
Negative automatic thoughts (NATs), 168
Neuhaus Education Center, 516
Neurofibromatosis, 97
Neurological impress method, 311–312
NICHCY, see National Dissemination Center for Children with Disabilities
NICHD, see National Institute of Child Health and Human Development
NJCLD, see National Joint Committee on Learning Disabilities
NLCD, see National Center for Learning Disabilities
NLD, see Nonverbal learning disabilities (NVLDs)
No Child Left Behind Act of 2001 (PL 107-110), 351, 525
Nonsense words, 221–222, 234–235, 257
Nonverbal block, 13, 369–377
   adaptation of the K-W-L (Know-Want-Learned) strategy, 374
   apps for, 399
   brainstorming, 374–376
   Building Blocks Questionnaire and, 18*f*, 21, 27, 369–370
   Cattell-Horn Carroll (CHC) theory and, 47–48, 47*t*
   characteristics, 369–370
   difficulties in learning math and, 319
   graphic organizers, 373
   instruction using visual imagery, 371–377
   interventions, 370–371
   keyword method, 372–373, 380
   mapping, 373
   Planning, Attention, Simultaneous, Successive (PASS) theory and, 44–46, 46*t*
   spatial outlining, 376–377
   visualization, 371–372
   see also Conceptual blocks; Nonverbal learning disabilities (NVLDs)
Nonverbal learning disabilities (NVLDs), 14, 21, 27, 369–371, 464
   incidence of, 42
   interventions for, 370–371
   rote memorization and, 369
   using visual imagery with, 373–377
   see also Dyscalculia; Nonverbal block
Noonan syndrome, 97
Norpramin (desipramine hydrochloride), 102–103
Nortriptyline hydrochloride (Pamelor), 103
Notetaking techniques, 381–382
   apps for, 399
   AWARE method, 382, 382*t*
   how teachers can assist students, 382
   laptop computers and, 381
   modeling proper techniques, 382
   three-column techniques, 376–377, 377*t*, 378*t*
Numeracy development, see Math knowledge

Occipitoparietal regions, 37
Occupational therapy, 9, 242–244, 247, 330
Office of Special Education Programs (OSEP), 523, 524
OHI, see Other health impairment
Onset Rime Cards, 516
Onsets, 220, 224, 227, 277, 295–296
Open Court Phonemic Awareness and Phonics Kits, 516
Oppositional and conduct disorders
   causes of, 126–127
   classroom interventions for, 127, 128*t*
   comorbid disorders with, 100–101, 125–126, 174
   Emotions block and, 126
   genetics and, 124
   incidence of, 81–82, 125–126
   parenting behaviors and, 127
   see also Attention-deficit/hyperactivity disorder (ADHD); Behavior modification; Challenging behaviors
Oppositional defiant disorder, 9, 33, 100, 125–126, 174
Organizational skills, see Time management and organizational strategies
Orthographic awareness, 228–231
   characteristics of poor, 230–231
   definition of, 228–230
   symbol recognition and recall, 229–230
   see also Grapheme–phoneme awareness; Orthographic awareness; Orthographic dyslexia
Orthographic block, 12, 37–38, 228–237
   Building Blocks Questionnaire and, 18*f*, 21, 25, 231, 232*f*
   Cattell-Horn Carroll (CHC) theory and, 47–48, 47*t*
   implications for intervention, 236–237, 238*f*
   orthographic dyslexia, 228, 231–236
   orthography defined, 228
   Planning, Attention, Simultaneous, Successive (PASS) theory and, 44–46, 46*t*
   process of orthographic coding, 228–229
   questionnaire, 231
   strengths and weaknesses as a predictor of school success, 233–235
   see also Orthographic awareness; Orthographic dyslexia; Processing blocks
Orthographic dyslexia, 228–236
   characteristics of individuals with, 229–230
   grapheme–phoneme awareness and, 234–235
   historical review of, 231–234
   impact on math skills, 231
   informal assessment of, 235–236, 236*t*
   irregular words and, 234
   popular oversimplification of, 236
   research on, 234–236
Orthography, see Orthographical dyslexia; Orthographic block
Orton Dyslexia Society, see International Dyslexia Association
Orton-Gillingham sequence, 291–294, 516
Other health impairment (OHI), 94

Paired-associate learning, see Rote memory
Palatal sounds, 266, 267*t*
PALS, see Peer Assisted Learning Strategies
Pamelor (nortriptyline hydrochloride), 103
Panic disorder, 172
Parents, see Student–parent interactions; Teacher–parent interactions
Paroxetine hydrochloride (Paxil), 103
PASS, see Phonological Awareness Skills Screener; Planning, Attention, Simultaneous, Successive (PASS) theory
Passive-aggressive behavior, 186
PATHS, see Promoting Alternative Thinking Strategies (PATHS)
Pattern of strengths and weaknesses (PSW) approach, 217–219
Patterns for Success in Reading and Spelling, 516
Paxil (paroxetine hydrochloride), 103
PBIS, see Positive behavior interventions and supports (PBIS) framework
PBS, see Public Broadcasting Service
Peer Assisted Learning Strategies (PALS), 516, 522
Peer comparison observation method, 136–137, 136*f*
Peer modeling, 147
Peer tutoring
   classwide, 66, 274–275, 313
   math skills and, 317
   reading fluency and, 274–275, 313
   self-advocacy skills and, 198
   test taking and, 254, 386
   usefulness for students with attention-deficit/hyperactivity disorder (ADHD), 111, 116, 118
Pemoline (Cylert), 102–103
Pencil grips, 253, 325–326, 329, 521
Perceptual speed, 47
Phobias, 172, 173
Phoneme blending, 256, 259, 260*f*
Phoneme deletion, 226, 259, 260*f*
Phoneme matching, 225
Phoneme recognition, 256, 258, 260*f*
Phoneme segmentation, 256, 259, 260*f*, 294
Phoneme substitution, 226
Phoneme–grapheme awareness, see Grapheme–phoneme awareness

537

Phonemes, 264, 356–357
   see also Grapheme–phoneme awareness; Phonological Awareness Skills Screener (PASS); Phonological awareness to print; Phonological block; Speech sounds; Spelling development
Phonemic Awareness in Young Children, 516
Phonic Reading Lessons, 292–293, 516
Phonics, 291–295
   analogy strategy, 295–296, 296*f*
   analytic, 295–299
   Glass Analysis Method for Decoding Only, 297, 514
   Language! The Comprehensive Literacy Curriculum, 293, 515
   Orton-Gillingham sequence, 291–294, 516
   phoneme–grapheme mapping and, 289–290
   Phonic Reading Lessons, 292–293, 516
   Reading Excellence: Word Attack and Rate Development Strategies (REWARDS), 298–299, 518
   Reading Lesson, The, 292, 517
   Reading Reflex, 292, 518
   Retrieval, Automaticity, Vocabulary, Engagement with Language, Orthography (RAVE-O), 299, 517
   Spalding Method, 293, 335, 519
   Specialized Program Individualizing Reading Excellence (S.P.I.R.E.), 293–294, 519
   spelling grids, 298, 298*f*
   synthetic, 291–295
   Wilson Reading System (WRS), 294–295, 519
   see also Grapheme–phoneme awareness; Phonological dyslexia; Phonological block
Phonics Q: The Complete Cueing System, 516–517
Phonological awareness
   blending (synthesizing sounds) and segmentation (analyzing sounds) in, 227
   defined, 220
   double-deficit hypothesis, 39–40
   informal assessment of, 224–226
   terminology, 220–221
   verbal short-term memory versus, 224
   see also Grapheme–phoneme awareness; Phonological awareness to print; Phonological block; Phonological dyslexia
Phonological Awareness Kit, 517
Phonological Awareness Skills Screener (PASS), 224, 256–263
   administration instructions, 256–259
   association with specific regions of the brain, 44
   letter–sound identification section, 259, 261*f*, 262–263
   materials, 256
   PASS Test Record, 260
   phoneme blending, 256, 259, 260*f*
   phoneme deletion, 226, 259, 260*f*
   phoneme recognition, 256, 258, 260*f*
   phoneme segmentation, 256, 259, 260*f*, 294
   rhyme production, 225, 256–257, 260*f*
   rhyme recognition, 224–225, 257, 260*f*
   syllable blending, 225, 256, 257, 260*f*
   syllable deletion, 256, 258, 260*f*
   syllable segmentation, 256, 258, 260*f*
   word discrimination, 256–257, 260*f*
Phonological awareness to print, 285–290
   adapted Elkonin procedure, 287–288
   auditory sequencing, 288
   invented or temporary spelling, 285–286
   Making Words task, 288–289, 515
   online reading programs, 290
   phoneme–grapheme mapping, 289–290
   reading pens, 290, 368, 521
   Road to the Code program, 289, 518
   talk-to-yourself chart, 286–287
   see also Grapheme–phoneme awareness; Reading comprehension; Reading fluency; Spelling development
Phonological block, 11–12, 37–38, 220, 219–228
   assessment and instructional activities, 224–227
   blending words, 227–228
   Building Blocks Questionnaire and, 18*f*, 21, 24, 220, 220*f*
   Cattell-Horn Carroll (CHC) theory and, 47–48, 47*t*
   developmental sequence, 223–224
   phonological dyslexia, 221–223
   phonology defined, 352
   Planning, Attention, Simultaneous, Successive (PASS) theory and, 44–46, 46*t*
   questionnaire, 219–220, 220*f*
   segmentation, 227
   see also Phonological awareness; Phonological Awareness Skills Screener (PASS); Phonological dyslexia; Processing blocks
Phonological dyslexia, 221–223, 235
   characteristics of, 39, 222
   history of, 223
   International Dyslexia Association (IDA) definition of, 222–223
   see also Dyslexia; Phonological awareness; Phonological block
Phonology, see Phonological awareness; Phonological block
Pinworms, 97
PIRATES test-taking strategy, 391, 392*t*
PL 94-142, see Education for All Handicapped Children Act of 1975 (PL 94-142)
PL 102-569, see Section 504 of the Rehabilitation Act Amendments of 1992 (PL 102-569)
PL 105-17, see amendments of 1997 (PL 105-17) *under* Individuals with Disabilities Education Improvement Act (IDEA) of 2004 (PL 108-446)
PL 107-110, see No Child Left Behind Act of 2001 (PL 107-110)
PL 108-446, see Individuals with Disabilities Education Improvement Act (IDEA) of 2004
Planning, Attention, Simultaneous, Successive (PASS) theory, 44–46, 46*t*
Planning processing, 45–46, 91–92
PMR, see Progressive muscle relaxation
Poems By Heart from Penguin Classics, 458, 459
PORPE (Predict, Organize, Rehearse, Practice, Evaluate) reading strategy, 417–418
Positive behavioral interventions and supports (PBIS) framework, 59, 525
Posttraumatic stress disorder (PTSD), 162*f*, 177–178
Poverty, 31–32, 70
POWER (Plan, Organize, Write, Edit, Revise) strategy, 422
Pragmatics, 352–353
Prefrontal cortex, 43, 45–46, 97
Premack principle, 110
Prevention-oriented approaches, 130, 130*t*
Print awareness, see Phonological awareness to print
Processing blocks, 10–13, 205–347
   Building Blocks Questionnaire and, 18*f*, 21, 24–26
   components of effective strategies for instruction in, 273
   Efficiency/Automaticity block, 13, 18*f*, 21, 26, 38, 248, 249*f*
   instruction for, 273–347
   Memory block, 12, 18*f*, 21, 25, 38, 241, 242*f*
   Motor block, 12, 18*f*, 21, 26, 38, 243–244, 244*f*
   Orthographic block, 12, 18*f*, 21, 25, 37–38, 231, 232*f*
   Phonological block, 11–12, 18*f*, 21, 24, 37–38, 220, 220*f*
   rationale for, 34–38
   as "secretarial" in nature, 10
   symbolic learning, 35, 273, 275–276
   see also Calculating; Decoding; Efficiency/Automaticity block; Encoding; Handwriting; Memory block; Motor block; Orthographic block; Phonological block; Reading fluency; Specific learning disabilities (SLD); Spelling development
Processing speed (Gs), 47, 252
Procrastination, 384–385
Professional development, 55, 57–60, 58*t*, 62, 524–426
Progressive muscle relaxation (PMR), 163, 165*f*–166*f*
Project Read, 517

Index

Promoting Alternative Thinking Strategies (PATHS), 57
Prozac (fluoxetine hydrochloride), 103
Psycholinguistic learning disabilities, *see* Specific learning disabilities (SLD)
P-type dyslexia, 223
Public Broadcasting Service (PBS), 525
Punishment, 148–153, 139*t*
   basic principles of, 137
   consequential versus rule-governed behavior, 152
   effective, 153
   response cost, 150–152
   see also Behavior modification; Challenging behaviors; Reinforcement

Questioning skills
   higher level, 368–369
   ReQuest (reciprocal questioning) reading procedure, 416
   story grammars and reading comprehension, 407–409
Quicktionary Reading Pens, 368, 521
Quitting and avoiding, 185

RAN, *see* Rapid automatized naming
RAP (Read, Ask, Put) reading strategy, 412
Rapid Alternating Stimulus Test, 249
Rapid automatized naming (RAN), 13, 39–40, 248–252
   brief history of, 249
   double-deficit hypothesis, 39–40
   existing research on, 251
   first documented test of, 249
   latency as predictor of reading-related difficulties, 249–250
   measures, 250–252
   phonological processing skills and, 250
   as predictor of academic performance, 249–250
   rate impairment, 250
   reading ability and, 250–251
   tests, 249
   word reading fluency versus accuracy, 251
Rapid word recognition chart, 310–311
RAPS 360, 290, 515–516
Rate-disabled dyslexia, 232
Rationalizing, 186
RAVE-O, *see* Retrieval, Automaticity, Vocabulary, Engagement with Language, Orthography
RCMAS, *see* Revised Children's Manifest Anxiety Scales
Reactive attachment disorder, 158, 179
Read, 180, 517
Read Naturally program, 314–315, 517
Read Well program, 301, 517
Read, Write, and Type program, 339, 517
Read, Write, Think, 525
Reading A–Z, 517

Reading comprehension, 403–418
   additional resources, 513–520
   apps for literacy instruction, 451–459
   categories of story elements, 406
   collaborative strategic reading (CSR), 412–414
   development of word consciousness and word-play activities, 366
   evidence-based strategies for English language learners (ELLs), 359
   explicit instruction in, 404
   expository text structure, 410–411
   intensive classroom or group-based strategy, 412
   interactive book apps, 458–459
   levels of reading material, 299
   metacognitive behaviors involved in, 44
   Multipass strategy, 416–417
   pointing out diagrams, charts, graphs, and illustrations, 372
   PORPE (Predict, Organize, Rehearse, Practice, Evaluate) strategy, 417–418
   RAP (Read, Ask, Put) strategy, 412
   reading fluency and, 306
   reciprocal teaching, 412
   repeated reading technique, 312–313, 312*f*, 364
   ReQuest (reciprocal questioning) procedure, 416
   "rule of thumb" for choosing student texts, 300
   shared storybook reading, 364
   SQ3R (Survey, Question, Read, Recite, and Review) strategy, 414–416
   story grammars, 404–410
   story retelling, 404
   strategies, 412–418
   summarization, 411
   symbolic learning and, 276
   vision problems and, 234
   weaknesses in verbal abilities, 352
   see also Dyslexia; Phonics; Reading disabilities; Reading fluency; Story grammars
Reading disabilities, 37
   cortical damage and, 232
   phonemes–grapheme awareness and, 37
   subtypes of, 39
   see also Dyslexia
Reading Excellence: Word Attack and Rate Development Strategies (REWARDS), 298–299, 518
Reading fluency, 306–315
   apps for word recognition skills, 452–453
   assessing progress in, 308
   backward spelling, 302
   basic skills necessary for academic performance, 49, 50*t*, 52*f*
   Carbo Method, 314
   cover-write methods, 305, 335
   curriculum-based measures (CBM) for reading, 308–309
   decodable text, 300–301

Fernald Method, 304–305
   flashcards and, 301–302
   Fry's 600 Instant Words, 301, 342–347, 455, 514
   Great Leaps Reading program, 311, 514
   high-frequency words, 301–302
   how skilled readers identify different words, 276
   instructional activities to improve, 310–315
   instructional level, 299–300
   multisensory procedures for reading and writing, 302–305
   neurological impress method (choral or concert reading), 311–312
   nonsense words, 221–222, 234–235, 257
   oral reading fluency rate, 306–308, 307*t*–308*t*
   persistence of difficulties into adulthood, 237
   personalized dictionaries, 302
   previewing, 313
   rapid word recognition chart, 310–311
   Read Naturally program, 314–315, 317
   Read Well program, 301, 517
   reading comprehension and, 306
   reading rate, 309–315
   recommendations for helping students to improve, 313
   recorded books, 214, 313–314, 521
   repeated reading, 312–313, 312*f*, 364
   self-monitoring, 302, 303*f*
   silent reading development, 227–228
   speed drills, 310
   symbolic learning and, 35, 273, 275–276
   types of text and, 299–305
   Wilson Fluency/Basic program, 311
   word game apps, 456–457
   see also High-frequency words; Multisensory techniques; Reading comprehension; Reading disabilities; Vocabulary instruction; Vocabulary knowledge
Reading Horizons, 517
Reading Lesson program, *The*, 292, 517
Reading Mastery Classic II 2008 Edition, 517–518
Reading Milestones, 518
Reading pens, 290, 368, 521
Reading Reflex program, 292, 518
Receptive language, *see* Decoding
Reciprocal teaching, 412
Rehabilitation Act Amendments of 1992 (PL 102-569), *see* Section 504 of the Rehabilitation Act Amendments of 1992 (PL 102-569)
Reinforcement, 137–148
   basic principles of, 137
   group examples, 132
   modeling, 146–147
   negative, 93, 139*t*, 143*t*, 145–146, 149
   positive, 132, 139–141, 139*t*, 143*t*
   schedules, 137–139
   selection of, 141–142

539

Reinforcement—*continued*
 shaping, 146–148
 timed writing exercises, 338
 token economies, 111, 130*t*, 142–145, 151
 see also Behavior modification; Challenging behaviors; Punishment
Relaxation exercises, 163, 165*f*–166*f*
Repeated reading, 312–313, 312*f*, 364
ReQuest (reciprocal questioning) reading procedure, 416
Resilience block, 10, 34, 181–203
 adolescence and, 189, 195, 198
 Building Blocks Questionnaire and, 18*f*, 21, 24, 185, 186*f*
 effective educators and student resilience, 184, 190–202
 nurturing in school environments, 60
 self-esteem and, 55–56, 194–196, 200–201
 student example of difficulties in, 10, 11*f*
 see also Foundational blocks
Response discrepancy observation method, 136*f*
Response to intervention (RTI), 215–217
 advantages of, 216
 ability–achievement discrepancy model versus, 216
 core concepts of, 215
 curriculum-based measures (CBM) and, 215
 evidence-based strategies, 218–219
 identification process, 217
 Individuals with Disabilities Education Improvement Act (IDEA) of 2004 (PL 108-446) and, 210, 214–215
 limits of, 215
 one-stage models and insufficient data, 216
 pattern of strength and weaknesses (PSW) approach, and, 218–219
 programs, 523
 small-group instruction and, 215
 specific learning disabilities (SLD) and, 214–217
 states implementing, 215
 tertiary system of intervention, 164
 unknowns of, 216
 see also Assessments; Instructional strategies; Interventions
Retrieval, Automaticity, Vocabulary, Elaboration, and Orthography (RAVE-O), 299, 517
Revised Children's Manifest Anxiety Scales (*RCMAS*), 162*f*
REWARDS, see *Reading Excellence: Word Attack and Rate Development Strategies*
Rhyming words, 220, 224
 analogy strategy and, 295–296, 296*f*
 nonsense words, 234–235, 257
 rhyme production, 225, 256–257, 260*f*
 rhyme recognition, 224–225, 257, 260*f*
 word segmentation and, 227
Rimes, *see* Rhyming words

Ritalin (methylphenidate hydrochloride), 83, 91, 102–104, 105*f*
Riverdeep, 444, 515
Road to the Code program, 289, 518
Role-playing, 114*t*, 133, 164*t*, 197–198
Rote memory, 4, 12
 academic performance and, 15, 35, 35*t*, 36*t*, 464, 473
 math knowledge and, 435
 nonverbal learning disabilities (NLVDs) and, 369
 spelling development and, 282
 see also Memory block

Saxon Phonics interventions, 520
Say It and Move It activity, 289
Scaffolding, 6, 67, 78, 188, 290, 341, 453
Scholastic Spelling, 520
School environments, 56–60, 58*t*
 characteristics of schools with outstanding achievement, 62
 Common Core State Standards (CCSS), 59–60
 effective teachers, 60–61
 elements of safe and healthy schools, 57
 individual value and shared purpose, 57
 nurturing resilience in, 60
 packaged programs to improve, 57
 positive and productive relationships among staff and students, 57
 positive behavior interventions and supports (PBIS), 57–59
 school climate and culture, 56–57
 sustainable, 76–77
 see also Classroom environments; Learning environment
School success, *see* Academic performance
Schwa sound, 269–270
Scott Foresman Early Reading Intervention, 518
Screening of Early Reading Processes, 259
SDOs, *see* Systematic direct observations
Second Step program, 57
Section 504 of the Rehabilitation Act Amendments of 1992 (PL 102-569), 94, 95*f*–97*f*
SEL, *see* Social and emotional learning
Selective mutism, 171–172
Selective serotonin reuptake inhibitors (SSRIs), 103
Self-advocacy skills, 106*t*, 197–198, 199*f*
Self-defeating behaviors, 184–189
Self-esteem, 182–184, 183*f*
 attribution theory and, 187–189, 200–202
 high, 184–185, 187, 195–196, 198, 200–201
 low, 170, 185–187, 190
 resilience and, 55–56, 194–196, 200–201
Self-harm, 157

Self-monitoring programs, 113, 114*t*, 115*f*, 302, 303*f*
Self-Regulation block, 9, 33, 81–121
 brain anatomy and, 97
 Building Blocks Questionnaire and, 18*f*, 21, 22, 101, 102*f*
 as a key component of executive functioning (EF), 33
 Planning, Attention, Simultaneous, Successive (PASS) theory and, 44–46, 46*t*
 see also Attention-deficit/hyperactivity disorder (ADHD); Behavior modification; Challenging behaviors; Foundational blocks; Self-monitoring programs
Self-talk, 164*t*, 371, 387
Semantic memory, 40–41
Semantics, 36*t*, 352
Sensory-motor integration impairment, 242
Separation anxiety disorder, 171, 178
Sequential mastery of topics, 66
SERI, *see* Special Education Resources on the Internet
Sertraline hydrochloride (Zoloft), 103
Short-term memory, 238
 poor, 36*t*, 240–241
 verbal, 12, 34, 224, 240, 254
 working memory and, 47, 47*t*, 240–241
 see also Memory block; Rote memory; Working memory
Sibilants, 267
Sight words, *see* High-frequency words
Simon S.I.O. (Sounds It Out), 518
Sitton Spelling Series, 520
Six-Minute Solution: A Reading Fluency Program, 518
SLD, *see* Specific learning disabilities
Slingerland, 518
Small-group instruction, 66–67, 130*t*, 159, 169
 dyslexia and, 274
 graphic organizers in, 373
 Great Leaps Reading program and, 311, 514
 K-W-L (Know-Want-Learned) strategy and, 363
 for math instruction, 318, 431
 reciprocal teaching and, 412
 response to intervention (RTI) and, 215
 Retrieval, Automaticity, Vocabulary, Engagement with Language, Orthography (RAVE-O) reading intervention, 299, 517
Social and emotional learning (SEL), 166
Social anxiety, 167–168, 172
Software, 338–340
 handwriting assistance, 338
 math related, 318, 444, 445*t*
 voice recognition software (VRS), 339–340, 521
 voice-activated software, 339–340
 see also Technology
Sonday System, 518

Index

Sound blending, 226
Sound counting, 226
Sound Partners, 519
Sounds Abound Interactive Software, 519
Sounds Abound Listening, Rhyming, and Reading, 518–519
Sounds Abound Program Teaching Phonological Awareness in the Classroom, 519
Sounds Great!, 519
Spalding method, 293, 335, 519
Spanish speakers, 356–357
Spatial organization, 35t, 41–42, 351, 369
Spatial outlining, 376–377
SpeakQ software program, 340, 521
Special Education Resources on the Internet (SERI), 525
Specialized Program Individualizing Reading Excellence (S.P.I.R.E.), 293–294, 519
Specialized vocabularies, 371–372, 419
Specific learning disabilities (SLD), 32, 34, 207–219
 alternative research-based methods, 217–219
 areas of impairment, 219
 assessment of and referral questions, 48
 broad groups of skills necessary for efficient learning, 34–35
 Building Blocks Questionnaire and, 48–49
 definitions, 207–210, 209t
 delayed services, 213
 distinction between processing linguistic and symbolic information, 252
 evidence-based differential diagnoses of, 219
 as a "hidden" disability, 192
 inclusion, 63–64, 184, 523
 Interagency Committee on Learning Disabilities definition of, 209
 legal definitions, 208–210, 209t
 levels of processing related to, 36t
 math-related subtypes of, 40–41
 misuse of the terms *category* and *diagnosis*, 35
 most widely accepted criterion for determination of, 212
 response to intervention (RTI), 214–217
 subtypes of in math, 40
 visual-motor skill accommodations, 247
 vocabulary instruction and, 364–365
 see also Accommodations; Ability-achievement discrepancy model; Dyscalculia; Dysgraphia; Dyslexia; Individuals with Disabilities Education Improvement Act (IDEA) of 2004 (PL 108-446); Interventions; Reading disabilities; Specific learning disabilities (SLD)

Speech sounds
 affricates, 266, 267, 268t
 alveolar, 266, 266t, 267t
 apps for spelling-sound correspondences, 453–455
 bilabial, 265, 266t, 267t
 classification of, 265
 closed versus open, 264
 consonants, 264–268
 dental, 267t
 digraphs, 269
 diphthongs, 267–267, 289, 294–295
 fricatives, 266, 267, 267t
 glides, 266, 267, 268t
 interdental, 266
 labiodental, 265, 267t
 liquids, 266, 268, 268t
 manner of articulation, 266
 nasals, 266, 267t
 nonsense words, 221–222, 234–235, 257
 palatal, 266, 267t
 place of articulation, 265–266
 schwa, 269–270
 short versus long vowel, 269
 sibilants, 267
 spelling development and, 264–270
 stops, 266, 266t, 267
 tense versus lax terminology, 268
 throat (glottal), 266
 trigraphs, 265
 velar, 266, 266t, 267t
 voicing, 265, 265t
 vowels, 268–270
 see also Grapheme–phoneme awareness; Language development; Spelling development
Spelling bank, 296
Spelling development
 apps for spelling, 453–457
 assessment and instruction, 277–285
 awareness of orthography and phonology, 285–286
 basic skills necessary for academic performance, 49, 50t, 52f
 curriculum-based measurement (CBM), 282
 difficulties into adulthood, 235–236, 238f, 279
 effective instruction focusing on language units, 296
 "equivalent index," 283
 grapheme–phoneme awareness and, 279
 impaired visual memory and, 231
 informal assessment of, 228
 invented spelling, 285–286
 metrics for scoring spelling, 283
 most common errors, 266, 336
 nonsense words, 221–222, 234–235
 partial credit for correct letter sequences (CLS), 282–283
 reading skills and, 274
 resources, 520
 rote memorization and, 282
 selecting spelling words, 284–285
 sequence of sounds, 288
 speech sounds and, 264–270
 spelling flow list, 280–281, 281f
 spelling rating scales, 283–284
 spelling rubric, 281–282
 Spelling Sensitivity Score (SSS), 283
 strategy approach to, 277
 symbolic learning and, 35, 273, 275–276
 temporary, 285–286
 theories of, 278–279
 when to assign memorization, 280
 see also Grapheme–phoneme awareness; Language development; Speech sounds; Verbal block
Spelling flow list, 280–281, 281f
Spelling grids, 298, 298f
Spelling rating scales, 283–284
Spelling rubric, 281–282
Spelling Sensitivity Score (SSS), 283
Spelling-sound correspondences, *see* Grapheme–phoneme awareness
Spellography, 520
S.P.I.R.E, *see* Specialized Program Individualizing Reading Excellence
SQ3R (Survey, Question, Read, Recite, and Review) reading strategy, 414–416
SSRIs, *see* Selective serotonin reuptake inhibitors
SSS, *see* Spelling Sensitivity Score
STAIC, *see* State-Trait Anxiety Inventory for Children
STAR mnemonic, 437
Start Write 6: The Handwriting Worksheet Wizard, 521
STATE the Story mnemonic, 408
Statement pie writing strategy, 425–426
State-Trait Anxiety Inventory for Children (STAIC), 162f
Stimulants, 102–104, 151
Stops, 266, 266t, 267
STORE the story strategy, 408–409, 409f
Story Grammar Marker, 519
Story grammars, 404–410
 character development, 406–407
 components of, 405–406
 C-SPACE mnemonic, 409–410
 elements of, 405–406
 questioning, 407–409
 simple, 404–405
 STORE the story mnemonic, 408–409, 409f
 story maps, 407
 W-W-W, What = 2, How = 2 mnemonic, 410
 see also Reading comprehension
Strategy instruction, 378–381
 cognitive behavior modification, 381
 core foundational teaching strategies, 378, 379t
 general principles of, 378
 math problem solving and, 437–442
 mnemonics, 380

541

Strategy instruction—*continued*
  self-regulated strategy development, 380
  think-alouds, 379
  see also Classroom activities; Instructional strategies
Strattera (atomoxetine), 103
Strephosymbolia ("twisted symbols"), *see* Specific learning disabilities (SLD)
Structural arithmetic, 320
Student engagement, 62–63, 140
  implementing audio and visual learning tools, 66
  selecting their own topics, 337
  student response systems, 65
  see also Classroom environments; Learning environments; Teacher–student interactions
Student–parent interactions
  developing reading skills, 470
  English language learners (ELLs) and potential embarrassment about parents, 359–360
  family problems, 471–472
  home environments, 126–127, 385–386, 471–472
  increased parental involvement, 75
Students
  basic needs of, 188–189
  qualities that predict classroom success, 469
  see also Academic performance; Student engagement; Student–parent interactions; Student–student interactions; Student–teacher interactions
Student–student interactions
  addressing classroom conflicts, 131–133
  aggressive behavior, 126
  cooperative time-outs, 133
  importance of socialization, 472
  mediation, 133
  peer modeling opportunities, 147
  proactive classroom management strategies, 130–131, 130*t*
  reflective listening, 133
  role-playing or role reversal, 133
  self-advocacy skills and improved, 197
  see also Behavior modification; Classroom environments; Learning environments; Peer tutoring; Teacher–student interactions
Student–teacher interactions, *see* Teacher–student interactions
Study buddies, 193
Substance/medication-induced disorders, 147, 173, 176
Suicide and suicidal thoughts, 157, 175
Surface dyslexia, 39, 232
Syllable blending, 225, 256, 257, 260*f*
Syllable counting, 225
Syllable deletion, 256, 258, 260*f*
Syllable segmentation, 256, 258, 260*f*

Symbol recognition and recall, 229–230
Symbolic learning, 35, 273, 275–276
Synonyms, 446–450
Syntax, 38, 45, 352–353, 359
Synthetic phonics, 291–295
Systematic direct observations (SDOs), 134–136, 135*f*

TACSEI, *see* The Technical Assistance Center on Social Emotional Intervention (TACSEI) for Young Children
Talk-to-yourself chart, 286–287
Teacher-Directed PALS: Path to Achieving Literacy Success, 519
Teacher–parent interactions
  assignment notebooks to facilitate, 117, 385
  behavior planning, 133–134
  monitoring medication in children, 104
  preventing challenging behaviors, 133–134
  see also Home environments; Student–parent interactions
Teachers, *see* Effective educators
Teacher–student interactions
  accepting students for who they are, 191–193
  attribution theory, 187–189, 200–202
  conflicts, 132
  developing a sense of responsibility in students, 193–195
  dominating behaviors, 149
  facilitating a "currency of caring" in, 147
  fear of failure and, 202
  general recommendations for addressing behavior problems, 128*t*
  helping students establish self-discipline, 196–197
  increasing students' sense of ownership, 189, 195–196
  orientation period, 190–191, 196–197
  positive feedback and encouragement, 60, 62, 64, 108, 198–199
  as a predictor of success, 56
  prevention-oriented approaches to promote positive, 130, 130*t*
  promoting self-advocacy skills, 197–198
  questions to encourage critical thinking and participation, 368
  teaching coping mechanisms to students, 199–202
  what students need from teachers, 469–471
  what teachers want from students, 468–469
  see also Classroom environments; Effective educators; Feedback; Individualized instruction; Small-group instruction; Student engagement; Teacher–parent interactions; Whole-class instruction
Teaching strategies, *see* Instructional strategies
Technical Assistance Center on Positive Behavioral Interventions and Supports, The, 525
Technical Assistance Center on Social Emotional Intervention (TACSEI) for Young Children, The, 525
Technology
  assistive, 218, 521, 524
  calculators, 321
  for handwriting, 338–340
  keyboarding, 339
  notetaking, 381
  reading pens, 290, 368, 521
  utility/presentation, 451–452
  web sites with reviews of apps, 460
  see also Apps; Software
Temporoparietal cortex, 37
Tenex (guanfacine hydrochloride), 103
Test of Awareness of Language Segments, 259
Test-taking, 386–387
  essay questions, 352, 387, 393–394, 417, 425
  fill-in-the-blank questions, 393
  Instructional Accommodations Survey and, 397
  matching questions, 393
  multiple-choice questions, 391–392, 398
  PIRATES test-taking strategy, 391, 392*t*
  recording answers, 391
  reducing test anxiety, 164*t*, 386, 387
  Scantron or bubble sheets, 231, 253, 391, 398
  Section 504 accommodations for, 95*f*
  short-answer questions, 393
  test formats, 391–394
  test preparation, 386–387, 400
  true/false questions, 393
  see also Executive Functions (EF) block
TF-CBT, *see* Trauma-focused cognitive-behavioral therapy
Theories of intelligence, 44–49
  Cattell-Horn-Carroll (CHC) theory, 46–49, 47*t*
  Planning, Attention, Simultaneous, Successive (PASS) theory, 44–46, 46*t*
Think sheets, 423–424
"Think time," 149–150
Think-alouds
  Cognitive Strategy in Writing (CSIW) program, 423
  for problem solving, 442
  major uses of, 379
  teacher–student, 423, 439–440
Three-column notetaking, 376–377, 377*t*, 378*t*
Throat (glottal) sounds, 266

Index

Time management and organizational strategies, 383–386
  apps for, 400
  color coding, 117, 120, 288, 295, 385, 414
  daily planner schedules, 117, 383–386
  getting organized, 385
  making lists, 383–384
  managing procrastination, 384–385
  organizing materials, 385–386
  schedules to manage challenging behaviors, 137–139
  to-do lists, 383, 400
  using time efficiently, 383–384
  see also Executive Functions (EF) block
Time Tables the Fun Way cards, 321, 522
Time-outs, 9–10, 69, 133, 148–149
To-do lists, 383, 400
Tofranil (imipramine), 102–103
Token economies, 111, 130*t*, 142–145, 151
Touch Points, 320
TouchMath, 320–321, 321*f*, 522
Trauma and stress-related disorders, 158, 177–179
  acute stress disorder, 158, 178
  adjustment disorders, 158, 178–179
  Diagnostic and Statistical Manual of Mental Disorders, Fifth Edition (*DSM-5*) on, 158, 177–179
  diagnostic criteria for various, 158, 162*f*, 177–179
  disinhibited social engagement disorder, 158, 179
  posttraumatic stress disorder (PTSD), 162*f*, 177–178
  reactive attachment disorder, 158, 179
  see also Cognitive behavioral therapy (CBT); Emotions block; Internalizing disorders; Trauma-focused cognitive-behavioral therapy (TF-CBT)
Trauma Symptom Checklist for Children, 162*f*
Trauma-focused cognitive-behavioral therapy (TF-CBT), 169–170
Tricyclic antidepressants, 102–103
Trigraphs, 265
Turner syndrome, 97
"Twisted symbols," *see* Specific learning disabilities (SLD)

Universal design for learning (UDL), 523
U.S. Department of Education, 523, 524

Variety (in the classroom), 104, 107
Vaughn Gross Center for Reading and Language Arts, University of Texas at Austin, 525–526
Velar sounds, 266, 266*t*, 267*t*
Verbal block, 13, 351–369
  Building Blocks Questionnaire and, 18*f*, 21, 27, 253, 253*f*
  Cattell-Horn Carroll (CHC) theory of intelligence and, 47–48, 47*t*
  Common Core State Standards (CCSS) English language arts/literacy (ELA) standards, 59, 403
  components of oral language, 352–354
  difficulties, 319, 351–352
  Executive Functions (EF) block and, 43
  expansion and elaboration, 361
  higher level questioning skills, 368–369
  instruction for developing, 361–369
  literacy instruction for English language learners (ELLs), 355–361
  math problem solving and, 319
  modeling, 361
  paraphrasing, 361–362
  receptive and expressive language, 354–355
  vocabulary, 363–368
  see also Background knowledge; Conceptual blocks; Language development; Reading comprehension; Reading fluency; Receptive language; Spelling development; Vocabulary instruction; Vocabulary knowledge; Written expression
Verizon Thinkfinity, 525
Visual defects, 234
Visual dyslexia, 231–232
Visual imagery
  apps for, 399
  brainstorming, 374–376
  graphic organizers, 373
  keyword method, 372–373, 380
  K-W-L (Know-Want-Learned) strategy, 374
  mapping, 373
  spatial outlining, 376–377
  visualization, 371–372
  see also Nonverbal block
Visual-perceptual impairment, 232
Visual-spatial impairment, 232
Visual-spatial thinking (Gv), 42, 47–48, 47*t*
Vocabulary instruction, 363–368
  apps for, 456–457
  components of effective, 364–366
  derivations of words, 367
  direct teaching, 364
  English language learners (ELLs) and, 364–365
  framework for choosing words, 365
  independent word-learning strategies, 366
  keyword method, 372
  prefixes/suffixes and word origins, 366–367
  resources, 520
  specific learning disabilities (SLD) and, 364–365
  studying specific words, 365
  word walls, 296, 368
  see also High-frequency words; Language development; Reading comprehension; Reading fluency; Spelling development; Vocabulary knowledge
Vocabulary knowledge
  academic language proficiency, 355, 357–358, 360
  assessing, 365
  background knowledge and, 223, 360, 362
  components of oral language, 352–354
  independent reading and increased, 365
  map of word derivations, 367*f*
  morphology, 8, 49, 274, 352
  pragmatics, 352–353
  self-selected words, 285
  semantics, 63*t*, 352
  specialized, 371–372, 419
  synonyms for words that children commonly use, 446–450
  syntax, 38, 45, 352–353, 359
  word recognition, 39, 310–311, 452–453
  see also High-frequency words; Language development; Reading comprehension; Reading fluency; Spelling development; Vocabulary instruction
Voice recognition software (VRS), 339–340, 521
Voice-activated software, 339–340
Vowels, 268–270
  digraphs, 269
  diphthongs, 267–267, 289, 294–295
  schwa, 269–270
  short versus long vowel sounds, 269
  see also Grapheme–phoneme awareness; Speech sounds
VRS, *see* Voice recognition software

Washington Educational Television Association, 524
WatchWord, 519
What Works Clearinghouse, 526
Whole word gestalts, 39
Whole-class instruction, 32, 62, 101, 130*t*, 136, 164–165
Williams syndrome, 97
Wilson Fluency/Basic program, 311
Wilson Reading System (WRS), 294–295, 519
WJ IV COG, *see* Woodcock-Johnson IV Tests of Cognitive Ability
Woodcock-Johnson IV Tests of Cognitive Ability (WJ IV COG), 48
Word blindness, 36*t*, 207, 209*t*, 232, 231–234
Word counting, 225
Word deafness, 209*t*, 223
Word discrimination, 256–257, 260*f*
Word identification, *see* Decoding; Vocabulary knowledge
Word knowledge, *see* Vocabulary knowledge

543

Word meanings, *see* Semantics
Word walls, 296, 368
Words read correctly (WRC), 306, 308
Working memory, 238, 240–241, 428–429
  attention-deficit/hyperactivity disorder (ADHD) and, 88, 92, 106*t*, 252
  backwards spelling and, 302
  capacity, 38
  contextual examples of, 238
  defined, 8, 12
  long-term, 240–241
  math problem solving and, 428–429
  models of, 240–241
  poor, 35, 40, 218–219, 241, 379
  short-term, 38, 47–48, 47*t*, 238
  see also Memory block; Rote memory; Short-term memory
Worksheets
  accommodations with, 118–120, 397
  color coding in, 120
  example planning facilitation for math, 112*f*
  handwriting instruction with, 338–339, 521
  individualized, 338–339
  K-W-L (Know-Want-Learned) strategy and, 363, 374
  math instruction with, 317–319, 397, 433, 443–444
  single-skill versus multiskill, 318–319
  for students with attention-deficit/hyperactivity disorder (ADHD), 118–120
  tools to create/use, 288, 338, 444, 452–453, 521
  see also Homework assignments
WRC, *see* Words read correctly
Wright Skills Decodable Books, 520
Writing styles
  choosing among, 329–330
  cursive writing, 329
  D'Nealian writing style, 330–334, 331*f*, 332*f*, 336, 456
  initial style for children, 330
  manucursive style, 326–327, 329–330, 336, 338
  manuscript writing, 329
  see also Handwriting; Letter formation
Written expression, 397, 403–404, 418–428
  basic skills necessary for, 49, 50*t*, 52*f*
  brainstorming and, 418–419
  Cognitive Strategy in Writing (CSIW) program, 423–424
  cohesion in, 424–425
  composing, 419
  dialogic and social nature of writing, 423
  Dinosaur for essay structure, 428, 429*f*
  editing and proofreading, 421–422
  essays, 426–428
  grammar, 38, 50*t*, 120, 290, 293, 340, 360–361
  Instructional Accommodations Survey and, 397
  Kerrigan's method for essays, 426–428
  outlining, 419
  paragraphs, 425–426
  POWER (Plan, Organize, Write, Edit, Revise) strategy, 422
  principles for teaching students expository writing, 423
  process approach to writing and revising, 421
  process of writing, 418–422
  research, 428
  resources, 520–521
  revising, 419–421
  self-regulated strategy development, 422–423
  software to assist, 520
  statement pie writing strategy, 425–426
  steps for theme organization and composition writing, 426–428
  synonyms for words that children commonly use, 446–450
  teacher modeling behaviors, 338
  timed writing exercises, 338
  weaknesses in verbal abilities and, 352
  writing instruction adjustments, 397
  see also Essay writing; Handwriting; Language development; Verbal block
WRS, *see* Wilson Reading System
W-W-W, What = 2, How = 2 mnemonic, 410

Zaner-Bloser writing speed proficiency scale, 245–246
Zoloft (sertraline hydrochloride), 103
Zone of proximal development, 388
Zoo-Phonics, 520